Modelling for Management
Volume I

The International Library of Management
Series Editor: Keith Bradley

Titles in the Series:

Performance Evaluation in Organizations
Walter C. Borman

Public Sector Management, Vols I & II
Sir John Bourn

Decision Science
Derek Bunn, et al.

Training and Development in Public and Private Policy
Peter Cappelli

Internal Auditing
A.D. Chambers

The Management of Banking and Finance
K. Alec Chrystal

Takeovers, Vols I, II & III
Andy Cosh and Alan Hughes

Ethics in Business and Economics, Vols I & II
Thomas Donaldson and Thomas W. Dunfee

Group Management
Connie Gersick

Career Development
Douglas T. Hall

Power and Politics in Organizations
Cynthia Hardy

Industrial Relations: Institutions and Organizational Performance
Morris M. Kleiner

Strategic Planning Process
Peter Lorange

Risk Management
Gerald Mars and David Weir

Management of Non-profit Organizations
Sharon M. Oster

International Cultural Differences
Gordon Redding

Modelling for Management, Vols I & II
George P. Richardson

Organizational Sociology
W. Richard Scott

Concepts of Leadership
Jeffrey A. Sonnenfeld

The Manager as a Leader
Jeffrey A. Sonnenfeld

Organizational Psychology
Philip Stone and Mark Cannon

Managerial Economics
Stefan Szymanski

International Management
Rosalie L. Tung

Management of Change and Innovation
Bengt-Arne Vedin

Management Accounting
Richard M.S. Wilson

Marketing Controllership
Richard M.S. Wilson

Strategic Cost Management
Richard M.S. Wilson

Management Buy-outs
Mike Wright

Venture Capital
Mike Wright and Ken Robbie

Modelling for Management Volume I

Simulation in Support of Systems Thinking

Edited by
George P. Richardson
*Associate Professor of Public Administration,
Public Policy and Information Science,
Nelson A. Rockefeller College of Public Affairs and Policy,
University at Albany, State University of New York*

Dartmouth
Aldershot · Brookfield USA · Singapore · Sydney

© George P. Richardson 1996. For copyright of individual articles please refer to the Acknowledgements.

All rights reserved. No part of this publication may be reproduced, stored in a retrieval system, or transmitted in any form or by any means, electronic, mechanical, photocopying, recording, or otherwise without the prior permission of Dartmouth Publishing Company Limited.

Published by
Dartmouth Publishing Company Limited
Gower House
Croft Road
Aldershot
Hants GU11 3HR
England

Dartmouth Publishing Company
Old Post Road
Brookfield
Vermont 05036
USA

British Library Cataloguing in Publication Data
Modelling for management : simulation in support of systems
 thinking. – (The international library of management)
 1. Management 2. Decision-making 3. Management – Simulation
methods
I. Richardson, George P.
658.4′032

Library of Congress Cataloging-in-Publication Data
Modelling for management : simulation in support of systems thinking /
 edited by George P. Richardson.
         p. cm. — (The international library of management)
   Includes bibliographical references and index.
   ISBN 1-85521-697-3 (set) hbk 1-85521-888-7 pbk
     1. Management—Simulation methods. 2. Strategic planning—
Simulation methods. 3. Decision-making—Simulation methods.
 4. System analysis. I. Richardson, George P. II. Series.
HD30.26.M63 1996
658.4′0352—dc20   95-52523
                                CIP

ISBN 1 85521 697 3 HBK
ISBN 1 85521 888 7 PBK

Printed in Great Britain at the University Press, Cambridge

Contents

Acknowledgements   vii
Series Preface   ix
Introduction   xi

PART I   MODELLING PERSPECTIVES

1. John D. Sterman (1988), 'A Skeptic's Guide to Computer Models' in Gerald O. Barney, W. Brian Kreutzer and Martha J. Garrett (eds), *Managing a Nation: The Microcomputer Software Catalog*, Boulder: Westview Press, pp. 209–29.   3
2. Barry Richmond (1993), 'Systems Thinking: Critical Thinking Skills for the 1990s and Beyond', *System Dynamics Review*, **9**, pp. 113–33.   25
3. George P. Richardson (1991), 'System Dynamics: Simulation for Policy Analysis from a Feedback Perspective' in P.A. Fishwick and P.A. Luker (eds), *Qualitative Simulation Modeling and Analysis*, New York: Springer Verlag, pp. 144–69.   47
4. John D.W. Morecroft (1984), 'Strategy Support Models', *Strategic Management Journal*, **5**, pp. 215–29.   73
5. John D. Sterman (1994), 'Learning in and about Complex Systems', *System Dynamics Review*, **10**, pp. 291–330.   89
6. Jay W. Forrester (1987), '14 "Obvious Truths"', *System Dynamics Review*, **3**, pp. 156–9.   129

PART II   SYSTEMS THINKING AND DYNAMIC DECISION MAKING

7. Peter M. Senge (1990), 'The Leader's New Work: Building Learning Organizations', *Sloan Management Review*, **32**, pp. 7–23.   135
8. Donella H. Meadows (1982), 'Whole Earth Models and Systems', *Coevolution Quarterly*, Summer, pp. 98–108.   153
9. Daniel H. Kim (1992), 'Systems Archetypes: Diagnosing Systemic Issues and Designing High-Leverage Interventions', *Toolbox Reprint Series: Systems Archetypes*, Cambridge: Pegasus Communications, pp. 3–26.   165
10. John D.W. Morecroft (1988), 'System Dynamics and Microworlds for Policymakers', *European Journal of Operational Research*, **35**, pp. 301–20.   189
11. John D. Sterman (1989), 'Modeling Managerial Behavior: Misperceptions of Feedback in a Dynamic Decision Making Experiment', *Management Science*, **35**, pp. 321–39.   209

12 Mark Paich and John D. Sterman (1993), 'Boom, Bust, and Failures to Learn in Experimental Markets', *Management Science*, **39**, pp. 1439–58. 229

PART III   CORPORATE POLICY AND MANAGEMENT

13 Roger I. Hall (1976), 'A System Pathology of an Organization: The Rise and Fall of the Old *Saturday Evening Post*', *Administrative Science Quarterly*, **21**, pp. 185–211. 251
14 John D.W. Morecroft, David C. Lane and Paul S. Viita (1991), 'Modeling Growth Strategy in a Biotechnology Startup Firm', *System Dynamics Review*, **7**, pp. 93–116. 279
15 Peter P. Merten, Reiner Löffler and Klaus-Peter Wiedmann (1987), 'Portfolio Simulation: A Tool to Support Strategic Management', *System Dynamics Review*, **3**, pp. 81–101. 303
16 Henry Birdseye Weil and Leon S. White (1994), 'Business Transformation: The Key to Long-Term Survival and Success', *Sloan School of Management*. 325
17 Glen L. Urban, John R. Hauser and John H. Roberts (1990), 'Prelaunch Forecasting of New Automobiles', *Management Science*, **36**, pp. 401–21. 339
18 Thomas D. Clark, Jr, Robert E. Trempe and Herbert E. Trichlin (1983), 'Complex Multiechelon Inventory System Management Using a Dynamic Simulation Model', *Decision Sciences*, **14**, pp. 389–407. 361
19 John D.W. Morecroft (1983), 'Concepts, Theory, and Techniques: A Systems Perspective on Material Requirements Planning', *Decision Sciences*, **14**, pp. 1–18. 381
20 Thomas D. Clark, Jr and Fred K. Augustine, Jr (1992), 'Using System Dynamics to Measure the Value of Information in a Business Firm', *System Dynamics Review*, **8**, pp. 149–73. 399
21 Kenneth G. Cooper (1980), 'Naval Ship Production: A Claim Settled and a Framework Built', *Interfaces*, **10**, pp. 20–36. 425
22 Tarek K. Abdel-Hamid and Stuart E. Madnick (1990), 'The Elusive Silver Lining: How We Fail to Learn from Software Development Failures', *Sloan Management Review*, **32**, pp. 39–48. 443
23 Jack B. Homer (1985), 'Worker Burnout: A Dynamic Model with Implications for Prevention and Control', *System Dynamics Review*, **1**, pp. 42–62. 453
24 Daniel H. Kim and Peter M. Senge (1994), 'Putting Systems Thinking into Practice', *System Dynamics Review*, **10**, pp. 277–90. 475

Name Index 489

Acknowledgements

The editor and publishers wish to thank the following for permission to use copyright material.

Administrative Science Quarterly for the essay: Roger I. Hall (1976), 'A System Pathology of an Organization: The Rise and Fall of the Old *Saturday Evening Post*', *Administrative Science Quarterly*, **21**, pp. 185–211.

Decision Sciences Institute for the essays: Thomas D. Clark, Jr, Robert E. Trempe and Herbert E. Trichlin (1983), 'Complex Multiechelon Inventory System Management Using a Dynamic Simulation Model', *Decision Sciences*, **14**, pp. 389–407; John D.W. Morecroft (1983), 'Concepts, Theory, and Techniques: A Systems Perspective on Material Requirements Planning', *Decision Sciences*, **14**, pp. 1–18.

Elsevier Science B.V. Amsterdam for the essay: John D.W. Morecroft (1988), 'System Dynamics and Microworlds for Policymakers', *European Journal of Operational Research*, **35**, pp. 301–20.

Institute for Operations Research and the Management Sciences for the essays: John D. Sterman (1989), 'Modeling Managerial Behavior: Misperceptions of Feedback in a Dynamic Decision Making Experiment', *Management Science*, **35**, pp. 321–39. Copyright © 1989, The Institute of Management Sciences. John D. Sterman and Mark Paich (1993), 'Boom, Bust, and Failures to Learn in Experimental Markets', *Management Science*, **39**, pp. 1439–58. Copyright © 1993, The Institute of Management Sciences. Glen L. Urban, R. Hauser and John H. Roberts (1990), 'Prelaunch Forecasting of New Automobiles', *Management Science*, **36**, pp. 401–21. Copyright © 1990, The Institute of Management Sciences. K.G. Cooper (1980), 'Naval Ship Production: A Claim Settled and Framework Built', *Interfaces*, **10**, pp. 20–36.

Donella H. Meadows (1982), 'Whole Earth Models and Systems', *Coevolution Quarterly* (now *Whole Earth Review*), Summer, pp. 98–108. Copyright © Donella H. Meadows.

Pegasus Communications for the essay: Daniel H. Kim (1992), 'Systems Archetypes: Diagnosing Systemic Issues and Designing High-Leverage Interventions', *Toolbox Reprint Series: Systems Archetypes*, pp. 3–26.

Sloan Management Review for the essays: Peter M. Senge (1990), 'The Leader's New Work: Building Learning Organizations', *Sloan Management Review*, **32**, pp. 7–23. Copyright © 1990 by the Sloan Management Review Association. All rights reserved. T.K. Abdel-Hamid and S. Madnick (1990), 'The Elusive Silver Lining: How We Fail to Learn from Software Development Failures', *Sloan Management Review*, **32**, pp. 39–48. Copyright 1990 by the Sloan Management Review Association. All rights reserved.

Springer-Verlag New York Inc. for the essay: George P. Richardson (1991), 'System Dynamics: Simulation for Policy Analysis from a Feedback Perspective' in P.A. Fishwick and P.A. Luker (eds), *Qualitative Simulation Modeling and Analysis*, pp. 144–69. Copyright © Springer-Verlag New York Inc.

John D. Sterman (1988), 'A Skeptic's Guide to Computer Models' in G.O. Barney et al. (eds), *Managing a Nation: The Microcomputer Software Catalog*, Boulder: Westview Press, pp. 209–29. Copyright © John D. Sterman.

John Wiley & Sons Limited for the essays: Barry Richmond (1993), 'Systems Thinking: Critical Thinking Skills for the 1990s and Beyond', *System Dynamics Review*, **9**, pp. 113–33. Copyright © 1993 by John Wiley & Sons Ltd. John D.W. Morecroft (1984), 'Strategy Support Models', *Strategic Management Journal*, **5**, pp. 215–29. Copyright © 1984 by John Wiley & Sons Ltd. John D. Sterman (1994), 'Learning in and about Complex Systems', *System Dynamics Review*, **10**, pp. 291–330. Copyright © 1994 by John Wiley & Sons Ltd. Jay W. Forrester (1987), '14 "Obvious Truths"', *System Dynamics Review*, **3**, pp. 156–9. Copyright © 1987 by the System Dynamics Society. John D.W. Morecroft, David C. Lane and Paul S. Viita (1991), 'Modeling Growth Strategy in a Biotechnology Startup Firm', *System Dynamics Review*, **7**, pp. 93–116. Copyright © 1991 by John Wiley & Sons Ltd. Peter P. Merten, Reiner Löffler and Klaus-Peter Wiedmann (1987), 'Portfolio Simulation: A Tool to Support Strategic Management', *System Dynamics Review*, **3**, pp. 81–101. Copyright © 1987 by the System Dynamics Society. Thomas D. Clark, Jr and Fred K. Augustine, Jr (1992), 'Using System Dynamics to Measure the Value of Information in a Business Firm', *System Dynamics Review*, **8**, pp. 149–73. Copyright © 1992 by John Wiley & Sons, Ltd. Jack B. Homer (1985), 'Worker Burnout: A Dynamic Model with Implications for Prevention and Control', *System Dynamics Review*, **1**, pp. 42–62. Copyright © 1985 by the System Dynamics Society. Daniel H. Kim and Peter M. Senge (1994), 'Putting Systems Thinking into Practice', *System Dynamics Review*, **10**, pp. 277–90. Copyright © 1994 by John Wiley & Sons Ltd. Reprinted by permission of John Wiley & Sons Limited.

Every effort has been made to trace all the copyright holders but if any have been inadvertently overlooked the publishers will be pleased to make the necessary arrangement at the first opportunity.

Series Preface

The International Library of Management brings together in one series the most significant and influential articles from across the whole range of management studies. In compiling the series, the editors have followed a selection policy that is both international and interdisciplinary. The articles that are included are not only of seminal importance today, but are expected to remain of key relevance and influence as management deals with the issues of the next millennium.

The Library was specifically designed to meet a great and growing need in the field of management studies. Few areas have grown as rapidly in recent years, in size, complexity, and importance. There has been an enormous increase in the number of important academic journals publishing in the field, in the amount published, in the diversity and complexity of theory and in the extent of cross-pollination from other disciplines. At the same time, managers themselves must deal with increasingly complex issues in a world growing ever more competitive and interdependent. These remarkable developments have presented all those working in the field, whether they be theorists or practitioners, with a serious challenge. In the absence of a core series bringing together this wide array of new knowledge and thought, it is becoming increasingly difficult to keep abreast of all new important developments and discoveries, while it is becoming ever-more vital to do so.

The International Library of Management aims to meet that need, by bringing the most important articles in management theory and practice together in one core, definitive series. The Library provides management researchers, professors, students, and managers themselves, with an extensive range of key articles which, together, provide a comprehensive basis for understanding the nature and importance of the major theoretical and substantive developments in management science. The Library is the definitive series in management studies.

In making their choice, the editors have drawn especially from the Anglo-American tradition, and have tended to exclude articles which have been widely reprinted and are generally available. Selection is particularly focused on issues most likely to be important to management thought and practice as we move into the next millennium. Editors have also prefaced each volume with a thought-provoking introduction, which provides a stimulating setting for the chosen articles.

The International Library of Management is an essential resource for all those engaged in management development in the future.

KEITH BRADLEY
Series Editor
The International Library of Management

Introduction

Setting the Stage for Volumes I and II

Systems Thinking and Simulation

Promising new lines of thinking are enriching corporate and public sector management. Prominent among them are various emphases on management for continuous improvement and quality tracing back to the corporate work of Deming[1] now appearing in the public sector,[2] and the systems thinking movement reflected in the work of Checkland[3] and the more recent publications of Senge[4] and Kim[5]. These lines of thinking are related. Peter Senge characterized systems thinking as the fifth and most central discipline in the development of learning organizations, organizations that can flourish because they have habits and skills that facilitate reflection and learning at all levels.[6]

Many of the insights that are emerging about systems thinking in the corporate and public sectors are grounded in modelling in simulation. This collection illustrates that grounding and extends the perspectives of systems thinking to complexities that cannot be understood without the aid of formal models. It contains some of the best recent and award-winning work in the use of modelling and simulation in support of systems thinking in industry and government.

Tools for Thinking

The goal of the modelling work presented in this collection is to provide cognitive support for management in planning, policy analysis, and strategic decision making. The premise these authors take is that such model-based support can significantly contribute to the potential insightfulness and effectiveness of management decisions.

Policy analysis and decision making in complex systems are difficult because of uncertainty, disagreement and complexity.[7] Managers and policy makers cope with uncertainty by acquiring information, generating and testing alternatives, consulting experts and striving to control consequences. They deal with disagreement by bargaining and compromise, persuasion, perhaps avoidance, and sometimes even by creating constructive, unifying crises. They strive to cope with complexity by formulating and analysing alternatives, aggregating information and preferences, and repeatedly diagnosing and rediagnosing the problem. Without formal models to aid in these processes, managers and policy makers must rely on mental models.

Formal quantitative tools – formal models – have the potential to contribute to the policy process by reducing uncertainty, disagreement and complexity. Different tools have different strengths. Uncertainty is mainly the domain of statistical and probabilistic models. Statistical estimation, time series analysis, statistical inference, risk analysis and the like can significantly reduce uncertainty about quantities and trends and can also shed some light on associations and linkages in complex systems. Disagreement can be addressed with formal models that aid in choosing among policy options. Familiar tools include decision trees, optimizing techniques such as linear and dynamic programming, and multicriteria decision models or MAU (multiattribute utility) models. These types of formal tools are treated elsewhere in the International Library of Management.

The kinds of formal models assembled in this volume primarily address the third problematic area of policy analysis and decision making – the problems of understanding, reducing and managing complexity. By themselves, the formal models and modelling techniques presented here can dramatically improve people's understanding of the structure and dynamic behaviour of complex systems. To some extent they can also contribute to reducing uncertainty and disagreement by helping people reach consensus on the most promising policy directions. Used jointly with other formal tools that can further aid in reducing uncertainty and disagreement, they contribute an essential dynamic perspective to a powerful team of formal techniques that can support management thinking and decision making.

Computer Simulation of Dynamic Feedback Systems

The essays in this collection are based on computer simulation models, crafted from an information feedback perspective and expressing an explicitly causal view of complex policy problems. Most are drawn from the literature of system dynamics, the field that had its origins in Jay W. Forrester's *Industrial Dynamics*.[8] Within ten years of the publication of that book, the applications of its perspective and methods had spread well beyond the problems of industry; thus the name evolved to the more general term 'system dynamics'. The label is not tightly descriptive and is actually somewhat misleading, suggesting incorrectly that the approach is linked to various systems philosophies such as General Systems Theory. System dynamics has its roots in four other traditions, which Forrester described in 1961 as

- advances in computing technology,
- growing experience with computer simulation,
- improved understanding of strategic decision making, and
- developments in the understanding of the role of feedback in complex systems.[9]

Modern developments in the field have improved its tools and techniques and have extended its application very widely, but these four traditions remain its foundations.

The fourth cornerstone – understanding the role of feedback in complex systems – deserves some comment. Although the word 'feedback' comes from the engineering literature dating from the 1920s,[10] its application to human systems should not conjure up images of stilted, distorted views of humans as machines. Information feedback and circular causality are natural parts of human, living systems, not of machines. People came to recognize that fact when they reflected on various attempts to make machines behave like people. 'Turn on the heat until the temperature is right.' How does a thermostat do that? 'Order sufficient production capacity.' How does a firm do that? Both processes involve a circular pattern in which current conditions (room temperature, corporate conditions such as delivery delay) are compared with a goal or target, and actions are initiated to close the gap. The circular causal loop in the lower right of Figure 1 shows such a self-adjusting process in which delivery delays longer than the target lead to decisions to increase production capacity to correct the imbalance. The figure, abstracted from a classic paper by Forrester on corporate growth,[11] also shows other circular causal feedback loops that were hypothesized to be present in the system and influential in the dynamics of the inconsistent corporate growth exhibited.

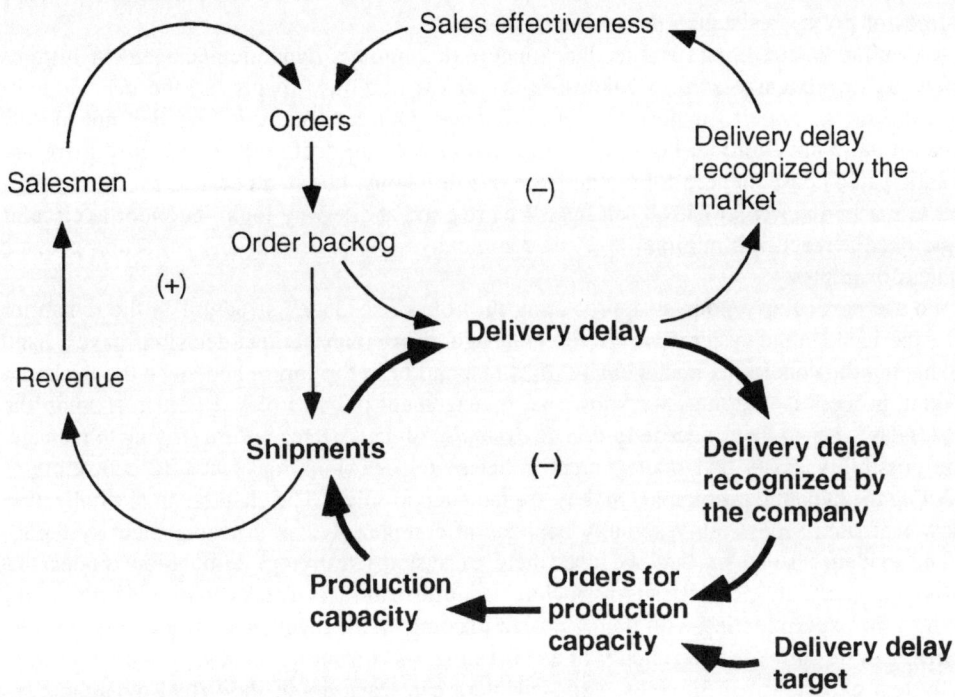

Figure 1: Feedback loops illustrated in a classic study of inconsistent corporate growth, simplified from Forrester (1968). The bold loop is an example of the generic goal-seeking negative feedback loop structure underlying all purposive action.

Only sometimes present in machines, and only in very smart ones at that, feedback loops are implicit and ubiquitous in all human activity. In particular, all management settings are characterized by circular causality and information feedback. The process is very familiar even if not frequently noted: information of various sorts and sources comes together to influence a policy and shape decisions whose effects ramify throughout the system and eventually return to the original decision point as new information with new implications for policies and decisions. Information thus emanates from a decision and feeds back to influence future decisions. In spite of our wish for clarity and simplicity, we are forced to recognize that causality in complex systems is circular. Rarely, if ever, does management have the luxury of being able to make a decision in which causality goes only outward and does not generate repercussions that feed back to influence or affect management. Management plans and decisions alter the management playing field, and consequently always have a hand in shaping the subsequent conditions to which management must respond.

Furthermore, management actions disturb the conditions other players are responding to in the same circular causal fashion, thus prompting natural feedback responses that can counteract or compensate for the initiatives. Thus advantages of a policy in the short run may dissipate over time as others reassert conditions they prefer. Circular causality and information feedback become vital concepts for perceiving and understanding the primary sources of policy resistance in complex systems.

Accepting the circular-causal feedback nature of complex, dynamic management systems forces us to recognize some weaknesses in our own abilities to predict the behaviour of the systems we hope to understand and influence. Our rationality is bounded not merely because there are limits to how much information we can deal with, or because there are unanticipated consequences following from our decisions, but also because we find it difficult to reason in circular causal settings. We are good at one-way logic, but poor at circular logic once it reaches a minimal level of complexity. The papers in this collection provide endless examples.

We are particularly poor at appreciating the role of feedback structure in the dynamics we experience in the systems we strive to manage. Since management decisions have a hand in shaping the conditions management must respond to in the future and since the decision-making process is ongoing, we know that management policies play a part in shaping the day-to-day, year-to-year, decade-to-decade *dynamics* of the systems we are striving to manage. The possibility exists that management policies and decisions may actually contribute to *creating* the dynamic problems that they are intended to solve. The chapters in this collection show that such a possibility actually happens in complex dynamic management systems.

The evidence suggests that we need help in systems thinking. Simulation models incorporating accurate circular causal structure and information feedback can provide laboratory settings for experimenting with policy design in complex management systems. Because the system can be simulated repeatedly in a short time, as if running through years or decades of system experience in minutes, experimenters can learn about the actual dynamic consequences of policy initiatives implemented in the simulated world. With care, extensive testing, comparison to real system data and structure, and much reflection, users of simulation models can gain confidence about policy initiatives in the real system they hope to improve.

There is much to be said about the design of models that can truly help and the testing that can build real confidence in model-based analyses; the reader will find both among the pages of this volume and the references the various authors cite.

Overview

The essays selected to appear in *Modelling for Management* are among the finest examples of recent work in dynamic modelling and model-based policy analysis. A number of them have earned their authors formal recognition (noted where they appear) in the form of awards for excellence from the System Dynamics Society and The Institute of Management Sciences. In the spirit of the commendable collection by Roberts,[12] the purpose of this volume is to show exemplary model-based work in a range of application areas, revealing a diversity of insights about complex dynamic management problems and opening avenues for further work supporting systems thinking in management planning, policy analysis and decision making.

Part I – Modelling Perspectives – contains papers that frame the perspectives and methods used in the rest of the book. The authors detail here the extent of the world of computer simulation modelling for management and then focus more closely on systems thinking and system dynamics modelling. Chapters 2 and 3 describe the essentials in philosophy and method of the system dynamics approach; Chapter 3 also contains an extensive bibliography for further study. Chapter 5 is a richly documented exposition of the barriers to learning in and about complex dynamic systems. It presents a carefully reasoned and well-grounded argument that simulation is necessary for learning when the systems we seek to understand are those that we ourselves live in and manage.

Part II – Systems Thinking and Dynamic Decision Making – documents the difficulties people encounter in making decisions in dynamic settings and captures a number of model-based insights in systems thinking archetypes. The dynamic decision-making research reported on here is carried out using sophisticated computer-based games – serious games. Two of the Jay Wright Forrester awards of the System Dynamics Society were given for breakthroughs that came from casting dynamic models in the form of serious games to create accessible computer-based learning environments and research platforms.

Parts III and IV address management problems in the private and public sectors. Part III – Corporate Policy and Management – investigates problems of corporate growth and collapse, strategic planning, operations management, project management, personnel and organizational learning. Part IV – Public Policy and Management (in Volume II) – includes studies on energy, the environment, third world development, welfare reform, health, and education finance.

Part V – Methods of Modelling *with* Management (Volume II) – addresses model conceptualization, the modelling process, modelling with groups, validation and reporting the results. An important idea here is that much of the learning about model-based analyses of complex systems comes from the modelling process itself. Involving management in that process – modelling *with* management – is often crucial for obtaining maximum understanding and implementation of model-supported insights.

A brief introduction to each major part of Volume I overviews its contents in more detail.

Notes

1 See e.g. S. Mizuno (1988), *Management for Quality Improvement: The Seven New QC Tools*, and M. Perigord (1990), *Achieving Total Quality Management: A Program for Action*, both published by Productivity Press in Portland (Oregon).
2 D.E. Osborne and T. Gaebler (1992), *Reinventing Government: How the Entrepreneurial Spirit is Transforming the Public Sector*, Reading, MA: Addison-Wesley.
3 P.B. Checkland (1981), *Systems Thinking, Systems Practice*, Chichester: Wiley; P.B. Checkland and J. Scholes (1990), *Soft Systems Methodology in Action*, Chichester: Wiley.

4   P.M. Senge (1990), *The Fifth Discipline: The Art and Practice of the Learning Organization*, New York: Doubleday/Currency.
5   D.H. Kim (ed.), *The Systems Thinker*, Cambridge, MA: Pegasus Communications.
6   See also C. Argyris and D. Schön (1978), *Organizational Learning: A Theory-in-Action Perspective*, Reading, MA: Addison-Wesley.
7   G.D. Brewer and P. deLeon (1983), *The Foundations of Policy Analysis*, Homewood, Illinois: Dorsey Press.
8   J.W. Forrester (1961), *Industrial Dynamics*, Cambridge, MA: MIT Press. Reprinted by Productivity Press, Portland (Oregon).
9   J.W. Forrester (1958), 'Industrial Dynamics: A Major Breakthrough for Decision Makers', *Harvard Business Review*, **36** (4), 37–66.
10 G.P. Richardson (1991), *Feedback Thought in Social Science and Systems Theory*, Philadelphia: University of Pennsylvania Press.
11 J.W. Forrester (1968), 'Market Growth as Influenced by Capital Investment', *Industrial Management Review*, **9** (2), 83–105.
12 E.B. Roberts (ed.) (1978), *Managerial Applications of System Dynamics*, Cambridge, MA: Productivity Press.

Part I
Modelling Perspectives

Modelling

The essays in this section frame the perspectives and methods used in the rest of this volume. We begin with John Sterman's overview of the world of computer simulation modelling, appropriately titled 'A Skeptic's Guide'. He begins with the observation that the use of models is inevitable; if we do not employ formal models we must be using mental models. After emphasizing the importance of purpose in modelling, he explores the strengths and weaknesses of three generic types of computer models: optimization models, simulation models and econometric models (as a type of simulation). The chapter ends with an illuminating checklist for the model consumer and an exhortation to view modelling as a *process* striving to aid human thought and foresight – fundamentally an educational rather than a predictive process.

System Dynamics Modelling

Barry Richmond, creator of the breakthrough iconographic modelling software STELLA and iThink,[1] then offers his view of the components of systems thinking. He identifies seven types which provide the foundation for simulation modelling from the system dynamics perspective: dynamic thinking, closed-loop thinking, generic thinking, structural thinking, operational thinking, continuum thinking and scientific thinking. Originally published in a special issue of the *System Dynamics Review* on education, Chapter 2 emphasizes teaching and learning. However, the framework of patterns of thought he presents applies universally and provides a smooth pathway into the system dynamics approach employed throughout this volume.

'System Dynamics: Simulation for Policy Analysis from a Feedback Perspective' then outlines the system dynamics approach. While touching on the structure of model equations and software environments, Richardson's emphasis is on the conceptual elements and phases of the approach: feedback thinking, nonlinearity and loop dominance, the field's characteristic 'endogenous point of view' and the particular conceptual distance from viewer to system for which the approach is most powerful. Various kinds of diagrams are illustrated for conceptualizing both stock-and-flow/feedback structure and the policy structure of complex systems. Accumulated modelling heuristics, principles of systems and generic simulation-based insights are overviewed. Chapter 3 ends with a sketch of a policy study (given in full in Chapter 12, Part IV of Volume II) and a rich bibliography.

Modelling as a Tool for Strategy and Learning

John Morecroft's 'Strategy Support Models' carries these ideas into the realm of strategy development. Chapter 4 is notable for the completeness of its overview of a strategy support modelling effort – from starting the project, through exposing policy structure (using Morecroft's innovative policy structure diagrams), to the use of the model in a dialectic process with management, and finally to an assessment of the impact of the model and the modelling process.

The last full article in Part I is Sterman's richly documented argument that learning in and about complex systems cannot be accomplished without simulation. Drawing on a number of research streams, he identifies nine barriers to learning about dynamics systems, outlines the requirements for successful learning processes, and includes an analysis of the promises and pitfalls of using simulated 'virtual worlds'. Extremely well-grounded and closely argued, Chapter 5 can be viewed as an apologia for the kinds of simulation-based efforts to aid management that are contained in the rest of this volume.

Part I ends with a punctuation mark: '14 "Obvious Truths"' is drawn from Jay W. Forrester's 1960 Distinguished Lecture of the Foundation for Instrumentation, Education, and Research. This little excerpt, reprinted in 1987 by the *System Dynamics Review*, is a list of tendencies that Forrester considered were misleading management science efforts. The list can be read as criticism, but its original intent, and its intent here, is to sketch by implication the opposite tendencies Forrester hoped to achieve in the system dynamics field he founded. Of particular significance for the studies in this volume are Forrester's emphases on nonlinearity, model purpose, the wide sources of knowledge appropriate for model building, the value of precision (unambiguity) and the subtle but insightful distinction between decisions and policies. Policies – 'the rules by which information sources are converted in a continuous flow of decisions' – are the principal focus of a system dynamics study.

Note

1. High Performance Systems, Hanover, NH.

14. A Skeptic's Guide to Computer Models

This chapter was written by Dr. John D. Sterman, Associate Professor, Sloan School of Management, Massachusetts Institute of Technology, 50 Memorial Drive, Cambridge, MA 02139, USA. Copyright © John D. Sterman, 1988. An earlier version of this paper also appeared in Foresight and National Decisions: The Horseman and the Bureaucrat *(Grant 1988). It is printed here with permission. The author wishes to acknowledge that many of the ideas expressed here emerged from discussions with or were first formulated by, among others, Jay Forrester, George Richardson, Peter Senge, and especially Donella Meadows, whose book* Groping in the Dark *(Meadows, Richardson, and Bruckmann 1982), was particularly helpful.*

> But Mousie, thou art no they lane
> In proving foresight may be vain;
> The best-laid schemes o' mice an' men
>   Gang aft a-gley,
> An lea'e us nought but grief an' pain,
>   For promis'd joy!
>   Robert Burns, "To a Mouse"

The Inevitability of Using Models

Computer modeling of social and economic systems is only about three decades old. Yet in that time, computer models have been used to analyze everything from inventory management in corporations to the performance of national economies, from the optimal distribution of fire stations in New York City to the interplay of global population, resources, food, and pollution. Certain computer models, such as *The Limits to Growth* (Meadows et al. 1972), have been front page news. In the U.S., some have been the subject of numerous congressional hearings and have influenced the fate of legislation. Computer modeling has become an important industry, generating hundreds of millions of dollars of revenues annually.

As computers have become faster, cheaper, and more widely available, computer models have become commonplace in forecasting and public policy analysis, especially in economics, energy and resources, demographics, and other crucial areas. As computers continue to proliferate, more and more policy debates—both in government and the private sector—will involve the results of models. Though not all of us are going to be model builders, we all are becoming model consumers, regardless of whether we know it (or like it). The ability to understand and evaluate computer models is fast becoming a prerequisite for the policymaker, legislator, lobbyist, and citizen alike.

During our lives, each of us will be faced with the result of models and will have to make judgments about their relevance and validity. Most people, unfortunately, cannot make these decisions in an intelligent and informed manner, since for them computer models are *black boxes*—devices that operate in completely mysterious ways. Because computer models are so poorly understood by most people, it is easy for them to be misused, accidentally or intentionally. Thus there have been many cases in which computer models have been used to justify decisions already made and actions already taken, to provide a scapegoat when a forecast turned out wrong, or to lend specious authority to an argument.

If these misuses are to stop and if modeling is to become a rational tool of the general public, rather than remaining the special magic of a technical priesthood, a basic understanding of models must become more widespread. This paper takes a step toward this goal by offering model consumers a peek inside the black boxes. The computer models it describes are the kinds used in foresight and policy analysis (rather than physical system models such as NASA uses to test the space shuttle). The characteristics and capabilities of the models, their advantages and disadvantages, uses and misuses are all addressed. The fundamental assumptions of the major modeling techniques are discussed, as is the appropriateness of these techniques for foresight and policy analysis. Consideration is also given to the crucial questions a model user should ask when evaluating the appropriateness and validity of a model.

Mental and Computer Models

Fortunately, everyone is already familiar with models. People use models—mental models—every day. Our decisions and actions are based not on the real world, but on our mental images of that world, of the relationships among its parts, and of the influence our actions have on it.

Mental models have some powerful advantages. A mental model is flexible; it can take into account a wider range of information than just numerical data; it can be adapted to new situations and be modified as new information becomes available. Mental models are the filters through which we interpret our experiences, evaluate plans, and choose among possible courses of action. The great systems of philosophy, politics, and literature are, in a sense, mental models.

But mental models have their drawbacks also. They are not easily understood by others; interpretations of them differ. The assumptions on which they are based are usually difficult to examine, so ambiguities and contradictions within them can go undetected, unchallenged, and unresolved.

That we have trouble grasping other peoples' mental models may seem natural. More surprising, we are not very good at constructing and understanding our own mental models—or using them for decision making. Psychologists have shown that we can take only a few factors into account in making decisions (Hogarth 1980; Kahneman, Slovic, and Tversky 1982). In other words, the mental models we use to make decisions are usually extremely simple. Often these models are also flawed, since we frequently make errors in deducing the consequences of the assumptions on which they are based.

Our failure to use rational mental models in our decision making has been well demonstrated by research on the behavior of people in organizations (e.g., families, businesses, the government). This research shows that decisions are not made by rational consideration of objectives, options, and consequences. Instead, they often are made by rote, using standard operating procedures that evolve out of tradition and adjust only slowly to changing conditions (Simon 1947, 1979). These procedures are determined by the role of the decision makers within the organization, the amount of time they have to make decisions, and the information available to them.

But the individual perspectives of the decision makers may be parochial, the time they have to weigh alternatives insufficient, and the information available to them dated, biased, or incomplete. Furthermore, their decisions can be strongly influenced by authority relations, organizational context, peer pressure, cultural perspective, and selfish motives. Psychologists and organizational observers have identified dozens of different biases that creep into human decision making because of cognitive limitations and organizational pressures (Hogarth 1980; Kahneman, Slovic, and Tversky 1982). As a result, many decisions turn out to be incorrect; choosing the best course of action is just too complicated and difficult a puzzle.

Hamlet exclaims (perhaps ironically) "What a piece of work is a man, how noble in reason, how infinite in faculties...!" But it seems that we, like Hamlet himself, are simply not capable of making error-free decisions that are based on rational models and are uninfluenced by societal and emotional pressures.

Enter the computer model. In theory, computer models offer improvements over mental models in several respects:

> They are explicit; their assumptions are stated in the written documentation and open to all for review.
>
> They infallibly compute the logical consequences of the modeler's assumptions.
>
> They are comprehensive and able to interrelate many factors simultaneously.

A computer model that actually has these characteristics has powerful advantages over a mental model. In practice, however, computer models are often less than ideal:

> They are so poorly documented and complex that no one can examine their assumptions. They are black boxes.

They are so complicated that the user has no confidence in the consistency or correctness of the assumptions.

They are unable to deal with relationships and factors that are difficult to quantify, for which numerical data do not exist, or that lie outside the expertise of the specialists who built the model.

Because of these possible flaws, computer models need to be examined carefully by potential users. But on what basis should models be judged? How does one know whether a model is well or badly designed, whether its results will be valid or not? How can a prospective user decide whether a type of modeling or a specific model is suitable for the problem at hand? How can misuses of models be recognized and prevented? There is no single comprehensive answer, but some useful guidelines are given on the following pages.

The Importance of Purpose

A model must have a clear purpose, and that purpose should be to solve a particular problem. A clear purpose is the single most important ingredient for a successful modeling study. Of course, a model with a clear purpose can still be incorrect, overly large, or difficult to understand. But a clear purpose allows model users to ask questions that reveal whether a model is useful for solving the problem under consideration.

Beware the analyst who proposes to model an entire social or economic system rather than a problem. Every model is a representation of a system—a group of functionally interrelated elements forming a complex whole. But for the model to be useful, it must address a specific problem and must simplify rather than attempting to mirror in detail an entire system.

What is the difference? A model designed to understand how the business cycle can be stabilized is a model of a problem. It deals with a part of the overall economic system. A model designed to understand how the economy can make a smooth transition from oil to alternative energy sources is also a model of a problem; it too addresses only a limited system within the larger economy. A model that claims to be a representation of the entire economy is a model of a whole system. Why does it matter? The usefulness of models lies in the fact that they simplify reality, putting it into a form that we can comprehend. But a truly comprehensive model of a complete system would be just as complex as that system and just as inscrutable. The map is not the territory—and a map as detailed as the territory would be of no use (as well as being hard to fold).

The art of model building is knowing what to cut out, and the purpose of the model acts as the logical knife. It provides the criterion about what will be cut, so that only the essential features necessary to fulfill the purpose are left. In the example above, since the purpose of the comprehensive model would be to represent the entire economic system, few factors could be excluded. In order to answer all questions about the economy, the model would have to include an immense range of long-term and short-term variables. Because of its size, its underlying assumptions would be difficult to examine. The model builders—not to mention the intended consumers—would probably not understand its behavior, and its validity would be largely a matter of faith.

A model designed to examine just the business cycle or the energy transition would be much smaller, since it would be limited to those factors believed to be relevant to the question at hand. For example, the business cycle model need not include long-term trends in population growth and resource depletion. The energy transition model could exclude short-term changes related to interest, employment, and inventories. The resulting models would be simple enough so that their assumptions could be examined. The relation of these assumptions to the most important theories regarding the business cycle and resource economics could then be assessed to determine how useful the models were for their intended purposes.

Two Kinds of Models: Optimization Versus Simulation

There are many types of models, and they can be classified in many ways. Models can be static or dynamic, mathematical or physical, stochastic or deterministic. One of the most useful classifications, however, divides models into those that optimize versus those that simulate. The distinction between optimization and simulation models is particularly important since these types of models are suited for fundamentally different purposes.

Optimization

The Oxford English Dictionary defines *optimize* as "to make the best of most of; to develop to the utmost." The output of an optimization model is a statement of the best way to accomplish some goal. Optimization models do not tell you what will happen in a certain situation. Instead they tell you what to do in order to make the best of the situation; they are normative or prescriptive models.

Let us take two examples. A nutritionist would like to know how to design meals that fulfill certain dietary requirements but cost as little as possible. A salesperson must visit certain cities and would like to know how to make the trip as quickly as possible, taking into account the available flights between the cities. Rather than relying on trial and error, the nutritionist and the salesperson could use optimization models to determine the best solutions to these problems.

An optimization model typically includes three parts. The *objective function* specifies the goal or objective. For the nutritionist, the objective is to minimize the cost of the meals. For the salesperson, it is to minimize the time spent on the trip. The *decision variables* are the choices to be made. In our examples, these would be the food to serve at each meal and the order in which to visit the cities. The *constraints* restrict the choices of the decision variables to those that are acceptable and possible. In the diet problem, one constraint would specify that daily consumption of each nutrient must equal or exceed the minimum requirement. Another might restrict the number of times a particular food is served during each week. The constraints in the travel problem would specify that each city must be visited at least once and would restrict the selection of routes to actually available connections.

An optimization model takes as inputs these three pieces of information—the goals to be met, the choices to be made, and the constraints to be satisfied. It yields as its output the best solution, i.e., the optimal decisions given the assumptions of the model. In the case of our examples, the models would provide the best set of menus and the most efficient itinerary.

Limitations of Optimization

Many optimization models have a variety of limitations and problems that a potential user should bear in mind. These problems are: difficulties with the specification of the objective function, unrealistic linearity, lack of feedback, and lack of dynamics.

Specification of the Objective Function: Whose Values? The first difficulty with optimization models is the problem of specifying the objective function, the goal that the model user is trying to reach. In our earlier examples, it was fairly easy to identify the objective functions of the nutritionist and the salesperson, but what would be the objective function for the mayor of New York? To provide adequate city services for minimal taxes? To encourage the arts? To improve traffic conditions? The answer depends, of course, on the perspective of the person you ask.

The objective function embodies values and preferences, but which values, whose preferences? How can intangibles be incorporated into the objective function? How can the conflicting goals of various groups be identified and balanced? These are hard questions, but they are not insurmountable. Intangibles often can be quantified, at least roughly, by breaking them into measurable components. For example, the quality of life in a city might be represented as depending on the rate of unemployment, air pollution levels, crime rate, and so forth. There are also techniques available for extracting information about preferences from interviews and other impressionistic data. Just the attempt to make values explicit is a worthwhile exercise in any study and may have enormous value for the clients of a modeling project.

It is important that potential users keep in mind the question of values when they examine optimization models. The objective function and the constraints should always be scrutinized to determine what values they embody, both explicitly and by omission. Imagine that a government employee, given responsibility for the placement of sewage treatment plants along a river, decides to use an optimization model in making the decision. The model has as its objective function the cheapest arrangement of plants; a constraint specifies that the arrangement must result in water quality standards being met. It would be important for the user to ask how the model takes into account the impacts the plants will have on fishing, recreation, wild species, and development potential in the areas where they are placed. Unless these considerations are explicitly incorporated into the model, they are implicitly held to be of no value.

Linearity. Another problem, and one that can seriously undermine the verisimilitude of optimization models, is their linearity. Because a typical optimization problem is very complex, involving hundreds or thousands of variables and constraints, the mathematical problem of finding the optimum is extremely difficult. To render such problems tractable, modelers commonly introduce a number of simplifications. Among these is the assumption that the relationships in the system are linear. In fact, the most popular optimization technique, linear programming, requires that the objective function and all constraints be linear.

Linearity is mathematically convenient, but in reality it is almost always invalid. Consider, for example, a model of a firm's inventory distribution policies. The model contains a specific relationship between inventory and shipments—if the inventory of goods in the warehouse is 10 percent below normal, shipment may be reduced by, say, 2 percent since certain items will be out of stock. If the model requires this relationship to be linear, then a 20 percent shortfall will reduce shipments by 4 percent, a 30 percent shortfall by 6 percent, and so on. And when the shortfall is 100 percent? According to the model, shipments will still be 80 percent of normal. But obviously, when the warehouse is empty, no shipments are possible. The linear relationship within the model leads to an absurdity.

The warehouse model may seem trivial, but the importance of non-linearity is well demonstrated by the sorry fate of the passenger pigeon, *Ectopistes migratorius*. When Europeans first colonized North America, passenger pigeons were extremely abundant. Huge flocks of the migrating birds would darken the skies for days. They often caused damage to crops and were hunted both as a pest and as food. For years, hunting had little apparent impact on the population; the prolific birds seemed to reproduce fast enough to offset most losses. Then the number of pigeons began to decline—slowly at first, then rapidly. By 1914, the passenger pigeon was extinct.

The disappearance of the passenger pigeons resulted from the non-linear relationship between their population density and their fertility. In large flocks they could reproduce at high rates, but in smaller flocks their fertility dropped precipitously. Thus, when hunting pressure was great enough to reduce the size of a flock somewhat, the fertility in that flock also fell. The lower fertility lead to a further decrease in the population size, and the lower population density resulted in yet lower birth rates, and so forth, in a vicious cycle.

Unfortunately, the vast majority of optimizations models assume that the world is linear. There are, however, techniques available for solving certain non-linear optimization problems, and research is continuing.

Lack of Feedback. Complex systems in the real world are highly interconnected, having a high degree of feedback among sectors. The results of decisions feed back through physical, economic, and social channels to alter the conditions on which the decisions were originally made. Some models do not reflect this reality, however. Consider an optimization model that computes the best size of sewage treatment plants to build in an area. The model will probably assume that the amount of sewage needing treatment will remain the same, or that it will grow at a certain rate. But if water quality improves because of sewage treatment, the area will become more attractive and development will increase, ultimately leading to a sewage load greater than expected.

Models that ignore feedback effects must rely on *exogenous variables* and are said to have a narrow boundary. Exogenous variables are ones that influence other variables in the model but are not calculated by the model. They are simply given by a set of numerical values over time, and they do not change in response to feedback. The values of exogenous variables may come from other models but are most likely the product of an unexaminable mental model. The *endogenous variables*, on the other hand, are calculated by the model itself. They are the variables explained by the structure of the model, the ones for which the modeler has an explicit theory, the ones that respond to feedback.

Ignoring feedback can result in policies that generate unanticipated side effects or are diluted, delayed, or defeated by the system (Meadows 1982). An example is the construction of freeways in the 1950s and 1960s to alleviate traffic congestion in major U.S. cities. In Boston it used to take half an hour to drive from the city neighborhood of Dorchester to the downtown area, a journey of only a few miles. Then a limited access highway network was built around the city, and travel time between Dorchester and downtown dropped substantially.

But there's more to the story. Highway construction led to changes that fed back into the system, causing unexpected side effects. Due to the reduction in traffic congestion and commuting time, living in outlying communities became a more attractive option. Farmland was turned into housing developments or paved over to provide yet more roads. The population of the suburbs soared, as people moved out of the center city. Many city stores followed their customers or were squeezed out by competition from the new suburban shopping malls. The inner city began to decay, but many people still worked in the downtown area—and they got there via the new highways. The result? Boston has more congestion and air pollution than before the highways were constructed, and the rush-hour journey from Dorchester to downtown takes half an hour, again.

In theory, feedback can be incorporated into optimization models, but the resulting complexity and non-linearity usually render the problem insoluble. Many optimization models therefore ignore most feedback effects. Potential users should be aware of this when they look at a model. They should ask to what degree important feedbacks have been excluded and how those exclusions might alter the assumptions and invalidate the results of the model.

Lack of Dynamics. Many optimization models are static. They determine the optimal solution for a particular moment in time without regard for how the optimal state is reached or how the system will evolve in the future. An example is the linear programming model constructed in the late 1970s by the U.S. Forest Service, with the objective of optimizing the use of government lands. The model was enormous, with thousands of decision variables and tens of thousands of constraints, and it took months just to correct the typographical errors in the model's huge database. When the completed model was finally run, finding the solution required full use of a mainframe computer for days.

Despite the gigantic effort, the model prescribed the optimal use of forest resources for only a single moment in time. It did not take into account how harvesting a given area would affect its future ecological development. It did not consider how land-use needs or lumber prices might change in the future. It did not examine how long it would take for new trees to grow to maturity in the harvested areas, or what the economic and recreational value of the areas would be during the regrowth period. The model just provided the optimal decisions for a single year, ignoring the fact that those decisions would continue to influence the development of forest resources for decades.

Not all optimization models are static. The MARKAL model, for example, is a large linear programming model designed to determine the optimal choice of energy technologies. Developed at the Brookhaven National Laboratory in the U.S., the model produces as its output the best (least-cost) mix of coal, oil, gas, and other energy sources well into the next century. It requires various exogenous inputs, such as energy demands, future fuel prices, and construction and operating costs of different energy technologies. (Note that the model ignores feedbacks from energy supply to prices and demand.) The model is dynamic in the sense that it produces a "snapshot" of the optimal state of the system at five-year intervals.

The Brookhaven model is not completely dynamic, however, because it ignores delays. It assumes that people, seeing what the optimal mix is for some future year, begin planning far enough in advance so that this mix can actually be used. Thus the model does not, for example, incorporate construction delays for energy production facilities. In reality, of course, it takes time—often much longer than five years—to build power plants, invent new technologies, build equipment, develop waste management techniques, and find and transport necessary raw materials.

Indeed, delays are pervasive in the real world. The delays found in complex systems are especially important because they are a major source of system instability. The lag time required to carry out a decision or to perceive its effects may cause overreaction or may prevent timely intervention. Acid rain provides a good example. Although there is already evidence that damage to the forests of New England, the Appalachians, and Bavaria is caused by acid rain, many scientists suspect it will take years to determine exactly how acid rain is formed and how it affects the forests. Until scientific and then political consensus emerges, legislative action to curb pollution is not likely to be strong. Pollution control programs, once passed, will take years to implement. Existing power plants and other pollution sources will continue to operate for their functional lifetimes, which are measured in decades. It will require even longer to change settlement patterns and lifestyles dependent on the automobile. By the time sulfur and nitrogen oxide emissions are sufficiently reduced, it may be too late for the forests.

Delays are a crucial component of the dynamic behavior of systems, but—like non-linearity—they are difficult to incorporate into optimization models. A common simplification is to assume that all delays in the model are of the same fixed length. The results of such models are of questionable value. Policymakers who use them in an effort to find an optimal course of action may discover, like the proverbial American tourist on the back roads of Maine, that "you can't get there from here."

When To Use Optimization

Despite the limitations discussed above, optimization techniques can be extremely useful. But they must be used for the proper problems. Optimization has substantially improved the quality of decisions in many areas, including computer design, airline scheduling, factory siting, and oil refinery operation. Whenever the problem to be solved is one of choosing the best from among a well-defined set of alternatives, optimization should be considered. If the meaning of *best* is also well defined, and if the system to be optimized is relatively static and free of feedback, optimization may well be the best technique to use. Unfortunately, these latter conditions are rarely true for the social, economic, and ecological systems that are frequently of concern to decision makers.

Look out for optimization models that purport to forecast actual behavior. The output of an optimization model is a statement of the best way to accomplish a goal. To interpret the results as a prediction of actual behavior is to assume that people in the real system will in fact make the optimal choices. It is one thing to say, "in order to maximize profits, people should make the following decisions," and quite another to say "people will succeed in maximizing profits, because they will make the following decisions." The former is a prescriptive statement of what to do, the latter a descriptive statement of what will actually happen.

Optimization models are valid for making prescriptive statements. They are valid for forecasting only if people do in fact optimize, do make the best possible decisions. It may seem reasonable to expect people to behave optimally—after all, wouldn't it be irrational to take second best when you could have the best? But the evidence on this score is conclusive: real people do not behave like optimization models. As discussed above, we humans make decisions with simple and incomplete mental models, models that are often based on faulty assumptions or that lead erroneously from sound assumptions to flawed solutions. As Herbert Simon puts it,

> The capacity of the human mind for formulating and solving complex problems is very small compared with the size of the problem whose solution is required for objectively rational behavior in the real world or even for a reasonable approximation to such objective rationality. (Simon 1957, p. 198)

Optimization models augment the limited capacity of the human mind to determine the objectively rational course of action. It should be remembered, however, that even optimization models must make simplifying assumptions in order to be tractable, so the most we can hope from them is an approximation of how people ought to behave. To model how people actually behave requires a very different set of modeling techniques, which will be discussed now.

Simulation

The Latin verb *simulare* means to imitate or mimic. The purpose of a simulation model is to mimic the real system so that its behavior can be studied. The model is a laboratory replica of the real system, a *microworld* (Morecroft 1988). By creating a representation of the system in the laboratory, a modeler can perform experiments that are impossible, unethical, or prohibitively expensive in the real world.

Simulations of physical systems are commonplace and range from wind tunnel tests of aircraft design to simulation of weather patterns and the depletion of oil reserves. Economists and social scientists also have used simulation to understand how energy prices affect the economy, how corporations mature, how cities evolve and respond to urban renewal policies, and how population growth interacts with food supply, resources, and the environment. There are many different simulation techniques, including stochastic modeling, system dynamics, discrete simulation, and role-playing games. Despite the differences among them, all simulation techniques share a common approach to modeling.

Optimization models are prescriptive, but simulation models are descriptive. A simulation model does not calculate what should be done to reach a particular goal, but clarifies what would happen in a given situation. The purpose of simulations may be *foresight* (predicting how systems might behave in the future under assumed conditions) or *policy design* (designing new decision-making strategies or organizational structures and evaluating their effects on the behavior of the system).

In other words, simulation models are "what if" tools. Often such "what if" information is more important than knowledge of the optimal decision. For example, during the 1978 debate in the U.S. over natural gas deregulation, President Carter's original proposal was modified dozens of times by Congress before a final compromise was passed. During the congressional debate, the Department of Energy evaluated each version of the bill using a system dynamics model (Department of Energy 1979). The model did not indicate what ought to be done to maximize the economic benefits of natural gas to the nation. Congress already had its own ideas on that score. But by providing an assessment of how each proposal would affect gas prices, supplies, and demands, the model generated ammunition that the Carter administration could use in lobbying for its proposals.

Every simulation model has two main components. First it must include a representation of the physical world relevant to the problem under study. Consider for example a model that was built for the purpose of understanding why America's large cities have continued to decay despite massive amounts of aid and numerous renewal programs (Forrester 1969). The model had to include a representation of the physical components of the city—the size and quality of the infrastructure, including the stock of housing and commercial structures; the attributes of the population, such as its size and composition and the mix of skills and incomes among the people; flows (of people, materials, money, etc.) into and out of the city; and other factors that characterize the physical and institutional setting.

How much detail a model requires about the physical structure of the system will, of course, depend on the specific problem being addressed. The urban model mentioned above required only an aggregate representation of the features common to large American cities. On the other hand, a model designed to improve the location and deployment of fire fighting resources in New York City had to include a detailed representation of the streets and traffic patterns (Greenberger, Crenson, and Crissey 1976).

In addition to reflecting the physical structure of the system, a simulation model must portray the behavior of the actors in the system. In this context, behavior means the way in which people respond to different situations, *how* they make decisions. The behavioral component is put into the model in the form of decision-making rules, which are determined by direct observation of the actual decision-making procedures in the system.

Given the physical structure of the system and the decision-making rules, the simulation model then plays the role of the decision makers, mimicking their decisions. In the model, as in the real world, the nature and quality of the information available to decision makers will depend on the state of the system. The output of the model will be a description of expected decisions. The validity of the model's assumptions can be checked by comparing the output with the decisions made in the real system.

An example is provided by the pioneering simulation study of corporate behavior carried out by Cyert and March (1963). Their field research showed that department stores used a very simple decision rule to determine the floor price of goods. That rule was basically to mark up the wholesale cost of the items by a fixed percentage, with the value of the markup determined by tradition. They also noted, however, that through time the traditional markup adjusted very slowly, bringing it closer to the actual markup realized on goods when they were sold. The actual markup could vary from the normal markup as the result of several other decision rules: When excess inventory piled up on the shelves, a sale was held and the price was gradually reduced until the goods were sold; if sales goals were exceeded, prices were boosted. Prices were also adjusted toward those of competitors.

Cyert and March built a simulation model of the pricing system, basing it on these decision-making rules. The output of the model was a description of expected prices for goods. When this output was compared with real store data, it was found that the model reproduced quite well the actual pricing decisions of the floor managers.

Limitations of Simulation
Any model is only as good as its assumptions. In the case of simulation models, the assumptions consist of the descriptions of the physical system and the decision rules. Adequately representing the physical system is usually not a problem; the physical environment can be portrayed with whatever detail and accuracy is needed for the model purpose. Also, simulation models can easily incorporate feedback effects, non-linearities, and dynamics; they are not rigidly determined in their structure by mathematical limitations as optimization models often are. Indeed, one of the main uses of simulation is to identify how feedback, non-linearity, and delays interact to produce troubling dynamics that persistently resist solution. (For examples see Sterman 1985, Morecroft 1983, and Forrester 1969.)

Simulation models do have their weak points, however. Most problems occur in the description of the decision rules, the quantification of soft variables, and the choice of the model boundary.

Accuracy of the Decision Rules. The description of the decision rules is one potential trouble spot in a simulation model. The model must accurately represent how the actors in the system make their decisions, even if their decision rules are less than optimal. The model should respond to change in the same way the real actors would. But it will do this only if the model's assumptions faithfully describe the decision rules that are used under different circumstances. The model therefore must reflect the actual decision-making strategies used by the people in the system being modeled, including the limitations and errors of those strategies.

Unfortunately, discovering decision rules is often difficult. They cannot be determined from aggregate statistical data, but must be investigated first hand. Primary data on the behavior of the actors can be acquired through observation of actual decision making in the field, that is, in the boardroom, on the factory floor, along the sales route, in the household. The modeler must discover what information is available to each actor, examine the timeliness and accuracy of that information, and infer how it is processed to yield a decision. Modelers often require the skills of the anthropologist and the ethnographer. One can also learn about decision making through laboratory experiments in which managers operate simulated corporations (Sterman 1989). The best simulation modeling draws on extensive knowledge of decision making that has been developed in many disciplines, including psychology, sociology, and behavioral science.

Soft Variables. The majority of data are soft variables. That is, most of what we know about the world is descriptive, qualitative, difficult to quantify, and has never been recorded. Such information is crucial for understanding and modeling complex systems. Yet in describing decision making, some modelers limit themselves to hard variables, ones that can be measured directly and can be expressed as numerical data. They may defend the rejection of soft variables as being more scientific than "making up" the values of parameters and relationships for which no numerical data are available. How, they ask, can the accuracy of estimates about soft variables be tested? How can statistical tests be performed without numerical data?

Actually, there are no limitations on the inclusion of soft variables in models, and many simulation models do include them. After all, the point of simulation models is to portray decision making as it really is, and soft variables—including intangibles such as desires, product quality, reputation, expectations, and optimism—are often of critical importance in decision making. Imagine, for example, trying to run a school, factory, or city solely on the basis of the available numerical data. Without qualitative knowledge about factors such as operating procedures, organizational structure, political subtleties, and individual motivations, the result would be chaos. Leaving such variables out of models just because of a lack of hard numerical data is certainly less "scientific" than including them and making reasonable estimates of their values. Ignoring a relationship implies that it has a value of zero—probably the only value known to be wrong! (Forrester 1980)

Of course, all relationships and parameters in models, whether based on soft or hard variables, are imprecise and uncertain to some degree. Reasonable people may disagree as to the importance of different factors. Modelers must therefore perform sensitivity analysis to consider how their conclusions might change if other plausible assumptions were made. Sensitivity analysis should not be restricted to uncertainty in parameter values, but should also consider the sensitivity of conclusions to alternative structural assumptions and choices of model boundary.

Sensitivity analysis is no less a responsibility for those modelers who ignore soft variables. Apparently hard data such as economic and demographic statistics are often subject to large measurement errors, biases, distortions, and revisions. Unfortunately, sensitivity analysis is not performed or reported often enough. Many modelers have been embarrassed when third parties, attempting to replicate the results of a model, have found that reasonable alternative assumptions produce radically different conclusions. (See the discussion below of the experiment conducted by the Joint Economic Committee with three leading econometric models.)

Model Boundary. The definition of a reasonable model boundary is another challenge for the builders of simulation models. Which factors will be exogenous, which will be endogenous? What feedbacks will be incorporated into the model? In theory, one of the great strengths of simulation models is the capacity to reflect the important feedback relationships that shape the behavior of the system and its response to policies. In practice, however, many simulation models have very narrow boundaries. They ignore factors outside the expertise of the model builder or the interests of the sponsor, and in doing so they exclude important feedbacks.

The consequences of omitting feedback can be serious. An excellent example is provided by the Project Independence Evaluation System (PIES) model, used in the 1970s by the U.S. Federal Energy Administration and later by the U.S. Department of Energy. As described by the FEA, the purpose of the model was to evaluate different energy strategies according to these criteria: their impact on the development of alternative energy sources, their impact on economic growth, inflation, and unemployment; their regional and social impacts; their vulnerability to import disruptions; and their environmental effects (Federal Energy Administration 1974, p. 1).

Surprisingly, considering the stated purpose, the PIES model treated the economy as exogenous. The economy—including economic growth, interest rates, inflation, world oil prices, and the costs of unconventional fuels—was completely unaffected by the U.S. domestic energy situation—including prices, policies, and production. The way the model was constructed, even a full embargo of imported oil or a doubling of oil prices would have no impact on the economy.

Its exogenous treatment of the economy made the PIES model inherently contradictory. The model showed that the investment needs of the energy sector would increase markedly as depletion raised the cost of getting oil out of the ground and synthetic fuels were developed. But at the same time, the model assumed that higher investment needs in the energy sector could be satisfied without reducing investment or consumption in the rest of the economy and without raising interest rates or inflation. In effect, the model let the economy have its pie and eat it too.

In part because it ignored the feedbacks between the energy sector and the rest of the economy, the PIES model consistently proved to be overoptimistic. In 1974 the model projected that by 1985 the U.S. would be well on the way to energy independence: energy imports would be only 3.3 million barrels per day, and production of shale oil would be 250,000 barrels per day. Furthermore, these developments would be accompanied by oil prices of about $22 per barrel (1984 dollars) and by vigorous economic growth. It didn't happen. In fact, at the time this paper is being written (1988), oil imports are about 5.5. million per day, and the shale oil industry remains a dream. This situation prevails despite the huge reductions in oil demand that have resulted from oil prices of over $30 per barrel and from the most serious economic recession since the Great Depression.

A broad model boundary that includes important feedback effects is more important than a great amount of detail in the specification of individual components. It is worth noting that the PIES model provided a breakdown of supply, demand, and price for dozens of fuels in each region of the country. Yet its aggregate projections for 1985 weren't even close. One can legitimately ask what purpose was served by the effort devoted to forecasting the demand for jet fuel or naphtha in the Pacific Northwest when the basic assumptions were so palpably inadequate and the main results so woefully erroneous.

In fairness it must be said that the PIES model is not unique in the magnitude of its errors. Nearly all energy models of all types have consistently been wrong about energy production, consumption, and prices. The evidence shows clearly that energy forecasts actually lag behind the available information, reflecting the past rather than anticipating the future (Department of Energy 1983). A good discussion of the limitations of PIES and other energy models is available in the appendix of Stobaugh and Yergin (1979).

Overly narrow model boundaries are not just a problem in energy analysis. *The Global 2000 Report to the President* (Barney 1980) showed that most of the models used by U.S. government agencies relied significantly on exogenous variables. Population models assumed food production was exogenous. Agriculture models assumed that energy prices and other input prices were exogenous. Energy models assumed that economic growth and environmental conditions were exogenous. Economic models assumed that population and energy prices were exogenous. And so on. Because they ignored important intersectoral feedbacks, the models produced inconsistent results.

Econometrics

Strictly speaking, econometrics is a simulation technique, but it deserves separate discussion for several reasons. First, it evolved out of economics and statistics, while most other simulation methods emerged from operations research or engineering. The difference in pedigree leads to large differences in purpose and practice. Second, econometrics is one of the most widely used formal modeling techniques. Pioneered by Nobel Prize-winning economists Jan Tinbergen and Lawrence Klein, econometrics is now taught in nearly all business and economics programs. Econometric forecasts are regularly reported in the media, and ready-to-use statistical routines for econometric modeling are now available for many personal computers. And third, the well publicized failure of econometric models to predict the future has eroded the credibility of all types of computer models, including those built for very different purposes and using completely different modeling techniques.

Econometrics is literally the measurement of economic relations, and it originally involved statistical analysis of economic data. As commonly practiced today, econometric modeling includes three stages—specification, estimation, and forecasting. First the structure of the system is specified by a set of equations. Then the values of the parameters (coefficients relating changes in one variable to changes in another) are estimated on the basis of historical data. Finally, the resulting output is used to make forecasts about the future performance of the system.

Specification

Specification is the description of the model's structure. This structure consists of the relationships among variables, both those that describe the physical setting and those that describe behavior. The relationships are expressed as equations, and a large econometric model may have hundreds or even thousands of equations reflecting the many interrelationships among the variables.

For example, an econometric model of the macroeconomy typically will contain equations specifying the relationship between GNP and consumption, investment, government activity, and international trade. It also will include behavioral equations that describe how these individual quantities are determined. The modeler may expect, for instance, that high unemployment reduces inflation and vice versa, a relationship known as the Phillips curve. One of the equations in the model will therefore express the Phillips curve, specifying that the rate of inflation depends on the amount of unemployment. Another equation may relate unemployment to the demand for goods, the wage level, and worker productivity. Still other equations may explain wage level in terms of yet other factors.

Not surprisingly, econometrics draws on economic theory to guide the specification of its models. The validity of the models thus depends on the validity of the underlying economic theories. Though there are many flavors of economics, a small set of basic assumptions about human behavior are common to most theories, including modern neoclassical theory and the "rational expectations" school. These assumptions are: optimization, perfect information, and equilibrium.

In econometrics, people (economic agents, in the jargon), are assumed to be concerned with just one thing—maximizing their profits. Consumers are assumed to optimize the "utility" they derive from their resources. Decisions about how much to produce, what goods to purchase, whether to save or borrow, are assumed to be the result of optimization by individual decision makers. Non-economic considerations (defined as any behavior that diverges from profit or utility maximization) are ignored or treated as local aberrations and special cases.

Of course, to optimize, economic agents would need accurate information about the world. The required information would go beyond the current state of affairs; it also would include complete knowledge about available options and their consequences. In most econometric models, such knowledge is assumed to be freely available and accurately known.

Take, for example, an econometric model simulating the operation of a firm that is using an optimal mix of energy, labor, machines, and other inputs in its production process. The model will assume that the firm knows not only the wages of workers and the prices of machines and other inputs, but also the production attainable with different combinations of people and machines, even if those combinations have never been tried. Rational expectation models go so far as to assume that the firm knows future prices, technologies, and possibilities, and that it can perfectly anticipate the consequences of its own actions and those of competitors.

The third assumption is that the economy is in or near equilibrium nearly all of the time. If disturbed, it is usually assumed to return to equilibrium rapidly and in a smooth and stable manner. The prevalence of static thinking is the intellectual legacy of the pioneers of mathematics and economics. During the late nineteenth century, before computers or modern cybernetic theory, the crucial questions of economic theory involved the nature of the equilibrium state for different situations. Given human preferences and the technological possibilities for producing goods, at what prices will commodities be traded, and in what quantities? What will wages be? What will profits be? How will a tax or monopoly influence the equilibrium?

These questions proved difficult enough without tackling the more difficult problem of dynamics, of the behavior of a system in flux. As a result, dynamic economic theory—including the recurrent fluctuations of inflation, of the business cycle, of the growth and decline of industries and nations—remained primarily descriptive and qualitative long after equilibrium theory was expressed mathematically. Even now, dynamic behavior in economics tends to be seen as a transition from one equilibrium to another, and the transition is usually assumed to be stable.

The rich heritage of static theory in economics left a legacy of equilibrium for econometrics. Many econometric models assume that markets are in equilibrium at all times. When adjustment dynamics are modeled, variables are usually assumed to adjust in a smooth and stable manner toward the optimal, equilibrium value, and the lags are nearly always fixed in length. For example, most macroeconometric models assume that capital stocks of firms in the economy adjust to the optimal, profit-maximizing level, with a fixed lag of several years. The lag is the same whether the industries that supply investment goods have the capacity to meet the demand or not. (See, for example, Eckstein 1983 and Jorgenson 1963).

Yet clearly, when the supplying industries have excess capacity, orders can be filled rapidly; when capacity is strained, customers must wait in line for delivery. Whether the dynamic nature of the lag is expressed in a model does make a difference. Models that explicitly include the determinants of the investment delay will yield predictions significantly different from models that assume a fixed investment lag regardless of the physical capability of the economy to fill the demand (Senge 1980). In general, models that explicitly portray delays and their determinants will yield different results from models that simply assume smooth adjustments from one optimal state to another.

Estimation

The second stage in econometric modeling is statistical estimation of the parameters of the model. The parameters determine the precise strengths of the relationships specified in the model structure. In the case of the Phillips curve, for example, the modeler would use past data to estimate precisely how strong the relationship between inflation and unemployment has been. Estimating the parameters involves statistical regression routines that are, in essence, fancy curve-fitting techniques. Statistical parameter estimates characterize the degree of correlation among the variables. They use historical data to determine parameter values that best match the data themselves.

All modeling methods must specify the structure of the system and estimate parameters. The use of statistical procedures to derive the parameters of the model is the hallmark of econometrics and distinguishes it from other forms of simulation. It gives econometricians an insatiable appetite for numerical data, for without numerical data they cannot carry out the statistical procedures used to estimate the models. It is no accident that the rise of econometrics went hand in hand with the quantification of economic life. The development of the national income and produce accounts by Simon Kuznets in the 1930s was a major advance in the codification of economic data, permitting consistent measures of economic activity at the national level for the first time. To this day all major macroeconometric models rely heavily on the national accounts data, and indeed macroeconomic theory itself has adapted to the national accounts framework.

Forecasting

The third step in econometric modeling is forecasting, making predictions about how the real system will behave in the future. In this step, the modeler provides estimates of the future values of the exogenous variables, that is, those variables that influence the other variables in the model but aren't themselves influenced by the model. An econometric model may have dozens of exogenous variables, and each must be forecast before the model can be used to predict.

Limitations of Econometric Modeling

The chief weak spots in econometric models stem from the assumptions of the underlying economic theory on which they rest: assumptions about the rationality of human behavior, about the availability of information that real decision makers do not have, and about equilibrium. Many economists acknowledge the idealization and abstraction of these assumptions, but at the same time point to the powerful results that have been derived from them. However, a growing number of prominent economists now argue that these assumptions are not just abstract—they are false. In his presidential address to the British Royal Economics Society, E. H. Phelps-Brown said:

> The trouble here is not that the behavior of these economic chessmen has been simplified, for simplification seems to be part of all understanding. The trouble is that the behavior posited is not known to be what obtains in the actual economy. (Phelps-Brown 1972, p. 4)

Nicholas Kaldor of Cambridge University is even more blunt:

> ...in my view, the prevailing theory of value—what I called, in a shorthand way, "equilibrium economics"—is barren and irrelevant as an apparatus of thought... (Kaldor 1972, p. 1237)

As mentioned earlier, a vast body of empirical research in psychology and organizational studies has shown that people do not optimize or act as if they optimize, that they don't have the mental capabilities to optimize their decisions, that even if they had the computational power necessary, they lack the information needed to optimize. Instead, they try to satisfy a variety of personal and organizational goals, use standard operating procedures to routinize decision making, and ignore much of the available information to reduce the complexity of the problems they face. Herbert Simon, in his acceptance speech for the 1978 Nobel Prize in economics, concludes:

> There can no longer be any doubt that the micro assumptions of the theory—the assumptions of perfect rationality—are contrary to fact. It is not a question of approximation; they do not even remotely describe the processes that human beings use for making decisions in complex situations (Simon 1979, p. 510).

Econometrics also contains inherent statistical limitations. The regression procedures used to estimate parameters yield unbiased estimates only under certain conditions. These conditions are known as *maintained hypotheses* because they are assumptions that must be made in order to use the statistical technique. The maintained hypotheses can never be verified, even in principle, but must be taken as a matter of faith. In the most common regression technique, ordinary least squares, the maintained hypotheses include the unlikely assumptions that the variables are all measured perfectly, that the model being estimated corresponds perfectly to the real world, and the random errors in the variables from one time period to another are completely independent. More sophisticated techniques do not impose such restrictive assumptions, but they always involve other a priori hypotheses that cannot be validated.

Another problem is that econometrics fails to distinguish between correlations and causal relationships. Simulation models must portray the causal relationships in a system if they are to mimic its behavior, especially its behavior in new situations. But the statistical techniques used to estimate parameters in econometric models don't prove whether a relationship is causal. They only reveal the degree of past correlation between the variables, and these correlations may change or shift as the system evolves. The prominent economist Robert Lucas (1976) makes the same point in a different context.

Consider the Phillips curve as an example. Though economists often interpreted the Phillips curve as a causal relationship—a policy trade-off between inflation and unemployment—it never did represent the causal forces that determine inflation or wage increases. Rather, the Phillips curve was simply a way of restating the past behavior of the system. In the past, Phillips said, low unemployment had tended to occur at the same time inflation was high, and vice-versa. Then, sometime in the early 1970s, the Phillips curve stopped working; inflation rose while unemployment worsened. Among the explanations given by economists was that the structure of the system had changed. But a modeler's appeal to "structural change" usually means that the inadequate structure of the model has to be altered because it failed to anticipate the behavior of the real system!

What actually occurred in the 1970s was that, when inflation swept prices to levels unprecedented in the industrial era, people learned to expect continuing increases. As a result of the adaptive feedback process of learning, they learned to deal with high inflation through indexing, COLAs, inflation-adjusting accounting, and other adjustments. The structure, the causal relationships of the system, did not change. Instead, causal relationships that had been present all along (but were dormant in an era of low inflation) gradually became active determinants of behavior as inflation worsened. In particular, the ability of people to adapt to continuing inflation existed all along but was not tested until inflation became high enough and persistent enough. Then the behavior of the system changed, and the historical correlation between inflation and unemployment broke down.

The reliance of econometric estimation on numerical data is another of its weaknesses. The narrow focus on hard data blinds modelers to less tangible but no less important factors. They ignore both potentially observable quantities that haven't been measured yet and ones for which no numerical data exist. (Alternatively, they may express an unmeasured factor with a proxy variable for which data already exists, even though the relationship between the two is tenuous—as when educational expenditure per capita is used as a proxy for the literacy of a population.)

Among the factors excluded from econometric models because of the hard data focus are many important determinants of decision making, including desires, goals, and perceptions. Numerical data may measure the results of human decision making, but numbers don't explain how or why people made particular decisions. As a result, econometric models cannot be used to anticipate how people would react to a change in decision-making circumstances.

Similarly, econometric models are unable to provide a guide to performance under conditions that have not been experienced previously. Econometricians assume that the correlations indicated by the historical data will remain valid in the future. In reality, those data usually span a limited range and provide no guidance outside historical experience. As a result, econometric models are often less than robust: faced with new policies or conditions, the models break down and lead to inconsistent results.

An example is the model used by Data Resources, Inc. in 1979 to test policies aimed at eliminating oil imports. On the basis of historical numerical data, the model assumed that the response of oil demand to the price of oil was rather weak—a 10 percent increase in oil price caused a reduction of oil demand of only 2 percent, even in the long run. According to the model, for consumption to be reduced by 50 percent (enough to cut imports to zero at the time), oil would have to rise to $800 per barrel. Yet at that price, the annual oil bill for the remaining 50 percent would have exceeded the total GNP for that year, an impossibility (Sterman 1981). The model's reliance on historical data led to inconsistencies. (Today, with the benefit of hindsight, economists agree that oil demand is much more responsive to price than was earlier believed. Yet considering the robustness of the model under extreme conditions could have revealed the problem much earlier.)

Validation is another problem area in econometric modeling. The dominant criterion used by econometric modelers to determine the validity of an equation or a model is the degree to which it fits the data. Many econometrics texts (e.g., Pindyck and Rubinfeld 1976) teach that the statistical significance of the estimated parameters in an equation is an indicator of the correctness of the relationship. Such views are mistaken. Statistical significance indicates how well an equation fits the observed data; it does not indicate whether a relationship is a correct or true characterization of the way the world works. A statistically significant relationship between variables in an equation shows that they are highly correlated and that the apparent correlation is not likely to have been the result of mere chance. But it does not indicate that the relationship is causal at all.

Using statistical significance as the test of model validity can lead modelers to mistake historical correlations for causal relationships. It also can cause them to reject valid equations describing important relationships. They may, for example, exclude an equation as statistically insignificant simply because there are few data about the variables, or because the data don't contain enough information to allow the application of statistical procedures.

Ironically, a lack of statistical significance does not necessarily lead econometric modelers to the conclusion that the model or the equation is invalid. When an assumed relationship fails to be statistically significant, the modeler may try another specification for the equation, hoping to get a better statistical fit. Without recourse to descriptive, micro-level data, the resulting equations may be ad hoc and bear only slight resemblance to either economic theory or actual behavior. Alternatively, the modelers may attempt to explain the discrepancy between the model and the behavior of the real system by blaming it on faulty data collection, exogenous influences, or other factors.

The Phillips curve again provides an example. When it broke down, numerous revisions of the equations were made. These attempts to find a better statistical fit met with limited success. Some analysts took another tack, pointing to the oil price shock, Russian wheat deal, or other one-of-a-kind events as the explanation for the change. Still others argued that there had been structural changes that caused the Phillips curve to shift out to higher levels of unemployment for any given inflation rate.

These flaws in econometrics have generated serious criticism from within the economic profession. Phelps-Brown notes that because controlled experiments are generally impossible in economics "running regressions between time series is only likely to deceive" (Phelps-Brown 1972, p. 6). Lester Thurow notes that econometrics has failed as a method for testing theories and is now used primarily as a "showcase for exhibiting theories." Yet as a device for advocacy, econometrics imposes few constraints on the prejudices of the modeler. Thurow concludes:

> By simple random search, the analyst looks for the set of variables and functional forms that give the best equations. In this context the best equation is going to depend heavily upon the prior beliefs of the analyst. If the analyst believes that interest rates do not affect the velocity of money, he find a 'best' equation that validates his particular prior belief. If the analyst believes that interest rates do affect the velocity of money, he finds a 'best' equation that validates this prior belief. (Thurow 1983, pp. 107-8)

But the harshest assessment of all comes from Nobel laureate Wassily Leontief:

> Year after year economic theorists continue to produce scores of mathematical models and to explore in great detail their formal properties; and the econometricians fit algebraic functions of all possible shapes to essentially the same sets of data without being able to advance, in any perceptible way, a systematic understanding of the structure and the operations of a real economic system. (Leontief 1982, p. 107; see also Leontief 1971.)

But surely such theoretical problems matter little if the econometric models provide accurate predictions. After all, the prime purpose of econometric models is short-term prediction of the exact future state of the economy, and most of the attributes of econometrics (including the use of regression techniques to pick the "best" parameters from the available numerical data and the extensive reliance on exogenous variables) have evolved in response to this predictive purpose.

Unfortunately, econometrics fails on this score also; in practice, econometric models do not predict very well. The predictive power of econometric models, even over the short-term (one to four years), is poor and virtually indistinguishable from that of other forecasting methods. There are several reasons for this failure to predict accurately.

As noted earlier, in order to forecast, the modeler must provide estimates of the future values of the exogenous variables, and an econometric model may have dozens of these variables. The source of the forecasts for these variables may be other models but usually is the intuition and judgment of the modeler. Forecasting the exogenous variables consistently, much less correctly, is difficult.

Not surprisingly, the forecasts produced by econometric models often don't square with the modeler's intuition. When they feel the model output is wrong, many modelers, including those at the "big three" econometric forecasting firms—Chase Econometrics, Wharton Econometric Forecasting Associates, and Data Resources—simply adjust their forecasts. This fudging, or add factoring as they call it, is routine and extensive. The late Otto Eckstein of Data Resources admitted that their forecasts were 60 percent model and 40 percent judgment ("Forecasters Overhaul Models of Economy in Wake of 1982 Errors," *Wall Street Journal*, 17 February 1983). *Business Week* ("Where Big Econometric Models Go Wrong," 30 March 1981) quotes an economist who points out that there is no way of knowing where the Wharton model ends and the model's developer, Larry Klein, takes over. Of course, the adjustments made by add factoring are strongly colored by the personalities and political philosophies of the modelers. In the article cited above, the *Wall Street Journal* quotes Otto Eckstein as conceding that his forecasts sometimes reflect an optimistic view: "Data Resources is the most influential forecasting firm in the country...If it were in the hands of a doom-and-gloomer, it would be bad for the country."

In a revealing experiment, the Joint Economic Committee of Congress (through the politically neutral General Accounting Office) asked these three econometric forecasting firms (DRI, Chase, and Wharton) to make a series of simulations with their models, running the models under different assumptions about monetary policy. One set of forecasts was "managed" or add factored by the forecasters at each firm. The other set consisted of pure forecasts, made by the GAO using the untainted results of the models. As an illustration of the inconsistencies revealed by the experiment, consider the following: When the money supply was assumed to be fixed, the DRI model forecast that after ten years the interest rate would be 34 percent, a result totally contrary to both economic theory and historical experience. The forecast was then add factored down to a more reasonable 7 percent. The other models fared little better, revealing both the inability of the pure models to yield meaningful results and the extensive ad hoc adjustments made by the forecasters to render the results palatable (Joint Economic Committee 1982).

Add factoring has been criticized by other economists on the grounds that it is unscientific. They point out that, although the mental models used to add factor are the mental models of seasoned experts, these experts are subject to the same cognitive limitations other people face. And whether good or bad, the assumptions behind add factoring are always unexaminable.

The failure of econometric models have not gone unnoticed. A representative sampling of articles in the business press on the topic of econometric forecasting include the following headlines:

"1980: The Year The Forecasters Really Blew It." (Business Week, 14 July 1980).

"Where The Big Econometric Models Go Wrong." (Business Week, 30 March 1981).

"Forecasters Overhaul Models of Economy in Wake of 1982 Errors." (Wall Street Journal, 17 February, 1983).

"Business Forecasters Find Demand Is Weak in Their Own Business: Bad Predictions Are Factor." (Wall Street Journal, 7 September 1984).

"Economists Missing The Mark: More Tools, Bigger Errors." (New York Times, 12 December 1984).

The result of these failures has been an erosion of credibility regarding computer models—all models no matter what their purpose, not just econometric models designed for prediction. This is unfortunate. Econometric models are poor *forecasting* tools, but well-designed simulation models can be valuable tools for *foresight* and *policy design*. Foresight is the ability to anticipate how the system will behave if and when certain changes occur. It is not forecasting, and it does not depend on the ability to predict. In fact, there is substantial agreement among modelers of global problems that exact, point prediction of the future is neither possible nor necessary:

> ...at present we are far from being able to predict social-system behavior except perhaps for carefully selected systems in the very short term. Effort spent on attempts at precise prediction is almost surely wasted, and results that purport to be such predictions are certainly misleading. On the other hand, much can be learned from models in the form of broad, qualitative, conditional understanding—and this kind of understanding is useful (and typically the only basis) for policy formulation. If your doctor tells you that you will have a heart attack if you do not stop smoking, this advice is helpful, even if it does not tell you exactly when a heart attack will occur or how bad it will be. (Meadows, Richardson, and Bruckmann 1982, p. 279)

Of course, policy evaluation and foresight depend on an accurate knowledge of the history and current state of the world, and econometrics has been a valuable stimulus to the development of much-needed data gathering and measurement by governments and private companies. But econometric models do not seem well-suited to the types of problems of concern in policy analysis and foresight. Though these models purport to simulate human behavior, they in fact rely on unrealistic assumptions about the motivations of real people and the information available to them. Though the models must represent the physical world, they commonly ignore dynamic processes, disequilibrium, and the physical basis for delays between actions and results. Though they may incorporate hundreds of variables, they often ignore soft variables and unmeasured quantities. In real systems the feedback relationships between environmental, demographic, and social factors are usually as important as economic influences, but econometric models often omit these because numerical data are not available. Furthermore, econometrics usually deals with the short term, while foresight takes a longer view. Over the time span that is of concern in foresight, real systems are likely to deviate from their past recorded behavior, making unreliable the historical correlations on which econometric models are based.

Checklist for the Model Consumer

The preceding discussion has focused on the limitations of various modeling approaches in order to provide potential model consumers with a sense of what to look out for when choosing a model. Despite the limitations of modeling, there is no doubt that computer models can be and have been extremely useful foresight tools. Well-built models offer significant advantages over the often faulty mental models currently in use.

The following checklist provides further assistance to decision makers who are potential model users. It outlines some of the key questions that should be asked to evaluate the validity of a model and its appropriateness as a tool for solving a specific problem.

What is the problem at hand? What is the problem addressed by the model?

What is the boundary of the model? What factors are endogenous? Exogenous? Excluded? Are soft variables included? Are feedback effects properly taken into account? Does the model capture possible side effects, both harmful and beneficial?

What is the time horizon relevant to the problem? Does the model include as endogenous components those factors that may change significantly over the time horizon?

Are people assumed to act rationally and to optimize their performance? Does the model take non-economic behavior (organizational realities, non-economic motives, political factors, cognitive limitations) into account?

Does the model assume people have perfect information about the future and about the way the system works, or does it take into account the limitations, delays, and errors in acquiring information that plague decision makers in the real world?

Are appropriate time delays, constraints, and possible bottlenecks taken into account?

Is the model robust in the face of extreme variations in input assumptions?

Are the policy recommendations derived from the model sensitive to plausible variations in its assumptions?

Are the results of the model reproducible? Or are they adjusted (add factored) by the model builder?

Is the model currently operated by the team that built it? How long does it take for the model team to evaluate a new situation, modify the model, and incorporate new data?

Is the model documented? Is the documentation publicly available? Can third parties use the model and run their own analyses with it?

Conclusions

The inherent strengths and weaknesses of computer models have crucial implications for their application in foresight and policy analysis. Intelligent decision making requires the appropriate use of many different models designed for specific purposes—not reliance on a single, comprehensive model of the world. To repeat a dictum offered above, "Beware the analyst who proposes to model an entire social or economic system rather than a problem." It is simply not possible to build a single, integrated model of the world, into which mathematical inputs can be inserted and out of which will flow a coherent and useful understanding of world trends.

To be used responsibly, models must be subjected to debate. A cross-disciplinary approach is needed; models designed by experts in different fields and for different purposes must be compared, contrasted, and criticized. The foresight process should foster such review.

The history of global modeling provides a good example. The initial global modeling efforts, published in *World Dynamics* (Forrester 1971) and *The Limits to Growth* (Meadows et al. 1972) provoked a storm of controversy. A number of critiques appeared, and other global models were soon developed. Over a period of ten years, the International Institute for Applied Systems Analysis (IIASA) conducted a program of analysis and critical review in which the designers of global models were brought together. Six major symposia were held, and eight important global models were examined and discussed. These models had different purposes, used a range of modeling techniques, and were built by persons with widely varying backgrounds. Even after the IIASA conferences, there remain large areas of methodological and substantive disagreement among the modelers. Yet despite these differences, consensus did emerge on a number of crucial issues (Meadows, Richardson, and Bruckmann 1982), including the following:

Physical and technical resources exist to satisfy the basic needs of all the world's people into the foreseeable future.

Population and material growth cannot continue forever on a finite planet.

Continuing "business as usual" policies in the next decades will not result in a desirable future nor even in the satisfaction of basic human needs.

Technical solutions alone are not sufficient to satisfy basic needs or create a desirable future.

The IIASA program on global modeling represents the most comprehensive effort to date to use computer models as a way to improve human understanding of social issues. The debate about the models created agreement on crucial issues where none had existed. The program helped to guide further research and provided a standard for the effective conduct of foresight in both the public and private sectors.

At the moment, model-based analyses usually take the form of studies commissioned by policymakers. The clients sit and wait for the final reports, largely ignorant of the methods, assumptions, and biases that the modelers put into the models. The policymakers are thus placed in the role of supplicants awaiting the prophecies of an oracle. When the report finally arrives, they may, like King Croesus before the Oracle at Delphi, interpret the results in accordance with their own preconceptions. If the results are unfavorable, they may simply ignore them. Policymakers who use models as black boxes, who accept them without scrutinizing their assumptions, who do not examine the sensitivity of the conclusions to variations in premises, who do not engage the model builders in dialogue, are little different from the Delphic supplicants or the patrons of astrologers. And these policymakers justly alarm critics, who worry that black box modeling abdicates to the modelers and the computer a fundamental human responsibility (Weizenbaum 1976).

No one can (or should) make decisions on the basis of computer model results that are simply presented, "take 'em or leave 'em." In fact, the primary function of model building should be educational rather than predictive. Models should not be used as a substitute for critical thought, but as a tool for improving judgment and intuition. Promising efforts in corporations, universities, and public education are described in Senge 1989; Graham, Senge, Sterman, and Morecroft 1989; Kim 1989; and Richmond 1987.

Towards that end, the role of computer models in policymaking needs to be redefined. What is the point of computer modeling? It should be remembered that we all use models of some sort to make decisions and to solve problems. Most of the pressing issues with which public policy is concerned are currently being handled solely with mental models, and those mental models are failing to resolve the problems. The alternative to continued reliance on mental models is computer modeling. But why turn to computer models if they too are far from perfect?

The value in computer models derives from the differences between them and mental models. When the conflicting results of a mental and a computer model are analyzed, when the underlying causes of the differences are identified, both of the models can be improved.

Computer modeling is thus an essential part of the educational process rather than a technology for producing answers. The success of this dialectic depends on our ability to create and learn from shared understandings of our models, both mental and computer. Properly used, computer models can improve the mental models upon which decisions are actually based and contribute to the solution of the pressing problems we face.

References

Barney, Gerald O., ed. 1980. *The Global 2000 Report to the President.* 3 vols. Washington, D.C.: U.S. Government Printing Office.

Business Forecasters Find Demand Is Weak in Their Own Business: Bad Predictions Are Factor. *Wall Street Journal*, 7 September 1984.

Cyert, R., and March, J. 1963. *A Behavioral Theory of the Firm.* Englewood Cliffs, N.J.: Prentice Hall.

Department of Energy. 1979. *National Energy Plan II.* DOE/TIC-10203. Washington, D.C.: Department of Energy.

_____. 1983. *Energy Projections to the Year 2000.* Washington, D.C.: Department of Energy, Office of Policy, Planning, and Analysis.

Eckstein, O. 1983. *The DRI Model of the US Economy.* New York, McGraw Hill.

Economists Missing the Mark: More Tools, Bigger Errors. *New York Times*, 12 December 1984.

Federal Energy Administration. 1974. *Project Independence Report.* Washington, D.C.: Federal Energy Administration.

Forecasters Overhaul Models of Economy in Wake of 1982 Errors. *Wall Street Journal*, 17 February, 1983.

Forrester, Jay W. 1969. *Urban Dynamics.* Cambridge, Mass.: MIT Press.

_____. 1971. *World Dynamics.* Cambridge, Mass.: MIT Press.

_____. 1980. Information Sources for Modeling the National Economy. *Journal of the American Statistical Association* 75(371):555-574.

Graham, Alan K.; Senge, Peter M.; Sterman, John D.; and Morecroft, John D. W. 1989. Computer Based Case Studies in Management Education and Research. In *Computer-Based Management of Complex Systems*, eds. P. Milling and E. Zahn, pp. 317-326. Berlin: Springer Verlag.

Grant, Lindsey, ed. 1988. *Foresight and National Decisions: The Horseman and the Bureaucrat.* Lanham, Md.: University Press of America.

Greenberger, M., Crenson, M. A., and Crissey, B. L. 1976. *Models in the Policy Process.* New York: Russell Sage Foundation.

Hogarth, R. M. 1980. *Judgment and Choice.* New York: Wiley.

Joint Economic Committee. 1982. *Three Large Scale Model Simulations of Four Money Growth Scenarios.* Prepared for subcommittee on Monetary and Fiscal Policy, 97th Congress 2nd Session, Washington, D.C.

Jorgenson, D. W. 1963. Capital Theory and Investment Behavior. *American Economic Review* 53:247-259.

Kahneman, D., Slovic, P., and Tversky, A. 1982. *Judgment Under Uncertainty: Heuristics and Biases.* Cambridge: Cambridge University Press.

Kaldor, Nicholas. 1972. The Irrelevance of Equilibrium Economics. *The Economic Journal* 82:1237-55.

Kim, D. 1989. Learning Laboratories: Designing a Reflective Learning Environment. In *Computer-Based Management of Complex Systems*, P. Milling and E. Zahn, eds., pp. 327-334. Berlin: Springer Verlag

Leontief, Wassily. 1971. Theoretical Assumptions and Nonobserved Facts. *American Economic Review* 61(1):1-7.

_____. 1982. Academic Economics. *Science* 217:104-107.

Lucas, R. 1976. Econometric Policy Evaluation: A Critique. In *The Phillips Curve and Labor Markets*, K. Brunner and A. Meltzer, eds. Amsterdam: North-Holland.

Meadows, Donella H.; Meadows, Dennis L.; Randers, Jorgen.; and Behrens, William W. 1972. *The Limits to Growth*. New York: Universe Books.

Meadows, Donella H. 1982. Whole Earth Models and Systems. *CoEvolution Quarterly*, Summer 1982, pp. 98-108.

Meadows, Donella H.; Richardson, John; and Bruckmann, Gerhart 1982. *Groping in the Dark*. Somerset, N.J.: Wiley.

Morecroft, John D. W. 1983. System Dynamics: Portraying Bounded Rationality. *Omega* II:131-142.

_____. 1988. System Dynamics and Microworlds for Policy Makers. *European Journal of Operational Research* 35(5):301-320.

1980: The Year The Forecasters Really Blew It. *Business Week*, 14 July 1980.

Phelps-Brown, E. H. 1972. The Underdevelopment of Economics. *The Economic Journal* 82:1-10.

Pindyck, R., and Rubinfeld, D. 1976. *Econometric Models and Economic Forecasts*. New York: McGraw Hill.

Richmond, B. 1987. *The Strategic Forum*. Lyme, New Hampshire (13 Dartmouth College Highway, Lyme, NH 03768, USA): High Performance Systems, Inc.

Senge, Peter M. 1980. A System Dynamics Approach to Investment Function Formulation and Testing. *Socioeconomic Planning Sciences* 14:269-280.

_____. 1989. Catalyzing Systems Thinking Within Organizations. In *Advances in Organization Development*, F. Masaryk, ed., forthcoming.

Simon, Herbert. 1947. *Administrative Behavior*. New York: MacMillan.

_____. 1957. *Models of Man*. New York: Wiley.

_____. 1979. Rational Decisionmaking in Business Organizations. *American Economic Review* 69:493-513.

Sterman, John D. 1981. The Energy Transition and the Economy: A System Dynamics Approach. Ph.D. dissertation, Massachusetts Institute of Technology, Cambridge.

_____. 1985. A Behavioral Model of the Economic Long Wave. *Journal of Economic Behavior and Organization* 6(1):17-53.

_____. 1989. Modeling Managerial Behavior: Misperceptions of Feedback in a Dynamic Decision Making Experiment. *Management Science* 35(3):321-339.

Stobaugh, Robert and Yergin, Daniel. 1979. *Energy Future*. New York: Random House.

Thurow, Lester. 1983. *Dangerous Currents*. New York: Random House.

Weizenbaum, J. 1976. *Computer Power and Human Reason: from Judgment to Calculation*. San Francisco: W. H. Freeman.

Where The Big Econometric Models Go Wrong. *Business Week*, 30 March 1981.

[2]

Systems thinking: critical thinking skills for the 1990s and beyond

Barry Richmond

The problems we face at all levels in the world today resist unilateral solutions. While the web of interdependencies tightens, our capacity for thinking in terms of dynamic interdependencies has not kept pace. As the gap between the nature of our problems and the ability to understand them grows, we face increasing perils on a multitude of fronts. Systems thinking and one of its subsets—system dynamics—are important for developing effective strategies to close this gap. Unfortunately, system dynamicists and systems thinkers have not effectively taught their framework, skills, and technologies to others. The door has not been opened wide enough to let others share our insights with respect to the workings of closed-loop systems. To transfer this understanding on a broad scale, we need a clearer view of its nature and of the education system into which it must be transferred. This article casts some

The problems that we currently face have been stubbornly resistant to solution, particularly unilateral solution. As we are painfully discovering, there is no way to unilaterally solve the problem of carbon dioxide buildup, which is steadily and inexorably raising the temperature around the globe. The problems of crack cocaine, ozone depletion, the proliferation of nuclear armaments, world hunger, poverty and homelessness, rain forest destruction, and political self-determination also fall into the category of "resistant to unilateral solution." Why is it no longer possible for some world power to pull out a big stick and beat a nasty problem into submission? The answer is that it probably never was. It's simply that the connections among the various subsystems conspiring to manifest a problem were less tight. Then, it was possible to score a Pyrrhic victory by essentially pushing a problem off into the future or into "someone else's backyard." Unfortunately, as Dana Meadows is fond of saying, "There is less and less space remaining to throw things away into." *Away* means both space and time. We have less and less space remaining to serve as a receptacle for our "garbage." And we have less and less time before we must endure "the morning after." Both are artifacts of sustained material growth in our finite earthly realm. Every generation of human beings has been subject to these rules, but our generation is the first to have to take them seriously.

System dynamics and systems thinking to the rescue?

If one accepts the argument that the primary source of the growing intractability of our problems is a tightening of the links between the various physical and social subsystems that make up our reality, one will agree that system dynamics and systems thinking hold great promise as approaches for augmenting our solution-generation capacity. The systems thinkers' forte is interdependence. Their specialty is understanding the dynamics generated by systems composed of closed-loop relations. Systems thinkers use diagraming languages to visually depict the feedback structures of these systems. They then use simulation to play out the associated dynamics. These tools give people the ability to "see" a neighbor's backyard—even if that backyard is thousands of miles away. They also confer the ability to "experience" the morning after—even if the morning after is tens of thousands of years hence.

Although the quality of the "seeing" and "experiencing" provided by the current systems thinking tools is improving, these tools remain quite primitive today. In three years, they will be much less so. In ten, available tools will be capable of effectively compressing space and time so as to produce "virtual light on what we have to bestow and on the education system that is to receive our bounty. Its intended audience is both system thinkers and educators, and the hope is to help eradicate the distinction between the two.

Barry Richmond is managing director and founder of High Performance Systems, an organization providing software and consulting services to build the capacity of people to understand and improve the workings of dynamic systems. Dr. Richmond is the impetus behind the iThink and STELLA II modeling and simulation software packages. He has taught at Thayer School of Engineering, Dartmouth College, and holds a Ph.D. degree in system dynamics from Sloan School of Management, MIT, and degrees from Syracuse, Columbia, and Case Western Reserve universities. *Address*: High Performance Systems, 45 Lyme Rd., Hanover, NH 03755, U.S.A.

realities." In these electronic realities, people will be able to participate in creating powerful, visceral experiences for themselves. But, no matter how advanced the technology gets, it will always be only part of the solution. If people are to make sense of their experiences in virtual realities, they must have the capacity for understanding the underlying closed-loop framework that is generating these experiences. They must be capable of thinking both systemically and dynamically. In short, they must be systems thinkers. This, in turn, brings us back to a long-unanswered question, which has plagued system dynamics from its outset some 30 years ago at that venerable technical university on the Charles River in Cambridge, Massachusetts. The question is, How can the framework, the process, and the technologies of systems thinking be transferred to the rest of the world in an amount of time that is considerably less than what it currently takes to get a master's or Ph.D. degree in our field?

I will argue that to successfully answer this question it is necessary to confront two aspects of the transfer process. We first must better understand the evolution of the education system into which the transfer must be made (this system offers the best potential for large-scale transfer). Second, we must better understand the "thing" we are seeking to transfer. Specifically, we must understand that this "thing" is multifaceted. As such, for people to swallow and digest it, it must be broken down into more consumable pieces.

Aspect 1: the evolution of the education system

Like any viable system, our system of formal education is evolving over time. The last several decades have seen numerous innovative experiments in educational progress and technology. Open classrooms, computer-aided instruction, and interdisciplinary course offerings are but a few of the initiatives that have been and are being tried. It is my perception that the time is now ripe for three evolutionary threads to come together to form a new learning gestalt. The three threads, illustrated in Figure 1, are educational process, thinking paradigm, and learning tools. The evolutionary fusing of these three threads can successfully create a permanent change in the way people learn. The evolution of each thread, taken independently, cannot.

Thread 1: educational process

I will refer to the newly emerging educational process as *learner-directed learning*. I like this phrase because it positions the process in sharp relief against the process that has dominated teaching for at least the last 200 years: *teacher-directed learning*.

Fig. 1. Three evolutionary threads in education

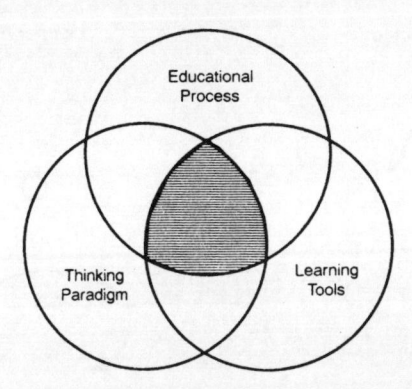

We are all, to varying degrees, products of a teacher-directed learning process. In this process, the classroom is arranged with students facing the front, in rows or nested U's. At the front is "Herr Professor." Herr Professor's job is to transmit what he or she knows to the students. The student's job is to take in as much of this transmission as possible. This is why it is important for students to "be quiet and pay attention" in the classroom. A schematic representation of the teacher-directed learning process appears at the left in Figure 2.

It is important to reveal the implicit assumption about learning that underlies a teacher-directed learning process. It is that learning is primarily an assimilation process. This assumption, in turn, defines appropriate roles for both teacher and student. Teacher is transmitter, or content dispenser. Student is receiver, or content receptacle. The objective of the educational process, then, is for the teacher to "fill up" the student. Measuring performance in this system is straightforward. Simply ask the student to retransmit what has previously been transmitted by the teacher. If the student can "dump" a full load, he is performing well. It's interesting to note that the teacher-directed learning process tacitly assumes that the students do not have much to contribute to each other's learning experience. Otherwise, they would not be arrayed in a physical arrangement in which they face the back of each other's heads.

Contrast the teacher-directed learning process with a learner-directed approach, illustrated at the right in Figure 2. The learner-directed approach assumes that learning is fundamentally a construction rather than an assimilation process. This means that to learn the student must reconstruct what is being taken in. Meaning and understanding are "making" processes, not "imbibing" processes. Extending this assumption leads to the conclusion that because there are many strategies for "making," learning cannot be standardized. People construct in different ways, at different paces, and in different

Fig. 2. Teacher-directed and learner-directed learning processes

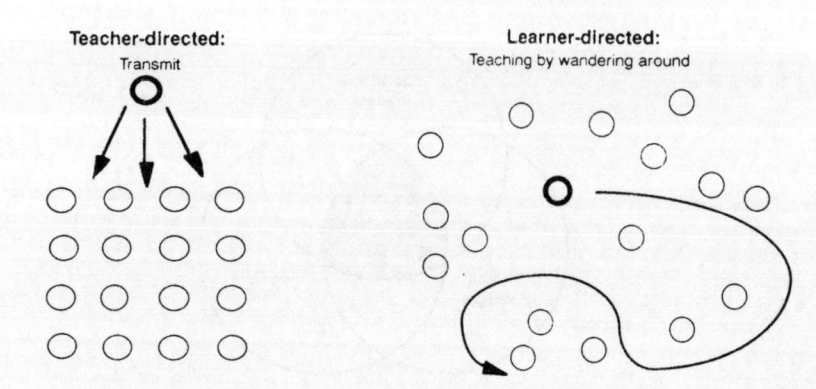

Teacher-directed: Transmit

Learner-directed: Teaching by wandering around

sequences. Construction also is an active process. Being quiet and listening often can be antithetical to construction activities. Both teacher and learner, in this process, have new roles. Teacher now is charged with providing materials and alternative strategies for constructing. In a sense, she creates the building environment. Once the building process begins, she wanders around, playing the role of project manager, keeping the process on track, but not doing the construction. Students are the construction workers. And, like construction crews, they often can accomplish more, reaping more enjoyment in the process, by working in teams rather than alone.

In order for a learner-directed approach to work, it is essential that both teachers and students rethink their roles and respective contributions to the learning process. Teachers must be willing to abdicate their position as all-knowing fonts of knowledge and wisdom. Students, in turn, must be willing to take personal responsibility for their learning. Students must also learn to cooperate with each other as learning partners rather than viewing fellow students as competitors in a zero-sum game. These are easy words to write, but the shifts in perspective and process needed to bring these changes about are quite profound. Fortunately, the benefits that appear to be achievable—from looking at the results of some experiments in several learner-directed processes—promise to be equally profound.

To begin with, the age-old question, Why do we have to learn this? is likely to cease reverberating through our schools. The active learning process will provide an outlet for the inherent need that all human beings have for activity. The cooperation involved will model the very processes needed to live in an increasingly interdependent world community. And all these gains can be achieved with no necessary forfeiture of content assimilation, because when students can see the "why," content assimilation becomes a means to an end

Fig. 3.
Overpopulation
laundry list

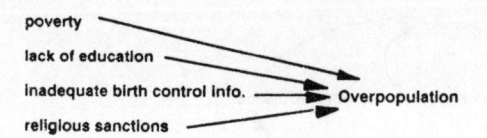

poverty
lack of education
inadequate birth control info. ⟶ Overpopulation
religious sanctions

rather than an end in itself. There are thus many "free lunches" to be eaten here. We have only to avail ourselves of the opportunity. Availing, however, will require not only the profound shifts in role, administrative structure, and performance measurement already alluded to but also that the two other threads—thinking paradigm and learning tools—also come together.

Thread 2: thinking paradigm

It is very difficult to see what you use for seeing. But that's what is involved in confronting your thinking paradigm. It's the water you swim in, so pervasive it's completely transparent. To bring it into view, try answering the following question: What is causing the overpopulation problem in so many countries in the world today? Take a moment to jot down a few thoughts before proceeding.

If you took the time to record your thoughts, I'll bet they took the form of a list. If you reflect on the structure of the mental modeling process that generated this "laundry list," I think you'll find that it looks something like Figure 3.

I like to refer to the mental modeling process that produces such lists as laundry list thinking. I believe it to be the dominant thinking paradigm in most of the Western world today. If one asks most Westerners (and many Easterners, too) a "what causes what?" type of question, one is likely to get a laundry list of causal factors in response. Implicitly, people also weight each factor in the list: this one is most important, this one is second; and so on. This kind of mental modeling has been given analytical expression as a multiple regression equation. Many of us are familiar with this type of expression:

$$y = a_0 + a_1X_1 + a_2X_2 + \ldots + a_nX_n$$

where
y = dependent variable
X_i = independent variables
a_i = coefficients (or weighting factors) for each of the independent variables

Notice that the implicit assumptions in the laundry list thinking process are that (1) each factor contributes as a cause to the effect, i.e., causality runs one way; (2) each factor acts independently; (3) the weighting factor of each is fixed;

Fig. 4. Overpopulation feedback loop

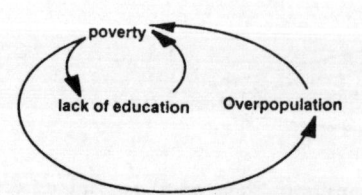

poverty → lack of education → Overpopulation → poverty (feedback loop diagram)

and (4) the way in which each factor works to cause the effect is left implicit (represented only by the sign of the coefficients, i.e., this factor has a positive or a negative influence).

The systems thinking paradigm offers alternatives to each of these assumptions. First, according to this paradigm, each of the causes is linked in a circular process to both the effect and to each of the other causes. Systems thinkers refer to such circular processes as feedback loops. Figure 4 illustrates two such loops. The shift from one-way to circular causality, and from independent factors to interdependent relations, is a profound one. In effect, it is a shift from viewing the world as a set of static, stimulus-response relations to viewing it as an ongoing, interdependent, self-sustaining, dynamic process. It will also cause students to think in a very different way about what is going on in the world around them.

The third assumption implicit in the laundry list paradigm is that factors have a static weighting. By contrast, in the systems thinking view, as Figure 4 suggests, the strength of the closed-loop relations is assumed to wax and wane over time. Some loops will dominate at first, other loops will then take over, and so on. Therefore, addressing a problem is not seen as a one-shot deal. Rather, it is considered necessary to think in terms of ongoing, interdependent relations whose strengths vary over time, partly in response to interventions that may have been implemented into the system.

The final assumption associated with laundry list thinking is that correlation is good enough for explaining how a system works. The systems thinking paradigm challenges this regression analysis approach, offering in its place operational models of how things work. Thus, for someone steeped in the systems thinking paradigm, it would not be enough to identify the factors that are correlated with overpopulation. Instead, it would be necessary to actually offer an operational explanation of how overpopulation is generated. The contrast between the correlational and operational models of the overpopulation process is illustrated in Figures 5 and 6.

The systems thinking paradigm, when combined with the learner-directed learning process, will breed students who are hungry to understand how things really work and who will continually be looking for how these workings might

Fig. 5. A correlational model

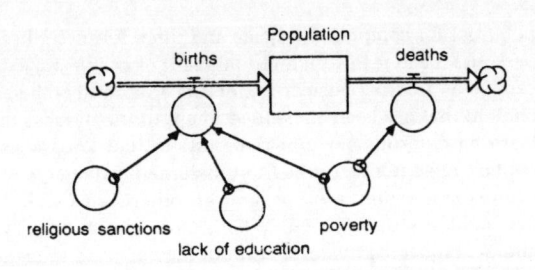

[Figure 5: stock-and-flow diagram with Population stock, births and deaths flows, influenced by religious sanctions, lack of education, and poverty]

Fig. 6. An operational model

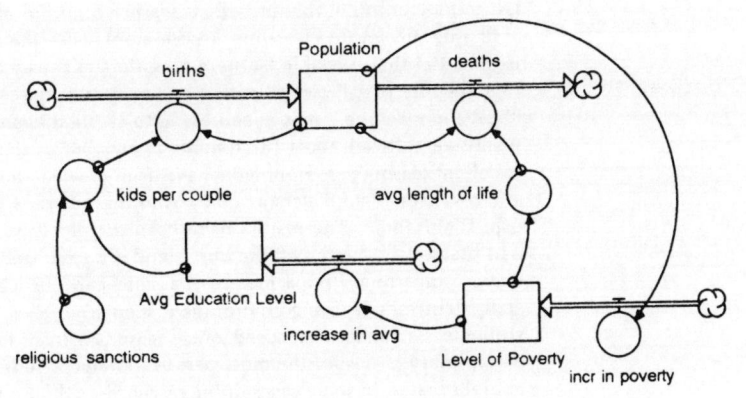

[Figure 6: operational stock-and-flow diagram with Population, births, deaths, kids per couple, avg length of life, Avg Education Level, increase in avg, religious sanctions, Level of Poverty, incr in poverty]

change over time as a consequence of shifts in the relative strengths of the underlying dynamic relations.

Thread 3: learning tools

To fully meld a learner-directed learning process with the systems thinking paradigm, it is essential to have the right set of learning tools available for classroom and out-of-classroom use. The tools of a teacher-directed, laundry list learning process—textbooks and blackboards—will play a smaller role in a nontransmit, active learning process. Textbooks operate, in effect, as purveyors of silent lectures. Students read them, for the most part, for the same reason they currently go to class—to assimilate content. On blackboards teachers can chart static relations and display lists. However, blackboards are not well suited to analyzing a system's dynamics. To support an inquiry-oriented, learner-directed learning process, textbooks and blackboards must share the stage with an emerging tool: the personal computer. The personal computer, with its rapidly expanding sound and graphic animation capabilities, holds the potential for compressing space and time. As such, these devices can serve as personal theaters in which virtual realities can be played out. Students literally can have the experience of wandering around in both space and time, stashing content that has been embedded in appropriate nooks in the electronics-based learning environment into their intellectual knapsacks as they go. And the content need not be limited to unadorned statements of fact. Video segments, sounds, animation, puzzles, and all other forms of intellectually stimulating presentations are fair game. What's more, the students' wandering need not be choreographed by the teacher. Both the pace and sequence of discovery can be left to the control of the individual learner or group of learners.

In order to elevate a learning environment above the status of a video game, it is essential that it enable learners to understand why things happen. Without this, the interplay between learner and computer can too easily deteriorate into "beat the machine." It is encouraging to see that even with today's relatively primitive software tools (Richmond et al. 1987; Peterson 1990), a few truly excellent learning environments have been created and are now in use (Draper and Swanson 1990; Peterson 1990). And the software tools are improving (see, e.g., Diehl 1990). The results have been extremely promising. Students who had previously "gotten off the bus," tended to get back on. The opportunity to design something (like a mammal, a state park, or a policy for managing an ecosystem) in a learning environment seemed to reset the counters, giving all students a chance to succeed once again. Motivation was high, and hence disciplinary issues for the most part evaporated. Students assimilated content at higher rates, in some cases doing research on their own in order to be able to do a better job in their design project. At the same time, depth of understanding of the concepts increased, and students' capacity for critical thinking was enhanced. Students began to think in terms of the long-run, as well as the immediate, implications of their decisions and actions. They began to anticipate the second- and third-order effects of their choices.

These results suggest what is possible when a new learning gestalt comes together. But even when all three threads—educational process, thinking paradigm, and learning tools—are ripe for fusion within a particular educational setting, there remains the issue of how to equip teachers with an understanding of the framework, processes, and technologies of systems thinking. Let's begin by emphasizing that it is not reasonable to expect teachers, on a wide scale, to stop what they're doing and move en masse to one or more of the institutions of higher learning that offer formal degrees in system dynamics. Teachers, like most other people, are very busy. And many could not secure the financial resources even if they did have the time. Furthermore, there is not sufficient system dynamics teaching capacity to process such demand. What, then, can be done to facilitate the fusion process when things are ready to fuse?

Aspect 2: transferring the systems thinking framework, process, and tools

I taught system dynamics in the Thayer School of Engineering at Dartmouth College for nine years. During this time, I experienced considerable frustration at the fact that after three or more courses even the good master's student ("good," in this case, being a pretty select breed!) often encountered considerable difficulty in constructing and analyzing a model from scratch come thesis time. This being the case, what hope was there, I used to muse, for any widespread dissemination of systems thinking?

Since leaving Dartmouth three years ago, my colleagues and I at High Performance Systems have embarked upon a mission designed to answer the question, Just how far is it possible to go in cutting the up-to-speed time for the serious, yet not whiz-bang, pilgrim? Now, after offering more than 50 workshops for educators, business folk, and all manner in between—both in the United States and abroad—I do believe that I can say, pretty far! In recent workshops, after two-and-a-half days, participants had produced models from scratch that addressed issues of their own choosing. The models were initialized in steady state, had been subjected to a rigorous testing program to establish robustness, and in many cases did a credible job of replicating the observed behavior pattern of interest. The quality of the better models in terms of "tightness" and insight-generation capacity was equivalent to what I used to receive from a good master's thesis effort. How was this achieved?

First, over the three-year period, we carefully monitored performance and continually fed back the results. We maintained no attachment to what we had done in previous workshops. Indeed, we turned over our curriculum materials at least 50 times each (and continue to do so). My intention here is not to summarize this closed-loop evolutionary process. Instead, I wish to stand back from the process and to focus on what we discovered to be the most fundamental barrier to learning productivity. Simply stated, it is cognitive overload.

What has become apparent over the course of the last three years of workshops is that doing good systems thinking means operating on at least seven thinking tracks simultaneously. This would be difficult even if these tracks were familiar ways of thinking. But they are not. And the result in the majority of cases is cognitive overload. Nevertheless, we've found that it is possible to take certain steps to prevent people from becoming overloaded. Specifically, (1) tell people that they're going to be asked to juggle multiple thinking tracks simultaneously; (2) be explicit about what these tracks are; and (3) align the curricular progression to emphasize development of only one thinking skill at a time.

It helps to begin placing the seven systems thinking skills into a broader

Fig. 7. Critical thinking skills: the systems thinking piece

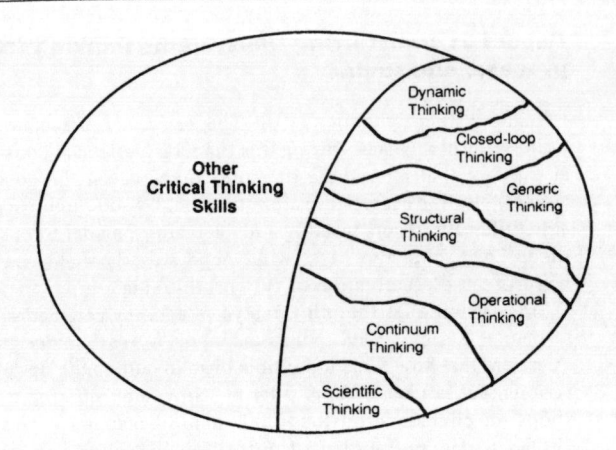

context. That context in education seems most appropriately labeled *critical thinking skills*. The seven tracks that I would construe as constituting systems thinking skills are depicted in Figure 7.

Skill 1: dynamic thinking

Dynamic thinking is the ability to see and deduce behavior patterns rather than focusing on, and seeking to predict, events. It's thinking about phenomena as resulting from ongoing circular processes unfolding through time rather than as belonging to a set of factors. Dynamic thinking skills are honed by having to trace out patterns of behavior that change over time and by thinking through the underlying closed-loop processes that are cycling to produce particular events. Having students think about everyday events or newspaper stories in terms of *graphs over time* would be good exercises for developing their abilities to think dynamically. Also very helpful is the use of simple models in real-time exercises in which students are asked to hypothesize what behavior pattern will result when a particular system is disturbed in a particular way. As an illustration of this kind of exercise, consider the simple system depicted in Figure 8.

In this system, mature trees are harvested. Each time a mature tree is removed via harvesting, a sapling is instantaneously planted to replace it. Saplings take exactly six time periods to pass through the Maturation Pipeline (entering the Mature Trees stock). All saplings mature (none die, all germinate). Given these structural assumptions, next assume the system is initially in steady state. This means that (1) mature trees are being harvested at the same rate that they're

Fig. 8. Maturation pipeline structure

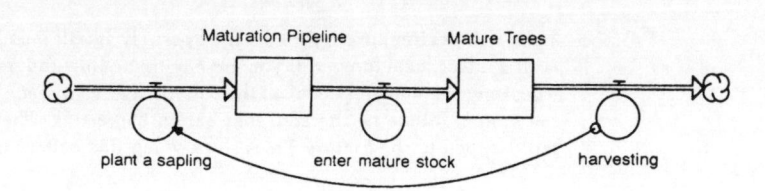

Fig. 9. Pattern of behavior

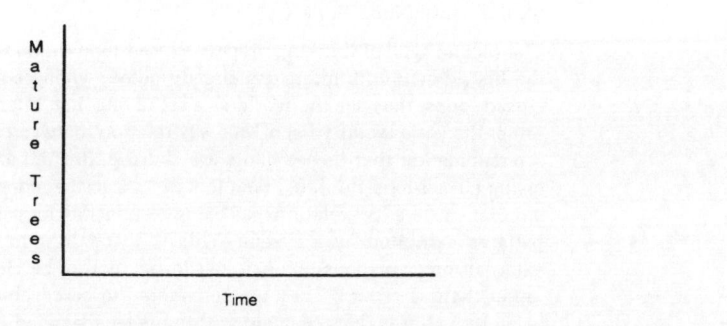

being planted (by definition, this is true), and (2) that the maturation pipeline is primed up such that trees are entering the Mature Trees stock at the same rate. Thus, both the stock of Mature Trees and the number of trees in the Maturation Pipeline are constant. Now, suppose that the harvest rate suddenly steps up to a new higher level and then remains there forever. What pattern do you think the stock of Mature Trees will trace over time in response to this permanent step increase in the harvest rate? Sketch your guess on the axis provided in Figure 9.

In our experience, with widely diverse audiences (across education level, occupation, age, and culture), only about 20 percent of people who guess at the answer guess correctly. This says something about the level of our dynamic thinking skills. It also says something about the potential for an extremely fruitful union of computer and human. Computers could never construct, or "understand," the preceding illustration. However, 100 percent of the computer population will correctly deduce the dynamic pattern of behavior that the Mature Trees stock will trace in response to the step increase in the harvest rate. Combining the human being's ability for making meaningful structure with the computer's ability for correctly tracing out the dynamic behavior patterns implied by that structure holds great promise for leveraging our capacity for addressing the set of intractable problems mentioned at the beginning of this article.

The correct answer to this illustration, by the way, is that the Mature Trees stock will decline linearly for six time periods. It will then level off and remain at this lower level forever. If you are having trouble understanding why this is true, I suggest that you trace out the pattern charted by each of the three flows in the system following the step increase in harvesting. Then think about what will happen to the Mature Trees stock when this pattern of flow unfolds.

Skill 2: closed-loop thinking

The second type of thinking process, closed-loop thinking, is closely linked to the first, dynamic thinking. As already noted, when people think in terms of closed loops, they see the world as a set of ongoing, interdependent processes rather than as a laundry list of one-way relations between a group of factors and a phenomenon that these factors are causing. But there is more. When exercising closed-loop thinking, people will look to the loops themselves (i.e., the circular cause-effect relations) as being responsible for generating the behavior patterns exhibited by a system. This is in contrast to holding some set of external forces responsible; external forces tend to be viewed as precipitators rather than as causes. They are considered to be capable of calling forth the behavior patterns that are latent within the feedback-loop structure of a system but not of causing these behaviors (in the sense of shaping their essential characteristics). This is a subtle, but extremely important, shift in viewpoint. It coincides, at the level of the individual, with adoption of an internal locus of responsibility. Such an adoption leads people to ask, How am I responsible for what transpired? rather than Why am I always the one who has it done to me? Making the system itself the cause of its behaviors, rather than a set of external forces places the burden of improving performance on relations that those within the system can manage. This perspective stands in sharp contrast to bemoaning "the slings and arrows of outrageous fortune."

There are numerous exercises available to build skill in identifying and representing the feedback-loop structure of a system as well as in viewing the dynamic behavior exhibited by that system as caused by its structure. See, e.g. Roberts et al. (1983) and Richmond et al. (1987).

Skill 3: generic thinking

Just as most people are captivated by events, they are generally locked into thinking in terms of specifics. Thus, for example, Gorbachev is seen as the man who brought glasnost and perestroika to the former Soviet Union. He's also the man who has allowed "freedom" to emerge in many of the former Soviet satellites. But is Gorbachev responsible, or was "freedom" an idea whose time had come? Similarly, was it Hitler, Napoleon, Joan of Arc, Martin Luther King who determined changes in history, or tides in history that swept these figures along on their crests? The notion of thinking generically rather than specifically applies not only to history. Apprehending the similarities in the underlying feedback-loop relations that generate a predator-prey cycle, a manic-depressive swing, the oscillation in an L-C circuit, and a business cycle can demonstrate how generic thinking can be applied to virtually any arena.

To develop generic thinking skills, people can work with a series of generic structures that progress from simple exponential growth and decay, through S-shaped growth, to overshoot/collapse and oscillation (Richmond et al. 1987). They also can do exercises with the classic policy insensitivity structures, e.g., Shifting the Burden to the Intervener, Floating Goal, First Response in the Wrong Direction, and Promotion Chain (Richmond 1985; Meadows 1982).

Skill 4: structural thinking

Structural thinking is one of the most disciplined of the systems thinking tracks. It's here that people must think in terms of units of measure, or dimensions. Physical conservation laws are rigorously adhered to in this domain. The distinction between a stock and a flow is emphasized.

To catch a glimmer of the kind of skill being developed here, consider the simple causal-loop diagram in Figure 10. The notion here is simple and intuitive, and it would work pretty well if one were proceeding along the dynamic thinking track. Beginning with births, the diagram says simply that as births increase, population increases. And, as population increases, births follow suit. This is a simple positive feedback-loop process. Left unchecked, it will generate an exponential increase in population over time.

When the same two variables are represented using a structural diagram (Fig. 11), a subtle but important dynamic distinction becomes apparent. The same positive feedback process depicted in Figure 10 is shown here, and again we see that if births increase, population follows suit.

Now, however, return to the causal-loop diagram (Fig. 10) and run the thought experiment in reverse. That is, begin by *decreasing* births. According to the causal-loop diagram, a decrease in births would result in a decrease in population. Clearly, this is not necessarily true. Population would only decrease following a decrease in births if births fell to a level *below* deaths. The causal-loop diagram, a tool for engaging in dynamic thinking, is not well suited to structural thinking (Richardson 1982). That's why the structural diagram was invented. As the structural diagram in Figure 11 shows, a decrease in births will only serve to slow the *rate* at which population is increasing. When one engages in structural thinking, such subtle distinctions (which can be very important in understanding dynamics) must be made.

Fig. 10. Population feedback loop

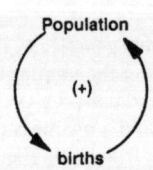

Fig. 11. Population structural diagram

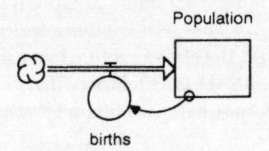

Another simple example will further illustrate the rigor associated with the structural thinking track. Consider the diagram in Figure 12, which provides an intuitive but structurally incorrect representation of a simple conveyor line process. Empty bottles flow along a conveyor, enter a filling station, and are filled with liquid that drains out of a vat. Filled bottles then exit the station and accumulate in a filled bottle inventory. Simple, intuitive and, as I said, not structurally correct.

To see why, examine the alternative representation of the process in Figure 13. In this alternative representation, notice that the flow of liquid and the flow of bottles are kept distinct. This is not the case in the first, more intuitive representation. If one took a snapshot of the actual process, the photograph would more closely resemble Figure 12. After all, liquid really does pour into bottles. However, liquid and bottle do not become one. We still have liquid (measured in liters) and bottles (measured in number of bottles). So, from a units-of-measure standpoint, we still have two quantities: number of bottles and number of liters. If one mixed the two units of measure, one would end up with a very strange quantity in the box labeled "Bottles being Filled," namely, bottle-liters.

When engaging in structural thinking, it is essential to maintain units-of-measure integrity within each stock-and-flow subsystem. Imprecise notions like "I put a lot of effort into the project" and "I'll give you all my love" simply "don't compute" when doing structural thinking. Quantities that flow into a stock must have the same units of measure as that stock. Maintaining unit integrity ensures the conservation of physical quantities. This, in turn, keeps one from getting something for nothing. It also infuses a very strong discipline and precision into the thinking process.

Fig. 12. Intuitive, structurally incorrect representation

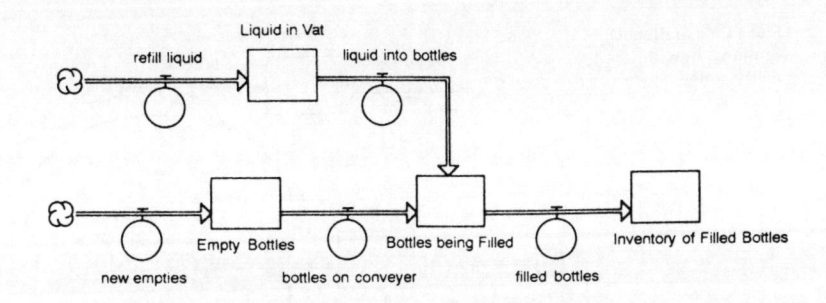

Fig. 13. Structurally correct: using distinct units of measure

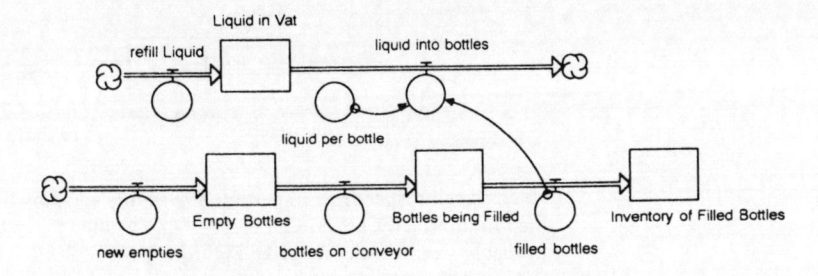

Skill 5: operational thinking

Operational thinking goes hand in hand with structural thinking. Thinking operationally means thinking in terms of how things really work—not how they theoretically work, or how one might fashion a bit of algebra capable of generating realistic-looking output. One of my favorite examples of the distinction between operational and nonoperational thinking is provided by the "universal soil loss equation." This equation expresses a "fundamental law" in soil physics. Used to predict the volume of erosion that will occur on a given parcel of land, it can be represented as

Erosion = RKLSCP

where
R = rainfall
K = soil erodability
L = slope length
S = slope gradient
C = vegetative coverage
P = erosion control practices

Fig. 14. Operational thinking: how it really works

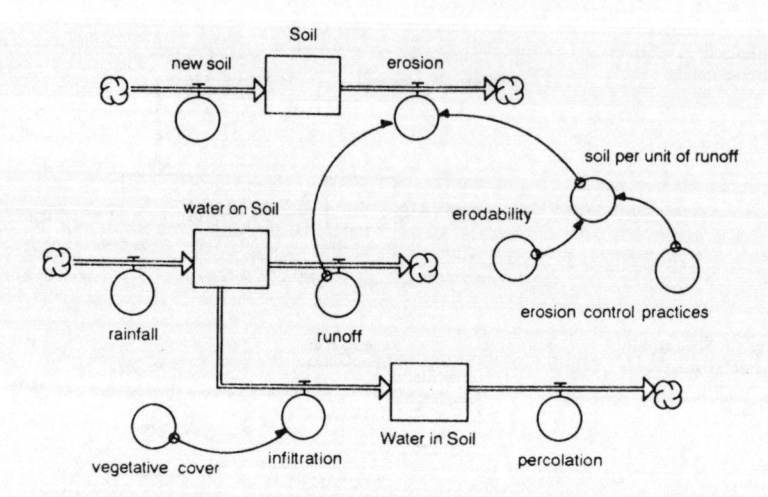

Now, no self-respecting soil particle solves this equation before it rolls on down the hill! In fact, the erosion process—if one wanted to see how it really works—probably would look more like Figure 14.

As the figure indicates, erosion is a process, not a string of factors. It is generated by water running off, with each unit of runoff carrying with it a certain quantity of soil. That quantity is, among other things, influenced by erosion control practices and by the characteristics of the soil itself. By looking at erosion in an operational way, it becomes possible to think more effectively about what the real levers are for managing the process.

A second brief example should further illustrate the notion of operational thinking. A popular economic journal published the research of a noted economist who had developed a very sophisticated econometric model designed to predict milk production in the United States. The model contained a raft of macroeconomic variables woven together in a set of complex equations. But nowhere in that model did cows appear. If one asks how milk is actually generated, one discovers that cows are absolutely essential to the process. Thinking operationally about milk production, one would focus first on cows, then on the rhythms associated with farmers' decisions to increase and decrease herd size, the relations governing milk productivity per cow, and so on.

Operational thinking grounds students in reality. It also tends to be perceived as relevant because the student is thinking about it *like it really is* rather than dealing with abstractions that may bear little relation to what's going on. It's easy to create exercises that develop operational thinking. Simply look around at real-world processes (like learning, becoming friends, experiencing peer pressure, pollution, drug or alcohol addiction) and ask, How do these processes really work? Let the students diagram their resulting observations. Then have them challenge each other's depictions, asking, Is this really how it works?

Skill 6: continuum thinking

Continuum thinking is nourished primarily by working with simulation models that have been built using a continuous, as opposed to discrete, modeling approach. Discrete models are distinguished by containing many "if, then, else" type of equations. In such models, for example, one might find that water consumption (the outflow from Available Water) is governed by some logic of the form IF Available Water >0 THEN Normal Water Consumption ELSE 0. The continuous version of this relation would begin with an operational specification of the water consumption process (e.g., Water consumption = Population × Water per person). Water per person (per year) then would be a continuous function of Available Water.

Unlike its discrete analog, the continuous formulation indicates that water consumption would be continuously affected as Available Water became depleted. That is, measures such as rationing, increases in water prices, or moratoriums on new construction would come into play as residents of the area began to detect less than adequate supplies of water. The discrete formulation, by contrast, implies "business as usual" right up to the point where Available Water falls to zero. At that point, consumption is zero. Although, from a mechanical standpoint, the differences between the continuous and discrete formulations may seem unimportant, the associated implications for thinking are quite profound.

An "if, then, else" view of the world tends to lead to "us versus them" and "*is* versus *is not*" distinctions. Such distinctions, in turn, tend to result in polarized thinking. Issues are seen as black or white; gray is not an option. Two examples should help make this point.

In the early 1970s, a Stanford University psychologist, Philip Zimbardo, conducted a now infamous experiment in which he randomly divided a group of undergraduate Stanford males into two groups. The first he classed as "prisoners," the second as "guards." The two groups, with little other direction, were told to "play prison" for a couple of weeks. Within two days, a student who had assumed the role of prisoner broke down and had to be released. The experiment was terminated prematurely (after six days) because two other "prisoners" had broken down, and others appeared to be on the verge of doing the same. In the postmortem discussion and analysis, one of the students was identified as having played the role of a "John Wayne" guard. He had shown considerable ingenuity in his forms of degradation and punishment. An interesting question was posed: If "John Wayne" could have been screened out before the experiment, would the results have been the same? Was the unexpectedly high level of brutality attributable to the tone being set by this one student guard?

From an "if, then, else" viewpoint, one might answer yes: screen out any "John Wayne" types, and you'll have a very different prison. From a continuum viewpoint, one might instead argue that people are not "John Wayne" or "not John Wayne." Rather, we each have the capacity for manifesting brutal and degrading behavior. This situation, demanding that guards "control" prisoners, can call forth this behavior. The individual most disposed to manifesting it, does so. Remove that individual, and the next most disposed will arise to assume this role. A STELLA model of this experiment, constructed using a continuous modeling process, did indeed show this result. The conclusion from the model, therefore, is that seeking to screen out "John Waynes" is not likely to be an effective intervention for improving the dynamic equilibrium (in real prisons or simulated ones) between prisoners and guards. Instead, some more fundamental change in the system is required.

A second brief example concerns the extreme positions on abortion taken by members of the pro-life and pro-choice camps. Who would want to be labeled anti-life or anti-choice? Yet that is how some in each camp see the other side. Once a debate becomes polarized in this fashion, it becomes extremely difficult to make any progress in resolving the issues. You're either "for me" or "against me." But, from a continuum standpoint, "us versus them" disappears. For example, even the most ardent pro-choice proponent would never claim it was all right to abort a fetus ten minutes before full-term delivery. And no pro-life adherent believes that the flushing of a live egg due to menstruation really is murder. By inventing these extreme conditions, it becomes clear that the real debate is not black and white. Pro-life people really are pro-choice people under certain circumstances, and pro-choice advocates really subscribe to a pro-life position in some cases. Given this perspective, the real issue is, Where is the common ground? When a piece of protoplasm should be considered to have achieved the status of a viable human life form is not so cut-and-dried after all. In place of "us versus them," there is a continuum.

The development of continuum thinking capability is closely related to the development of generic thinking skills. Both emphasize the ability to recognize the familiar in what appears diverse or distinct. It's the ability to see connections and interdependencies rather than sharp boundaries and disconnections. Many continuous models exist that can be used to develop the sense of continuum. Using these models is a powerful process for building continuum thinking capability.

Skill 7: scientific thinking

The final component of systems thinking that we have identified is scientific thinking. Let me begin by saying what scientific thinking is *not*. My definition of scientific thinking has virtually nothing to do with absolute numerical measurement. Too often, science is taken to be synonymous with "measuring precisely." To me, scientific thinking has more to do with quantification than measurement. Again, the two are not synonymous. There are very few things that can be measured unambiguously, for instance, length, width, height, concentration, magnitude, and velocity. But think of all the things that cannot be measured precisely: how much wisdom you possess; how nice a person you are; what it feels like to go to a particular high school; how hungry you are; how much you love someone; how much self-esteem you have; how frustrated you feel.

I think most people would agree that all these nonmeasurable things are important. None can be gauged on any absolute numerical scale, but all of them can be quantified. It's simple. Pick a scale—for example, 0–100—and assign a value. Zero means "the absence of." One hundred means "maximum possible amount." Establishing a scale does not mean one can specify exactly what any of these values are in the real system. It means only that one has established a rigorous convention for thinking about the dynamics of the variable. Now one can ask questions like, What keeps self-confidence from rising above 100? Since 100 has been defined as "maximum possible amount," some processes must exist in the real system that prevent this accumulation from overflowing! Having been rigorous (scientific) about the quantification, one can then think rigorously about the dynamics of the variable.

Thinking scientifically also means being rigorous about testing hypotheses. This process begins by always ensuring that students in fact have a hypothesis to test. Once again, in the absence of an a priori hypothesis, the experimentation process can easily degenerate into a video game. People will simply flail away trying to get one of the Super Mario Brothers to the Princess. Having an explicit hypothesis to test before engaging in any simulation activity helps guard against the video game syndrome. The hypothesis-testing process itself also needs to be informed by scientific thinking. People thinking scientifically modify only one thing at a time and hold all else constant. They also test their models from steady state, using idealized inputs to call forth "natural frequency responses." This set of rigorous hypothesis-testing concepts really is at the heart of what I mean by scientific thinking.

The seven-track melee

When one becomes aware that good systems thinking involves working on at least these seven tracks simultaneously, it becomes a lot easier to understand why people trying to learn this framework often go on overload. When these tracks are explicitly organized, and separate attention is paid to develop each skill, the resulting bite-sized pieces make the fare much more digestible. We've found that explicitly separating these seven tracks, then attending to skill development in each, greatly increases learning productivity.

Summary

The connections among the various physical, social, and ecological subsystems that make up our reality are tightening. There is indeed less and less "away," both spatially and temporally, to throw things into. Unfortunately, the evolution of our thinking capabilities has not kept pace with this growing level of interdependence. The consequence is that the problems we now face are stubbornly resistant to our interventions. To "get back into the foot race," we will need to coherently evolve our educational system along three dimensions: educational process, thinking paradigm, and learning tools. At the nexus of these three threads is a learner-directed learning process in which students will use computer-based learning environments to build their intuition and understanding of complex interdependent systems by participating in virtual reality experiences. One of the principal barriers to this exciting prospect is the currently limited capacity for transferring the systems thinking framework to educators and their students. By viewing systems thinking within the broader context of critical thinking skills, and by recognizing the multidimensional nature of the thinking skills involved in systems thinking, we can greatly reduce the time it takes for people to apprehend this framework. As this framework increasingly becomes the context within which we think, we will gain much greater leverage in addressing the pressing issues that await us in the 1990s. The time is now!

References

Diehl, E. W. 1990. MicroWorlds Creator 2.0. MicroWorlds, Inc., 47 Third St. #200, Cambridge, MA 02141, U.S.A.
Draper, F., and M. Swanson. 1990. Learner-Directed Systems Education: A Successful Example. *System Dynamics Review* 6(2): 209-213.
Meadows, D. H. 1982. Whole Earth Models and Systems. *The CoEvolution Quarterly* (summer): 98-108.
Peterson, S. 1990. *A User's Guide to STELLAStack*. 2d ed. High Performance Systems, 45 Lyme Rd., Hanover, NH 03755, U.S.A.

Richardson, G. P. 1982. Problems with Causal-Loop Diagrams. *System Dynamics Review* 2(2): 158–170. Original paper 1976.

Richmond, B. 1985. *Designing Effective Policy: A Conceptual Foundation*. Thayer School of Engineering, Dartmouth College, Hanover, NH 03755, U.S.A.

Richmond, B., S. Peterson, and P. Vescuso. 1987. *An Academic User's Guide to STELLA*. High Performance Systems.

Roberts, N., D. F. Andersen, R. M. Deal, M. S. Garet, and W. A. Shaffer. 1983. *Introduction to Computer Simulation: A System Dynamics Modeling Approach*. Reading, Mass.: Addison-Wesley.

[3]

CHAPTER 7

System Dynamics: Simulation for Policy Analysis from a Feedback Perspective

George P. Richardson

Abstract

System dynamics is a computer-aided approach to policy analysis and design. With origins in servomechanisms engineering and management, the approach uses a perspective based on information feedback and circular causality to understand the dynamics of complex social systems.

The loop concept underlying feedback and circular causality is not sufficient by itself, however. The explanatory power and insightfulness of feedback understandings also rest on the notions of active system structure and loop dominance, concepts that arise only in nonlinear systems. Computer simulation is the tool that makes it possible to trace the dynamic implications of nonlinear systems. The system dynamicist's feedback perspective is strengthened further by approaching complex problems from a particular conceptual distance, one that blurs discrete events and decisions into continuous patterns of behavior. This continuous view, expressed in stocks, flows, and information links, focuses not on discrete decisions but on the policy structure underlying decisions.

This chapter describes the system dynamics approach and provides an entry into the literature in the field. It explores the wide range of diagramming tools used to conceptualize and explain the stock-and-flow feedback structure responsible for observed behavior. It discusses several simulation environments that are increasing our conceptual and technical modeling abilities and points to principles of systems that facilitate the formulation of insightful models.

An example of policy analysis in school finance is sketched. The insights dervied from that study are linked to a growing list of generic simulation-based policy insights in complex systems.

The background of the field of system dynamics and its current directions are contained in an extensive bibliography.

1. Introduction

System dynamics is a computer-aided approach to policy analysis and design. It applies to *dynamic* problems—problems that involve change over time—arising in complex social, managerial, economic, or ecological systems—liter-

7. System Dynamics

ally any dynamic systems characterized by interdependence, mutual interaction, information feedback, and circular causality.

The field developed from the work of Jay W. Forrester (1958). His seminal book *Industrial Dynamics* [14] is still a significant statement of philosophy and methodology in the field. Within ten years of its publication, the span of applications grew from corporate and industrial problems to include the management of research and development, urban stagnation and decay [1, 17], commodity cycles, and the dynamics of growth in a finite world. It is now applied in economics, public policy, environmental studies, defense, theory-building in social science, and others, as well as in management. The name *industrial dynamics* no longer does justice to the breadth of the field, so it has become generalized to *system dynamics*.[1]

The system dynamics approach involves

—defining problems dynamically, in terms of graphs over time;
—striving for an endogenous, behavioral view of the significant dynamics of a system, a focus inward on the characteristics of a system that themselves generate or exacerbate the perceived problem;
—thinking of all concepts in the real system as continuous quantities interconnected in loops of information feedback and circular causality;
—identifying independent stocks or accumulations (levels) in the system and their inflows and outflows (rates);
—formulating a behavioral model capable of reproducing, by itself, the dynamic problem of concern—the model is usually a computer simulation model expressed in nonlinear equations, but is occasionally left unquantified as a diagram capturing the stock-and-flow/causal feedback structure of the system;
—deriving understandings and applicable policy insights from the resulting model;
—implementing changes resulting from model-based understandings and insights.

This is a skeletal list. The field is broad, and there are practitioners worldwide who would add to or alter these emphases. Mathematically, the basic structure of a formal system dynamics computer simulation model is easily, if not very helpfully, described as a system of coupled, nonlinear, first-order differential (or integral) equations,

$$\frac{d}{dt}\mathbf{x}(t) = \mathbf{f}(\mathbf{x}, \mathbf{p}),$$

where **x** is a vector of levels (stocks or state variables), **p** is a set of parameters,

---

[1] The modern name suggests links to other systems methodologies, but the links are weak and misleading. System dynamics emerges out of servomechanisms engineering, not general systems theory or cybernetics [38, 39].

and **f** is a nonlinear vector-valued function.[2] Some practitioners in the field work on the mathematics of such structures, including the theory and mechanics of computer simulation (e.g., [35]), analysis and simplification of dynamic systems (e.g., [22]), policy optimization (e.g., [24, 26, 61]), dynamical systems theory (e.g., [3, 31]), and complex nonlinear dynamics and deterministic chaos.[3]

Although recognizing these important mathematical directions within the field and not wanting to slight them, here we shall limit our focus to the core of the field that studies perceived problems in complex systems and presses toward qualitative understandings and policy insights. This chapter begins with a broad view of some of the characteristics of the system dynamics approach, discussing in turn feedback thinking, loop dominance in dynamic feedback systems, and the system dynamicist's endogenous point of view. The discussion then focuses on some of the details, including the concept of levels and rates, continuity, diagrams for conceptualization and communication, and existing simulation languages for system dynamics modeling. At the end of the chapter, we drop back from the details to consider broader modeling heuristics and principles of systems, a policy analysis example, generic simulation-based policy insights, and directions for further reading.

2. Feedback Thinking

Conceptually, the feedback concept is at the heart of the system dynamics approach. Diagrams of loops of information feedback and circular causality are tools for conceptualizing the structure of a complex system and for communicating model-based insights. Intuitively, a feedback loops exists when information resulting from some action travels through a system and eventually returns in some form to its point of origin, potentially influencing future action. If the tendency in the loop is to reinforce the initial action, the loop is called a *positive* feedback loop; if the tendency is to oppose the initial action, the loop is called a *negative* feedback loop. The sign of the loop is called its *polarity*. Negative loops can be variously characterized as goal-seeking, equilibrating, or stabilizing processes. They can sometimes generate oscillations, as a pendulum seeking its equilibrium goal gathers momentum and overshoots it. Positive loops are sources of growth or accelerating collapse; they are disequilibrating and destabilizing. Combined, positive and negative circular causal feedback loops can generate all manner of dynamic patterns.

The loop concept is familiar to readers of this volume. It finds expression in a number of qualitative approaches presented here. Its attractiveness as a

---

[2] Such a system has been variously called a *state-determined system* in the engineering literature, an *absolute system* [4], an *equifinal system* [57], and a *dynamical system* [32].

[3] See *System Dynamics Review* 4, 1–2 (1988), a special issue on chaos.

basis for modern qualitative technologies is no accident, for feedback thought has been present implicitly or explicitly for hundreds of years in the social sciences [38, 39, 55]. We have the vicious circle originating in classical logic, the invisible hand of Adam Smith, Malthus's correct observation of population growth as a self-reinforcing process, Keynes's consumption multiplier, the investment accelerator of Hicks and Samuelson, compound interest or inflation, the biological concepts of proprioception and homeostasis [7], Gregory Bateson's schismogenesis (the generation and maintenance of a split between cultures in contact) [5, 6], Festinger's cognitive dissonance, the bandwagon effect, Myrdal's principle of cumulative causation, Venn's idea of a suicidal prophecy, Merton's related notion of a self-fulfilling prophecy, and so on. Each of these ideas can be concisely and insightfully represented as one or more loops of causal influences with positive or negative polarities. Great social scientists are feedback thinkers; great social theories are feedback thoughts.

3. Loop Dominance

The loop concept underlying feedback and circular causality by itself is not enough, however. The explanatory power and insightfulness of feedback understandings also rest on the notions of active structure and loop dominance.

We know that social systems change over time. What focuses concern in one period is overshadowed by other concerns at other times and conditions. There are discernible patterns in newspaper headlines and legislative efforts as pressures shift from national affairs to international affairs, defense, or the balance of payments. Goals and negative feedback structures that dominate governmental efforts in times of persistent inflation change and evolve as the main economic problems are perceived to shift to, say, persistently high unemployment. No static view of the structure of a dynamic social system is likely to be perceived to be powerful. A crucial requirement for a powerful feedback view of a dynamic system is the ability of a mental or formal model to change the strengths of influences as conditions change, that is to say, the ability to shift *active* or *dominant structure*.

An overly simplified example can make the concept clear. Consider the life cycle of a finite resource, such as global petroleum. Figure 7.1 shows two highly aggregated feedback loops that can describe the dynamics of the life cycle. As oil is discovered and production begins, economies find uses for the resource and demand for it increases. Furthermore, accumulating experience with discovery, recovery, and production leads to more sophisticated and efficient technologies, further accelerating the rate at which the resource can be produced. The feedback loop on the right side of Figure 7.1 is a positive loop. In this highly simplified view, the self-reinforcing tendencies this loop represents are responsible for the growth of the use of the resource. Oil production would

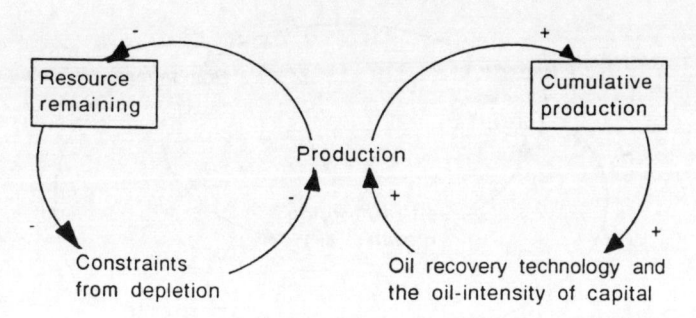

FIGURE 7.1. Positive and negative feedback loops in the life cycle of a finite resource such as petroleum.

increase, and its rate of increase would also increase; a graph of oil production and cumulative oil production would curve upward, looking like exponential growth.

The left side of Figure 7.1 is a negative loop representing the effects of the depletion of this finite resource. In the early stages of the petroleum life cycle, this loop is not influential. It might not even be perceived to exist. Whatever minor effects it might have are completely overshadowed by the growth-producing self-reinforcing processes aggregated in the right-side loop. However, under the assumption that the resource is finite, this negative loop must eventually become the dominant factor in our ability to produce and consume petroleum. Eventually, as the resource becomes scarce, the difficulties and costs of discovery and production will slow production and pull supply below the growing demand. Toward the end of the life cycle, the price of the resource will have risen well beyond the price of substitute energy sources, and substitution will increasingly occur.

The graph of production will rise, peak, and eventually enter a persistent though noisy decline. Cumulative production over time will show a more-or-less S-shaped pattern. The upward curving period of exponential growth changes to a still-increasing but downward-curving pattern that eventually comes into equilibrium by the end of the life cycle. The pattern of cumulative production shifts from accelerating, limitless growth to a decelerating approach to a limit. The change in the pattern is insightfully seen as a *shift in dominance* from self-reinforcing positive loop processes to constraining, equilibrating, negative loop processes.

The qualitative notion of a shift in loop dominance can be made rigorous in such a simple system, and an important modeling understanding emerges. Consider the Verhulst equation (the logistic equation) for population growth: $dP/dt = aP - bP^2$. Verhulst intended the term aP to represent the self-reinforcing growth tendencies of the population, while the term bP^2 is to represent the constraints on growth that would come from human interaction (assumed proportional to $P*P$). Thus, the system can be viewed as a pair of feedback loops, as shown in Figure 7.2.

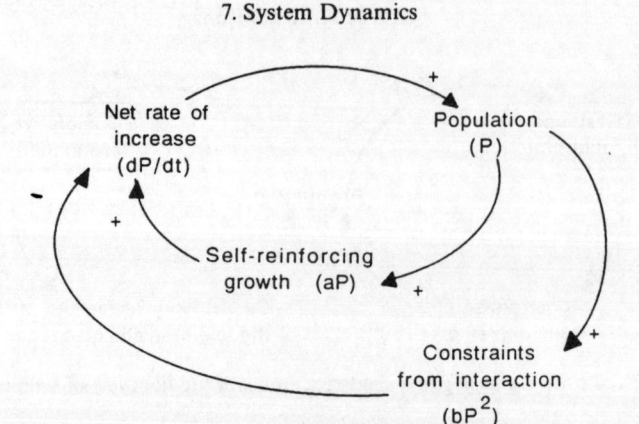

FIGURE 7.2. Feedback loops in the Verhulst (logistic) equation.

The dominant polarity of this system can be defined as the sign of dP'/dP, where $P' = dP/dt$. Intuitively, we trace the aggregate effect in this system of a small increase dP in population. If the effect is positive and so self-reinforcing, the positive polarity dominates; if it is negative, the negative polarity dominates.

Since $P' = dP/dt = aP - bP^2$, we compute $dP'/dP = a - 2bP$, which is positive for $P < a/(2b)$ and negative for $P > a/(2b)$. Noting that population growth halts when P reaches a/b, we conclude that the positive loop dominates until the population size reaches half its maximum and from there on the negative loop dominates. Thus, the classic logistic growth pattern can be seen as the consequence of a shift in loop dominance from a positive feedback loop to a negative feedback loop.

Two things about this example are critically important and generalizable to a feedback view of dynamic systems. First, the shift in loop dominance comes as a consequence of the *nonlinearity* of the Verhulst equation. If the equation were $dP/dt = aP - bP$, no such shift in loop dominance would occur. If $a > b$, the positive loop would always dominate, and the system would show limitless exponential growth; if $a < b$, the negative loop would always dominate, and the system would exhibit exponential decline to the goal of zero. Furthermore, if the system were $dP/dt = aP - bP^3$ or $aP - bP \ln P$ (the Gompertz curve), it would show qualitatively the same behavior as the classic logistic equation, for in either of these equations the negative, nonlinear constraint term can start small and then overtake the positive, self-reinforcing growth term. Thus, *nonlinear* models have the property that they can exhibit shifts in loop dominance. Linear models cannot.

From a feedback perspective, the ability of nonlinearities to generate shifts in loop dominance is the fundamental reason for advocating nonlinear models of social system behavior. Real systems are perceived to change their active or dominant structure over time. Only nonlinear models can do that, so the best mathematical models of dynamic social systems must be nonlinear. In fact, without the concept of shifting loop dominance—without nonlinearities in formal models of complex systems—the feedback concept is justifiably perceived to be a weak tool incapable of capturing important dynamics in real systems.

4. The Endogenous Point of View

A second but even more powerful insight is that a shift in loop dominance in these nonlinear models comes about *endogenously*. The shift from positive loop to negative loop in the Verhulst equation is not engineered from outside the system; it happens *internally* as the system plays itself out over time. The system changes its own dominant structure as it evolves. Yet we could easily imagine an exogenous intervention—a random blip, a switch, even the re-writing of an equation part way through—that could produce fundamental changes in structure and dynamics. We really must qualify the strong conclusion previously reached: Nonlinearities in a formal dynamic model are essential if one wishes to obtain changes in active structure *endogenously*.

The concept of endogenous change is fundamental to the system dynamics approach. Practitioners strive for an *endogenous point of view*. The goal is to derive the essential dynamic characteristics of a system from the inner workings of the system itself. It is an inward-looking perspective. Look for sources of urban decay within the structure and policies of the city itself; look for sources of cyclical customer orders in the inventory and production policies of the company itself. The goal is to view problems as consequences of a complex system of interacting subsystems, not as the unavoidable result of exogenous disturbances.

The endogenous point of view is variously expressed. Forrester [15, 17] signaled it when he outlined his general hierarchical theory of system structure:

Closed boundary
  Feedback loops
    Levels
    Rates
      Goal
      Observed condition
      Discrepancy
      Desired action

The *closed boundary* in this hierarchy is not "closed" in the general system theory sense [57]. A system dynamics model—of a company, an urban area, a school district—interchanges material (orders, people, money) with its environment, so it is not closed in the general system theory sense. Forrester intended the word here to mean *causally* closed:

> The boundary encloses the system of interest. It states that the modes of behavior under study are created by the interaction of the system compo-

7. System Dynamics

nents within the boundary. The boundary implies that no influences from outside of the boundary are necessary for generating the particular behavior being investigated. [15, 16, p. 84]

The modeler's goal is to assemble a formal structure that can, *by itself*, without exogenous explanations, reproduce the essential characteristics of a dynamic problem.[4]

The importance of the endogenous point of view must not be underestimated. It dictates aspects of model formulation: exogenous disturbances are seen at most as *triggers* of system behavior (like displacing a pendulum); the *causes* are contained within the structure of the system itself (like the interaction of a pendulum's position and momentum that produces oscillations). Corrective responses are also not modeled as functions of time, but are dependent on conditions within the system. Time by itself is not seen as a cause.

But, more importantly, theory building and policy analysis are significantly affected by this endogenous perspective. Taking an endogenous view changes the focus of policymakers from trying to anticipate a whimsical environment to trying to understand the inner workings of the system that create or amplify perceived problems. It exposes the natural *compensating* tendencies in social systems that conspire to defeat many policy initiatives.

It is seen as an essential foundation of good theory. Exogenous explanations of system behavior are simply not as interesting. They can even be misleading: There are no exogenous events that cause the turnaround in the swing of a pendulum, and perhaps none in the peak or trough of the business cycle.

Finally, the endogenous point of view is an empowering perspective that focuses attention on aspects of the system over which people may hope to have some control. If the cause of urban decay is seen as not enough federal funding, then restoring urban health lies outside the control of urban actors. But, if urban decay is seen to have components that are internal to the city, then local policymakers can strive to improve matters no matter what the federal government decides to do. The effort to find endogenous sources of dynamic problems is essential if endogenous solutions are to be found.

The endogenous point of view is the feedback view pressed to an extreme. In fact, the feedback view can be seen as a *consequence* of the effort to capture dynamics within a closed causal boundary. Without causal loops, all variables must trace the sources of their variation ultimately outside a system. Without loops we are forced to an exogenous view of the causes of system behavior. Assuming instead that the causes of all significant behavior in the system are contained within some closed causal boundary forces causal influences to feed back upon themselves, forming causal loops. Feedback loops enable the endogenous point of view and give it structure.

This endogenous point of view has come to be summarized in a shorthand

---

[4] There is some debate about the practicality of creating endogenous models of real policy problems. Fundamentally, the debate concerns the appropriate model boundary for a given policy analysis.

tenet: *Behavior is a consequence of structure.* Behavior here means dynamic behavior, phrased in terms of graphs over time. Structure refers to feedback structure: a circular causal complexity composed of stocks (levels), flows (rates), and information links. The phrase is, at the same time, a grand conjecture, an article of faith, and a proposition repeatedly verified in the practice of building and simulating models of social systems.

5. Levels and Rates

Stocks and the flows that affect them are essential components of system structure. A map of causal influences and feedback loops is not enough to determine the dynamic behavior of a system. Stocks—accumulations—are the memory of a dynamic system and are the sources of disequilibrium. An inventory, for example, exists to decouple the flow of the production from the flow of shipments. If shipments exceed production, inventory absorbs the inequity by declining. A population similarly absorbs inequity between births per year and deaths per year. And changes in such levels generate other changes. A rising population would produce more births per year, for example, which would in turn push population still higher, ceteris paribus. A declining inventory would eventually generate pressures to slow shipments or increase production. Stocks, or *levels* in the system dynamicist's intuitive terminology, and the rates that affect them are the sources of dynamic behavior.[5]

Levels also persist through time. If time were to stop, it is the levels, the conceptual and physical stocks in the system, that would still exist and be in some sense measurable. We could tell the size of inventories and the work force, for example, but we could not know the rate of production.

6. Continuity and Conceptual Distance

The importance of levels and rates appears most clearly when one takes a *continuous* view of structure and dynamics. Although a discrete view, focusing on separate events and decisions, is entirely compatible with an endogenous feedback perspective, the system dynamics approach emphasizes a continuous view. System dynamics models are continuous representations of system structure and dynamics.[6]

---

[5] In engineering terminology, levels are the *state* variables; rates are the components of the derivatives or rates of change of the system states.

[6] To be excruciatingly precise, a system dynamics model simulated on a digital computer is a discrete approximation of a continuous system. For computation purposes, model TIME is segmented into short chunks of length *DT*, and the model is stepped discretely through TIME. However, this discreteness is an unavoidable accident of digital simulation; it has nothing to do with the intent or perspective of the modeler. A system dynamics model is most properly seen as a continuous system composed of differential equations (really integral equations), not a discrete system made up of difference equations.

The continuous view has several advantages and one or two disadvantages. Its major disadvantage is that it is hard to achieve. In daily, lifelong experience, we see discrete events and make discrete decisions. Forrester [14] argued, however, that a continuous view helps to focus us on what is most important in dynamic social systems. He cautioned us to be "on guard against unnecessarily cluttering our formulation with the detail of discrete events that only obscure the momentum and continuity" of social systems [14].[7] The continuous view strives to look beyond events to see the dynamic patterns underlying them. Model not the appearance of a discrete new housing unit, but focus instead on the rise and fall of aggregate numbers of housing units. Moreover, the continuous view focuses not on discrete decisions but on the *policy structure* underlying decisions: not why this particular apartment building was constructed but what persistent pressures exist in the urban system that produce decisions that change housing availability in the city. Events and decisions are seen as surface phenomena that ride on an underlying tide of system structure and behavior. It is that underlying tide of policy structure and continuous behavior that is the system dynamicist's focus.

There is thus a *distancing* inherent in the system dynamics approach, not so close as to be confused by discrete decisions and myriad operational details, but not so far away as to miss the critical elements of policy structure and behavior. Events are deliberately blurred into dynamic behavior. Decisions are deliberately blurred into perceived policy structures. Insights into the connections between system structure and behavior come from this particular distance of perspective.[8]

7. Modeling Tools: Diagrams

Diagrams are essential for conceptualizing system structure and communicating model-based insights about feedback structure and dynamic behavior. We will mention four kinds that prove useful in various stages of a policy simulation study.

The kind of diagram that contains the greatest amount of information about system structure is exemplified in Figure 7.3; it is perhaps best referred to as a *stock-and-flow/feedback diagram*. Each symbol in such a detailed diagram refers to a unique equation in the formal model the diagram represents. Types of equations are distinguished: levels are rectangles and auxiliaries (algebraic computations or relationships expressed graphically) are circles: constants are marked with a line; rates are shown with a symbol representing a valve that controls a flow. The arrows also convey information: Conserved flows, shown as solid or double arrows, are distinguished from information links, which are identified with dotted arrows. There is such a lack of ambiguity in such

---

[7] See also [10, p. 64], [33], and [34, p. 21].
[8] For further comments on conceptual distance, see [11, p. 377], [14, p. 96], and [39, p. 508].

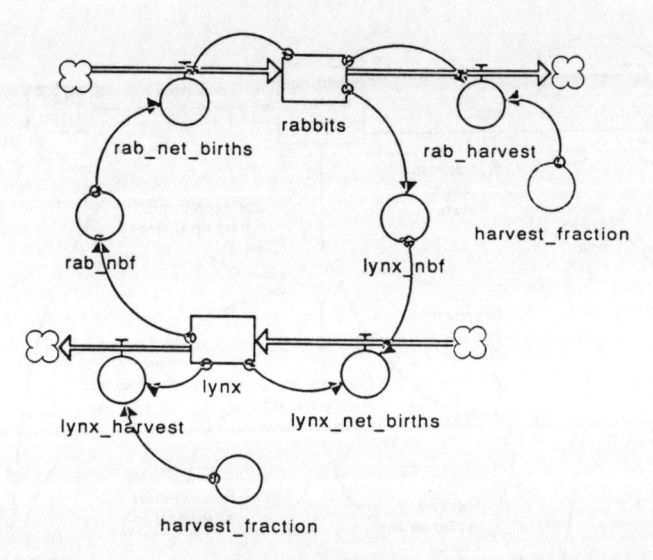

FIGURE 7.3. Stock-and-flow/feedback structure diagram of a simple predator–prey system.

diagrams that one can come close to recreating a model's equations (without parameters) from well-drawn stock-and-flow/feedback structure diagrams. Their very detail and precision, however, limits the audiences to which they communicate well.

A much simpler diagram at the same structural level is a picture of a feedback system consisting simply of words and arrows, so-called *causal-loop diagrams* or *influence diagrams* (Figure 7.2, or Figures 7.1 and 7.7 without the rectangles, would be examples). Frequently, causal-loop diagrams are suggested as the first step in model conceptualization [20, 42, 47]. Their greatest strength—simplicity—is also their greatest weakness. They omit the critical distinction between material flows and information links and consequently obscure the accumulations in a system. Furthermore, they make it easy to draw a picture of systemic interactions that focuses on sequences of events. The arrows can come to mean sequence ("and then ..."), not causal influence. An event orientation severely inhibits formulating a quantitative model of a complex system, particularly one striving to capture the fundamental structure and pressures present in the system that persist through time.[9]

The troubles simple influence diagrams and causal loops can cause in the

---

[9] The flexibility of the technique of *cognitive mapping* frequently results in word-and-arrow diagrams that mix causal structure with sequences of events; see, for example, some of the cognitive maps in [13]. For the kinds of translations event-oriented diagrams require, see [42].

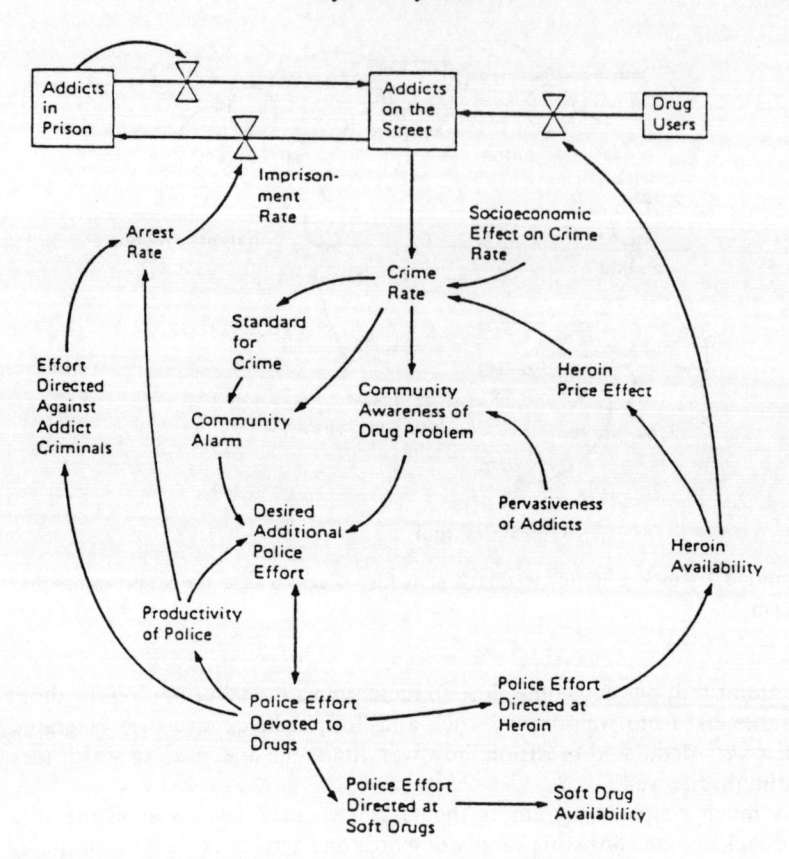

FIGURE 7.4. An example of a causal-loop or influence diagram modified to show the distinctions between accumulations (levels) and other variables and between information links and material flows [25, p. 27]. (See, also, [62, Figs. 1 and 7] for other approaches.)

conceptualization stages of a simulation study have prompted most practitioners to find ways to modify them to show levels and rates. Figures 7.4 and 7.7 show examples. Suffice it to say, experience suggests that simple word-and-arrow diagrams are best reserved for communicating system structure and insights toward the *end* of a study, not as a step in model conceptualization or formulation. In the formulation phase, there appears to be no substitute for trying to identify important accumulations and the rates that change them.

A powerful extension of influence diagrams with explicit rates and levels is Morecroft's notion of policy structure diagrams [29, 30]. Figure 7.5 shows an example.

These diagrams focus on the important levels and rates in a portion or *sector* of a complex system, along with an aggregated view of important information

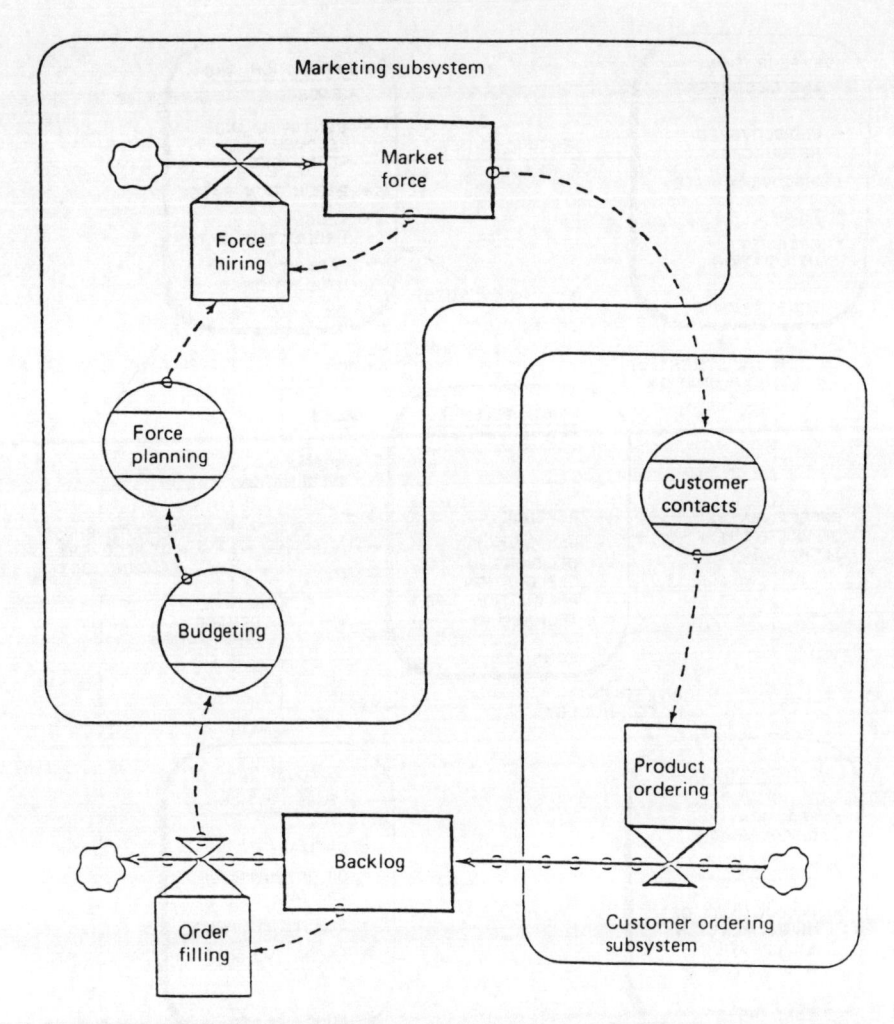

FIGURE 7.5. A policy structure diagram [29]. The diagram presents a view of part of Forrester's market growth model [15].

connections among those levels and rates. They highlight the key policy areas in the sector and show the information streams that combine to produce decisions under those policies. Some of the information streams would be deliberate components of policy, while others would be unavoidable pressures on policy decisions from various parts of the system. The advantages of policy structure diagrams are an appropriate level of detail for clients; explicit representation on stocks and flows, which helps to sensitize clients to the importance of accumulations in the dynamics of the system; and a focus on policy, which matches the client's locus of concern. Their main disadvantage

7. System Dynamics

[Figure 7.6 diagram: An overview of model and sector boundaries, showing five interconnected sectors:

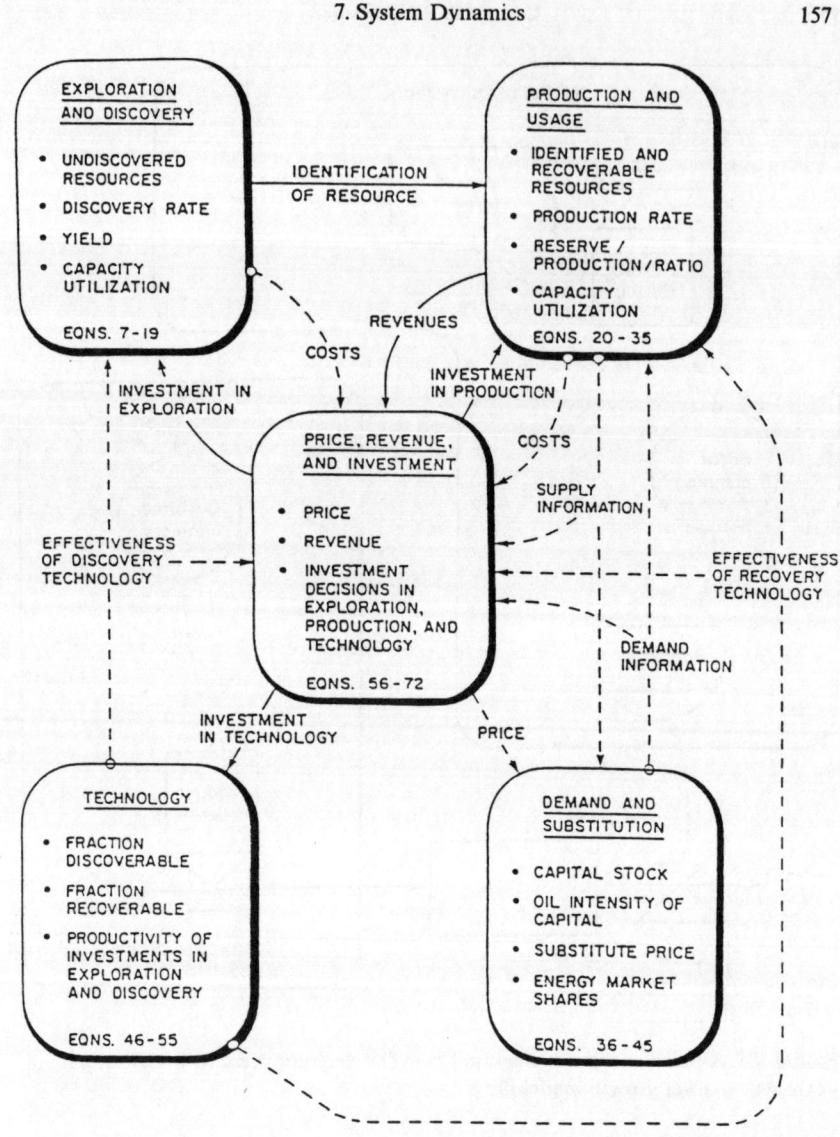

- **EXPLORATION AND DISCOVERY**: UNDISCOVERED RESOURCES; DISCOVERY RATE; YIELD; CAPACITY UTILIZATION. EQNS. 7–19
- **PRODUCTION AND USAGE**: IDENTIFIED AND RECOVERABLE RESOURCES; PRODUCTION RATE; RESERVE/PRODUCTION/RATIO; CAPACITY UTILIZATION. EQNS. 20–35
- **PRICE, REVENUE, AND INVESTMENT**: PRICE; REVENUE; INVESTMENT DECISIONS IN EXPLORATION, PRODUCTION, AND TECHNOLOGY. EQNS. 56–72
- **TECHNOLOGY**: FRACTION DISCOVERABLE; FRACTION RECOVERABLE; PRODUCTIVITY OF INVESTMENTS IN EXPLORATION AND DISCOVERY. EQNS. 46–55
- **DEMAND AND SUBSTITUTION**: CAPITAL STOCK; OIL INTENSITY OF CAPITAL; SUBSTITUTE PRICE; ENERGY MARKET SHARES. EQNS. 36–45

Flows include: IDENTIFICATION OF RESOURCE, REVENUES, COSTS, INVESTMENT IN EXPLORATION, INVESTMENT IN PRODUCTION, INVESTMENT IN TECHNOLOGY, EFFECTIVENESS OF DISCOVERY TECHNOLOGY, EFFECTIVENESS OF RECOVERY TECHNOLOGY, SUPPLY INFORMATION, DEMAND INFORMATION, PRICE.]

FIGURE 7.6. An example of an overview of model and sector boundaries [54].

is their tendency to obscure the existence and the character of feedback loops in the system. Their use in the system dynamics literature is limited. Nonetheless, for system conceptualization and for communication about model structure, policy structure diagrams have considerable promise.

A fourth kind of diagram useful for both conceptualization and communication is an *overview of model and sector boundaries*. Figure 7.6 shows an example. Such diagrams strive to capture the organization of a simulation model, to show a summary of what is included and what is excluded, and to show the main interconnections among the identifiable sectors in the system. Such a diagram is really a visual outline of the system and the model formulated to represent it for policy analysis. Formulated and presented at the outset of a study, an overview of model and sector boundaries helps to orient and join (if different) the modeler and the client. Throughout a study, such diagrams provide quick introductions and summaries of the scope of the study.

Rarely, however, can a study of policy alternatives in a complex social system stop at the level of diagrams.[10] Our means of making reliable deductions about the dynamic implications of a complex stock-and-flow/feedback structure is computer simulation.

8. Modeling Tools: Simulation Environments

As could be expected, there have been and continue to be dramatic developments in the software available to support system dynamics modeling. Many languages have the capabilities to represent and simulate dynamic systems; even general-purpose languages like BASIC or Pascal suffice. But special-purpose languages make the modeling task far easier. The original simulation language in the field was called SIMPLE, a cute acronym standing for Simulating Industrial Management Problems with Lots of Equations. It was followed quickly by DYNAMO [36, 42], for DYNAmic MOdels, which is still the language of choice for a majority of practitioners in the field. DYNAMO relieves the modeler from thoughts about *programming*. To a remarkable extent, it leaves one free to concentrate on the real system. The order of equations in a model, for example, can be arranged to suit the tastes and understandings of the modeler and the audience or clients. The equations can be arranged to tell a sensible story; DYNAMO handles the task of putting them in a computable order a machine can execute.

DYNAMO provides timescripts J, K, and L, analogous to subscripts, that make clear what is being computed when. K is "now," the time of the current computation; J is the previous moment, the time of the previous computation; and L is the time of the next computation. A level equation for population, for example, might look like

$$L \quad POP.K = POP.J + DT*(BIRTHS.JK - DEATHS.JK)$$

Here,

---

[10] An example of system dynamics studies that did is [62]. The potential for flawed conclusions from causal-loop diagrams without simulation is shown by [58], for example, who rests some of his analysis on the false claim that an even number of negative loops in a system creates a "deviation amplifying system" (see, e.g., [58, p. 133]).

POP.K	represents population at time K (current population);
POP.J	represents population at the previous computation;
DT	represents the length of simulated time between times J and K; and
BIRTHS.JK	represents the number of births per year that occurred in the time interval from time J to K.

DEATHS.JK represents the number of deaths per year that occurred from J to K. The L tells DYNAMO to expect a level equation in more or less this form. The language has extensive error-checking capabilities that can signal the user when unusual formats (errors usually) are encountered. The form of this level equation shows that the variable POP accumulates BIRTHS and DEATHS over time.[11]

Rearranging slightly, we see that the level equation is equivalent to the statement that

$$\frac{\Delta POP}{\Delta T} = \frac{POP.K - POP.J}{DT} = BIRTHS.JK - DEATHS.JK,$$

that is, that the net rate of change of population is births per year minus deaths per year, as we would require.

The computation interval DT in such equations is a fiction. The modeler's intent, in this case, is to capture population growth as a continuous process. To simulate a continuous process, we break simulated $TIME$ into discrete chunks and *step* the model through time, one discrete DT at a time. The modeler chooses DT small enough so that it has no discernible effect on model behavior. Calculus and derivatives and integrals are lurking in the not-so-distant background here, but simulation relieves the practitioner from concentrating on them. In fact, simulation makes possible the creation and use of models that can not be solved in closed form. Simulation expands the range of problems we can model, the complexity of models we formulate, and the number of people who can build and understand them.

Several other languages, including NDTRAN[12] and DYSMAP [8], have been developed that have the look and feel of DYNAMO with various other capabilities. All of these have recently been migrated to IBM-compatible personal computers.[13] For further information about these simulation

---

[11] It also tells advanced simulation modelers that DYNAMO's default integration scheme is Euler integration. In social systems, modeling that conceptually simple approach is computationally accurate enough for almost all purposes [35]. Most simulation languages, including DYNAMO, provide more accurate integration options (e.g., Runge-Kutta) that a knowledgeable user can invoke.

[12] W. Davisson and J. Uhran, University of Notre Dame, Notre Dame, Indiana.

[13] Professional DYNAMO and Professional DYNAMO Plus, Pugh-Roberts Associates, Cambridge, MA. 02139; DYSMAP2, University of Salford, M5 4WT Salford, England.

environments, the reader should consult the references in the notes. However, it is worth repeating a frequently heard but vital warning: Even the most detailed knowledge of a simulation language is little assurance of readiness to formulate and analyze insightful simulation models of social system dynamics. Knowledge of vocabulary and syntax are only meager first steps toward writing that is worth reading. Like a writer, a modeler must have something to say, born of intimate knowledge of the subject and great skill in translating that understanding into a form that a machine can simulate and people can learn from.

A recent breakthrough in simulation software that extends modeling capabilities still further is STELLA™ on the Macintosh [43, 44]. In this simulation environment, the modeler concentrates on *drawing* in a structured way the stock-and-flow feedback structure of the system on the computer screen, and the software writes the model equations in the background. Figure 7.3 is an example of a STELLA diagram. Each icon in the figure represents an equation in the system that must be carefully thought about, but the modeler concentrates most on the interconnected structure. STELLA (an acronym that stands for Structural Thinking, Experiential Learning Laboratory with Animation) is a major step toward making quantitative dynamic modeling qualitative. The manual with the language is really an excellent state-of-the-art text in modeling.

9. Modeling Heuristics and Principles of Systems

Forrester [16] distilled a number of mathematical formalisms and system insights into a set of *principles of systems*. Quite literally, they are an enlightened collection of biases about good modeling practice. Some examples follow:

1. A feedback loop consists of two distinctly different types of variables: the levels (states) and the rates (actions). Except for constants, these two are sufficient to represent a feedback loop. Both are necessary.
2. Levels integrate (or accumulate) the results of action in a system. ...
3. Levels are changed only by the rates ....
4. Levels and rates are not distinguished by units of measure.[14] ... The identification must recognize the difference between a variable created by integration and one that is a policy statement in the system.
5. Rates [are] not instantaneously measurable. ... No rate can, in principle, control another rate without an intervening level variable.
6. Level variables and rate variables [in a feedback loop] must alternate. ...
7. Levels completely describe the system condition.

---

[14] "People per year" could be the units of a rate (births or deaths) or an *average rate* over a period of time, which would be a level since an average involves an accumulation. Velocity could be a level in a model of pendulum dynamics.

7. System Dynamics

8. Levels exist in conservative subsystems; they can be changed only by moving the contents between levels (or to or from a source or sink).
9. Information is not a conservative flow; information is not depleted by its use.[15]
10. Decisions (rates) are based only on available information.

... and so on.

In Forrester [16] there are more than 30 such principles. Some constitute a verbal description, in largely nonmathematical terms, of the engineer's and mathematician's notion of a *state-determined* system. Others, such as (5) and (6) above, reflect qualitative wisdom about social systems, often stemming from an endogenous point of view or a particular conceptual distance. Still others, such as (10), are explicit biases about what may and may not be assumed in a formal model of a social system. Some scholars have chosen explicitly or implicitly to ignore some of these principles.[16] That is a possible but perilous course. Far better is to understand deeply the principle and its rationale, to be always alert for errors related to it, and to know under what conditions it may be violated. It takes a good acrobat to be a clown.

There are some circumstances, for example, when one rate can instantaneously influence another (see (5) above). An example occurs in the dynamics of financial systems, where the rate of flow of payments into assets is also the rate at which the stock of payments due are reduced. But the principle that information about one rate cannot instantaneously be used to govern another rate is an extremely good one; information almost always takes time to be collected and transmitted from one part of a system to another. It is almost always an error to formulate one rate as an instantaneous function of another rate. What we usually know in social systems is not the current value of a rate (such as GNP or highway accidents) but a recent *average* rate, and an average is actually a level, as it involves a sum—an accumulation.

Many of Forrester's principles have found their way into the simulation languages system dynamicists use. DYNAMO and DYSMAP, for example, will respond with a warning if a level equation is written to say the level is changed by something that does not look like a rate. STELLA will simply not let the modeler draw a causal link directly to a level—the link evaporates. Both languages will refuse to accept a feedback loop that does not contain at

---

[15] The distinction between information and material (conserved) flows is a critical insight of the information age. An information link from, say, the rabbit population to the lynx growth rate in Figure 7.3 does not subtract from the rabbit population, but the material flow of the "rabbit harvest" does. Unlike material, information is not a conserved quantity: Using it does not deplete it.

[16] See, for example, [4, p. 54] and [9, p. 21]; both stumble because they use a difference equation representation, which allows them to violate the principle of at least one accumulation in every feedback loop. Hanneman [23], advocating DYNAMO simulation in sociology, explicitly rejects what he calls the "conceptual baggage" of system dynamics. In the process he leaves behind some powerful modeling heuristics that would have improved his sociological model building.

least one level [in violation of (1), (7), and implicitly, (10)]. Such a loop implies that information travels instantaneously around the loop, creating a simultaneity that is both philosophically and computationally troublesome. There are no such simultaneous loops in continuous systems, so there are none in system dynamics models.

Others have added to Forrester's list, often identifying generalizations repeatedly seen in past work. Model a *problem*, not a *system*. Have a clear purpose for the effort (a model without a purpose is like a ship without a sail, a boat without a rudder, a hammer without a nail ...). Distinguish desired quantities from obtainable quantities, and perceived quantities from actual ones. And so on.

Although these principles and heuristics, and the modeling guidelines built into the languages we use, are enormously helpful, they are still not enough to guarantee that people who know the languages will build good models. In spite of people's attempts to embed expert knowledge in simulation languages and to formulate wise modeling heuristics, modeling is still an art.

10. Policy Analysis Based on System Dynamics Simulation

The goal of a system dynamics policy study is understanding: understanding the interactions in a complex system that are conspiring to create a problem, and understanding the structure and dynamic implications of policy changes intended to improve the system's behavior.

It is useful to distinguish two kinds of policy insights that can come from simulation studies. Some insights are system specific, applying to a particular company, government, or ecosystem during a particular period. As an example, consider the following simulation-based analysis of state aid to local school districts.

The problem the study addressed dealt with inequities in per-pupil expenditures among rich and poor school districts. Like many other states, Connecticut had pursued a particular funding policy known as a Guaranteed Wealth or Guaranteed Tax Base formula. In theory the formula would bring all school districts up to the same level of wealth, so that if they taxed themselves the same, there would be the same amount of money available to fund school systems across the state. The court-mandated goal of equal expenditures per pupil among rich and poor school districts in a state would be achieved.

Figure 7.7 shows an overview of the theory of local district planning captured in the simulation model in this study. The darker loops in the upper part of the figure show a simplified view of the the process a local district follows to set staffing levels. Presuming there are sufficient funds, staffing levels are set to achieve a desired staff-per-pupil ratio. This goal for staff-per-pupil is presumed to be strongly influenced by the district's traditional staff-per-pupil ratio, as both the literature and anecdotal evidence suggest. The traditional staff-per-pupil ratio leads to a desired staff level that functions as an "anchor" (see [49] and [56]) in the policy process that finally results in a decision about planned tax rates and planned staff. Given a tight budgetary

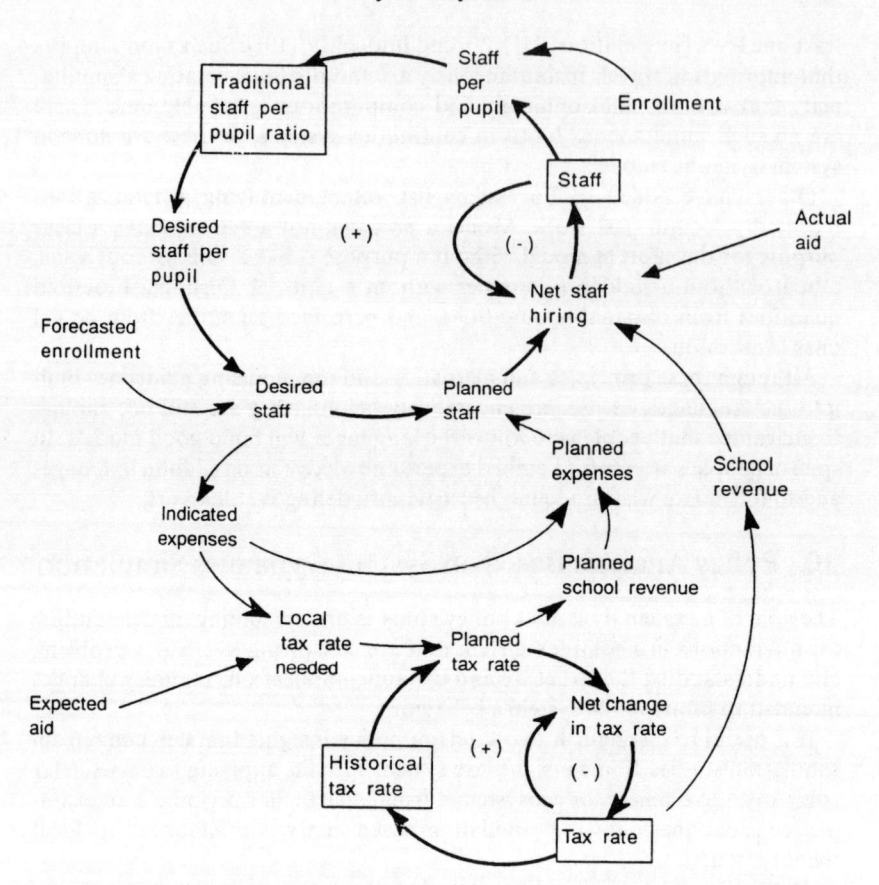

FIGURE 7.7. A simplified overview of the policy structures of local school district planning, captured in a simulation model of state aid to education. The rectangles identify levels (states) in the system.

year, the planned staff might be adjusted somewhat below this anchor, the desired staff level. Or, given unexpected revenues or other sources of slack in a town's budget, the planned staff level could rise above the traditionally desired level of staff.

When goals are anchored on historical or traditional achievements, it follows that the goals themselves may slowly change over time. If pressures combine to drag down staff-per-pupil ratios, and the lowered levels of staffing continue over a long period of time, then lower staff-per-pupil ratios can become the new standard, the new goal in the staffing policy process. Goals based on traditional achievements can slide.[17] They can gradually drift up, as

---
[17] The feedback structure underlying the phenomenon of adaptive or sliding goals was first described in [15].

well as slide down, if unexpected revenues or other positive pressures combine to produce increases in staffing levels that are then sustained over a sufficiently long period of time to change the way people think about standards.

On the tax side of this policy picture, an analogous sliding goals structure is responsible for the potential of local districts to become *addicted* to state aid. Tax planning comes to be based on, or anchored on, a traditional tax rate structure. A sustained period of state aid results in a historical or traditional tax rate structure in a local district that is lower than would be required without the aid. The school and tax traditions in the local district in effect are addicted to the continuation of state aid.

The structure shown in Figure 7.7 and captured in the simulation model provides an explanation of why the state's Guaranteed Wealth formula failed. A local district, planning and budgeting as shown in the diagram, would initially set staffing goals based on recent levels of staffing within its locale. Expected state aid would be incorporated into the planning process. The local district can respond to anticipated aid to education by putting more of its local money into other pressing demands. Untargeted aid-to-education that can be anticipated and planned for can indirectly be used to fill potholes in neighborhood streets. The implication is that local goals can frustrate state goals in the way local districts use general, anticipated grants. The study concluded that general, anticipated grants, GAGs, will not work.

The direct opposite of GAGs, the study suggested, are TUGs—*targeted, unanticipated grants*. The structure of local budgeting behavior in the simulation model and its resulting behavior suggest that states should try TUGing local districts to achieve the aims of state aid-to-education. The extent to which aid can be targeted to fulfill the purposes intended by state policy, the more likely that aid will not be used for other purposes. Still, there is the potential that, if the aid can be anticipated in the local budget and tax planning process, relief of the need for school revenues in may translate into tax savings or increased expenditures elsewhere. The greatest potential, then, according to this reasoning, would come from *unanticipated* grants—state aid-to-education that local districts do not know is coming or cannot rely on fully. The study pushed these simulation-based feedback insights further to discuss the potential of SLUGs (short-lived unanticipated grants) and concluded that TUGing and SLUGing in state aid-to-education may work, where other approaches have not.

11. Generic Simulation-Based Policy Insights

Other simulation-based policy insights have a more generic character and apply to a wide range of systems in a wide variety of circumstances. Two interesting collections in the system dynamics literature of these more general policy insights about complex dynamic feedback systems are contained in [17] and [27]. In both collections the sliding goals structure shown in the school finance study above was identified. In addition, we have

—*insensitivity*: complex systems are remarkably insensitive to changes in many system parameters;
—*compensating feedback*: complex systems counteract and compensate for externally applied corrective efforts;
—*policy resistance*: complex systems resist most policy changes;
—*leverage points*: complex systems contain influential pressure points, often in unexpected places, from which forces will radiate to alter system balance;
—*worse-before-better and better-before-worse behavior*: complex systems often react to a policy change in the long run in a way opposite to how they react in the short run;
—*drift to low performance*: complex social systems tend toward a condition of poor performance;
—*addiction*: action in complex social systems may appear to make the system better and create the apparent need for the continuation of the action, while actually over the long term it is making matters worse; and
—*shifting the burden to the intervener* (*official addiction*): action improving the behavior of a complex social system may lead to the atrophy of endogenous mechanisms striving for the same goals.

The reader should consult [17] and [27] for further discussion of these generic simulation-based insights about complex dynamic feedback systems.

Suffice it to say here, deriving deep insights about system structure and behavior is one of the tantalizing goals of dynamic feedback simulation. Success requires technical and conceptual skills and very good simulation models, of course, but also a drive to strive for lessons that go beyond the limits of the particular. The best system dynamics work ultimately leaves the equations behind and pushes toward qualitative and conceptual statements of the implications of computer simulations. The goal is understanding.

12. Directions for Further Reading

This brief overview of system dynamics as a qualitative modeling methodology has, of necessity, selected a small number of topics for discussion and ignored many others. Several additional topic areas particularly deserve the attention of interested readers:

—Good sources of classic applications and examples include [18] and [46].
—The modeling stages of problem definition and system conceptualization are particularly difficult. Andersen and Richardson [2] surveyed the state of the art. The best sources of advice since then are [37], [42], [44], [47], [60], and [62]. Wolstenholme and Coyle (1983). Focusing exclusively on urban dynamics, [1] also manages to be an excellent general introduction to system dynamics modeling.
—Model evaluation (validation) in system dynamics differs considerably from

other quantitative methodologies in the range and depth of its qualitative criteria. The emphasis is on building confidence in the suitability of the model for its intended purposes and its consistency with observed reality. Forrester and Senge [19] detail 17 rigorous tests for building confidence in system dynamics models, which deserve careful study (see also [42, pp. 310–320]).

—Implementation of model-based policy insights should be an early concern in a simulation-based study of policy options. Roberts [45] and Weil [59] describe why implementation is difficult and how to improve its chance of success. Stenberg [48] discusses the problem in the context of public policy.

—Finally, current directions in the field reveal a diversity of interests. Traditional policy simulation studies remain a central focus, but increasingly, practitioners are turning to the potential of simulation games for communicating insights about dynamic feedback systems [28, 53]. Computerized case studies appear to hold considerable promise in that regard [21]. Efforts are under way to provide greater computer support in the search for model-based understanding and optimal policies in exceedingly complex systems [24, 61]. Complex nonlinear dynamics and chaos are naturally of interest (e.g., [31] and *System Dynamics Review 4*, 1–2 (1988)—special issue on chaos). Sterman [49, 50] has shown that policies people actually follow in some limited contexts produce deterministic chaos when simulated. The even greater significance of that research line [51, 52] may be in the extensions it provides to our understandings of patterned weaknesses in human dynamic decision-making complicated by feedback effects.

References

1. Alfeld, L.E., and Graham, A.K. MIT Press, Cambridge, Mass., 1976.
2. Andersen, D.F., and Richardson, G.P. Toward a pedagogy of system dynamics. *TIMS Studies Manage. Sci. 14* (System Dynamics) (1980), 91–106.
3. Aracil, J. Qualitative analysis and bifurcations in system dynamics models. *IEEE Trans. Syst., Man, Cybern. SMC-14*, 4 (1984), 688–696.
4. Ashby, W.R. *Introduction to Cybernetics.* Wiley, New York, 1956.
5. Bateson, G. Culture contact and schismogenesis. *Man 35* (1935), 178–183. (Reprinted in Bateson, G., *Steps to an Ecology of Mind*, Ballantine Books, New York, 1972.)
6. Bateson, G. *Naven.* Cambridge University Press. Cambridge, Mass., 1936. (2nd ed., Stanford University Press, Stanford, Calif., 1958.)
7. Cannon, W.B. *The Wisdom of the Body.* W.W. Norton, New York, 1932.
8. Cavana, R.Y., and Coyle, R.G. *DYSMAP User Manual.* System Dynamics Research Group, Univ. of Bradford, England, 1982.
9. Culbertson, J.M. *Macroeconomic Theory and Stabilization Policy.* McGraw-Hill, New York, 1968.
10. Dewey, J. The reflex arc concept in psychology. *Psychol. Rev. 3* (1896), 357–370.
11. Easton, D. *A Systems Analysis of Political Life.* Prentice-Hall, Englewood Cliffs, N.J., 1965.

12. Easton, D. Simplification and understanding of models. *Sys. Dynamics Rev.* 5, 1 (Winter 1989), 51–68.
13. Eden, C., Jones, S., and Sims, D. *Messing About in Problems.* Pergamon Press, Oxford, 1983.
14. Forrester, J.W. *Industrial Dynamics.* MIT Press, Cambridge, Mass., 1961.
15. Forrester, J.W. Market growth as influenced by capital investment. *Industrial Manage. Rev.* (now the *Sloan Manage. Rev.*) 9, 2 (Winter 1968), 83–106.
16. Forrester, J.W. *Principles of Systems.* MIT Press, Cambridge, Mass., 1968.
17. Forrester, J.W. *Urban Dynamics.* MIT Press, Cambridge, Mass., 1969.
18. Forrester, J.W. *Collected Papers of Jay W. Forrester.* MIT Press, Cambridge, Mass., 1975.
19. Forrester, J.W., and Senge, P.M. Tests for building confidence in system dynamics models. *TMS Stud. Manage. Sci. 14* (System Dynamics) (1980), 209–228.
20. Goodman, M.R. *Study Notes in System Dynamics.* MIT Press, Cambridge, Mass., 1974.
21. Graham, A.K. Generic models as a basis for computer-based case studies. In *Proceedings of the 1988 International System Dynamics Conference* (San Diego, Calif.). 1988.
22. Graham, A.K., and Pugh, A.L., III. Behavior analysis software for large Dynamo models. In *Proceedings of the 1983 International System Dynamics Conference* (Chestnut Hill, Mass.). 1983.
23. Hanneman, R. *Computer-Assisted Theory Building: Modeling Dynamic Social Systems.* Sage Publications, Newbury Park, Calif., 1989.
24. Kelóharju, R. *Relativity Dynamics.* The Helsinki School of Economics, Helsinki, 1983.
25. Levin, G., Hirsch, G.B., and Roberts, E.B. *The Persistent Poppy: A Computer Aided Search for Heroin Policy.* Ballinger, Cambridge, Mass., 1975.
26. Macedo, J. A reference approach for policy optimization in system dynamics models. *Syst. Dynamics Rev. 5* 2 (Summer 1989).
27. Meadows D.H. Whole earth models and systems. *Coevolution Q.* (Summer 1981), 98–108.
28. Meadows, D.L. *Strategem I.* Resource Policy Center, Dartmouth College, Hanover, N.H., 1988.
29. Morecroft, J.D.W. A critical review of diagramming tools for system dynamics. *Dynamica 8,* 2 (Summer 1982), 20–29.
30. Morecroft, J.D.W. Rationality in the analysis of behavioral simulation models. *Manage. Sci. 31,* 7 (July 1985), 900–916.
31. Mosekilde, E., Aracil, J., and Allen, P.M. Instabilities and chaos in nonlinear dynamic systems. *Syst. Dynamics Rev. 4,* 1–2 (1988), 14–55.
32. Nicholis, G., and Prigogine, I. *Self-Organization in Nonequilibrium Systems: From Dissipative Structures to Order Through Fluctuations.* Wiley, New York, 1977.
33. Phillips, A.W. Stabilization policy in a closed economy. *Econ. J.* (June 1954), 290–305.
34. Powers, W.T. *Behavior: The Control of Perception.* Aldine, Chicago, 1973.
35. Pugh, A.L. Integration method: Euler or other for system dynamics. *TIMS Stud. Manage. Sci. 14* (System Dynamics) (1980), 179–188.
36. Pugh, A.L. *DYNAMO User's Manual.* 6th ed. MIT Press, Cambridge, Mass., 1983.
37. Randers, J. Guidelines for model conceptualization. In *Elements of the System*

Dynamics Method: Proceedigs of the 1976 International System Dynamics Conference, J. Randers, Ed. (Geilo, Norway). MIT Press, Cambridge, Mass., 1980.
38. Richardson, G.P. The evolution of the feedback concept in American social science, with implications for system dynamics. Plenary paper. In *Proceedings of the 1983 International System Dynamics Conference* (Chestnut Hill, Mass.). 1983.
39. Richardson, G.P. The evolution of the feedback concept in American social science. Ph.D. dissertation, Sloan School of Management, MIT Press, Cambridge, Mass., 1985.
40. Richardson, G.P. Problems with causal-loop diagrams. *Syst. Dynamics Rev. 3*, 2 (Summer 1986), 158–170.
41. Richardson, G.P. *Feedback Thought in Social Science*. To be published.
42. Richardson, G.P., and Pugh, A.L., III. *Introduction to System Dynamics Modeling with DYNAMO*. MIT Press, Cambridge, Mass., 1981.
43. Richmond, B., Peterson, S., and Vescuso, P. *STELLA^{TM} for Business*. High Performance Systems, Inc., Lyme, N.H., 1985.
44. Richmond, B., Peterson, S., and Vescuso, P. *An Academic User's Guide to STELLA^{TM}*. High Performance Systems, Inc., Lyme, N.H., 1987.
45. Roberts, E.B. Strategies for effective implementation of complex corporate models. *Interfaces 8*, 1 (1977), Part I.
46. Roberts, E.B., Ed. *Managerial Applications of System Dynamics*. MIT Press, Cambridge, Mass., 1978.
47. Roberts, N., Andersen, D.F., Deal, R., Garet, M., and Shaffer, W. *Introduction to Computer Simulation: A System Dynamics Modelling Approach*. Addison-Wesley, Reading, Mass., 1983.
48. Stenberg, L. A modeling procedure for public policy. In *Elements of the System Dynamics Method: Proceedings of the 1976 International System Dynamics Conference*, J. Randers, Ed. (Geilo, Norway). MIT Press, Cambridge, Mass., 1980.
49. Sterman, J.D. 1987. Testing behavioral simulation models by direct experiment. *Manage. Sci. 33*, 12 (1987), 1572–1592.
50. Sterman, J.D. Deterministic chaos in models of human behavior: Methodological issues and experimental results. *Syst. Dynamics Rev. 4* 1–2 (1988), 148–178.
51. Sterman, J.D. Misperceptions of feedback in dynamic decision making. *Organ. Behav. Human Dec. Proc. 43* (June 1989).
52. Sterman, J.D. Modeling managerial behavior: Misperceptions of feedback in a dynamic decision making experiment. *Manage. Sci. 35*, 3 (Mar. 1989).
53. Sterman, J.D., and Meadows, D.L. Strategem-2: A microcomputer simulation game of the Kondratiev cycle. *Sim. Games 16* (1985), 174–202.
54. Sterman, J.D., and Richardson, G.P. An experiment to evaluate methods of estimating fossil fuel resources. *J. Forecasting 4* (1985), 197–226.
55. Stinchcomb, A.L. *Constructing Social Theories*. Harcourt, Brace and World, New York, 1968.
56. Tversky, A., and Kahneman, D. Judgement under uncertainty: Heuristics and biases. *Science 185* (1974), 1124–1131.
57. von Bertalanffy, L. *General Systems Theory: Foundations, Develpment, Applications*. George Braziller, New York, 1968.
58. Weick, K.E. *The Social Psychology of Organizing*. 2nd ed. Addison-Wesley, Reading, Mass., 1979.
59. Weil, H.B. The Evolution of an approach for achieving implemented results from system dynamics projects. In *Elements of the System Dynamics Method: Proceedings*

of the 1976 International System Dynamics Conference, J. Randers, Ed. (Geilo, Norway). MIT Press, Cambridge, Mass., 1980.
60. Wolstenholme, E.F. A methodology for qualitative system dynamics. In *Proceedings of the 1985 International System Dynamics Conference* (Keystone, Colo.). 1985.
61. Wolstenholme, E.F., and Al-Alusi, A.S. System dynamics and heuristic optimization in defense analysis. *Syst. Dynamics Rev. 3*, 2 (Summer 1987), 102–115.
62. Wolstenholme, E.F., and Coyle, R.G. The development of system dynamics as a methodology for system description and qualitative analysis. *J. Oper. Res. 34*, 7 (1983), 569–581.

Strategy Support Models

JOHN D. W. MORECROFT
Sloan School of Management, Massachusetts Institute of Technology, Cambridge, Massachusetts, U.S.A.

Summary
A major challenge in strategy development is to deduce the consequences of the interacting programmes underlying strategy. The paper argues that behavioural simulation models can help meet this challenge by acting out the consequences of strategy proposals in their full organizational setting. However, the real key to effective strategy support is not simply having a model, but using it in a structured dialogue with executives. To illustrate the idea, the paper presents a system dynamics simulation model used to aid executives of an advanced office equipment firm in setting their marketing strategy. The paper describes the process by which the model was created and brought to the attention of executives. Several examples are provided of the dialectical use of the model, showing how differences in management intuition and model-generated opinion led to improved insight into the consequences of strategy.

INTRODUCTION

The concept of support
Over the past decade considerable attention has been given to advanced computational aids used in support, rather than replacement, of managerial judgement. Here, computational aid includes not only rapidly advancing computer hardware but also the algorithms and numerical methods that have become feasible with the existence of the hardware. Underlying the concept of management support is the recognition that the human mind is itself a very powerful, flexible, and agile problem-solving and decision-making 'machine', and should remain an integral part of the decision-making process. The key to support is to identify the activities in which our built-in, flesh-and-blood computers are weakest and remedy the weakness with our new, chip-and-board computers.

The field of management information systems has clearly identified one weakness of our flesh-and-blood computers — their ability to collect and process information. Decision support systems (Keen and Scott-Morton, 1978) come to the rescue by massaging business information, making it more compact, easy to access and absorb so that managers can be better informed and therefore, presumably, better able to make decisions.

This paper extends the notion of support to strategy support, in which a man/machine combination is used to provide more effective assessment of strategic proposals.[1] But what

---
[1] The term strategy support was coined by my colleague Dr. Alan K. Graham of the M.I.T. System Dynamics Group.

0143-2095/84/030215-15$01.50
©1984 by John Wiley & Sons, Ltd.

Received 19 April 1983
Revised 22 August 1983

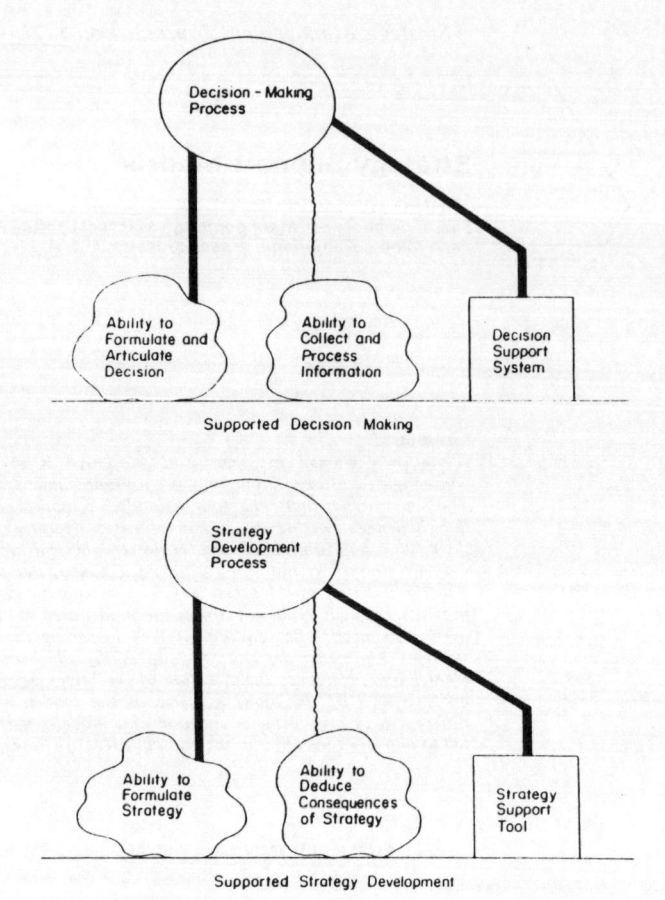

Figure 1. The analogy between decision support and strategy support

kind of support can be usefully brought to bear on highly unstructured strategy questions? Here we suggest that management intuition and experience must serve as the primary architects of strategy, to bring form and substance to otherwise unstructured issues. The initiative for defining alternative markets to be served, resources to be deployed, organizational responsibilities, and allocation of budgets must lie with senior management. Strategy support can be provided by a tool that provides sharper insights into the *consequences* of pursuing strategy proposals once formulated.

Figure 1 illustrates the analogy between decision and strategy support. The Figure shows both the human and machine components of decision making and strategy development. The decision-making process is depicted as being strongly supported by natural human ability to formulate, articulate, and communicate a decision. However, it is much less strongly supported by the ability of the human mind to collect and process information (Simon, 1971). A decision-support system provides reinforcement by storing relevant information, reworking and condensing it, indexing it and providing easy access. By analogy, the strategy development process is depicted as being supported by natural managerial ability to formulate strategy, to set a course for the corporation, and create the administrative structure necessary to implement strategy. But it is much less strongly supported by the ability of the human mind to deduce the consequences of the strategy (Cyert, Simon and Trow, 1956). A strategy support tool should reveal flaws and inconsistencies in proposals that might not otherwise come to light until the proposals are implemented and under way.

Strategy support, the dialectic method and the role of models

A common approach to the evaluation of strategy in business and government institutions is argument and debate. From this method we can learn much about the way a strategy support tool should interact with executives. If the consequences of a given proposal are difficult to assess, it is certain there will be widely differing opinions on the outcome. Debating these opinions in a meeting will force people to scrutinize and justify their reasoning and will provide clearer insight into the viability of the proposal. This process may be usefully summarized as the dialectic method, defined in *Webster's Twentieth Century Dictionary* as

> The art or practice of examining opinions or ideas logically, often by the method of question and answer, so as to determine their validity.

Successful formalizations of the approach have been described by Mason (1969) and Mitroff and Emshoff (1979) for corporate planning, and by Schon (1983) for urban planning.[2]

A most natural extension of the dialectic method is the introduction of a formal model into the discussion with which to temper the prevailing opinions. In the standard dialectic method, debate and discussion draw on opinion from the 'mental models' of a management team. A formal model merely adds another viewpoint, which, though perhaps more carefully formulated, is nevertheless an opinion.

To be effective, the model must be seen as a vehicle for extending argument and debate—quite different from the customary role of models. The model must be brought down from the pedestal of the infallible black box (where it is often ignored) to occupy a more modest position as a complement to the thinking and deducing powers of management. The model must be seen as a generator of opinions, not answers. Executives must be encouraged to challenge and debate model conclusions, and members of the modelling team must be capable of engaging in executive, non-technical argument.

The use of system dynamics

The remainder of this paper will illustrate the use of system dynamics simulation modelling (Forrester, 1961; Lyneis, 1980) as a strategy support tool. System dynamics is an appropriate tool for a number of reasons. First, it provides effective graphic display methods for illustrating the policy structure of an organization. A management team can easily relate to these graphics. They can see the range of interlinked policies that constitute their organization. They can see the complex network of communication and control through which strategic initiatives must filter to bring about change in organizational performance.

---
[2] Some recent theoretical advances in the formal analysis of the logic of policy are described by Mitroff, Mason and Barabba (1982).

J. D. W. Morecroft

A system dynamics model is descriptive of the way a company functions; it does not contain idealized decision-making processes (Morecroft, 1983). It shows the division of responsibilities, the goal and reward structure of the organization, as well as the inconsistencies of policy that are a part of any real organization (Hall, 1976). It reveals the limitations on information flow that can produce distorted or even conflicting images of performance at different parts of the organization. Together, these descriptive features of the model lend a realism necessary to good communication as the model comes to be used in a discussion.

The simulation analysis methods of system dynamics are very effective in argument and debate. Simulation can be used to create clear strategy scenarios to challenge the collective intuition of a management team. Simulation runs create time charts of important business variables that bring to life the consequences of policy change and bring discipline to the subsequent discussion (Probert, 1982).

CREATING A STRATEGY SUPPORT MODEL—AN EXAMPLE

A strategy support model is intended to influence executive opinion in a company. To do this it must be aimed at a problem that engages the executives' attention, it must have political support within the organization, and its structure and insights must be widely communicated (Roberts, 1977).

In this section we will use a case study to illustrate how a strategy support model is created. The example is based on the analysis of marketing strategy for a supplier of advanced office equipment.[3] To retain anonymity the company is referred to as Datacom Corporation.

Starting the project

At the start of the modelling project a small project team was assembled that included a senior and a junior manager, an M.I.T. consultant, and several staff analysts. The managers involved in the project both had some prior exposure to system dynamics modelling.

Preliminary discussions between the managers and consultant revealed that Datacom was faced with an important strategic problem, common in high-technology industries, of managing a market conversion from a base of old-technology equipment to a new generation of more advanced equipment. This issue certainly had executive attention. The company had experienced loss of market share during the early stages of the transition. There was uncertainty over how rapidly the conversion should take place and over the combination of sales efforts and price incentives that would be most effective at bringing about the conversion. The modelling project was, therefore, addressed to this problem.

The next step was to sketch a conceptual model showing key elements of the existing decision-making structure of the market and the sales organization. In the market, we wanted to understand what induces customers to switch from old- to new-technology equipment and how they make the choice between equipment offered by Datacom and the competition. In the sales organization, we wanted to look at factors affecting selling effort and its allocation to different activities in the market. At an early stage we ruled out the need to consider factors such as product development, production, and delivery. The new-

---

[3] For a more detailed account of the case study and subsequent policy analysis, see Morecroft (1982).

technology equipment was already developed, and there was adequate capacity to meet projected market needs.

Round-table meetings were held by the project team and subject area experts. On the table we had our sketch of the decision-making processes in the market and sales organization. We discussed how these processes worked and how they are linked, using the descriptive knowledge of company participants and the structuring principles of system dynamics.

The diagram served as the focal point for meetings. It was very useful as a communication tool to management and staff, pointing out internal linkages between company programmes and procedures, and external linkages to the market. There were frequent revisions to the diagram as our understanding of the system improved. The diagram also served to generate a feeling of involvement and commitment in the project by the numerous people who contributed to its construction, thereby aiding the communication process. Finally, the diagram served as a valuable interface between the formal mathematical model ultimately developed, and the mental models of the various project participants.

Policy structure of the market
Figure 2 shows the conceptual model of the market that was arrived at in meetings with the project team and subject area experts from the sales force and marketing staff. Notice first the heavy black lines showing the installed base of systems. The installed base is divided into three categories shown as system levels. At the top of Figure 2 there are old systems, all of which have been sold by Datacom and reflect the company's strong initial market position. As times goes by, old systems are upgraded until, eventually, all have been converted either to new Datacom or new competitor systems. Ownership of the installed base is, therefore, gradually redistributed between Datacom and the competition. Notice that in this particular market (uncharacteristic of many high-technology markets) the size of the total installed base is fixed. All business customers who need the equipment offered by Datacom already have it, at least in its old-technology form. Thus, the only way to sell new equipment is to exchange it for old. Finally, the reader should also note that Datacom leases much of its equipment to the market. Sales revenues are, therefore, generated both by the base of installed systems (old and new) and by the conversion from old to new systems.

The remainder of Figure 2 shows how a customer decided to convert. By talking with members of the sales force, we learned that the first step is simply one of making the customer aware of the new technology. Customers must be contacted, talked to, and convinced that the switch to new technology is worth while. In Figure 2 this process is called acceptance. The number of acceptances depends primarily on proactive sales effort, where the sales force takes the initiative in contacting the customer. Acceptances depend also on price. If old prices are low in relation to new-equipment prices, acceptance will be less likely. Acceptances further depend on the number of old systems that remain to be converted. As the base of old systems is depleted, there are fewer and fewer customers to contact, until only the diehards are left.

Customers convert to new systems only after they have accepted the usefulness of new technology. Figure 2, therefore, shows conversions dependent on acceptances. Interestingly, Datacom conversions depend not only on acceptances generated by Datacom sales effort, but also to some degree on acceptances generated by competitor sales effort. Customers who are aware of the new-technology option may choose to obtain their equipment from any of the system vendors in the market. Some cross-talk between

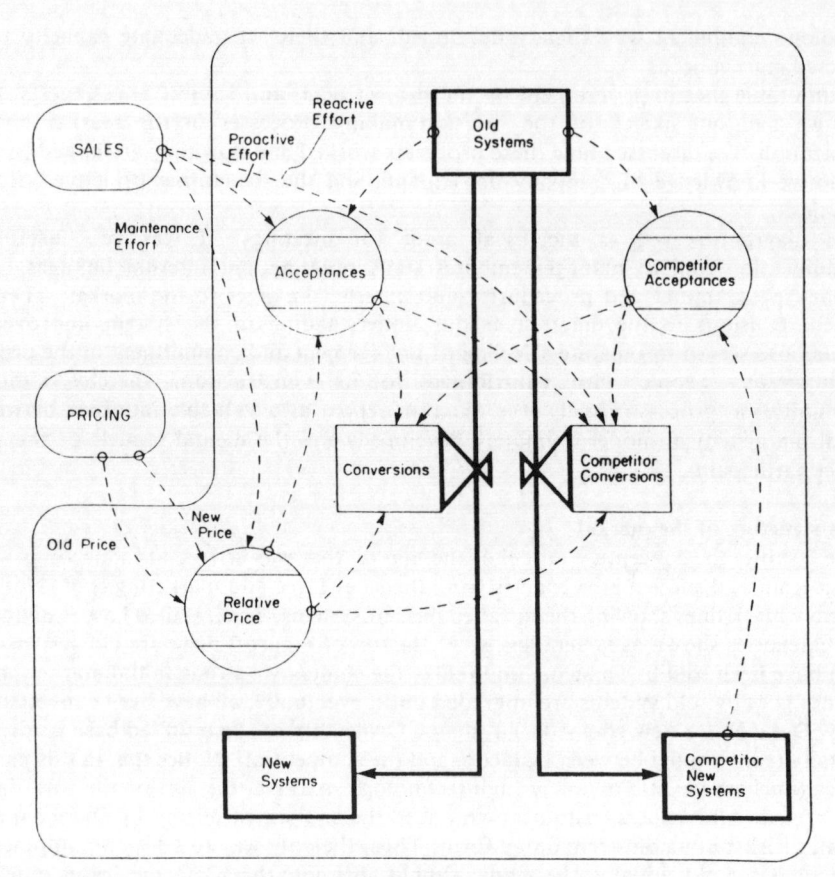

Figure 2. Policy structure of the market

competitor sales effort and Datacom, and vice versa conversions is, therefore, a natural and very important feature of the market. The degree of cross-talk depends on the relative price of Datacom and competitor systems. If Datacom prices rise in relation to competitor prices, the company wins fewer conversions, and a correspondingly greater number go to the competition.

Discussions with the sales force indicated that relative price should be viewed as a rather subtle decision-making process in its own right. Price perception in the office-equipment market is quite complex. There are lease and purchase options to consider. There are price/performance characteristics to judge. There are new, old, and competitive prices to consider. The customer does not make price judgements in a highly objective way but is swayed by general sales effort (labelled maintenance effort in Figure 2), by price reputation, and by other subjective factors. Figure 2 captures these intangibles in price perception by showing that old and new prices first pass through a decision-making process labelled relative price before they affect acceptance or conversion.

Competition is treated in a simplified way that focuses on the growth capability of competitive firms as a whole. Competitor acceptances depend, in the aggregate, on the installed base of competitor systems. In general, the more installed systems there are, the greater the revenue base and the greater the competition's ability to support marketing effort. Competitor conversions depend on competitor *and* Datacom acceptances modified by relative price and Datacom's reactive sales effort. If competitor prices are relatively low, competitor share of conversions will be high. Such price advantages can be counteracted to some extent by Datacom's reactive sales effort. Datacom knows about competitor attempts to win customers and can respond by putting in sales time to lure customers away from the competition.

Policy structure of the sales organization
The conceptual model of the sales organization focuses on policies that can affect sales capability and its allocation among three principal market activities: proactive sales effort, reactive sales effort, and market maintenance. Figure 3 shows the structure that emerged from round-table discussions between the project team and subject area experts from the sales force and the market planning area.

The size of the sales force is a key determinant of overall sales capability. The sales force, which is shown by heavy black lines at the top of the figure, is increased through hiring and

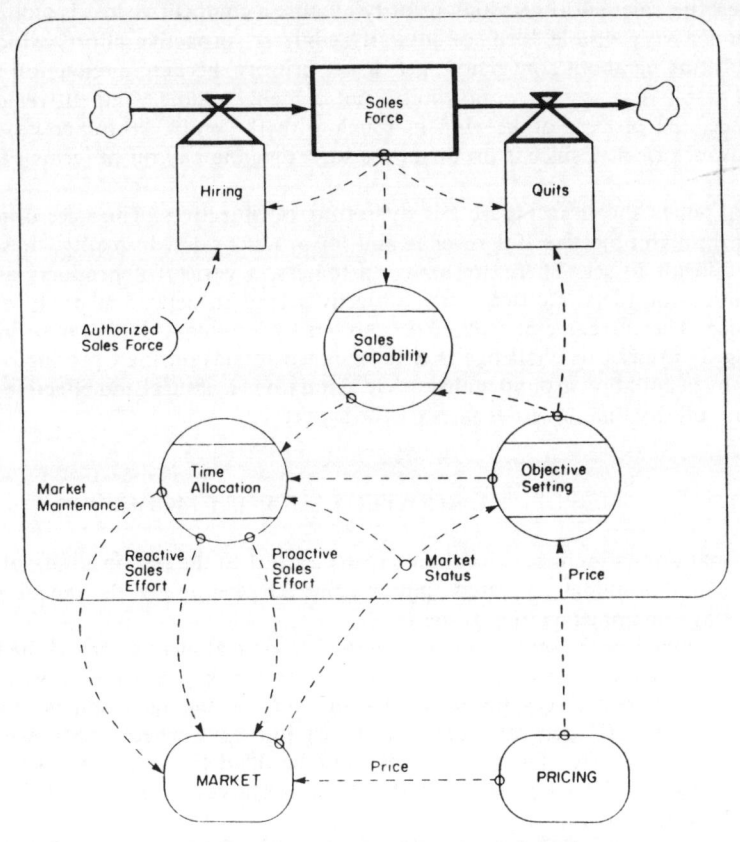

Figure 3. Policy structure of the sales organization

decreased through quits. Hiring adjusts the sales force to an authorized level, which can be varied experimentally in the formal model. Sales capability is also affected by overtime and by the motivation of the sales force, which in turn depend on sales objectives. By raising objectives, overtime and sales capability may be increased. But sustained periods of high overtime or poor performance that result from overly ambitious sales objectives can lower motivation and ultimately lower the capability of the sales organization. Our conceptual model shows this fluid, variable nature of the output of the sales force.

Sales capability is a measure of the total effective effort that the sales organization can bring to bear on the market. This total effort is allocated among different marketing activities according to the time-allocation policy of individual salesmen. Discussion with salesmen revealed that there is a natural hierarchy in the allocation of time. The highest priority goes to reactive sales efforts, the process of responding to competitor attempts to win Datacom customers. The rest of the time is split between proactive sales effort, the process of converting existing old-technology customers, and general market maintenance. Second highest priority goes to proactive effort, unless the product sales objective has been completely satisfied.

This allocation of time is probably not optimal in an economic sense, but it is a very natural and powerful hierarchy from the salesman's viewpoint within the sales incentive system. Reactive sales effort gets high priority because a competitive loss is a direct threat to revenue and a very visible form of loss. By contrast, proactive effort, which is highly effective at bringing about conversion, gets lower priority, because a reduction in proactive effort will result in a loss of opportunity, not a highly visible competitive loss. Market maintenance, the process of keeping in touch with the entire customer base, naturally receives lowest priority, since it produces the least tangible pay-off in terms of revenue or sales.

The final policy shown in Figure 3 is the setting of objectives. The sales organization is motivated through objectives for revenue and for product sales. In reality, these objectives are quite difficult to set. There are many customers, a variety of products and different types of price contracts. Consequently, objectives tend to depend strongly on historical performance. The current year's objectives are set by looking at last year's objectives and negotiating a 'stretch' or challenge that is intended to sustain high productivity. Setting objectives by negotiation around an historical standard is a natural and effective way to deal with the complexity that underlies sales performance.

USE OF THE STRATEGY SUPPORT MODEL

Once a formal simulation model has been created, it is then the responsibility of the project team to ensure that model-generated opinion gains the attention of the executives involved in formulating and implementing strategy.

In the Datacom case the senior manager in the project team was aware of the issues being debated in the market conversion strategy and of the key executives who should be influenced. He played a very important liaison role, arranging meetings, sounding out executive response and generally creating an environment where model-based opinion would be taken seriously. The liaison role must be filled by a person who has political insight, the respect of colleagues and higher-level executives, and a high level of comfort with modelling methods.

The project team should arrange meetings in which the model is used for debate and argument, in order to challenge the preconceptions of management. This dialectic use of the model is at the heart of strategy support, but does not happen automatically. It is essential that model runs be organized around clear scenarios, that executives be encouraged to challenge and debate model conclusions, and that members of the project team be capable of engaging in executive, non-technical argument. With these conditions satisfied, it is possible for both executives and modellers to clarify their understanding of the consequences of strategy.

Steps in the dialectic

Figure 4 illustrates the use of a model as practised at Datacom for six high-level meetings. The first step is to select a proposal that is already under active discussion in the company. The former model is then run and analysed to render an opinion on the consequences of the proposal. This kind of analysis should not be done at the meeting, but rather beforehand, when there is adequate time to diagnose and understand the simulation runs. It is essential to develop a clear intuitive explanation for simulation runs, and this always takes time.

In the next step managerial opinion and model opinion are brought together in debate and discussion. Meetings can last as long as 2 or 3 hours. Modellers should be expected to provide a clear explanation of why the model behaves as it does and why it differs from executive expectation (if it does). Executives should feel free to point out when their intuitive opinion on the proposal differs from model-generated opinion. The explanation of

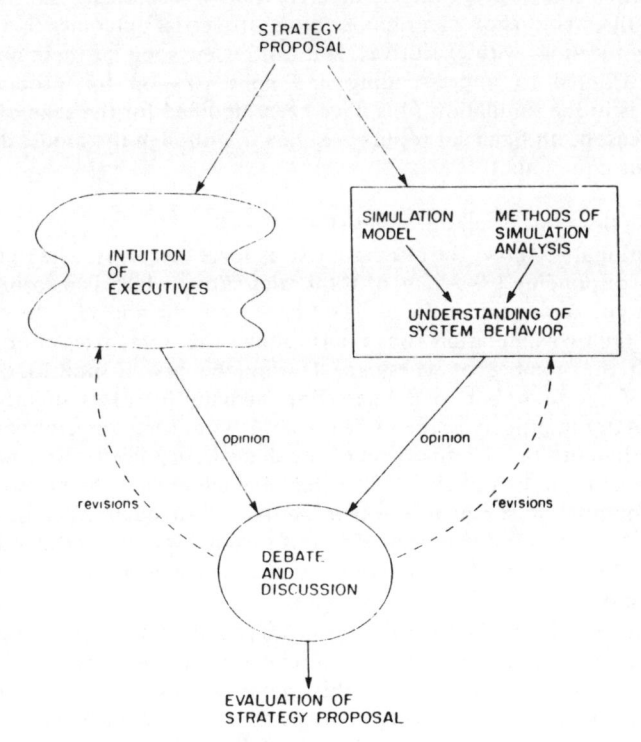

Figure 4. Using a system dynamics model to evaluate strategy proposals

differences will lead to revisions and clarifications in both executive intuition and the formal model that will ultimately improve the evaluation of the strategy proposal. The central role of the model, then, is to clarify the consequences of the proposal and to anticipate surprises. As Mass (1981) has pointed out:

> Some of the most important insights into real system behavior can arise from model results that at first appear to be at odds with knowledge of the real system, but which in fact suggest important new interpretations of perceived facts.

THE PROCESS IN ACTION—INSIGHTS FROM THE MODEL

The conceptual model described above was translated into a formal simulation model using the DYNAMO simulation language. It took 4 months to assemble and test a first model worthy of executive attention. The model was then used for about 8 months, first to examine the effectiveness of force additions in the market conversion strategy, then later to explore pricing policy. It is interesting to note that, during the 8 months of model use, time spent on the project was about equally divided between model development and the elucidation and communication of results.

To illustrate the use of the model, we will concentrate on the evaluation of the proposal to change sales force size. We compare two alternatives: a 20 per cent force addition versus a 10 per cent force reduction. What would the market and financial consequences be of pursuing the conversion strategy under these alternative scenarios? The formal model was run for 40 months, and it showed a number of controversial outcomes that became a focus of discussion in meetings with executives. We will review some of these outcomes to show how they contributed to understanding and consensus on the proposal. (Note that numerical values in the simulation runs have been modified for the sake of confidentiality. For the same reason, no financial results are shown, although the model did include a full set of accounting equations.)

Sales force reductions lower sales productivity

The left half of Figure 5 shows the alternative sales force scenarios. The right half of Figure 5 shows the corresponding behaviour of total sales effort, which is measured in thousands of hours per month and includes the effect of both overtime and sales force motivation. A comparison of the two simulation runs clearly shows that total sales effort is not perfectly correlated with the number of salesmen. During the first 6 months of the reduction scenario, sales force falls, but total sales effort actually increases slightly and only then begins to fall. After month six in the same scenario, sales force remains constant, but total sales effort continues to fall. Comparison of the shaded areas in the two runs shows that the force reduction causes a loss of sales effort that is much greater than can be accounted for by the smaller number of salesmen. In other words, force reductions cause the productivity of individual salesmen to fall, whereas additions sustain high sales productivity. This result ran counter to the opinion of some members of management and, therefore, demanded further explanation.

The model suggested that the behaviour of sales productivity could be explained in terms of sales force motivation, which was in turn related to the performance of the sales force against sales objectives. To illustrate this point we examined a simulation run of performance against product and revenue objectives, as shown in Figure 6. Under both scenarios performance against revenue objective falls as the size of the revenue-generating

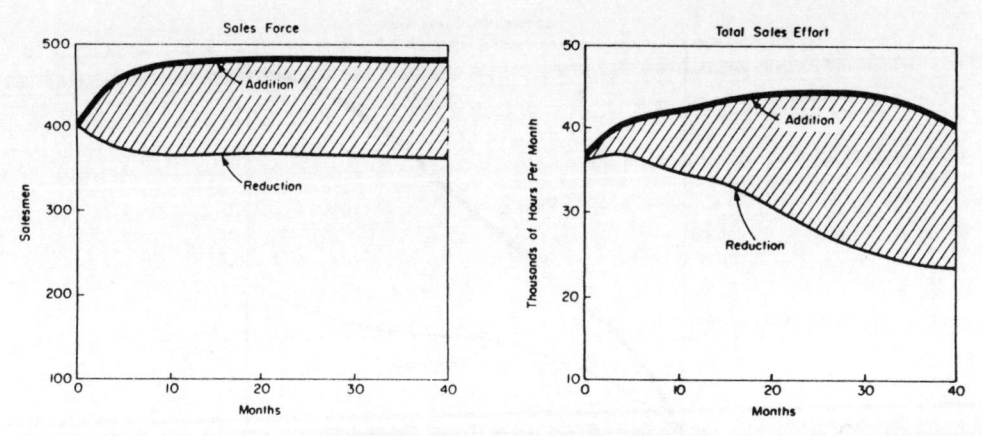

Figure 5. Force size and sales effort

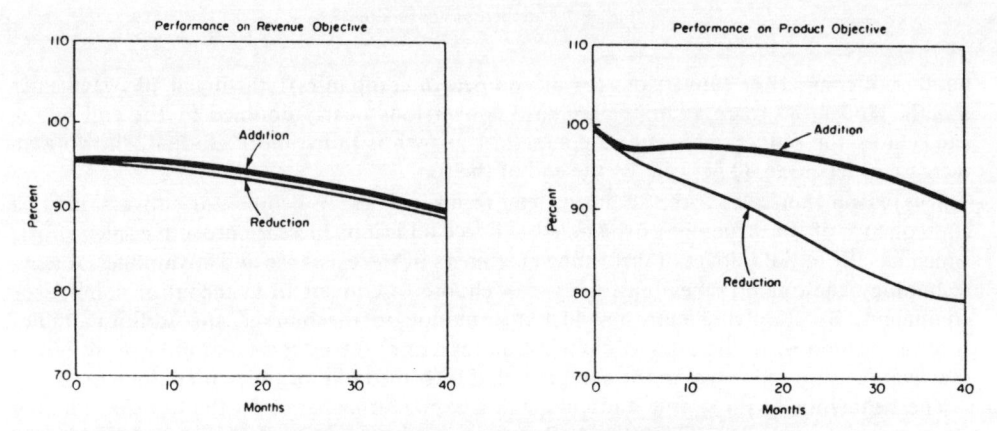

Figure 6. Performance against product and revenue objectives

base is eroded by competition. Erosion makes it progressively more difficult to repeat the revenue performance achieved in the past, thereby creating the potential for demotivation and lowered productivity. Force reductions exacerbate the motivation problems. Not only is it difficult to attain revenue objective but also product objective. Poor performance on both measures leads to a decline in motivation, a decline in sales effort, and a further deterioration in performance. By contrast, force additions relieve the danger of becoming trapped in this downward spiral by making it easier to attain the product objective.[4]

Sales force additions encourage the growth of competition
This result was particularly surprising to management, who had intuitively expected that sales force additions would act as a brake on competitive growth. Figure 7 shows the

---
[4] The lesson from the simulation runs has one subtle twist. It says, *given* that objectives are set on past performance, and *given* that the revenue-generating base is being eroded, force reductions will precipitate spiral decline in performance and motivation. However, changes in the objective-setting procedure introduced simultaneously with force reductions may overcome the difficulty, but that is another issue and was not an explicit part of the force reduction plans.

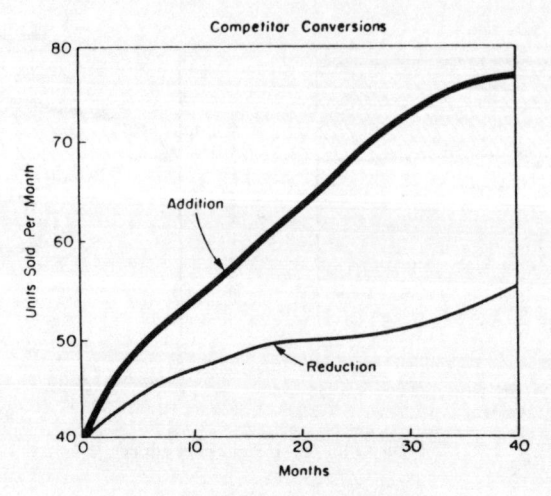

Figure 7. Competitor conversions

number of competitor conversions (by all competitor companies), starting at 40 systems per month. Under the force additions scenario conversions nearly doubled by the end of the run. Under the reductions scenario competitor growth is much more gradual, showing an increase of less than 40 per cent by the end of the run.

The reason that sales force additions lead to an increase in competitor conversions is a consequence of the structure of the market. Force additions increase proactive sales effort, which has the initial impact of informing customers of the existence and advantages of new-technology equipment. These customers can choose to convert to Datacom *or* competitor equipment. By supplying more product information to the market, the additional sales force gives a boost to the sales of competition (except in the extreme and unlikely situation that every customer is loyal to the company that informed him of the new equipment).

The behaviour has a simple and compelling explanation based on the decision-making structure of the market. Once the explanation has been given, it seems almost trivially obvious. Yet in the real strategy-evaluation process, it was surprising at first. The explanation provided sharper insight into the role of the sales force in market conversion.

Sales force additions depress market share
Market-share behaviour was another surprising result that ran counter to initial management intuition. Figure 8 shows Datacom's market share under the two sales force scenarios. Share starts above 90 per cent and in both cases declines to below 70 per cent by the end of the simulation run. With force additions, market share actually declines more quickly, because additions *accelerate* the conversion process. Customers convert sooner to new-technology equipment, and inevitably some of them go to the competition.

Intuition suggests there should be a market advantage from additional sales effort. The advantage, however, is one of completing the conversion process rapidly and, thereby, gaining a larger share of the new-technology base. Total market share (share of old *and* new systems) hides the advantage because it obscures the larger share of the *new* base resulting from force additions. Only when the conversion process is complete under both scenarios will market share properly reflect the advantage of the additions scenario. But the

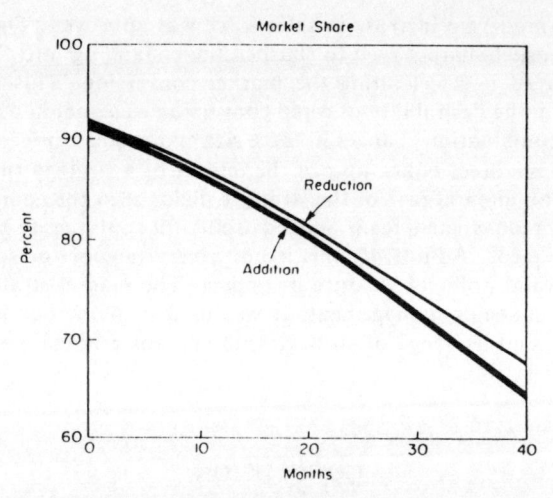

Figure 8. Market share

conversion takes more than 3 years! The simulation brings this fact to life, and dispels the expectation that force additions and market share are closely correlated.[5]

ASSESSING THE IMPACT OF THE MODEL

The impact of a strategy support model is often intangible. It is an insight generator and, therefore, differs from many common business models such as financial-planning and econometric models. The model does not get implemented in the sense that it is run weekly or monthly to produce a particular report or to execute a particular decision. By its very nature a strategy support model is involved in the amorphous to-and-fro of managerial and political debate. If it generates an insight, the insight can often quickly be absorbed into managerial thinking (mental models are, after all, much more agile than any formal simulation model, which is, by comparison, a rather cumbersome piece of intellectual infrastructure). The insight becomes part of intuition, particularly if it was backed with clear simulation analysis. Sometimes the model will form the basis for a specific recommendation but, usually, it will not contain the detail needed to state precisely how the recommendation should be translated into operating procedures. Like any strategic recommendation, it will need to pass through the usual communication and administrative channels to be fleshed out and receive operational identity.[6]

In the market-strategy case it was clear that the model had an impact on management opinion in a number of areas. For example, the insight that force reductions can precipitate a spiral of declining productivity and motivation eroded executive enthusiasm for such a

---

[5] It should be added that neither scenario shows very attractive market-share behaviour. Further simulation experiments show that combination policies involving price initiatives, force additions, and more flexible objective setting can restrict market-share erosion to less than 10 per cent.

[6] Lyneis (1981) has made the point that system dynamics models used for strategy purposes should be constructed at a level of detail that enables them to interact with the detailed planning procedures of an organization. In that way they become more tangibly integrated into company operations and are in a sense implemented. Although there is satisfaction in such tangible outcomes, the formal model loses its agility and becomes less effective as a basis for argument.

measure. In fact, a moderate increase in sales force was approved. The insight that force additions depress market share served to sharpen understanding into the short- and long-run trade-offs involved in accelerating the market conversion. This new understanding brought into question the desirability of rapid conversion as a goal in its own right, and led to further work on combination changes in force size and product price.

There are other, less direct indications of the impact of a strategy support model. Since the model becomes an integral part of the strategic dialogue in the company, it is, like any other member of the management team, judged useful if it continues to hold the interest and attention of management. Admittedly this is not a very tangible or scientific measure of impact, but it is a valid political measure of impact. The market-strategy model received ample attention from senior management. It was used in numerous high-level meetings, spanning 6 months, and its range of strategic enquiry was gradually expanded to include pricing and objective setting.

CONCLUSION

Strategy development remains an intuitive, intangible activity that is still a long way from yielding to formal analysis. Executives must be the primary architects of strategy. Where formal analysis can play a role is in strategy support—providing support in deducing the consequences of particular strategic proposals. It is in deducing consequences that the human mind is often inaccurate and misleading, even when starting from a clear understanding of the organizational elements of the strategy.

We have suggested that a valuable tool for strategy support is a formal simulation model that can act out the consequences of a new strategy in its full organizational setting. The formal model should contain the policies and communication and control structure of the organization through which strategy will be implemented.

However, the real key to effective strategy support is not simply *having* a formal model, but using it in dialogue and discussion with the managers responsible for the strategy. The formal model is used in interactive support or challenge of managerial intuition. In this dialectic role, the model is removed from the pedestal of the infallible black box to occupy a more modest (and appropriate) position as a complement to the powers of deductive thinking of a management team. The formal model should be used to set up scenarios. Managers should be challenged to think through the consequences of the scenarios for themselves. Their intuitive deductions and the formal deductions of the model can then be played off one against the other in discussion. Any differences in deduced outcome should be seized upon as opportunities for improving insight or correcting the formal model.

ACKNOWLEDGEMENTS

The author thanks David F. Andersen, Alan K. Graham and Nathaniel J. Mass for helpful comments received on an earlier draft of this paper, and Andrew M. Plummer for valuable editorial assistance. He also thanks James P. Cleary and William D. Kastning of the sponsoring company both for their comments on the paper and their enthusiastic support of the modelling project. Funds for the preparation of the paper were provided by the System Dynamics Corporate Research Program of the Sloan School of Management, M.I.T.

REFERENCES

Cyert, R. M., H. A. Simon and D. B. Trow. 'Observations of a business decision', *Journal of Business*, **29**, 1956, pp. 237-248.
Forrester, Jay W. *Industrial Dynamics*, The MIT Press, Cambridge, 1961.
Hall, R. I. 'A system pathology of an organization: the rise and fall of the old Saturday Evening Post', *Administrative Science Quarterly*, **21** (2), June 1976, pp. 185-211.
Keen, P. G. W. and M. S. Scott-Morton. *Decision Support Systems*, Addison-Wesley, Reading, Massachusetts, 1978.
Lyneis, J. M. *Corporate Planning and Policy Design—A System Dynamics Approach*, The MIT Press, Cambridge, 1980.
Lyneis, J. M. 'Increasing the effectiveness of corporate policy models', *Proceedings of the 1981 System Dynamics Research Conference*, Rensselaerville, NY, 14-17 October 1981, pp. 204-213.
Mason, R. O. 'A dialectical approach to strategic planning', *Management Science*, **15** (8), 1969, pp. B403-B414.
Mass, N. J. 'Diagnosing surprise model behavior: a tool for evolving behavioral and policy insight', *Proceedings of the 1981 System Dynamics Research Conference*, Rensselaerville, NY, 14-17 October 1981, pp. 254-272. Also available as *M.I.T. System Dynamics Group Working Paper D-3323*, M.I.T. Sloan School of Management, Cambridge, MA 02139, 1981.
Mitroff, I. I. and J. R. Emshoff. 'On strategic assumption-making: a dialectical approach to policy and planning', *Academy of Management Review*, **4**, 1979, pp. 1-12.
Mitroff, I. I., R. O. Mason and V. P. Barabba. 'Policy as argument—a logic for ill-structured decision problems', *Management Science*, **28** (12), December 1982, pp. 1391—1404.
Morecroft, J. D. W. 'System dynamics: portraying bounded rationality', *Omega*, **11** (2), March 1983, pp. 131-142.
Morecroft, J. D. W. 'Aspects of marketing strategy in the office equipment market', *System Dynamics Group Working Paper D-3352*, Sloan School of Management, M.I.T., Cambridge, MA 02139, August 1982.
Probert, D. E. 'System dynamics modeling within the British telecommunications business', *Dynamica*, **8** (Part II), Winter 1982, pp. 69-81.
Roberts, E. B. 'Strategies for effective implementation of complex corporate models', *Interfaces*, **8** (1), November 1977.
Schon, D. A. 'Conversational planning', forthcoming in Bennis, W. G., K. D. Benne and R. Chin (eds), *The Planning of Change*, Holt, Reinhart and Winston, New York, 1983.
Simon, H. A. 'Designing organizations for an information rich world', in Greenburger, M. (ed.) *Computer Communications and Public Interest*, The John Hopkins Press, Baltimore, 1971, pp. 38-52.

[5]

Learning in and about complex systems

John D. Sterman

Change is accelerating, and as the complexity of the systems in which we live grows, so do the unanticipated side effects of human actions, further increasing complexity. Many scholars call for the development of systems thinking to improve our ability to manage wisely. But how do people learn in and about complex dynamic systems? Learning is a feedback process in which our decisions alter the real world, we receive information feedback about the world and revise the decisions we make and the mental models that motivate those decisions. Unfortunately, in the world of social action various impediments slow or prevent these learning feedbacks from functioning, allowing erroneous and harmful behaviors and beliefs to persist. The barriers to learning include the dynamic complexity of the systems themselves; inadequate and ambiguous outcome feedback; systematic misperceptions of feedback; inability to simulate mentally the dynamics of our cognitive maps; poor interpersonal and organiza-

The greatest constant of modern times is change. Accelerating changes in technology, population, and economic activity are transforming our world, from the prosaic—the effect of information technology on the way we use the telephone—to the profound—the effect of greenhouse gases on the global climate. Some of the changes are desirable; others defile the planet, impoverish the human spirit, and threaten our survival. All challenge traditional institutions, practices, and beliefs. Most important, most of the changes we now struggle to comprehend arise as consequences, intended and unintended, of humanity itself.

The dizzying effects of accelerating change are not new. Henry Adams, a perceptive observer of the great changes wrought by the Industrial Revolution, formulated a "Law of Acceleration" to describe the exponential growth of technology, production, and population that made the legacy of colonial America he inherited irrelevant (Adams 1918, 490, 496):

> Since 1800 scores of new forces had been discovered; old forces had been raised to higher powers.... Complexity had extended itself on immense horizons, and arithmetical ratios were useless for any attempt at accuracy.
> ... If science were to go on doubling or quadrupling its complexities every ten years, even mathematics should soon succumb. An average mind had succumbed already in 1850; it could no longer understand the problem in 1900.

Adams believed the radical changes in society induced by these forces "would require a new social mind." With uncharacteristic, and perhaps ironic, optimism, he concluded, "Thus far, since five or ten thousand years, the mind had successfully reacted, and nothing yet proved that it would fail to react—but it would need to jump."

A steady stream of philosophers, scientists, and management gurus have since echoed Adams, lamenting the acceleration and calling for similar leaps to fundamental new ways of thinking and acting. Many advocate the development of systems thinking—the ability to see the world as a complex system, in which we understand that "you can't just do one thing," that "everything is connected to everything else." If people had a holistic worldview, it is argued, they would then act in consonance with the long-term best interests of the system as a whole. Indeed, for some, the development of systems thinking is crucial for the survival of humanity.

There are many schools of systems thinking (for surveys, see Richardson 1991 and Lane 1993). Some emphasize qualitative methods, others formal modeling. As sources of method and metaphor they draw on fields as diverse as

This work was supported by the MIT System Dynamics Group and the MIT Organizational Learning Center.

System Dynamics Review Vol. 10, nos. 2–3 (Summer–Fall 1994): 291–330   Received February 1994
© 1994 by John Wiley & Sons, Ltd. CCC 0883–7066/94/030291–40

291

tional inquiry skills; and poor scientific reasoning skills. To be successful, methods to enhance learning about complex systems must address all these impediments. Effective methods for learning in and about complex dynamic systems must include (1) tools to elicit participant knowledge, articulate and reframe perceptions, and create maps of the feedback structure of a problem from those perceptions; (2) simulation tools and management flight simulators to assess the dynamics of those maps and test new policies; and (3) methods to improve scientific reasoning skills, strengthen group process, and overcome defensive routines for individuals and teams.

John D. Sterman is professor of management science and director of the System Dynamics Group at the MIT Sloan School of Management. Address: Sloan School of Management, MIT, 50 Memorial Drive, Cambridge, MA 02142, U.S.A.

anthropology, biology, engineering, linguistics, psychology, physics, and Taoism, and seek applications in fields still more diverse. All agree, however, that a systems view of the world is still rare.

The challenge facing all is how to move from generalizations about accelerating learning and systems thinking to tools and processes that help us understand complexity, design better operating policies, and guide organization- and society-wide learning. However, learning about complex systems when you also live in them is difficult. We are all passengers on an aircraft we must not only fly but redesign in flight. In this article, I review what we know about how people learn in and about complex dynamic systems. Such learning is difficult and rare because a variety of structural impediments thwart the feedback processes required for learning to occur. I argue that successful approaches to learning about complex dynamic systems require (1) tools to articulate and frame issues, elicit knowledge and beliefs, and create maps of the feedback structure of an issue from that knowledge; (2) formal models and simulation methods to assess the dynamics of those maps, test new policies, and practice new skills; and (3) methods to sharpen scientific reasoning skills, improve group processes, and overcome defensive routines for individuals and teams, that is, in the words of Don Schön (1983a), to raise the quality of the "organizational inquiry that mediates the restructuring of organizational theory-in-use." Systems approaches that fail on any of these dimensions will not prove useful in enhancing the capabilities of individuals or organizations to understand, operate effectively in, or improve the design of the systems we have created and in which we live, nor can they form the basis for the scientific study of complexity.[1]

Learning is a feedback process

All learning depends on feedback. We make decisions that alter the real world; we receive information feedback about the real world, and using the new information, we revise our understanding of the world and the decisions we make to bring the state of the system closer to our goals (Fig. 1).

The feedback loop in Figure 1 appears in many guises throughout the social sciences. George Richardson (1991), in his history of feedback concepts in the social sciences, shows how beginning in the 1940s leading thinkers in economics, psychology, sociology, anthropology, and other fields recognized that the engineering concept of feedback applied not only to servomechanisms but to human decision making and social settings as well. Forrester, in *Industrial Dynamics* (1961), asserted that all decisions (including learning) take place in the context of feedback loops. Later, Powers (1973, 351) wrote:

Fig. 1. Learning is a feedback process.

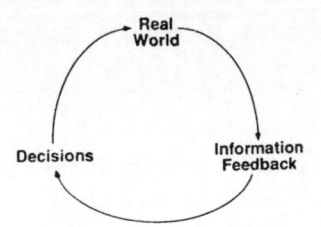

> Feedback is such an all-pervasive and fundamental aspect of behavior that it is as invisible as the air that we breathe. Quite literally it is behavior—we know nothing of our own behavior but the feedback effects of our own outputs. To behave is to control perception.

These feedback thinkers followed in the footsteps of John Dewey, who recognized the feedback-loop character of learning around the turn of the century when he described learning as an iterative cycle of invention, observation, reflection, and action (Schön 1992). Explicit feedback accounts of behavior and learning have now permeated most of the social and management sciences. Learning as an explicit feedback process has even appeared in practical management tools such as Total Quality Management, where the so-called Shewhart-Deming PDCA cycle (Plan-Do-Check-Act) lies at the heart of the improvement process in TQM (Shewhart 1939; Walton 1986; Shiba et al. 1993).

The single feedback loop shown in Figure 1 describes the most basic type of learning. The loop is a classical negative feedback whereby decision makers compare quantitative and qualitative information about the state of the real world to various goals, perceive discrepancies between desired and actual states, and take actions that (they believe will) cause the real world to move toward the desired state. Even if the initial choices of the decision makers do not close the gaps between desired and actual states, the system might eventually reach the desired state as subsequent decisions are revised in light of the feedback received (see Hogarth 1981). When driving, I may turn the steering wheel too little to bring the car back to the center of the lane, but as visual feedback reveals the error, I continue to turn the wheel until the car returns to the straight and narrow. If the current price for products of my firm is too low to balance orders with production, depleted inventories and long delivery delays cause me to gradually raise price until I discover a price that clears the market.[2]

The feedback loop shown in Figure 1 obscures an important aspect of the learning process. Information feedback about the real world is not the only input to our decisions. Decisions are the result of applying a decision rule or policy to information about the world as we perceive it (see Forrester 1961; 1992). The policies are themselves conditioned by institutional structures,

Fig. 2. The learning feedback operates in the context of existing decision rules, strategies, culture, and institutions, which are derived from our prevailing mental models.

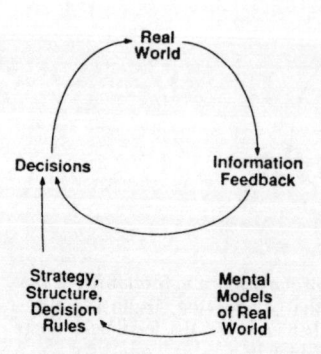

organizational strategies, and cultural norms. These in turn are governed by the mental models of the real world we hold (Fig. 2). As long as the mental models remain unchanged, the feedback loop in Figure 2 represents what Argyris (1985) calls single-loop learning, a process whereby we learn to reach our current goals in the context of our existing mental models. Single-loop learning does not result in deep change to our mental models—our understanding of the causal structure of the system, the boundary we draw around the system, the time horizon we consider relevant, or our goals and values. Single-loop learning does not alter our worldview.

Mental models are widely discussed in psychology and philosophy. Different theorists describe mental models as collections of routines, scripts, or schemata for selecting possible actions, cognitive maps of a domain, typologies for categorizing experience, pointers from instances of a phenomenon to analogous instances, logical structures for the interpretation of language, or attributions about individuals we encounter in daily life (Axelrod 1976; Bower and Morrow 1990; Cheng and Nisbett 1985; Gentner and Stevens 1983; Halford 1993; Johnson-Laird 1983; Schank and Abelson 1977; Vennix 1990). The concept of the mental model has been central to system dynamics from the beginning of the field. Forrester (1961) stresses that all decisions are based on models, and provides a typology classifying models into formal or mental, analytic or simulation, and so forth. In system dynamics, the term *mental model* stresses the implicit causal maps of a system we hold, our beliefs about the network of causes and effects that describe how a system operates, the boundary of the model (the exogenous variables) and the time horizon we consider relevant—our framing or articulation of a problem.

Most people do not appreciate the ubiquity and invisibility of mental models, instead believing naively that their senses reveal the world as it is. On the contrary, our world is actively constructed—modeled—by our sensory and

Fig. 3. Kanizsa triangle.

Fig. 4. Diagram of a company's supply chain.

Manufacturing Lead Time	Order Fulfillment Lead Time	Customer Acceptance Lead Time
75 Days	22 Days	85 Days

|← 182 Days →|

cognitive structures. Figure 3 shows a Kanizsa triangle, after the Yugoslav psychologist Gaetano Kanizsa. Most people see a white triangle whose corners cover part of three dark circles and whose body rests on top of a second triangle with black edges. The illusion is extremely powerful. Recent research shows that the neural structures responsible for the ability to see illusory contours such as the white triangle exist between the optic nerve and the areas of the brain responsible for processing visual information.[3] Active modeling occurs well before sensory information reaches the areas of the brain responsible for conscious thought. Powerful evolutionary pressures are responsible: our survival depends so completely on the ability to rapidly interpret reality that we (and other species) long ago evolved structures to build these models automatically. Usually we are totally unaware these mental models even exist. It is only when a construction such as the Kanizsa triangle reveals the illusion that we become aware of our mental models.[4]

The Kanizsa triangle illustrates the necessity of active and unconscious mental modeling, or the construction of "reality," at the level of visual perception. Modeling of higher-level knowledge is similarly unavoidable and often equally unconscious. Figure 4 shows a mental model elicited during a meeting between my colleague Fred Kofman and a team from a large global corporation. The company worked with the Organizational Learning Center at MIT to explore ways to reduce the total cycle time for their supply chain. At that time the cycle time was 182 days, and they sought to reduce it by half, to 90 days. The company viewed reductions in cycle time as essential for continued competitiveness and even corporate survival. With the support of senior management, they assembled a team to address these issues. At the first meeting the team presented background information, including Figure 4. The figure shows the current cycle time divided into three intervals along a line: manufacturing lead time; order fulfillment lead time; and customer acceptance lead time.[5] Order fulfillment, which then required 22 days, occupies more than half of the total length of the line, while the manufacturing lead time, then requiring 75 days (70 days due to suppliers), receives about one quarter of the length. Customer acceptance, then requiring 85 days, occupies only about one eighth of the total length. What the figure reveals is the prominence of order fulfillment operations in the mental models of the people on the team and the insignificance in their minds of vendors and customers. It will come as no surprise to the reader that the members of the team all worked in functions contributing to order fulfillment. There was not a single person at the meeting representing procurement, nor a single supplier representative, nor anyone from accounting, nor a single customer. Until Kofman pointed out this distortion, the members of the group were as unaware of the illusory character of their image of the supply line as we normally are of the illusory contours we project onto the sense data transmitted by our optic nerves. The distorted mental model of the supply chain significantly constrained the company's ability to achieve cycle time reduction: even if order fulfillment could be accomplished instantly, the organization would fall well short of its cycle time goal.

The type of reframing stimulated by Kofman's intervention, denoted double-loop learning by Argyris (1985), is illustrated in Figure 5. Here information feedback about the real world not only alters our decisions within the context of existing frames and decision rules but feeds back to alter our mental models. As our mental models change, we create different decision rules and change the strategy and structure of our organizations. The same information, filtered and

Fig. 5. Feedback from the real world can cause changes in mental models.

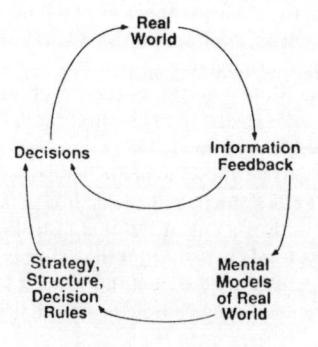

processed through a different decision rule, now yields a different decision. The development of systems thinking is a double-loop learning process in which we replace a reductionist, partial, narrow, short-term view of the world with a holistic, broad, long-term, dynamic view and then redesign our policies and institutions accordingly. Such learning involves new articulations of our understanding, or reframing of a situation, and leads to new goals and new decision rules, not just new decisions.

Barriers to learning

For learning to occur, each link in the two feedback loops must work effectively, and we must be able to cycle around the loops quickly relative to the rate at which changes in the real world render existing knowledge obsolete. Yet, in the real world, particularly the world of social action, these feedbacks often do not operate well. Figure 6 shows the main ways in which each link in the learning feedbacks can fail. These include dynamic complexity, imperfect information about the state of the real world, confounding and ambiguous variables, poor scientific reasoning skills, defensive routines and other barriers to effective group processes, implementation failure, and the misperceptions of feedback that hinder our ability to understand the structure and dynamics of complex systems.

Dynamic complexity

Much of the literature in psychology and other fields suggests learning proceeds via the simple negative feedback loops described in Figure 5. Implicitly, the loops are seen as effectively first-order, linear negative feedbacks that produce stable convergence to an equilibrium or optimal outcome. The real world is not so simple. From the beginning, system dynamics emphasized the multiloop, multistate, nonlinear character of the feedback systems in which we live (Forrester 1961). The decisions of any one agent form but one of many feedback loops that operate in any given system. These loops may reflect both anticipated and unanticipated side effects of the decision maker's actions; there may be positive as well as negative feedback loops; and these loops will contain many stocks (state variables) and many nonlinearities. Natural and human systems have high levels of dynamic complexity.

Time delays between taking a decision and its effects on the state of the system are common and particularly problematic. Most obviously, delays reduce the number of times one can cycle around the learning loop, slowing the ability to accumulate experience, test hypotheses, and improve. Schneiderman

Fig. 6. Impediments to learning.

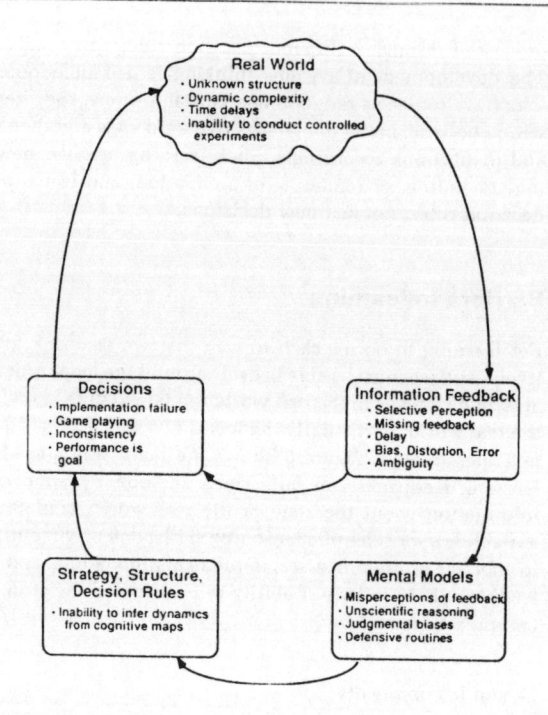

Real World
- Unknown structure
- Dynamic complexity
- Time delays
- Inability to conduct controlled experiments

Decisions
- Implementation failure
- Game playing
- Inconsistency
- Performance is goal

Information Feedback
- Selective Perception
- Missing feedback
- Delay
- Bias, Distortion, Error
- Ambiguity

Strategy, Structure, Decision Rules
- Inability to infer dynamics from cognitive maps

Mental Models
- Misperceptions of feedback
- Unscientific reasoning
- Judgmental biases
- Defensive routines

(1988) estimated the improvement half-life—the time required to cut defects in half—in a wide range of manufacturing firms. He found improvement half-lives as short as a few months for processes with short delays, for example, reducing operator error in a job shop, while complex processes with long time delays, such as product development, had improvement half-lives of several years or more. Kofman et al. (1994) show how these differential improvement rates led to difficulty at a leading semiconductor manufacturer.

Dynamic complexity not only slows the learning loop but reduces the learning gained on each cycle. In many cases, controlled experiments are prohibitively costly or unethical. More often, it is simply impossible to conduct controlled experiments. Complex systems are in disequilibrium and evolve. Many actions yield irreversible consequences. The past cannot be compared well to current circumstance. The existence of multiple interacting feedbacks means it is difficult to hold other aspects of the system constant to isolate the effect of the variable of interest; as a result, many variables simultaneously change, confounding the interpretation of changes in system behavior and reducing the effectiveness of each cycle around the learning loop.

Delays also create instability in dynamic systems. Adding time delays to the negative feedback loops increases the tendency for the system to oscillate.[6] Systems from driving a car to drinking alcohol to raising hogs to construction of office buildings all involve time delays between the initiation of a control action (accelerating/braking, deciding to "have another," choosing to breed more hogs, initiating development of a new building) and its effects on the state of the system. As a result, decision makers often continue to intervene to correct apparent discrepancies between the desired and actual state of the system even after sufficient corrective actions have been taken to restore the system to equilibrium, leading to overshoot and oscillation. The result is stop-and-go traffic, drunkenness, commodity cycles, and real estate boom-and-bust cycles (see Sterman 1989b for discussion). Oscillation and instability reduce our ability to control for confounding variables and discern cause and effect, further slowing the rate of learning.

Limited information

We experience the real world through filters. No one knows the current sales rate of their firm, the current rate of production, or the true value of the order backlog at any given time. Instead we receive estimates of these data, based on sampled, averaged, and delayed measurements. The act of measurement introduces distortions, delays, biases, errors, and other imperfections, some known, others unknown and unknowable. Above all, measurement is an act of selection. Our senses and information systems select but a tiny fraction of possible experience. Some of the selection is "hard-wired" (we cannot see in the infrared or hear ultrasound). Some results from our own decisions. We define gross domestic product so that extraction of nonrenewable resources counts as production of goods rather than as depletion of natural capital stocks and so that medical care to treat pollution-induced disease is counted as goods and services that add to GDP but the production of the pollution itself does not reduce GDP. Because the prices of most goods in our economic system do not include the costs of resource depletion or waste disposal, these 'externalities' receive little weight in decision making (see Cobb and Daly 1989 for thoughtful discussion of alternative measures of economic welfare).

Of course, the information systems governing the feedback we receive and its characteristics can change as we learn. They are part of the feedback structure of our systems. Through our mental models we define constructs such as 'GDP' or 'scientific research', create metrics for these constructs, and design information systems to evaluate and report them. These then condition the perceptions we form. Changes in our mental models are constrained by what we previously chose to define, measure, and attend to. Seeing is believing, and believing is seeing.[7]

In a famous experiment, Bruner and Postman (1949) showed playing cards to people using a tachistoscope to control exposure time to the stimuli. Most subjects could identify the cards rapidly and accurately. They also showed subjects anomalous cards, such as a black three of hearts, or a red ten of spades. Subjects took on average four times as long to judge the anomalous cards. Many misidentified them (e.g., they said "three of spades" or "three of hearts" when shown a black three of hearts). Some could not identify the card at all, even with very long exposure times, and grew anxious and confused. Only a small minority correctly identified the cards. Bruner and Postman concluded, "Perceptual organization is powerfully determined by expectations built upon past commerce with the environment." The self-reinforcing feedback between expectations and perceptions has been repeatedly demonstrated in a wide variety of experimental studies (see Plous 1993 for excellent discussion). Sometimes the positive feedback assists learning by sharpening our ability to perceive features of the environment, as when an experienced naturalist identifies a bird in a distant bush where the novice birder sees only a tangled thicket. Often, however, the mutual feedback of expectations and perceptions limits learning by blinding us to the anomalies that might challenge our mental models. Thomas Kuhn (1970) cited the Bruner-Postman study to argue that a scientific paradigm suppresses the perception of data inconsistent with the paradigm, making it hard for scientists to perceive anomalies that might lead to scientific revolution. Sterman (1985) developed a formal model of Kuhn's theory, which showed the positive feedback between expectations and perceptions suppressed the recognition of anomalies and the emergence of new paradigms.

Two recent cases, one a global environmental issue, the other the fight against AIDS, show the mutual dependence of expectation and perception is no laboratory artifact but a phenomenon with potentially grave consequences for humanity.

The first scientific papers describing the ability of chlorofluorocarbons (CFCs) to destroy atmospheric ozone were published in 1974 (Stolarski and Cicerone 1974; Molina and Rowland 1974). Yet much of the scientific community remained skeptical, and despite a ban on CFCs as aerosol propellants, global production of CFCs remained near its all-time high. It was not until 1985 that evidence of a deep ozone hole in the Antarctic was published (Farman et al. 1985). As described by Meadows, Meadows, and Randers (1992, 151–152):

> The news reverberated around the scientific world. Scientists at [NASA] ... scrambled to check readings on atmospheric ozone made by the Nimbus 7

satellite, measurements that had been taken routinely since 1978. Nimbus 7 had never indicated an ozone hole.

Checking back, NASA scientists found that their computers had been programmed to reject very low ozone readings on the assumption that such low readings must indicate instrument error.

The NASA scientists' belief that low ozone readings must be erroneous led them to design a measurement system that made it impossible to detect low readings that might have invalidated their models. Fortunately, NASA had saved the original, unfiltered data and later confirmed that total ozone had indeed been falling since the launch of Nimbus 7. Because NASA created a measurement system immune to disconfirmation, the discovery of the ozone hole and resulting global agreements to cease CFC production were delayed by as much as seven years. Those seven years could be significant: ozone levels in Antarctica dropped to less than one third of normal in 1993, and current models show atmospheric chlorine will not begin to fall until the year 2000, and then only slowly. Recent measurements show thinning of the ozone layer is a global phenomenon, not just a problem for penguins. Measurements taken near Toronto show a 5 percent increase in cancer-causing UV-B ultraviolet radiation at ground level: ozone depletion now affects the agriculturally important and heavily populated northern hemisphere.[8]

The second example comes from the fight against AIDS. Until recently AIDS vaccine research was dominated by the search for sterilizing immunity—a vaccine that could prevent a person's becoming infected with HIV altogether rather than merely preventing the disease. Potential vaccines are administered to monkeys, who are then challenged with SIV, the simian analogue of HIV. The blood and lymph systems of the monkeys are then tested to see if they become infected. Despite early promise, the candidate vaccines tried so far have failed: the vaccinated monkeys became infected at about the same rate as the unvaccinated controls. As each trial vaccine failed, researchers moved on to other candidates. The experimenters often killed the monkeys from the failed trial to free up lab space for the next trial. A few researchers, however, continued to observe their monkeys. They were surprised to find that even though their vaccine did not prevent infection, the vaccinated monkeys survived longer, were healthier, and had lower concentrations of virus in their blood than the controls. These results are stimulating interest in a model of disease prevention rather than prevention of infection. However, evaluation of, and thus resources to support, work in the new approach have been delayed because so many of the monkeys that received trial vaccinations were killed after blood tests revealed they had become infected, denying the researchers the opportunity to observe whether the vaccine helped prevent AIDS. Patricia Fast, a researcher with the U.S. National Institute on AIDS, lamented, "A lot of monkeys have been killed because it seemed like the experiment was over.... In retrospect, we wish we would have kept them alive" (quoted in Cohen 1993). Just as NASA's belief that ozone concentrations could not be low prevented them from learning that ozone concentrations were low, the belief that only sterilizing immunity could stop AIDS prevented researchers from discovering another promising therapy as early as they might have.[9]

Confounding variables and ambiguity

To learn we must use the limited and imperfect feedback available to us to understand the effects of our own decisions, so we can adjust our decisions to align the state of the system with our goals (single-loop learning) and so we can revise our mental models and redesign the system itself (double-loop learning). Yet much of the outcome feedback we receive is ambiguous. Ambiguity arises because changes in the state of the system resulting from our own decisions are confounded with simultaneous changes in a host of other variables, both exogenous and endogenous. The number of variables that might affect the system vastly overwhelms the data available to rule out alternative theories and competing interpretations. This identification problem plagues both qualitative and quantitative approaches. In the qualitative realm, ambiguity arises from the ability of language to support multiple meanings. In the opening soliloquy of Richard III (I, i, 28–31), the hump-backed Richard laments his deformity:

> And therefore, since I cannot prove a lover
> To entertain these fair well-spoken days,
> I am determined to prove a villain
> And hate the idle pleasures of these days.

Does Richard celebrate his free choice to be evil or resign himself to a predestined fate? Did Shakespeare intend the double meaning? Rich, ambiguous texts with multiple layers of meaning often make for beautiful and profound art, along with employment for literary critics, but also make it hard to know the minds of others, rule out competing hypotheses, and evaluate the impact of our past actions so we can decide how to act in the future.

In the quantitative realm, econometricians have long struggled with the problem of uniquely identifying the structure and parameters of a system from its observed behavior. Elegant and sophisticated theory exists to delimit the conditions in which one can identify a system. In practice the data are too scarce and the plausible alternative specifications too numerous for econometric methods to discriminate among competing theories. The same data often support wildly divergent models equally well, and conclusions based on such models are not robust. As Leamer (1983) put it in an article entitled "Let's take the 'con' out of Econometrics,"

> In order to draw inferences from data as described by econometric texts, it is necessary to make whimsical assumptions.... The haphazard way we individually and collectively study the fragility of inferences leaves most of us unconvinced that any inference is believable.[10]

Misperceptions of feedback

Effective management is difficult in a world of high dynamic complexity. Our decisions may create unanticipated side effects and delayed consequences. Our attempts to stabilize the system may destabilize it. Our decisions may provoke reactions by other agents seeking to restore the balance we upset. Our decisions may move the system into a new regime of behavior where unexpected and unfamiliar dynamics arise because the dominant feedback loops have changed. Forrester (1971) calls such phenomena the "counterintuitive behavior of social systems." It often leads to "policy resistance," the tendency for interventions to be delayed, diluted, or defeated by the response of the system to the intervention itself (Meadows 1982). No less an organizational theorist than Machiavelli discussed policy resistance at length, observing in *The Discourses* (1979, 240–241):

> ... when a problem arises either from within a republic or outside it, one brought about either by internal or external reasons, one that has become so great that it begins to make everyone afraid, the safest policy is to delay dealing with it rather than trying to do away with it, because those who try to do away with it almost always increase its strength and accelerate the harm which they feared might come from it.

Recent experimental studies confirm these observations. Human performance in complex dynamic environments is poor relative to normative standards, and even compared to simple decision rules:

- Subjects, including experienced managers, in a simple production-distribution system (the Beer Distribution Game) generate costly fluctuations even when consumer demand is constant. Average costs were more than ten times greater than optimal (Sterman 1989c).
- Subjects responsible for capital investment in a simple multiplier-accelerator model of the economy generate large amplitude cycles even though consumer demand is constant. Average costs were more than 30 times greater than optimal (Sterman 1989b).
- Subjects managing a firm in a simulated consumer product market generate the boom-and-bust, price war, and shakeout characteristic of industries from video games to chain saws (Paich and Sterman 1993).
- Participants in experimental asset markets repeatedly bid prices well above fundamental value, only to see them plummet when a "greater fool" can no

longer be found to buy. These speculative bubbles do not disappear when the participants are investment professionals, when monetary incentives are provided, or when short-selling is allowed (Smith et al. 1988).
- In a forest fire simulation, many people allow their headquarters to burn down despite their best efforts to put out the fire (Brehmer 1989).
- In a medical setting, subjects playing the role of doctors order more tests while the (simulated) patients sicken and die (Kleinmuntz and Thomas 1987).

These studies and many others (Brehmer 1992 provides a recent review; Funke 1991 reviews the large literature of the "German School" led by Dörner, Funke, and colleagues) show that performance is far from optimal—often far from reasonable—in a wide range of tasks, from managing an ecosystem to governing a town to controlling a factory.

In the Beer Distribution Game, for example, subjects seek to minimize costs as they manage the production and distribution of a commodity (Sterman 1989c; 1992). Though simplified compared to real firms, the task is dynamically complex because it includes multiple feedbacks, time delays, nonlinearities, and accumulations. Average costs were ten times greater than optimal. The subjects generated costly oscillations with consistent amplitude and phase relations, even though demand was essentially constant. Econometric analysis of subjects' decisions showed that people were insensitive to the time delays in the system. People did not account well, and often not at all, for the supply line of orders that had been placed but not yet received, causing them to overcompensate for inventory shortfalls. Facing an inventory shortfall, many subjects order enough beer to close the gap. Because of the delay in filling orders, inventory remains depressed, and the next period they order more beer. Still deliveries are insufficient, and they order more beer. Finally, the first order arrives, inventory rises to the desired level, and the subjects cut their orders. But the beer in the supply line continues to arrive, swelling their inventory many times above the desired levels and causing emotional reactions from anxiety to anger to chagrin. Significantly, subjects often blame their difficulty on exogenous events. When asked to sketch the pattern of customer demand, for example, most draw a large amplitude fluctuation similar to the oscillation they generated. When it is revealed that customer demand was in fact constant, many voice disbelief.

In a second experiment (Sterman 1989b), subjects exhibited the same behavior in a simulated macroeconomy representing the capital investment multiplier-accelerator. Analysis of the subjects' decision rules showed they used essentially the same rule as subjects in the Beer Distribution Game. The estimated parameters again showed most people ignored the time delays and feedback structure of the task, even though each subject was the only decision maker and the structure was completely revealed.

Simulation of the decision rules estimated for the subjects in both experiments showed that approximately one third were intrinsically unstable, so that the system never reached equilibrium. About one quarter of the estimated rules yield deterministic chaos (Sterman 1988; 1989a). The heuristics people used interacted with the feedback structure of these systems to yield severe, persistent, and costly oscillations.

These studies led me to suggest that the observed dysfunction in dynamically complex settings arises from misperceptions of feedback. I argued that the mental models people use to guide their decisions are dynamically deficient. Specifically, people generally adopt an event-based, open-loop view of causality, ignore feedback processes, fail to appreciate time delays between action and response and in the reporting of information, do not understand stocks and flows, and are insensitive to nonlinearities that may alter the strengths of different feedback loops as a system evolves.

Subsequent experiments show that the greater the dynamic complexity of the environment, the worse people do relative to potential. Diehl and Sterman (1993) examined the performance of MIT undergraduates in a simple one-person inventory management task. Time delays and side effect feedbacks were varied from trial to trial as experimental treatments. We compared subject performance against two benchmarks: optimal behavior and the behavior of a do-nothing rule. The results strongly supported the misperceptions of feedback hypothesis. Overall, subject costs were more than four times greater than optimal, despite financial incentives, training, and repeated play. In the easy conditions (no time delays or feedback effects) subjects dramatically outperformed the do-nothing rule, but in the difficult conditions many were bested by the do-nothing rule—their attempts to control the system were counterproductive. Regression models of subject decision rules showed little evidence subjects adapted their decision rules as the complexity of the task changed. Indeed, when the environment was complex, subjects seemed to revert to simple rules that ignored the time delays and feedbacks, leading to degraded performance. There was no significant difference in the time taken to make decisions across the different complexity levels, even though the number of variables to consider is much greater in the difficult conditions.

Paich and Sterman (1993) showed that learning in situations of dynamic complexity is often poor. We designed a management flight simulator representing a common and realistic corporate strategy setting.[11] The simulation portrays the market for a consumer durable product that the subjects manage through the full product life cycle, from launch through decline. The simulation includes realistic features of such markets, including price elasticity effects, marketing, word of mouth, original and replacement demand, competition, learning curves, and capacity acquisition delays. Subjects make price and capacity expansion decisions each quarter for ten simulated years. The subjects played five such trials, each with different characteristics of the market and product. As treatments we varied the strength of the key feedback loops in the simulated market. Results show patterns characteristic of many real consumer durable markets, including boom-and-bust, overcapacity, price war, and shakeout. We contrast subject performance against a simple decision rule embodying a naive strategy. The naive strategy does not engage in any strategic or game theoretic reasoning. Indeed, it is insensitive to the feedback structure of the market and the behavior of the competitor. Yet the naive strategy outperforms nearly 90 percent of the subjects. Performance relative to potential is degraded significantly as the feedback complexity of the environment grows, consistent with the misperceptions of feedback hypothesis.

Though subjects improved with experience, they learned little. Subjects accumulated 50 years of simulated experience in an environment with perfect, immediate outcome feedback. Yet in the last trial the naive strategy still outperformed 83 percent of the subjects. Most important, subjects did not learn how to improve their performance in the dynamically complex conditions. Even in the last trial, the stronger the feedback complexity of the environment, the lower profits were relative to potential. The degradation of performance relative to potential caused by high feedback complexity is not moderated by experience. Estimation of subject decision rules showed subjects actually became less responsive to critical variables and more vulnerable to forecasting errors—their learning hurt their ability to perform well in the complex conditions.

Other experiments show the misperceptions of feedback are robust to experience, incentives, opportunities for learning, and the presence of market institutions. Kampmann and Sterman (1994) designed an experiment where subjects managed a firm in an experimental economy under various market institutions and feedback complexity conditions. The high feedback complexity condition included production delays and a multiplier feedback from production to aggregate demand; the simple condition had neither. Three market institutions were tested: fixed prices, posted prices, and market clearing prices. Subjects were mostly MIT and Harvard graduate students in economics and were paid in proportion to their profits in the experiment.

In the constant price dynamically complex condition, subjects created the same unstable fluctuations observed in the other experiments discussed. In the simple market clearing condition with no feedback complexity, subjects generally converged to the predicted equilibrium, replicating prior studies in experimental economics.

However, performance relative to optimal in all three price institutions was significantly worse in the complex condition than in the simple condition. Even in perfectly functioning markets, modest levels of dynamic complexity caused large and systematic deviations from rational behavior. Complexity reduced subjects' ability to reach and maintain the cooperative equilibrium, slowed learning, and reduced the consistency of decisions. In the complex conditions, most subjects created sustained "business cycles" even though the environment was unchanging. As in the Beer Distribution Game, they attributed these cycles to exogenous changes in consumer demand.

Process data and regression models of subject decisions showed people used only a few cues, tended to ignore time delays and feedbacks, and forecasted by averaging past values and extrapolating past trends. Subjects actually spent less time making their decisions in the complex markets than in the simple ones. Simulations of the estimated rules replicated the aggregate dynamics of the experimental markets with surprising fidelity. Thus, while markets may reduce the magnitude of errors caused by the misperceptions of feedback, they do not eliminate them. Even well-functioning markets do not render the bounds on human rationality irrelevant.

The robustness of the misperceptions of feedback and the poor performance they lead us to create across many domains result from two basic and related deficiencies in our mental models of complexity. First, our cognitive maps of the causal structure of systems are vastly simplified compared to the complexity of the systems themselves. Second, we are unable to infer correctly the dynamics of all but the simplest causal maps. Both are direct consequences of bounded rationality (Simon 1979; 1982); that is, the many limitations of attention, memory, recall, information processing, and time that constrain human decision making.

Flawed cognitive maps of causal relations

Causal attributions are a central feature of mental models. People create, update, and maintain cognitive maps of causal connections among entities and actors, from the prosaic—"If I touch a flame, I will be burned"—to the grand— "The larger the government deficit, the higher interest rates will be." Studies of cognitive maps show that few incorporate any feedback loops. Axelrod (1976) found virtually no feedback processes in studies of the cognitive maps of political elites; rather, people tended to formulate intuitive decision trees relating possible actions to probable consequences—an event-level representation. Hall (1976) reports similar open-loop mental maps in a study of the publishing industry. Dörner (1980) found that people tend to think in single-strand causal series and have difficulty in systems with side effects and multiple causal pathways (much less feedback loops). Similarly, experiments in causal attribution show people tend to assume each effect has a single cause and often cease their search for explanations when a sufficient cause is found; usually base rates and situational factors are ignored (see the discussion in Plous 1993).

The heuristics we use to judge causal relations lead systematically to cognitive maps that ignore feedbacks, multiple interconnections, nonlinearities, time delays, and the other elements of dynamic complexity. The "causal field" or mental model of the stage on which the action occurs is crucial in framing people's judgments of causation (Einhorn and Hogarth 1986). Within a causal field, people use various cues to causality, including temporal and spatial proximity of cause and effect, temporal precedence of causes, covariation, and similarity of cause and effect. These heuristics lead to difficulty in complex systems, where cause and effect are often distant in time and space, actions have multiple effects, and the delayed and distant consequences are often different from and less salient than proximate effects—or simply unknown.

The multiple feedbacks in complex systems cause many variables to be correlated with one another, confounding the task of judging cause. However, people are poor judges of correlation. In the widely studied "multiple cue probability learning" paradigm, subjects seek to discover the relation between a criterion and various cues upon which it depends (along with a random error) by predicting the criterion from the cues and then receiving outcome feedback on the accuracy of their judgment. People can generally detect linear, positive correlations given enough trials if the outcome feedback is accurate enough. However, they have great difficulty in the presence of random error, nonlinearity, and negative correlations, often never discovering the true relation (Brehmer 1980).

A fundamental principle of system dynamics states that the structure of the system gives rise to its behavior. However, people have a strong tendency to attribute the behavior of others to dispositional rather than situational factors— the so-called fundamental attribution error (see Ross 1977). In complex systems, the same policy (decision rule) can lead to very different behavior (decisions) as the state of the system changes. When we attribute differences in behavior to differences in personality, we lose sight of the role of system structure in shaping our choices. The attribution of behavior to individuals and special circumstances rather than to system structure systematically diverts our attention from the high-leverage points where redesign of the system or governing policy can have significant, sustained, beneficial effects on performance (Forrester 1969, ch. 6; Meadows 1982). When we attribute behavior to people rather than to system structure, the focus of management becomes the search for extraordinary people to do the job rather than designing the job so that ordinary people can do it.

Erroneous inferences about dynamics

Even if our cognitive maps of causal structure were perfect, learning, especially double-loop learning, would still be difficult. In order to use a mental model to design a new strategy or organization we must make inferences about the consequences of decision rules that have never been tried and for which we have no data. To do so requires intuitive solution of high-order nonlinear differential equations, a task far exceeding human cognitive capabilities in all but the simplest systems (Forrester 1971; Simon 1982). In several of the experiments discussed, including the inventory management task in Diehl and Sterman (1993) and the multiplier-accelerator task in Sterman (1989b), subjects were given complete knowledge of all structural relations and parameters, along with perfect, comprehensive, and immediate outcome feedback. The subjects were the only players. Further, the systems were simple enough that the number of cues to consider was small: the multiplier-accelerator task involved only three state variables. Poor performance in these tasks seems to arise from the inability of the subjects to use their perfect knowledge to make reasonable inferences about the dynamics of the system or its response to possible decisions they might make.

People cannot simulate mentally even the simplest possible feedback system, the first-order linear positive feedback loop. The differential equation $dx/dt = gx$ yields pure exponential growth $x = x_0 \exp(gt)$. Such positive feedback processes are commonplace, from the compounding of interest to the growth of populations. Wagenaar and Sagaria (1975) and Wagenaar and Timmers (1978; 1979) showed that people significantly underestimate exponential growth, tending to extrapolate linearly rather than exponentially. Using more data points or graphing the data did not help, and mathematical training did not improve performance.

Thus, bounded rationality simultaneously constrains the complexity of our cognitive maps and our ability to use them to anticipate the system dynamics. Schemata where the world is seen as a sequence of events and where feedback, nonlinearity, time delays, and multiple consequences are lacking lead to poor performance in settings where these elements of dynamic complexity are prevalent. Dysfunction in complex systems can arise from the misperception of the feedback *structure* of the environment. But schemata that do account for complexity cannot be used reliably to understand the dynamics. Dysfunction in complex systems can arise from faulty mental simulation—the misperception of feedback *dynamics*. These two different bounds on rationality must both be overcome for effective learning to occur. Perfect maps without a simulation capability yield little insight; a calculus for reliable inferences about dynamics yields systematically erroneous results when applied to simplistic maps.

Unscientific reasoning; judgmental errors and biases

To learn effectively in a world of dynamic complexity and imperfect information people must develop what Davis and Hogarth (1992) call insight skills—the skills that help people learn when feedback is ambiguous:

> [T]he interpretation of feedback in the form of outcomes needs to be an *active* and *disciplined* task governed by the rigorous rules of scientific inference. Beliefs must be actively challenged by seeking possible disconfirming evidence and asking whether alternative beliefs could not account for the facts. (emphasis in original)

Unfortunately, people are poor intuitive scientists, generally failing to reason in accordance with the principles of scientific method. For example, they do not generate sufficient alternative explanations or consider enough rival hypotheses. They generally do not adequately control for confounding variables when they explore a novel environment. People's judgments are strongly affected by the frame in which the information is presented, even when the objective information is unchanged. People suffer from overconfidence in their judgments (underestimating uncertainty), wishful thinking (assessing desired outcomes as more likely than undesired outcomes), and the illusion of control (believing one can predict or influence the outcome of random events). They violate basic rules of probability, believe in the "law of small numbers," do not understand basic statistical concepts such as regression to the mean, and do not update beliefs according to Bayes' rule. Memory is distorted by hindsight, the availability and salience of examples, and the desirability of outcomes. And so on. Hogarth (1987) discusses 30 different biases and errors documented in decision-making research and provides a good guide to the literature (see also Kahneman et al. 1982). The research convincingly shows that scientists and professionals, not only laypeople, suffer from many of these judgmental biases.

Among the failures of scientific reasoning most inimical to learning is the tendency to seek evidence consistent with current beliefs rather than potential disconfirmation (Einhorn and Hogarth 1978; Klayman and Ha 1987). In a famous series of experiments, Wason and colleagues presented people tasks of the sort shown in Figure 7.[12] In one version you are shown one side of four cards, each with a letter on one side and a number on the other, say E, K, 4, and 7. You are told that "if a card has a vowel on it, then it has an even number on the other side." You must then identify the smallest set of cards to turn over to see if the proposed rule is correct. Wason and Johnson-Laird (1972) found that most of the subjects selected "E" or "E and 4" as the answers. Less than 4 percent gave the correct answer, "E and 7." The rule has the logical form "if p then q." Falsification requires observation of "p and not-q." The only card showing p is the E card, so it must be examined—the back of the E card must be

Fig. 7. Wason card task. What is the smallest number of cards you should turn over to test the rule that "cards with vowels on one side have even numbers on the reverse", and which are they?

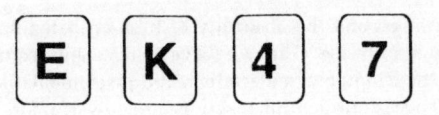

[E] [K] [4] [7]

an even number if the rule holds. The only card showing "not-q" is the 7 card, so it must be examined. The K and 4 cards are irrelevant. Yet people consistently choose the card showing q, a choice that can only provide data consistent with the theory but cannot test it—if the back of the 4 card is a consonant, you have learned nothing, since the rule is silent about the numbers associated with consonants. Experiments show the tendency to seek confirmation is robust in the face of training in logic, mathematics, and statistics. Search strategies that focus only on confirmation of current beliefs slow the generation and recognition of anomalies that might lead to learning, particularly double-loop learning (see also Davis and Hogarth 1992 for examples and discussion).

Some argue that while people err in applying the principles of logic, at least they are rational in the sense that they appreciate the desirability of scientific explanation. Unfortunately, the situation is far worse. The rational, scientific worldview is a relatively recent development in human history and remains rare. Many people place their faith in what Dostoyevsky's Grand Inquisitor called "miracle, mystery, and authority," for example, astrology, ESP, UFOs, creationism, conspiracy theories of history, channeling of past lives, cult leaders promising Armageddon, and Elvis sightings. The persistence of such superstitious beliefs depends partly on the bias toward confirming evidence. Wade Boggs, the former Red Sox batting champion, ate chicken every day for years because he once had a particularly good day at the plate after a dinner of lemon chicken (Shaughnessy 1987). During this time Boggs won five batting championships, "proving" the wisdom of the "chicken theory." Consider the continued popularity of astrology, psychics, and economic forecasters, who publicize their successes and suppress their (more numerous) failures. Remember that less than a decade ago the President of the United States and his wife managed affairs of state on the basis of astrology (Robinson 1988). And it worked: he was reelected in a landslide.

Such lunacy aside, there are deeper and more disturbing reasons for the prevalence of these learning failures and the superstitions they engender. Human beings are more than cognitive information processors. We have a deep need for emotional and spiritual sustenance. But from Copernican heliocentrism through evolution, relativity, quantum mechanics, and Gödelian uncertainty, science stripped away ancient and comforting structures that placed humanity at the center of a rational universe designed for us by a supreme authority. For many people scientific thought leads not to enlightenment but to existential angst and the absurdity of human insignificance in an incomprehensibly vast universe. Others believe science and technology were the shock troops for the triumph of materialism and instrumentalism over the sacred and spiritual. These antiscientific reactions are powerful forces. In many ways, they are important truths. They have led to many of the most profound works of art and literature. But they can also lead to mindless new-age psychobabble.

The reader should not conclude I am a naive defender of science as it is practiced, nor an apologist for the real and continuing damage done to the environment and to our cultural, moral, and spiritual lives in the name of rationality and progress. On the contrary, I have stressed the research showing that scientists are often as prone to the judgmental errors and biases discussed above as laypeople. It is precisely because scientists are subject to the same cognitive limitations and moral failures as others that we experience abominations such as U.S. government-funded research in which plutonium was injected into seriously ill patients and radioactive calcium was fed to retarded children, all without their knowledge or consent (Mann 1994). A central principle of the systems view of the world is to examine issues from multiple perspectives; to expand the boundaries of our mental models to consider the long-term consequences and side effects of our actions, including their environmental, cultural, and moral implications (Meadows, Richardson, and Bruckmann 1982).

Defensive routines and interpersonal impediments to learning

Learning by groups can be thwarted even if the system provides excellent information feedback and the decision makers reason well as individuals. We rely on our mental models to interpret the language and acts of others, construct meaning, and infer motives. However, as Forrester (1971) argues,

> The mental model is fuzzy. It is incomplete. It is imprecisely stated. Furthermore, within one individual, a mental model changes with time and even during the flow of a single conversation. The human mind assembles a few relationships to fit the context of a discussion. As the subject shifts so does the model.... [E]ach participant in a conversation employs a different mental model to interpret the subject. Fundamental assumptions differ but are never brought into the open.

Argyris (1985), Argyris and Schön (1978), Janis (1982), Schein (1969; 1985; 1987), and others document the defensive routines and cultural assumptions people rely on, often unknowingly, to interact with and interpret their experience of others. We use defensive routines to save face, assert dominance over others, make untested inferences seem like facts, and advocate our positions while appearing to be neutral. We make conflicting, unstated attributions about the data we receive, fail to distinguish between the sense data of experience and the attributions and generalizations we readily form from them. We avoid publicly testing our hypotheses and beliefs, and avoid threatening issues. Above all, defensive behavior involves covering up the defensiveness and making these issues undiscussable, even when all parties are aware they exist.

Defensive routines are subtle. They often arrive cloaked in apparent concern and respect for others. Consider the strategy of "easing-in" (Argyris et al. 1985, 83, 85):

> If you are about to criticize someone who might become defensive and you want him to see the point without undue resistance, do not state the criticism openly; instead, ask questions such that if he answers them correctly, he will figure out what you are not saying.... [But easing-in often] ... creates the very defensiveness that it is intended to avoid, because the recipient typically understands that the actor is easing-in. Indeed, easing-in can be successful only if the recipient understands that he is supposed to answer the questions in a particular way, and this entails the understanding that the actor is negatively evaluating the recipient and acting as if this were not the case.

Defensive behavior, in which the "espoused theories" we offer to others differ from our "theories-in-use," prevents learning by hiding important information from others, avoiding public testing of important hypotheses, and tacitly communicating that we are not open to having our mental models challenged. Defensive routines often yield "groupthink" (Janis 1982), where members of a group mutually reinforce their current beliefs, suppress dissent, and seal themselves off from those with different views or possible disconfirming evidence. Defensive routines ensure that the mental models of team members remain hidden, ill formed, and ambiguous. Thus learning by groups can suffer even beyond the impediments to individual learning.

Implementation failure

In the real world, decisions are often implemented imperfectly, further hindering learning. Even if a team agreed on the proper course of action, the implementation of these decisions can be delayed and distorted as the actual organization responds. Local incentives, asymmetric information, and private agendas can lead to game playing by agents throughout a system. Obviously implementation failures can hurt the organization. Imperfect implementation can defeat the learning process as well, because the management team evaluating the outcomes of their decisions may not know the ways in which the decisions they thought they were implementing were distorted.

Finally, in the real world of irreversible actions and high stakes the need to maintain performance often overrides the need to learn by suppressing new strategies for fear they would cause present harm even though they might yield great insight and prevent future harm.

Requirements for successful learning in complex systems

Thus, we face grave impediments to learning in complex systems like a nation, firm, or family. Every link in the feedback loops by which we might learn can be weakened or cut by a variety of structures. Some of these are physical or institutional features of the environment—the elements of dynamic complexity that reduce opportunities for controlled experimentation, prevent us from learning the consequences of our actions, and distort the outcome feedback we do receive. Some are consequences of our culture, group process, and inquiry skills. Still others are fundamental bounds on human cognition, particularly the poor quality of our mental maps and our inability to make correct inferences about the dynamics of complex nonlinear systems.

When can evolution overcome the impediments to learning?

Given the many impediments to learning, how is it possible that people walked on the moon, or even get through the day without grave injury? Reflecting on this paradox, Toda (1962, 165) wrote:

> Man and rat are both incredibly stupid in an experimental room. On the other hand, psychology has paid little attention to the things they do in their normal habitats; man drives a car, plays complicated games, and organizes society, and rat is troublesomely cunning in the kitchen.

Many scholars resolve the paradox by arguing that evolution can lead to high performance without the improvement of our causal maps or accurate mental simulation. Consider learning to ride a bicycle. Few people can write, let alone solve, the equations of motion for the bicycle, yet many master bicycling by the age of six. Such examples—others include billiards (Friedman 1953)—are often cited by economists who believe that human systems rapidly approach optimality through evolution (Lucas 1987). In this view, learning does not require good mental models of the environment. All we require is the ability to generate new candidate decision rules sufficiently different from current procedures and the ability to recognize and reward those that improve performance. Selection of the best performing rules over time will lead to high performance without the need to understand how or why something works.

Evolution does occur, both in the biological world and in the social world. Recent work with genetic algorithms and other simulated evolutionary processes (Nelson and Winter 1982; Anderson et al. 1988) shows that these "blind" processes often lead to rapid improvements in system performance. However, evolution leads to improvement only to the extent that (1) the processes for generating new candidate rules provide for sufficient variety; (2) the better-performing rules are rewarded by more frequent use; and (3) evolution proceeds rapidly compared to changes in the system itself.[13] Dynamic complexity and the misperceptions of feedback, however, reduce the effectiveness of all three.

Contrast learning to ride a bicycle with learning to invest successfully in real estate. The real estate industry suffers from chronic cycles of boom and bust. Low vacancy rates lead to high rents and rising prices, causing many new projects to be initiated. Development continues until prices fall as the stock of buildings increases enough to bring the vacancy rate up. However, projects under construction continue to add to the stock of buildings for several years after new development ceases. The stock of buildings overshoots, prices fall, and new construction remains low until vacancies drop, initiating the next cycle. (Bakken 1993; Hernandez 1990; and Thornton 1992 describe field studies of successful and unsuccessful developers that verify the account here.) The equations of motion for the real estate cycle are much simpler than those governing the bicycle. A simple, low-dimensional system dynamics model replicates the real estate cycle well (Jarmain 1963; Bakken 1993). Yet the boom-and-bust cycles in real estate persist over centuries (Hoyt 1933), while novice riders quickly learn to pilot their bicycles smoothly. The differences must be sought in the effects of dynamic complexity on the efficacy of the feedbacks governing learning and evolution.

Consider first the bicycle. The conditions for learning are excellent: outcome feedback is available continuously with but short time delays between action and result. Feedback is salient and accurate. There are few confounding variables (what others in the neighborhood are doing is irrelevant). One can cycle around the driveway—and the learning loop—dozens of times in an afternoon. Thus one can try many different ways to ride (variety is easily generated) and can easily determine which work best (thus effectively selecting those that improve performance). In the next round of trials, one generates new experience similar to what worked best before, and selects from these the best-performing ways to ride. Furthermore, the laws of physics and equations of motion for the bicycle do not change in response to the rider's decisions, so what is learned does not become obsolete. Thus evolution can work well.[14]

Consider now the problem of successful investing in the real estate industry. Time lags are substantial—it takes two to five years between the decision to develop a property and the completion of the project, still more time to cash out, and the buildings last at least 50 years. Even seasoned developers experience only one or at most two cycles in their career, and so much will change over those decades it is difficult to draw general conclusions about the symptoms, much less the causes, of the dynamics. Information about rents, prices, construction costs, vacancies, migration patterns, and many other relevant variables is extremely limited, incomplete, noisy, and ambiguous. Current prices and stories of successful deals are highly salient and concrete but misleading, while the critically important supply pipeline and plans of other developers are abstract and unpersuasive. It is extremely difficult to relate current prices and costs to likely future costs and returns. It is not possible to conduct controlled experiments. As developers begin new projects, their actions alter a host of variables, including the availability and cost of construction crews, migration patterns, and business location decisions, all of which feed back to alter vacancies and prices and thus future development decisions. Unlike the bicycle case, in real estate what others in the neighborhood are doing matters a great deal: success in the market rapidly attracts new entrants, who then contribute to overbuilding and lower prices.

Evolution functions poorly in the real estate market both because there is much less variation in behavior and because selection is less effective. The slow dynamics mean there are fewer decisions than for the bicycle. Variation and experimentation are reduced because of the strong herd instinct in the industry. Groupthink and strong networks of communication among developers, bankers, and others lead to common knowledge and expectations. The costs of error are also asymmetric: it is better to be wrong with the crowd than wrong alone. Even if a developer wished to follow a contrarian strategy by buying properties when prices are depressed and pessimism reigns, few investors would be willing to lend the needed funds. Experimentation is also reduced because errors are punished much more severely (by bankruptcy and loss of reputation) than the skinned knees typical in bicycling. Without variation in developer strategy, meaningful performance differentials cannot arise, and selection will operate on noise. Finally, the feedbacks among market participants are so strong that evolution itself introduces variation in the environment that makes current knowledge obsolete (that is, the players, their strategies, and their environment are coevolving).

More important, evolution selects according to whatever fitness function is used to evaluate different strategies. Different fitness functions—values— reward different behaviors. When short-run performance is rewarded, strategies yielding superior quarterly or annual results proliferate even though they may cause long-run ruin for all. The bias toward reward of short-run results is reinforced by the misperceptions of feedback, which make it hard to assign credit for long-term results to particular strategies or people. Most developers and bankers find the structure and dynamics of the industry so hard to understand that the effectiveness of strategies is evaluated well before the full consequences are observed. The short time horizon for performance evaluation is reinforced by perverse incentives whereby deals that ultimately lose money generate fees up front. These incentives are themselves devices to reduce uncertainty about short-term cash flow. Thus during booms strategies based on maximum financial leverage and building "on spec" work best, while conservative investors lag far behind. Aggressive strategies proliferate as the apparent success of players like Donald Trump makes still more capital available to them and draws in a host of imitators. Selection thus rewards strategies that worsen the bust. Rather than leading to stability, evolution may select against conservative investors and increase the prevalence of speculators who destabilize the industry.

Improving the learning process

What then are the requirements for successful learning in complex systems? If we are to create useful protocols and tools for learning effectively in a world of dynamic complexity, we must attend to all the impediments to learning. Figure 8 shows how the learning feedbacks would operate when all the impediments to learning are addressed. The diagram features a new feedback loop created by the use of virtual worlds.

Effective learning involves continuous experimentation in both virtual worlds and real worlds, with feedback from both informing development of the mental models, the formal models, and the design of experiments.

Virtual worlds—the term is Schön's (1983b)—are formal models, or microworlds (Papert 1980), in which the decision makers can refresh decision-making skills, conduct experiments, and play. They can be physical models, role plays, or computer simulations. In systems with significant dynamic complexity, computer simulation will typically be needed, although there are notable exceptions, such as the Beer Distribution Game and the Du Pont Maintenance Game (Carroll et al. 1994), and role-play/computer hybrids such as Fish Banks, Ltd. (Meadows, Fiddaman, and Shannon 1993).

Virtual worlds have several advantages. First, they provide low-cost laboratories for learning. The virtual world allows time and space to be compressed or dilated. Actions can be repeated under the same or different conditions. One can stop the action to reflect. Decisions that are dangerous, infeasible, or unethical in the real system can be taken in the virtual world. Thus controlled experimentation becomes possible, and the time delays in the learning loop through the real world are dramatically reduced. In the real world the irreversibility of many actions and the need to maintain high performance often override the goal of learning by preventing experiments with untried possibilities ("if it ain't broke, don't fix it"). In the virtual world one can try strategies that one suspects will lead to poor performance or even (simulated) catastrophe. Often pushing a system into extreme conditions reveals more about its structure and dynamics than incremental adjustments to successful strategies.

Fig. 8. Idealized learning loops.

Real World
- Unknown structure
- Dynamic complexity
- Time delays
- Inability to conduct controlled experiments

Virtual World
- Known structure
- Variable level of complexity
- Controlled experiments

Decisions

Real World:
- Implementation failure
- Game playing
- Inconsistency
- Performance is goal

Virtual World:
- Perfect Implementation
- Consistent Incentives
- Consistent application of decision rules
- Learning can be goal

Information Feedback

Virtual World:
- Complete, accurate, immediate feedback

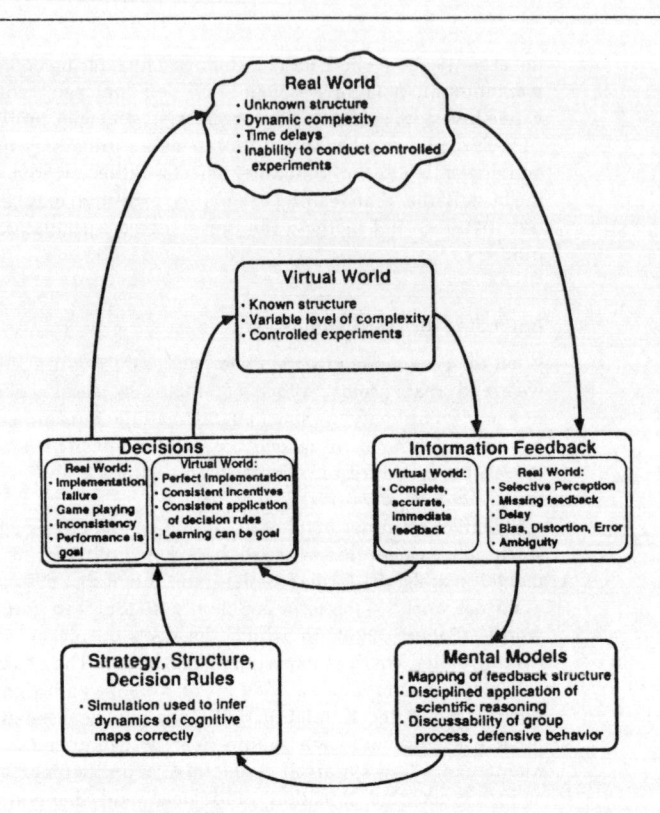

Real World:
- Selective Perception
- Missing feedback
- Delay
- Bias, Distortion, Error
- Ambiguity

Strategy, Structure, Decision Rules
- Simulation used to infer dynamics of cognitive maps correctly

Mental Models
- Mapping of feedback structure
- Disciplined application of scientific reasoning
- Discussability of group process, defensive behavior

Virtual worlds are the only practical way to experience catastrophe in advance of the real thing. Thus a great deal of the time pilots spend in flight simulators is devoted to extreme conditions such as engine failure or explosive decompression.

Virtual worlds provide high-quality outcome feedback. In the People Express Management Flight Simulator (Sterman 1988), for example, and similar system dynamics simulations, players receive perfect, immediate, undistorted, and complete outcome feedback. In an afternoon one can gain years of simulated experience. The degree of random variation in the virtual world can be controlled. Virtual worlds offer the learner greater control over strategy, leading to more consistency of decision making, avoiding implementation failure, and game playing. In contrast to the real world, which, like a black box, has a poorly resolved structure, virtual worlds can be open boxes whose assumptions are fully known and can even be modified by the learner.

Virtual worlds for learning and training are commonplace in the military, in pilot training, in power plant operations, and in many other real-time tasks where human operators interact with complex technical systems. Virtual worlds are also common in professions such as architecture (Schön 1983b). The use of virtual worlds in managerial tasks, where the simulation compresses into a day or an hour dynamics extending over years or decades, is more recent and less widely adopted. Yet these are precisely the settings where dynamic complexity is more problematic and the learning feedbacks least effective. Many virtual worlds for the study of dynamically complex settings have now been developed, and while further evaluative research is needed, they have enjoyed great success in precollege education, universities, and corporations (see Gould-Kreutzer 1993; Graham et al. 1992; Morecroft and Sterman 1994; and Mandinach and Cline 1994).

Pitfalls of virtual worlds

Virtual worlds are effective when they engage people in what Dewey called "reflective thought" and what Schön (1992) calls "reflective conversation with the situation." While the use of virtual worlds may be necessary for effective learning in dynamically complex systems, this does not guarantee that virtual worlds overcome the flaws in our mental models, scientific reasoning skills, and group process.

Obviously, while the virtual world enables controlled experimentation, it does not require the learner to apply the principles of scientific method. Many participants in model-based workshops lack training in scientific method and awareness of the pitfalls in the design and interpretation of experiments. A commonly observed behavior in workshops using management flight simulators is "trial and trial again" where players make incremental adjustments to their last strategy, then try again. Participants do not take time to reflect on the outcomes, identify discrepancies between the outcomes and their expectations, formulate hypotheses to explain the discrepancies, and then devise experiments to discriminate among the competing alternatives (Mass 1991 gives guidelines for effective experimentation in simulation models.) Effective learning in virtual worlds will often require training for participants in scientific method. Protocols for the use of simulations should be structured to encourage proper procedure, such as keeping laboratory notebooks, explicitly formulating hypotheses and presenting them to the group, and so on.

Defensive routines and groupthink can operate in the learning laboratory just as in the real organization. Indeed, protocols for effective learning in virtual worlds, such as public testing of hypotheses, accountability, and comparison of different strategies can be highly threatening, inducing defensive reactions that prevent learning (Isaacs and Senge 1992). The use of virtual worlds to stimulate learning in organizations often requires that group members spend time addressing their own defensive behavior. Managers unaccustomed to disciplined scientific reasoning and an open, trusting environment with learning as its goal will have to build these basic skills before a virtual world can prove useful. Developing these skills takes effort and practice.

Still, settings with high dynamic complexity can garble the reflective conversation between the learner and the situation. Long time delays, causes and effects that are distant in time and space, and the confounding effects of multiple nonlinear feedbacks can slow learning even for people with good insight and group process skills. Learning in virtual worlds can be accelerated when the protocols for simulator use help people learn how to represent complex feedback structures and understand their implications. To learn when dynamic complexity is high, participants must have confidence in the external validity of the virtual world. They must believe it mimics the relevant parts of the real world well enough that the lessons emerging from the virtual world apply to the real one. To develop such confidence, the virtual world must be an open box whose assumptions are accessible and modifiable. To learn from the open box, participants must become modelers, not merely players in a simulation.

In practice, effective learning from models occurs best, and perhaps only, when the decision makers participate actively in the development of the model. Modeling here includes the elicitation of the participants' existing mental models, including articulating the issues (problem structuring), selecting the model boundary and time horizon, and mapping the causal structure of the relevant system. Researchers in the soft operations research tradition have pioneered many methods to facilitate the elicitation and mapping process. Along with techniques developed in system dynamics, many tools and protocols for group model building are now available, including causal-loop diagrams, policy structure diagrams, hexagon modeling, interactive computer mapping, and various problem structuring and soft systems methods (see, for instance, Checkland 1981; Eden et al. 1983; Lane 1993; Morecroft 1982; Morecroft and Sterman 1994; Reagan-Cirincione et al. 1991; Richmond 1987; 1993; Rosenhead 1989; Senge and Sterman 1992; and Wolstenholme 1990).

Why simulation is essential

Eliciting and mapping the participants' mental models, while necessary, is far from sufficient. As discussed, the temporal and spatial boundaries of our mental models tend to be too narrow. They are dynamically deficient, omitting feedbacks, time delays, accumulations, and nonlinearities. The great virtue of many protocols and tools for elicitation is their ability to improve our models by encouraging people to identify the elements of dynamic complexity normally absent from mental models. However, most problem-structuring methods yield qualitative models showing causal relations but omitting the parameters, functional forms, exogenous variables, and initial conditions needed to fully specify and test the model. Regardless of the form of the model or technique used, the result of the elicitation and mapping process is never more than a set of causal attributions, initial hypotheses about the structure of a system, which must then be tested.

Simulation is the only practical way to test these models. The complexity of the cognitive maps produced in an elicitation workshop vastly exceeds our capacity to understand their implications. Qualitative maps are simply too ambiguous and too difficult to simulate mentally to provide much useful information on the adequacy of the model structure or guidance about the future development of the system or the effects of policies.

Without simulation, even the best maps can only be tested and improved by relying on the learning feedback through the real world. As we have seen, this feedback is very slow and often rendered ineffective by dynamic complexity, time delays, inadequate and ambiguous feedback, poor reasoning skills, defensive reactions, and the cost of experimentation. In these circumstances simulation becomes the only reliable way to test the hypotheses emerging from elicitation techniques and other problem-structuring methods.

Some scholars argue that it is not possible to create valid formal models of human systems; that formal modeling can at best provide quantitative precision within preexisting problem definitions but cannot lead to fundamentally new conceptions (for various views, see Dreyfus and Dreyfus 1986 and the discussion in Lane 1993). On the contrary, formalizing qualitative models and testing them via simulation often leads to radical changes in the way we construe reality and carve problems out of "messes" (Ackoff 1979). Simulation speeds and strengthens the learning feedbacks. Discrepancies between the formal and mental models stimulate improvements in both, including changes in basic assumptions, such as model boundary, time horizon, and dynamic hypotheses (see Forrester 1985 and Homer 1990 for philosophy and an example). Without the discipline and constraint imposed by the rigorous testing enabled by simulation, it becomes all too easy for mental models to be driven by unconscious bias or deliberate ideology.

Some argue that formalization forces the modeler to omit important aspects of the problem to preserve tractability and enable theorems to be proved, or to omit soft variables for which no numerical data exist. These are indeed dangers. The literature of the social sciences is replete with models in which elegant theorems are derived from questionable axioms, where simplicity dominates utility, and where variables known to be important are ignored because data to estimate parameters are unavailable. System dynamics was designed specifically to overcome these limitations and from the beginning stressed the development of useful, realistic models, models unconstrained by the demands of analytic tractability, based on realistic assumptions about human behavior, grounded in field study of decision making, and utilizing the full range of available data, not only numerical data, to specify and estimate relations (see Forrester 1987).

As to the notion that useful and valid formal models of human behavior cannot be developed, space does not permit full rebuttal of this position here. However, as Kenneth Boulding points out, "Anything that exists is possible," and many formal models of human behavior in systems with soft variables exist (see, for instance, the models in Levine and Fitzgerald 1992; Roberts 1978; Langley et al. 1987; Sterman 1985; Homer 1985; and many of the models cited in Sastry and Sterman 1993).

Is it possible to learn effectively in complex settings without simulation? Can the use of problem-structuring methods, elicitation techniques, and other qualitative systems methods overcome the impediments to learning? If intuition is developed highly enough, if systems thinking is incorporated in precollege education early enough, or if we are taught how to recognize a set of "system archetypes" (Senge 1990), will we be able to improve our intuition about complex dynamics enough to render simulation unnecessary?

The answer is clearly no. It is true that systems thinking techniques, including system dynamics and qualitative methods such as soft systems analysis, can enhance our intuition about complex situations, just as studying physics can improve our intuition about the natural world.[15] As Wolstenholme (1990) argues, qualitative systems tools should be made widely available so that those with limited mathematical background can benefit from them. I am a strong advocate for the introduction of system dynamics and related methods at all levels of the educational system. Yet even if children began serious study of physics in kindergarten, and continued it through a doctorate, it is ludicrous to suggest that they could predict the track of a hurricane or understand what happens when two galaxies collide by intuition alone. Many human systems are just as complex. Even if children learn to think in systems terms—a goal I believe is vitally important—it will still be necessary to develop formal models, solved by simulation, to learn about such systems.

Most important, when experimentation in the real system is infeasible, simulation becomes the main, and perhaps the only, way learners can discover *for themselves* how complex systems work. The alternative is rote learning based on the authority of the teacher and textbook, a pedagogy that dulls creativity and stunts the development of the scientific reasoning skills needed to learn about complexity.

Conclusion

Complex dynamic systems present multiple barriers to learning. The challenge of bettering the way we learn about these systems is itself a classic systems problem. Overcoming the barriers to learning requires a synthesis of many methods and disciplines, from mathematics and computer science to psychology and organizational theory. Theoretical studies must be integrated with field work. Interventions in real organizations must be subjected to rigorous follow-up research.

There are many reasons for hope. Recent advances in interactive modeling, tools for representation of feedback structure, and simulation software make it possible for anyone to engage in the modeling process. Corporations, universities, and schools are experimenting vigorously. Much further work is needed to test the utility of the tools and protocols, evaluate their impact on individual and organizational learning, and develop effective ways to train others to use them. The more rigorously we apply the principles discussed here to our own theories and our own practices, the faster we will learn how to learn in and about complex systems.

Notes

1. By *scientific* I mean an endeavor much like the "normal science" of Thomas Kuhn (1970), i.e., the disciplined activity of a community that builds a cumulative stock of knowledge according to certain principles, including documentation and publication of methods and results, replicability, and transferability (the knowledge can be learned and used by others).
2. Depending on the time delays and other elements of dynamic complexity in the system, these examples may not converge. It takes but little ice, fog, fatigue, or alcohol to cause an accident, and equilibrium eludes many industries that experience chronic business cycles.
3. See *Science* 256 (June 12, 1992): 1520–1521.
4. Even more obviously, our ability to see a three-dimensional world is the result of extensive modeling by the visual processing system, since the retina images a planar projection of the visual field.
5. Note that the time intervals in Figure 4 do not map onto the lengths of the segments representing those intervals. The figure has been simplified compared to the actual chart supplied, to protect confidential company information, but it is drawn to scale.

6. Technically, negative loops with no time delays are first-order; the eigenvalue of the linearized system can only be real, and oscillation is impossible. Adding delays (state variables) allows the eigenvalues to become complex conjugates, yielding oscillatory solutions. Whether the oscillations of the linearized system are damped or expanding depends on the parameters. All else equal, the more phase lag in a control loop, the less stable the system will be.
7. Philosophers have long noted the critical role of beliefs in conditioning perception. A brief summary is provided in Sterman (1985).
8. These data are summarized in Culotta and Koshland (1993).
9. The example is not merely an example of hindsight bias. Given the weak theoretical basis for the null results of the sterilizing immunity approach, it does not seem reasonable to design vaccination trials so that the experiments could generate data only on the one hypothesis of sterilizing immunity. Far from illustrating hindsight bias, the example illustrates the overconfidence bias (too much faith that sterilizing immunity would work) and the failure to generate sufficient alternative hypotheses. It is too soon to know which approach will work, if either, and the example does not imply that work on sterilizing immunity should stop. But the favored hypothesis led to experimental protocols that precluded the observation of data that might have led to other possibilities, thus slowing learning.
10. Despite its difficulties, I am not arguing that econometrics should be abandoned. On the contrary, wise use of statistical estimation is important to good system dynamics practice, and more effort should be devoted to the use of these tools in simulation model development and testing.
11. This and other management flight simulators are available from the author.
12. The summary of the Wason test is drawn from Plous (1993, ch. 20).
13. Of course, in systems such as an ecosystem or market, evolution is itself a source of change. Such systems involve populations of entities all mutually coevolving, so that the evolutionary landscape shifts because of the evolutionary process itself.
14. Perhaps most important, bicycling is a motor skill drawing on neural and sensory systems that evolved to provide accurate feedback about and control of balance, position, and motion. Balancing and pedaling require little conscious effort. The decision to invest in real estate, in contrast, is largely conscious and cognitive (though emotions often loom large as well). High survival value over millions of years caused excellent motor skills to evolve, while the cognitive skills required to understand the assumptions behind a spreadsheet or the dynamic complexity of a market have led to reproductive advantage only recently, if at all.
15. Such education is desperately needed. When asked the question, "If a pen is dropped on the moon, will it (a) float away; (b) float where it is; (c) fall to the surface of the moon?" 48 out of 168 students in physics courses at Iowa State University gave incorrect answers. A typical student explanation was, "The gravity of the moon can be said to be negligible, and also the moon is a vacuum, so there is no external force on the pen. Therefore it will float where it is" (Partee 1992).

References

Ackoff, R. 1979. The Future of Operational Research Is Past. *Journal of the Operational Research Society* 30: 93–104.

Adams, H. 1918. *The Education of Henry Adams*. Boston: Houghton Mifflin.

Anderson, P., K. Arrow, and D. Pines, eds. 1988. *The Economy as an Evolving Complex System*. Redwood City, Calif.: Addison-Wesley.

Argyris, C. 1985. *Strategy, Change, and Defensive Routines*. Boston: Pitman.

Argyris, C., R. Putnam, and D. Smith. 1985. *Action Science*. San Francisco: Jossey-Bass.

Argyris, C., and D. Schön. 1978. *Organizational Learning: A Theory of Action Perspective*. Reading, Mass.: Addison-Wesley.

Axelrod, R. 1976. *The Structure of Decision: The Cognitive Maps of Political Elites*. Princeton, N.J.: Princeton University Press.

Bakken, B. 1993. Learning and Transfer of Understanding in Dynamic Decision Environments. Ph.D. dissertation, Sloan School of Management, MIT, Cambridge MA 02142, U.S.A.

Bower, G., and D. Morrow. 1990. Mental Models in Narrative Comprehension. *Science* 247 (5): 44–48.

Brehmer, B. 1980. In One Word: Not from Experience. *Acta Psychologica* 45: 223–241.

———. 1989. Feedback Delays and Control in Complex Dynamic Systems. In *Computer-Based Management of Complex Systems*, ed. P. Milling and E.O.K. Zahn, 189–196. Berlin: Springer-Verlag.

———. 1992. Dynamic Decision Making: Human Control of Complex Systems. *Acta Psychologica* 81: 211–241.

Bruner, J. S., and L. J. Postman. 1949. On the Perception of Incongruity: A Paradigm. *Journal of Personality* 18: 206–223.

Carroll, J. S., J. D. Sterman, and A. A. Marcus. 1994. Playing the Maintenance Game: How Mental Models Drive Organizational Decisions. In *Nonrational Elements of Organizational Decision Making*, ed. R. R. Stern and J. J. Halpern. Ithaca, N.Y.: ILR Press.

Checkland, P. 1981. *Systems Thinking, Systems Practice*. Chichester, U.K.: Wiley.

Cheng, P., and R. Nisbett. 1985. Pragmatic Reasoning Schemas. *Cognitive Psychology* 17: 391–416.

Cobb, J., and H. Daly. 1989. *For the Common Good*. Boston: Beacon Press.

Cohen, J. 1993. A New Goal: Preventing Disease, Not Infection. *Science* 262 (December 17): 1820–1821.

Culotta, E., and D. Koshland. 1993. Molecule of the Year. *Science* 262 (December 24): 1960.

Davis, H., and R. Hogarth. 1992. Rethinking Management Education: A View from Chicago. Selected Paper 72, Graduate School of Business, University of Chicago.

Diehl, E., and J. D. Sterman. 1993. Effects of Feedback Complexity on Dynamic Decision Making. Working Paper, Sloan School of Management, MIT, Cambridge, MA 02142, U.S.A.

Dörner, D. 1980. On the Difficulties People Have in Dealing with Complexity. *Simulations and Games* 11 (1): 87–106.

Dreyfus, H. L., and S. E. Dreyfus. 1986. *Mind over Machine*. New York: Free Press.

Eden, C., S. Jones, and D. Sims. 1983. *Messing About in Problems*. Oxford: Pergamon.
Einhorn, H., and R. Hogarth. 1978. Confidence in Judgment: Persistence of the Illusion of Validity. *Psychological Review* 85: 395–476.
———. 1986. Judging Probable Cause. *Psychological Bulletin* 99: 3–19.
Farman, J., B. Gardiner, and J. Shanklin. 1985. Large Losses of Total Ozone in Antarctica Reveal Seasonal ClO/NO$_2$ Interaction. *Nature* 315: 207.
Forrester, J. W. 1961. *Industrial Dynamics*. Portland, Ore.: Productivity Press.
———. 1969. *Urban Dynamics*. Portland, Ore.: Productivity Press.
———. 1971. Counterintuitive Behavior of Social Systems. *Technology Review* 73 (January): 52–68.
———. 1985. "The" Model Versus a Modeling "Process". *System Dynamics Review* 1 (1): 133–134. Original paper 1971.
———. 1987. 14 "Obvious Truths." *System Dynamics Review* 3 (2): 156–159. Original paper 1960. Also in *Collected Papers of Jay W. Forrester* (Portland, Ore.: Productivity Press, 1975).
———. 1992. Policies, Decisions, and Information Sources for Modeling. *European Journal of Operational Research* 59 (1): 42–63.
Friedman, M. 1953. The Methodology of Positive Economics. In *Essays in Positive Economics*, ed. M. Friedman. Chicago: University of Chicago Press.
Funke, J. 1991. Solving Complex Problems: Exploration and Control of Complex Systems. In *Complex Problem Solving: Principles and Mechanisms*, ed. R. Sternberg and P. Frensch. Hillsdale, N.J.: Erlbaum.
Gentner, D., and A. Stevens. 1983. *Mental Models*. Hillsdale, N.J.: Erlbaum.
Gould-Kreutzer, J. 1993. System Dynamics in Education. *System Dynamics Review* 9 (2): 101–112.
Graham, A. K., J. D. Morecroft, P. M. Senge, and J. D. Sterman. 1992. Model-Supported Case Studies for Management Education. *European Journal of Operational Research* 59 (1): 151–166.
Halford, G. 1993. *Children's Understanding: The Development of Mental Models*. Hillsdale, N.J.: Erlbaum.
Hall, R. I. 1976. A System Pathology of an Organization: The Rise and Fall of the Old Saturday Evening Post. *Administrative Science Quarterly* 21 (2): 185–211.
Hernandez, K. 1990. Learning in Real Estate: The Role of the Development System in Creating Oversupply. M.S. thesis, Sloan School of Management, MIT, Cambridge, MA 02142, U.S.A.
Hogarth, R. 1981. Beyond Discrete Biases: Functional and Dysfunctional Aspects of Judgmental Heuristics. *Psychological Bulletin* 90: 197–217.
———. 1987. *Judgement and Choice*. 2d ed. Chichester, U.K.: Wiley.
Homer, J. B. 1985. Worker Burnout: A Dynamic Model with Implications for Prevention and Control. *System Dynamics Review* 1 (1): 42–62.
———. 1990. Cocaine Use in America: The Evolution of a Dynamic Model. In *Proceedings of the 1990 International System Dynamics Conference* (Chestnut Hill, Mass.), 495–510.
Hoyt, H. 1933. *One Hundred Years of Land Values in Chicago*. Chicago: University of Chicago Press.
Isaacs. W. N., and P. Senge. 1992. Overcoming Limits to Learning in Computer-

Based Learning Environments. *European Journal of Operational Research* 59 (1): 183–196.

Janis, I. L. 1982. *Groupthink: Psychological Studies of Policy Decisions and Fiascoes*. 2d ed. Boston: Houghton Mifflin.

Jarmain, W. E. 1963. *Problems in Industrial Dynamics*. Cambridge, Mass.: MIT Press.

Johnson-Laird, P. 1983. *Mental Models: Toward a Cognitive Science of Language, Inference, and Consciousness*. Cambridge: Cambridge University Press.

Kahneman, D., P. Slovic, and A. Tversky. 1982. *Judgment under Uncertainty: Heuristics and Biases*. Cambridge: Cambridge University Press.

Kampmann, C., and J. Sterman. 1994. Feedback Complexity, Bounded Rationality, and Market Dynamics. Working paper, System Dynamics Group, Sloan School of Management, MIT, Cambridge MA 02142, U.S.A.

Klayman, J., and Y. Ha. 1987. Confirmation, Disconfirmation, and Information in Hypothesis Testing. *Psychological Review* 94: 211–228.

Kleinmuntz, D., and J. Thomas. 1987. The Value of Action and Inference in Dynamic Decision Making. *Organizational Behavior and Human Decision Processes* 39 (3): 341–364.

Kofman, F., N. Repenning, and J. D. Sterman. 1994. Unanticipated Side Effects of Successful Quality Programs: Exploring a Paradox of Organizational Improvement. Working Paper D-4390, System Dynamics Group, Sloan School of Management, MIT, Cambridge MA 02142, U.S.A.

Kuhn, T. 1970. *Structure of Scientific Revolutions*. 2d ed. Chicago: University of Chicago Press.

Lane, D. C. 1993. With a Little Help from Our Friends: How Third-Generation System Dynamics and Issue-Structuring Techniques of "Soft" OR Can Learn from Each Other. In *System Dynamics 1993*, ed. E. Zepeda and J.A.D. Machuca, 235–244. System Dynamics Society, 49 Bedford Road., Lincoln, MA 01773, U.S.A. Published in expanded form as City University Business School Discussion Paper ITM/93/DCL2.

Langley, P., H. A. Simon, G. L. Bradshaw, and J. M. Zytkow. 1987. *Scientific Discovery: Computational Explorations of the Creative Processes*. Cambridge, Mass.: MIT Press.

Leamer, E. 1983. Let's Take the Con out of Econometrics. *American Economic Review* 73 (1): 31–43.

Levine, R., and H. Fitzgerald. 1992. *Analysis of Dynamic Psychological Systems*. New York: Plenum.

Lucas, R. 1987. Adaptive Behavior and Economic Theory. In *Rational Choice: The Contrast Between Economics and Psychology*, ed. R. Hogarth and M. Reder. Chicago: University of Chicago Press.

Machiavelli, N. (1519) 1979. The Discourses. In *The Portable Machiavelli*, ed. and trans. P. Bondanella and M. Musa. New York: Viking Press.

Mandinach, E. B., and H. F. Cline. 1994. *Classroom Dynamics: Implementing a Technology-Based Learning Environment*. Hillsdale, N.J.: Lawrence Erlbaum Associates.

Mann, C. 1994. Radiation: Balancing the Record. *Science* 263 (January 28): 470–473.

Mass, N. 1991. Diagnosing Surprise Model Behavior: A Tool for Evolving Behavioral and Policy Insights. *System Dynamics Review* 7 (1): 68–86. Original paper 1981.

Meadows, D. H. 1982. Whole Earth Models and Systems. *CoEvolution Quarterly* (Summer): 98–108.

Meadows, D. H., D. L. Meadows, and J. Randers. 1992. *Beyond the Limits*. Post Mills, Vt.: Chelsea Green Publishing Co.

Meadows, D. H., J. Richardson, and G. Bruckmann. 1982. *Groping in the Dark*. Chichester, U.K.: Wiley.

Meadows, D. L., T. Fiddaman, and D. Shannon. 1993. *Fish Banks, Ltd. A Microcomputer-Assisted Group Simulation That Teaches Principles of Sustainable Management of Renewable Natural Resources*. 3d ed. Laboratory for Interactive Learning, Hood House, University of New Hampshire, Durham, NH 03824, U.S.A.

Molina, M., and F. S. Rowland. 1974. Stratospheric Sink for Chlorofluoromethanes: Chlorine Atomic Catalysed Destruction of Ozone. *Nature* 249: 810.

Morecroft, J.D.W. 1982. A Critical Review of Diagramming Tools for Conceptualizing Feedback Models. *Dynamica* 8 (1): 20–29.

Morecroft, J.D.W., and J. D. Sterman, eds. 1994. *Modeling for Learning*. Portland Ore.: Productivity Press.

Nelson, R., and S. Winter. 1982. *An Evolutionary Theory of Economic Change*. Cambridge, Mass.: Harvard University Press.

Paich, M., and D. Sterman. 1993. Boom, Bust, and Failures to Learn in Experimental Markets. *Management Science* 39 (12): 1439–1458.

Papert, S. 1980. *Mindstorms*. New York: Basic Books.

Partee, J. 1993. Heavy Boots. E-mail from partee@iastate.edu.

Plous, S. 1993. *The Psychology of Judgment and Decision Making*. New York: McGraw-Hill.

Powers, W. 1973. Feedback: Beyond Behaviorism. *Science* 179: 351–356.

Reagan-Cirincione, P., S. Schuman, G. P. Richardson, and S. A. Dorf. 1991. Decision Modeling: Tools for Strategic Thinking. *Interfaces* 21 (6): 52–65.

Richardson, G. P. 1991. *Feedback Thought in Social Science and Systems Theory*. Philadelphia: University of Pennsylvania Press.

Richmond, B. 1987. *The Strategic Forum: From Vision to Operating Policies and Back Again*. High Performance Systems, 45 Lyme Rd., Hanover, NH 03755, U.S.A.

———. 1993. Systems Thinking: Critical Thinking Skills for the 1990s and Beyond. *System Dynamics Review* 9 (2): 113–134.

Roberts, E. B., ed. 1978. *Managerial Applications of System Dynamics*. Portland, Ore.: Productivity Press.

Robinson, J. 1988. A Day for the Capital to Consider Its Stars. *Boston Globe* (May 4): 1.

Rosenhead, J., ed. 1989. *Rational Analysis for a Problematic World: Problem Structuring Methods for Complexity, Uncertainty, and Conflict*. Chichester, U.K.: Wiley.

Ross, L. 1977. The Intuitive Psychologist and His Shortcomings: Distortions in the Attribution Process. In *Advances in Experimental Social Psychology*, vol. 10, ed. L. Berkowitz. New York: Academic Press.

Sastry, A., and J. D. Sterman. 1993. Desert Island Dynamics: An Annotated Guide to the Essential System Dynamics Literature. In *Proceedings of the 1993 International System Dynamics Conference* (Cancún, Mexico), 466–475.

Schank, R., and R. Abelson. 1977. *Scripts, Plans, Goals, and Understanding.* Hillsdale, N.J.: Erlbaum.

Schein, E. 1969. *Process Consultation: Its Role in Organization Development.* Reading, Mass.: Addison-Wesley.

———. 1985. *Organizational Culture and Leadership.* San Francisco: Jossey-Bass.

———. 1987. *Process Consultation.* Vol. 2. Reading, Mass.: Addison-Wesley.

Schneiderman, A. 1988. Setting Quality Goals. *Quality Progress* (April): 55–57.

Schön, D. 1983a. Organizational Learning. In *Beyond Method*, ed. G. Morgan. London: Sage.

———. 1983b. *The Reflective Practitioner.* New York: Basic Books.

———. 1992. The Theory of Inquiry: Dewey's Legacy to Education. *Curriculum Inquiry* 22 (2): 119–139.

Senge, P. 1990. *The Fifth Discipline.* New York: Doubleday/Currency.

Senge, P., and J. D. Sterman. 1992. Systems Thinking and Organizational Learning: Acting Locally and Thinking Globally in the Organization of the Future. *European Journal of Operational Research* 59 (1): 137–150.

Shaughnessy, D. 1987. Bogged Down. *Boston Globe* (March 15): III, 20.

Shewhart, W. 1939. Statistical Method from the Viewpoint of Quality Control. Washington, D.C.: U.S. Department of Agriculture.

Shiba, S., A. Graham, and D. Walden. 1993. *A New American TQM: Four Practical Revolutions in Management.* Portland, Ore.: Productivity Press.

Simon, H. A. 1979. Rational Decision Making in Business Organizations. *American Economic Review* 69: 493–513.

———. 1982. *Models of Bounded Rationality.* Cambridge: MIT Press.

Smith, V., G. Suchanek, and A. Williams. 1988. Bubbles, Crashes, and Endogenous Expectations in Experimental Spot Asset Markets. *Econometrica* 56 (5): 1119–1152.

Sterman, J. D. 1985. The Growth of Knowledge: Testing a Theory of Scientific Revolutions with a Formal Model. *Technological Forecasting and Social Change* 28 (2): 93–122.

———. 1988. *People Express Management Flight Simulator.* Software and briefing book. Available from J. D. Sterman, Sloan School of Management, 50 Memorial Drive, MIT, Cambridge, MA 02142, U.S.A.

———. 1989a. Deterministic Chaos in an Experimental Economic System. *Journal of Economic Behavior and Organization* 12: 1–28.

———. 1989b. Misperceptions of Feedback in Dynamic Decision Making. *Organizational Behavior and Human Decision Processes* 43 (3): 301–335.

———. 1989c. Modeling Managerial Behavior: Misperceptions of Feedback in a Dynamic Decision-Making Experiment. *Management Science* 35 (3): 321–339.

———. 1992. Teaching Takes Off: Flight Simulators for Management Education. *OR/MS Today* (October): 40–44.

Stolarski, R., and R. Cicerone. 1974. Stratospheric Chlorine: A Possible Sink for Ozone. *Canadian Journal of Chemistry* 52: 1610.

Thornton, L. 1992. Real Estate Development Firms as Learning Organizations: Systems Thinking as a Methodology for Strategic Planning. M.S. thesis, Sloan School of Management, MIT, Cambridge, MA 02142, U.S.A.

Toda, M. 1962. The Design of a Fungus-Eater: A Model of Human Behavior in an Unsophisticated Environment. *Behavioral Science* 7: 164–183.

Vennix, J.A.M. 1990. Mental Models and Computer Models: Design and Evaluation of a Computer-Based Learning Environment for Policy Making. Ph.D. dissertation, Catholic University of Nijmegen, Netherlands.

Wagenaar, W., and S. Sagaria. 1975. Misperception of Exponential Growth. *Perception and Psychophysics* 18: 416–422.

Wagenaar, W., and H. Timmers. 1978. Extrapolation of Exponential Time Series Is Not Enhanced by Having More Data Points. *Perception and Psychophysics* 24: 182–184.

———. 1979. The Pond and Duckweed Problem: Three Experiments in the Misperception of Experimental Growth. *Acta Psychologica* 43: 239–251.

Walton, M. 1986. *The Deming Management Method*. New York: Dodd, Mead.

Wason, P., and P. Johnson-Laird. 1972. *Psychology of Reasoning: Structure and Content*. Cambridge, Mass.: Harvard University Press.

Wolstenholme, E. F. 1990. *System Enquiry: A System Dynamics Approach*. Chichester, U.K., Wiley.

[6]

ARCHIVES

14 "obvious truths"

Jay W. Forrester

Founded in the mid-1950s, the field of system dynamics has intellectual roots reaching much further into the past. The Archives section of the *Review* seeks to publish material from that past which can contribute to current theory and practice. The section welcomes previously unpublished but deserving system dynamics work, classics from past system dynamics literature that should receive renewed attention, and previously published articles from other disciplines of particular significance to current system dynamicists. Contributions emphasizing the philosophy and theory of model building, validation, implementation, education, and generic structures are particularly encouraged. Submissions may range in length from notes to main articles but may be edited. Send suggested material, together with a brief introduction placing it in historical and current contexts, to John D. Sterman, System Dynamics Group, M.I.T. E40-294, Cambridge, MA 02139, U.S.A.

The following "14 points" first appeared in "The Impact of Feedback Control Concepts on the Management Sciences," originally delivered as the 1960 Distinguished Lecture of the Foundation for Instrumentation, Education, and Research and reprinted in The Collected Papers of Jay W. Forrester *(Cambridge, Mass.: MIT Press, 1975). The paper is nearly 30 years old, but it is remarkable how many of its points remain relevant today, despite tremendous progress in some areas (such as the recognition of unstable behavior in many systems). Such continuing relevance arises in large measure from Forrester's vision of system dynamics as a pragmatic tool whose ultimate purpose is to improve the functioning of social and economic systems. The different goals of the "operator," such as a manager, who must choose a course of action now, and the "observer," such as the academic, who seeks to add to the stockpile of knowledge, account for much of the persistence of the viewpoints and methods Forrester criticizes here. While not all modelers will (or should) agree with each of the following points, it is useful, from time to time, to raise unquestioned assumptions to the surface, where they can be examined, debated, and revised.*

John D. Sterman

A number of "obvious truths" seem to have been accepted in varying degrees as the philosophical guidelines for much of the search for a scientific foundation underlying management and economics. All of the following appear to be given at least some credence, and all seem to me to be misleading:

1. Linear analysis

That a linear analysis is an adequate representation of industrial and economic systems. Almost every factor in these systems is nonlinear. Much of the important behavior is a direct manifestation of the nonlinear characteristics. The amplitude of excursion of system variables is so large that "small signal" linear analysis is not suitable.

2. Stable systems

That our social systems are inherently stable and can be attacked with methods that are valid only for stable systems that tend toward equilibrium. There seems ample evidence that much of our industrial and economic behavior shows the characteristics of an unstable system. Many industries are characterized by an unstable, nonlinear, self-limiting systems behavior.

3. Prediction function

That the obvious purpose and test of a model of an industrial system is its ability to predict specific future action. We should use a model to predict the character and the nature of a system and for the design of the kind of system that we desire. This is far different, less stringent, and much more useful than the prediction of the specific future times of peaks and valleys in a sales curve.

4. Data

That the construction of a model must be limited to those variables for which numerical time-series data exists. A model of system behavior must deal with those variables which are thought to control system action. If data has not been collected in the past, best guesses must be substituted until measurements are taken.

5. Accepted definitions

That a model must be limited to considering those variables which have generally accepted definitions. Many undefined concepts are known to be of major importance. Integrity, hope, research output, quality, customer satisfaction, and confidence must all be given definitions and be incorporated in those system models where they are presumed to be important.

6. Descriptive knowledge

That our vast body of descriptive knowledge is unsuitable for use in model formulations. Just as formal numerical data has been the preferred ingredient for model making, so has the wealth of information in the business press been rejected. *Business Week* and *The Wall Street Journal* lack academic stature even though they may contain the clearest and most perceptive published insights into the reasons for industrial managers' decisions.

7. Exact versus social

That there is a sharp distinction between the "exact" and the social sciences. At the most this is but a quantitative distinction and at the least there is no distinction at all. Exactness and accuracy must be measured not in terms of the number of decimal digits. This accuracy of measurement has been developed because it was needed. The next advancement is based on the preceding level of accuracy. Dramatic progress is possible in the dynamic behavior of industrial systems using parameters which may be in error by a factor of 3—which are not even correct in the first decimal place.

8. Source of analogy

That the physical and genetic sciences provide the proper analogy for model building in the social sciences. The "laws" of physics usually relate to open systems rather than to information-feedback systems. Furthermore, they relate to fragments of systems rather than to entire systems. A much better analogy exists in the engineering and military models—models of telephone systems, of aircraft, of military systems, and of missile controls.

9. Accuracy of structure

That accuracy of parameters is more important than system structure. A great deal of time and effort in social science is devoted to the measurement of parameters. Yet these parameters are put into models which I believe do not belong to the general class to which the actual systems themselves belong. Correct parameters can hardly succeed in a grossly incorrect model structure. Here I refer to the failure to deal adequately with those factors that give information-feedback systems their characteristic behavior.

10. Accuracy versus precision

That accuracy must be achieved before precision is useful. The ability to precisely state a hypothesis and to examine its consequences can be tremendously revealing even though the accuracy of the statement is low. A precise and explicit statement with assumed numerical values will tell us the kinds of things which can happen. Should these things be important we can later devote attention to improving the accuracy of their statement.

11. Optimum solutions

That it is necessary to find optimum solutions to managerial questions. Tremendous gains lie ahead in systems management. Mere improvement will often be dramatic even when it falls short of some optimum. Optimum solutions are generally possible only for naively simple questions. More is to be gained by improving areas of major opportunity than by optimizing areas of minor importance.

12. Controlled experiments

That the social sciences differ fundamentally from the physical sciences by inability to conduct "controlled experiments." Again, this is not more than a matter of degree. Controlled experiments in engineering are done with models. The models are as complete and realistic as our knowledge permits. The same concepts in using a model are possible in management and economics. Effective models are entirely feasible with present technical resources. We have only to construct the models and then the laboratory experimental stage can begin.

13. Human decisions

That human decision making is obscurely subtle and impenetrable. The major factors to which a decision is responsive are relatively few in number. They are usually subject to clarification if properly approached. Once we have dealt with a relatively few properly selected factors, the remaining ones can be relegated to a noise and uncertainty category.

14. Decision versus policy

That emphasis in models should be on decision making. The sharp distinction between policy and decision has been obscured. Too much attention has been concentrated on the individual decisions and not enough on the policy which governs how the decisions are made. Models of industrial systems should be directed toward policy. In other words, what are the rules by which information sources are converted into a continuous flow of decisions? The present-day emphasis on the management game as a training device arises from a misplaced concentration on decisions rather than on policies.

Part II
Systems Thinking and Dynamic Decision Making

This section brings together essays focusing on people's abilities to reason in complex dynamic systems. The first three chapters focus on qualitative statements concerning insightful feedback structures that can enhance thinking about complex managerial systems. The next three present the framework and results of empirical, model-based investigations revealing limitations of our decision-making abilities in complex dynamic systems. Together these papers present a sobering picture of our systems thinking abilities and a promising direction for improvements.

Systems Thinking

There are many systems thinkers and many styles of systems thinking.[1] The phrase 'systems thinking' has emerged within the system dynamics modelling community relatively recently in order to capture what modellers are striving to facilitate. System dynamics models are seen as *aids for reflection* on the structure and dynamics of complex systems: they facilitate a kind of systems thinking.

In *The Fifth Discipline*,[2] Peter Senge identified systems thinking in the system dynamics tradition as the fifth of five disciplines of the learning organization. Chapter 7, 'The Leader's New Work: Building Learning Organizations', is an elegantly concise statement from Senge about this development in management thinking. The list of system archetypes sketched there had its origins in Forrester's 'Notes on Complex Systems',[3] the result of years of experience and reflection on system dynamics models. In a real sense they are empirical results – generalizations from themes that have surfaced repeatedly in the structure and behaviour of dynamic feedback simulation models of serious policy problems. The list of these generic structures was first brought to a wider audience in the essay of Donella Meadows reprinted as Chapter 8 in this section. The most current and complete statement of these insightful system archetypes appears in the next chapter, authored by Daniel Kim and taken from the Toolbox Reprint Series of Pegasus Communications, publishers of *The Systems Thinker*.

Decision Making in Dynamic Environments

John Morecroft's chapter on 'Microworlds for Policymakers' outlines recent developments in the field of system dynamics that have extended its accessibility to managers. He traces innovations in software and diagramming tools that have greatly facilitated both the modelling process and management's active participation in it. His overview of the development and use of model-based serious games as learning laboratories creates links between systems thinking, simulation modelling for management and research in dynamic decision making.

That research is the subject of the remaining two chapters in Part II. John Sterman's path-breaking 'Misperceptions of Feedback in a Dynamic Decision Making Experiment' won the System Dynamics Society's Jay Wright Forrester award for the overall excellence of its research and for the significance of its documentation of common flaws in dynamic decision making. Sterman's work led to a line of research within the system dynamics community using simulated microworlds to extend our understanding of consistent weaknesses in human decision making in dynamic systems complicated with time lags, feedback loops, accumulations and nonlinearities.

In the last paper in this sequence, Paich and Sterman investigated managerial decision making in a realistic 'management flight simulator', capturing the structure and dynamics of the 'boom and bust' pattern common in new products. Particularly significant are their demonstrations that performance varies systematically with the strength of particular feedback loops and that repeated play is not sufficient to bring performance up to potential.

Learning in complex, dynamic, circular-causal management settings appears certain to require more than experience. Crucial as well are the capacities and tendencies to map complexity, to reflect on structure and behaviour, and to test understandings through reflective conversation or simulation.

Notes

1 For a view of the diversity of approaches and contributions, see 'Systems Thinkers, Systems Thinking', a special 1994 issue of the *System Dynamics Review*, **10** (2–3), Summer–Fall, edited by G.P. Richardson, E.F. Wolstenholme and J.D.W. Morecroft.
2 P.M. Senge (1990), *The Fifth Discipline: The Art and Practice of the Learning Organization*, New York: Doubleday/Currency.
3 J.W. Forrester (1969), *Urban Dynamics*, Cambridge, MA: MIT Press; reprinted by Productivity Press, Portland (Oregon).

[7]

The Leader's New Work: Building Learning Organizations

Peter M. Senge   *MIT Sloan School of Management*

OVER THE PAST two years, business academics and senior managers have begun talking about the notion of the learning organization. Ray Stata of Analog Devices put the idea succinctly in these pages last spring: "The rate at which organizations learn may become the only sustainable source of competitive advantage." And in late May of this year, at an MIT-sponsored conference entitled "Transforming Organizations," two questions arose again and again: *How can we build organizations in which continuous learning occurs?* and, *What kind of person can best lead the learning organization?* This article, based on Senge's recently published book, *The Fifth Discipline: The Art and Practice of the Learning Organization*, begins to chart this new territory, describing new roles, skills, and tools for leaders who wish to develop learning organizations.

Sloan Management Review

7

Fall 1990

HUMAN BEINGS are designed for learning. No one has to teach an infant to walk, or talk, or master the spatial relationships needed to stack eight building blocks that don't topple. Children come fully equipped with an insatiable drive to explore and experiment. Unfortunately, the primary institutions of our society are oriented predominantly toward controlling rather than learning, rewarding individuals for performing for others rather than for cultivating their natural curiosity and impulse to learn. The young child entering school discovers quickly that the name of the game is getting the right answer and avoiding mistakes—a mandate no less compelling to the aspiring manager.

"Our prevailing system of management has destroyed our people," writes W. Edwards Deming, leader in the quality movement.[1] "People are born with intrinsic motivation, self-esteem, dignity, curiosity to learn, joy in learning. The forces of destruction begin with toddlers—a prize for the best Halloween costume, grades in school, gold stars, and on up through the university. On the job, people, teams, divisions are ranked—reward for the one at the top, punishment at the bottom. MBO, quotas, incentive pay, business plans, put together separately, division by division, cause further loss, unknown and unknowable."

Peter M. Senge is Director of the Systems Thinking and Organizational Learning program at the MIT Sloan School of Management.

Ironically, by focusing on performing for someone else's approval, corporations create the very conditions that predestine them to mediocre performance. Over the long run, superior performance depends on superior learning. A Shell study showed that, according to former planning director Arie de Geus, "a full one-third of the Fortune '500' industrials listed in 1970 had vanished by 1983."[2] Today, the average lifetime of the largest industrial enterprises is probably less than *half* the average lifetime of a person in an industrial society. On the other hand, de Geus and his colleagues at Shell also found a small number of companies that survived for seventy-five years or longer. Interestingly, the key to their survival was the ability to run "experiments in the margin," to continually explore new business and organizational opportunities that create potential new sources of growth.

If anything, the need for understanding how organizations learn and accelerating that learning is greater today than ever before. The old days when a Henry Ford, Alfred Sloan, or Tom Watson *learned for the organization* are gone. In an increasingly dynamic, interdependent, and unpredictable world, it is simply no longer possible for anyone to "figure it all out at the top." The old model, "the top thinks and the local acts," must now give way to integrating thinking and acting at all levels. While the challenge is great, so is the potential payoff. "The per-

Learning Organizations

8

Senge

son who figures out how to harness the collective genius of the people in his or her organization," according to former Citibank CEO Walter Wriston, "is going to blow the competition away."

Adaptive Learning and Generative Learning

The prevailing view of learning organizations emphasizes increased adaptability. Given the accelerating pace of change, or so the standard view goes, "the most successful corporation of the 1990s," according to *Fortune* magazine, "will be something called a learning organization, a consummately adaptive enterprise."[3] As the Shell study shows, examples of traditional authoritarian bureaucracies that responded too slowly to survive in changing business environments are legion.

But increasing adaptiveness is only the first stage in moving toward learning organizations. The impulse to learn in children goes deeper than desires to respond and adapt more effectively to environmental change. The impulse to learn, at its heart, is an impulse to be generative, to expand our capability. This is why leading corporations are focusing on *generative* learning, which is about creating, as well as *adaptive* learning, which is about coping.[4]

The total quality movement in Japan illustrates the evolution from adaptive to generative learning. With its emphasis on continuous experimentation and feedback, the total quality movement has been the first wave in building learning organizations. But Japanese firms' view of serving the customer has evolved. In the early years of total quality, the focus was on "fitness to standard," making a product reliably so that it would do what its designers intended it to do and what the firm told its customers it would do. Then came a focus on "fitness to need," understanding better what the customer wanted and then providing products that reliably met those needs. Today, leading edge firms seek to understand and meet the "latent need" of the customer — what customers might truly value but have never experienced or would never think to ask for. As one Detroit executive commented recently, "You could never produce the Mazda Miata solely from market research. It required a leap of imagination to see what the customer *might* want."[5]

Generative learning, unlike adaptive learning, requires new ways of looking at the world, whether in understanding customers or in understanding how to better manage a business. For years, U.S. manufacturers sought competitive advantage in aggressive controls on inventories, incentives against overproduction, and rigid adherence to production forecasts. Despite these incentives, their performance was eventually eclipsed by Japanese firms who saw the challenges of manufacturing differently. They realized that eliminating delays in the production process was the key to reducing instability and improving cost, productivity, and service. They worked to build networks of relationships with trusted suppliers and to redesign physical production processes so as to reduce delays in materials procurement, production set up, and in-process inventory — a much higher-leverage approach to improving both cost and customer loyalty.

As Boston Consulting Group's George Stalk has observed, the Japanese saw the significance of delays because they saw the process of order entry, production scheduling, materials procurement, production, and distribution *as an integrated system*. "What distorts the system so badly is time," observed Stalk — the multiple delays between events and responses. "These distortions reverberate throughout the system, producing disruptions, waste, and inefficiency."[6] Generative learning requires seeing the systems that control events. When we fail to grasp the systemic source of problems, we are left to "push on" symptoms rather than eliminate underlying causes. The best we can ever do is adaptive learning.

The Leader's New Work

"I talk with people all over the country about learning organizations, and the response is always very positive," says William O'Brien, CEO of the Hanover Insurance companies. "If this type of organization is so widely preferred, why don't people create such organizations? I think the answer is leadership. People have no real comprehension of the type of commitment it requires to build such an organization."[7]

Our traditional view of leaders — as special people who set the direction, make the key decisions, and energize the troops — is deeply rooted in an individualistic and nonsystemic worldview. Especially in the West, leaders are *heroes* — great men (and occasionally women) who rise to the fore in times of crisis. So long as such myths prevail, they reinforce a focus on short-term events and charismatic heroes rather than on systemic forces and collective learning.

Leadership in learning organizations centers on subtler and ultimately more important work. In a learning organization, leaders' roles differ dramatically from that of the charismatic decision maker. Leaders are designers, teachers, and stewards. These roles require new skills: the ability to build shared vision, to bring to the surface and challenge prevailing mental models, and to foster more systemic patterns of thinking. In short, leaders in learning organizations are responsible for *building organizations* where people are continually expanding their capabilities to shape their future—that is, leaders are responsible for learning.

Creative Tension: The Integrating Principle

Leadership in a learning organization starts with the principle of creative tension.[8] Creative tension comes from seeing clearly where we want to be, our "vision," and telling the truth about where we are, our "current reality." The gap between the two generates a natural tension (see Figure 1).

Creative tension can be resolved in two basic ways: by raising current reality toward the vision, or by lowering the vision toward current reality. Individuals, groups, and organizations who learn how to work with creative tension learn how to use the energy it generates to move reality more reliably toward their visions.

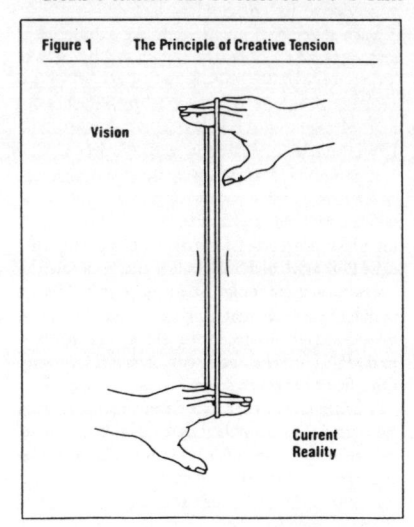

The principle of creative tension has long been recognized by leaders. Martin Luther King, Jr., once said, "Just as Socrates felt that it was necessary to create a tension in the mind, so that individuals could rise from the bondage of myths and half truths . . . so must we . . . create the kind of tension in society that will help men rise from the dark depths of prejudice and racism."[9]

Without vision there is no creative tension. Creative tension cannot be generated from current reality alone. All the analysis in the world will never generate a vision. Many who are otherwise qualified to lead fail to do so because they try to substitute analysis for vision. They believe that, if only people understood current reality, they would surely feel the motivation to change. They are then disappointed to discover that people "resist" the personal and organizational changes that must be made to alter reality. What they never grasp is that the natural energy for changing reality comes from holding a picture of what might be that is more important to people than what is.

But creative tension cannot be generated from vision alone; it demands an accurate picture of current reality as well. Just as King had a dream, so too did he continually strive to "dramatize the shameful conditions" of racism and prejudice so that they could no longer be ignored. Vision without an understanding of current reality will more likely foster cynicism than creativity. The principle of creative tension teaches that *an accurate picture of current reality is just as important as a compelling picture of a desired future.*

Leading through creative tension is different than solving problems. In problem solving, the energy for change comes from attempting to get away from an aspect of current reality that is undesirable. With creative tension, the energy for change comes from the vision, from what we want to create, juxtaposed with current reality. While the distinction may seem small, the consequences are not. Many people and organizations find themselves motivated to change only when their problems are bad enough to cause them to change. This works for a while, but the change process runs out of steam as soon

Figure 1   The Principle of Creative Tension

Vision

Current Reality

as the problems driving the change become less pressing. With problem solving, the motivation for change is extrinsic. With creative tension, the motivation is intrinsic. This distinction mirrors the distinction between adaptive and generative learning.

New Roles

The traditional authoritarian image of the leader as "the boss calling the shots" has been recognized as oversimplified and inadequate for some time. According to Edgar Schein, "Leadership is intertwined with culture formation." Building an organization's culture and shaping its evolution is the "unique and essential function" of leadership.[10] In a learning organization, the critical roles of leadership—designer, teacher, and steward—have antecedents in the ways leaders have contributed to building organizations in the past. But each role takes on new meaning in the learning organization and, as will be seen in the following sections, demands new skills and tools.

Leader as Designer

Imagine that your organization is an ocean liner and that you are "the leader." What is your role?

I have asked this question of groups of managers many times. The most common answer, not surprisingly, is "the captain." Others say, "The navigator, setting the direction." Still others say, "The helmsman, actually controlling the direction," or, "The engineer down there stoking the fire, providing energy," or, "The social director, making sure everybody's enrolled, involved, and communicating." While these are legitimate leadership roles, there is another which, in many ways, eclipses them all in importance. Yet rarely does anyone mention it.

The neglected leadership role is the *designer* of the ship. No one has a more sweeping influence than the designer. What good does it do for the captain to say, "Turn starboard 30 degrees," when the designer has built a rudder that will only turn to port, or which takes six hours to turn to starboard? It's fruitless to be the leader in an organization that is poorly designed.

The functions of design, or what some have called "social architecture," are rarely visible; they take place behind the scenes. The consequences that appear today are the result of work done long in the past, and work today will show its benefits far in the future. Those who aspire to lead out of a desire to control, or gain fame, or simply to be at the center of the action, will find little to attract them to the quiet design work of leadership.

But what, specifically, is involved in organizational design? "Organization design is widely misconstrued as moving around boxes and lines," says Hanover's O'Brien. "The first task of organization design concerns designing the governing ideas of purpose, vision, and core values by which people will live." Few acts of leadership have a more enduring impact on an organization than building a foundation of purpose and core values.

In 1982, Johnson & Johnson found itself facing a corporate nightmare when bottles of its bestselling Tylenol were tampered with, resulting in several deaths. The corporation's immediate response was to pull all Tylenol off the shelves of retail outlets. Thirty-one million capsules were destroyed, even though they were tested and found safe. Although the immediate cost was significant, no other action was possible given the firm's credo. Authored almost forty years earlier by president Robert Wood Johnson, Johnson & Johnson's credo states that permanent success is possible only when modern industry realizes that:

- service to its customers comes first;
- service to its employees and management comes second;
- service to the community comes third; and
- service to its stockholders, last.

Such statements might seem like motherhood and apple pie to those who have not seen the way a clear sense of purpose and values can affect key business decisions. Johnson & Johnson's crisis management in this case was based on that credo. It was simple, it was right, and it worked.

If governing ideas constitute the first design task of leadership, the second design task involves the policies, strategies, and structures that translate guiding ideas into business decisions. Leadership theorist Philip Selznick calls policy and structure the "institutional embodiment of purpose."[11] "Policy making (the rules that guide decisions) ought to be separated from decision making," says Jay Forrester.[12] "Otherwise, short-term pressures will usurp time from policy creation."

Traditionally, writers like Selznick and Forrester have tended to see policy making and implementation as the work of a small number of senior managers. But that view is changing. Both the dynamic business environment and the mandate of the learning organization to engage people at all levels now make it clear that this second design task is more subtle. Henry Mintzberg has argued that strategy is less a rational plan arrived at in the abstract and implemented throughout the organization than an "emergent phenomenon." Successful organizations "craft strategy" according to Mintzberg, as they continually learn about shifting business conditions and balance what is desired and what is possible.[13] The key is not getting the right strategy but fostering strategic thinking. "The choice of individual action is only part of . . . the policymaker's need," according to Mason and Mitroff.[14] "More important is the need to achieve insight into the nature of the complexity and to formulate concepts and world views for coping with it."

Behind appropriate policies, strategies, and structures are effective learning processes; their creation is the third key design responsibility in learning organizations. This does not absolve senior managers of their strategic responsibilities. Actually, it deepens and extends those responsibilities. Now, they are not only responsible for ensuring that an organization have well-developed strategies and policies, but also for ensuring that processes exist whereby these are continually improved.

In the early 1970s, Shell was the weakest of the big seven oil companies. Today, Shell and Exxon are arguably the strongest, both in size and financial health. Shell's ascendance began with frustration. Around 1971 members of Shell's "Group Planning" in London began to foresee dramatic change and unpredictability in world oil markets. However, it proved impossible to persuade managers that the stable world of steady growth in oil demand and supply they had known for twenty years was about to change. Despite brilliant analysis and artful presentation, Shell's planners realized, in the words of Pierre Wack, that they "had failed to change behavior in much of the Shell organization."[15] Progress would probably have ended there, had the frustration not given way to a radically new view of corporate planning.

As they pondered this failure, the planners' view of their basic task shifted: "We no longer saw our task as producing a documented view of the future business environment five or ten years ahead. Our real target was the microcosm (the 'mental model') of our decision makers." Only when the planners reconceptualized their basic task as fostering learning rather than devising plans did their insights begin to have an impact. The initial tool used was "scenario analysis," through which planners encouraged operating managers to think through how they would manage in the future under different possible scenarios. It mattered not that the managers believed the planners' scenarios absolutely, only that they became engaged in ferreting out the implications. In this way, Shell's planners conditioned managers to be mentally prepared for a shift from low prices to high prices and from stability to instability. The results were significant. When OPEC became a reality, Shell quickly responded by increasing local operating company control (to enhance maneuverability in the new political environment), building buffer stocks, and accelerating development of non-OPEC sources—actions that its competitors took much more slowly or not at all.

Somewhat inadvertently, Shell planners had discovered the leverage of designing institutional learning processes, whereby, in the words of former planning director de Geus, "Management teams change their shared mental models of their company, their markets, and their competitors."[16] Since then, "planning as learning" has become a byword at Shell, and Group Planning has continually sought out new learning tools that can be integrated into the planning process. Some of these are described below.

Leader as Teacher

"The first responsibility of a leader," writes retired Herman Miller CEO Max de Pree, "is to define reality."[17] Much of the leverage leaders can actually exert lies in helping people achieve more accurate, more insightful, and more *empowering* views of reality.

Leader as teacher does *not* mean leader as authoritarian expert whose job it is to teach people the "correct" view of reality. Rather, it is about helping everyone in the organization, oneself included, to gain more insightful views of current reality. This is in line with a popular emerging view of leaders as coaches, guides, or facilitators.[18] In learning organizations, this teaching role is developed further by virtue of explicit attention to people's mental models and by the influence of the systems perspective.

The role of leader as teacher starts with bringing to the surface people's mental models of important issues. No one carries an organization, a market, or a state of technology in his or her head.

Learning Organizations

12
Senge

What we carry in our heads are assumptions. These mental pictures of how the world works have a significant influence on how we perceive problems and opportunities, identify courses of action, and make choices.

One reason that mental models are so deeply entrenched is that they are largely tacit. Ian Mitroff, in his study of General Motors, argues that an assumption that prevailed for years was that, in the United States, "Cars are status symbols. Styling is therefore more important than quality."[19] The Detroit automakers didn't say, "We have a *mental model* that all people care about is styling." Few actual managers would even say publicly that all people care about is styling. So long as the view remained unexpressed, there was little possibility of challenging its validity or forming more accurate assumptions.

But working with mental models goes beyond revealing hidden assumptions. "Reality," as perceived by most people in most organizations, means pressures that must be borne, crises that must be reacted to, and limitations that must be accepted. Leaders as teachers help people *restructure their views of reality* to see beyond the superficial conditions and events into the underlying causes of problems—and therefore to see new possibilities for shaping the future.

Specifically, leaders can influence people to view reality at three distinct levels: events, patterns of behavior, and systemic structure.

Systemic Structure
(Generative)
↓
Patterns of Behavior
(Responsive)
↓
Events
(Reactive)

The key question becomes *where do leaders predominantly focus their own and their organization's attention?*

Contemporary society focuses predominantly on events. The media reinforces this perspective, with almost exclusive attention to short-term, dramatic events. This focus leads naturally to explaining what happens in terms of those events: "The Dow Jones average went up sixteen points because high fourth-quarter profits were announced yesterday."

Pattern-of-behavior explanations are rarer, in contemporary culture, than event explanations, but they do occur. "Trend analysis" is an example of seeing patterns of behavior. A good editorial that interprets a set of current events in the context of long-term historical changes is another example. Systemic, structural explanations go even further by addressing the question, "What causes the patterns of behavior?"

In some sense, all three levels of explanation are equally true. But their usefulness is quite different. Event explanations—who did what to whom—doom their holders to a reactive stance toward change. Pattern-of-behavior explanations focus on identifying long-term trends and assessing their implications. They at least suggest how, over time, we can respond to shifting conditions. Structural explanations are the most powerful. Only they address the underlying causes of behavior at a level such that patterns of behavior can be changed.

By and large, leaders of our current institutions focus their attention on events and patterns of behavior, and, under their influence, their organizations do likewise. That is why contemporary organizations are predominantly reactive, or at best responsive—rarely generative. On the other hand, leaders in learning organizations pay attention to all three levels, but focus especially on systemic structure; largely by example, they teach people throughout the organization to do likewise.

Leader as Steward

This is the subtlest role of leadership. Unlike the roles of designer and teacher, it is almost solely a matter of attitude. It is an attitude critical to learning organizations.

While stewardship has long been recognized as an aspect of leadership, its source is still not widely understood. I believe Robert Greenleaf came closest to explaining real stewardship, in his seminal book *Servant Leadership*.[20] There, Greenleaf argues that "The servant leader *is* servant first. . . . It begins with the natural feeling that one wants to serve, to serve *first*. This conscious choice brings one to aspire to lead. That person is sharply different from one who is leader first, perhaps because of the need to assuage an unusual power drive or to acquire material possessions."

Leaders' sense of stewardship operates on two levels: stewardship for the people they lead and stewardship for the larger purpose or mission that underlies the enterprise. The first type arises from a keen appreciation of the impact one's leadership can have on others. People can suffer economically, emotionally, and spiritually under inept leadership. If anything, people in a learning organization are more vulnerable because of their commitment and sense of shared ownership. Appreciating this naturally instills a sense of responsibility in leaders. The second type of stewardship arises from a leader's sense of personal purpose and commitment to the organization's larger mission. People's natural impulse to learn is unleashed when they are engaged in an endeavor they consider worthy of their fullest commitment. Or, as Lawrence Miller puts it, "Achieving return on equity does not, as a goal, mobilize the most noble forces of our soul."[21]

Leaders engaged in building learning organizations naturally feel part of a larger purpose that goes beyond their organization. They are part of changing the way businesses operate, not from a vague philanthropic urge, but from a conviction that their efforts will produce more productive organizations, capable of achieving higher levels of organizational success and personal satisfaction than more traditional organizations. Their sense of stewardship was succinctly captured by George Bernard Shaw when he said,

> This is the true joy in life, the being used for a purpose you consider a mighty one, the being a force of nature rather than a feverish, selfish clod of ailments and grievances complaining that the world will not devote itself to making you happy.

New Skills

New leadership roles require new leadership skills. These skills can only be developed, in my judgment, through a lifelong commitment. It is not enough for one or two individuals to develop these skills. They must be distributed widely throughout the organization. This is one reason that understanding the *disciplines* of a learning organization is so important. These disciplines embody the principles and practices that can widely foster leadership development.

Three critical areas of skills (disciplines) are building shared vision, surfacing and challenging mental models, and engaging in systems thinking.[22]

Building Shared Vision

How do individual visions come together to create shared visions? A useful metaphor is the hologram, the three-dimensional image created by interacting light sources.

If you cut a photograph in half, each half shows only part of the whole image. But if you divide a hologram, each part, no matter how small, shows the whole image intact. Likewise, when a group of people come to share a vision for an organization, each person sees an individual picture of the organization at its best. Each shares responsibility for the whole, not just for one piece. But the component pieces of the hologram are not identical. Each represents the whole image from a different point of view. It's something like poking holes in a window shade; each hole offers a unique angle for viewing the whole image. So, too, is each individual's vision unique.

When you add up the pieces of a hologram, something interesting happens. The image becomes more intense, more lifelike. When more people come to share a vision, the vision becomes more real in the sense of a mental reality that people can truly imagine achieving. They now have partners, co-creators; the vision no longer rests on their shoulders alone. Early on, when they are nurturing an individual vision, people may say it is "my vision." But, as the shared vision develops, it becomes both "my vision" and "our vision."

The skills involved in building shared vision include the following:

- **Encouraging Personal Vision.** Shared visions emerge from personal visions. It is not that people only care about their own self-interest—in fact, people's values usually include dimensions that concern family, organization, community, and even the world. Rather, it is that people's capacity for caring is *personal*.
- **Communicating and Asking for Support.** Leaders must be willing to continually share their own vision, rather than being the official representative of the corporate vision. They also must be prepared to ask, "Is this vision worthy of your commitment?" This can be difficult for a person used to setting goals and presuming compliance.
- **Visioning as an Ongoing Process.** Building shared vision is a never-ending process. At any one point there will be a particular image of the future that is predominant, but that image will evolve. Today, too many managers want to dispense with the "vision business" by going off and writing the Official Vision Statement. Such statements almost always lack the vitality, freshness, and excitement

Learning Organizations

14

Senge

of a genuine vision that comes from people asking, "What do we really want to achieve?"
• **Blending Extrinsic and Intrinsic Visions.** Many energizing visions are extrinsic—that is, they focus on achieving something relative to an outsider, such as a competitor. But a goal that is limited to defeating an opponent can, once the vision is achieved, easily become a defensive posture. In contrast, intrinsic goals like creating a new type of product, taking an established product to a new level, or setting a new standard for customer satisfaction can call forth a new level of creativity and innovation. Intrinsic and extrinsic visions need to coexist; a vision solely predicated on defeating an adversary will eventually weaken an organization.
• **Distinguishing Positive from Negative Visions.** Many organizations only truly pull together when their survival is threatened. Similarly, most social movements aim at eliminating what people don't want: for example, anti-drugs, anti-smoking, or anti-nuclear arms movements. Negative visions carry a subtle message of powerlessness: people will only pull together when there is sufficient threat. Negative visions also tend to be short term. Two fundamental sources of energy can motivate organizations: fear and aspiration. Fear, the energy source behind negative visions, can produce extraordinary changes in short periods, but aspiration endures as a continuing source of learning and growth.

Surfacing and Testing Mental Models

Many of the best ideas in organizations never get put into practice. One reason is that new insights and initiatives often conflict with established mental models. The leadership task of challenging assumptions without invoking defensiveness requires reflection and inquiry skills possessed by few leaders in traditional controlling organizations.[23]
• **Seeing Leaps of Abstraction.** Our minds literally move at lightning speed. Ironically, this often slows our learning, because we leap to generalizations so quickly that we never think to test them. We then confuse our generalizations with the observable data upon which they are based, treating the generalizations *as if they were data*. The frustrated sales rep reports to the home office that "customers don't really care about quality, price is what matters," when what actually happened was that three consecutive large customers refused to place an order unless a larger discount was offered. The sales rep treats her generalization, "customers care only about price," as if it were absolute fact rather than an assumption (very likely an assumption reflecting her own views of customers and the market). This thwarts future learning because she starts to focus on how to offer attractive discounts rather than probing behind the customers' statements. For example, the customers may have been so disgruntled with the firm's delivery or customer service that they are unwilling to purchase again without larger discounts.
• **Balancing Inquiry and Advocacy.** Most managers are skilled at articulating their views and presenting them persuasively. While important, advocacy skills can become counterproductive as managers rise in responsibility and confront increasingly complex issues that require collaborative learning among different, equally knowledgeable people. Leaders in learning organizations need to have both inquiry *and* advocacy skills.[24]

Specifically, when advocating a view, they need to be able to:
— explain the reasoning and data that led to their view;
— encourage others to test their view (e.g., Do you see gaps in my reasoning? Do you disagree with the data upon which my view is based?); and
— encourage others to provide different views (e.g., Do you have either different data, different conclusions, or both?).

When inquiring into another's views, they need to:
— actively seek to understand the other's view, rather than simply restating their own view and how it differs from the other's view; and
— make their attributions about the other and the other's view explicit (e.g., Based on your statement that . . . ; I am assuming that you believe . . . ; Am I representing your views fairly?).

If they reach an impasse (others no longer appear open to inquiry), they need to:
— ask what data or logic might unfreeze the impasse, or if an experiment (or some other inquiry) might be designed to provide new information.
• **Distinguishing Espoused Theory from Theory in Use.** We all like to think that we hold certain views, but often our actions reveal deeper views. For example, I may proclaim that people are trustworthy, but never lend friends money and jealously guard my possessions. Obviously, my deeper mental model (my theory in use), differs from my espoused theory. Recognizing gaps between espoused views and theories in use (which

often requires the help of others) can be pivotal to deeper learning.
- **Recognizing and Defusing Defensive Routines.** As one CEO in our research program puts it, "Nobody ever talks about an issue at the 8:00 business meeting exactly the same way they talk about it at home that evening or over drinks at the end of the day." The reason is what Chris Argyris calls "defensive routines," entrenched habits used to protect ourselves from the embarrassment and threat that come with exposing our thinking. For most of us, such defenses began to build early in life in response to pressures to have the right answers in school or at home. Organizations add new levels of performance anxiety and thereby amplify and exacerbate this defensiveness. Ironically, this makes it even more difficult to expose hidden mental models, and thereby lessens learning.

The first challenge is to recognize defensive routines, then to inquire into their operation. Those who are best at revealing and defusing defensive routines operate with a high degree of self-disclosure regarding their own defensiveness (e.g., I notice that I am feeling uneasy about how this conversation is going. Perhaps I don't understand it or it is threatening to me in ways I don't yet see. Can you help me see this better?)

Systems Thinking

We all know that leaders should help people see the big picture. But the actual skills whereby leaders are supposed to achieve this are not well understood. In my experience, successful leaders often *are* "systems thinkers" to a considerable extent. They focus less on day-to-day events and more on underlying trends and forces of change. But they do this almost completely intuitively. The consequence is that they are often unable to explain their intuitions to others and feel frustrated that others cannot see the world the way they do.

One of the most significant developments in management science today is the gradual coalescence of managerial systems thinking as a field of study and practice. This field suggests some key skills for future leaders:
- **Seeing Interrelationships, Not Things, and Processes, Not Snapshots.** Most of us have been conditioned throughout our lives to focus on things and to see the world in static images. This leads us to linear explanations of systemic phenomenon. For instance, in an arms race each party is convinced that the other is *the cause* of problems. They react to each new move as an isolated event, not as part of a process. So long as they fail to see the interrelationships of these actions, they are trapped.
- **Moving beyond Blame.** We tend to blame each other or outside circumstances for our problems. But it is poorly designed systems, not incompetent or unmotivated individuals, that cause most organizational problems. Systems thinking shows us that there is no outside—that you and the cause of your problems are part of a single system.
- **Distinguishing Detail Complexity from Dynamic Complexity.** Some types of complexity are more important strategically than others. Detail complexity arises when there are many variables. Dynamic complexity arises when cause and effect are distant in time and space, and when the consequences over time of interventions are subtle and not obvious to many participants in the system. The leverage in most management situations lies in understanding dynamic complexity, not detail complexity.
- **Focusing on Areas of High Leverage.** Some have called systems thinking the "new dismal science" because it teaches that most obvious solutions don't work—at best, they improve matters in the short run, only to make things worse in the long run. But there is another side to the story. Systems thinking also shows that small, well-focused actions can produce significant, enduring improvements, if they are in the right place. Systems thinkers refer to this idea as the principle of "leverage." Tackling a difficult problem is often a matter of seeing where the high leverage lies, where a change—with a minimum of effort—would lead to lasting, significant improvement.
- **Avoiding Symptomatic Solutions.** The pressures to intervene in management systems that are going awry can be overwhelming. Unfortunately, given the linear thinking that predominates in most organizations, interventions usually focus on symptomatic fixes, not underlying causes. This results in only temporary relief, and it tends to create still more pressures later on for further, low-leverage intervention. If leaders acquiesce to these pressures, they can be sucked into an endless spiral of increasing intervention. Sometimes the most difficult leadership acts are to refrain from intervening through popular quick fixes and to keep the pressure on everyone to identify more enduring solutions.

While leaders who can articulate systemic ex-

Learning Organizations

16

Senge

planations are rare, those who *can* will leave their stamp on an organization. One person who had this gift was Bill Gore, the founder and long-time CEO of W.L. Gore and Associates (makers of Gore-Tex and other synthetic fiber products). Bill Gore was adept at telling stories that showed how the organization's core values of freedom and individual responsibility required particular operating policies. He was proud of his egalitarian organization, in which there were (and still are) no "employees," only "associates," all of whom own shares in the company and participate in its management. At one talk, he explained the company's policy of controlled growth: "Our limitation is not financial resources. Our limitation is the rate at which we can bring in new associates. Our experience has been that if we try to bring in more than a 25 percent per year increase, we begin to bog down. Twenty-five percent per year growth is a real limitation; you can do much better than that with an authoritarian organization." As Gore tells the story, one of the associates, Esther Baum, went home after this talk and reported the limitation to her husband. As it happened, he was an astronomer and mathematician at Lowell Observatory. He said, "That's a very interesting figure." He took out a pencil and paper and calculated and said, "Do you realize that in only fifty-seven and a half years, everyone in the world will be working for Gore?"

Through this story, Gore explains the systemic rationale behind a key policy, limited growth rate — a policy that undoubtedly caused a lot of stress in the organization. He suggests that, at larger rates of growth, the adverse effects of attempting to integrate too many new people too rapidly would begin to dominate. (This is the "limits to growth" systems archetype explained below.) The story also reaffirms the organization's commitment to creating a unique environment for its associates and illustrates the types of sacrifices that the firm is prepared to make in order to remain true to its vision. The last part of the story shows that, despite the self-imposed limit, the company is still very much a growth company.

The consequences of leaders who lack systems thinking skills can be devastating. Many charismatic leaders manage almost exclusively at the level of events. They deal in visions and in crises, and little in between. Under their leadership, an organization hurtles from crisis to crisis. Eventually, the worldview of people in the organization becomes dominated by events and reactiveness. Many, especially those who are deeply commited, become burned out. Eventually, cynicism comes to pervade the organization. People have no control over their time, let alone their destiny.

Similar problems arise with the "visionary strategist," the leader with vision who sees both patterns of change and events. This leader is better prepared to manage change. He or she can explain strategies in terms of emerging trends, and thereby foster a climate that is less reactive. But such leaders still impart a responsive orientation rather than a generative one.

Many talented leaders have rich, highly systemic intuitions but cannot explain those intuitions to others. Ironically, they often end up being authoritarian leaders, even if they don't want to, because only they see the decisions that need to be made. They are unable to conceptualize their strategic insights so that these can become public knowledge, open to challenge and further improvement.

New Tools

Developing the skills described above requires new tools — tools that will enhance leaders' conceptual abilities and foster communication and collaborative inquiry. What follows is a sampling of tools starting to find use in learning organizations.

Systems Archetypes

One of the insights of the budding, managerial systems-thinking field is that certain types of systemic structures recur again and again. Countless systems grow for a period, then encounter problems and cease to grow (or even collapse) well before they have reached intrinsic limits to growth. Many other systems get locked in runaway vicious spirals where every actor has to run faster and faster to stay in the same place. Still others lure individual actors into doing what seems right locally, yet which eventually causes suffering for all.[25]

Some of the system archetypes that have the broadest relevance include:

• **Balancing Process with Delay.** In this archetype, decision makers fail to appreciate the time delays involved as they move toward a goal. As a result, they overshoot the goal and may even produce recurring cycles. Classic example: Real estate developers who keep starting new projects until the market has gone soft, by which time an even-

tual glut is guaranteed by the properties still under construction.
- **Limits to Growth.** A reinforcing cycle of growth grinds to a halt, and may even reverse itself, as limits are approached. The limits can be resource constraints, or external or internal responses to growth. Classic examples: Product life cycles that peak prematurely due to poor quality or service, the growth and decline of communication in a management team, and the spread of a new movement.
- **Shifting the Burden.** A short-term "solution" is used to correct a problem, with seemingly happy immediate results. As this correction is used more and more, fundamental long-term corrective measures are used less. Over time, the mechanisms of the fundamental solution may atrophy or become disabled, leading to even greater reliance on the symptomatic solution. Classic example: Using corporate human resource staff to solve local personnel problems, thereby keeping managers from developing their own interpersonal skills.
- **Eroding Goals.** When all else fails, lower your standards. This is like "shifting the burden," except that the short-term solution involves letting a fundamental goal, such as quality standards or employee morale standards, atrophy. Classic example: A company that responds to delivery problems by continually upping its quoted delivery times.
- **Escalation.** Two people or two organizations, who each see their welfare as depending on a relative advantage over the other, continually react to the other's advances. Whenever one side gets ahead, the other is threatened, leading it to act more aggressively to reestablish its advantage, which threatens the first, and so on. Classic examples: Arms race, gang warfare, price wars.
- **Tragedy of the Commons.**[26] Individuals keep intensifying their use of a commonly available but limited resource until all individuals start to experience severely diminishing returns. Classic examples: Sheepherders who keep increasing their flocks until they overgraze the common pasture; divisions in a firm that share a common salesforce and compete for the use of sales reps by upping their sales targets, until the salesforce burns out from overextension.
- **Growth and Underinvestment.** Rapid growth approaches a limit that could be eliminated or pushed into the future, but only by aggressive investment in physical and human capacity. Eroding goals or standards cause investment that is too weak, or too slow, and customers get increasingly unhappy, slowing demand growth and thereby making the needed investment (apparently) unnecessary or impossible. Classic example: Countless once-successful growth firms that allowed product or service quality to erode, and were unable to generate enough revenues to invest in remedies.

The Archetype template is a specific tool that is helping managers identify archetypes operating in their own strategic areas (see Figure 2).[27] The template shows the basic structural form of the archetype but lets managers fill in the variables of their own situation. For example, the shifting the burden template involves two balancing processes ("B") that compete for control of a problem symptom. The upper, symptomatic solution provides a short-term fix that will make the problem symptom go away for a while. The lower, fundamental solution provides a more enduring solution. The side effect feedback ("R") around the outside of the diagram identifies unintended exacerbating effects of the symptomatic solution, which, over time, make it more and more difficult to invoke the fundamental solution.

Several years ago, a team of managers from a leading consumer goods producer used the shifting the burden archetype in a revealing way. The problem they focused on was financial stress, which

Figure 2 "Shifting the Burden" Archetype Template

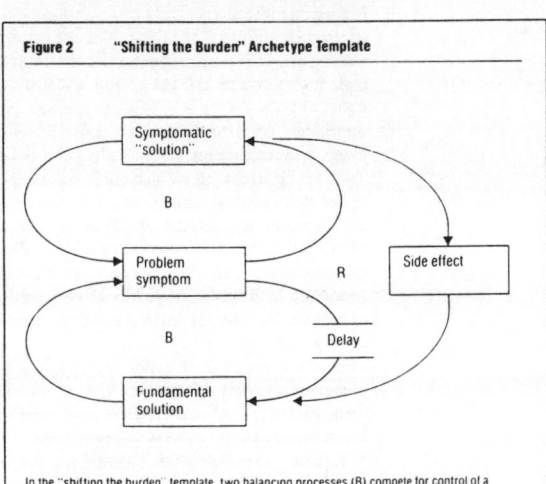

In the "shifting the burden" template, two balancing processes (B) compete for control of a problem symptom. Both solutions affect the symptom, but only the fundamental solution treats the cause. The symptomatic "solution" creates the additional side effect (R) of deferring the fundamental solution, making it harder and harder to achieve.

Learning Organizations
18
Senge

could be dealt with in two different ways: by running marketing promotions (the symptomatic solution) or by product innovation (the fundamental solution). Marketing promotions were fast. The company was expert in their design and implementation. The results were highly predictable. Product innovation was slow and much less predictable, and the company had a history over the past ten years of product-innovation mismanagement. Yet only through innovation could they retain a leadership position in their industry, which had slid over the past ten to twenty years. What the managers saw clearly was that the more skillful they became at promotions, the more they shifted the burden away from product innovation. But what really struck home was when one member identified the unintended side effect: the last three CEOs had all come from advertising function, which had become the politically dominant function in the corporation, thereby institutionalizing the symptomatic solution. Unless the political values shifted back toward product and process innovation, the managers realized, the firm's decline would accelerate—which is just the shift that has happened over the past several years.

Charting Strategic Dilemmas

Management teams typically come unglued when confronted with core dilemmas. A classic example was the way U.S. manufacturers faced the low cost-high quality choice. For years, most assumed that it was necessary to choose between the two. Not surprisingly, given the short-term pressures perceived by most managements, the prevailing choice was low cost. Firms that chose high quality usually perceived themselves as aiming exclusively for a high quality, high price market niche. The consequences of this perceived either-or choice have been disastrous, even fatal, as U.S. manufacturers have encountered increasing international competition from firms that have chosen to consistently improve quality *and* cost.

In a recent book, Charles Hampden-Turner presented a variety of tools for helping management teams confront strategic dilemmas creatively.[28] He summarizes the process in seven steps:
- **Eliciting the Dilemmas.** Identifying the opposed values that form the "horns" of the dilemma, for example, cost as opposed to quality, or local initiative as opposed to central coordination and control. Hampden-Turner suggests that humor can be a distinct asset in this process since "the admission that dilemmas even exist tends to be difficult for some companies."
- **Mapping.** Locating the opposing values as two axes and helping managers identify where they see themselves, or their organization, along the axes.
- **Processing.** Getting rid of nouns to describe the axes of the dilemma. Present participles formed by adding "ing" convert rigid nouns into processes that imply movement. For example, central control versus local control becomes "strengthening national office" and "growing local initiatives." This loosens the bond of implied opposition between the two values. For example, it becomes possible to think of "strengthening national services from which local branches can benefit."
- **Framing/Contextualizing.** Further softening the adversarial structure among different values by letting "each side in turn be the frame or context for the other." This shifting of the "figure-ground" relationship undermines any implicit attempts to hold one value as intrinsically superior to the other, and thereby to become mentally closed to creative strategies for continuous improvement of both.
- **Sequencing.** Breaking the hold of static thinking. Very often, values like low cost and high quality appear to be in opposition because we think in terms of a point in time, not in terms of an ongoing process. For example, a strategy of investing in new process technology and developing a new production-floor culture of worker responsibility may take time and money in the near term, yet reap significant long-term financial rewards.
- **Waving/Cycling.** Sometimes the strategic path toward improving both values involves cycles where both values will get "worse" for a time. Yet, at a deeper level, learning is occurring that will cause the next cycle to be at a higher plateau for both values.
- **Synergizing.** Achieving synergy where significant improvement is occurring along all axes of all relevant dilemmas. (This is the ultimate goal, of course.) Synergy, as Hampden-Turner points out, is a uniquely systemic notion, coming from the Greek *syn-ergo* or "work together."

"The Left-Hand Column": Surfacing Mental Models

The idea that mental models can dominate business decisions and that these models are often tacit and even contradictory to what people espouse can be very threatening to managers who pride themselves on rationality and judicious decision making. It is important to have tools to help managers discover for themselves how their mental models operate to undermine their own intentions.

One tool that has worked consistently to help managers see their own mental models in action is the "left-hand column" exercise developed by Chris Argyris and his colleagues. This tool is especially helpful in showing how we leap from data to generalization without testing the validity of our generalizations.

When working with managers, I start this exercise by selecting a specific situation in which I am interacting with other people in a way that is not working, that is not producing the learning that is needed. I write out a sample of the exchange, with the script on the right-hand side of the page. On the left-hand side, I write what I am thinking but not saying at each stage in the exchange (see sidebar).

The left-hand column exercise not only brings hidden assumptions to the surface, it shows how they influence behavior. In the example, I make two key assumptions about Bill: he lacks confidence and he lacks initiative. Neither may be literally true, but both are evident in my internal dialogue, and both influence the way I handle the situation. Believing that he lacks confidence, I skirt the fact that I've heard the presentation was a bomb. I'm afraid that if I say it directly, he will lose what little confidence he has, or he will see me as unsupportive. So I bring up the subject of the presentation obliquely. When I ask Bill what we should do next, he gives no specific course of action. Believing he lacks initiative, I take this as evidence of his laziness; he is content to do nothing when action is definitely required. I conclude that I will have to manufacture some form of pressure to motivate him, or else I will simply have to take matters into my own hands.

The exercise reveals the elaborate webs of assumptions we weave, within which we become our own victims. Rather than dealing directly with my assumptions about Bill and the situation, we talk around the subject. The reasons for my avoidance are self-evident: I assume that if I raised my doubts, I would provoke a defensive reaction that would only make matters worse. But the price of avoiding the issue is high. Instead of determining how to move forward to resolve our problems, we end our exchange with no clear course of action. My assumptions about Bill's limitations have been reinforced. I resort to a manipulative strategy to move things forward.

The exercise not only reveals the need for skills in surfacing assumptions, but that we are the ones most in need of help. There is no one right way to handle difficult situations like my exchange with Bill, but any productive strategy revolves around a high level of self-disclosure and willingness to have my views challenged. I need to recognize my own leaps of abstraction regarding Bill, share the events

---

The Left-Hand Column: An Exercise

Imagine my exchange with a colleague, Bill, after he made a big presentation to our boss on a project we are doing together. I had to miss the presentation, but I've heard that it was poorly received.
Me: How did the presentation go?
Bill: Well, I don't know. It's really too early to say. Besides, we're breaking new ground here.
Me: Well, what do you think we should do? I believe that the issues you were raising are important.
Bill: I'm not so sure. Let's just wait and see what happens.
Me: You may be right, but I think we may need to do more than just wait.

Now, here is what the exchange looks like with my "left-hand column":

What I'm Thinking	What Is Said
Everyone says the presentation was a bomb.	*Me:* How did the presentation go?
Does he really not know how bad it was? Or is he not willing to face up to it?	*Bill:* Well, I don't know. It's too early to say. Besides, we're breaking new ground here.
	Me: Well, what do you think we should do? I believe that the issues you were raising are important.
He really is afraid to see the truth. If he only had more confidence, he could probably learn from a situation like this.	*Bill:* I'm not so sure. Let's just wait and see what happens.
I can't believe he doesn't realize how disastrous that presentation was to our moving ahead.	*Me:* You may be right, but I think we may need to do more than just wait.
I've got to find some way to light a fire under the guy.	

Learning Organizations

20 Senge

Learning at Hanover Insurance

Hanover Insurance has gone from the bottom of the property and liability industry to a position among the top 25 percent of U.S. insurance companies over the past twenty years, largely through the efforts of CEO William O'Brien and his predecessor, Jack Adam. The following comments are excerpted from a series of interviews Senge conducted with O'Brien as background for his book.

Senge: Why do you think there is so much change occurring in management and organizations today? Is it primarily because of increased competitive pressures?

O'Brien: That's a factor, but not the most significant factor. The ferment in management will continue until we find models that are more congruent with human nature.

One of the great insights of modern psychology is the hierarchy of human needs. As Maslow expressed this idea, the most basic needs are food and shelter. Then comes belonging. Once these three basic needs are satisfied, people begin to aspire toward self-respect and esteem, and toward self-actualization—the fourth- and fifth-order needs.

Our traditional hierarchical organizations are designed to provide for the first three levels, but not the fourth and fifth. These first three levels are now widely available to members of industrial society, but our organizations do not offer people sufficient opportunities for growth.

Senge: How would you assess Hanover's progress to date?

O'Brien: We have been on a long journey away from a traditional hierarchical culture. The journey began with everyone understanding some guiding ideas about purpose, vision, and values as a basis for participative management. This is a better way to begin building a participative culture than by simply "letting people in on decision making." Before there can be meaningful participation, people must share certain values and pictures about where we are trying to go. We discovered that people have a real need to feel that they're part of an enobling mission. But developing shared visions and values is not the end, only the beginning.

Next we had to get beyond mechanical, linear thinking. The essence of our jobs as managers is to deal with "divergent" problems—problems that have no simple answer. "Convergent" problems—problems that have a "right" answer—should be solved locally. Yet we are deeply conditioned to see the world in terms of convergent problems. Most managers try to force-fit simplistic solutions and undermine the potential for learning when divergent problems arise. Since everyone handles the linear issues fairly well, companies that learn how to handle divergent issues will have a great advantage.

The next basic stage in our progression was coming to understand inquiry and advocacy. We learned that real openness is rooted in people's ability to continually inquire into their own thinking. This requires exposing yourself to being wrong—not something that most managers are rewarded for. But learning is very difficult if you cannot look for errors or incompleteness in your own ideas.

What all this builds to is the capability throughout an organization to manage mental models. In a locally controlled organization, you have the fundamental challenge of learning how to help people make good decisions without coercing them into making *particular* decisions. By managing mental models, we create "self-concluding" decisions—decisions that people come to themselves—which will result in deeper conviction, better implementation, and the ability to make better adjustments when the situation changes.

Senge: What concrete steps can top managers take to begin moving toward learning organizations?

O'Brien: Look at the signals you send through the organization. For example, one critical signal is how you spend your time. It's hard to build a learning organization if people are unable to take the time to think

> through important matters. I rarely set up an appointment for less than one hour. If the subject is not worth an hour, it shouldn't be on my calendar.
> **Senge**: Why is this so hard for so many managers?
> **O'Brien**: It comes back to what you believe about the nature of your work. The authoritarian manager has a "chain gang" mental model: "The speed of the boss is the speed of the gang. I've got to keep things moving fast, because I've got to keep people working." In a learning organization, the manager shoulders an almost sacred responsibility: to create conditions that enable people to have happy and productive lives. If you understand the effects the ideas we are discussing can have on the lives of people in your organization, you will take the time. ∎

and reasoning that are leading to my concern over the project, and be open to Bill's views on both. The skills to carry on such conversations without invoking defensiveness take time to develop. But if both parties in a learning impasse start by doing their own left-hand column exercise and sharing them with each other, it is remarkable how quickly everyone recognizes their contribution to the impasse and progress starts to be made.

Learning Laboratories: Practice Fields for Management Teams

One of the most promising new tools is the learning laboratory or "microworld": constructed microcosms of real-life settings in which management teams can learn how to learn together.

The rationale behind learning laboratories can best be explained by analogy. Although most management teams have great difficulty learning (enhancing their collective intelligence and capacity to create), in other domains team learning is the norm rather than the exception — team sports and the performing arts, for example. Great basketball teams do not start off great. They learn. But the process by which these teams learn is, by and large, absent from modern organizations. The process is a continual movement between practice and performance.

The vision guiding current research in management learning laboratories is to design and construct effective practice fields for management teams. Much remains to be done, but the broad outlines are emerging.

First, since team learning in organizations is an individual-to-individual and individual-to-system phenomenon, learning laboratories must combine meaningful business issues with meaningful interpersonal dynamics. Either alone is incomplete.

Second, the factors that thwart learning about complex business issues must be eliminated in the learning lab. Chief among these is the inability to experience the long-term, systemic consequences of key strategic decisions. We all learn best from experience, but we are unable to experience the consequences of many important organizational decisions. Learning laboratories remove this constraint through system dynamics simulation games that compress time and space.

Third, new learning skills must be developed. One constraint on learning is the inability of managers to reflect insightfully on their assumptions, and to inquire effectively into each other's assumptions. Both skills can be enhanced in a learning laboratory, where people can practice surfacing assumptions in a low-risk setting. A note of caution: It is far easier to design an entertaining learning laboratory than it is to have an impact on real management practices and firm traditions outside the learning lab. Research on management simulations has shown that they often have greater entertainment value than educational value. One of the reasons appears to be that many simulations do not offer deep insights into systemic structures causing business problems. Another reason is that they do not foster new learning skills. Also, there is no connection between experiments in the learning lab and real life experiments. These are significant problems that research on learning laboratory design is now addressing.

Developing Leaders and Learning Organizations

In a recently published retrospective on organization development in the 1980s, Marshall Sashkin and N. Warner Burke observe the return of an emphasis on developing leaders who can develop or-

Learning Organizations

22

Senge

ganizations.[29] They also note Schein's critique that most top executives are not qualified for the task of developing culture.[30] Learning organizations represent a potentially significant evolution of organizational culture. So it should come as no surprise that such organizations will remain a distant vision until the leadership capabilities they demand are developed. "The 1990s may be the period," suggest Sashkin and Burke, "during which organization development and (a new sort of) management development are reconnected."

I believe that this new sort of management development will focus on the roles, skills, and tools for leadership in learning organizations. Undoubtedly, the ideas offered above are only a rough approximation of this new territory. The sooner we begin seriously exploring the territory, the sooner the initial map can be improved—and the sooner we will realize an age-old vision of leadership:

> The wicked leader is he who the people despise.
> The good leader is he who the people revere.
> The great leader is he who the people say, "We did it ourselves."
>
> — Lao Tsu ■

References

1
P. Senge, *The Fifth Discipline: The Art and Practice of the Learning Organization* (New York: Doubleday/Currency, 1990).

2
A.P. de Geus, "Planning as Learning," *Harvard Business Review*, March-April 1988, pp. 70–74.

3
B. Domain, *Fortune*, 3 July 1989, pp. 48–62.

4
The distinction between adaptive and generative learning has its roots in the distinction between what Argyris and Schon have called their "single-loop" learning, in which individuals or groups adjust their behavior relative to fixed goals, norms, and assumptions, and "double-loop" learning, in which goals, norms, and assumptions, as well as behavior, are open to change (e.g., see C. Argyris and D. Schon, *Organizational Learning: A Theory-in-Action Perspective* (Reading, Massachusetts: Addison-Wesley, 1978)).

5
All unattributed quotes are from personal communications with the author.

6
G. Stalk, Jr., "Time: The Next Source of Competitive Advantage," *Harvard Business Review*, July-August 1988, pp. 41–51.

7
Senge (1990).

8
The principle of creative tension comes from Robert Fritz' work on creativity. See R. Fritz, *The Path of Least Resistance* (New York: Ballantine, 1989) and *Creating* (New York: Ballantine, 1990).

9
M.L. King, Jr., "Letter from Birmingham Jail," *American Visions*, January-February 1986, pp. 52–59.

10
E. Schein, *Organizational Culture and Leadership* (San Francisco: Jossey-Bass, 1985).
Similar views have been expressed by many leadership theorists. For example, see:
P. Selznick, *Leadership in Administration* (New York: Harper & Row, 1957);
W. Bennis and B. Nanus, *Leaders* (New York: Harper & Row, 1985); and
N.M. Tichy and M.A. Devanna, *The Transformational Leader* (New York: John Wiley & Sons, 1986).

11
Selznick (1957).

12
J.W. Forrester, "A New Corporate Design," *Sloan Management Review* (formerly *Industrial Management Review*), Fall 1965, pp. 5–17.

13
See, for example, H. Mintzberg, "Crafting Strategy," *Harvard Business Review*, July-August 1987, pp. 66–75.

14
R. Mason and I. Mitroff, *Challenging Strategic Planning Assumptions* (New York: John Wiley & Sons, 1981), p. 16.

15
P. Wack, "Scenarios: Uncharted Waters Ahead," *Harvard Business Review*, September-October 1985, pp. 73–89.

16
de Geus (1988).

17
M. de Pree, *Leadership Is an Art* (New York: Doubleday, 1989) p. 9.

18
For example, see T. Peters and N. Austin, *A Passion for Excellence* (New York: Random House, 1985) and
J.M. Kouzes and B.Z. Posner, *The Leadership Challenge* (San Francisco: Jossey-Bass, 1987).

19
I. Mitroff, *Break-Away Thinking* (New York: John Wiley & Sons, 1988), pp. 66–67.

20
R.K. Greenleaf, *Servant Leadership: A Journey into the Nature of Legitimate Power and Greatness* (New York: Paulist Press, 1977).

21
L. Miller, *American Spirit: Visions of a New Corporate Culture* (New York: William Morrow, 1984), p. 15.

22
These points are condensed from the practices of the five disciplines examined in Senge (1990).

23
The ideas below are based to a considerable extent on the work of Chris Argyris, Donald Schon, and their Action Science colleagues:
C. Argyris and D. Schon, *Organizational Learning: A Theory-in-Action Perspective* (Reading, Massachusetts: Addison-Wesley, 1978);
C. Argyris, R. Putnam, and D. Smith, *Action Science* (San Francisco: Jossey-Bass, 1985);
C. Argyris, *Strategy, Change, and Defensive Routines* (Boston: Pitman, 1985); and
C. Argyris, *Overcoming Organizational Defenses* (Englewood Cliffs, New Jersey: Prentice-Hall, 1990).

24
I am indebted to Diana Smith for the summary points below.

25
The system archetypes are one of several systems diagraming and communication tools. See D.H. Kim, "Toward Learning Organizations: Integrating Total Quality Control and Systems Thinking" (Cambridge, Massachusetts: MIT Sloan School of Management, Working Paper No. 3037-89-BPS, June 1989).

26
This archetype is closely associated with the work of ecologist Garrett Hardin, who coined its label: G. Hardin, "The Tragedy of the Commons," *Science*, 13 December 1968.

27
These templates were originally developed by Jennifer Kemeny, Charles Kiefer, and Michael Goodman of Innovation Associates, Inc., Framingham, Massachusetts.

28
C. Hampden-Turner, *Charting the Corporate Mind* (New York: The Free Press, 1990).

29
M. Sashkin and W.W. Burke, "Organization Development in the 1980s" and "An End-of-the-Eighties Retrospective," in *Advances in Organization Development*, ed. F. Masarik (Norwood, New Jersey: Ablex, 1990).

30
E. Schèin (1985).

Reprint 3211

WHOLE SYSTEMS

WHOLE EARTH MODELS & SYSTEMS

by Donella H. Meadows

I WANT to describe here just one paradigm or way of looking that reveals just some aspects of reality. I do not believe it is the right or best way, since I cannot settle on any one way as right or best. But it is a perspective that is unfamiliar and thus revealing to most people. And it is, I believe, a useful way of looking at some of humankind's most persistent problems — hunger, poverty, environmental degradation, and war — problems that do not seem to be solvable when looked at from older and more familiar viewpoints.

This paradigm has many names. I will call it the "systems paradigm," knowing that the word *systems* has disparate meanings but intending to clarify what I mean primarily through examples throughout this paper.

I will begin with what might be considered the state of the art — the seven complex computer models of the global system that have been constructed and documented so far. I will describe how the world system looks when it is seen from the comprehensive and sophisticated viewpoint of those models. Then I will backtrack to the very beginning, to what any schoolchild can see and know about complex systems and to the kinds of examples I use to teach systems thinking. Having completed the introductory course, I will progress immediately to more advanced but still computer-free systems insights that any adult can carry in his or her head to deal with the persistent, system-dependent malfunctions of a complicated society. And finally I will come back to an overview of the entire planet and speculate on how it would be different if more of its inhabitants saw it from a systems point of view.

The Globe as Seen through Computer Models

To most people the word *systems* implies massive computers containing vast arrays of information about everything there is to know. But the first well-known computer simulation on a global, long-term scale was in fact relatively simple. It was published only about ten years ago by M.I.T.'s Jay Forrester.[1] Since then seven other widely recognized "global" models have been completed, with at least 20 more still under development. Some major characteristics of the completed models are summarized in **Figure 1**.

As you can see, global models have been made in many parts of the world, using many different techniques, to answer quite different questions. Even with a computer a modeler is severely limited in the amount of information that he or she can include, and each of these models contains only a fraction of what is known about the world. Most of them focus on

---

1. Jay W. Forrester, *World Dynamics*, MIT Press, Cambridge, Massachusetts, 1971.

To my surprise it appears that systems and computer modeling lore is moving rapidly beyond smart toward wise. A coauthor of the famed **The Limits to Growth** *(with Dennis Meadows and Jay Forrester), Dana Meadows gave this paper at an education and environment conference in Budapest, Hungary, in November 1980. She updated the material for CQ and at our request expanded the systems-perversities section at the end. For still further expansion see her new book* **Groping in the Dark** *(The First Decade of Global Modeling), coauthored with John Richardson and Gerhart Bruckmann; $29.50 postpaid from John Wiley and Sons, One Wiley Drive, Somerset, NJ 08873. The Meadows family works a small farm near Dartmouth College, New Hampshire, where they also teach. —Stewart Brand*

About one-fifth of the complete diagram of a computer-model of the world. This one, from Forrester's **World Dynamics**, shows negative loops which adjust population levels to the maximum number of people who can survive their own pollution.

Figure 1
CHARACTERISTICS OF GLOBAL COMPUTER MODELS

Model	Institution Where Constructed	Major Modeling Technique	Basic Problem Focus	Principal References
World 2 World 3	Massachusetts Institute of Technology (USA)	System dynamics	The pattern of approach of the growing population and economy to the limited physical carrying capacity of the planet	Forrester, World Dynamics, MIT Press, 1971. Meadows et al., The Limits to Growth, Universe Books, 1972. Meadows et al., The Dynamics of Growth in a Finite World, MIT Press, 1974.
WIM (World Integrated Model)	Case Western University (USA) and Technical University, Hannover (Federal Republic of Germany)	Multilevel hierarchical systems theory, components include simulation, input-output, econometrics	Global interdependence, population and economic growth, resource depletion	Mesarovic & Pestel, Mankind at the Turning Point, Dutton, 1974.
Latin American World Model	Fundacion Bariloche (Argentina)	Optimization	Maximization of basic human needs, improvement of quality of life of the poor	Herrera et al., Catastrophe or New Society?, International Development Research Centre, 1976.
MOIRA (Model of International Relations in Agriculture)	Free University of Amsterdam and Agricultural University of Wageningen (Netherlands)	Econometrics, optimization	World food trade patterns, policies to eliminate hunger	Buringh et al., Computation of the Absolute Maximum Food Production of the World, Wageningen, 1975. Linnemann et al., MOIRA — Model of International Relations in Agriculture, North-Holland, 1979.
SARUM (Systems Analysis Research Unit Model)	Department of the Environment (U.K.)	Simulation, system dynamics, econometrics	Consequences of and stresses on economic development	Roberts et al., SARUM 76 — Global Modelling Project, UK Departments of Environment and Transport, 1977.
FUGI (Future of Global Interdependence)	Tokyo University, Soka University (Japan)	Input/output, econometrics	Co-development of industrial and industrializing economies	Kaya et al., Future of Global Interdependence, IIASA, 1977.
United Nations World Model	New York University Brandeis University (USA)	Input/output	Effect of development policies on equity and the environment.	Leontief et al., The Future of the World Economy, Oxford, 1977.
	All-Union Institute for System Studies (USSR)		Effect of social and political factors on global development	(still in progress)
GLOBUS	Wissenschaftszentrum Berlin (Federal Republic of Germany)		International relations, trade, and conflict	(still in progress)

economic factors, population, and agricultural production. Only two of the seven contain any mention of resources or the environment. None say anything about war, politics, new ideas, or natural disasters. Most assume either that technology does not change or that it changes automatically, exponentially, and without cost, to allow more and more to be produced from less and less. Some of the models represent the world as a single unit, others divide it into 10 to 15 regions or as many as 106 separate nations. Some run into the future as far as the year 2100, others only to 1985. Several, especially the first ones, have been highly controversial, and some of the later models were made expressly to refute or improve upon earlier ones.

I am introducing you to these models to make several basic points that are often misunderstood by a public that is either too easily awed or too easily cynical about computer technologies.

1 The models are highly diverse. They were made by people with different political and cultural persuasions and all are extremely biased, but in very different ways. There is no such thing as an "objective" socioeconomic model.

2 Simultaneously, the models are tremendously complicated in what they represent (detailed population age structures, multiple economic sectors, complex trade patterns, various income classes) and surprisingly simplistic in what they omit (armaments, capital age structures, nearly all values, motivations, social norms, political structures, the sources and sinks of most material flows).

3 No model is (or is claimed to be) a predictive tool. At best each one is a very explicit mathematical rendering of someone's view of the world, tied down as much as possible with statistical data, logically consistent, and able to produce statements of this sort: "*If* all these assumptions are correct, complete, and extended into the future,

> **The modelers themselves, who generally started out hostile and critical of one another, have been surprised at the extent to which their conclusions overlapped.**

then the logical consequences will be . . ."

To me these models are instructive not singly but as a set. Although they were made by people of different continents and ideologies, the nature of the exercise forced those people to a similar and not-very-ordinary viewing point. All were looking at the globe as a whole and at the relatively long-term implications of the interconnecting web of population, capital, and economic production that links all nations. All were immersed in the global statistics and had to construct a model that captured the global situation with fullness and consistency — every seller must have a buyer, every birth must eventually be matched by a death, once productive capital is in place it cannot shift its purpose from a tractor factory to a hospital. Despite many differences in emphasis and detail, viewing the closed system somehow produced some basic findings that are common to every one of the models. The modelers themselves, who generally started out hostile and critical of one another, have been surprised at the extent to which their conclusions overlapped. The following statements would be agreed upon, I believe, by everyone involved in global modeling so far:[2]

1 There is no known physical or technical reason why basic needs cannot be supplied for all the world's people into the foreseeable future. These needs are not

[2]. The list is taken from **Groping in the Dark: The First Decade of Global Modeling**, Donella Meadows et al., Editors (1982: $26.95 postpaid from John Wiley and Sons, 1 Wiley Drive, Somerset, NJ 08873).

being met now because of social and political structures, values, norms, and world views, not because of physical scarcities.

2 Population and physical (material) capital cannot grow forever on a finite planet.

3 There is, quite simply, no reliable and complete information about the degree to which the earth's physical environment can absorb and meet the needs of further growth in population, capital, and the things that this population will generate. There is a great deal of partial information, which optimists read optimistically and pessimists read pessimistically.

4 Continuing "business-as-usual" policies through the next few decades will not lead to a desirable future — or even to meeting basic human needs. It will result in an increasing gap between the rich and the poor, problems with resource availability and environmental destruction, and worsening economic conditions.

5 Because of these difficulties, continuing current trends is not a likely future course. Over the next three decades the world socioeconomic system will be in a period of transition to some state that will be not only quantitatively but also qualitatively different from the present.

6 The exact nature of this future state, and whether it will be better or worse than the present, is not predetermined, but is a function of

Some problems consistently resist solution in many cultures and over long periods of time. These are the problems for which a new way of looking is required.

decisions and changes being made now.

7 Owing to the momentum inherent in the world's physical and social processes, policy changes made soon are likely to have more impact with less effort than the same set of changes made later. By the time a problem is obvious to everyone, it is often too late to solve it.

8 Although technical changes are expected and needed, no set of purely technical changes tested in any of the models was sufficient in itself to bring about a desirable future. Restructuring social, economic, and political systems was much more effective.

9 The interdependencies among peoples and nations across time and space are greater than commonly imagined. Actions taken at one time and on one part of the globe have far-reaching consequences that are impossible to predict intuitively, and probably impossible to predict (totally, precisely, maybe at all) with computer models.

10 Because of these interdependencies, single, simple measures intended to reach narrowly defined goals are likely to be counterproductive. Decisions should be made within the broadest possible context, across space, time, and areas of knowledge.

11 Cooperative approaches to achieving individual or national goals often turn out to be more beneficial in the long run to all parties than competitive approaches.

12 Many plans, programs, and agreements, particularly complex international ones, are based on assumptions about the world that are either mutually inconsistent or inconsistent with physical reality. Much time and effort is spent designing and debating policies that are, in fact, simply impossible.

To nearly anyone with the education and time to think about the world as a whole, these statements are not surprising. We all have an intuitive feel for how the complex systems in which we are embedded work, and the statements above are about the working of a complex system. Many of them follow directly from general systems theory. They were *bound* to emerge from any systematic look at the global economy.

What is surprising is the lack of congruence between these descriptions of the world and the view of the world reflected in policy — nearly every policy of every nation, enterprise, and individual. Those policies are virtually all based on such implicit assumptions as:

There is not enough of anything to go around.

We know that any physical or environmental limits are far away and can be ignored.

Competition works better than cooperation; if everyone looks out for her or himself, the result will be satisfactory.

Any change in policy should be postponed as long as possible.

The future will be very much like the past, only bigger and better.

The poor will catch up with the rich someday if we pursue business as usual.

The bottom line message of the global models is quite simple: *The world is a complex, interconnected, finite, ecological-social-psychological-economic system. We treat it as if it were not, as if it were divisible, separable, simple, and infinite. Our persistent, intractable, global problems arise directly from this mismatch.* No one wants or works to generate hunger, poverty, pollution, or the elimination of species. Very few people favor arms races or terrorism or alcoholism or inflation. Yet those results are consistently produced by the system-as-a-whole, despite many policies and much effort directed against them. Many social policies work: they solve problems permanently. But some problems consistently resist solution in many cultures and over long periods of time. Those are the problems for which a new way of looking is required.

A Child's Guide to the Systems Viewpoint

So what is this "systems viewpoint" – what can you see from it that you can't see from anywhere else?

1 **The Concept of a System.** A system is any set of interconnected elements. In our usual reductionist-scientific view of things the emphasis is on the *elements*. To understand things, we take them apart and study the pieces. In the systems view the *interrelationships* are important. A corporation is a corporation even when every person and machine in it changes, as long as the hierarchies, purposes, and punishments remain the same. You can't understand the essence of a symphony orchestra just by looking at the instruments and players – it is also the set of relationships that causes it to produce beautiful music. The human body, the nation of Hungary, the ecosystem of a coral reef are all more than the sum of their parts. As an ancient Sufi sage said, "You think because you understand *one* you must understand *two* because one and one

When you see whole systems, you start noticing where things come from and where they go. You begin to see that there is no "away" to throw things to.

make two. But you must also understand *and*."

To see not only things but also relationships opens your vision immensely. You never confuse hastily constructed government apartment blocks with real communities. You never make an urban policy separate from a rural policy. You begin to lose the distinction between humanity and nature or between economic benefits and environmental ones. You also begin to see new solutions — the traffic problem may be affected by the housing sector, economic growth may be enhanced through increasing capital lifetimes, cancer may be prevented by protecting the integrity of the cell membrane and the whole tissue, not the individual nucleus. It is often easier and more effective to act on system relationships rather than on system elements.

2 The Limiting Factor. Growth in a complex system may require hundreds of inputs, but at any given time only one input is important — the one that is most limiting. Bread will not rise without yeast, and adding more flour will not help. Corn will not grow without phosphate no matter how much nitrogen is present. This concept is childishly simple and widely ignored. American economists have claimed that energy cannot be an important factor of production because it accounts for less than 10 percent of the GNP (yeast accounts for much less than 10 percent of the bread — that doesn't make it unimportant). Agronomists assume they know what to put in fertilizer because they have identified the 20 major chemicals in good soil (how many chemicals have they not identified?). Rich countries transfer food or capital or technology to poor ones and wonder why they don't grow. In each case attention may be on every major factor but the crucial one — the limiting one.

Real insight comes not only from recognizing that the important factor is the limiting one, but from seeing that *growth itself depletes and enhances factors.* The interplay between a growing plant and the soil or a growing economy and its resource base is dynamic, everchanging. Whenever one factor ceases to be limiting, growth occurs and changes the relative scarcity of factors until another becomes limiting. To shift attention from the abundant factors to the *next potential limiting one* is to gain real understanding of and control over the growth process.

3 Boundaries. When you see whole systems, you start noticing where things come from and where they go. You begin to see that there is no "away" to throw things to. You can no longer ignore the connectedness between an automobile's exhaust and your nose. You see that the products of a coal-burning electric plant are electricity, fly ash, particulates, SO_2, CO_2, NO_x, and heavy-metal aerosols and that there is no real boundary between the economic product and the "byproducts." You wonder why some effects of a policy are called "side effects" when they are as real and direct as the "main effects." You notice how beautifully designed natural systems are so that the outputs and wastes of one process are always inputs to another process, and you begin to think of new designs for industrial systems.

4 Feedback. Whenever you postulate that A causes or affects B

$$A \rightarrow B$$

look for all the ways that B in turn affects A.

$$A \rightleftarrows B$$

When you turn a faucet to control the level of water in a glass

FAUCET POSITION → WATER FLOW → WATER IN GLASS

notice how the level of water determines how you turn the faucet, so that the level comes to just where you wanted it.

DESIRED AMOUNT OF WATER IN GLASS → FAUCET POSITION → WATER FLOW → WATER IN GLASS → (back to faucet)

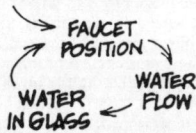

A closed chain of causal relationships that feeds back on itself is called a feedback loop. The water-glass system is a *negative* feedback loop that draws the system to a goal (desired amount of water). Negative loops act to adjust systems toward equilibrium points or goals, just as a thermostat loop adjusts room temperature to a desired setting.

When your country acquires more armaments to catch up with the competition

ARMS IN COUNTRY A → A'S ARMS AS PERCEIVED BY COUNTRY B → ARMS IN COUNTRY B

it effectively generates more armaments for the competition.

ARMS IN COUNTRY A → A'S ARMS AS PERCEIVED BY COUNTRY B → ARMS IN COUNTRY B → B'S ARMS AS PERCEIVED BY COUNTRY A → (back)

This is a *positive* feedback loop, a vicious circle that builds upon itself more and more. Positive loops cause growth, evolution, and also collapse in systems.

Of course most systems, especially socioeconomic ones, are made of hundreds of interconnected positive and negative feedbacks and their behavior becomes very complicated.

The concept of feedback is a powerful one because it allows one to link causal structure to dynamic behavior. If a system persistently oscillates or equilibrates or fails to grow, one can identify the structural reasons for that behavior and learn how to intervene in the feedback loops to alter it. That is what I do for a living, and my colleagues and I have applied these concepts to problems as varied as fluctuating inventory, unstable grain prices, diabetes and cancer, rising oil prices, and economic development.

But the most powerful aspect of the feedback concept, a truly profound and different insight, is the way you begin to see that *the system causes its own behavior.* Country A perceives the arms race as "caused" by country B and vice versa, but one could equally well claim that country A causes its own arms buildup by stimulating the buildup of country B. Or, more accurately, there is no single cause, no credit or blame. The relationships in the system make an arms race inevitable, and A and B are helpless puppets (until they decide to redesign the system). Similarly oil-price rises that are blamed on OPEC could equally be blamed on the heavy consumption of the non-OPEC countries, but more accurately, the price rises are an inevitable result of a growing economic system dependent on a depleting nonrenewable resource base. Similarly, from a systems point of view, businesses make up a system that is structured to generate recessions and depressions, the decisions of farmers make fluctuating commodity prices inevitable, and the flu doesn't invade you — you invite it.

Seeing the source of a problem within the system that suffers the problem is never politically popular. It is much more appealing to find a "cause" for your problems somewhere "out there" than to contemplate changing the relationships between the elements "in here." It is comforting to view something outside the system as the problem, but it isn't very effective. There is real opportunity for action in learning to view every system as the cause of its behavior. First of all, if the entire concept of blame is removed, you can stop arguing about who is at fault and get on with solving the problem. And second, if a system is the source of a problem, it is also the mechanism for a solution. To demonstrate that, I would like to proceed to the advanced-level systems course and talk about multiple-feedback systems.

Advanced Understanding — Making Complex Systems Work

1 **Policy Resistance.** Why do some problems persist in spite of continuous efforts to solve them?

A systems analyst would explain it this way (see **Figure 2**). Any social system is made up of hundreds of actors, each with his or her (or its in the case of an institution) own goals. Each actor monitors the state of the system with regard to any important variable, income or prices or housing or whatever, and compares that state with his, her, or its goal. If there is a discrepancy, if the system is not meeting the goal, each actor does something concrete to correct the situation. Usually the greater the discrepancy between the goal and the actual situation for any actor, the more emphatic will be the action taken on the system. The combination of all actors trying to adjust the system to achieve all the different goals produces a system state that is often not what anybody wants. And yet everyone is putting great effort into keeping it there, because if any single actor lets up the effort, the others will drag the system closer to their goals and farther from his/hers.

Examples of such system configurations come to mind far too readily. Farmers, consumers, and farm suppliers pursue various income goals and produce economic conditions unfavorable for production and also unfavorable for protection of the soils and

Figure 2 Policy Resistance

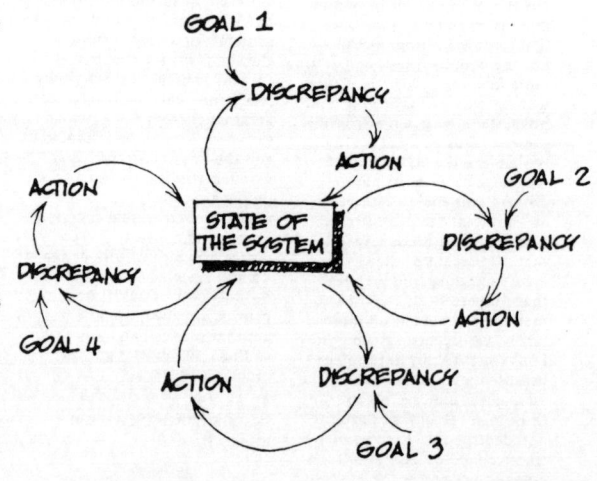

waters. Government, laborers, and producers act together to produce inflation that damages everyone. Rich and poor nations trade basic commodities, each nation pursuing overriding domestic political and economic goals, with a resultant instability on the world market that systematically penalizes the poor. Or, closer to home, individual members of a family or of a working group, each concentrating on personal goals, can produce an uncoordinated or disconnected entity that furthers the goals of no one.

Suppose a government intervenes in such a system with a strong policy that actually moves the state of the system toward the government's goal. That will open up greater discrepancies for other actors with different goals, which will cause them to redouble their efforts. If they are successful, the system is likely to equilibrate very near its previous state, but with everyone working harder to keep it there. Think, for example, of efforts to improve traffic flow (by widening streets or adding control lights or building mass transit systems) that eventually result in the same traffic densities as before. Or look at the results of one country's attempt to raise its birth rate by prohibiting abortions (Figure 3). Abortions were legal until 1967, when they became unavailable. The birth rate rapidly tripled, but then came slowly back down nearly to its previous level. The individual families, pursuing their own family-size goals, found some other way to achieve them, perhaps through dangerous illegal abortions.

This systems view of policy resistance suggests some interesting new approaches to previously intractable problems. At the very least, it suggests letting up on an ineffective policy, so that all the resources and energy spent on enforcing and resisting the policy could be released for some more constructive purpose. One might also look more closely at the goals and actions within the system, to understand them and to look for a way they could be used instead of being combatted or subjugated. The principle is similar to that of karate: use the force and energy of your opponent instead of resisting it. For example, a nation wishing to increase its birth rate might study the reasons for families to want few children, discover that cramped housing conditions may be a prime motivating factor, and devise a housing policy that allows young couples to achieve their goals for peace and privacy while also achieving the national goal of more births. This policy has been followed in Hungary, with much better results than those of Romania's policy of abortion restrictions.

The most effective way of dealing with policy resistance is to find an alignment of the goals in the system, so that all actors are working harmoniously and naturally toward the same outcome. If this can be done, the results can be amazing. The most familiar examples of this are mobilization of economies during wartime or recovery after war or natural disaster. Another example was Sweden's population policy during the 1930s, when the Swedish birth rate dropped below replacement. The government assessed its goals and those of its population carefully and decided that the real basis of goal-agreement was not the size of the population but its *quality*.[3] Every child should be wanted and cared for, preferably in a strong, stable family, with access to excellent education and health care. The government and the Swedish people could align on that goal. The resulting policies included free contraceptives and abortions, sex and family education, easier divorce laws, free obstetrical care, support for families with children not in cash but in kind (toys, clothing, etc.), and increased investment in education and medical facilities. Some of these policies looked strange in a time when birth rates were thought to be too low, but they were implemented anyway, and since then birth rates have risen, fallen, and risen again.

2 Drift to Low Performance. Some systems not only resist policy and stay in their normal state, they actually worsen gradually over time, despite efforts at improvement. Examples could be falling productivity or market share of a business enterprise, reduced quality of service at a repair shop or hospital, continuously dirtier rivers or air, or increased fat on a person in spite of periodic diets.

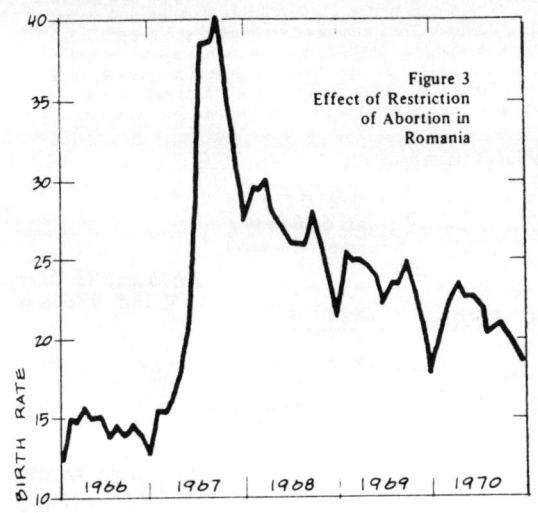

---

[3] See Alva Myrdal, Nation and Family, MIT Press, 1968 (reprint).

Figure 3
Effect of Restriction of Abortion in Romania

A system that takes its goal from its own performance is very likely to drift downhill.

The structure that produces such a behavior is shown in Figure 4. The actor in this system (enterprise, repair station, environmental agency, fat person) has a performance goal (desired state) that is compared to the actual state. If there is a discrepancy, action is taken to restore the system state to the goal. So far that is a simple negative feedback loop that should keep performance at a constant, high level.

The problem comes in the connection between the actor's perception of the system state and his or her desired state. If for some reason performance falters, and *if the lower performance becomes the standard*, then less corrective action is taken for any given discrepancy and the system state is permanently lowered. Another shortfall can produce another drop in standards, and so on until performance is nearly totally degraded. A system that takes its goals from its own performance is very likely to drift downhill.

Some examples: In the U.S. 4 percent inflation used to be considered unacceptable and would generate strong corrective action. That standard has slowly changed so that now inflation below 10 percent looks good, 12 percent is almost normal, and it takes rates of 20 percent or more to raise great public concern (and we're beginning to get used to those). Also, in the U.S. air quality standards are set at different levels for different areas; places with dirty air have far less stringent standards. Another example: I live in a beautiful rural area where the streets of the small village are kept quite clean and unlittered. I find myself bothered when I go to big cities and see all the trash littering the streets. My friends who live there are almost unconscious of the trash — and after a few days there I am too.

An obvious antidote to the drift to low performance is to keep standards absolute — never let past performance become a guide to present goals. Another is to make goals sensitive to *over*performance as well as underperformance. The same set of feedback loops could actually pull the system state to better and better levels, if *good* performance were taken as reason to reset standards but bad performance were considered only bad luck, not to be taken seriously.

3 Addiction. The structure of a system that produces addiction is shown in **Figure 5**. Again the actor has a goal and compares the goal with a perception of the actual state to determine what action to take. But here the action chosen has the effect of making the system appear better to the actor, while actually over the long term it is making it worse. As the effect of this action wears off, the problem reappears, probably more insistently, so the actor applies even more of the "solution," thereby worsening the problem and making it necessary to use more "solution" in the future.

Consumption of alcohol, nicotine, heroin, caffeine, and sugar are obvious examples of addictive actions. A less obvious example is the use of pesticides (removing the immediate pest, but also eliminating natural control mechanisms, so that the pest is likely to surge back in the future). Another is the pricing of a depleting resource such as oil at average rather than replacement costs (thereby keeping price artificially low and postponing the pain but also encouraging further use and more rapid depletion and discouraging the shift to other resources that will eventually be necessary).

Policy choices with addictive effects are insidious because they look good in the short term, but once chosen they are very difficult to reverse. Obviously, the best procedure is to be alert for options that improve the symptoms but worsen the problem and to avoid them, whatever their political appeal. Once caught in the addictive cycle, one must

Fig. 4 Drift to Low Performance

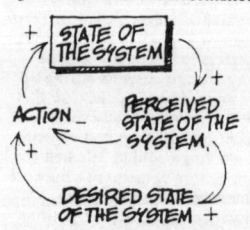

Figure 5 Addiction

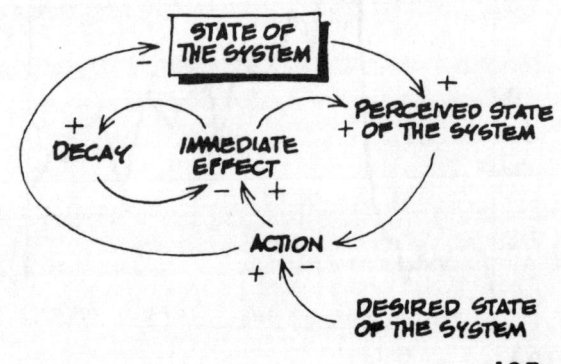

almost inevitably prepare to suffer short-term difficulties in order to get out, whether that means the physical pain of heroin withdrawal, a sudden sharp price rise to reduce oil consumption, or an invasion of pests while natural predator populations are being restored. Sometimes the reversal can be done gradually, or an alternative nonaddictive policy can be put in place first to restore the system state with a minimum of turbulence (psychiatric help to restore the self-image of the addict, home insulation to reduce oil expense, crop rotation and multiculture to reduce vulnerability to pests). But it is always less expensive to avoid the addiction in the first place than to get out of it once it has started — as anyone with a long-term systems viewpoint can see.

4 Official Addiction — Shifting the Burden to the Intervener.
As I grew older and spent most of my time reading, I slowly became more and more near-sighted. Finally I couldn't read writing on a blackboard or slides on a screen anymore. So I got contact lenses. Within a year my uncorrected vision deteriorated far more than it had in the previous 30 years. Now the lenses are necessary not only for reading distant fine print but for everyday navigation. Apparently the muscles around my eyes had been doing a fair job of compensating for an increasingly misshaped natural lens. But when they no longer had to do that job, they lost their tone, their ability to do it. Soon I needed a newer, stronger prescription.

That is a classic case of shifting the burden to the intervener— a benevolent form of addiction (Figure 6). In this sort of system a natural corrective force is doing only a so-so job of maintaining the system state. A well-meaning, benevolent, and very efficient intervener decides to help out by taking on some of the load. A new mechanism is established to bring the system to the state everybody wants it to be in. This new mechanism works beautifully.

But in the process, whether by active destruction or simple neglect and atrophy, the original corrective forces within the system are weakened. The system slips away from the desired state. So the intervener increases his, her, or its efforts. The natural system weakens or atrophies still more. The intervener picks up the slack. And so forth. Finally, most or all of the original job carried out by the natural system has, gladly or reluctantly, been accepted by the intervening system. The ability of the original system to do the job has been severely and perhaps irreversibly weakened.

Finding examples of burden-shifting systems is easy and fun and sometimes horrifying. Here is a beginning of a list, to which everyone will be able to add.

Shifting a burden to an intervener is not necessarily a bad thing. It is usually done willingly, and the result is often an increased tendency for the system to achieve desired states. But this system characteristic can be problematic, for two reasons. First, the intervener may not realize that the initial urge to help out a bit can start a whole chain of events that leads to ever-heavier loads on the intervening system. The American social security system is now experiencing the strains of that chain of events. Second, the community that is being helped may not think through the long-term loss of control and the increased vulnerability that may go along with the opportunity to shift a burden to a more able and powerful intervener.

burden	original system	intervening system
care of the aged	families, communities, accumulation of personal wealth	social security
bread-making	households, local millers, small bakeries	multinational corporations
smallpox prevention	natural resistance, accidental cowpox infection	vaccination
long-distance transportation	railroads	interstate highways, trucks
arithmetic	mental training	personal calculators
grain storage	households, farmers, local merchants	grain trading companies, international reserve agreements

Figure 6 Shifting the Burden to the Intervener

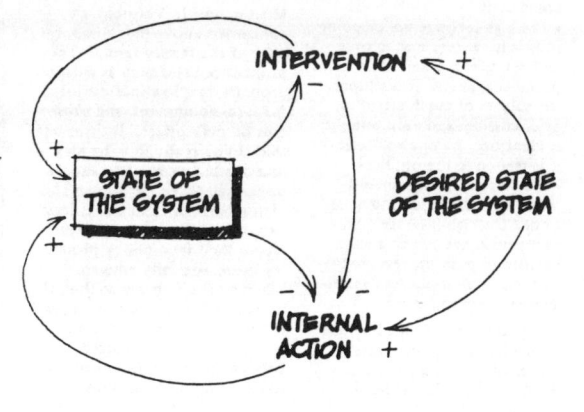

Rebuilding a decayed system of self-reliance and private enterprise that long ago stopped handling its own burdens is a long, difficult process, something no Republican administration seems to understand. Sudden removal of an intervening system does not necessarily shift the burden back; it may drop the burden because there is little left to shift it back to. Intervening in such a way as to *strengthen the ability of the system to shoulder its own burdens* is very possible and often cheap and easy, something no Democratic administration seems to realize. The secret is to begin not by taking over, but by asking why the natural correction mechanisms are failing to handle the problem, and how the obstacles to handling it could be removed.

5 **High Leverage, Wrong Direction.** Jay Forrester, my systems guru, likes to tell of working with corporations to establish a systems view of management. He has often discovered, in modeling the feedback loop structure of a corporation's decision processes, that:

• Whatever the problem is (falling market share, unstable inventory, inadequate quality control), it is nearly always traceable to the way the *corporation* does things — not to the customers, the competitors, the regulators, or any other convenient scapegoats.
• Often one small change, in one or a few simple policies, will solve the problem easily and completely.
• The high-leverage policy point is usually far removed in time and place from where the problem appears. It is seldom the subject of much attention or discussion, and even when it is identified, no one will believe it is related to the problem.
• If it happens that someone has indeed identified and questioned the high-leverage policy, that person has almost always decided to push the lever in the *wrong direction*, thereby intensifying the problem.

The peculiarity of high-leverage points lurking in unexpected places and inviting counterproductive policies is not one I can illustrate with a simple feedback diagram. It seems to occur in just about any system that contains enough interlocking feedback loops to boggle one's capacity for mental analysis (for me that means more than four feedback loops).

Here are a few examples of systems with high-leverage points pushed the wrong direction.

A large engine company had a problem with falling market share. Every four years or so, it would lose sales to the competition, and the lost customers rarely returned. The problem was finally traced to the firm's *inventory* policy. The company was reluctant to build large, expensive engines on speculation to accumulate an inventory. It preferred to build only on definite orders. This policy saved a lot of money, but on the upturn of each business cycle, the company was swamped by new orders, which it could deliver only after a long delay. Customers turned to the competition who could supply engines quickly "off the shelf." The firm habitually responded to the loss in sales by cost-cutting measures, including *decreases* in its inventory.

Most people in Vermont are concerned about the "disappearance of the family farm." They propose policies such as cuts in property tax, low-interest loans for farm equipment, and subsidies on milk prices. It turns out that if you really like the idea of lots of small farms, you should oppose all those measures. The major cause of farm loss is farm expansion. Farmers try to increase their incomes by producing more, logically enough. When all the farmers do that, the market is flooded with milk, and the price goes down (the price is not currently subsidized enough to hold constant regardless of supply — if it were, it

Policy choices with addictive effects are insidious because they look good in the short term, but once chosen they are very difficult to reverse.

would shift the burden to an intervener!). Since the profit per unit of milk has gone down, each farmer must produce more *even to keep the same income.* Some do. Others don't, and eventually their incomes drop so low that they quit farming.

The leverage point in this system is the farmers' ability to increase their production. Given the treadmill of the system, they will have to use any break that gives them more cash to expand their output. And that drives prices, profits, and farm numbers down still faster. The best way to stabilize farm numbers would be to restrict total production in some way. If that could be done, all farmers would have higher and more stable incomes (as many industrial sectors have discovered).

One of the leverage points in any growing economy is the lifetime of the capital plant. The easiest way to stimulate economic growth is to increase the useful lifetime of capital (by better design, or better maintenance). Yet the policy of planned obsolescence is promoted and defended for the sake of economic growth.

The way to revitalize the economy of a city and create more upward mobility for the poor is not to build subsidized housing in the inner city. It is to demolish substandard and abandoned housing, creating open space for the establishment of more businesses, so the job/population balance can be restored.

I wish I could provide here some simple rules for finding high-leverage points and for knowing what direction to push them. Some of my professional colleagues would argue that this is the point where I should stop relying on innate systems understanding and start hiring them.

BOX 428 SAUSALITO CA 94966

Indeed, all of the examples I have given here came from formal computerized analyses. I do respect and use the computer as a handy tool to help learn about complex systems, but I also think one can go a long way without it.

One's rational, figuring-out ability seems to be a bad guide for finding leverage points. It leads one to look at pieces of systems, and to make judgements based on short-term and incomplete information. It would lead a company to cut back on inventory when sales are down, the state of Vermont to reduce farmers' property taxes, or a nation to invest in new machines instead of repairing old ones. All very *reasonable* policies. And yet there is something in all of us that might lead us to notice the customers' dissatisfaction with long delivery delays, or to wonder why farmers always complain about the pressure to expand, or to feel that replacing a machine that is still productive somehow doesn't make sense.

I think we do have within us the ability to see whole systems and to sense leverage points. What we don't seem to have is the ability to win arguments, even within ourselves, with that "reasonable" side of us. We keep expecting a solution to be near a symptom, a long-term gain to start off with a short-term gain, or a winning strategy to produce instant gratification for all players. We know complex systems don't behave like that. But something within us keeps insisting somehow that they should. And so we pursue difficult policies that can't work, and miss seeing rather simple policies that can. We try to compete instead of cooperating, to push against environmental limits instead of noticing that there is already enough, to hang on to a deteriorating status quo instead of welcoming changes that take us where we really want to go. The results are hunger, weapons, pollution, depletion. And just within our grasp, accessible through our innate systems understanding, are sufficiency, peace, equity, and sustainability.

We keep expecting a solution to be near a symptom, a long-term gain to start off with a short-term gain, or a winning strategy to produce instant gratification for all players.

Back to the Globe

It is impossible to lay out a whole new way of viewing the world in a short paper — it is like trying to describe everything that can be seen through a telescope and comparing it systematically to what can be seen through a microscope. I could go on about the role of delays and nonlinearity in systems, about the structural homologies across systems, about other behavioral properties such as the tragedy of the commons or the worse-before-better syndrome. One could create whole undergraduate and graduate curricula on the subject, and of course I and many other people have done so.

It should be clear that I am excited by what I can see from the new viewpoint of systems. I find my entire sense of what is happening, what is possible, what I identify with, and what is important is shifting. I want to take others by the hand and say "Look at that" — which I do in my teaching. I believe that if more people could learn to see the world as a system, *in addition to, not in place of,* the ways they already see the world, some remarkable things would happen. At the very least, like the global modelers who started from very different positions, they would find a common ground of understanding and would find that many current proposals that are the source of argument and divisiveness simply cannot be effective. They would find themselves losing interest in simple notions of fault or blame. And then they would start seeing whole new kinds of policies.

What would these policies look like? Some people expect that policies arising from systems views and computer analysis should be precise, absolute, certain, and a bit inhuman. In my own experience, however, after ten years of trying to simulate social systems, I find myself becoming more humble, less certain, more experimental, and acutely aware of the unique and wonderful complications human beings add to complex systems. I am finding that policies consistent with the systems view would be:

1 **Respectful of the system** — designed to aid and encourage those forces within the system that help it to run itself, rather than imposing on it from "outside" or "above."

2 **Responsible** for the system's behavior, rather than trying to blame or control outside influences.

3 **Experimental** — recognizing that nature is complex beyond our ability to understand; therefore careful experiment and constant monitoring are more appropriate than certain, undeviating directives.

4 **Attentive to the system as a whole** and to total system properties such as growth, oscillation, equilibrium, or resilience, rather than trying to maximize the performance of parts.

5 **Attentive to the long term**, realizing that in fact there is no long-term short-term distinction; that actions taken now have effects for decades to come and that we experience now the results of actions taken decades ago.

6 **Comprehensive** — above all, the systems view, as demonstrated by the global models, makes clear that no part of the human race is really separate either from other human beings or from the global ecosystem. We all rise or fall together. ∎

[9]

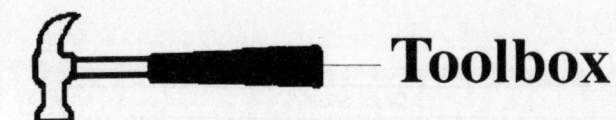

Toolbox

A Palette of Systems Thinking Tools

In this *Toolbox* it may be helpful to lay out the full array of systems thinking tools from which this column draws. You can think of these tools like a painter views colors—many shades can be created out of three primary colors, but having a full range of colors ready-made makes painting much easier.

There are at least ten distinct types of systems thinking tools (a full-page summary diagram appears on the next page). They fall under four broad categories: I. Brainstorming Tools, II. Dynamic Thinking Tools, III. Structural Thinking Tools, and IV. Computer-Based Tools. Although each of the tools is designed to stand alone, they also build upon one another and can be used in combination to achieve deeper insights into dynamic behavior.

Brainstorming Tools

The *Double-Q (QQ) Diagram* is based on what is commonly known as a fishbone or cause-and-effect diagram. The Q's stand for *qualitative* and *quantitative*, and the technique is designed to help participants begin to see the whole system. During a structured brainstorming session with the QQ diagram, both sides of an issue remain equally visible and properly balanced, avoiding a "top heavy" perspective. The diagram also provides a visual map of the key factors involved. Once those factors are pinpointed, Behavior Over Time Diagrams and/or Causal Loop Diagrams can be used to explore how they interact.

A QQ diagram begins with a heavy horizontal arrow that points to the issue being addressed. Major "hard" (quantitative) factors branch off along the top and "soft" (qualitative) factors run along the bottom. Arrows leading off of the major factors represent sub-factors. These sub-factors can in turn have *sub* sub-factors leading off of them. However, many layers of nesting may be a sign that one of the sub-factors should be turned into a major factor.

Although QQ diagramming may sound like a very rigid process, it can help give form and structure to "fuzzy" problems. It can be likened to the free flowing visualization process that an artist uses—it encourages creativity while still conforming to artistic "rules."

Dynamic Thinking Tools

Behavior Over Time (BOT) Diagram. BOT diagrams are more than simple line projections—they require an understanding of the dynamic relationships among the variables being drawn. For example, say we were trying to project the relationship between sales, inventory, and production. If sales jump 20%, production cannot jump instantaneously to match the new sales number. In addition, inventory must drop below its previous level while production catches up with sales. By sketching out the behavior of different variables on the same graph, we can gain a more explicit understanding of how these variables interrelate.

Causal Loop Diagram (CLD). The Causal Loop Diagram provides a useful way to represent dynamic interrelationships. CLD's make explicit one's understanding of a system structure, provide a visual representation with which to communicate that understanding, and capture complex dynamics in a succinct form. CLD's can be combined with BOT's to form structure-behavior pairs which provide a rich framework for describing complex dynamic phenomena (see *Toolbox*, Vol. 1, No. 1, "Reinforcing and Balancing Loops: Building Blocks of Dynamic Systems" and "Balancing Loops with Delays: Teeter Tottering on Seesaws," page 9). The CLD's are the systems thinker's equivalent of the artist's primary colors.

System Archetypes is the name given to certain common dynamics that seem to recur in many different situations. These archetypes, consisting of various combinations of balancing and reinforcing loops, are the systems thinker's "paint-by-numbers" set—users can take real-world examples and fit them into the appropriate archetype. Specific archetypes include: "Drifting Goals," "Shifting the Burden," "Limits to Success," "Success to the Successful," "Fixes that Backfire," "Tragedy of the Commons," and "Escalation."

Structural Thinking Tools

Graphical Function Diagrams, Structure-Behavior Pairs, and Policy Structure Diagrams can be viewed as the building blocks for computer models. Graphical Functions are useful for clarifying nonlinear relationships between variables. Structure-Behavior Pairs link a specific structure with its corresponding behavior. Policy Structure Diagrams represent the decision-making processes that drive policies. In a sense, when we use these tools we are moving from painting on canvas to sculpting with hammer and chisel.

Computer-Based Tools

This class of tools, including computer models, management flight simulators, and learning laboratories, demands the highest level of technical proficiency to *create*. On the other hand, very little advance training is required to *use* them once they are developed. We will discuss these tools in future issues from the perspective of pre-designed packages—art appreciation versus art creation.

Toolbox

	Tool		Description
Brainstorming	I 1. Double-Q Diagram	"hard" variables / issue focus / "soft" variables	A brainstorming tool for capturing free-flowing thoughts in a structured manner and distinguishing between hard and soft variables that affect the issue of interest.
Dynamic Thinking	II 2. Behavior Over Time Diagram		Using some of the main branch variables from the Double-Q diagram, the behavior of each one can be graphed over time, taking into account any inter-relatedness in their behavior. (Also called reference modes).
	3. Causal Loop Diagram		Drawing out causal relationships using the Double-Q and behavior over time diagrams helps identify reinforcing (R) and balancing (B) processes.
	4. Systems Archetypes		Helps in recognizing common system behaviors that fit one of the recurring system archetypes such as "Eroding Goals," "Shifting the Burden," "Limits to Growth," "Fixes that Fail," etc. Captures compelling "stories" about organizational dynamics.
Structural Thinking	III 5. Graphical Function Diagram		Captures the way in which one variable affects another by graphically plotting the relationship between the two over the entire range of relevant values.
	6. Structure-Behavior Pairs		A library of simple structure-behavior pairs consists of the basic dynamic structures that can serve as building blocks for developing computer models (e.g. exponential growth, delays, smooths, S-shaped growth, oscillations, etc.)
	7. Policy Structure Diagram		A conceptual map of the decision making process that is embedded in the organization. Focuses on the factors which are weighed for each decision point. Helps build library of generic structures.
Computer-Based	IV 8. Computer Model		Allows you to map all the relationships that have been identified as relevant and important to an issue in terms of mathematical equations. You can then run policy analyses through multiple simulations.
	9. Management Flight Simulator		Provides "flight" training for managers through the use of interactive computer games based on a computer model. Through formulating strategies and by making decisions based on those strategies, management flight simulators help users recognize long-term consequences of their decisions.
	10. Learning Laboratory	Reflection / Experimentation	A manager's practice field. It is equivalent to a sports team's experience, where active experimentation is blended with reflection and discussion. Uses all the systems thinking tools, from Double-Q diagrams to MFS's.

TOOLBOX REPRINT SERIES

Toolbox

Systems Archetypes at a Glance

Archetype	Description	Guidelines
Drifting Goals	In a "Drifting Goals" archetype, a gap between the goal and current reality can be resolved by taking corrective action (B1) or lowering the goal (B2). The critical difference is that lowering the goal immediately closes the gap, whereas corrective actions usually take time. (See *Toolbox*, October 1990).	• Drifting performance figures are usually indicators that the "Drifting Goals" archetype is at work and that real corrective actions are not being taken. • A critical aspect of avoiding a potential "Drifting Goals" scenario is to determine what drives the setting of the goals. • Goals located outside the system will be less susceptible to drifting goals pressures.
Escalation	In the "Escalation" archetype, one party (A) takes actions that are perceived by the other as a threat. The other party (B) responds in a similar manner, increasing the threat to A and resulting in *more* threatening actions by A. The reinforcing loop is traced out by following the outline of the figure-8 produced by the two balancing loops. (See *Toolbox*, November 1991).	To break an escalation structure, ask the following questions: • What is the relative measure that pits one party against the other and can you change it? • What are the significant delays in the system that may distort the true nature of the threat? • What are the deep-rooted assumptions that lie beneath the actions taken in response to the threat?
Fixes that Fail	In a "Fixes that Fail" situation, a problem symptom cries out for resolution. A solution is quickly implemented that alleviates the symptom (B1), but the unintended consequences of the "fix" exacerbate the problem (R1). Over time, the problem symptom returns to its previous level or becomes worse. (See *Toolbox*, November 1990).	• Breaking a "Fixes that Fail" cycle usually requires two actions: acknowledging that the fix is merely alleviating a symptom, and making a commitment to solve the real problem now. • A two-pronged attack of applying the fix and planning out the fundamental solution will help ensure that you don't get caught in a perpetual cycle of solving yesterdays "solutions."
Growth and Underinvestment	In a "Growth and Underinvestment" archetype, growth approaches a limit that can be eliminated or pushed into the future if capacity investments are made. Instead, performance standards are lowered to justify underinvestment, leading to lower performance which further justifies underinvestment. (See *Toolbox*, June/July 1992).	• Dig into the assumptions which drive capacity investment decisions. If past performance dominates as a consideration, try to balance that perspective with a fresh look at demand and the factors that drive its growth. • If there is a potential for growth, build capacity in anticipation of future demand.

Archetype	Description	Guidelines
Limits to Success	In a "Limits to Success" scenario, continued efforts initially lead to improved performance. Over time, however, the system encounters a limit which causes the performance to slow down or even decline (B1), even as efforts continue to rise. (See *Toolbox*, December 1990/January 1991).	• The archetype is most helpful when it is used well in advance of any problems, to see how the cumulative effects of continued success might lead to future problems. • Use the archetype to explore questions such as "What kinds of pressures are building up in the organization as a result of the growth?" • Look for ways to relieve pressures or remove limits *before* an organizational gasket blows.
Shifting the Burden/Addiction	In a "Shifting the Burden" archetype, a problem is "solved" by applying a symptomatic solution (B1) which diverts attention away from more fundamental solutions (R1). (See *Toolbox*, September 1990). In an "Addiction" structure, a "Shifting the Burden" degrades into an addictive pattern in which the side-effect gets so entrenched that it overwhelms the original problem symptom. (See *Toolbox*, April 1992).	• Problem symptoms are usually easier to recognize than the other elements of the structure. • If the side-effect has become the problem, you may be dealing with an "Addiction" structure. • Whether a solution is "symptomatic" or "fundamental" often depends on one's perspective. Explore the problem from differing perspectives in order to come to a more comprehensive understanding of what the fundamental solution may be.
Success to the Successful	In a "Success to the Successful" archetype, if one person or group (A) is given more resources, it has a higher likelihood of succeeding than B (assuming they are equally capable). The initial success justifies devoting more resources to A than B (R1). As B gets less resources, its success diminishes, further justifying more resource allocations to A. (See *Toolbox*, March 1992).	• Look for reasons why the system was set up to create just one "winner." • Chop off one half of the archetype by focusing efforts and resources on one group, rather than creating a "winner-take-all" competition. • Find ways to make teams collaborators rather than competitors.
Tragedy of the Commons	In a "Tragedy of the Commons" structure, each person pursues actions which are individually beneficial (R1 and R2). If the amount of activity grows too large for the system to support, however, the "commons" becomes overloaded and everyone experiences diminishing benefits (B1 and B2). (See *Toolbox*, August 1991).	• Effective solutions for a "Tragedy of the Commons" scenario never lie at the individual level. • Ask questions such as: "What are the incentives for individuals to persist in their actions?" and "Can the long-term collective loss be made more real and immediate to the individual actors?" • Find ways to reconcile short-term individual rewards with long-term cumulative consequences.

Toolbox
Organizational Addictions: Breaking the Habit

It's 6:00 a.m. on a Monday morning. The alarm clock blares, jolting you out of bed. You shuffle down to the kitchen and grab a cup of fresh coffee. A few gulps and...ahh. Your eyes start to open; the fog begins to clear.

10:30 a.m.—time for the weekly staff meeting. "I gotta have something to keep me awake through this one," you think to yourself as you grab a cup of coffee and head into the conference room.

By 3:30 p.m. you start to feel that mid-afternoon energy low, so you head down toward the crowded coffee machine for another cup. "I really gotta cut down on this stuff," you comment to the guy behind you in line. He nods. "I'm a five-cup-a-day guy," he confesses. "I just can't give it up."

Caffeine Addiction

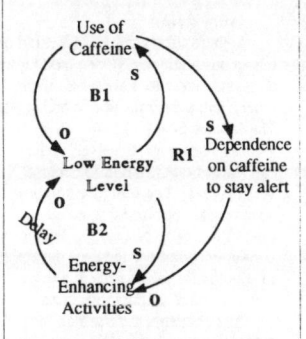

Low energy can be counteracted by more sleep or exercise—but that takes time (B2). A cup of coffee immediately restores energy (B1). But it also leads to a dependence on caffeine to stay alert, which takes attention away from long-term energy-boosters (R1).

Addiction

For most of us, the word "addiction" conjures up images of alcoholism and drug abuse or more "acceptable" habits such as coffee drinking—dependencies which are rooted in physical and neurological processes. It is not usually viewed as a social or organizational phenomena. But from a systemic perspective, addiction is a very generic structure which is quite prevalent in both social and organizational settings.

As a systemic structure, the "Addiction" archetype is a special case of "Shifting the Burden" (see p. 21 "Shifting the Burden: The Helen Keller Loops"). "Shifting the Burden" usually starts with a problem symptom that cries out for attention. The solution that is most obvious and easy to implement usually relieves the problem symptom very quickly. But the symptomatic solution has a long-term side effect that diverts attention away from the more fundamental solution to the problem (see "Addiction: A Special Case of 'Shifting the Burden'").

What makes the "Addiction" archetype special is the nature of the side-effect. In an "Addiction" structure, a "Shifting the Burden" situation degrades into an addictive pattern in which the side-effect gets so entrenched that it overwhelms the original problem symptom—the addiction becomes "the problem."

With coffee drinking, the problem symptom usually is that you feel tired (see "Caffeine Addiction"). When you drink a cup of coffee, the caffeine raises your metabolism, stimulating the body and making the mind more alert. But in doing this, it forces your body to deplete its reserves of energy faster than usual. When the effects of the caffeine wear off in a few hours, you have even less energy than before. You feel sluggish again and reach for another cup of coffee to get a jump start. Over time, your body begins to rely on the caffeine at regular intervals in order to regulate your energy and metabolism.

Organizational Addictions

In organizational settings, addiction can take the form of a dependence on certain policies, procedures, departments, or individuals. The way we think about problems, or the policies that we pursue, can become addictions when we use them without consideration or choice, as an auto-

Addiction: A Special Case of "Shifting the Burden"

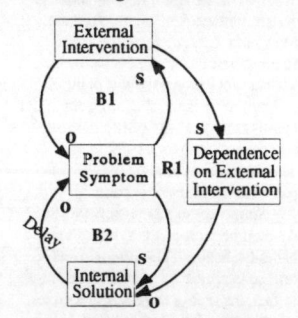

The "Addiction" archetype is a special case of "Shifting the Burden." In both cases, a problem symptom is "solved" by applying a symptomatic solution (B1), but the solution has a side-effect which diverts attention away from the fundamental solution (R1). This side-effect—the dependence on an external intervention—eventually overwhelms the original problem.

Toolbox

matic knee-jerk response to a particular situation.

Hooked on Heroics

A common yet very subtle example of addiction in companies is "crisis management"—fire-fighting. Most managers *say* they abhor fire-fighting because it wreaks havoc on normal work processes and makes it difficult to focus on the long-term. Yet fire-fighting is a way of life in most companies. Its pervasiveness and persistence is a clue that maybe it is part of an addictive structure.

Suppose you have a new product development project that has fallen behind schedule. The timing of its release is critical to its market success. In fact, the delays have reached crises proportions. You decide to make it a high priority project and assign a "crisis manager" to do what it takes to get that product out on time. This new manager suddenly has enormous flexibility in what he can do to get the product out. When the product is launched on time, he is touted as the hero of the day.

If we look at crisis management from the "Addiction" archetype, the symptomatic problem is the prevalence of crises that occur in the company (see "Hooked on Heroics"). When a crisis occurs, someone practices great heroism and "saves the day." The problem is solved and the person receives praise for doing a fine job. But what happens to the rest of the organization in the meantime? Oftentimes the solution causes a lot of disruptions which form the seeds of the next problems and perpetuate the crisis cycle.

The insidious side-effect of crisis management is that over time, as crisis management becomes the operating norm, managers begin to become dependent on the use of heroics—the need to have recognition and a feeling of accomplishment in an otherwise paralyzing institution. Usually there are roadblocks to taking action in the company: formalities and rules that say "No, you can't do this," "You have to do it this way," or "We don't have the resources." Suddenly when there's a crisis, people are given tremendous freedom and leeway and are allowed to do what they couldn't do before. Once it's over, there is tremendous fanfare: the hero is rewarded or promoted. Over time, the company becomes addicted to continually creating crises, pulling the organization through tremendous turmoil, and creating new heroes.

Breaking the Addiction Cycle

To identify "Addiction" dynamics at work, use the "Shifting the Burden" archetype as a diagnostic to ask questions such as: "What was the addiction responding to?" "Why did we feel a need to engage in this behavior or create this institution in the first place?" and "What are the problem symptoms that we were responding to?"

"Addiction" structures can be much more difficult to reverse than "Shifting the Burden" because they are more deeply ingrained. Just as you can't cure alcoholism by simply removing the alcohol, you can't attempt a frontal assault on an organizational addiction because it is so rooted in what else is going on in the company.

If your company is addicted to fire-fighting, declaring that there will be no more heroics may be the worst thing you can do. If heroics were the only way your organization knew how to release the accumulated pressures produced by ineffective processes, ending that practice may lead to an eventual explosion or systemic breakdown. To break the addictive pattern, you need to explore what it is about the organizational system that created the crisis and left fire-fighting as the only option.

Innovation

Is there such a thing as a benign or innocuous addiction? One could argue that some addictions are worse than others, and some may not be bad at all. The fundamental problem with *any* addictive behavior, however, is that it can lead an organization to become very myopic. The addictive solution becomes so ingrained that no other possibility seems necessary. Preventing corporate addictions requires the ability to continually see choices in a fresh way—to shun habitual responses.

The challenge for the learning organization is to get all the members of the organization to continually look at things with fresh eyes. That's the essence of discovery...and the essence of innovation.

Hooked on Heroics

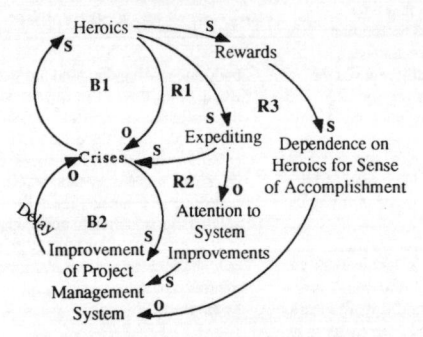

Crises can be solved either through short-term "heroics" (B1) or long-term improvements in management systems (B2). "Crisis management" tactics such as expediting projects not only propagate more crises, but they also take attention away from fundamental system improvements (loops R1 and R2). Over time, managers can become "hooked" on heroics to give them a sense of accomplishment in an otherwise disempowering situation (R3).

Toolbox

Balancing Loops with Delays: Teeter-Tottering on Seesaws

Most of us have played on a seesaw at one time or another and can recall the up and down motion as the momentum shifted from one end to the other. The more equal the weights of both people, the smoother the ride. At a very basic level, a free market economy is a lot like a seesaw with supply at one end and demand on the other end. Prices indicate the imbalance between the two, like a needle positioned at the pivot point of the seesaw.

The goal of a seesaw ride is to always keep things in a state of imbalance (it would be pretty boring to sit on a perfectly balanced one). But the goal in the marketplace is exactly the opposite—to bring supply in balance with demand. Unfortunately, the supply and demand balancing process feels a lot more like a seesaw ride than a smooth adjustment to a stable equilibrium. As shown in a causal loop diagram, the dynamics of this adjustment process are produced by two balancing loops that try to stabilize on a particular price. But the process is complicated by the presence of significant delays.

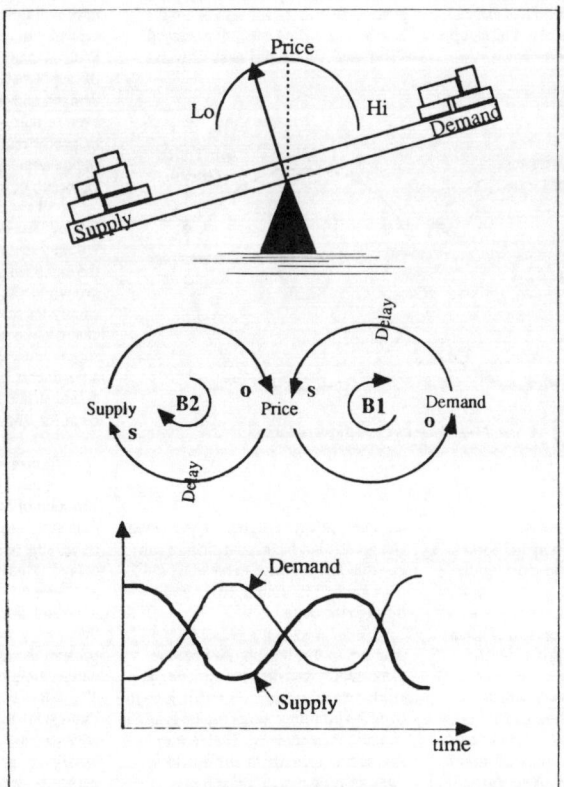

A free market economy is a lot like a see-saw with supply at one end and demand on the other. The dynamics that result from trying to balance supply and demand are produced by two balancing loops that try to stabilize on a particular price. Due to the presence of significant delays, a cycle of overshoot and collapse occurs.

Balancing Supply and Demand

Tracing through the loops we see that if demand rises, price tends to go up (all else remaining the same), and as price goes up, demand tends to go down (Cabbage Patch dolls notwithstanding). If there is enough inventory or capacity in the system to absorb the increased demand, prices may not go up immediately. As demand outstrips supply, however, price will rise.

On the supply side of the seesaw, an increase in price provides a profit incentive for firms to produce more. Of course, it takes time for firms to expand. The length of the delay depends on how close they already are to full capacity and how quickly they can add additional capacity to produce more. Hiring new workers may only take a few days while obtaining additional capital equipment or factory floor space may take months or even years. While firms are making supply adjustments, the gap between supply and

Toolbox

demand widens and price goes even higher. The higher price spurs companies to increase their production plans even more.

As supply eventually expands and catches up with demand, price begins to fall. By this time, firms have overexpanded their production capacity and supply overshoots demand, causing price to fall. When the price falls low enough, the product becomes more attractive again and demand picks up, starting the cycle all over again.

buying rates in the industry, the total number of airplanes is expected to increase by 50% over the next five years. But in the meantime air traffic growth has been slowing during the last three years. The leasing companies, however, do not seem too worried.

According to the article, "eight years of unbroken prosperity have created the illusion that many cyclical businesses aren't cyclical any longer." But, as one airline executive warned, "This is a cyclical business. Always

airplane orders. Since airplanes take many months to build, the supply of leasable airplanes did not adjust right away, making lease rates go even higher. This led to higher profits which attracted more capital which was plowed into even more orders for airplanes.

As the supply catches up to demand, however, the airplane lease rates will fall (the slowing of air traffic growth will accelerate this process). With so many airplanes in the pipeline, the supply will begin to outstrip demand and drive lease rates down even further. This will put a squeeze on profits and force marginal firms out of business. Some orders will be canceled; others will be renegotiated.

All the pieces of the airline leasing industry seem to be operating within a seesaw structure. Although the extended period of air traffic growth has kept demand ahead of supply for several years, it has not changed the nature of the delays in the supply line. When the supply adjustments bring the seesaw back down, airline leasing companies could be in for a bumpy landing.

A causal loop diagram of the airplane leasing industry shows the same seesaw structure at work.

Airplanes on Seesaws

The supply and demand seesaw is played out in all but the most tightly regulated markets. A good example of this balancing act is described in a recent *Forbes* article entitled "Fasten seat belts, please" (April 2, 1990), about airplane leasing companies.

Leasing companies, which account for roughly 20% of all commercial jet aircraft currently on order, have enjoyed enormous profits during the latest boom in air travel. One carrier alone has put in an order to lease 500 planes. Based on leasing and

has been, always will be. With a small change in load factor, the airlines can go from spilling cash to bleeding red ink like the Mississippi River going through the delta."

If we draw out a causal loop diagram of this industry, we see the same supply and demand structure at work. An increase in air traffic growth over the past three years fueled a strong demand for airplanes. That in turn sparked an increase in airplane lease rates as airlines scrambled for additional airlines. The high lease rates led to increased profits and a surge in

Summary

In this *Toolbox*, we focused on a variation of one of the basic feedback loop structures covered in the last issue—the balancing loop—with delays. This structure is at once simple and complex: simple, because it seems to be an innocuous single loop structure that is easy to comprehend; complex because the resulting behavior is neither simple nor easily predictable. The delays in a typical system are rarely consistent or well-known in advance, and the cumulative effects are usually beyond the control of any one person or firm.

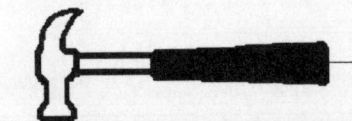

Toolbox
Drifting Goals: The "Boiled Frog" Syndrome

It's becoming an old story in the systems thinking field: If you drop a frog into a pot of boiling water, he will immediately hop out and save himself. But, if you put him in a pot of lukewarm water and slowly turn up the heat, something different happens. The frog swims around contentedly for a while, even enjoying the balmy water. As the temperature rises, however, he becomes more groggy and lethargic until finally, he dies.

The frog may not have known it, but he was a victim of a drifting goals scenario. "Drifting Goals" is a structure that leads to poorer and poorer performance and/or lower and lower expectations (or in the frog's case, higher and higher temperature). In a company setting, this structure may take the form of slipped delivery schedules, where a once-intolerable eight-week delivery delay becomes the accepted goal; or lower quality standards, as everyone focuses on decreasing backlogs and delivery delays by just getting the product "out the door."

Making adjustments to initial goals is not inherently wrong. Sticking to the original goal purely for its own sake is as misdirected as changing the goal at every whim. But distinguishing between legitimate goal adjustments and the "Drifting Goals" structure can be very difficult—it is easy to rationalize adjustments as "needed corrections."

The Boiled Frog Structure

The archetype works in the following manner (see "Drifting Goals Template" diagram). There is a certain goal—implicit or explicit—which is compared to the current state of affairs. If a gap persists, corrective actions are taken to improve the current state and bring it in line with the goal. This forms the basic balancing loop (B1) at the heart of any system that strives for equilibrium. A delay between corrective action and actual state represents the fact that results may take from minutes to years to materialize, depending on the specific situation.

Of course, there is more than one way to close the gap. In the "Drifting Goals" archetype, a second balancing loop is driven by pressure to lower the goal. As the gap increases (or persists over a period of time), the pressure to lower the goal increases. If the pressure is high and persistent, the goal may be lowered, thereby decreasing the gap (loop B2). The critical difference between the two loops is that lowering the goal immediately closes the gap, whereas corrective actions usually take time.

In the frog's case, the goal is a desired body temperature. If the gap between this desired temperature and the water temperature is large, the frog will immediately take a corrective action and jump out of the water. But, if the temperature increases gradually, the gap between his ideal temperature and the water temperature widens slowly. As this happens, the frog's perceived desired temperature may gradually drift higher. This closes the gap between desired and actual temperature, negating the need to take corrective action until it is too late.

The reason drifting goals is labeled the "boiled frog" syndrome is that goals, like the frog's ideal temperature, tend to drift slowly and usually go unnoticed. Similar to the frog that doesn't recognize a gradual rise in temperature, organizations are often unalarmed by deteriorating performance if it occurs over a long period of time.

Budget Deficits, Drifting Goals

The federal budget deficit is a good example of the "Drifting Goals" archetype at work (see "Budget Deficit" diagram). If there is a gap between the previously stated acceptable deficit level and the actual deficit, it can be closed by either reducing government spending (B3) or increasing tax revenues (B4). Bipartisan compromises, however, have usually resulted in *increased* government spending, mixed results in terms of taxes, and, consequently, higher deficits. The rising deficits created an intolerable gap between the actual and stated maximum acceptable deficit, creating pressure to raise deficit targets, and eventually resulting in higher maximum acceptable deficits (B5).

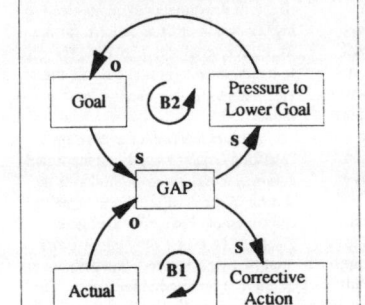

Drifting Goals Template

In a Drifting Goals archetype, a gap between the goal and current reality can be resolved by taking corrective action (B1) or lowering the goal (B2).

Toolbox

The Gramm-Rudman-Hollings bill (GRH) was seen as the answer to the growing budget deficit. By making deficit reductions a law, it was intended to force bipartisan cooperation to eliminate deficit spending. If GRH target numbers are not met, mandatory cuts go into effect, indiscriminately cutting billions of dollars from federal government programs and services. The GRH targets were meant to set a standard that lay outside of the current deficit-reinforcing system—a standard that would not succumb to the internal pressures.

In an article in *Barron's* magazine ("Rudman on Gramm-Rudman" July 16, 1990), Senator Rudman reacted to pressures to lower the goal by suggesting that GRH targets may be changed as "long as they are accompanied by a major deficit reduction." Rudman's new proposal would re-introduce GRH targets into the very drifting goals archetype it was intended to change (B6).

Using the Archetype

Drifting performance figures usually are a quick clue that this dynamic is occurring and that real corrective actions necessary to meet the targets are not being taken. It may also mean current targets are being set more by past levels of performance than by some absolute standard (zero defects) or by something outside of the system (customer requirements).

The flipside is also true: a steady pattern of improvement can mean that the goal is continually being adjusted upwards. Total Quality (TQ), Kaizen, and other continuous improvement efforts are examples of the "Drifting Goals" structure being used in a positive manner to drive goals higher.

The "Quality Improvement" diagram provides a useful framework for applying the "Drifting Goals" structure to other organizational issues. The lower loop (B7) represents improvements, while the upper loop (B8) represents ever-present pressures to lower the goal. TQ works well, in part, due to the reinforcing loop (R1): improvements in quality lead to higher customer expectations, raising the quality goal and increasing the gap. In a company committed to TQ, this gap leads to further quality improvements.

A critical aspect of evaluating a "Drifting Goals" scenario in an organization is to determine what drives the setting of the goal(s). In the "Quality Improvement" diagram, the Quality Goal can be affected by competitors' quality, by customers' expectations of quality, or by internal pressures. The relative strength of each potential influence will determine whether the quality will drift up, down, or oscillate. Goals located outside the system, like the original GRH targets, will be less susceptible to drifting goals pressures.

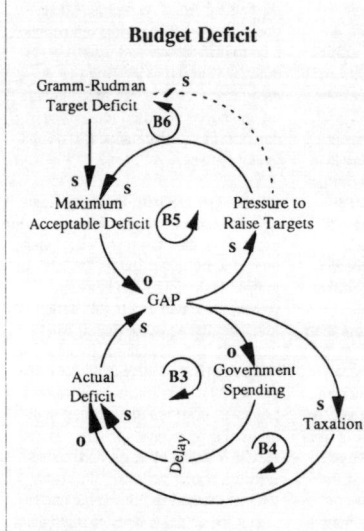

Budget Deficit

Rudman's new proposal would re-introduce GRH targets into the very drifting goals situation it was intended to change (B6).

Quality Improvement

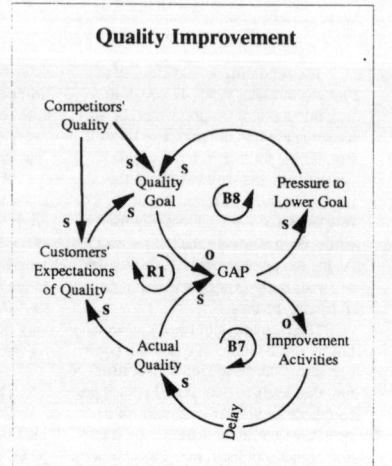

In a quality improvement scenario, the quality goal can be affected by competitors' quality, customers' expectations of quality, or internal pressures.

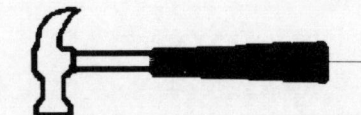

Toolbox
Escalation: The Dynamics of Insecurity

Have you ever been caught in a situation where you felt that things were going well beyond what you intended, but you felt powerless to stop it? As a child, perhaps, in the playground at school—a classmate makes a snide comment, and you counter with a sharp retort. The next round of insults gets uglier and louder. You each stick your neck out further and further with every remark. Classmates gather around and egg on the escalation of hostilities. Pretty soon, you are so far out on a limb that there is little else left to do but succumb to the chanting that has begun all around you—"Fight! Fight! Fight!"

The Dynamics of Insecurity

At the heart of an escalation dynamic are two (or more) parties, each of whom feels threatened by the actions of the other (see "Escalation Archetype"). Each side attempts to keep things under control by managing its own balancing process. Actions taken by A, for example, improve A's result relative to B. This decreases A's feeling of threat, so A eases off its activities (B1). B, on the other hand, now feels threatened by A's relative advantage and increases its activities in order to improve its result over A (B2). The interaction of the two parties trying to unilaterally maintain control produces a reinforcing spiral in which nobody feels in control.

In school, a few harsh words can quickly lead to a playground brawl. In a more deadly confrontation, the escalation structure can lead to catastrophic consequences. The Cuban Missile Crisis in October of 1962, for example, caught U.S. President Kennedy and Soviet Chairman Khrushchev in an escalation structure that led their countries to the brink of nuclear war.

The crisis began with the discovery of offensive nuclear weapons being constructed in Cuba—contrary to repeated public assurances by the Soviet chairman. The U.S. called for complete dismantling and withdrawal of the missiles. The Soviets first denied the existence of any such missiles. Then they acknowledged the missiles but refused to remove them, claiming they were defensive. Kennedy responded by ordering a naval blockade around Cuba to prevent more missiles from being shipped. Tensions were high. The Soviets pressed for accelerated construction of the missiles already in Cuba. The United States massed over 200,000 troops in Florida to prepare for an invasion.

When a United States U2 reconnaissance plane was shot down over Cuba, Kennedy's advisors unanimously proposed launching a retaliatory strike. But Kennedy stopped short. "It isn't the first step that concerns me," he said, "but both sides escalating to the fourth and fifth step. And we won't go to the sixth because there [will be] no one around to do so." Had Kennedy not broken the escalation structure at that juncture, the forces unleashed might have been beyond anyone's control to stop.

De-escalation

The Cuban missile crisis was one incident in a larger dynamic—the Cold

---

Escalation Archetype and Price Wars

In the "Escalation" archetype (top), one party takes actions that are perceived by the other as a threat. The other party responds in a like manner, increasing the threat to the first party, resulting in <u>more</u> threatening actions by the first party. The reinforcing loop is traced out by following the outline of the figure-8 produced by the balancing loops. In the case of the U.S./Soviet arms race (bottom), each country felt threatened by the arms stockpile of the other, leading to massive buildups in both countries.

Toolbox

War. Although that particular crisis was resolved, it did nothing to defuse the mutual distrust between the two countries, so the arms race continued (see "Arms Race" diagram). The balance of power shifted over time as each side built more arms in response to a perceived threat from the other. Yet, the very act of building arms to "balance" the situation only led to further threat, which strengthened the other side's "need" for even more arms.

It takes two to have an arms race, but only one to stop it. Unilateral action can break the escalation dynamic by robbing it of its legitimacy. If one side stops building arms, the source of threat diminishes, giving the other side less reason to invest in more arms. The escalation can then run in reverse. A recent newspaper headline, "Gorbachev escalates arms *cuts*," shows how the arms race is now being driven rapidly in reverse.

Wars on Many Fronts

Escalation dynamics, because they thrive in a competitive environment, are pervasive in business. The common logic is that whenever your competitor gains, you lose (and vice-versa). That logic leads to all kinds of "wars"—price wars, advertising wars, rebate and promotion wars, salary and benefit wars, labor and management wars, divisional wars, marketing vs. manufacturing department wars, and so on.

At the core of each of these wars is a set of relative measures that pits one group against another in a zero-sum game. In a typical price war, company A wants to "buy" market share by cutting its price (see "Price Wars"). As its sales and market share increase, B's market share decreases. B retaliates by slashing its prices, generating more sales for B at the expense of A's sales. In the short run, consumers may benefit from low prices. But in the long term, everyone may lose, since depressed prices mean less ability to invest in new product development, customer service, and overall attractiveness for the next round of competition.

Reversing or stopping such price wars is difficult. As competitors, A and B cannot collude to set prices. Nor is either company likely to stop unilaterally, since in the absence of other distinguishing features, the market usually favors the one with the lower price. In the heat of battle, a company can easily get locked into one competitive variable, such as price, and neglect to emphasize other strengths. Texas Instruments learned that lesson the hard way. Even though Texas Instruments had a superior technical product, it had to write off its entire personal computer business (the TI99/4A) as a result of a vicious price war with Commodore.

Insecurity

As the term "threat" suggests, the escalation archetype is about insecurity. In our playground example, the name-calling threatens our reputation and makes us insecure about our identity. The Cuban Missile Crisis and the arms race threatened the national security of both countries. Engaging in a price war reveals each company's insecurity about its ability to hold on to customers on a basis other than price.

If you find yourself caught in an escalation dynamic, drawing out the archetype can help you gain some perspective. The following questions are useful for identifying escalation structures. With advance knowledge, you can design strategies around them or use them to your advantage:

• Who are the parties whose actions are perceived as threats?

• What is being threatened, and what is the source of that threat?

• What is the relative measure that pits one party against the other—and can you change it?

• What are the significant delays in the system that may distort the true nature of the threat?

• Can you identify a larger goal that will encompass the individual goals?

• What are the deep-rooted assumptions that lie beneath the actions taken in response to the threat?

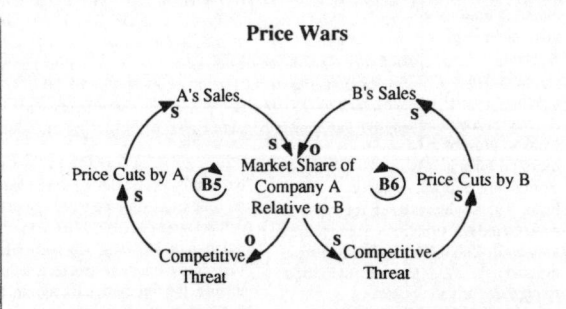

Price Wars

In a price war, company A slashes its price in order to gain market share (B5). This poses a threat to company B, who then retaliates by cutting its price (B6). The result is a zero-sum game for all involved: companies will have less revenue to invest in new products and customer service, and customers will ultimately feel the effects of those cutbacks.

Toolbox

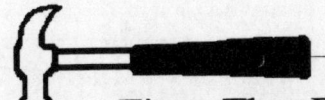

Fixes That Fail: Oiling the Squeaky Wheel— Again and Again...

How many times have you heard the saying "the squeaky wheel gets the oil?" Most people agree that whoever or whatever makes the most "noise" grabs our attention and will presumably be attended to first. The problem with following this adage is that it leads to operating in a reactive mode, continually "fighting fires" rather than making fundamental improvements.

To make matters worse, in our haste to grab the oil, we often mistakenly pick up a can of water and splash it on the squeaky wheel. The squeaking stops momentarily, only to return more loudly as the air and water join forces to rust the joint. We can stay very busy running about splashing water on all the squeaky wheels. But when there are finally no more squeaks, we may discover that instead of having fixed all the problems, we have encased the wheels in rust.

Better before Worse

In our search for the quick fix, we often rush into "solutions" without taking the time to understand the full impact of our actions. One of the tricky things about systems is that they usually point our attention toward short-term fixes and away from fundamental solutions.

In a typical "Fixes that Fail" situation (see "'Fixes that Fail' Template"), a problem symptom cries out (squeaks) for resolution. A solution is quickly implemented that alleviates the symptom (loop B1). The relief is usually temporary, however, and the symptom returns, often worse than before. This happens because there are unintended consequences of the solution that unfold over a long period of time (loop R1) or as an accumulated consequence of repeatedly applying the solution.

In the case of the squeaky wheel, the noise attracts our attention and we grab the nearest (easiest, most available, previously used, organizationally accepted, etc.) "fix" we can get our hands on and apply it. In the short term, even water will act as a lubricant and stop the squeaking. If we do not know anything about oxidation, we might assume that the water did, in fact, solve the squeaking problem. As the water evaporates and the metal oxidizes, however, the wheel begins to squeak again. So we reach for the water again, since it worked the last time.

Of course we all know that oil or grease, not water, should be used to lubricate a squeaky wheel. But suppose the squeaky wheel is a customer screaming for a product that is two weeks late—how do we know whether we are applying the oil or the water when we respond? Do we understand enough about this situation's "chemical reaction" to take appropriate actions? Or, in our frenzy of fighting fires and oiling squeaky wheels, are we throwing oil on fires and applying water to the wheels?

Expediting Customer Orders

Expediting customer orders, a common practice in many manufacturing firms, illustrates the "Fixes that Fail" archetype. A large semiconductor manufacturer, for example, is experiencing some

"Fixes that Fail" Template

In a typical "Fixes that Fail" situation, a problem symptom cries out for resolution. A solution is quickly implemented that alleviates the symptom (B1), but the unintended consequences of the "fix" exacerbate the problem (R1). Over time (right), the problem symptom returns to its previous level or becomes worse (dotted line).

Toolbox

production problems and is running behind schedule on some shipments. They know if their customers do not receive their orders on time, the customers literally will have to shut down their production lines until they receive the chips. So what happens?

Company A calls and demands that its chips be delivered immediately. The semiconductor company responds by assigning an expediter to track down A's order and push it through the line (see "Expediting Customer Orders"). Of course it's not simply a matter of finding one item and escorting it to the loading docks. The company produces over a hundred different kinds of integrated circuits, and Company A has many different types on order. What's worse, the production steps from silicon wafers to final packaged circuits can number 50 or more. Finding and expediting A's order may mean wading through the entire factory and causing disruptions throughout the production line. Finally Company A's order is rushed through, resulting in a satisfied customer (loop B2).

But no sooner has A's order left the warehouse when company B calls demanding to receive *its* orders immediately, and the process begins all over again. At the same time, somebody *else* is expediting for company C. The squeaky wheels are getting oiled, but the number of squeaking wheels is rapidly increasing. As a result, the production line is continually being disrupted—leading to more missed delivery dates and more customer calls (loop R2).

New Product Releases

Similarly, in a consumer electronics company, when one new product development project is in danger of missing its release date, resources are often diverted from other projects to give it a final "push." The product is released, but at a much higher cost. And as a result of all the shifting around, all the other neglected projects are more likely to need the same extra "push" in order to finish them on time.

Both in the semiconductor company and the electronics company, the quickest solution was to attend to each crisis as it happened. The specific problems were resolved, but at what expense?—a guarantee of more problems in the future.

Using the Archetype

In most instances of "Fixes That Fail," people are usually aware of the negative consequences of applying a quick fix. But the pain of not doing something right away is often more real and immediate than the delayed negative effects. If the long-term/short-term tradeoff was indeed one-for-one, where solving one problem today would create another one tomorrow, this strategy might be tolerable. But the reinforcing nature of unintended consequences ensures that tomorrow's problems will multiply faster than today's solutions.

Breaking the "Fixes that Fail" cycle usually requires two actions: acknowledging up front that the fix is merely alleviating a symptom, and making a commitment to solve the real problem now. Launching a two-pronged attack of applying the fix *and* planning out the fundamental solution will help ensure that you don't get caught in a perpetual cycle of solving yesterday's "solutions."

Expediting Customer Orders

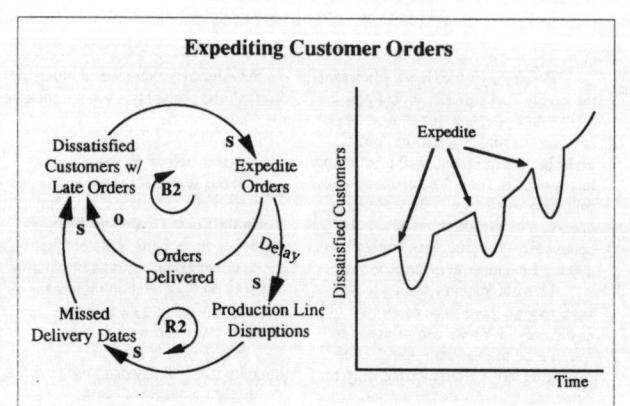

Expediting a late order ensures that the order will be processed immediately, reducing the number of dissatisfied customers (B2). But the product line disruptions that can result will lead to more missed delivery dates and, ultimately, more unhappy customers (R2).

Toolbox

Growth and Underinvestment: Is Your Company Playing with a Wooden Racket?

Do you recall the first time you picked up a tennis racket? Perhaps it was an old wooden racket you found in your garage, or one a friend had outgrown. You weren't really sure you had it "in you" to play—you didn't even know if you would like the sport. But you tried playing a couple of games a week with the beat-up racket, picking up some of the basic moves and even sustaining a volley for a few rounds. After a month or so, however, you couldn't seem to improve your play beyond a certain level.

If you were a *little* bit better, you might have been willing to invest in a new high-performance racket. But you decide that tennis is really not for you. Besides, another friend has just given you a pair of ski boots. They're a little beat up and a bit tight at the toes, but then again you don't know whether you'll like skiing....

Growth and Underinvestment

The above scenario is an example of the "Growth and Underinvestment" archetype at work. At its core is a reinforcing loop that drives the growth of a performance indicator and a balancing force which opposes that growth (loops R1 and B1 in "Growth and Underinvestment Archetype"). An additional loop (B2) links performance to capacity investments, and shows how deteriorating performance can justify underinvesting in capacity needed to *lift* the limit to growth. This propensity to underinvest in the face of growth makes "Growth and Underinvestment" a special case of the "Limits to Success" archetype (see p. 19 "Limits to Success: When the 'Best of Times' Becomes the 'Worst of Times'").

In the tennis example, the reinforcing process is practice, which improves performance (loop R1 in "Practice Makes Perfect?"). Improvement slows, however, as you reach the point at which the equipment limits your ability (loop B1). If your decision to purchase better equipment is dependent on your past performance, you may fall victim to this archetype. Without investing in better equipment, your performance will likely plateau—or even decline as you become frustrated and spend less time practicing. The result then justifies your decision not to invest in a new racket.

Legacy of the Past

Often in a "Growth and Underinvestment" situation, ghosts of past failures remain as a systemic legacy, influencing current decisions. A classic example is the story of a capital equipment manufacturer. The company's CEO had seen an industry downturn in which the company had been saddled with too much capacity, so he was cautious about expanding. The company's product was selling well, however, and a backlog began to pile up—three months' worth of orders, then four, then five. The CEO continued to believe that it was just a temporary spurt. When the backlog grew to six months, he finally agreed to expand production capacity.

It took about a year and a half for the additional capacity to come on-line. In the meantime, demand trailed off as people found alternative sources. The company gradually worked off the backlog, and orders started to pick up again. After a couple of years they were in a similar backlog, but the CEO was even more reluctant to invest in new capacity because of what appeared to be a continual cycle of growing and falling demand.

The "Growth and Underinvestment" archetype reveals that the company's slow response may actually

Growth and Underinvestment Archetype

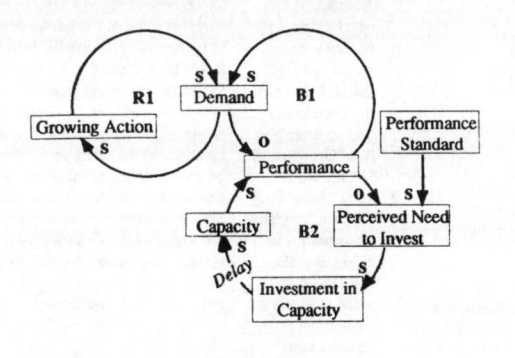

"*Growth and Underinvestment*" has at its core a "*Limits to Success*" archetype (loops R1 and B1). The additional loop (B2) shows how deteriorating performance can justify underinvesting in the very capacity that is needed to forestall the limit to growth.

have created the cyclical demand. The reinforcing action of marketing activities, coupled with the balancing action of delivery delays, trace out a "Limits to Success" archetype in which the limit is production capacity (loops R1 and B1 in "Capacity Delays and Underinvestment"). As performance declined relative to performance standards, the perceived need to invest increased, until investments were finally made (loop B2).

Because of the delay in capacity coming on-line, however, delivery performance continued to decline for a while, hurting new orders. In the meantime, deliveries began to increase and the company crawled out of backlog. This led the CEO once again to question the need to invest in capacity, making him even more conservative the next time they were in a backlog situation.

Downward Spiral

If this dynamic continues through many cycles, customers are not likely to keep coming back. The result may be a downward spiral of cutting back on investments: the two balancing loops lock into a figure eight dynamic in which the effects of the reinforcing loop no longer have much impact on growth, while the combined balancing loops create a counter-reinforcing process of continual cutbacks. As demand goes down, delivery performance goes back up, creating less need for capacity investments. If capacity dips below the level needed to service incoming orders, performance will go down again, reducing demand even further. Perceived need to invest will decrease, so investments will drop, leading to even less capacity over time (as older equipment depreciates or is taken off-line). Thankfully, the reverse situation can also be true: the two balancing loops can trace out a reinforcing loop that continues to expand demand and performance.

Breaking the Cycle

To determine whether a "Growth and Underinvestment" structure is at work, start by looking for patterns of oscillations in customer demand. If you overlay that with capacity investments and find that they follow the same pattern, you're probably in a "Growth and Underinvestment" situation.

If a company waits until it receives signals from the marketplace to invest in capacity, it may be too late to prevent some fall-off

Capacity Delays and Underinvestment

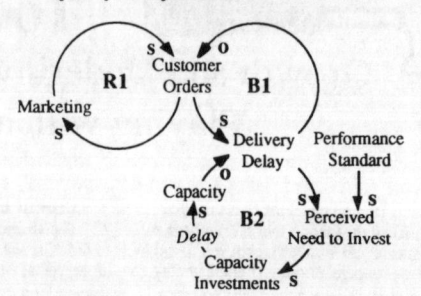

Marketing efforts produce more customer orders (R1)—but increasing demand also causes a longer delivery delay (B1). As the delay increases, the company realizes its need for capacity investment. However, delays in implementation further lengthen the delivery delay (B2) and in the end, affect future customer orders.

Practice Makes Perfect?

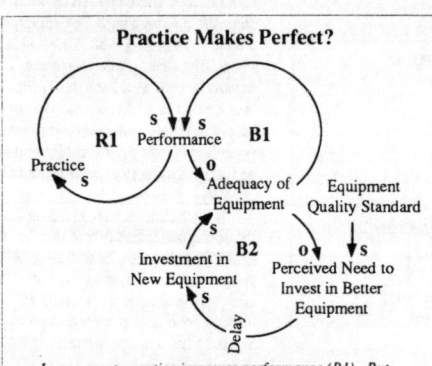

In any sport, practice improves performance (R1). But performance is also affected by the adequacy of equipment (B1). If performance is not improving or actually decreases, the perceived need to invest in new equipment also decreases, leading to underinvestment which further affects performance (B2).

in demand that will result because of the delay between investment decisions and capacity coming on-line. The key is to develop a way of assessing capacity needs relative to demands *before* the performance indicator starts to suffer.

Take some time early in the growth phase to determine what the limits may be, especially with respect to capacity. Studying the market response and characteristics of your target customers during an upswing can help you anticipate future capacity needs.

Also make sure internal systems are set up to deal with growth: if you have an aggressive growth strategy but a sluggish internal system for responding to performance shortfalls, then you might have created a structural inability to handle continued growth.

Most importantly, explore the assumptions driving your capacity investment decisions. Past performance may be a consideration, but it should not dominate your decisions. Instead, identify the marketplace factors that are driving growth. Otherwise you may end up with investment decisions that are too dependent on past experience and not on present (and future) needs.

Toolbox
Limits to Success: When the "Best of Times" Becomes the "Worst of Times"

"It was the best of times, it was the worst of times, it was the age of wisdom, it was the age of foolishness..." wrote Charles Dickens in *A Tale of Two Cities*. Life often seems full of such paradoxes. When we are busy earning lots of money, we have little time to enjoy it. When we do have time available, it seems we don't have much money to spend. A rapidly growing company finds itself too busy to invest its profits in internal development, but when sales begin to slow, it no longer has the resources (money and people) to spend on needed improvements. The "best of times" for investing in resource development always seems like the "worst of times" for actually carrying out such plans, and vice-versa.

The Structure

Recognizing this paradox can help individuals and companies avoid the "Limits to Success" trap. In a typical scenario (see "Limits to Success Template"), a system's performance continually improves as a direct result of certain efforts. As performance increases, the efforts are redoubled, leading to even further improvement (loop R1). When the performance begins to plateau, the natural reaction is to increase the same efforts that led to past gains. But the harder one pushes, the harder the system seems to push back: it has reached some limit or resistance which is preventing further improvements in the system (loop B1). The real leverage in a "Limits to Success" scenario doesn't lie in pushing on the "engines of growth," but in finding and eliminating the factor(s) that are limiting success while you still have time and money to do so.

In a rapidly-growing company, for example, initial sales are spurred by a successful marketing program. As sales continue to grow, the company redoubles its marketing efforts and sales rise even further. But after a point, pushing harder on the marketing has less and less effect on sales—the company has hit some limit, such as market saturation or production capacity. To continue its upward path, the company may need to invest in new production capacity or explore new markets.

Diets and Weight Loss

Examples abound where rapid success is followed by a slowdown or decline in results. Dieters usually find that losing the first ten pounds is a lot easier than losing the last two, and losing weight the first time around is a lot easier than losing it the next time.

On a diet, eating less leads to weight loss, which encourages the person to continue to eat less (loop R2 in the "Dieting Bind" diagram). But, over time, the body adjusts to the lower intake of food by lowering the rate at which it burns the calories. Eventually the weight loss slows or even stops. The limit here is the body's metabolic rate—how fast it will burn the food. To continue losing weight, the person needs to increase the metabolic rate by combining exercise with dieting.

But pushing equally hard on exercising isn't the full answer either, since intense exercise burns simple sugars and not the stored fat that is the real tar-

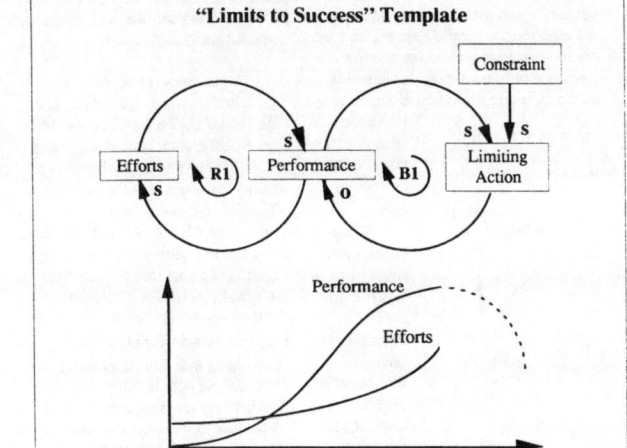

"Limits to Success" Template

In a "Limits to Success" scenario, continued efforts initially lead to improved performance. Over time, however, the system encounters a limit which causes the performance to slow down or even decline (B1). Once the system has hit a limit, performance begins to level off (or "crash"), even as efforts continue to rise (bottom).

Toolbox

get for weight loss. Intense exercise is counterproductive towards the dieter's goal because it *increases* appetite while only temporarily raising the metabolism. The real leverage is to engage in steady exercise such as long, brisk walks that will increase the metabolic rate to a permanently higher level.

Service Capacity Limit

People Express airlines is one of the best-known casualties of the "Limits to Success" archetype (see "'Flying' People Express Again," November, 1990). Its tremendous growth was fueled by a rapid expansion of fleet and routes along with unheard-of low airfares. As the fleet capacity grew, People Express was able to carry more passengers and boost revenues, allowing it to expand fleet capacity even more (loop R3). The quality of its service was initially very good, so the positive experience of many fliers increased word-of-mouth advertising and the number of passengers.

The "engine of growth" at People Express was its physical capacity—expanding fleet size, employees and routes. But its "limit to success" was service capacity—the ability to invest time and money in training its employees—which became more difficult to sustain as the company grew (loop R4).

The number of passengers eventually outstripped the airline's capacity to provide good service. As a result, quality suffered and it began losing passengers (loop B3). When competitors began matching low rates on selected routes, People Express' market competitiveness suffered even more. Focusing only on the reinforcing side of the structure turned rapid growth into a tailspin, contributing to the airline's demise.

Simply hiring more employees was not the answer to People Express' service capacity problems. Similar to the dieter's reliance on intense exercise, it only masked the real need for the steady long-term commitment to hire and train the necessary people to bring service quality up to a high and sustainable level.

Using the Archetype

The "Limits to Success" archetype should not be seen as a tool to be applied only when something "stalls out." It is most helpful when it is used in advance to see how the *cumulative* effects of continued success might lead to future problems. When the times are good and everything is growing rapidly, we tend to operate with an "if it ain't broke, don't fix it" attitude. By the time something breaks, however, it may be too late to apply a fix.

Using the "Limits to Success" template can help highlight potential problems by raising questions such as "what kind of pressures are building in the organization as a result of the growth?" By tracing through their implications, you can then plan for ways to release those pressures *before* an organizational gasket blows.

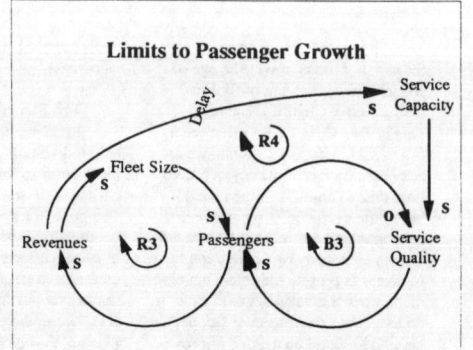

Limits to Passenger Growth

At People Express, physical capacity—fleet size, routes, and employees—were seen as the "engine of growth" (R3). The limit to that growth was its service capacity (R4).

The Dieting Bind

On a diet, an individual's metabolic rate becomes the limiting factor for weight loss. The leverage point lies in boosting the metabolism to a permanently higher level through slow, steady exercise.

Toolbox

Shifting the Burden: The "Helen Keller" Loops

Most of us know the story of Helen Keller and have probably sympathized with her and her parents, whose actions to protect their handicapped daughter seemed not only compassionate but necessary. After all, how could a blind and deaf child ever be expected to take care of herself? But if it had not been for the determined efforts of her teacher, Ann Sullivan, who refused to let Helen's handicaps prevent her from becoming self-reliant, Helen probably never would have achieved her real potential. She went on to graduate from Radcliffe College and become an author as well as spokesperson and role model for many of the nation's handicapped.

Helen Keller's story is much more than an inspirational human interest story; it illustrates a pervasive dynamic that is rooted in an archetypal structure. The well-intentioned actions of her parents shifted the burden of responsibility for Helen's welfare to them. Every problem or failure on Helen's part brought the parents rushing to her aid. Helen learned that no matter what she did, her parents would accommodate her. And each incident reinforced her parents' belief that she was indeed helpless. All three were caught in a system that was eroding Helen's ability (and desire) to cope with the world and shifting the responsibility for her well-being to her parents.

The Structure

The basic structure of this archetype is shown in the diagram labeled "Shifting the Burden Template." The archetype usually begins with a problem symptom that prompts someone to intervene and "solve" it. The solution (or solutions) that are obvious and immediately implementable usually relieve the problem symptom very quickly. But these symptomatic solutions have two specific negative effects. First, they divert attention away from the real or fundamental source of the problem. More subtly, symptomatic solutions cause the viability of the fundamental solution to deteriorate over time, reinforcing the perceived need for more of the symptomatic solution.

In the Helen Keller story, her parents' intervention is the symptomatic solution, Helen's failure to cope with real world is the problem symptom, the development of Helen's own abilities to care for herself is the fundamental solution, and the side effect is that her parents assume increasing responsibility for her well-being. This particular type of "Shifting the Burden" structure, in which responsibility is shifted to a third party, is known as "Shifting the Burden to the Intervener." Over time, the role of the

Shifting The Burden Template

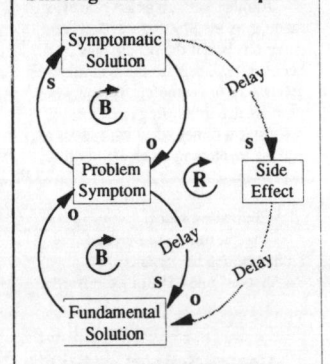

In the "Shifting the Burden" Template, a problem symptom is "solved" by applying a symptomatic solution which diverts attention away from a more fundamental solution.

Shifting the Burden Examples

Problem Symptom	Symptomatic Solution	Fundamental Solution	Side Effect(s)
Slow/declining revenue growth	Increased Marketing	New Products	Diverts resources away from R&D; increased reliance on marketing
Bank Failures	FDIC, FSLIC	Prudent Banking Practices	Responsibility for protecting deposits is shifted to government
Employee Performance Problem	Manager "Provides" Solution	Necessary Training for Employee	Growing dependence on manager; decreasing confidence of employee
Low Self-Esteem	Drug Use	Invest time in personal development	Drug Addiction; further debilitation of personal development

Toolbox

intervener increases, until it becomes an essential part of the system. In Helen's case, her parents' actions reinforced the underdevelopment of her abilities and therefore strengthened their role as "protectors."

Another very common side effect that occurs in "Shifting the Burden" situations is that the person may become "addicted" to the symptomatic solution. For example, a person who turns to alcohol or drugs to boost his self-esteem or help deal with stress may end up developing an alcohol or drug dependency.

Central vs. Local

The "Shifting the Burden" archetype and its variants—"Addiction" and "Shifting the Burden to the Intervener"—comprise perhaps the single most pervasive systems structure. The diagram labeled "Central Support vs. Branch Capability" illustrates a classic example of this dynamic.

A claims office in a local branch of a large insurance company is faced with a large, complex claim that requires more expertise than it possesses. The central office responds by sending out its corps of experts who take care of the complex claim while the branch office goes about its other, more routine business. Although the occurrence of large claims may be infrequent—making it hard to justify keeping such experts in every branch—over time the interventions can result in deteriorating branch capability.

The reason is that after a while, an implicit operating norm develops that says if a person wants to handle complex, technically challenging claims she has to either join the central office or move to a different firm. Gradually, the most talented people take either of the two options. Unless these people can be replaced by equally capable adjusters, the talent of the branch office gradually erodes, making it rely even more on central support. The cycle is reinforcing— as the central staff becomes better at intervening, the branch seeks their help more often.

Using the Archetype

Templates—causal loop diagrams that trace out generic dynamic structures—serve as a useful guide for mapping out archetypes. The basic "Shifting the Burden" Template serves as a starting point, but templates are not meant to be rigid structures in which we must "fit" a specific case. Tracing out the fundamental solution in the Central vs. Local situation, for example, requires more than a single variable—"Branch attempts to settle claims," "Learning," and "Branch ability" are all part of the fundamental solution.

In theory, any one of the four elements of the template—problem symptom, symptomatic solution, side effect, and fundamental solution—can help us identify a "Shifting the Burden" structure at work. Side effects, however, are usually very subtle and difficult to detect from inside the system. Solutions such as alcohol use, increased marketing, oil imports, or federal insurance are more readily identified, but there may not be complete agreement on whether they are "symptomatic" or "fundamental." Identifying problem symptoms such as high stress, falling revenues, energy shortage, or bank failures (see "Table of Shifting the Burden Examples") is probably the easiest way to begin filling out a "Shifting the Burden" template.

Keeping in mind that the "rightness" of a solution depends on one's perspective, it can be helpful to ask whether we are seeing the situation from the parents', Helen Keller's, or Ann Sullivan's point of view. Examining a problem or issue from these different viewpoints can help us understand why a "Shifting the Burden" archetype is operating and discover a solution that is fundamental, not symptomatic.

Central Support vs. Branch Capability

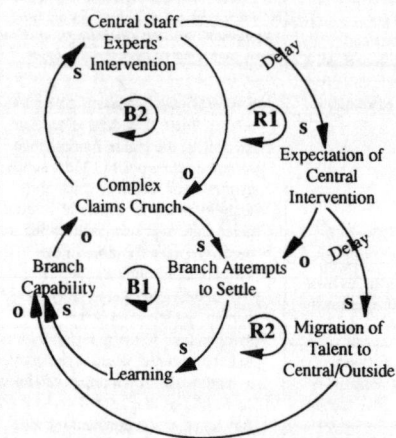

In this example of a "Shifting the Burden" archetype, the symptomatic problem is a complex claim that the branch cannot handle alone. Experts from the central office help out, but over time the branch's ability to handle difficult claims atrophies.

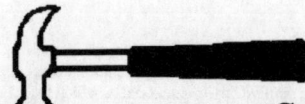

Toolbox
Success to the Successful: Self-Fulfilling Prophecies

Imagine you have two new direct reports, Stan and Frank. Both seem equally qualified—a degree from a good school, a couple of years of solid business experience, and youthful enthusiasm. You want to fill an upcoming opening in a management position, but you aren't quite sure which one is the best candidate. You want to be as objective as possible in your recommendation, so you decide to encourage both of them and see which one demonstrates the most ability.

After a couple of weeks, Stan has gotten a jump start on the latest assignment and is doing a stellar job. Frank was out with the flu, so when he comes back, he's a little bit behind. You keep your eye on him and continue to encourage him, but you really start to focus on Stan. Before you know it, you're giving him more and more responsibility, and he does exceedingly well each time. Frank is doing adequately, but for some reason, you just don't feel like he has that extra "umph." Since you already have a "hot one" on your hands, you feel it's not as necessary to invest as much time and energy in him.

In time, you promote Stan into the management position and pat yourself on the back for having picked the right person from the beginning. Frank, in your assessment, turned out to be just an average performer. But is that really the case?

Self-Fulfilling Prophecies

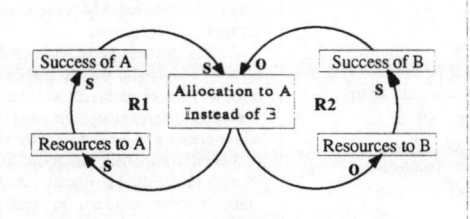

The "Success to the Successful" archetype suggests that success may depend as much on structural forces as innate ability or talent (see "Success to the Successful Template"). The performance of individuals or teams is often the result of the structure they are put in which forces them to compete for a limited resource such as a manager's time, a company's investments, or training facilities.

Assuming both groups (or individuals) are equally capable, if one person or group (A) is given more resources, it has a higher likelihood of succeeding than B. That initial success justifies devoting more resources to A and robs B of further resources (R1). As B gets less resources, its success diminishes, which further reinforces the "bet on the winner" allocation of resources (R2). The structure continues to reinforce the success of one, and the eventual demise of the other.

"Success to the Successful" is an archetypal case of self-fulfilling prophecies. The outcome of a situation is highly dependent on the initial conditions (or expectations) and whether they favor one party or the other. If B had received more resources in the beginning, the roles would be reversed: B's success would increase, and A would suffer.

In effect, our mental model of what we believe will determine success shapes the very success we seek to assess. In the case of Stan and Frank, the manager may not have had a strong feeling either way in the beginning. But initial events—Stan's success with the first project and Frank's illness—quickly became the shaper of his expectations and actions, reinforcing what he later believed to be an objective assessment that Stan was "right" for the job.

Balancing Work and Family

The tension between work and family is another example of the "Success to the Successful" archetype (see "Balancing Work and Family" diagram). We each have a certain amount of time and attention available. The more we devote to work, the more successful we may become, which fuels the desire to put more time into work (R3). A similar result occurs if we devote our energy to our family (R4). Most of us struggle to maintain a balance between the two.

Suppose, however, that a large project forces you to put in long hours

---

Success to the Successful Template

Success of A ← s → Allocation to A Instead of B ← s → Success of B
R1 / R2
Resources to A ← s o → Resources to B

The "Success to the Successful" archetype suggests that success may depend as much on structural forces as talent. If one person or group (A) is given more resources, it has a higher likelihood of succeeding than B (assuming their are equally capable). The initial success justifies devoting more resources to A than B (R1). As B gets less resources, its success diminishes, further justifying more resource allocations to A (R2).

Toolbox

at work for an extended period of time. The time away from the family begins to create tension at home. Your family complains that you are never around. But when you do come home, you get hit with all of the problems that have been accumulating. So you withdraw further from your family, devoting yourself even more to the project. Your work on the project is starting to generate interest throughout the company. At the same time that praise at work is building, the complaints at home are piling up, driving you further from your family. The two situations mutually feed each other—the downward spiral of one, and the upward spiral of the other.

Rewriting the Prophecies

The "Success to the Successful" archetype highlights how success can be determined by initial chance and how the structure can systematically eliminate the other possibilities that may have been equally viable (or even superior). If we are not conscious of being in this archetype, we become a victim of its structure, which continually pushes us to do whatever has been successful in the past. After a while, the choice between work and family doesn't seem like a choice anymore—the structure has determined the outcome.

As in most of the archetypes, managing a "Success to the Successful" situation requires looking at it from a more macro level and asking ourselves "what is the larger goal within which the situation is embedded?" In the case of work vs. family, a larger goal that includes both of them, such as, "I seek a balance between my success at work and time with my family," must guide the daily decisions. In the case of the two protégés, the goal might be to provide an environment in which the full potential of both employees can be developed. Without the guidance of a larger goal, the structure will continue to dictate your actions.

Creating Environments for Success

At the heart of the "Success to the Successful" archetype lies the competitive model of Western economies which is characterized by a win-lose philosophy. An implicit assumption of the competitive model is that whoever wins must, by default, be the best. In reality, however, it may not be the individuals, but the structure they are in that determines the "winner." The assumption here is that you need a competitive environment out of which the best candidates will somehow surface.

A fundamental question that the archetype begs us to ask is why put two groups or individuals into the structure in the first place? If we want a single "winner," why not put our energies towards understanding what it takes to develop such a winner? We can then focus our energy and resources on that person or project from the beginning rather than waste time, money, and morale by stringing along multiple people and projects. We can, in effect, lop off the other half of the "Success to the Successful" archetype. Instead of diverting resources and systematically letting other groups to fail, we can focus all our efforts and resources on finding ways to build a supportive environment for success.

A way to break out of the "Success to the Successful" archetype is to get rid of its competitive structure and find ways to make teams collaborators rather than competitors. Many Japanese companies, for example, often have multiple project teams working on the same design. Unlike American companies, however, the goal is *not* to compete against each other and have one team's design win. All of the teams are seen as part of the same larger effort to develop the best design for the company. The teams collaborate with each other, sharing ideas and information, and produce a design that may be a combination of innovations from each of the groups.

The "Success to the Successful" archetype highlights the need for creating a win-win environment where cooperation replaces competition and where creating an environment for success is more important than trying to identify successful individuals. In fact, that's what good academic institutions provide, and ultimately what good corporate environments should provide—an environment in which all their people can thrive and contribute their unique talents.

Balancing Work and Family

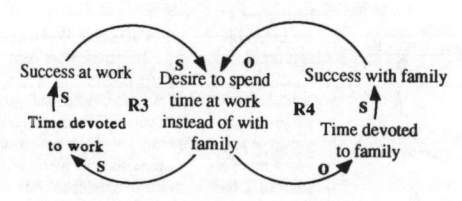

Success at work — s → Desire to spend time at work instead of with family — o → Success with family
↑s R3 R4 s↑
Time devoted to work ← s Time devoted to family ← o

If not carefully managed, the allocation of time between work and family can fall into a "Success to the Successful" trap. Extended time away from the family (due to a large project, for example) can create tension at home, making it more desirable to spend time at work. As job success and time at work continue to build, family relationships can suffer.

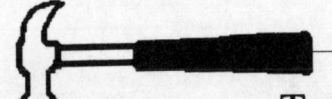

Toolbox
Tragedy of the Commons: All for One & None for All

Do you recall any hot summer days when you and your family decided to spend a relaxing day at the local swimming pool? You loaded up the car and arrived at the pool, only to discover that every other family had the same idea. So instead of the relaxing outing each family anticipated, everyone ended up spending a nerve-wracking day dodging running children and trying to cool off in a pool filled with wall-to-wall people. In many similar situations, people hoping to maximize individual gain end up diminishing the benefits for everyone involved. What was a great idea for each person or family becomes a collective nightmare for them all.

Individual Gain, Collective Pain

At the heart of the "Tragedy of the Commons" structure lies a set of reinforcing actions that make sense for each individual player to pursue (see "Tragedy of the Commons Template"). As each person continues his individual action, he gains some benefit. For example, each family heading to the pool will enjoy cooling off in the swimming area. If the activity involves a small number of people relative to the amount of "commons" (or pool space) available, each individual will continue to garner some benefit. However, if the amount of activity grows too large for the system to support, the commons becomes overloaded and everyone experiences diminishing benefits.

Traffic jams in L.A. are a classic example of how a "public" good gets overused and lessened in value for everyone. Each individual wishing to get to work quickly uses the freeway because it is the most direct route. In the beginning, each additional person on the highway does not slow down traffic because there is enough "slack" in the system to absorb the extra users. At some critical level, however, each additional driver brings about a decrease in the average speed. Eventually, there are so many drivers that traffic crawls at a snail's pace. Each person seeking to minimize driving time has in fact conspired to guarantee a long drive for everyone.

This structure also occurs in corporate settings all too frequently. A company with a centralized salesforce, for example, will suffer from the "Tragedy of the Commons" archetype as each autonomous division requests that more and more efforts be expended on its behalf. The division A people know that if they request "high priority" from the central sales support they will get a speedy response, so they label more and more of their requests as high priority. Division B, C, D, and E all have the same idea. The net result is that the central sales staff grows increasingly burdened by all the field requests and the net gains for each division are greatly diminished. The same story can be told about centralized engineering, training, maintenance, etc. In each case, either an implicit or explicit limit is keeping the resource constrained at a specific level, or the resource cannot be added fast enough to keep up with the demands.

Brazil's Inflation Game

When the shared commons is a small, localized resource, the consequences of a "Tragedy of the Commons" scenario are more easily contained. At a national level, however, the "Tragedy of the Commons" archetype can wreak havoc on whole economies. Take inflation in Brazil, for example. Their inflation was 367% in 1987, 933% in 1988, 1,764% in 1989, and 1,794% in 1990. With prices rising so rapidly, each seller expects inflation to continue, therefore seller B will raise his price to keep up with current inflation and hedge against future inflation.

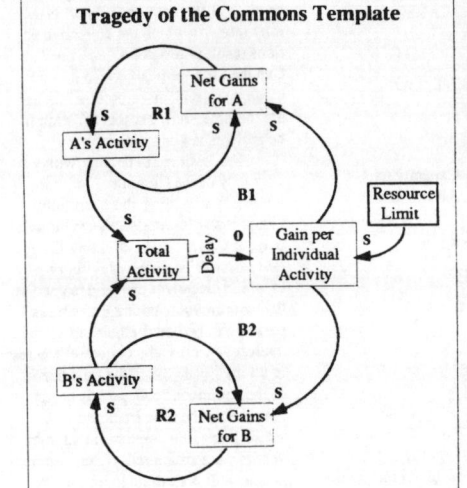

Tragedy of the Commons Template

In a "Tragedy of the Commons" structure, each person pursues actions which are individually beneficial (R1 & R2), but eventually result in a worse situation for everyone (B1 & B2).

🔨 Toolbox

With thousands of seller B's doing the same thing, inflation increases and reinforces expectations of continued inflation, leading to another round of price increases (R1 in "Brazil's Inflation 'Tragedy'").

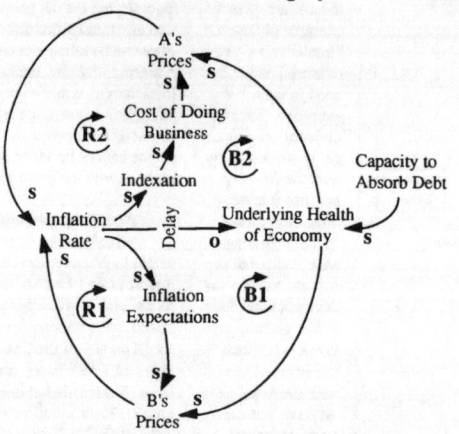

Inflation also leads to indexation of wages, which increases the cost of doing business. In response to rising business costs, Seller A raises her price, which fuels further inflation (R2). Since there are thousands of Seller A's doing the same thing, their collective action creates runaway inflation. The underlying health of the economy steadily weakens as the government and businesses perpetuate endless cycles of deficit spending to keep up with escalating costs. Over time, everyone grows increasingly preoccupied with using price increases to make profits rather than investing in ways to be more productive. Eventually the economy may collapse due to high debts and loss of global competitiveness, resulting in dramatic price adjustments (B1 & B2).

Common "Commons"

Perhaps the trickiest part of identifying a "Tragedy of the Commons" archetype at work is coming to some agreement on exactly what is the commons that is being overburdened. If no one sees how his or her individual action will eventually reduce everyone's benefits, the level of debate is likely to revolve around why individual A should stop doing what she is doing and why individual B is entitled to do what he is doing. Debates at that level are rarely productive because effective solutions for a "Tragedy of the Commons" situation never lie at the individual level.

In the sales force situation, for example, as long as each division defines the commons to include only its performance, there is little motivation for anyone to address the real issue—that the collective, not individual, action of each division vying for more sales support is at the heart of the problem. Only when there is general agreement that managing the commons requires coordinating everyone's actions can issues of resource allocation be settled equitably.

Managing the Commons

Identifying the commons is just the beginning. Other questions that help define the problem and identify effective actions include: What are the incentives for individuals to persist in their actions? Who, if anybody, controls the incentives? What is the time frame in which individuals reap the benefits of their actions? What is the time frame in which the collective actions result in losses for everyone? Can the long-term collective loss be made more real, more present? What are the limits of the resource? Can it be replenished or replaced?

The leverage in dealing with a "Tragedy of the Commons" scenario involves reconciling short-term individual rewards with long-term cumulative consequences. Evaluating the current reward system may highlight ways in which incentives can be designed so that coordination among the various parties will be both in their individual interest as well as the collective interest of all involved. Since the time frame of the commons "collapse" is much longer than the time frame for individual gains, it is important that interventions are structured so that current actions will contribute to long-term solutions. ✍

Brazil's Inflation "Tragedy"

Brazil's runaway inflation shows how the "Tragedy of the Commons" archetype can play out on a national level. As companies raise prices in order to offset rising costs and inflation expectations, they simply add more fuel to the fire of rising inflation.

Invited Review

System dynamics and microworlds for policymakers

John D.W. MORECROFT
Business Policy Group, London Business School, Sussex Place, Regent's Park, London NW1 4SA, United Kingdom

Abstract: In the past ten years, system dynamics has become more accessible to policymakers and to the academic community. The paper reviews four major developments in the subject that have brought about this change. There have been improvements in the symbols and software used to map and model system structure. New ideas have been adopted from behavioural decision theory which help to transfer policymakers' knowledge into computer models. There have been improvements in methods of simulation analysis that enable modelers and model users to gain better insight into dynamic behaviour. Greater emphasis has been placed on small transparent models, on games and on dialogue between 'mental models' and computer simulations. Together these developments allow modelers to create computer-based learning environments (or microworlds) for policymakers to 'play-with' their knowledge of business and social systems and to debate policy and strategy change. The paper concludes with some thoughts on future research.

Keywords: Strategic modeling, system dynamics, mapping and simulation, gaming, behavioural decision making, group strategy support

Introduction [1]

In the past ten years there have been several important developments in system dynamics which

---

[1] The paper explores recent developments in system dynamics for policymaking. I have tried to provide a broad survey of these developments. However, one's knowledge of even specialised topics is always incomplete, and is conditioned by his/her institutional and geographical setting. I have spent more than 10 years in the United States at MIT's Sloan

The author is grateful to Tony Cornford, Kees van der Heijden, Donald Kalff, Linda Morecroft and Jane Varley for comments and editorial suggestions received on an earlier draft of the paper. The author is also grateful to Arie de Geus for his support and for his commitment to the concept of microworlds for policymakers.

Received September 1987

School of Management and returned to the UK in mid 1986 to join the London Business School. My knowledge of system dynamics for policy-making is therefore heavily influenced by what I have seen at close hand in North America and most particularly at MIT. I am aware of several developments in system dynamics for policymaking in the UK and some in the rest of Europe, but I apologise for omissions that European readers may detect. They are not intentional. Important developments in mathematical methods of model analysis and estimation are excluded from the paper by design, since they are contributions to basic technical methodology and not to the practice of policymaking. The conceptual developments in system dynamics inspired by work on self-organising systems (from the so-called 'Brussels school') are also excluded because the theoretical ties between the Brussels school and traditional system dynamics have only recently been examined closely. As a result, the contribution of self-organising system concepts to the practice of traditional policy modeling, though potentially significant, is not yet clear.

make the subject more accessible to policymakers, more communicable to the academic community and more challenging for research.[2] There have been improvements in the symbols and software used to map and model system structure. New ideas have been adopted from behavioural decision theory which help to capture policymakers' knowledge in computer models. There have been improvements in methods of simulation analysis that enable modelers and model users to gain better insight into dynamic behaviour. Greater emphasis has been placed on small, transparent models and dialogue between 'mental models' and computer simulation models.

As a result of these developments, system dynamics can now be used, with a management team, to structure informed debate about strategic change, in a process where models and computer simulations are an integral part of management dialogue. The paper explores each of the major developments in more depth in order to show readers the range of ideas and concepts that system dynamics now encompasses. The paper concludes with some thoughts on future research to improve model supported policy dialogue and the mapping of policymakers' knowledge.

System dynamics—A microworld for policy debate

What is a 'microworld'[3] for policy debate? Figure 1 shows the elements in the microworld

---

[2] In addition there is now an international System Dynamics Society. The Society runs an annual international conference and publishes a bi-annual journal, the *System Dynamics Review*, containing articles on the theory and applications of system dynamics, research problems, reports of meetings and book reviews. The Society also distributes a newsletter listing the universities and colleges around the world that offer courses in system dynamics. Readers should contact the System Dynamics Society, Principal Office MIT E40-294, Cambridge, MA 02139, USA.

[3] The term 'microworld' comes from Seymour Papert in a fascinating book called *Mindstorms* [45]. Papert is a mathematician and computer scientist at MIT who has devoted his energy to exploring how computers can help people to learn. A fundamental premise of his work is that people learn effectively when they have transitional objects to 'play with' in order to develop their understanding of a particular subject or issue. The writer has pen, paper and word processor with which to hone his skill of composition. The very young child has building blocks to learn about sizes, sorting and

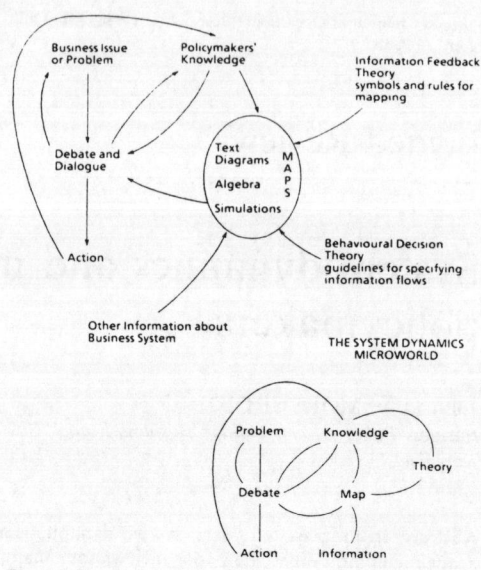

Figure 1. The microworld for policy debate provided by system dynamics

provided by system dynamics. At the top left is a problem or issue facing policymakers which initiates debate and dialogue. The debate leads to clarification of the problem or issue and eventually to recommendations for action. The microworld contains all the factors that impinge on the debate. A most important factor is the policymakers' own knowledge (or mental model) of the business or social system they manage. This knowledge provides the raw material for debate and discussion. In conventional policymaking (by argument) it is the interplay between the knowledge base and the debate that produces a consensus for action.

---

simple construction. The combination of transitional objects, learner and learning process is what Papert calls a microworld or 'incubator for knowledge'. But what transitional objects can one provide for learning about 'intangible' topics like motion, geometry, mathematics and (for our purpose) policymaking? Papert suggests the computer and simulation: "The computer is the Proteus of machines. Its essence is its universality, its power to simulate. Because it can take on a thousand forms and can serve a thousand functions, it can appeal to a thousand tastes."

The combination of computer, simulation language, learner and learning process is a computer-based microworld.

When modeling and simulation enter the debate (or for that matter any other framework for policymaking) the picture becomes more complex as the interplay of knowledge, information and debate becomes richer. Policymakers' knowledge, and other information about the business or social system, (staff reports, financial documents etc.) are converted into text, diagrams, algebra and simulations. The process of mapping knowledge and information is guided by theory and concepts of system dynamics. The figure shows two main inputs from theory. The first input, from information feedback theory, provides symbols for diagramming a business or social system and rules for mapping. As explained in more detail later, these symbols include levels, action flows, flow regulators, converters and information flows to represent physical, financial and decisionmaking processes. The rules for mapping include rules for connecting the symbols, guidelines for equation formulation and guidelines for simulation testing and behaviour analysis.[4] The second input, from behavioural decision theory, improves the 'fidelity' of models. Behavioural decision theory provides the modeler with guidelines for specifying a model's information flows. It helps modelers to ask the 'right' questions of policymakers and it helps modelers to represent an organisation's decision processes accurately.

The microworld includes knowledge (K), information (I), theory (T), maps (M), debate (D) and the interplay of these factors as summarised in the inset of Figure 1. The scope of policy debate is larger (in principle) than can be achieved with conventional argument. The maps (text, diagrams, algebra, and simulations) provide policymakers with a variety of perspectives on their pooled knowledge. The maps also draw information from reports and staff specialists. So the interplay of debate and knowledge is enhanced through increased variety of representation, more information, and additional paths of interaction. Moreover, the maps themselves are created with the specialist knowledge supplied by theory.

Now let us turn to the developments in system dynamics which have made possible this microworld for policy debate.

Improvements in mapping methods and software

The origin of system dynamics can be traced to engineering control systems and the theory of information feedback systems. Indeed courses with the title system dynamics are offered in many engineering schools. But, in the setting of engineering, the subject has a rather mathematical flavour. One of the major contributions to modeling made by Forrester was to reshape sophisticated modeling and analysis methods from control engineering into a flexible form suited to modeling and debate in the business/social arena. One can think of this reshaping as a change in the 'technology' for mapping knowledge of systems into algebra and differential equations. In *Industrial Dynamics* Forrester [11] offered symbols for diagramming feedback systems and rules for connecting the symbols. Together these symbols and rules produce a diagram that shows the interconnectedness of a business or social system, that highlights feedback paths and that guides equation formulation. In addition Forrester devised a special purpose simulation language for coding symbols from diagrams into algebraic equations. Forrester's reshaping of methods from control engineering led to a visual representation of feedback systems, and through simulations, to a visual representation of feedback dynamics. These graphics provide a conduit for policymaker's knowledge and a basis for policy debate.

In the past ten years there has been renewed interest in the symbols used in system dynamics (Morecroft [38], Richardson [51], Richmond [52]). They have been simplified visually and can now be manipulated on graphical computers.

Let us review the symbols and rules of connection, and then talk about software. Figure 2 shows the main symbols. At the top of the figure, shown as a circle, is a decision function or converter. The function receives information, shown as dotted lines, processes it and generates an output in the form of action or more information (such as a command transmitted elsewhere in the system). For example, one might think of a hiring function in a sales organisation, receiving information on both the current size of the salesforce and the

---

[4] I am using the term 'mapping here to mean all stages in the conversion of mental models into computer simulation models, including diagrams, text, algebra, programmed algebra, and even simulations.

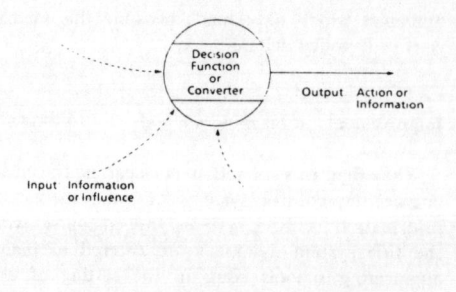

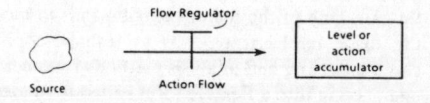

Figure 2. Symbols for mapping

decision making 'players' whose decisions and actions are coupled (Forrester [11, Chapter 10]). Each 'player', or centre of responsibility, is represented by a decision function with information inputs and an output which is either information or action. For example, players in a sales organisation might be business planners (setting sales objectives), compensation planners (adjusting the commission paid on different product lines), salespeople (deciding how to allocate their selling time to product lines), force planners (adjusting the size of the salesforce) and customers (being influenced by salespeople to buy). But how are the decision functions and actions coupled? Here is where the remaining symbols and rules of connection are useful.

In the lower half of Figure 2 there are three symbols. The box on the right is a level that accumulates action. In the centre is a composite symbol that represents an action flow (shown as an arrow) and a flow regulator (shown as a 'T') which controls the size or volume of the flow. Finally, on the left is a source (shown as an irregular 'blob') which supplies the action flow. (If the action flow is reversed, then the source becomes a sink and the flow drains the level). In order to understand the symbols, again imagine the process of hiring in a sales organisation. The level is the number of salespeople currently employed, which accumulates the flow of people being hired. The hiring flow is controlled by the flow regulator, (which as we shall see later, is connected to the hiring function). Salespeople are hired from the labour market which is therefore the source of the flow.

System dynamics provides rules for connecting the symbols so that one can construct a network of decision functions of arbitrary complexity and thereby map and mimic an organisation. Figure 3 shows many symbols connected. The sequence of connection is: level–information (or influence)–decision function (or converter)–action–level. This is a feedback representation. A decision function (say hiring) leads to action (the arrival of salespeople). New recruits accumulate in the level of salespeople. Information from the level (the size of the salesforce) is an input to the hiring function.

The arrival of graphic computers has now made it possible to map symbols directly onto a computer screen and to benefit from interactive mapping and high quality graphics. The new modelling

force size authorised by the budget. Force planners (or a hiring committee/manager) process this information periodically in order to adjust the size of the salesforce (an action). The circular function symbol is usually identified with a specific decision making process or centre of responsibility in an organisation.[5] Within each symbol there can be quite complex information processing and therefore quite complex algebra.

The decision function or converter is a *general* function of its inputs. The detail of the function is not specified by the symbol, and this is deliberate, because a diagram made of such symbols retains a lot of flexibility in discussion—it is not overly defined and it is not too 'close' to the final algebra. The decision function or converter may contain within it 'subsymbols' such as constants, auxiliaries and information levels. The function symbol is therefore a quite-compact visual representation of the decisionmaking process under study.

A business or social system is viewed as a set of

---

[5] Sometimes a function may represent a physical process or behavioural process such as motivation. In the case of production, the function combines inputs of material, labour and capital and converts them into (say) finished goods. There is no conscious decisionmaking or information processing involved. Similarly, in the case of motivation, the function combines inputs of say stress, workload, and goal achievement and converts them into an index of individual or group motivation. In such physical or behavioural processes, the inputs to the function are best thought of as influences rather than information flows.

Figure 3. Rules for symbol connection

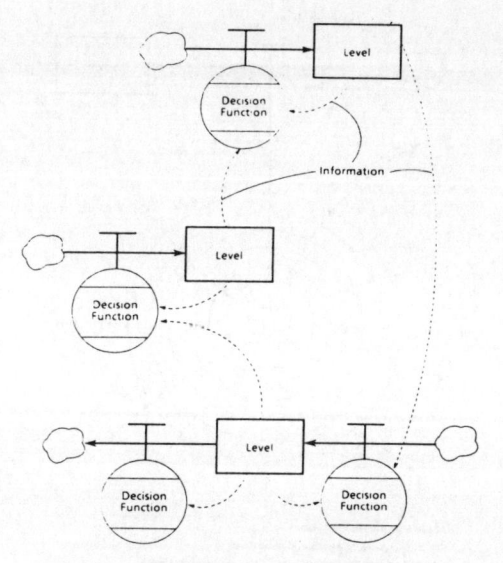

- Sequence of connection: level - information - decision function - action - level

and simulation package STELLA (Richmond [53] and Richmond et al. [54]) includes very effective mapping software. STELLA provides the modeler with a menu of symbols for creating a diagram on an 'electronic' worksheet. The symbols include those shown in Figure 2 and several others (hand, ghost and dynamite) that help in editing and organising the diagram. One can select symbols from the menu, move them onto the computer screen (a small part of the available electronic worksheet) and connect them. The software 'knows' the connection rules, so modelers are constrained to produce diagrams which connect symbols in the sequence: level–information flow (or influence)–converter–action flow–level. The software provides a very effective (and entertaining) medium for mapping policymakers' knowledge of a business or social system. [6]

---

[6] There is one symbol provided by the STELLA software, the converter, that differs from the function symbol in Figure 2. The function symbol is a 'high level' symbol that can contain many subsymbols. In STELLA, the converter is just like a traditional 'auxiliary' symbol in system dynamics. In practice this difference is important. It causes STELLA diagrams to be more visually complex than policy structure diagrams (or policy maps). The increase in visual complexity is more noticeable the larger the model. Moreover it is difficult to identify in STELLA diagrams the major 'players' and centres of decisionmaking responsibility. However, there is no technical reason why a graphic modeling package could not employ a high-level general function symbol.

In addition to symbols, system dynamics provides guidelines for equation formulation. These guidelines can be thought of as rules for converting symbols, text and words into algebra. There is not the space here to examine the guidelines in depth. [7] However, let us take just a couple of examples to illustrate how methods of developing algebra are improving with the help of software.

Consider first the simple but crucial issue of naming symbols and variables. Names are chosen to fit closely with the terminology and concepts used by policymakers. Models often go through major revisions of terminology as concepts become clearer and more precisely defined. The objective is to make diagrams and algebra readable and easy to relate to people's mental models.

Modeling software gives good support to users who wish to create readable models. For example, the modeling and simulation package Professional DYNAMO [49] has a documentation module that provides clear visual display of algebra, automatic translation of algebraic names into plain language (using a file of definitions supplied by the modeler) and comprehensive cross indexing of variables, equations and manually-prepared diagrams. STELLA allows the modeler to specify long (17 character) labels for symbols in diagrams. Once the labels are entered into a diagram they are available for use in equation writing without being retyped. Moreover, modelers must write equations that combine the inputs to symbols as specified on the diagram, otherwise the software will reject the equations. The result is a diagram with understandable labels that always match exactly with the variables used in equations.

Consider next the issue of dimensional balance in equations. The units of measure on the left-hand side of an equation should match those on the right, and any conversion coefficients (such as productivity that relates a workforce to a produc-

---

[7] Readers who would like to know more about guidelines for equation formulation are referred to Forrester [12, Chapters 3–9], Richardson and Pugh [50, Chapter 4], Coyle [6, Chapter 5] and Richmond et al. [54, pp 2.72–2.74].

tion rate) should have real meaning in the system. Dimensional analysis, if thorough, is a powerful method of rooting-out errors in formulation and for pinpointing confusion in the conversion of diagrams and verbal descriptions into algebra.

Software packages help modelers with dimensional analysis. DYSMAP (Cavana and Coyle [3], Vapenikova and Dangerfield [72]) includes a full dimensional analysis module. Professional DYNAMO and STELLA encourage dimensional analysis in that they allow one to supply dimension labels that appear in equation listings.

New concepts from behavioural decision theory

With the symbols and mapping rules of system dynamics it is possible to create quite complex networks of decision functions, actions and levels. But there are innumerable ways to link the symbols which all obey the connection rules of feedback systems. However, *only some symbol configurations* correspond to realistic organisational systems. There is a need for modelers to be quite discriminating in their choice of information links and influences if they are to produce plausible and insightful policy models.

Recently, system dynamics has adopted concepts from behavioural decision theory that are useful for specifying information links among decision functions. (Hall [25,26,27], Morecroft [39,41], Sterman [66,68,69]). Behavioural decision theory focuses on the information and heuristics in real-life decisionmaking. What information receives attention in organisational decisions? What information is ignored, and why? What factors condition the quantity and quality of this information? Behavioural decision theory concludes (with plenty of empirical evidence) that people make choices using only a few sources of information processed with simple rules of thumb. So the network of information flows in a realistic organisation is quite sparse relative to the network that would exist if each decisionmaker used information from every source in the system.

Figure 4 shows how behavioural decision theory guides the mapping of decision functions and therefore complements the rules from information feedback theory. One can see in the figure the standard feedback representation: decision function–action flow–level–information–decision

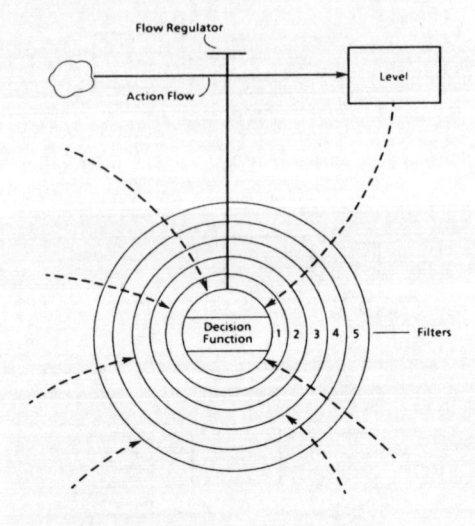

1. People's cognitive limitations
2. Operating goals, rewards and incentives
3. Information, measurement and communication systems
4. Organisational and geographical structure
5. Tradition, culture, folklore, leadership.

Figure 4. The behavioural decision function—Decision making and information filters

function. In addition there are many other information flows and influences (originating from other levels in the system) which are shown on the outer boundaries of the decision function. Only a few of the information flows actually penetrate to the heart of the decision function where they influence the choices and actions of the 'players' (individuals, groups, subunits) represented by the function. The concentric circles surrounding the decision function represent organisational and cognitive filters which select or limit the information made available to different decisionmakers.

The composite symbol comprising the decision function and concentric circles (filters) is a behavioural decision function. It is a visual representation of ideas first developed by Simon [61], and the Carnegie School (summarised in Allison [1, Chapter 3] and captures aspects of modern behavioural decision theory by Hogarth [28], Tversky and Kahnemann [71].

There are five information filters surrounding a decision function. The first filter represents people's cognitive limits and Simon's notion of bounded rationality (Simon [60,62,64]). People are unable to process all the information that a business or social system may present them. They make their judgements on the basis of a few sources of information processed according to quite simple rules of thumb.

The outer filters (2, 3, 4 and 5) in Figure 4 represent the ways in which an organisation conditions the information made available to decisionmakers. This part of the figure draws particularly on Simon's *Administrative Behavior* which explains how organisations may display effective decisionmaking despite people's cognitive limits and an over-abundance of information. [8] Executives and managers (and in fact all employees) make their judgements and decisions in a 'psychological environment' provided by the organisation. The psychological environment limits the range of factors they consider and, in principle, supplies only the relevant information (a tiny subset of the total information available in the organisation) for making the correct choices at a given centre of responsibility. The filters show the components of the 'psychological environment' and they also provide a convenient basis for questioning policymakers.

Filter number 2 represents the influence of operating goals, rewards and incentives on information flow. Decisions and actions in business and social systems depend on the operating goals and rewards faced by the key players in the system. One can only understand organisational choice and action relative to these goals and rewards. So, for example, it is well-known that factory managers who are held accountable for a specific end-of-year inventory target will drastically curtail or boost production to meet the target, in defiance of 'rational' cost-minimizing scheduling criteria. For these factory managers, information about the status of inventory easily penetrates filter number 2. The filter excludes other information on future expected demand, cost structure and capacity constraints, which together with information on inventory would be required to set an 'objectively rational' production schedule. The modeler must ask questions which elicit policymakers' knowledge of goals and rewards.

Filter number 3 represents the influence of information, measurement and communication systems on information flow. To take another production example, a 'good' production schedule for a microcomputer manufacturer might require information on the status of inventory in all retail outlets. If there is no information system capable of monitoring and reporting retail inventory, then the production schedule must make do with factory information on the size of the order backlog, the amount of finished inventory and the recent shipping rate.

Filter 4 represents the influence of organisational and geographical structure on information flow. As a decisionmaker, one's position in an organisation (both geographical location and position on the organisational chart) have a profound influence on the information sources one is exposed to.

Filter 5 represents the influence of tradition, culture, folklore and leadership on information flow. Filter 5 is quite intangible yet very important in determining the factors that get the attention of decisionmakers in business and social systems. For example, suppose one is modeling the service division of a computer company and wants to understand the quality of service provided to customers. Quality of service depends on the speed with which servicemen fix customer problems. The division can respond quickly if its servicemen receive information promptly from customers. But the company also needs a 'service culture'. A customer problem which is known to a serviceman will get attention (i.e. bring about some action) if the company's 'culture' encourages good service. A culture for good service may derive from quite intangible factors such as stories and folklore which circulate the company. The stories and folklore underpin the attitudes of individuals in the service division, and condition the attention they pay to customer problems (in other words, the weight they give to information from customers requiring service).

What guidance do the filters provide the modeler? Principally they help modelers to map organisational systems accurately by forcing them to pay close attention to the information sources that are *actually used* by decisionmakers (as opposed to the information sources that are available

---

[8] Therefore policy modelers and policymakers would benefit from reading books like *Administrative Behaviour* (Simon [58]), *The Functions of the Executive* (Barnard [2]) *Essence of Decision* (Allison [1] and *Judgement and Choice* (Hogarth [28]), in order to cull some basic principles of human and organisational decisionmaking.

or that seem, at a distance, to be the most 'sensible') and to be aware that information deficiencies, bias and error are commonplace. [9,10] Also, the filters focus attention on the modeling of decision processes, not just causal links or influences. [11]

By being aware of the filters, modelers can ask more precise questions to draw out policymakers' knowledge, and to better specify decision functions. The result is realistic feedback structure that comes from linking well-specified decision functions.

Influence of behavioural decision theory on system dynamics

Besides helping modelers to specify decision functions and map feedback structure, the ideas adopted from behavioural decision theory have improved communication with academics, added some momentum to the 'soft-modeling' movement, and stimulated new research in gaming and the experimental study of organisational decisionmaking. These influences are examined in more detail below, particularly as they relate to policy modeling and policymaking.

---

[9] Forrester [11] stresses the need to model real-life decisionmaking processes and to pay attention to the information sources that are influential at different points in an organisation (see particularly Chapter 10, 'Policies and Decisions'). But *Industrial Dynamics* gives little explicit guidance to the modeler on how to select the information flows that should enter decision functions and later books by other authors give no guidance at all (because the later books show how to model causal loops, not decisionmaking processes). Behavioural decision theory (particularly from Carnegie literature) provides some conceptual apparatus for discriminating influential information sources.

[10] During the 1970's, many system dynamics models were mapped in terms of causal loop diagrams or influence diagrams without explicit representation of decisionmaking. In the case of policy models, it is much better to map decision processes, actions and levels (rather than simple influences) in order to build credible feedback structure (see Forrester [11], Chapters 6-10, and Morecroft [38]).

[11] Interestingly, the outer filters owe very little to modern behavioural decision theory, because modern theory deals principally with individual or group decisionmaking in a *given* organisational setting. The outer filters represent the conditioning of information by the organisation or, in other words, the organisational setting itself.

Communication with the academic community

Behavioural decision theory clarifies and amplifies the conceptual content of system dynamics and provides new vocabulary for communicating with academics. System dynamics models can now be described as 'behavioural simulation models' that 'portray bounded rationality in organisations'. The models represent organisations as decisionmaking/information processing systems involving many players, with multiple (often conflicting) goals and limited information processing capability. The feedback structure of the models emerges from the assumptions one makes about decisionmakers' access to information, the weight that decisionmakers place on different information sources and the rules of thumb they use to make judgements. Dynamic behaviour (which is often economically 'inefficient' from a system-wide perspective) is a consequence of the feedback structure and can therefore be traced to assumptions about behavioural decisionmaking. With these labels to describe models it is possible to write articles of direct interest to (and to converse with) academic economists (Sterman [66],) organisational and policy theorists (Hall [24,25,27], Morecroft [41,42], and behavioural scientists (Sterman [68,69]). Moreover, policymakers also relate to models which capture explicitly the multiple operating goals, administrative procedures and information deficiencies of real organisations.

Momentum to the soft-modeling movement

Recently interest has grown in system dynamics as a soft-modeling methodology. Work in this area has been spearheaded by Wolstenholme [73, 74 (with Coyle), 75] and is related to work in the general systems area by Checkland [4] and in cognitive mapping by Eden [7,8,9]. The thrust of the soft modeling movement in system dynamics can be seen in a portion of Figure 1 which is reproduced in Figure 5 below for convenience. The idea is to emphasize the 'front-end' of system dynamics modeling before one invokes the use of algebra or simulation. Wolstenholme and Coyle [74] distinguish 'qualitative' and 'quantitative' models and argue that 'qualitative' modeling is quite useful to policymakers in its own right, if the modeler uses the symbols and structuring rules of

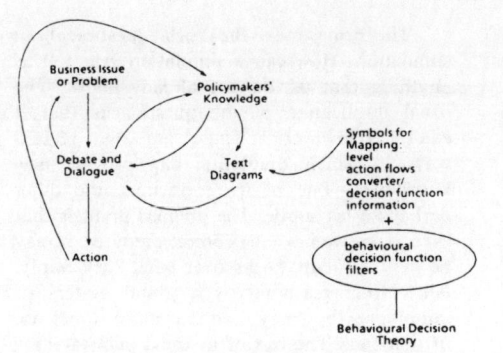

Figure 5. The soft modeling movement and the influence of behavioural decision theory

system dynamics to full advantage.

In Figure 5, a 'qualitative' model is the text and diagrams that result from mapping policymakers' knowledge into the symbols provided by system dynamics. Wolstenholme suggests a number of guidelines to enhance the mapping. Behavioural decision theory adds more symbols (the behavioural decision function and associated filters) to the qualitative modeler's graphic menu. These extra symbols enrich the diagrams, draw in more of the policymakers' knowledge, and broaden the scope of policy debate and dialogue.

Research in gaming and experimental study of organisational decisionmaking

Gaming has long been a branch of system dynamics. Recently, Meadows [35] has revitalised the topic, principally as a means of improving communication between models and policymakers. His work is reviewed later. However, building on Meadow's work, and injecting behavioural decision theory, Sterman has opened gaming as a fascinating new branch of research that promises to forge closer ties to modern behavioural decision theory and to yield new experimental methods for the study of organisational decisionmaking.

An example of Sterman's work is a behavioural simulation model of capital investment in an economy [12] (Sterman [66]). Included in the model are aggregate decision functions for production planning, inventory control, backlog control, capital ordering and capital supply, linked together by information flows, action flows and levels representing the aggregate stock of capital equipment on-hand and on-order in the economy. Sterman and Meadows [67] have converted the model into a role-playing simulation game by replacing the decision function for capital ordering with a 'decision shell' which provides to real human subjects the same information used in the capital ordering function of the full model. The design of the decision shell is guided by considering the behavioural and organisational filters in the original model's capital ordering function. Gameplayers manage a simulated economy in which they must order sufficient capital plant and equipment to satisfy aggregate demand. They have complete and perfect information on demand, backlog, delivery time and capital stock. They can view the structure of the simulated economy on a video display generated by the microcomputer-based game, and they can call up screens of information which show the past history of the system. When the game is played, the overwhelming majority of subjects generate significant and costly oscillations in capital stock and capital orders quite similar to those generated by the full model. The behaviour of subjects is far from optimal and Sterman [68] suggests that the decision-making heuristic they are following is captured by a simple decision rule which is consistent with the notion of bounded rationality.

In business policy modeling, similar gaming work has been carried out by Flint [10] who constructed a role-playing simulation game of sales planning and control for a multiproduct salesforce. Flint's game links decision functions for salesforce time allocation (salespeople's choice of the proportion of selling time they allocate to different product lines), customer ordering, sales forecasting and objective setting, to a decision shell for compensation planning. Subjects in the game play the role of compensation planners, adjusting the commission on product lines according to sales performance. Flint describes the design

---

[12] Sterman's model is a much simplified version of a system dynamics model of aggregate production activity in the U.S. economy, developed over the past ten years by MIT's System Dynamics Group. For more information on the model see Forrester [15,16] and Forrester et al. [18].

of the decision shell and the results of playing the game with managers and compensation planners in companies with a multi-product salesforce.

Emphasis on learning and reasoning—the microworld concept

People frequently ask what new insight can be gained into business and social problems from modeling and simulation that cannot be obtained from conventional written and verbal argument? Forrester and Simon have both made interesting statements on this question which serve to underscore the new emphasis in system dynamics on learning and reasoning. Forrester organises his paper 'Counterintuitive Behavior of Social Systems' [14] on "the basic theme that the human mind is not adapted to interpreting how social systems behave". He suggests that people misjudge the dynamic behaviour of social systems because there are:

"...orderly processes at work in the creation of human judgement and intuition, which frequently lead people to wrong decisions when faced with complex and highly interacting systems."

He then goes on to contrast a computer simulation model with a mental model:

"...the most important difference between the properly conceived computer model and the mental model is in the ability to determine the dynamic consequences when the assumptions within the model interact with one another. The human mind is not adapted to sensing correctly the consequences of a mental model. The mental model may be correct in structure and assumptions but, even so, the human mind—either individually or as a group consensus—is most apt to draw the wrong conclusions. There is no doubt about the digital computer routinely and accurately tracing through the sequences of actions that result from following the statements of behavior for individual points in the model system."

Simon [63] devotes pages 17 to 22 of his book *The Sciences of the Artificial* to the topic 'Simulation as a Source of New Knowledge':

"...This brings me to the crucial question about simulation. How can a simulation ever tell us anything that we do not already know? The usual implication of the question is that it can't...[However]...There are two related ways in which simulation can provide new knowledge—one of them obvious, the other perhaps a bit subtle. The obvious point is that even when we have the correct premises, it may be very difficult to discover what they imply. All correct reasoning is a grand system of tautologies, but only God can make direct use of that fact. The rest of us must painstakingly and fallibly tease out the consequences of our assumptions... The more interesting and subtle question is whether simulation can be of any help to us when we do not know very much initially about the laws that govern the behavior of the inner system?... [The question can also be answered in the affirmative]... if the aspects in which we are interested arise out of the *organization* of the parts, independent of all but a few properties of the individual components."

Increasingly system dynamicists view their models as 'sources of new knowledge' or as tools for *learning* about business and social systems. (See de Geus [21], for the views of a senior planning executive on corporate learning and the role of models). This emphasis on learning is reflected in several trends and topics: generating dialogue between mental models and simulations, using workshops and role-playing simulation games, and finally generic models.

Generating dialogue between mental models and simulations

How can one generate a dialogue between a mental model and a simulation model? In system dynamics the process for doing so was first spelled out by Mass [34] in a paper with the title 'Diagnosing Surprise Model Behavior: A Tool for Evolving Behavioral and Policy Insights'. Mass begins with the observation (like Simon) that simulations can provide new knowledge:

"...some of the most important insights into real system behavior can arise from model results that at first appear to be at odds with knowledge of the real system, but which in fact suggest important new interpretations of perceived facts."

He then goes on to propose ten guidelines and tests for resolving surprise behaviour. I will not list all ten here but instead pick three which are especially relevant to starting a dialogue. First, and most important, policymakers and modelers should establish an a priori expectation of system behaviour:

"Appearance of 'surprise' behavior implies a discrepancy between results actually produced and previous expectations of those results. Thus, it is absolutely essential that the model builder have a strong a priori expectation of model outcomes, to establish a baseline against which surprise model behavior can be recognised through the appearance of a discrepancy."

Once an expectation of model behavior is established then the second guideline is to follow up all unanticipated behaviour to an appropriate resolution:

"The model builder must adopt a perspective that views the encountering of surprise model behaviour as a significant opportunity to be capitalized upon ... [rather than] ... to pursue parameter combinations that make the anomalous behavior less evident or to dismiss the behavior as being outside the intended use of the model."

The third guideline is to confirm all hypotheses about surprise dynamic behaviour with appropriate model tests:

"When surprise model behavior is encountered, the model builder must identify why the model produces the unexpected results. The question of why a model produces certain patterns of dynamic behavior can always be answered with enough time and effort relative to the model framework. Once the model behavior is understood, the realism of both the behavior and the underlying mechanisms must be challenged against corresponding behavior and structure in real life."

Mass's guidelines provide a protocol for generating dialogue that many system dynamicists have since adopted. The protocol has evolved to suit the needs of policymakers (in addition to modelers) and to suit new software. Morecroft [40] describes the process of generating policy dialogue and debate by contrasting executive opinion (about the outcome of a proposed strategic move) with model-generated 'opinion'. Models which are built to facilitate this 'dialectic' are described as 'strategy support models'. Similarly, Richmond's [53] model-testing guidelines require modelers to state a hypothesis (about dynamic behaviour) before simulating, in order to 'squeeze the maximum learning' out of simulations.

For people to engage in dialogue with a model, simulation runs must readily relate to their intuition. In other words, simulation runs should be designed to correspond to scenarios whose outcome policymakers and modelers can readily imagine (express an opinion on) using their knowledge of the system.

Morecroft [41] and Sterman [66] suggest the use of partial model tests that expose the 'intended rationality' of decisionmaking in complex systems. This testing strategy is particularly effective for communicating models that exhibit counterintuitive dynamic behaviour (e.g. long term cycles in capital equipment in Sterman's model of capital investment and a productivity trap in Morecroft's model of a sales organisation). Partial model tests show that decisions and actions of players in a system are 'sensible' (intendedly rational) when the feedback setting for the players' decisions is simple. Dynamic behaviour which arises from 'sensible' decisions and actions is usually intuitively clear, and therefore conducive to dialogue.

Partial model tests are designed by cutting feedback loops in the full model (or by building a deliberately simple, incomplete model) in order to isolate a subset of the system's interacting behavioural decision functions. The simplification is carried out in such a way that one can construct plausible scenarios (scenarios that policymakers can identify with) from simulations of the partial structure. For example, Sterman conducts a test of capital ordering in an aggregate economy in which production of capital equipment is unconstrained by the economy's stock (or level) of capital equipment. Of course, in the real economy, and in the full model, the stock of capital equipment *does* constrain production. Nevertheless, removing the constraint does not alter the logic or inputs to the model's decision function for capital ordering. But it does simplify the feedback network in which the function is embedded. Two feedback loops are cut. One cut eliminates capital self-ordering, the boostrapping process in capital investment whereby, in order to boost production of capital equipment, the sector must first increase its stock of capital equipment. The other cut eliminates hoarding, the tendency for producers to order more equipment when equipment delivery time is rising. [13]

Simulations of the partial model show that capital orders and capital stock adjust in a straightforward (easy-to-understand) way to a step increase in demand for capital goods. By contrast, simulations of the full model show that capital orders and capital stock fluctuate with a long 50 year period in response to the same step increase in demand. Sterman uses several partial model tests to build a clear explanation for the complex (non-intuitive) behaviour of the full model.

Richmond et al. [54] also talk about partial model testing under the heading of 'conducting a sanity check'. Step one of the process is to construct a simple 'open-loop' model (the equivalent of a partial model). As Richmond explains, the open-loop model stimulates thinking:

"Open loop, in this context, really means 'free lunch' i.e. you can get what you want simply by asking for it. Clearly, such an open loop model is not intended to be realistic. Rather, it is designed to indicate what's possible (under the most ideal circumstances), and also to acquaint the group of managers involved in the sanity check exercise with the basic framework and technology that will be used in the analysis. The idea is to begin simple... Then, as the exercise proceeds, the 'freebies' will be systematically removed. The operative question throughout is always the same: can we still get there from here?"

Using workshops and role-playing simulation games

It used to be common in policy modeling to develop models containing several hundred or even several thousand equations. These large models (which are still built today and have an important role to play in policymaking) are large because their creators want them to accurately replicate historical time series and to provide good short-term predictions, in addition to generating dialogue. It usually takes lots of equations to write a model that will accurately simulate history.

Now, much smaller models of thirty, forty or fifty equations are commonly presented to policymakers. The purpose of these models is to 'prime' policymakers' for debate. Much less emphasis is given to replicating time series.

In order to stimulate debate, a model should be transparent so that policymakers can see their knowledge reflected in the model's assumptions. The model should also be presented in a way that dramatises its assumptions and relates them to policymakers' experience.

The idea of 'dramatising' a model has led to the development of 'policy workshops' and has brought renewed interest in role-playing simulation games. [14] In both cases the modeler (perhaps best thought of as a facilitator/modeler) creates a 'learning environment' for policymakers that makes them feel part of the model situation. In principle, policymakers who are placed in such an environment come to relate their own experience more closely to the model than they would in a conventional model presentation. They also internalise more readily the 'lessons' about dynamic behaviour that the model contains.

There are several people paying close attention to workshops and games who are discovering how to design effective learning environments. Kreutzer

---

[13] Strictly speaking, the hoarding loop is not cut but instead neutralized, because equipment delivery time stays constant in the partial model.

[14] Another way to provide a context of drama and realism for a policy model is to integrate it with a conventional case study. The case, which let us suppose is a business policy case, provides general information on a selected company: the situation or problems it faces; the industry it competes in, its products and markets, its history, its organisation and administration and the personalities of its leaders (see for example Christensen, Andrews and Bower [6]). The model provides discussants with additional information on the business which may include maps, descriptions of policy functions, algebra and simulations. The case and model are complementary. The case reveals the strategy, structure and operational decisionmaking of the business, while the model shows graphically (with maps and simulations) how the company's resistance to strategic change arises from its structure and the inertia of its operational decisionmaking. The case/model combination can help probe the crucial (and often weak) link between strategy and operating policies. Work in this interesting area is only just beginning.

[30] has developed a workshop for educators and students to explore the dynamics of an arms-race. The workshop builds on a small (20 equation) dynamic model of an arms-race created by Forrester [19]. Forrester's model represents in outline the decisionmaking processes used by two countries, X and Y, for estimating their opponent's stock of arms, for judging the adequacy of their own stock of arms and for procuring arms from industrial military suppliers. The model also includes levels that represent the stock of existing arms and new arms under development. The decisionmaking network of the model captures in very interesting ways the lags, distortions and biases that occur in the transmission and processing of sensitive military and political information. The model's treatment of information flow is a fascinating example of bounded rationality in the military and political domain. The dynamic properties of the model (exponential growth in the stock of arms of both countries X and Y) arise from the imperfections assumed in the system's decisionmaking processes.

Kreutzer's workshop immerses participants in the realities of military and political decisionmaking. They are provided with articles on the arms-race from magazines like *Newsweek* and the *Economist*. They are presented with charts showing the history of the Soviet–U.S. arms race. They are given cartoon illustrations from magazines like *Punch* or the *New Yorker* which portray (in amusing but memorable and usually realistic ways) the imperfections of military intelligence (for example, an illustration showing large crates being shipped to Cuba on anonymous freighters, and two military officers debating the likely contents of the still-closed crates). All this material activates participants' mental models of the arms-race and highlights the role of information processing and information feedback in arms control. With this preparation participants are able to relate their knowledge and experience to the model and to appreciate the assumptions that underlie the model's feedback structure and dynamic behaviour.

In his workshop, Kreutzer also uses a series of partial model tests to show how the decisionmaking processes that generate an arms-race are quite 'sensible and benign' when the imperfections and biases in information processing are eliminated. (e.g. simulations which assume that decisionmakers in countries X and Y have perfect knowledge of their opponent's stock of arms (both installed and in development) exhibit much slower exponential growth, or in some cases, no growth at all.

Role-playing games fulfill a very similar function to workshops by providing a context of realism and drama to relate policymakers' knowledge to simulation models. In the case of games the drama is provided by making participants play the role of a selected decisionmaker/s in the model system.

The production distribution 'hand simulation' game is a good example of a game that promotes learning and policy debate. It is a board game played by teams of four players. Each player takes a role as either retailer, wholesaler, distributor or manufacturer in a vertically integrated manufacturing and supply system (a beer production and distribution system is usually selected). A player is responsible for managing inventories and backlogs at one point in the system (e.g. wholesaler) and for placing orders with the adjacent player downstream (e.g. distributor) in the supply chain. The objective of the players is to minimise the team's inventory and backlog costs in the face of exogenous customer orders. The volume of orders is not known in advance by any player, and is revealed week-by-week to only the retailer. The game shows the difficulty of coordinating decisionmaking and action in a system with decentralised decisionmaking and imperfect information processing. Almost all teams that play the game incur inventory and backlog costs which are much higher than the 'theoretical' cost minimum. Recently, Senge [15] and Sterman [65] have refined the game instructions, improved the board layout and documented an effective protocol for debriefing so that the game now serves as a general purpose introduction to feedback systems and modeling.

The production-distribution game uses coins, paper, and a plastic printed board. But many new electronic or semielectronic role-playing games are being developed. Meadows is spearheading the development of games for policymakers and has

---

[15] Senge uses the game regularly with chief executives in a short course on Systems Thinking. The game materials (board, cards, instructions, debriefing protocol) are available from Innovation Associates, PO Box 2008, Framingham MA 01701, USA.

devoted much of his research effort to the topic. His games are aimed not only at policymakers in business, but also public policymakers as for example with the game STRATAGEM 1 (Meadows [35]). He has also collaborated with Sterman to produce STRATAGEM 2, the role-playing simulation game of economic investment cycles mentioned earlier [67].

More policy games have been developed such as Hall's magazine publishing game [23], Flint's multi-product salesforce game [10] and Habibe's arms-race game [22]. The management consulting company Pugh-Roberts Associates has developed a role-playing game for managers of large-scale projects (based on a comprehensive simulation model of project management [48]). Further games are under development at several modeling centres both as learning environments and as laboratories for research in behavioural decisionmaking.

Generic policy models

Generic policy models are (usually small) models which display important dynamic processes that occur frequently in business and social systems. In addition generic policy models often encapsulate some 'managerial wisdom' in the form of 'principles' for effective policymaking in situations like the one represented by the model.

Examples of important and general dynamic processes are captured in such words and phrases as growth, decline, saturation, goal-seeking, fluctuation, goal erosion, worse-before-better, better-before-worse, vicious cycle, snowball effect, bandwagon, productivity trap, poverty trap, policy resistance, compensating feedback and others. For each dynamic process there is a corresponding feedback structure. For example, Forrester's 'market growth model' [14] contains three important feedback loops that interrelate production capacity, salesforce size and customer orders in a growth company (or business unit). One loop—which combines policies for budgeting, salesforce hiring and customer ordering—generates exponential growth in sales. A second loop—which combines policies for capacity expansion and for control of delivery time—adjusts production capacity to changes in customer orders. The third loop–which links customer's ordering and company production—ensures a long run balance between customer orders and production capacity. The complete model can exhibit dynamic behaviour ranging from exponential growth in sales and capacity, to stagnation and decline. This range of dynamic behaviour comes from combining dynamic processes (and associated feedback structures) of growth, saturation, fluctuation and goal erosion.

Generic models offer modelers and policymakers a way of collecting and storing knowledge about feedback structure and dynamics of social and business systems. [16] Each generic model is a self-contained 'behavioural theory' of the dynamic processes it illustrates. Because generic models store dynamic theories (and 'insight' into dynamic behaviour) they have attracted research effort, especially in the last five years. But, progress so far has been disappointingly slow, partly because it is difficult to prove that a given model is truly general, and partly because the word 'generic' means different things to different people. [17]

Despite these problems, research on generic models remains an important topic, (see for example Paich [44]) particularly given the growing emphasis on models and simulations for learning and reasoning. A comprehensive 'library' of generic models (Forrester [17]) would help modelers organise descriptive information about a system. One could identify important feedback loops in policy diagrams and then, from knowledge of simulations of similar structures in the 'library', analyse growth, fluctuations, decline and saturation in system performance.

---

[16] Lyneis' book *Corporate Planning and Policy Design* [33] contains several well-documented generic models of manufacturing systems.

[17] Some modelers think of generic models in terms of feedback structures, dynamic behaviour and insights which are of use *across the board* in social, physical, ecological and biological systems. These people tend to focus on patterns and types of interacting feedback loops, and on abstract dynamic behaviour. Others think of generic models in terms of policy structure, dynamic behaviour and insights which are of use in *many policymaking situations*. These people tend to focus on policy interactions and feedback loops that arise from connecting policy functions, and on managerial principles that stem from dynamic behaviour.

Future research—Improving model supported 'dialogue' and the mapping of policymakers' knowledge

An important objective of future policy-related research in system dynamics is to improve the quality of dialogue and debate among policymakers and between policymakers and models. Better dialogue comes from capturing accurately in maps and models policymakers' knowledge of business, and from strengthening the influence of model-generated opinion in policy debate. Many research paths are open to improve model-supported dialogue. They include field experiments, behavioural decisionmaking, game design and mapping technology.

Field experiments

Field experiments are already underway to explore the process for generating effective model supported policy dialogue. The experiments are taking place in both large and small business organisations in the United States and Europe. Researchers and consultants are experimenting with the content and sequence of model development to better understand which modeling activities should be conducted during meetings and which beforehand; to better understand what balance to strike between qualitative mapping and simulation; and to better understand how to use partial model tests and simple scenarios to challenge policymakers' intuition.

Researchers and consultants are also experimenting with the composition of the project team (the mix of policymakers, modelers and facilitators), [18] the format of meetings (how frequent, how long, and what mix of discussants), and the 'technology' for presenting and recording policy debate (flip-charts, blackboards, paper, overheads, video projectors and computers (with word-processing, diagramming and modeling software)).

Several recent papers describe the style and direction of the field work. Richmond [55] and Senge [59] describe a 'Strategic Forum' which they view as a 'process' to enable a cross-functional management team to improve the match between operating policies and stated strategic objectives. [19] A forum involves several work steps for a management team: articulating current vision and strategy, developing simple 'reality check' models, developing more complex models by closing feedback loops, conducting 'what-if' policy testing and defining action steps. Morecroft [40,42,43] describes 'strategy support models' which are intended to 'provide executives with insight into whether the policies and programs (of a business strategy) are properly coordinated and whether they are in fact capable of achieving the market and financial objectives called for by the strategy'. He describes two phases of modeling, a first qualitative mapping phase to identify 'players', policies, and feedback structure, and a second simulation modeling phase to develop equations and concepts and to debate the outcome of simple simulated scenarios.

It is interesting to note that research and consulting on the process of model-building with management teams is already well-established outside the system dynamics field. Well-known work has been carried out by Phillips [46,47] and Eden [8,9] and the topic is receiving increasing attention in the area of decision support systems (Land et al. [31]), Keen and Scott-Morton [29], Lorange et al. [32]). Some cross-fertilisation of research and methods would likely be fruitful.

Behavioural decisionmaking and gaming

The value of behavioural decision theory to system dynamics is clear enough: its ideas can help modelers to ask better questions of policymakers, to specify decision processes more accurately, and to capture more or policymakers' knowledge in maps and algebra. It is likely that modelers can pull still more ideas from the combined literature of the Carnegie school and mod-

---

[18] Roberts [56] wrote an influential paper in 1972 that highlights several key issues in the modeling process: project selection, project team composition, pace of model development, model detail and communication/implementation of model-based recommendations. New field research in system dynamics is examining these issues in more depth.

[19] Senge is using the strategic forum in a research program at MIT's Sloan School of Management called 'Systems Thinking and the New Management Style'. The program, which involves leaders of some of America's most innovative corporations, is exploring how systems thinking can be developed within the participating organisations (Senge [57,58]).

ern behavioural decision theorists. An important extension to this bridge-building is to embody the new ideas explicitly into symbols for mapping (say by including information filters in maps) and into protocols for questioning policymakers.

Another significant area for research is game design. Behavioral decision theory gives some guidance to game design by focussing the game-builders' attention on the design of the 'decision-shell' in which human subjects will role-play. Immediately one thinks of 'designing a decision shell' then game-building takes on many interesting research dimensions (that go well beyond the purely technical issue of outfitting a simulation model with the capability for occasional human intervention). There is the question of how one 'replicates' the organisational, cultural and administrative filters (of information) that condition choice and action. What information (from the vast matrix of simulated data available) should be presented to gameplayers? How should screens of information be organised? What balance of graphic, verbal and visual displays is appropriate? How much leakage of information between players should be allowed in multi-player games? What is an appropriate protocol for gaming-decisions? How should one gauge the adequacy and fidelity of the decision-shell? The research questions are numerous. At a more technical level one might consider the merits of different programming environments and computers for developing behavioural decision shells.

Finally, there is a challenging, and potentially large, research topic in the use of gaming to *link experimentally* the behavioural decisionmaking of individuals and groups to the dynamics of large organisations. In this kind of research a simulation game becomes a laboratory for 'testing' cognitive limitations of individuals and groups in environments that 'simulate' large organisations. Subjects make choices in an experimentally controlled setting (the decision shell) that provides operating information. The operating information is generated by a simulation model that 'surrounds' the decision shell. Subjects are free to make any choice they consider appropriate, given the available operating information, their knowledge of operating goals and incentives, their 'mental model' of how the rest of the organisation operates, and also given their own cognitive limitations. The actions and reactions of the rest of the organisation (comprising several behavioural decision functions, actions and levels) are represented by algebraic functions and simulated during the game. Since the business situation is entirely experimental, one can replace the decision shell and human decisionmaker/s with an algebraic decision rule and discover (through analysis or simulation) an 'optimal' decision rule. Knowing an optimal decision rule and the results of many game trials with many different players, one can discover if and when people use systematically poor decisionmaking heuristics. One can also 'model' the players' heuristics and compare them with the optimal decision rule in order to probe the link between cognitive limits and observed dynamic behaviour.

Research along these lines is being carried out by Sterman [69]. It is a fascinating area that promises to yield better understanding of the reasons for (economically) inefficient dynamic behaviour in business and social systems; experimental methods for validating model assumptions; and new insights into the design of roleplaying simulation games.

Better mapping technology

There is a large potential for research which leads to better mapping technology and therefore to a richer flow of policymakers' knowledge into maps and models. The most direct research path leads straight to improvements in software. A more ambitious research path leads into aspects of modern computer science and artificial intelligence.

Software for mapping, modeling and simulation has improved over the past five years, as outlined earlier. However, there is room for still more improvement. Mapping (of the kind allowed by STELLA) should permit word-and-picture maps to be built at the level of policies (Morecroft [38]) rather than at the present level of algebraic converters. Word-and-picture maps would allow better communication with policymakers (because the maps are readable, visually compact and easily changeable) and would guide equation formulation without constraining conversation (because they stand in a natural hierarchy above equation formulation). The needed software should combine the flexibility of drawing and writing packages (say like MacDraw and MacWrite) with the modeling capability of STELLA.

New software should also help modelers write good clear algebra that a policymaker can (almost literally) read! A simple step is to allow much longer labels so that equations look like sentences. Also needed, but more difficult to provide, is guidance for equation formulation—a computer environment for developing equations that weeds-out poor formulations. Here is an ambitious but clear research challenge: to capture in a software package (at least some of) the expert modelers' rules of formulation (for example, dimensional consistency checks and extreme-condition tests).

Finally, new software should give modelers more simulation power and flexibility. Given a credible model, one should be able to probe 'policy parameter' space as quickly as one can envisage and articulate meaningful policy scenarios. The required flexibility here is not only for rapid re-simulation, but more important, for rapid reformating and reorganisation of simulated graphs and charts. Some original thinking on the 'visual display of quantitative information' (Tufte [70]) is called for.

The most ambitious research path leads into modern computer science and artificial intelligence. Here I will speculate from the perspective of a knowledgeable modeler and policy analyst but a relative novice in modern computer science.

The challenge is to better understand how to elicit and reconstruct policymakers' broad business knowledge into meaningful word-and-picture maps, algebraic 'sentences', models and simulations. It seems to me that an important prerequisite is to discover more precisely what we mean by the phrase 'policymakers' knowledge'. Branches of Artificial Intelligence (AI) may provide some answers (for an eloquent and authoritative introduction to AI see Minsky's *Society of Mind* [36]). However, there is a need for focus. The likely criterion for achieving focus is to select the work that is most informative on how symbols (words, charts, pictures, etc.) can be used to provide a 'framework' on which to hang policymakers' knowledge. [20]

---

[20] A recent article by Geoffrion [20] on structured modeling provides some stimulating ideas on frameworks for modeling and representation schemes (the use of graphs, charts, text-based schema and 'elemental detail tables'). The article also provides references to AI literature on knowledge representation.

I do not know which branch of artificial intelligence/computer science would be most useful though I can think of areas that are related. For example, the branch of expert systems has made headway in coding specialists' (narrow domain) knowledge into collections of facts and inference engines for relating the facts. One might say that expert system designers have created frameworks that help (narrow domain) experts articulate their specialist knowledge and transfer it into computer models. In addition one might note that the structure of the frameworks (the facts and the rules of inference) both guides *and limits* the form in which knowledge is articulated and collected. Expert systems then provide examples of frameworks for mapping knowledge. I expect that deliberately designed frameworks to capture policymakers' knowledge will differ radically in content and structure from expert systems (since policymakers' judgements draw on broad (rather than specialist) experience and knowledge). Nevertheless some clues to the design of policy frameworks might emerge from expert systems. Almost certainly there are other branches of research in artificial intelligence which could offer more (and perhaps more relevant) clues.

Let us suppose now that there exist powerful qualitative frameworks to capture policymakers' knowledge in words-and-pictures. Now consider the more specific research issue of converting words-and-pictures into simulations that can be used to challenge policymakers' intuition. System dynamics has a particular 'conversion technology'. It is quite effective, but it has remained fundamentally unchanged for the past twenty five years. Is there room for improvement, and where should one look for new ideas?

In my view, a weakness in the existing conversion technology is in the link between word-and-picture maps and algebra. It is difficult to write good algebra that means mathematically what you intend with words, and some ideas just don't seem to fit very well into the mould of algebra and differential equations. Are there alternatives to algebraic equations and would they be better? I don't pretend to know the answer to this question, but I think it is worth exploring as a research topic. Moreover, new programming/modeling approaches from modern computer science may prove helpful.

I have some familiarity with the programming

language LOGO (Papert [45]). LOGO is used to create learning environments (microworlds) to help schoolchildren (and university students) to understand 'difficult' or abstract concepts such as force, momentum and energy in physics. A LOGO microworld is built using LOGO primitive commands each labeled in plain English. LOGO commands can be grouped together and given a name to form a new command. New commands built in this way can be abstractions for complex concepts. For example, if one is learning about relative motion one can use a relative-motion microworld (Linda E. Morecroft [37]). Such a microworld is constructed from a set of commands that simulate motion. The commands are used to set objects in motion on a computer screen and then combined to study relative motion. Thus, objects set in circular motion can be used to investigate complex patterns of relative motion that occur when one object moving in a circle is viewed from another. The point here is to show that the structure of the programming language allows the construction of micro-worlds in which complex situations can be studied by playing with and combining simple building blocks. I do not know what the structure of an analogous language for policy systems might be, but I am sure it differs from conventional simulation modeling languages.

I have outlined some promising paths for future research in system dynamics. A lot has been accomplished over the last ten years, but the remaining opportunities and challenges are enormous. Future research should provide the technology, theory and group processes for policy microworlds which will (in Richmond's words) 'help organisations design their own future'.

References

[1] Allison, Graham, T., *Essence of Decision*, Little Brown, Boston, MA, 1971.
[2] Barnard, Chester I., *The Functions of the Executive*, 29th printing, Harvard University Press, Cambridge MA, 1982.
[3] Cavana, Robert Y., and Coyle, R. Geoffrey, *Dysmap User Manual*, University of Bradford Publications, Bradford, Yorkshire, UK, 1982.
[4] Checkland, Peter, *Systems Thinking, Systems Practice*, Wiley, Chichester, 1981.
[5] Christensen, C. Roland, Andrews Kenneth R. and Bower, Joseph L., *Business Policy: Text and Cases*, Irwin, Homewood, IL, 1978.
[6] Coyle, R. Geoffrey, *Management System Dynamics*, Wiley, Chichester, UK, 1977.
[7] Eden, Colin, Jones, Sue, and Sims, David, *Messing About in Problems*, Pergamon Press, Oxford, 1983.
[8] Eden, Colin, "Perish the Thought", *Journal of the Operational Research Society* 36(9) (1985) 808–819.
[9] Eden, Colin, "Managing Strategic Ideas: The Role of the Computer", *ICL Technical Journal* 5/2 (1986) 173–183.
[10] Flint, Brilsford, B., "A role-playing simulation for sales planning and control", Unpublished Master's Thesis, Sloan School of Management, MIT, Cambridge, MA, May 1986.
[11] Forrester, Jay W., *Industrial Dynamics*, The MIT Press, Cambridge MA, 1961.
[12] Forrester, Jay W., *Principles of Systems*, The MIT Press, Cambridge MA, 1969.
[13] Forrester, Jay W., "Market growth as influenced by capital investment", *Sloan Management Review* 9/2 (1968) 83–105. Also in *Collected Papers of Jay W. Forrester*, pp 111–132, MIT Press, Cambridge, MA, 1975.
[14] Forrester, Jay W., "Counterintuitive behavior of social systems", pp. 211–237 in *Collected Papers of Jay W. Forrester*, MIT Press, Cambridge, MA, 1975.
[15] Forrester, Jay W., "Business structure, economic cycles and national policy", *Futures* 8 (1976) 195–214.
[16] Forrester, Jay W., "An alternative approach to economic policy: Macrobehavior from microstructure" in: N. Kamrany and R. Day (eds.), *Economic Issues of The Eighties*, Johns Hopkins University Press, Baltimore, MD, 1979.
[17] Forrester, Jay W., "System dynamics—Future opportunities", in *System Dynamics, TIMS Studies in the Management Sciences*, Vol. 14, North-Holland, New York, 1980, 7–21.
[18] Forrester, Jay W., Graham, A., Senge, P., and Sterman, J., "An integrated approach to the economic long wave", Working paper D-3447-1, System Dynamics Group, MIT, Cambridge, MA, 1983.
[19] Forrester, Jay W., "Dynamic modeling of the arms race", System Dynamics Group Working Paper D-3684-3, Sloan School of Management, MIT, Cambridge, MA, 1985.
[20] Geoffrion, Arthur M., "An introduction to structured modeling", *Management Science* 33/5 (1987) 547–588.
[21] Geus, Arie P. de, "Planning as learning: The adaptive corporation", presentation paper from the *Shell Planning Conference*, Banff, Alberta, Canada, May 1986.
[22] Habibe, Tommy O., "The arms race game", System Dynamics Group Working Paper D-3836, Sloan School of Management, MIT, Cambridge, MA, June 1986.
[23] Hall, Roger I., "Managing a magazine publishing company: A decision making game", in: T. Carney (ed.), *Constructing Instructional Simulation Games*, University of Manitoba, Winnipeg, Manitoba, 1974, 22–29.
[24] Hall, Roger I., "A system pathology of an organization: The rise and fall of the old Saturday Evening Post", *Admin. Sci. Quart.* 21 (1976) 185–211.
[25] Hall, Roger I., "Decision making in a complex organization", in: G.W. England, A. Neghandi and B. Wilpert (eds.), *The Functioning of Complex Organizations*, Oelgeschlager, Gunn and Hain, Cambridge, MA, Chapter 5, 1981, 111–144.

[26] Hall, Roger I., and Menzies William, "A corporate system model of a sports club: Using simulation as an aid to policy making in a crisis", *Management Science* 29 (1983) 52-64.
[27] Hall, Roger I., "The natural logic of management policy making: Its implications for the survival of an organization, *Management Science* 30/8, (1984).
[28] Hogarth, Robin M., *Judgement and Choice*, Wiley, New York, 1980.
[29] Keen, Peter G.W., and Scott-Morton, Michael S., *Decision Support Systems*, Addison-Wesley, Reading, MA, 1978.
[30] Kreutzer, David P., "A microcomputer workshop exploring the dynamics of arms races", System Dynamics Group Working Paper D-3689-1, Summer 1985.
[31] Land, Frank, Gall, Michael, Hawgood, John, Miller, Gordon, and Mundle, Fred, (editors and organisers) "Knowledge Based Management Support Systems", *Proceedings of International Business Schools Computer User's Group and Information Systems Association*, Joint European Meeting, London Business School, April 1987.
[32] Lorange, Peter, Scott-Morton, Michael S., and Ghoshal, Sumantra, *Strategic Control Systems*, West Publishing Company, St. Paul, MN, 1986.
[33] Lyneis, James M., *Corporate Planning and Policy Design: A System Dynamics Approach*, MIT Press, Cambridge, MA, 1980.
[34] Mass, Nathaniel, J. "Diagnosing surprise model behavior: A tool for evolving behavioral and policy insight", *Proceedings of the 1981 System Dynamics Research Conference*, Rensselaerville, NY, 14-17 October 1981, 254-272. Also available as *MIT System Dynamics Group Working Paper D-3323*, MIT Sloan School of Management, Cambridge, MA 02139, 1981.
[35] Meadows, Dennis L., "STRATAGEM I: A resource planning game", *Environmental Education Report and Newsletter* 14/2 (1985) 9-13.
[36] Minsky, Marvin, *The Society of Mind*, Simon and Schuster, New York, 1986.
[37] Morecroft, Linda E., "A relative-motion microworld", SM Thesis, Laboratory for Computer Science, Publication no. MIT/LCS/TR-347, MIT, Cambridge, MA, September 1985.
[38] Morecroft, John D.W., "A critical review of diagramming tools for conceptualizing feedback system models", *Dynamica* 8, Part I (1982) 20-29.
[39] Morecroft, John D.W., "System dynamics: Portraying bounded rationality", *Omega* 11/2 (1983) 131-142.
[40] Morecroft, John D.W., "Strategy support models", *Strategic Management Journal* 5/3 (1984) 215-229.
[41] Morecroft, John D.W., "Rationality in the analysis of behavioral simulation models", *Management Science* 31/7 (1985) 900-916.
[42] Morecroft, John D.W., "The feedback view of business policy and strategy", *System Dynamics Review* 1/1 (1985) 4-19.
[43] Morecroft, John D.W. and Paich, Mark, "System dynamics for reasoning about business policy and strategy", Centre for Business Strategy Working Paper 30, London Business School, Regent's Park, London, UK, March 1987.
[44] Paich, Mark, "Generic structures", Research problems section *System Dynamics Review* 1/1 (1985) 126-132.

[45] Papert, Seymour, *Mindstorms*, Basic Books, New York, 1980.
[46] Phillips, Lawrence, D., 'Computing to consensus', *Datamation* 68 (1986) 2-6.
[47] Phillips, Lawrence D., "Decision support for managers", forthcoming in: Harry J. Otway and Malcolm Peltu (eds.), *The Managerial Challenge of New Office Technology*, Butterworths, London, 1987.
[48] Pugh-Roberts Associates, *Project Management Modeling System PMMS*, Pugh-Roberts Associates, Five Lee Street, Cambridge, MA, 1986.
[49] Pugh-Roberts Associates, *Professional DYNAMO Introductory Guide and Tutorial*, and *Professional DYNAMO Reference Manual*, Pugh-Roberts Associates, Five Lee Street, Cambridge, MA, 1986.
[50] Richardson, George P. and Alexander L. Pugh, *Introduction to System Dynamics Modeling with DYNAMO*, MIT Press, Cambridge, MA, 1981.
[51] Richardson, George, P., "Problems with causal loop diagrams", Archives section, *System Dynamics Review*, 2/2 (1986) 158-170.
[52] Richmond, Barry M., "STELLA: Software for bringing system dynamics to the other 98%", *Proceedings of the 1985 International Conference of the System Dynamics Society*, Keystone, CO, July 1985.
[53] Richmond, Barry M., *A Users Guide to STELLA* (2nd printing), High Performance Systems Inc., 13 Dartmouth College Highway, Lyme, NH, November 1985.
[54] Richmond, Barry M., Peter Vescuso and Steven Peterson, *STELLA for Business*, High Performance Systems, 13 Dartmouth College Highway, Lyme, NH, 1987.
[55] Richmond, Barry M., "The strategic forum: From vision to operating policies and back again", High Performance Systems Publications, 13 Dartmouth College Highway, Lyme, NH, 1987.
[56] Roberts, Edward B., "Strategies for effective implementation of complex corporate models", in: Edward B. Roberts (ed.), *Managerial Applications of System Dynamics*, Chapter 4, MIT Press, Cambridge, MA, 1978, 77-85.
[57] Senge, Peter M., "Systems thinking in business: An interview with Peter Senge", *ReVISION* 7/2 (1984).
[58] Senge, Peter M., "Systems principles for leadership", in J. Adams (ed.), *Transforming Leadership*, Miles River Press, Alexandria, VA, 1986.
[59] Senge, Peter M., "Catalyzing systems thinking within organizations", System Dynamics Group Working Paper D-3877-2, Sloan School of Management, MIT, Cambridge, MA, March 1987.
[60] Simon, Herbert A., "Rationality and Decisionmaking", in: *Models of Man*, Wiley, New York, 1957.
[61] Simon, Herbert A., *Administrative Behavior*, third edition, The Free Press, New York, 1976.
[62] Simon, Herbert A., "Rational decision making in business organizations", *The American Economic Review* 69/4 (1978).
[63] Simon, Herbert A., *The Sciences of the Artificial*, MIT Press, Cambridge, MA, 1982.
[64] Simon, Herbert A., *Models of Bounded Rationality Vol. 2: Behavioral Economics and Business Organization*, MIT Press, Cambridge, MA, 1982.
[65] Sterman, John D., "Instructions for running the beer

distribution game", System Dynamics Group Working Paper D-3679, October 1984.

[66] Sterman, John D., "A Behavioral Model of the Economic Long Wave", *Journal of Economic Behavior and Organization* 6/1 (1985) 17–53.

[67] Sterman, John D. and Meadows, Dennis L., "STRATAGEM-2: A microcomputer simulation game of the kondratiev cycle", *Simulation and Games* 16/2 (1985) 174–202.

[68] Sterman, John D., Testing behavioral simulation models by direct experiment", System Dynamics Group Working Paper D-3783-1, Sloan School of Management, MIT, March 1986, forthcoming in *Management Science*.

[69] Sterman, John D., "Misperceptions of feedback in dynamic decisionmaking", System Dynamics Group Working Paper, D-3876-1, Sloan School of Management, MIT, May 1987.

[70] Tufte, E.R., *The Visual Display of Quantitative Information* Graphics Press, Cheshire, CT, 1983.

[71] Tversky, A., and Kahneman, D., "Judgement under uncertainty: Heuristics and biases", *Science* 185 (1974) 1124–1131.

[72] Vapenikova, O. and Dangerfield, B., *DYSMAP2 User Manual*, University of Salford, 1987.

[73] Wolstenholme, E.F., "System dynamics in perspective", *The Journal of the Operational Research Society* 33/6 (1982) 547–566.

[74] Wolstenholme, E.F. and Coyle, R.G., "The development of system dynamics as a methodology for system description and qualitative analysis", *The Journal of the Operational Research Society* 34/7 (1983) 569–581.

[75] Wolstenholme, E.F., "System dynamics: A system methodology or a system modeling technique?", *Dynamica* 9, Part II (1983) 84–90.

MODELING MANAGERIAL BEHAVIOR: MISPERCEPTIONS OF FEEDBACK IN A DYNAMIC DECISION MAKING EXPERIMENT*

JOHN D. STERMAN
Sloan School of Management, Massachusetts Institute of Technology, Cambridge, Massachusetts 02139

Studies in the psychology of individual choice have identified numerous cognitive and other bounds on human rationality, often producing systematic errors and biases. Yet for the most part models of aggregate phenomena in management science and economics are not consistent with such micro-empirical knowledge of individual decision-making. One explanation has been the difficulty of extending the experimental methods used to study individual decisions to aggregate, dynamic settings. This paper reports an experiment on the generation of macrodynamics from microstructure in a common managerial context. Subjects manage a simulated inventory distribution system which contains multiple actors, feedbacks, nonlinearities, and time delays. The interaction of individual decisions with the structure of the simulated firm produces aggregate dynamics which systematically diverge from optimal behavior. An anchoring and adjustment heuristic for stock management is proposed as a model of the subjects' decision processes. Econometric tests show the rule explains the subjects' behavior well. The estimation results identify several 'misperceptions of feedback' which account for the poor performance of the subjects. In particular, subjects are shown to be insensitive to the feedbacks from their decisions to the environment. Finally, the generality of the results is considered and implications for behavioral theories of aggregate social and economic dynamics are explored.
(BEHAVIORAL DECISION THEORY; DYNAMIC DECISION-MAKING; EXPERIMENTAL ECONOMICS; INVENTORY MANAGEMENT; SYSTEM DYNAMICS)

1. Introduction

Experimental studies in economics and the psychology of individual choice have identified numerous cognitive, informational, temporal, and other limitations which bound human rationality, often producing behavior which differs from the predictions of rational models (Simon 1979, Kahneman, Slovic, and Tversky 1982, Plott 1986, Smith 1986, Hogarth and Reder 1987). Yet for the most part models of aggregate phenomena in management science and economics are not consistent with such micro-empirical knowledge of individual decision-making. In a 1981 review Hogarth laments the "insufficient attention" paid "to the effects of feedback between organism and environment." By feedback is meant not merely outcome feedback but changes in the environment, in the conditions of choice, which are caused, directly and indirectly, by an agent's past actions. For example, a firm's decision to increase production feeds back through the market to influence the price of goods, profits, and demand; greater output may tighten the markets for labor and materials; competitors may react—all influencing future production decisions. Such multiple feedbacks are the norm rather than the exception in real problems of choice. Consequently, the focus of much research in behavioral decision theory on individual choice in static and discrete tasks has limited the penetration of psychological perspectives in theories of aggregate dynamics such as the behavior of firms, industries, and the economy. In response, many call for renewed empirical investigation designed to "secure new kinds of data at the micro level, data that will provide direct evidence about the behavior of economic agents and the ways in which they go about making their decisions". (Simon 1984, p. 40). Though crucial, securing such micro-level data is

---

* Accepted by Robert L. Winkler, former Departmental Editor; received September 21, 1987. This paper has been with the author 3 months for 1 revision.

not sufficient. Coleman (1987) argues that the greatest progress in coupling economics and psychology lies in understanding the "apparatus for moving from the level of the individual actor to the behavior of the system," that is, the generation of macrobehavior from microstructure.

This paper applies the experimental methods used so effectively in the study of individual behavior to the generation of macrodynamics from microstructure in a common managerial context. In the experiment subjects manage a simulated industrial production and distribution system, the "Beer Distribution Game". The decision-making task is straightforward: subjects seek to minimize total costs by managing their inventories appropriately in the face of uncertain demand. But the simulated environment is rich, containing multiple actors, feedbacks, nonlinearities, and time delays. The interaction of individual decisions with the structure of the simulated firm produces aggregate dynamics which diverge significantly and systematically from optimal behavior. An anchoring and adjustment heuristic for stock management is proposed as a model of the subjects' decision processes. Econometric tests show the rule explains the subjects' behavior well. Analysis of the results shows that the subjects fall victim to several 'misperceptions of feedback.' Specifically, subjects failed to account for control actions which had been initiated but not yet had their effect. Subjects were insensitive to feedbacks from their decisions to the environment. The majority attributed the dynamics they experienced to external events, when in fact these dynamics were internally generated by their own actions. Further, the subjects' open-loop mental model, in which dynamics arise from exogenous events, is hypothesized to hinder learning and retard evolution towards greater efficiency. Finally, the generality of the results is considered and implications for behavioral theories of aggregate social and economic dynamics are discussed.

2. The Stock Management Problem

One of the most common dynamic decision-making tasks is the regulation of a stock or system state. In such a task, the manager seeks to maintain a quantity at a particular target level, or at least within an acceptable range. Stocks cannot be controlled directly but rather must be influenced by changes in their inflow and outflow rates. Typically, the manager must set the inflow rate so as to compensate for losses and usage and to counteract disturbances which push the stock away from its desired value. Often there are lags between the initiation of a control action and its effect, and/or lags between a change in the stock and the perception of that change by the decision maker. The duration of these lags may vary and may be influenced by the manager's own actions.

Stock management problems occur at many levels of aggregation. At the level of a firm, managers must order parts and raw materials so as to maintain inventories sufficient for production to proceed at the desired rate, yet prevent costly inventories from accumulating. They must adjust for variations in the usage and wastage of these materials and for changes in their delivery delays. At the level of the individual, people regulate the temperature of the water in their morning shower, guide their cars down the highway, and manage their checking account balances. At the macroeconomic level, the Federal Reserve seeks to manage the stock of money to stimulate economic growth and avoid inflation, while compensating for variations in credit demand, budget deficits, and international capital flows.

The generic stock management control problem may be divided into two parts: (i) the stock and flow structure of the system; and (ii) the decision rule used by the manager (Figure 1). Considering first the stock and flow structure, the stock S is the accumulation of the acquisition rate A less the loss rate L:

$$S_t = \int_{t_0}^{t} (A_\tau - L_\tau)d\tau + S_{t_0}. \tag{1}$$

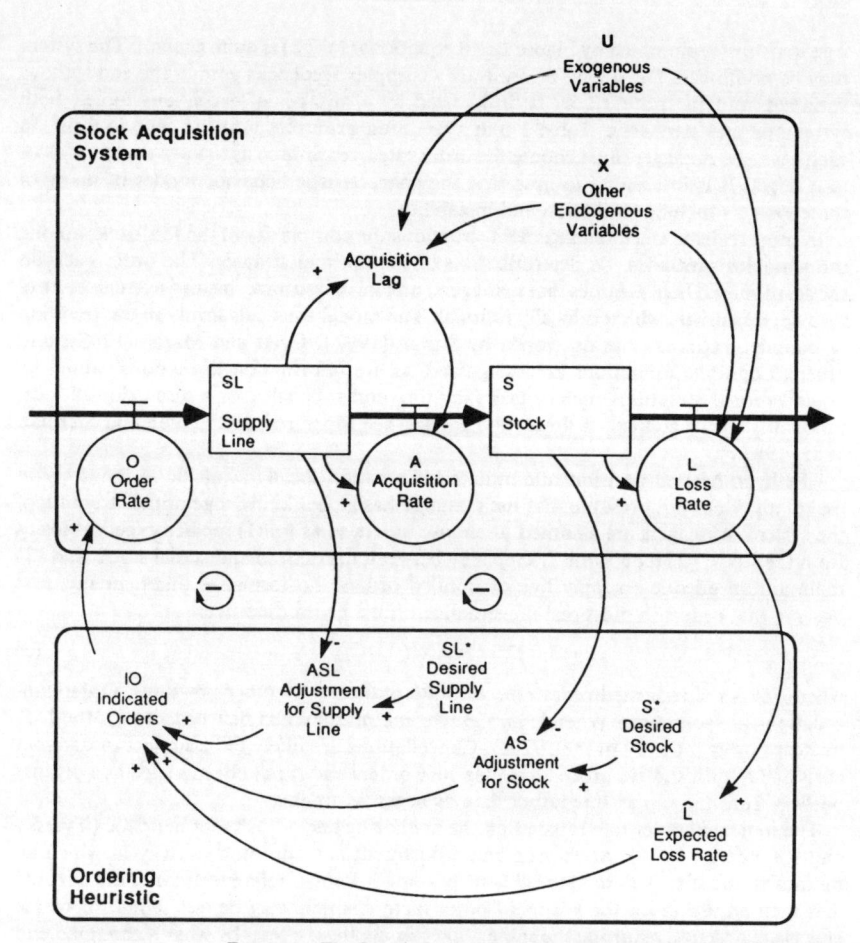

FIGURE 1. The Generic Stock-Management System.
Rectangles denote state variables; heavy arrows and 'valves' denote rates of flow (see equations (1)–(2)). The polarity of the information feedbacks denotes the sign of the relationship between independent and dependent variables, e.g., $X \to {}^+Y \Rightarrow (\partial Y/\partial X) > 0$.

Losses here include any outflow from the stock and may arise from usage (as in a raw material inventory) or decay (as in the depreciation of plant and equipment). The loss rate must depend on the stock itself—losses must approach zero as the stock is depleted—and may also depend on other endogenous variables X and exogenous variables U. Losses may be nonlinear and may depend on the age distribution of the stock.

The acquisition rate depends on the supply line SL of units which have been ordered but not yet received, and the average acquisition lag λ. In general, λ may depend on the supply line itself and on the other endogenous and exogenous variables. The supply line is simply the accumulation of the orders which have been placed O less those which have been delivered:

$$SL_t = \int_{t_0}^{t} (O_\tau - A_\tau) d\tau + SL_{t_0}. \qquad (2)$$

The structure represented by Figure 1 and equations (1)–(2) is quite general. The system may be nonlinear. There may be arbitrarily complex feedbacks among the endogenous variables, and the system may be influenced by a number of exogenous forces, both systematic and stochastic. Table 1 maps common examples into the generic form. In each case, the manager must choose the order rate over time so as to keep the stock close to a target. It is interesting to note that the characteristic behavior modes of many of these systems include oscillation and instability.

In most realistic stock management situations the complexity of the feedbacks among the variables precludes the determination of the optimal strategy. The order decision model proposed here assumes that managers, unable to optimize, instead exercise control through a heuristic which is locally rational. The model thus falls firmly in the tradition of bounded rationality as developed by Simon (1982), Cyert and March (1963), and others. Cognitive limitations are recognized, as are information limitations caused by organizational structures such as task factoring and subgoals (for a discussion of local rationality in the context of simulation models see Morecroft 1983, 1985 and Sterman 1985, 1987a).

The hypothesized decision rule utilizes information locally available to the decision maker and does not presume that the manager has global knowledge of the structure of the system. Managers are assumed to choose orders so as to: (1) replace expected losses from the stock; (2) reduce the discrepancy between the desired and actual stock; and (3) maintain an adequate supply line of unfilled orders. To formalize this heuristic, first observe that orders in most real-life situations must be nonnegative:

$$O_t = \text{MAX}(0, IO_t) \tag{3}$$

where IO is the indicated order rate, the rate indicated by other pressures. Order cancellations are sometimes possible and may sometimes exceed new orders (e.g. the U.S. nuclear power industry in the 1970s). Cancellations are likely to be subject to different costs and administrative procedures than new orders and should be modeled as a distinct outflow from the supply line rather than as negative orders.

The indicated order rate is based on the anchoring and adjustment heuristic (Tversky and Kahneman 1974). Anchoring and adjustment is a common strategy in which an unknown quantity is estimated by first recalling a known reference point (the anchor) and then adjusting for the effects of other factors which may be less salient or whose effects are obscure, requiring the subject to estimate these effects by what Kahneman and Tversky (1982) call 'mental simulation.' Anchoring and adjustment has been shown to apply to a wide variety of decision-making tasks (Einhorn and Hogarth 1985, Davis et al. 1986, Johnson and Schkade 1987, Hines 1987). Here the anchor is the expected loss rate $\hat{L}$. Adjustments are then made to correct discrepancies between the desired and actual stock (AS), and between the desired and actual supply line (ASL):

$$IO_t = \hat{L}_t + AS_t + ASL_t. \tag{4}$$

Expected losses may be formed in various ways. Common formulations include static expectations $\hat{L}_t = L^*$ (a constant or equilibrium value), regressive expectations $\hat{L}_t = \gamma L_{t-1} + (1 - \gamma)L^*$, $0 \leq \gamma \leq 1$, adaptive expectations $\hat{L}_t = \theta L_{t-1} + (1 - \theta)\hat{L}_{t-1}$, $0 \leq \theta \leq 1$, and extrapolative expectations, $\Delta\hat{L}_t = \Sigma \omega_i \cdot \Delta L_{t-i}$, where Δ is the first difference operator and $\omega_i \geq 0$.

The feedback structure of the heuristic is shown in the bottom part of Figure 1. The adjustment for the stock AS creates a negative feedback loop which regulates the stock. For simplicity the adjustment is linear in the discrepancy between the desired stock S^* and the actual stock:

$$AS_t = \alpha_S(S_t^* - S_t), \tag{5}$$

MODELING MANAGERIAL BEHAVIOR

TABLE 1
Examples of Stock-Management Systems

System	Stock	Supply Line	Loss Rate	Acquisition Rate	Order Rate	Typical Behavior
Inventory Management	Inventory	Goods on Order	Shipments to Customers	Arrivals from supplier	Orders for goods	Business cycles
Capital investment	Capital Plant	Plant under construction	Depreciation	Construction completion	New contracts	Construction cycles
Equipment	Equipment	Equipment on order	Depreciation	Equipment delivery	New equipment orders	Business cycles
Human Resources	Employees	Vacanies & trainees	Layoffs and quits	Hiring rate	Vacancy creation	Business cycles
Cash Management	Cash balance	Pending loan applications	Expenditures	Borrowing rate	Loan application rate	?
Marketing	Customer Base	Prospective customers	Defections to competitors	Recruitment of new customers	New customer contacts	?
Hog farming	Hog stock	Immature and gestating hogs	Slaughter rate	Maturation rate	Breeding rate	Hog cycles
Agricultural commodities	Inventory	Crops in the field	Consumption	Harvest rate	Planting rate	Commodity cycles
Commercial construction	Building stock	Buildings under development	Depreciation	Completion rate	Development rate	15–25 year cycles
Cooking on electric range	Temperature of pot	Heat in coils of range	Diffusion to air	Diffusion from coils to pot	Setting of burner	Overcooked dinner
Driving	Distance to next car	Momentum of car	Friction	Velocity	Gas and Brake pedals	Stop-and-go traffic
Showering	Water Temperature	Water Temp. in pipes	Drain rate	Flow from showerhead	Faucet settings	Burn-then-freeze
Personal energy level	Glucose in bloodstream	Sugar and starch in GI tract	Metabolism	Digestion	Food consumption	Cycles of energy level
Social drinking	Alcohol in blood	Alcohol in stomach	Metabolism of alcohol	Diffusion from stomach to blood	Drinking rate	Drunkenness

where the stock adjustment parameter α_S is the fraction of the discrepancy ordered each period. The adjustment for the supply line is formulated analogously as

$$ASL_t = \alpha_{SL}(SL_t^* - SL_t), \qquad (6)$$

where SL^* is the desired supply line and α_{SL} is the fractional adjustment rate for the supply line. The desired supply line in general is not constant but depends on the desired throughput Φ^* and the expected lag between ordering and acquisition of goods:

$$SL_t^* = \hat{\lambda}_t \cdot \Phi_t^*. \qquad (7)$$

The longer the expected delay in acquiring goods or the larger the throughput desired, the larger the supply line must be. For example, if a retailer wishes to receive 1,000 widgets per week from the supplier and delivery requires 6 weeks, the retailer must have 6000 widgets on order to ensure an uninterrupted flow of deliveries. The adjustment for the supply line creates a negative feedback loop which adjusts orders so as to maintain an acquisition rate consistent with the desired throughput and the acquisition lag. Without such a feedback orders would be placed even after the supply line contained sufficient orders to correct stock shortfalls, producing overshoot and instability. The supply line adjustment also compensates for changes in the acquisition lag. If the acquisition lag doubled, for example, the supply line adjustment would induce sufficient additional orders to restore the desired throughput. As in the formation of expected losses, there are a variety of possible representations for $\hat{\lambda}$ and Φ^*, ranging from constants through sophisticated forecasts.

In terms of anchoring and adjustment, expected losses form an easily anticipated and relatively stable starting point for the determination of orders. Loss rate information will typically be locally available and highly salient to the decision maker. Replacing losses will keep the stock constant at its current level. Adjustments are then made in response to the adequacy of the stock and supply line. No assumption is made that these adjustments are optimal or that managers actually calculate the order rate using the equations (Einhorn, Kleinmuntz, and Kleinmuntz 1979). Rather, pressures arising from the discrepancies between desired and actual quantities cause managers to adjust the order rate above or below the level that would maintain the status quo.

3. A Stock Management Experiment

The "Beer Distribution Game" is a role-playing simulation of an industrial production and distribution system developed at MIT to introduce students of management to the concepts of economic dynamics and computer simulation. In use for nearly three decades, the game has been played all over the world by thousands of people ranging from high school students to chief executive officers and government officials.

The game is played on a board which portrays the production and distribution of beer (Figure 2). Orders for and cases of beer are represented by markers and pennies which are manipulated by the players. Each brewery consists of four sectors: retailer, wholesaler, distributor, and factory (R, W, D, F). One person manages each sector. A deck of cards represents customer demand. Each week, customers demand beer from the retailer, who ships the beer requested out of inventory. The retailer in turn orders beer from the wholesaler, who ships the beer requested out of the wholesaler's inventory. Likewise the wholesaler orders and receives beer from the distributor, who in turn orders and receives beer from the factory. The factory produces the beer. At each stage there are shipping delays and order receiving delays. These represent the time required to receive, process, ship, and deliver orders, and as will be seen play a crucial role in the dynamics.

The subjects' objective is to minimize total company costs during the game. Inventory holding costs are $.50/case/week, and stockout costs (costs for having a backlog of

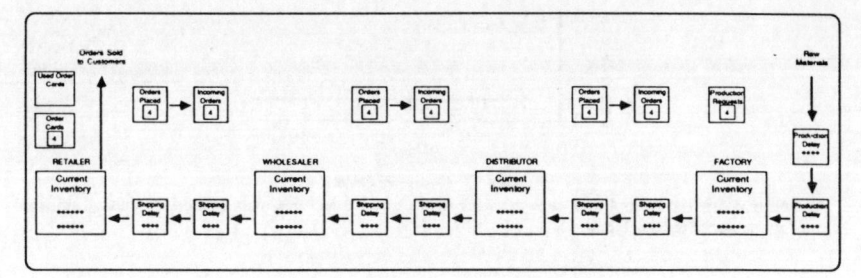

FIGURE 2. "Beer Distribution Game" Board.
Initial conditions are shown: each inventory contains 12 pennies; each shipping/production delay contains 4. Orders are 4 throughout the distribution chain. During actual play the order cards are face down at all times. Each simulated week requires all subjects to carry out five steps:

1. *Receive inventory and advance shipping delays*. The contents of the shipping delay immediately to the right of the inventory are added to the inventory; the contents of the shipping delay on the far right are moved into the delay on the near right. The factory advances the production delays.

2. *Fill orders*. Retailers take the top card in the customer order deck, others examine the contents of "Incoming Orders". Orders are always filled to the extent inventory permits. Unfilled orders add to the backlog, if any. The number of orders to fill is the incoming order plus any backlog from the prior week.

3. *Record inventory or backlog on the record sheet*.

4. *Advance the order slips*. Order slips in the "Orders Placed" box are moved to the "Incoming Orders" box on the immediate right. Factories introduce the contents of "Production Requests" into the top production delay.

5. *Place orders*. Each player decides what to order, records the order on the record sheet and on an order slip which is placed face down in the "Orders Placed" box. Factories place their orders in "Production Requests."

Note that only step 5, Place Orders, involves a decision on the part of the subject. Steps 1–4 handle bookkeeping and other routine tasks.

unfilled orders) are $1.00/case/week. Costs are assessed at each link of the distribution chain.

The decision task of each subject is a clear example of the stock management problem. Subjects must keep their inventory as low as possible while avoiding backlogs. Inventory must be ordered, and the delivery lag is potentially variable (that lag is never less than 4 weeks but may be longer if upstream inventories are insufficient).

Experimental Protocol

Typical sessions involve three to eight teams of four players. Subjects are randomly assigned roles as retailer, wholesaler, etc. Each subject is asked to place $1 in a kitty to be wagered against the other teams. The kitty goes to the team with the lowest total costs, winner take all.[1] Next, the steps of the game are explained (Figure 2). The game is initialized in equilibrium. Each inventory contains 12 cases and initial throughput is four cases per week (Figure 2). Customer demand likewise begins at four cases per week. The first four weeks of play are used to familiarize the subjects with the mechanics of filling orders, recording inventory, etc. During this time customer demand remains constant, and each player is directed to order four cases, maintaining the initial equilibrium. Beginning with week four the players are allowed to order any nonnegative quantity they wish. There is an unannounced, one-time increase in customer demand to eight cases

---

[1] Protocols for experimental economics (e.g. Smith 1982) call for monetary rewards geared to performance. However, a number of experiments have shown performance is not significantly improved and may be worsened by higher reward levels (e.g. Grether and Plott 1979, Slovic and Lichtenstein 1983, Tversky and Kahneman 1981). Here subjects wager $1 for a chance to win about $4. Though small, these rewards emphasize the goal of minimum *team* costs and appear to have a powerful motivating effect.

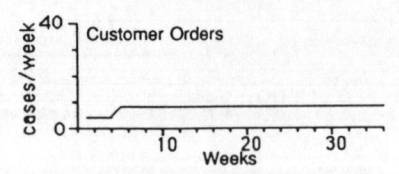

FIGURE 3. Customer Orders.
Customer orders rise from 4 to 8 cases per week in week 5. Vertical tick-marks denote 10 units. Compare against the subjects' orders (Figure 4).

per week in week 5 (Figure 3). The step creates a disequilibrium disturbance to which the subjects must react while facilitating subsequent analysis.

During the sessions questions concerning rules, procedures, or interpretation are answered; questions concerning strategy or customer demand are not. Subjects are told the game will run for 50 simulated weeks, but play is actually halted after 36 weeks to avoid horizon effects. Typically the game is introduced and played in 90 minutes, followed by a debriefing session.

Information Availability

The game is designed so that each subject has good local information but severely limited global information. Each maintains a record sheet which includes their inventory or backlog and orders placed with their supplier for each week. However, subjects are directed not to communicate with one another, either across or within a game. Customer demand is not known to any of the subjects in advance. Retailers are the only subjects who discover customer demand as the game proceeds. The others learn only what their own customer orders, and only after a delay of one week. The players do sit next to one another, and some crosstalk is unavoidable. Each can readily inspect the board to see how large the inventories of beer are at the other stations, thus gleaning information potentially useful in ordering. Game play is usually quite lively and the subjects' outbursts may also convey information.

These information limitations imply that the subjects are unable to coordinate their decisions or jointly plan strategy, even though the objective of each team is to minimize total costs. As in many real situations, the problem of global optimization must be factored into subgoals which are distributed throughout the organization.

The Sample

The results reported here were drawn from 48 trials (192 subjects) collected over a period of four years. Since the subjects keep the records manually there are occasional accounting errors. Trials in which any of the four subjects made significant errors were discarded. Eleven trials were retained (44 subjects). That sample consists of undergraduate, MBA, and Ph.D. students at MIT's Sloan School of Management, executives from a variety of firms participating in short courses on computer simulation, and senior executives of a major computer firm. Analysis showed the trials with the highest costs to be most prone to accounting errors. Thus the final sample of eleven is biased towards those who understood and performed best in the game. The effect is modest, however, and reinforces the conclusions drawn below.

4. Results

The complexity of the system—it is a 23rd order nonlinear difference equation—renders calculation of the optimal behavior intractable. However, a benchmark for evaluating the performance of the subjects was obtained through computer simulation. As

MODELING MANAGERIAL BEHAVIOR

TABLE 2
Comparison of Experimental and Benchmark Costs. Benchmark costs are the minimum costs produced by simulation of the proposed decision rule and are an upper bound estimate of optimal performance in the experiment

	Team Total	Retailer	Wholesaler	Distributor	Factory
Mean ($N = 11$)	$2028	$383	$635	$630	$380
Benchmark	$204	$46	$50	$54	$54
Ratio	9.9	8.3	12.7	11.7	7
t-statistic:	8.7	4.9	5.9	6.9	9.7
H_0: Mean cost = Benchmark	$p < 0.000+$	$p < 0.001$	$p < 0.000+$	$p < 0.000+$	$p < 0.000+$

implemented below, the proposed decision rule involves four parameters. The parameters which produce minimum total costs were calculated by simulation of the game over the plausible parameter space.[2] The benchmark costs were computed subject to the same information limitations faced by the subjects. Benchmark costs are shown in Table 2 compared to actual costs for the eleven trials. The average team cost is ten times greater than the benchmark. The individual sectors exceed the benchmark costs by similar ratios. The differences between actual and benchmark costs are highly significant.

More interesting is the character of the departures from optimality. Are the subjects behaving in similar ways? Do their errors arise from common sources? Figure 4 shows several typical trials; Table 3 summarizes key indicators of the behavior for the full sample. Examination of the order pattern reveals several regularities.

1. *Oscillation*. The trials are all characterized by instability and oscillation. Orders and inventory are dominated by large amplitude fluctuations, with an average of 21 weeks required to recover initial inventory levels. In virtually all cases, the inventory levels of the retailer decline, followed in sequence by a decline in the inventory of the wholesaler, distributor, and factory (Figure 4). As inventory falls, subjects tend to increase their orders. 'Effective inventory' (inventory less any backlog of unfilled orders) generally becomes significantly negative, indicating the sectors have backlogs. The maximum backlog averages 35 cases, and occurs between weeks 20 and 25. As additional product

TABLE 3
Summary of Experimental Results. Averages of 11 Trials

	Customer	Retailer	Wholesaler	Distributor	Factory
Periodicity (weeks)					
Time to recover initial inventory	N/A	24	23	22	16
Date of Minimum Inventory	N/A	20	22	20	22
Date of Maximum Inventory	N/A	28	27	30	26
Amplification					
Peak Order Rate (cases/week)	8	15	19	27	32
Variance of Order Rate (cases/week)^2	1.6	13	23	45	72
Peak Inventory (cases)	N/A	20	41	49	50
Minimum Inventory (cases)	N/A	−25	−46	−45	−23
Range (cases)	N/A	45	88	94	73
Phase Lag					
Date of Peak Order Rate (week)	5	16	16	21	20

---

[2] To reduce the search space the same parameters are used in each sector. The optimal parameters are $\theta = 0$, $\alpha_S = 1$, $\beta = 1$, and $S' = 28$ (20 for the factory).

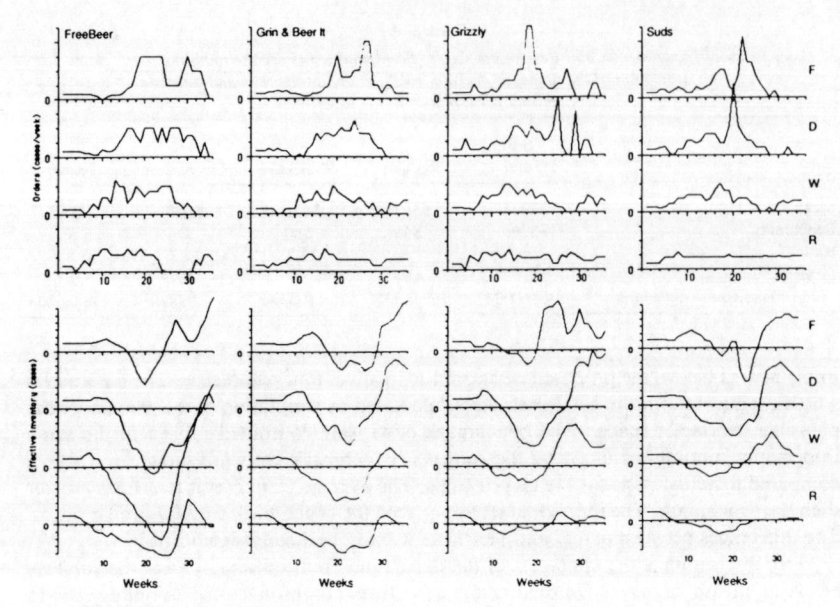

FIGURE 4. Experimental Results for Four Typical Trials.
Top: Orders; bottom: inventory (from bottom to top, Retailer; Wholesaler, Distributor, Factory). Tick-marks on y-axes denote 10 units. Note the oscillation, amplification, and phase lag as the change in customer orders propagates from retailer to factory.

is brewed and shipped inventory levels surge. Inventory in many cases substantially overshoots its initial levels. The inventory peak averages 40 cases and occurs between weeks 25 and 30. Orders fall off rapidly as inventory builds up.

2. *Amplification.* The amplitude and variance of orders increases steadily from customer to retailer to factory. The peak order rate at the factory is on average more than double the peak order rate at retail. Customer orders increase from 4 to 8 cases per week; by the time the disturbance has propagated to the factory the order rate *averages* a peak of 32 cases, an amplification factor of 700%.[3] Amplification in inventory excursions is also apparent. Note that the average period and excursion of factory inventories are somewhat less than those of the distributor and wholesaler. The factory, as primary producer, faces a shorter and constant delay in acquiring beer and can therefore correct inventory discrepancies faster and more reliably than the other sectors. This subtlety in the outcomes illustrates the extent to which the feedback structure of the task shapes the behavior of the subjects.

3. *Phase lag.* The order rate tends to peak later as one moves from the retailer to the factory. Customer orders increase from 4 to 8 in week 5. Retailer orders do not reach their peak until week 16, on average. Factory orders lag behind still further, peaking at week 20 on average. The phase lag is not surprising since the disturbance in customer orders must propagate through decision-making and order delays from retailer to wholesaler and so on.[4]

---

[3] Amplification is a rough measure of closed-loop gain and is measured as the excursion in the output variable relative to that of the input, in this case $\Delta(\text{Factory Orders})/\Delta(\text{Customer Orders}) = (32 - 4)/(8 - 4) = 7$.

[4] There is no apparent lag between retailer and wholesaler or between distributor and factory, perhaps indicating that subjects used information outside their own sector.

Thus while the behavior of the subjects is plainly far from optimal, their behavior exhibits significant regularities, suggesting the subjects used similar heuristics to determine their orders. The pervasiveness and qualitative similarity of the oscillations is particularly noteworthy since the customer order rate, the only external disturbance, does not oscillate and is in fact virtually constant. The oscillation is endogenously produced by the interaction of the subjects' decisions with the feedback structure of the system. Explaining the origin of the cycle and the determinants of its period and amplitude are major tasks for any theory of dynamic decision-making behavior.

5. Testing the Theory

The decision rule must next be adapted to the particulars of the beer game and cast in a form suitable for estimation of the parameters. In the experiment, the stock S corresponds to the effective inventory of the subject and the supply line SL to the sum of orders in the mail delays, the backlog of the subject's supplier (if any), and the beer in the shipping delays. The loss rate is the rate at which each subject receives orders. To test the rule it is necessary to specify expected losses $\hat{L}$, the desired stock S^*, and the desired supply line SL^*.

Expected losses from the stock are the rate at which each subject expects their immediate customer to place orders, that is, the retailer's forecast of the customer order rate, the factory's forecast of the distributor's order rate, etc. Adaptive expectations are postulated. Adaptive expectations are widely used in simulation modeling of economic systems, are often a good model of the evolution of expectations in the aggregate (Sterman 1987b, Frankel and Froot 1987), and are one of the simplest formulations for expectations suitable for nonstationary processes.

Theory suggests the desired stock should be chosen to minimize expected costs given the cost function and expected variability of deliveries and incoming orders. However, the subjects have neither the time nor information to determine optimal inventory levels. The asymmetry of the cost function does suggest desired inventory should be greater than zero. In the absence of a procedure to calculate optimal inventory levels, however, one might expect the subjects' choice of S^* to be anchored to the initial level of 12 units. This hypothesis is tested below.

In general the desired supply line is variable and depends on the anticipated delay in receiving orders. However, subjects lack the means to determine the current lag in receiving orders. That lag is never less than four weeks but may be longer if the supplier has insufficient inventory to fill incoming orders. The desired supply line SL^* is therefore assumed to be constant.

The generic decision rule of equations (3)–(7) then becomes:

$$O_t = \text{MAX}(0, \hat{L}_t + AS_t + ASL_t), \tag{8}$$

$$\hat{L}_t = \theta L_{t-1} + (1 - \theta)\hat{L}_{t-1}, \quad 0 \leq \theta \leq 1, \tag{9}$$

$$AS_t = \alpha_S(S^* - S_t), \tag{10}$$

$$ASL_t = \alpha_{SL}(SL^* - SL_t), \tag{11}$$

where S^* and SL^* are constants. Defining $\beta = \alpha_{SL}/\alpha_S$ and $S' = S^* + \beta SL^*$, collecting terms, and allowing for an additive disturbance term ϵ yields

$$O_t = \text{MAX}[0, \hat{L}_t + \alpha_S(S' - S_t - \beta SL_t) + \epsilon_t]. \tag{12}$$

Note that since S^*, SL^*, α_{SL} and α_S are all ≥ 0, $S' \geq 0$. Further, subjects are unlikely to place more emphasis on the supply line than on inventory itself: the supply line does not directly enter the cost function nor is it as salient as inventory. Therefore it is probable that $\alpha_{SL} \leq \alpha_S$, meaning $0 \leq \beta \leq 1$. Thus β can be interpreted as the fraction of the supply line taken into account. If $\beta = 1$, the subjects fully recognize the supply line and do not overorder. If $\beta = 0$, goods on order are ignored.

The decision rule contains four parameters to be estimated (θ, α_S, S', and β) and is nonlinear. The disturbance ϵ is assumed to be Gaussian white noise. In this case, maximum likelihood estimates are found by minimizing the sum of squared errors $\Sigma\ e_i^2$. The estimated parameters of such nonlinear models are consistent and asymptotically efficient, and the usual measures of significance such as the t-test are asymptotically valid (Judge et al. 1980).[5] The Durbin-Watson test showed no significant residual autocorrelation for 23 of 44 subjects. Monte Carlo simulations showed the estimation procedure was not significantly degraded by autocorrelation in the disturbance as high as $\rho = 0.9$.

Table 4 shows the estimated parameters together with R^2 and root mean square errors. The mean R^2 is 71%; R^2 is less than 50% for only 6 of 44 subjects. A large majority of the estimated parameters are significant. Only 7 values of α_S, 4 values of S', and 15 values of β are not significantly different from zero. Of course any of these parameters could legitimately take on a value of zero. Zero is in fact the estimated value for 14 of the 26 insignificant estimates, and the standard errors of these estimates are smaller, on average, than those for the rest of the sample. However, two-thirds of the estimated values of θ are not significant. It appears that there is insufficient variation in incoming orders to determine if the expectation formation process is misspecified for these subjects.[6]

As a further test the game was simulated using the decision rule with the estimated parameters for each sector. Note that the costs incurred by a sector depend not only on the behavior of that sector but on all the other sectors in the distribution chain, and thus on the vectors of parameters θ, α_S, S', and β for the entire chain. If the rule were perfect, simulated and actual costs would be equal, and regression of the simulated costs on the actual costs would produce a slope of unity (t-statistic in parentheses):

$$\text{Costs}_{i,j} = 1.11 * \text{Simulated Costs } (\theta_j, \alpha_{S_j}, S'_j, \beta_j)_i; \quad i = R, W, D, F; \quad j = 1, \ldots, 11,$$

(16.7)

$N = 44, \quad R^2 = 0.40.$

The slope is less than two standard errors from unity and highly significant, indicating an excellent correspondence between actual and simulated costs.

There is, however, a modest bootstrapping effect. Replacing the subjects with the model of their behavior improves performance. The average improvement is about 5% of actual costs. The improvement arises from the consistency of the decision rule compared to the subjects, who often changed orders from week to week, introducing high-frequency noise (Figure 4). The magnitude of the bootstrapping effect is comparable to that found in many prior studies of bootstrapping (reviewed in Camerer 1981) even though these studies involved linear models of clinical judgments where there were in general no significant

---

[5] Estimates were found by grid search of the parameter space subject to the constraints $0 \leq \theta \leq 1$ and α_S, S', $\beta \geq 0$. θ, α_S, β, and S' were estimated to the nearest 0.1, 0.05, 0.05, and 1 units, respectively. The search space was large enough to ensure capturing the global minimum of $\Sigma\ e_i^2$. The data and computer programs are available from the author. Because the ordering function does not contain a regression constant, the residuals need not satisfy $\Sigma\ e_t = 0$ (estimated and actual orders need not have a common mean) and the conventional R^2 is not an appropriate measure of fit. The alternative $R^2 = r^2$ is used, where r is the simple correlation between estimated and actual orders (Judge et al. 1980).

[6] θ can only be identified if L_t and $\hat{L}_t$ differ. Since $\hat{L}_t$ approaches L_t over time, a tight estimate of θ requires large variation in incoming orders from period to period. For all the retailers and several other sectors the variation in incoming orders is slight (recall that retailers face virtually constant demand). In fact, the 6 largest standard errors for θ are retailers. The hypothesis that expectations of customer demand adapt to past orders for these subjects cannot therefore be rejected; for one third of the sample it is supported.

MODELING MANAGERIAL BEHAVIOR

TABLE 4
Estimated Parameters

Trial & Position	θ	α_s	β	S'	R^2	RMSE
Bassbeer						
R	0.90	0.10	0.65 a	20 a	0.20	3.13
W	0.00	0.25 a	0.50 a	27 a	0.86	1.99
D	0.15	0.05 a	0.35	14	0.74	2.76
F	1.00 a	0.65 a	0.40 a	15 a	0.84	4.56
Budweiser						
R	0.00	0.40 a	0.10 a	7 a	0.67	2.60
W	0.00	0.40 a	0.75 a	30 a	0.92	1.32
D	0.00	0.30 a	0.10 a	10 a	0.88	2.09
F	0.25 c	0.25 a	0.10	9 a	0.87	2.52
Coors						
R	0.00	0.20 a	0.00	25 a	0.57	1.60
W	0.00	0.15 a	0.50 a	38 a	0.11	2.84
D	0.90 a	0.30 a	0.20 a	10 a	0.61	2.84
F	0.25	0.30 a	0.00	18 a	0.73	4.07
Freebeer						
R	0.40	0.35 a	0.45 a	15 a	0.43	4.29
W	0.30	0.05 a	0.00	30 c	0.76	3.57
D	0.05	0.35 a	1.00 a	18 a	0.86	2.72
F	0.25	0.25 a	0.00	19 a	0.89	3.82
Grin & Beer It						
R	0.10	0.35 a	0.65 a	13 a	0.60	1.79
W	0.95 a	0.15 a	0.55 a	14 a	0.79	2.24
D	0.20 b	0.20 a	0.30 a	19 a	0.94	1.75
F	0.25	0.35 a	0.55 a	24 a	0.73	5.02
Grizzly						
R	0.05	0.30 a	0.65 a	31 a	0.58	1.88
W	0.30	0.20 a	0.35 a	27 a	0.82	2.32
D	0.15	0.05	0.25	15	0.32	7.47
F	0.55 a	0.65 a	0.00	9 a	0.75	5.93
Heineken1						
R	0.95	0.15 a	0.00	9 a	0.75	1.92
W	0.50 a	0.00	N/D	N/D	0.87	1.25
D	0.20 a	0.30 a	0.05 a	8 a	0.98	0.96
F	0.80 b	0.00	N/D	N/D	0.60	3.70
Heineken2						
R	0.50	0.05	0.60	6	0.10	4.08
W	0.40 a	0.10 a	0.30 a	16 a	0.81	2.18
D	1.00 a	0.15 a	0.80 a	14 a	0.73	3.26
F	0.55 a	0.80 a	0.00	9 a	0.87	3.08
Heineken3						
R	0.05	0.30 a	0.45 a	5 a	0.89	0.97
W	0.20	0.00	N/D	N/D	0.23	3.17
D	0.30 a	0.10 a	0.90 a	12 a	0.94	0.83
F	0.00	0.30 a	0.15 c	17 a	0.87	1.46
Suds						
R	1.00	0.00	N/D	N/D	0.76	0.85
W	0.05	0.30 a	0.20 a	20 a	0.76	2.23
D	0.15	0.60 a	0.35 a	0	0.69	5.19
F	0.40 a	0.35 a	1.05 a	32 a	0.95	2.06
Twoborg						
R	0.75	0.35 a	0.00	4 a	0.83	1.53
W	0.00	0.25 a	0.05	18 a	0.72	2.65
D	0.05	0.50 a	0.00	15 a	0.84	3.80
F	0.95 a	0.30 b	0.20	26 a	0.66	5.42
Minimum	0.00	0.00	0.00	0	0.10	0.83
Maximum	1.00	0.80	1.05	38	0.98	7.47
Mean	0.36	0.26	0.34	17	0.71	2.86

N/D: Not Defined
Significant at a: 0.005; b: 0.01; c: 0.025 level (1-tailed *t*-test [since parameters must be ≥ 0]).

feedbacks or dynamics. The improvement is consistent as well with the results of Bowman's (1963) application of similar rules to inventory management data for actual firms.

6. Misperceptions of Feedback

The results strongly support the hypothesis that subjects use the proposed heuristic to manage their inventories. Several issues may now be addressed. What do the estimated parameters reveal about the causes of the severely dysfunctional performance of the subjects? To what causes do subjects attribute the dynamics they experience, and how do these attributions affect the potential for learning? Finally, why do subjects use a rule that produces such poor results? The results reveal several distinct misperceptions of the feedback structure of the simulated environment. These misperceptions are responsible for the poor performance of the subjects.

Anchoring in the Choice of the Desired Stock

How do subjects select the desired stock? Because the complexity of the system and limited time available make calculation of optimal inventory levels infeasible, it is hypothesized that the subjects' choice of S^* is anchored to the initial level of 12 units. Since $S' = S^* + \beta SL^*$, S^* and SL^* may be estimated by regression of the estimated values of β on S':

$$S' = 13.9 + \beta*8.4, \qquad N = 40, \qquad R^2 = 0.09. \tag{14}$$
$$(6.9) \quad (2.8)$$

The low R^2 indicates, as one might expect, that individual differences in S^* and SL^* account for most of the variance in S'. The estimated value of SL^*, significant at the 10% level, is considered below. The estimated value of the desired stock S^*, that is, the value of S' when $\beta = 0$, is not significantly different from the initial level of 12 units. It appears that in the absence of a calculus to determine optimal inventories, subjects strongly anchor desired stocks on their initial level.

Misperception of Time Lags

To understand the source of the oscillations it is necessary to consider how the subjects dealt with the long time lags between placing and receiving orders—the supply line. The results show that most subjects failed to account adequately for the supply line. The evidence takes two forms. First, the small estimate of SL^* found in equation (14) indicates that the subjects underestimated the lag between placing and receiving orders. To ensure an appropriate acquisition rate the supply line must be proportional to the lag in acquiring beer (equation (7)). The acquisition lag is never less than 4 weeks (3 for the factory). Even if subjects' expectations of demand (and thus desired throughput) remained at the initial level of 4, the required supply line would be 16 cases, far greater than the estimated value of 8.4 cases. Thus it appears that subjects failed to allow for sufficient beer in the pipeline to achieve their desired inventory level.

More significant is the extent to which subjects responded to the supply line itself, as indicated by the estimated values of β. The optimal value of β is unity: subjects should fully account for the goods in the supply line to prevent overordering. But the mean value of β is just 0.34; only five subjects (11%) accounted for more than two-thirds of the supply line. The result is overordering and instability. For example, consider the Grizzly factory (Figure 4; $R^2 = 0.75$). As in most trials, the distributor begins to place substantially higher orders around week 15. These orders deplete the factory's inventory and build up a backlog of unfilled orders, encouraging the factory to boost orders. However, α_S for the Grizzly factory is 0.65 while $\beta = 0$, meaning the subject ordered two-thirds of the discrepancy between S' and S each period, and completely ignored the supply line.

Since the factory's supply line is three weeks long, the subject orders two-thirds of the stock shortfall for three successive weeks before receiving any of these new orders, overordering by a factor of two. Thus factory orders reach a peak of 50 units in weeks 18 and 19, coincident with the largest backlog. Inventory then rises toward the desired level and the subject cuts orders back. But the orders already in the pipeline continue to arrive, ultimately swelling inventory to a peak of 69 units. Because the distributor also acquired excess inventory (the distributor's $\beta = 0.25$), the factory finds incoming orders plummet to an average of just 5 cases per week after week 25, and ends the trial with high inventory, no way to unload it, and considerable frustration. The factory's ordering policy significantly amplifies the distributor's orders: incoming orders rise from 4 to 20 units; the factory responds by raising orders from 4 to 50 units, an amplification factor of 290%. By ignoring the supply line the factory's ordering policy is highly destabilizing.

In contrast, consider the Suds factory (Figure 4, $R^2 = 0.95$). Here $\beta \approx 1$ while $\alpha_S = 0.35$, indicating the subject fully accounts for the supply line and seeks to correct 35% of any inventory discrepancy each period. Because the Suds factory accounted for the supply line, orders peak and fall *before* the backlog reaches its maximum since the subject realized that sufficient orders to correct the problem were already in the pipeline. The Suds factory actually stabilizes the system: the amplification factor is 85%, meaning the factory's ordering policy attenuates demand shocks rather than exacerbating them.

"*Open-Loop*" Explanations of Dynamics

At the end of the game subjects are debriefed. Emotions run high. The majority express frustration at their inability to control the system. Many report feelings of helplessness—they feel themselves to be at the mercy of forces outside their control. Subjects are then asked to sketch their best estimate of the pattern of customer demand, that is, the contents of the customer order deck. Only the retailers have direct knowledge of that demand. Figure 5 shows a typical set of responses. Invariably the majority of subjects judge that customer demand was oscillatory, first rising from the initial level of 4 cases per week to a peak anywhere from 12 to 40 cases, and then dropping to the neighborhood of 0 to 12 cases per week. Factories and distributors tend to draw the largest excursion; wholesalers tend to draw smaller fluctuations. Only a small fraction suggest that customer demand was essentially constant. It may seem obvious that subjects' judgments of customer demand reflect their experiences during the game: after all, customer demand in reality does fluctuate. Yet these beliefs are revealing. Most subjects attribute the cause of the dynamics they experienced to external events. Most blame their own poor performance on what they see as a perverse pattern of customer demand: the customers increased their demand, encouraging them to order additional beer, but suddenly stopped ordering

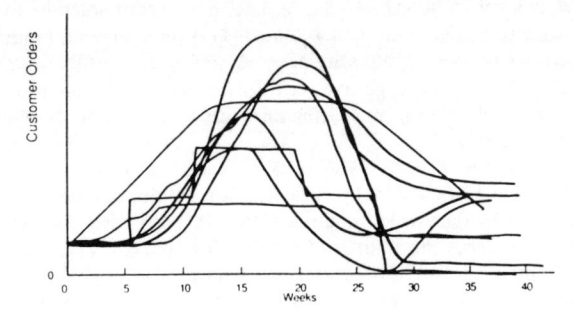

FIGURE 5. Typical Sample of Subjects' Post-Play Judgments of Customer Orders. Compare against actual customer orders (Figure 3).

just when the tap began to flow. Many participants are quite shocked when the actual pattern of customer orders is revealed; some voice strong disbelief. Few ever suggest that their own decisions were the cause of the behavior they experienced. Fewer still explain the pattern of oscillation in terms of the feedback structure, time delays, or stock and flow structure of the game.

Most subjects attribute the dynamics to external variables which they believe to be closely correlated in time and space with the phenomenon to be explained. These explanations reflect an 'open-loop' conception of the origin of dynamics, as opposed to a mode of explanation in which change is seen as arising from the endogenous interactions of decision makers with their environment. Learning from experience may be hindered by such misperceptions of the origins of dynamic behavior. When asked how they could improve their performance, many call for better forecasts of customer demand. The erroneous open-loop attribution of dynamics to exogenous events thus draws subjects' efforts to learn away from the high leverage point in the system (the stock management policy) and towards efforts to anticipate and react to external shocks. While better forecasts are likely to help, the key to improved performance lies within the policy individuals use to manage the system and not in the external environment. Even a perfect forecast will not prevent a manager who ignores the supply line from overordering.

7. Discussion and Conclusions

The experiment, despite its rich feedback structure, is vastly simplified compared to the real world. To what extent do the experimental conditions and results apply? First, would subjects' behavior differ if customer demand followed a more realistic pattern, e.g. noise or seasonality? The order decisions of many subjects were in fact noisy and cyclic (Figure 4). Therefore subjects upstream of these noisy individuals did in fact experience realistic demands. The behavior of these subjects is not statistically different from that of the retailers, indicating that the use of a step input does not reduce the generality of the results.

More fundamentally, are the main features of the experimental behavior observed in real production-distribution systems? It has long been recognized that production-distribution networks in the real economy exhibit the three aggregate behaviors generated in the experiment, i.e. oscillation, amplification from retail sales to primary production, and phase lag (T. Mitchell 1923, Hansen 1951, W. Mitchell 1971, Zarnowitz 1973). Is it plausible that managers in the real economy fall victim to the same misperceptions of feedback which plague subjects of the experiment? After all, in reality managers have access to more information than is available in the experiment. More time is available to gather intelligence and deliberate. Decision aids may be used. On the other hand information in the real world is often out of date, noisy, contradictory and ambiguous. Managers struggle to balance competing demands on their time and must make many additional decisions besides the quantity of goods to order. Consultants and models are subject to many of the same cognitive, informational, and temporal limitations, and there is no accepted calculus for integrating numerous and possibly conflicting positions and information sources.

The hypothesis that managers in real stock management contexts use a rule like the proposed anchoring and adjustment heuristic does not require equivalence of the decision-making tasks but only the weaker condition that in both cases the determination of optimal quantities exceeds the abilities of the decision makers. The virtue of the rule is its simplicity. It requires no knowledge of the dynamics or general equilibrium of the system. It is self-correcting—the feedback structure of the rule ensures that forecast errors, changes in the structure of the environment, and even self-generated overreactions can eventually be corrected. The benchmark costs (Table 2) show the rule can, with reasonable parameters, produce excellent results. As argued in Sterman (1987a), the decision rule characterizes actual decisions well because it captures the essential attributes of any minimally sensible stock management procedure. These are replacement of expected losses, correction of discrepancies between the desired and actual stock, and an accounting for the supply line of unfilled orders.

Of course individual managers do not ignore the goods they have on order. The problem in the real economy is one of aggregation. There are many examples of stock management situations in which the aggregate supply line is distributed among individual competitors and largely unknown to each. It is interesting to note that many of the markets most prone to instability such as agricultural commodities, commercial construction, machine tools, electronic components, and other durable goods are characterized by both significant delays in bringing investments to fruition and imperfect knowledge of the plans, commitments, and pending investments of the participants (Meadows 1970, Hoyt 1933, Commodity Research Bureau, various years). Verification of the supply line hypothesis requires further empirical work focussed not only on the decision processes of individual firms but also on the availability, timeliness, salience, and perceived accuracy of supply line information.

The robustness of the stock management heuristic is illuminating here. An earlier experiment tested the heuristic in a macroeconomic context (Sterman 1987a, 1989). Subjects were responsible for capital investment decisions in a simulated multiplier-accelerator economy. In contrast to the beer game, with its complex structure, multiple players, and time pressure, the macroeconomic system was rather simple. Perfect information was available to the subjects. There were no other participants to consider. The cost function was symmetric. There was no time limit. Yet as in the beer game, the results strongly supported the proposed rule. The rule explained an average of 85% of the variance of the subjects' decisions, and the estimated parameters were generally highly significant. As in the beer game, performance was decidedly suboptimal. Subjects produced large amplitude cycles in response to nonoscillatory inputs. The same misperceptions of feedback were apparent. In particular, subjects were insensitive to the presence of feedback from their decisions to the environment, underestimated the time lag between action and response, and failed to account for the supply line.

Though the stock-management task investigated here has wide applicability, there are many dynamic decision-making tasks which cannot be described by that framework (e.g. price-setting behavior). However, the results suggest the method used here may be helpful in explaining how unintended and dysfunctional results may be produced by apparently reasonable decision processes in diverse systems (e.g. Hall's account (1976, 1984) of the *Saturday Evening Post* and other organizations). Morecroft (1985) suggests the use of simulation to test the intended rationality of the decision rules in simulation models. The experimental approach used here allows direct investigation of the decision processes of real managers, and provides a technique to relate these decision rules to performance. Normative use of the techniques appears also holds some promise.[7]

Future work should apply the experimental method used here to other dynamic decision tasks and should consider the processes by which the parameters of the heuristics are modified or the heuristics themselves revised or replaced by learning and the selective pressures of the market. Tversky and Kahneman (1987) and Hogarth (1981) have stressed ways in which inadequate outcome feedback may hinder learning and efficiency. The

---

[7] In a study in progress, a similar game has been developed for an insurance company. Like the beer game, it appears that similar underperformance and misperceptions arise. After estimating the parameters of the managers' decision rules, the sources of poor performance will be discussed in training sessions. It is hoped that such training will help managers develop more appropriate heuristics by improving their mental models of the feedback environment.

results here suggest that outcome feedback alone is not sufficient: by attributing the source of change to external factors, people's mental models lead them away from the true source of difficulty. Efforts to improve performance may therefore have little leverage and experience may not lead rapidly to improved mental models, allowing dysfunctional performance to persist.

These results reinforce and extend prior work in dynamic decision-making (Brehmer 1987, Hogarth 1981, Kleinmuntz 1985, MacKinnon and Wearing 1985, Remus 1978). The efficacy and robustness of decision strategies lies not only in the availability of *outcome* feedback, but depends crucially on the nature of the *action* feedback between decisions and changes in the environment which condition future decisions. A heuristic may produce stable behavior in one setting and oscillation in another solely as a function of the feedback structure in which it is embedded. That structure consists of the stock and flow structure, information networks, time delays, and nonlinearities which characterize the organization. The magnitude of the oscillations despite a virtually constant external environment suggests the powerful role of action feedback in the genesis of dynamics. Further, the qualitative behavior of the different teams is strikingly similar despite wide variation in individual responses (as represented by the diverse parameters which characterize different subjects). As a result, the aggregate dynamics of an organization may be relatively insensitive to the decision processes of the individual agents, suggesting the importance in both descriptive and normative work of research methods which integrate individual decision-making with theories of feedback structure and dynamics. In that spirit the results show how experimental methods may be coupled with simulation to form a useful part of the "apparatus for moving from the level of the individual actor to the behavior of the system," ultimately yielding testable theories to explain the endogenous generation of macrobehavior from the microstructure of human systems.[8]

[8] The comments of John Carroll, Richard Day, James Hines, Robin Hogarth, Don Kleinmuntz, Robert Winkler, and anonymous referees are gratefully acknowledged. Daniel Ryu provided invaluable assistance.

References

BOWMAN, E. H., "Consistency and Optimality in Managerial Decision Making," *Management Sci.*, 9 (1963), 310–321.
BREHMER, B., "Systems Design and the Psychology of Complex Systems," in J. Rasmussen and P. Zunde (Eds.), *Empirical Foundations of Information and Software Science III*, Plenum, New York, 1987.
CAMERER, C., "General Conditions for the Success of Bootstrapping Models," *Organizational Behavior and Human Performance*, 27 (1981), 411–422.
COLEMAN, J. S., "Psychological Structure and Social Structure in Economic Models," in R. Hogarth and M. Reder (Eds.), *Rational Choice: The Contrast Between Economics and Psychology*, University of Chicago Press, Chicago, 1987.
COMMODITY RESEARCH BUREAU, *Commodity Year Book*, Commodity Research Bureau, Inc., New York, various years.
CYERT, R. AND J. MARCH, *A Behavioral Theory of the Firm*, Prentice Hall, Englewood Cliffs, NJ, 1963.
DAVIS, H. L., S. J. HOCH AND E. K. EASTON-RAGSDALE, "An Anchoring and Adjustment Model of Spousal Predictions," *J. Consumer Res.*, 13 (1986), 25–37.
EINHORN, H. J. AND R. M. HOGARTH, "Ambiguity and Uncertainty in Probabilistic Inference," *Psychological Rev.*, 92 (1985), 433–461.
———, D. KLEINMUNTZ AND B. KLEINMUNTZ, "Linear Regression and Process-Tracing Models of Judgment," *Psychological Rev.*, 86 (1979), 465–485.
FRANKEL, J. A. AND K. A. FROOT, "Using Survey Data to Test Standard Propositions Regarding Exchange Rate Expectations," *Amer. Economic Rev.*, 77 (1987), 133–153.
GRETHER, D. AND C. PLOTT, "Economic Theory of Choice and the Preference Reversal Phenomenon," *Amer. Economic Rev.*, 69 (1979) 623–638.
HALL, R. I., "The Natural Logic of Management Policy Making: Its Implications for the Survival of an Organization," *Management Sci.*, 30 (1984), 905–927.
———, "A System Pathology of an Organization: The Rise and Fall of the Old Saturday Evening Post," *Admin. Sci. Quart.*, 21 (1976), 185–211.

HANSEN, A. H., *Business Cycles and National Income*, W. W. Norton, New York, 1951.
HINES, J. H., "A Behavioral Theory of Interest Rate Mechanics," *Essays in Behavioral Economic Modeling*, PhD dissertation, Sloan School of Management, MIT, 1987.
HOGARTH, R. M., "Beyond Discrete Biases: Functional and Dysfunctional Aspects of Judgmental Heuristics," *Psychological Bulletin*, 90 (1981), 197–217.
────── AND M. W. REDER (Eds.), *Rational Choice: The Contrast Between Economics and Psychology*, University of Chicago Press, Chicago, 1987.
HOYT, H. *One Hundred Years of Land Values in Chicago*, University of Chicago Press, Chicago, 1933.
JOHNSON, E. J. AND D. A. SCHKADE, "Heuristics and Bias in Utility Assessment," unpublished manuscript, Wharton School, University of Pennsylvania, Philadelphia, 1987.
JUDGE ET AL., *"The Theory and Practice of Econometrics*, Wiley, New York, 1980.
KAHNEMAN, D. AND A. TVERSKY, "The Simulation Heuristic," in Kahneman, D. et al., *Judgment Under Uncertainty: Heuristics and Biases*, Cambridge University Press, Cambridge, 1982.
──────, P. SLOVIC AND A. TVERSKY, *Judgment Under Uncertainty: Heuristics and Biases*, Cambridge University Press, Cambridge, 1982.
KLEINMUNTZ, D. N., "Cognitive Heuristics and Feedback in a Dynamic Decision Environment," *Management Sci.*, 31, 6 (1985), 680–702.
MACKINNON, A. AND A. WEARING, "Systems Analysis and Dynamic Decision Making," *Acta Psychologica*, 58 (1985), 159–172.
MEADOWS, D. L., *Dynamics of Commodity Production Cycles*, MIT Press, Cambridge, MA, 1970.
MITCHELL, T. W., "Competitive Illusion as a Cause of Business Cycles," *Quart. J. Economics*, 38 (1923), 631–652.
MITCHELL, W. C., *Business Cycles and their Causes*, Univ. of California Press, Berkeley, 1971.
MORECROFT, J., "System Dynamics: Portraying Bounded Rationality," *Omega*, 11 (1983), 131–142.
──────, "Rationality in the Analysis of Behavioral Simulation Models," *Management Sci.*, 31 (1985), 900–916.
PLOTT, C. R., "Laboratory Experiments in Economics: The Implications of Posted Price Institutions," *Science*, 232 (9 May 1986), 732–738.
REMUS, W. E., "Testing Bowman's Managerial Coefficient Theory Using a Competitive Gaming Environment," *Management Sci.*, 24 (1978), 827–835.
SIMON, H. A., "Rational Decisionmaking in Business Organizations," *Amer. Economic Rev.*, 69 (1979), 493–513.
SIMON, H. A., *Models of Bounded Rationality*, The MIT Press, Cambridge, MA, 1982.
──────, "The Behavioral and Rational Foundations of Economic Dynamics," *J. Economic Behavior and Organization*, 5 (1984), 35–55.
SLOVIC, P. AND S. LICHTENSTEIN, "Preference Reversals: A Broader Perspective," *Amer. Economic Rev.*, 73 (1983), 596–605.
SMITH, V. L., "Experimental Methods in the Political Economy of Exchange," *Science*, 234 (10 October 1986), 167–173.
──────, "Microeconomic Systems as an Experimental Science," *Amer. Economic Rev.*, 72 (1982), 923–955.
STERMAN, J. D., "A Behavioral Model of the Economic Long Wave," *J. Economic Behavior and Organization*, 6 (1985), 17–53.
──────, "Testing Behavioral Simulation Models by Direct Experiment," *Management Sci.*, 33 (1987a), 1572–1592.
──────, "Expectation Formation in Behavioral Simulation Models," *Behavioral Sci.*, 32 (1987b), 190–211.
──────, "Misperceptions of Feedback in Dynamic Decisionmaking," *Organizational Behavior and Human Decision Processes*, forthcoming 1989.
TVERSKY, A. AND D. KAHNEMAN, "Judgment Under Uncertainty: Heuristics and Biases," *Science*, 185 (27 September 1974), 1124–1131.
────── AND ──────, "The Framing of Decisions and the Psychology of Choice," *Science*, 211 (30 January 1981), 453–458.
────── AND ──────, "Rational Choice and the Framing of Decisions," in R. Hogarth and M. Reder (Eds.), *Rational Choice: The Contrast Between Economics and Psychology*, University of Chicago Press, Chicago, 1987.
ZARNOWITZ, V., *Orders, Production, and Investment—A Cyclical and Structural Analysis*, National Bureau of Economic Research, New York, 1973.

[12]

Boom, Bust, and Failures to Learn in Experimental Markets

Mark Paich • John D. Sterman
Department of Economics, Colorado College, Colorado Springs, Colorado 80903
Sloan School of Management, Massachusetts Institute of Technology, 50 Memorial Drive,
Cambridge, Massachusetts 02142

Boom and bust is a pervasive dynamic for new products. Word of mouth, marketing, and learning curve effects can fuel rapid growth, often leading to overcapacity, price war, and bankruptcy. Previous experiments suggest such dysfunctional behavior can be caused by systematic "misperceptions of feedback," where decision makers do not adequately account for critical feedbacks, time delays, and nonlinearities which condition system dynamics. However, prior studies often failed to vary the strength of these feedbacks as treatments, omitted market processes, and failed to allow for learning. A decision making task portraying new product dynamics is used to test the theory by varying the strength of key feedback processes in a simulated market. Subjects performed the task repeatedly, encouraging learning. Nevertheless, performance relative to potential is poor and is severely degraded when the feedback complexity of the environment is high, supporting the misperception of feedback hypothesis. The negative effects of feedback complexity on performance were not moderated by experience, even though average performance improved. Models of the subjects' decision making heuristics are estimated; changes over trials in estimated cue weights explain why subjects improve on average but fail to gain insight into the dynamics of the system. Though conditions for learning are excellent, experience does not appear to mitigate the misperceptions of feedback or systematic dysfunction they cause in dynamic decision making tasks. We discuss implications for educational use of simulations and games.
(*Decision Making; Simulation; Feedback; Experimental Economics; System Dynamics*)

Boom and bust is a pervasive dynamic for new products. Sales of new products often grow rapidly as word of mouth, advertising, and falling prices attract new buyers. New producers tend to enter the market. But eventually the stock of potential purchasers is depleted and sales fall to an equilibrium determined by replacement needs. During the transition to replacement demand producers often suffer large losses due to excess capacity and falling prices, stimulating exit (Gort and Klepper 1982, Klepper and Graddy 1990).

As a typical example, Figure 1 shows the sales and profits of Atari, the leader of the first wave of video games. Atari, then a division of Warner Communications, roughly doubled its sales each year, from $35 million in 1976 to over $2 billion in 1983. Operating profit reached $323 million in 1983. Yet within a year sales plummeted as both home and arcade markets became glutted. Atari lost $539 million in 1983, and was sold for just $160 million in debt, a 32% equity stake, and no cash (Petre 1985). Warner took an additional $592 million charge against 1984 earnings for losses related to the sale.

Porter (1980) describes this pattern of boom, bust, price war and shakeout as a generic feature of industrial dynamics:

> As [a maturing industry] adjusts to slower growth, the rate of capacity addition in the industry must slow down as well or overcapacity will occur. Thus companies' orientations toward

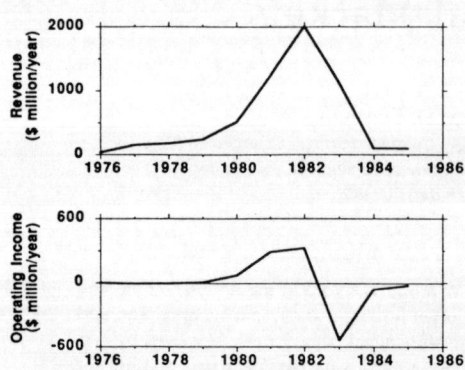

Figure 1. Boom and Bust: Sales and Operating Income of Atari, Inc.

adding capacity and personnel must fundamentally shift and be disassociated from the euphoria of the past. . . . These shifts in perspective rarely occur in maturing industries, and overshooting of industry capacity relative to demand is common. Overshooting leads to a period of overcapacity, accentuating the tendency during transition toward price warfare. (p. 239)

Boom and bust occurs in diverse industries. "Snowmobiles, hand calculators, tennis courts and equipment, and integrated circuits are just a few" examples cited by Porter (1980). To these can be added VCRs and other consumer electronics, personal computers, toys and games (Beinhocker 1991), bicycles and chain saws (Porter 1983), home furnishings (Salter 1969), fiberglass sailboats (Carlson 1990) and many others. This study explores the role of cognitive misperceptions and decision-making errors in the genesis and persistence of the boom and bust phenomenon.

The boom and bust dynamic exemplifies a dynamic decision making system. Decisions made today alter the environment, giving rise to information upon which tomorrow's decisions are based—the evolution of the system is strongly conditioned by the behavior of the decision makers. Recent studies show, with few exceptions, that decision making in complex dynamic environments is poor relative to normative standards or even relative to simple heuristics, especially when decisions have indirect, delayed, nonlinear, and multiple feedback effects (Diehl 1992; Sterman 1989a, 1989b; Kleinmuntz and Thomas 1987; Brehmer 1990, 1992; Smith et al. 1988; Funke (1991) reviews the large literature of the "German School" led by Dörner, Funke, and colleagues). Sterman (1989a, 1989b) argued that the mental models people use to guide their decisions are dynamically deficient. People generally adopt an event-based, "open-loop" view of causality, ignore feedback processes, fail to appreciate time delays between action and response and in the reporting of information, do not understand stocks and flows, and are insensitive to nonlinearities which may alter the strengths of different feedback loops as a system evolves. Sterman argued that such "misperceptions of feedback" cause systematically dysfunctional behavior in dynamically complex settings.

The term "misperceptions of feedback" covers more than simple perception. At the most basic level, poor performance can arise because decision makers do not attend to or perceive helpful outcome feedback. For example, real estate developers tend to start new projects when rents are high and prices are rising, and ignore the supply line of buildings under construction (Bakken 1993, Hoyt 1933). By the time their projects are completed the market is glutted and prices have fallen. The information needed for high performance is available but not heeded: a misperception of (outcome) feedback. Why? Failure to utilize important cues can result from dynamically deficient mental models. Decision makers who do not understand feedback concepts are unlikely to perceive the feedback loops, time delays, and nonlinearities that create the system's dynamics and so may not see the relevance of a critical cue: a misperception of feedback *structure*. At a still deeper level, even given perfect information and complete knowledge of system structure people are not able to infer the resulting dynamics. To do so requires intuitive solution of high-order nonlinear differential equations, a task far exceeding human cognitive capabilities in all but the simplest systems (Forrester 1971, Simon 1982).

Winston Churchill, commenting on the design of the House of Commons, wrote "We shape our buildings, and then our buildings shape us." Similarly, the different threads of the misperceptions of feedback phenomenon are themselves entwined in feedback loops. These interactions have not received sufficient attention in dynamic decision making research. In many studies feedback complexity was not varied as an experimental treatment; other factors might have been responsible for subjects' poor performance. Market institutions, argued by many to provide incentives and means to overcome individual departures from rationality (Hogarth and Reder 1987), have not been included in most studies of dynamic decision making (but see Kampmann and Sterman 1992). Many studies report the results of first trials in which subjects had little opportunity for learning. In others (Brehmer 1990, Kleinmuntz and Thomas 1987, Broadbent and Aston 1978 and many of the studies surveyed in Funke 1991), subjects had little or no prior training or experience relevant to the task (fighting forest fires, treating disease, running a national economy or managing an ecosystem). While good arguments can be made that "real life" is more like the first trial in such experiments than the last (Camerer 1987), the robustness of the misperception of feedback phenomenon to opportunities for learning has largely gone untested.

This study addresses many of the limitations of earlier work. The task—the management of a new product—is realistic and well matched to the interests of the management school subjects, most with several years of business experience. The simulated environment includes market forces. Powerful incentives are used to motivate performance. The misperception of feedback (MOF) hypothesis is tested directly by varying the strength of key feedback processes across experimental conditions. If subjects are prone to misperceptions of feedback, performance relative to potential should be systematically worse under high feedback complexity, since these feedbacks will produce consequences unaccounted for by subjects' mental models, and better in environments with low complexity, since these environments will more closely coincide with their mental models. Further, the subjects performed the task repeatedly, creating opportunities for learning which might improve performance. We describe the task, protocol, and results, analyze the nature of the learning process, and close with implications for educational use of simulations and games.

The Task: Managing a New Product

We developed an interactive computer game or "management flight simulator" (Senge and Sterman 1992,

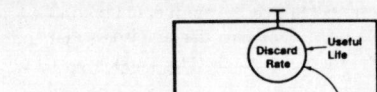

Figure 2 Causal Structure of the Market Sector

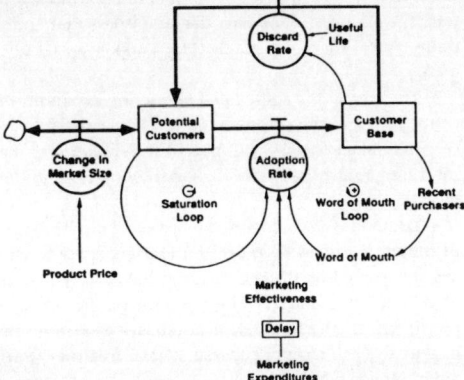

Graham et al. 1992, Sterman 1988 and 1992 discuss design principles and give examples). The flight simulator embodies a model representing a firm, its market, and its competition. Subjects manage a new product from launch through maturity, making price and capacity decisions each quarter year through a ten-year simulation.[1]

Market Sector

The market model is based on well known diffusion models in the tradition of Bass (1969), Kalish and Lilien (1986), Mahajan and Wind (1986), Homer (1987), and Mahajan et al. (1990). The essence of these models is the feedback structure through which potential purchasers become aware of and choose to buy the product (Figure 2). Adoption increases the customer base, generating word of mouth which leads to additional sales (a positive feedback), but also depleting the pool of potential customers (a negative feedback). The customer base follows an s-shaped pattern, while sales rise exponentially, then peak and decline to the rate of replacement purchases as the market saturates.[2]

---

[1] See Paich (1993) for documentation of the model, methods and results. The game, revised for educational use with user's guide and instructor's manual, is available from John Sterman.

[2] In reality additional feedbacks exist involving, e.g., changes in technology, line extensions, cannibalization of sales by new generations of the product, network externalities, and so on. To keep the task manageable these effects are not treated.

Key features of the market sector include:
- Product price affects the number of potential adopters. The elasticity of industry demand is less than unity, quite typical for many goods (Hauthakker and Taylor 1970).
- The greater the aggregated marketing expenditures of the firm and the competition, the larger the fraction of potential customers who purchase each quarter. Diminishing returns set in for high marketing expenditure levels.
- Demand is also generated by word of mouth. Word of mouth is driven by recent purchasers (people who are still excited by the product and have not yet come to take it for granted). The strength of the word of mouth effect (the number of purchases generated per quarter by each recent purchaser) was a treatment variable in the experiment.
- A fraction of the customer base re-enters the market each quarter to replace worn or obsolete units. The repurchase fraction was a treatment variable in the experiment.
- Total orders for the product are divided between the firm and the competition in proportion to the attractiveness of each product. Attractiveness depends on price, availability (measured by delivery delay), and marketing expenditure. Firm demand is highly but not infinitely elastic—price is important to consumers but availability and marketing can differentiate the two products.

Firm Sector

While many diffusion models implicitly equate shipments with orders, the model here explicitly represents the supply side of the market. The key assumptions of the firm sector are:
- Product is built to order. Customer orders flow into a backlog until they are produced and shipped.[3] The firm will ship the current backlog within one period unless capacity is inadequate, in which case the backlog and delivery delay rise, reducing the attractiveness of the firm's product and the share of orders it receives.

- Subjects set a capacity target each quarter. Actual capacity adjusts to the target with a delay representing the time required to plan for, acquire, and ramp up new production facilities. Capacity adjustments follow a distributed lag with a mean of four quarters. Some investments can be realized sooner than four quarters (purchasing equipment), while some take longer (building a new plant). For simplicity the delay is symmetrical in the case of capacity reduction.
- The firm benefits from a learning curve which reduces unit costs as cumulative production experience grows. A standard "80%" learning curve is assumed— each doubling of cumulative production reduces unit variable costs by 20%. The competitor's learning curve has identical strength. Learning is assumed to be fully appropriable.
- Profit is revenue less total costs. Total costs consist of fixed and variable costs, marketing expenditures, and investment costs. Revenues are determined by the quantity shipped in the current quarter and the average price received for those units. Customers pay the price in effect when they booked their order, even if the price has changed in the interim.
- Fixed Costs are proportional to current capacity. Unit fixed costs are constant. Variable costs are proportional to output. Unit variable costs fall as cumulative production increases. Marketing expenditures are set to 5% of revenues.
- Investment costs represent administrative, installation, training, and other costs of increasing capacity. Symmetric decommissioning costs are incurred whenever capacity is decreased. Investment costs are proportional to the magnitude of the rate of change of capacity.
- Subjects may lose as much money as they like without facing bankruptcy. The task is therefore more forgiving than reality since losses leading to bankruptcy in real life can in the game be offset by subsequent profits.

Competitor Structure and Strategy

The subject's firm faces competition from another firm which has launched a similar product at the same time. The playing field is level—the structure and parameters for the firm and its competitor are identical. But while the subjects make price and target capacity decisions

---

[3] Experimental evidence shows that inventories would substantially destabilize the system and make the player's task much harder (Sterman 1989b, Diehl 1992).

for their firm, the competitor's price and target capacity decisions are simulated.

The competitor sets target capacity to meet expected orders and maintain normal capacity utilization. Expected orders are determined by the competitor's current order rate and the expected growth rate of orders. Extrapolative expectations are assumed: the recent growth rate of orders is projected four quarters ahead—the length of the capacity acquisition lag—to account for the growth in demand likely to occur while awaiting delivery of capacity ordered today. The forecast of future demand is adjusted in proportion to the balance between desired production and capacity. If desired production exceeds current capacity, additional capacity is ordered to reduce the backlog, and vice-versa. The decision rule for competitor capacity acquisition is extensively used in simulation models and is well supported empirically and experimentally (Senge 1980; Sterman 1987a, 1987b). Competitor price is set to equal unit costs multiplied by a fixed margin to cover marketing and investment costs, and to provide a normal return when capacity is well utilized. As production experience grows, unit costs fall, and competitor price falls proportionally.

These decision rules are extremely simple. Consistent with theories of bounded rationality (Simon 1982, Morecroft 1985) and the experimental evidence cited above, the competitor relies on locally available information and uses simple rules of thumb. The competitor does not optimize, nor engage in any strategic or game-theoretic reasoning. One might expect that subjects would easily find ways to exploit the competitor and achieve excellent results. On the other hand, Hogarth and Makridakis (1981) found that subjects in a management game could not differentiate between simulated and human competitors and attributed complex strategic reasoning to "players" whose decisions were largely random.

Hypotheses and Experimental Design

The central issue is the extent to which subject behavior depends on the feedback complexity of the environment. In markets for new products two critical feedback processes involve word of mouth and the average lifetime of the product. Word of mouth creates a powerful positive feedback loop by which recent purchasers of the product generate new purchasers. The stronger the word of mouth feedback, the faster demand grows, the higher it peaks, and the sooner and more suddenly the market declines as the nonlinear transition to saturation sets in. The longer the lifetime of the product, the lower the replacement demand and the larger the "bust" as demand falls from its peak to equilibrium value. We seek to understand whether subjects employ capacity expansion and pricing strategies that are internally consistent and that function well in the rich feedback environment surrounding the diffusion of new products.

Obviously, changes in feedback complexity change potential performance. Strengthening the word of mouth feedback or lengthening product lifetimes makes the task objectively more difficult, reducing potential profit. But prior work (Sterman 1989a, 1989b; Diehl 1992) predicts that performance *relative to potential* should deteriorate as the word of mouth feedback increases in strength and as the product lifetime lengthens. Performance relative to potential is hypothesized to decline as dynamic complexity increases because subjects will approach the decision task with mental models that are insufficiently sensitive to these feedbacks, nonlinearities and delays, leading to decisions that intensify the problems created by strong word of mouth and long lifetimes.

To illustrate, consider a mental model many student subjects bring to the task: the learning curve strategy. A firm facing a strong learning curve can achieve sustained cost advantage by setting prices lower than the competition and aggressively expanding capacity. If such aggressive tactics give the firm a market share lead, its costs will fall faster than the competitors', allowing it to gain still more market share while remaining profitable. The learning curve strategy is widely preached in the business literature, consulting world and management schools (Oster 1990, Porter 1980, Hax and Majluf 1984). Not surprisingly, many subjects, noting the presence of a strong learning curve, choose to pursue the learning curve strategy in the experiment.

However, the effectiveness of the learning curve strategy is contingent on the feedback complexity of the environment. When word of mouth is weak and replacement demand strong peak demand overshoots equilibrium only slightly. Capacity planning is straightforward, and an aggressive player runs little risk of excess capacity when the market saturates. However, when these feedbacks are strong the same strategy might lead to disaster. Low prices and aggressive expansion will lead to a large overshoot if the market saturates unexpectedly. The resulting excess capacity and losses may overwhelm the cost advantages of rapid learning (Beinhocker et al. 1993). Furthermore, the aggressive strategy feeds back to exacerbate the boom and bust dynamic. Low prices induce more customers to enter the market, accelerating demand growth. Aggressive capacity expansion speeds growth of the customer base, strengthening the word of mouth feedback. By augmenting the growth-generating feedbacks, the learning curve strategy increases peak demand and forces saturation to occur more rapidly. Forecasting becomes more difficult. Firms are more likely to experience excess capacity, undercutting the benefits of market share advantage.

Thus managers may intensify or moderate the boom and bust dynamic, depending on how well they understand the feedback structure of their environment. The misperceptions of feedback hypothesis thus predicts strong main effects of the treatments, with performance relative to potential degraded significantly by stronger word of mouth and longer product lifetimes.

Yet performance should improve with experience. Improvement might arise for two reasons with quite different implications. First, all features of the task other than the treatment variables remain constant over successive trials. Subjects can be expected to improve simply because they become increasingly familiar with the task and information display. Later trials will be informed by knowledge of the magnitudes and timing the variables achieved in prior trials. Beyond learning from these surface features, however, we hope and expect subjects will gain a deeper appreciation for the dynamics of the system and the feedback processes that produce them, allowing them to perform better in complex feedback environments. The distinction between these two modes of learning is critical. Since real situations vary in more dimensions than the task, improvement based on knowledge that, say, "last time demand reached about two million units/quarter" will not transfer well from one actual new product setting to another. Insight into the system's feedback structure and dynamics, however, can be applied to situations with very different numerical outcomes. Learning derived from surface features of the task is expected to improve performance on average, but differences in performance across feedback conditions would remain. Insight into the feedback structure of the task, in contrast, should help subjects improve performance more in conditions of high feedback complexity. Such deep learning would manifest as a significant interaction between the treatments and trial in which the negative effects of strong word of mouth and long product lifetimes are moderated by experience.

We created five scenarios identical except for the strength of the word of mouth feedback and replacement fraction. These parameters were varied from half to double their base case values to produce five scenarios with orthogonal (log) values of the two treatments. Figure 3 shows the pattern market demand would take in

Figure 3 Experimental Treatments and Resulting Market Dynamics

Note: Assumes no capacity constraints and constant margin pricing. Actual demand patterns also depend on subject decisions.

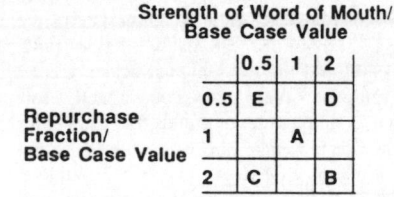

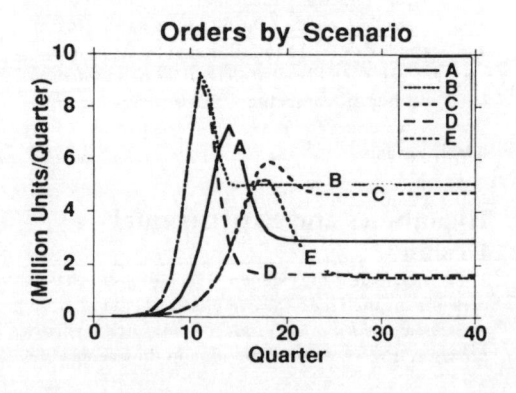

Strength of Word of Mouth/
Base Case Value

	0.5	1	2
Repurchase Fraction/ Base Case Value 0.5	E		D
1		A	
2	C		B

Orders by Scenario

1444

the five scenarios assuming no capacity constraints and assuming price equals unit costs plus a fixed gross margin of 25%. When word of mouth is strong demand grows rapidly, peaks at a large value, and declines sharply compared to those cases where word of mouth is weak. When the replacement interval is long, the drop to equilibrium is large, while frequent replacement leads to modest declines. Of course, the actual order pattern is also influenced by the subject's decisions, both directly, through the influence of price and capacity on demand, and indirectly, through the subject's influence on competitor behavior.

The 122 subjects were students in two sections of an elective class on system dynamics at MIT's Sloan School of Management. About 35% and 40% were first and second year MBA students, respectively. Roughly 10% were mid-career managers in an executive MBA program, 7% were undergraduates and the rest were graduate students from other MIT departments. We used a Latin square design with five sequences of the five scenarios. Subjects were randomly assigned to one of the five sequences by randomizing the floppy disks prior to distribution. Though a few subjects failed to complete all five trials, the design was quite well balanced. The number of trials in each of the 25 cells of the design ranged from 19 to 27, with a mean of 23.

The task was assigned as homework to be done individually within ten days. Subjects received a detailed written description of the firm, market, competitor, cost structure, information available, and so on (Paich 1993). The software was demonstrated in class, and the simulated environment discussed. Subjects could take as much time as they wished for each decision, and could suspend play between trials, resuming it later, moderating fatigue effects and encouraging reflection between trials. Subjects were instructed to keep a log during each trial, including the strategy they intended to follow and evaluation of their results. Subjects were told these write-ups would be graded for the quality of the analysis, providing an incentive to formulate a sensible strategy and evaluate its effects carefully.[4] Subjects also received "bonus points" in proportion to their cumulative profits for all five trials (grades were never reduced no matter how poorly subjects did). Students' evident concern with grades and the large number of questions received about the bonus point system suggest the bonus provided a powerful incentive to perform well.[5]

A disadvantage of the protocol is the lack of control over the time spent by each subject. Allowing subjects to work at their own pace over an extended period meant individual effort could vary, introducing additional between-subject variance. On the other hand, the design increased the incentives and opportunity for subjects to perform well and learn. Further, many protocols for the use of simulations in university and executive education closely parallel the design used here. The experiment thus offers a chance to examine how people learn from simulation games.

Each trial consisted of a 40 quarter market. The first two quarters of data were provided to orient the subjects, who then made 38 sets of target capacity and price decisions. After each decision, outcome feedback was provided showing the results for the quarter. A spreadsheet display was used since the subject pool, management students with excellent computer skills, were all experienced in interpreting such displays. The screen presented 19 variables, including a complete description of the firm's operations and finances, extensive market data and competitor intelligence. The display normally showed the current and three prior quarters. Subjects could at any time scroll through the entire history with a few clicks of the mouse. In addition, subjects could select up to four variables to display graphically the entire history of the trial to date. Any of the variables in the spreadsheet could be so displayed; graphs could be constructed at any time and as often as desired. The software automatically recorded the results.

Results

Before presenting the statistical results it is useful to examine the dynamics generated by the subjects. Figure

---

[4] The purpose of the logs was to encourage reflection and learning. We note, however, that the logs consist primarily of retrospective reports by the subjects who knew they would be graded, perhaps leading to ex post rationalization.

[5] The role of incentives in decision making performance is complex (see Hogarth et al. (1991) for a review and experimental evidence). There is no evidence to suggest subjects did not take the task seriously or attempt to do their best.

4 shows a typical first trial (overall this subject's profits were 114% of the grand mean). The subject's log (Table 1) records his strategy before playing: "grow at market pace. Price follower." However, the subject faced the condition with highest feedback complexity (Scenario D: strong word of mouth; low repurchase fraction). Orders grow rapidly. The subject comments at time two "Need much more capacity" and raises target capacity. However, due to the acquisition lag, capacity constrains shipments, backlog grows, and delivery delay rises. The subject tends to follow competitor price moves with a lag, even though he is unable to fill incoming orders throughout the growth phase. The subject continues to increase target capacity to a peak of 5 million units in quarter 16—reflecting rapid industry growth and the large backlog of unfilled orders. However, orders peak in quarter 12 at about 2.7 million units, and by quarter 14 capacity has risen enough to work off the backlog. Shipments fall precipitously to the rate of new orders. Commenting "I've gotta cut fixed costs," he slashes target capacity, but again capacity lags behind, peaking at 3.7 million units in quarter 18 just as orders fall to their low point. Unable to cover fixed costs he experiences large losses. He writes "fire the CEO" as cumulative losses reach $475 million in period 21. By quarter 25 orders stabilize at the replacement equilibrium. The

Figure 4 Behavior of Typical Subject in the First Trial

Compare to Figure 1.

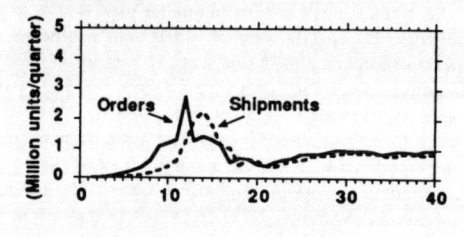

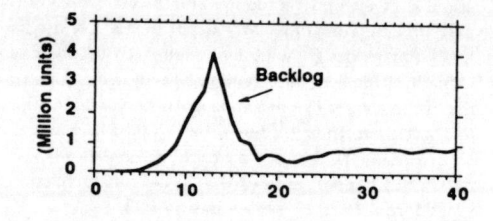

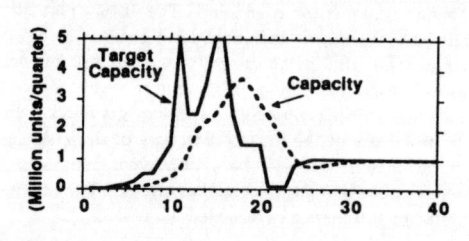

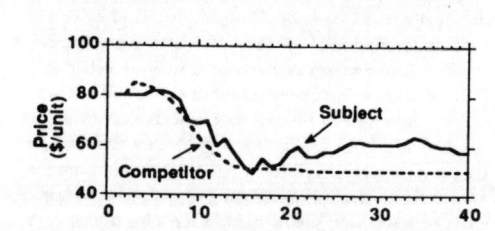

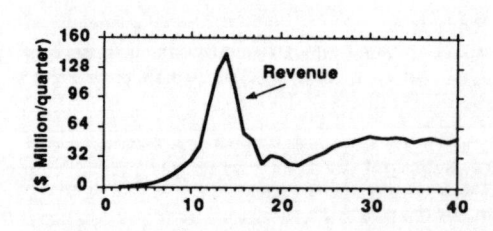

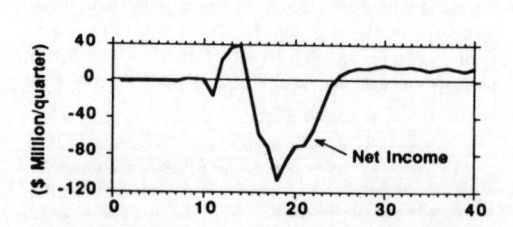

Table 1   Typical Log, as Typed by Subject: Trial 1, Scenario D: Strong Word of Mouth, Low Repurchase Rate

Q	Comments Before Entering Decisions	Comments After Entering Decisions
1	Strategy: grow @ market pace; price follower; assume capacity growth is linear.	Sales WAY up!!!!!
2	Grow faster than the market. Need much more capacity. Expand to 55,000. P[rice] constant.	Sales WAY up!!!!! Try and be patient.
3	Hold capacity target fixed. P to 81 to follow competitor.	Sales WAY up! Way above capacity. Behind. EXPAND!!!
4	Want 50% of market. Build to 150,000. Believe market max. = 300,000.	Sales WAY up! Way above capacity. Behind.
5	Want more. Build to 250,000 NOW. P up to 82.	
6		
7	Revise market max est. Build to 500,000 and vow never to add.	
8		
9	Build to 1,000,000 & vow never to add again.	Sales flattening therefore drop price.
10	Build to 1,500,000 & vow never to add again. P to 70.	Market demand up to 7,000,000.
11	Build to 5,000,000.	Sales fell. HELP!!!!!!
12	Destroy CAPACITY to 2,500,000. P to 65 to up demand.	LOOK AT NET INC[OME]. I got suckered!!!!
13		
14	P to 55.	
15		
16	Target capacity = 90,000 ONLY. I've gotta cut fixed costs.	
17	P to 52.	
18		
19		
20		
21	Capacity "OK." P up to 56.	A new high in lows. Fire the CEO.
22		
23		
24		
25	Capacity = orders = backlog GOOD.	Let's fool around with Price.
26	P to 58.	
27	P to 60.	
28	P to 62.	
29	P to 62.	
30	P to 61.	Zero-sum game.
⋮		
40		That's all folks. This was humiliating.

subject gradually reduces capacity and uses price to manage utilization. Profitability is restored, and the cumulative loss is cut to "only" $268 million by the end of the trial.

Performance Measures

Since the profit potential of each scenario depends on the strength of word of mouth and the product lifetime, subjects' raw performance—cumulative profit—confounds their relative ability to manage the situation with absolute profit potential.[6] We therefore assess subject performance relative to benchmarks to remove the effect of the treatments on potential profits. Profit equals the

[6] Theoretically, the net present value of profits should be the performance measure. However, experimental studies (see Prelec and Loewenstein (1991) and references therein) show people's subjective time preferences often do not follow standard discounted utility models. We therefore used undiscounted cumulative profits to simplify the cognitive burden of the task and to avoid confounding the results with various anomalies in intertemporal choice.

product of unit sales and the profit margin (price − unit costs). Sales depend multiplicatively on the strength of word of mouth w, and the replacement fraction r. Thus cumulative profit is a multiple of a function of w and r, and the appropriate performance measure Π, is the ratio of cumulative profit for each subject i in each trial t, $\pi_{it}\{w, r\}$, to cumulative benchmark profit $\pi^*\{w, r\}$:[7]

$$\Pi_{it}\{w, r\} = \pi_{it}\{w, r\}/\pi^*\{w, r\}. \quad (1)$$

Π adjusts raw profit for the intrinsic profit potential of the task, allowing us to measure the effects of the experimental treatments beyond changes in objective difficulty. The benchmark reported here is provided by simple behavioral rules for both price and target capacity:[8]

$$C_t^* = s^* D_{t-1}(1 + g_{t-1})^{\alpha_1}(B_t/C_t)^{\alpha_2}, \quad (2)$$

$$g_{t-1} = (D_{t-1} - D_{t-2})/D_{t-2}. \quad (3)$$

where C^* is target capacity, s^* is target market share, D is total industry sales, g is the fractional growth rate of industry sales over the most recently available period, B is the current backlog and C is current capacity. The target market share is set to 50%, with $\alpha_1 = 2.88$ and $\alpha_2 = 0.83$.[9] The capacity rule seeks to capture 50% of expected demand, where demand is forecast by extrapolating current industry sales at the current growth rate. Target capacity is increased (decreased) relative to the demand forecast when capacity is insufficient (excessive) relative to desired production.

The benchmark strategy assumes cost-plus pricing with a constant gross margin:

$$P_t = (1 + m)c_t, \quad (4)$$

where c = unit costs and m = gross margin, set to 0.25. Price in the benchmark strategy simply follows costs down the learning curve, with a markup sufficient to cover marketing expense, investment costs, and provide a reasonable profit (at normal capacity utilization).

The behavioral benchmark is a simple, even naive, rule. It utilizes only four cues (costs, industry sales, backlog, and current capacity) rather than full information. The rule naively extrapolates demand growth even though the subjects know the product will go through a lifecycle of growth, saturation, and decline. It does not use pricing to clear the market, control profitability, or signal intentions. It involves no game-theoretic reasoning. There is no explicit consideration of investment costs, no anticipation of market saturation and no response to competitor price or capacity, much less the competitor's strategy. The rule cannot learn. The rule is much less sophisticated than the decision making typically presumed in economic models and strategy texts. Subjects should be able to outperform the benchmark quite easily.

We next estimate general linear models to test the hypotheses above. We first tested for the effect of the sequence of scenarios. No sequence effect was found ($p = 0.27$ with trial T, word of mouth w, and replacement fraction r, as explanatory variables). Sequence was therefore not included in subsequent models. We next estimated a model with subject S, trial T, w, and r as explanatory variables along with the interactions $w \times r$, $T \times w$, $T \times r$, and $T \times w \times r$ (Table 2).

Overall, subjects performed very poorly relative to the benchmark. Despite the naiveté of the benchmark rule, the estimated mean ratio of profit to benchmark profit was under 24%. The benchmark outperforms the subjects in 87% of the cases (492 trials to 73).

The main effects of the treatments are highly significant and consistent with the MOF hypothesis. Over and above changes in intrinsic profit potential, performance relative to the benchmark is severely degraded as feedback complexity increases (Table 2, Figure 5).

---

[7] Consider equilibrium, when sales = orders ≈ capacity and $\pi(w, r)$ ≈ orders*(price − unit costs). In equilibrium orders are determined by the product of total market size and the replacement purchase fraction. Thus both subject profit and benchmark profit are multiples of the replacement fraction, and the ratio then allows comparison of profit relative to potential across scenarios with different repurchase fractions.

[8] We have also analyzed other benchmarks, including a "perfect foresight" rule in which target capacity is always set to provide capacity exactly equal to desired production (but maintaining the naive pricing strategy). This rule substantially outperforms the behavioral rule and dominates the subjects in 98% of the trials. Cumulative profit relative to cumulative sales was also used to remove the effect of the treatments on total market size. The statistical significance and magnitudes of the treatment and learning effects are robust to these alternative benchmarks (Paich 1993).

[9] The values of α_1 and α_2 were found by grid search of the parameter space to maximize cumulative profit over the five scenarios conditional on the assumption that target market share is 50%. We stress, however, that the simplistic behavioral benchmark rule is far from optimal.

PAICH AND STERMAN
Boom, Bust, and Failures to Learn in Experimental Markets

Table 2a Analysis of Cumulative Profit Relative to the Behavioral Benchmark

Explanatory Variable	SS	df	Mean Square	F	prob.
Subject	182.13	121	1.51	1.26	0.05
Trial	30.29	4	7.57	6.31	0.000+
w (log Word of Mouth)	14.07	1	14.07	11.73	0.001
r (log Replacement Fraction)	79.51	1	79.51	66.29	0.000+
w × r	9.93	1	9.93	8.28	0.004
Trial × w	3.87	4	0.97	0.81	0.52
Trial × r	2.38	4	0.60	0.50	0.74
Trial × w × r	4.73	4	1.18	0.99	0.42
Error	508.52	424	1.20		

$N = 565$.
$\bar{R}^2 = 0.39$.
Note: Dependent Variable: $\Pi_n(w, r)$ = cumulative subject profit relative to benchmark profit.

Specifically, the stronger the positive feedback loops that produce growth (the stronger the word of mouth effect; Figure 5a), the worse people do even relative to the naive benchmark. Why? The faster the growth in orders the harder it is for subjects to match capacity with demand. Excess backlogs build up, increasing delivery delays and reducing market share, all reducing profit. The stronger the positive growth loop, the sooner and higher demand will peak and the larger the decline when demand drops to replacement rates. The larger the drop, the larger the losses when the fixed costs of peak capacity cannot be covered by low demand. Also consistent with the MOF hypothesis, the longer the useful life of the product the worse subjects perform

Table 2b Estimated Treatment and Trial Effects

Constant	0.235				
Trial:	1	2	3	4	5
	−0.353	−0.118	−0.053	0.216	0.308
w	−0.257				
r	0.613				
w × r	0.313				

Note: The interactions of trial with treatments are not shown as they are not significant.

Figure 5a Effect of Word of Mouth on Profit Relative to Benchmark

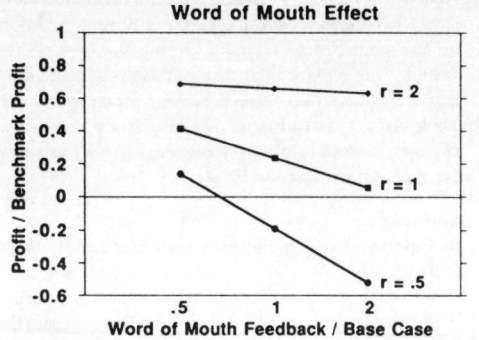

relative to the benchmark (Figure 5b). The longer the useful life, the steeper and deeper the drop in orders as the market saturates. Subjects are not able to track demand even as well as the naive strategy which forecasts by univariate extrapolation and has no knowledge of the life cycle.

The highly significant interaction between word of mouth and product lifetime shows that the negative effects of feedback complexity on performance are compounded when the word of mouth feedback is strong *and* the replacement fraction small. Frequent repurchase implies demand overshoots its equilibrium value only slightly—the nonlinear transition from

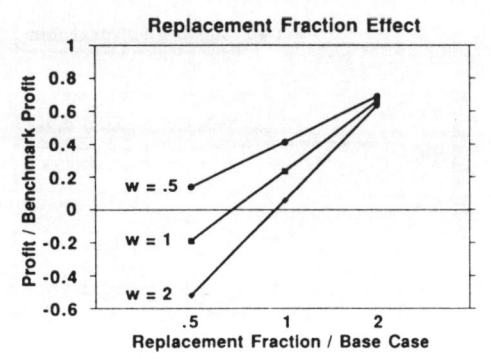

Figure 5b Effect of Replacement Fraction on Profit Relative to Benchmark

growth-generating positive feedback to the negative feedback of market saturation is gradual and mild. Subjects who aggressively build capacity during the boom are not punished too harshly during the bust. When there is little replacement demand, however, the nonlinear transition from boom to bust is sudden and severe. Thus average performance is significantly worse and changes in word of mouth have stronger effects when the replacement fraction is low.

Learning

As expected, subjects improve with experience. Mean performance is just 13% of the benchmark in trial 1 but rises to 63% in trial 5 (Figure 6). The fraction of trials in which the subjects outperform the benchmark (the "win ratio") rises from under 4% in trial 1 to 17% in trial five. However, improvement is slowing by the final trial. Mean profits in trial 5 are the same as in trial 4, and the win ratio actually drops between trials 4 and 5. Performance seems to be saturating well below even the naive benchmark.

We had hoped that, beyond the general improvement shown by the main effect of trial on performance, subjects would be improving their understanding of the environment with experience and so would develop heuristics that produce better relative performance in the conditions with high feedback complexity. Such learning would be reflected in significant interactions between the treatments and trial. However, none of the interactions between treatments and trial are even remotely significant. Though subjects improve on average there is no evidence to suggest they are learning to cope better with environments involving strong feedback processes.

The failure of subjects to improve their ability to manage complex feedback environments is an important and somewhat unexpected result. The conditions for learning are excellent: subjects receive immediate, comprehensive and accurate outcome feedback. In the course of their five trials they made nearly 200 sets of decisions, were under no time pressure, and faced strong incentives for performance. While prior research shows that learning from outcome feedback is difficult in the presence of noise (e.g., Brehmer 1980), the present task is completely deterministic and subjects had extensive knowledge of the causal structure of the system. Yet performance after five trials remains significantly worse than the naive benchmark.

Modeling Subjects' Decision Rules

To understand both the weak overall learning effect and the failure of subjects to improve in the difficult feedback conditions we next test several behavioral decision rules for target capacity and price. The rules postulated here were suggested by the subjects' written reports of their strategies, prior models of similar decisions in the literature, and the feedback structure of the task. Other rules are of course possible. The estimated rules reveal the cues subjects used, how cue weights relate to performance, and how the weights change with the experimental treatments. Changes in cue weights across trials yield insight into learning and its limitations, but do not constitute models of the subjects' decision process (Einhorn et al. 1979).

Generalizing the behavioral benchmark, we postulate that subjects select the share of the market they seek to capture, estimate future market demand from prior information, current demand, and recent demand growth, and invest to balance capacity with demand. The rule thus combines feedforward or forecasting (estimation of future demand) with a feedback component to correct

Figure 6 Effect of Experience on Profit Relative to Benchmark

Note: The "perfect foresight" benchmark assumes perfect knowledge of future demand in the capacity decision. The slight variation in the values of the benchmarks over trials arises because the design was not perfectly balanced.

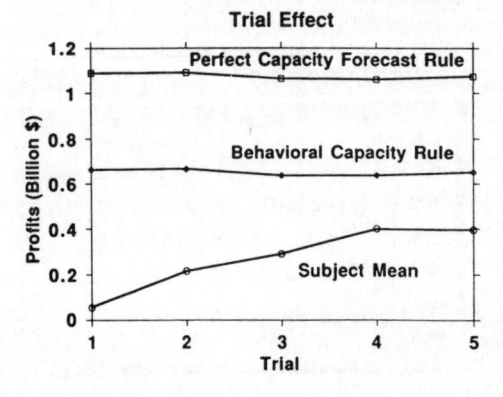

errors in the forecasts (the response to excess or insufficient capacity). Specifically,

$$C_t^* = s^*[D_0^{e(1-\alpha_0)} D_{t-1}^{e\alpha_0}](1 + g_{t-1})^{\alpha_1}(B_t/C_t)^{\alpha_2}, \quad (5)$$

$$g_{t-1} = (D_{t-1} - D_{t-2})/D_{t-2}, \quad (6)$$

where s^* is target market share (assumed constant), D_0^e is the prior expectation of average industry demand, D is actual demand, g_t is the expected fractional growth rate of demand, B is the backlog (desired production), and C is actual capacity. The rule assumes subjects seek to capture a certain share of the forecasted market demand. Forecasted demand is modeled as a weighted geometric average of current demand and a prior expectation. That prior belief is likely to be strongly conditioned by the demand observed in earlier trials. Subjects with little initial idea of market potential, as before the first trial, would most likely follow a demand tracking strategy with a high α_0. Subjects whose prior expectation is never modified by actual experience would have $\alpha_0 = 0$, while $0 \le \alpha_0 \le 1$ indicates a conservative strategy in which target capacity falls increasingly short if orders exceed the subject's prior expectation for demand. Such behavior could be intentional, if subjects fear overshooting the equilibrium as demand becomes large, or the result of inadvertent anchoring on prior beliefs. In addition to estimating current demand, the capacity acquisition lag requires subjects to account for likely growth in demand. Both demand and demand growth rate were reported on the information display and are commonly available in actual markets. Subjects who forecast by extrapolating recent changes in demand would have $\alpha_1 > 0$. To correct any forecast errors target capacity should also respond to the demand/supply balance, measured by the ratio of backlog (desired production) to production capacity.

The proposed decision rule for price P assumes subjects use markup pricing:

$$P_t = UVC_t \cdot M_t^*, \quad (7)$$

where UVC = unit variable cost and M^* = gross margin. Gross margin depends on the subject's response to demand/supply balance and the policy for passing cost reductions on to the consumer:

$$M_t^* = M_0(UVC_t/UVC_0)^{\beta_1}(B_t/C_t)^{\beta_2}. \quad (8)$$

As the firm moves down the learning curve, the subject must decide how much of the cost reduction to pass on to consumers. All cost reductions are passed into price when $\beta_1 = 0$, while $-1 \le \beta_1 \le 0$ indicates price falls less than costs. Positive values of β_1 indicate price falls faster than costs, perhaps indicating an attempt to build market share and move more rapidly down the learning curve than the competitor.[10] We further expect that the gross margin will increase when desired production is high relative to capacity ($\beta_2 > 0$).

Collecting constant terms, assuming independent multiplicative errors, and taking logs yields the form in which the decision rules were estimated:

$$\log(C_t^*) = c + a_0 \log(D_{t-1})$$
$$+ a_1 \log(1 + g_{t-1})$$
$$+ a_2 \log(B_t/C_t) + \epsilon_1, \quad (9)$$
$$\log(P_t) = b_0 + b_1 \log(UVC_t)$$
$$+ b_2 \log(B_t/C_t) + \epsilon_2. \quad (10)$$

Each rule was estimated separately for each of the five trials of each subject. OLS regression revealed positive autocorrelation in the residuals, so the Cochrane-Orcutt procedure (first-order autocorrelation correction) was used.

The proposed rules capture the bulk of the variance in subject's decisions (Table 3). For target capacity the mean $\bar{R}^2$ is 0.87, exceeds 0.90 for more than two-thirds of the trials, and is less than 0.50 for only 5%. The mean $\bar{R}^2$ is 0.95 for price, with $\bar{R}^2 > 0.90$ for more than 87% of the trials and less than 0.50 for just 1%. The coefficients generally have the expected signs. The mean estimate of the elasticity of capacity with respect to demand, α_0, is 0.38, indicating subjects based their capacity decisions primarily on their prior estimate of market demand and only secondarily on actual market demand. To assess the prior expectation of market demand, we note from Equations (5) and (9) that $c = (1 - \alpha_0) \ln(s^*D^e)$. After obvious outliers are elimi-

---

[10] Gross margin should also depend on competitor price. However, competitor cost (and therefore price, since competitor margin is constant) is highly correlated with the firm's own costs. Therefore subjects' responses to costs and competition cannot be independently estimated.

Table 3 Means and Standard Deviations of Estimated Parameters for Subjects' Capacity and Pricing Rules (Eq. 9-10)

Parameter	Mean	Std. Dev.	% NS
Capacity Rule:			
c	8.414	6.450	22
a_0	0.383	0.433	30
a_1	0.036	0.533	56
a_2	0.318	0.715	43
ρ	0.560	0.328	21
$\bar{R}^2$	0.872	0.183	
Pricing Rule:			
b_0	3.125	2.553	3
b_1	0.259	0.337	28
b_2	0.016	0.067	62
ρ	0.781	0.215	3
$\bar{R}^2$	0.947	0.095	

Note: The parameter ρ is the estimate of the first-order autoregressive term. The final column shows the percentage of estimates which were not significantly different from zero (% NS).

nated,[11] the mean value of $\ln(s^*D^e) = 13.3$, indicating subjects' initial goal for capacity averaged roughly 600,000 units. In contrast, the estimates of α_1 and α_2 are generally small—roughly half are not statistically different from zero—showing subjects are quite insensitive to the recent growth of demand and the demand/supply balance. For price, the estimate of the response to unit costs, β_1, is usually statistically significant while the response to the demand/supply balance, β_2, is very small and not significant in nearly two-thirds of the cases. Subjects generally price slightly above costs (or competitor price) as they move down the learning curve. The demand/supply balance has but little effect.

The estimated decision rules provide insight into subjects' poor overall performance relative to the benchmark rule. Subjects generally set target capacity equal to their initial goal for capacity, are only partially

[11] Values such that $0 \leq \ln(s^*De) \leq \ln(20e6)$ were retained (410 out of 565). This range easily encompassed all actual market demand levels attained in the task.

responsive to actual market demand, and are quite insensitive to the growth in demand. Given the capacity acquisition lag such conservative forecasts ensure that actual capacity will be grossly inadequate during the boom phase, causing high backlogs, long delivery delays, and market share erosion. The subjects' insensitivity to growth is consistent with prior work (Wagenaar and Timmers 1979). However, the low weight on the demand/supply balance in both the capacity and pricing decisions is quite surprising.

Hogarth (1981) argues that dynamic decision making might be better than one-shot static decision making, since subjects can review and revise prior decisions as outcome feedback becomes available, gradually correcting errors. Here, however, this postulated adaptation does not operate well. Subjects fail to increase target capacity sufficiently as backlogs accumulate, and they fail to cut target capacity aggressively when faced with excess capacity. The result is lost profit during the growth phase and larger losses during the bust phase. Similarly the near-zero weight on the demand/supply balance in the pricing rule shows that subjects price too low during the boom phase, even though they cannot possibly satisfy the current demand; likewise, subjects generally fail to cut prices to stimulate demand during the bust despite huge amounts of excess capacity. Not only are subjects insufficiently adaptive, but their capacity and pricing decisions are inconsistent.

We next seek to understand the nature of the learning process. Why was learning so poor overall? Why didn't experience help subjects learn to handle the complex feedback conditions better? To do so we investigate how subjects' decision weights change by estimating models for each estimated parameter with subject, trial, and the word of mouth and replacement fraction treatments as explanatory variables (Table 4).

All the coefficients of the target capacity rule change significantly over the five trials, indicating experience caused subjects to alter their forecasts of demand and their responsiveness to market growth and demand/supply balance. The estimated elasticity of target capacity with respect to current market demand (α_0) falls from 0.49 in trial one to 0.32 by trial five. Before their first trial subjects have little knowledge of likely demand, so have little choice but to follow actual demand (even so there is substantial conservatism in their fore-

Table 4 Dependence of Estimated Parameters on Trial and Treatments

Parameter	w	r	w•r	Constant + Trial Effect 1	2	3	4	5	$\bar{R}^2$
Capacity Rule:									
$\ln(s^*D^e)$§	.077 (.55)	.453 (.000+)	.35 (.06)	12.6	13.3	13.6 (.000+)	13.5	13.7	.36
a_0	.006 (.82)	−.032 (.22)	−.06 (.14)	0.49	0.39	0.40 (.011)	0.33	0.32	.40
a_1	.171 (.000+)	.038 (.26)	.08 (.115)	−0.06	−0.02	0.05 (.018)	0.14	0.09	.36
a_2	.003 (.94)	−.031 (.47)	.05 (.43)	0.18	0.40	0.34 (.000+)	0.57	0.43	.40
Pricing Rule:									
b_0	−.126 (.42)	.288 (.07)	.08 (.72)	3.39	3.01	3.00 (.502)	3.27	2.92	.39
b_1	−.004 (.86)	−.028 (.18)	.01 (.76)	0.26	0.27	0.24 (.489)	0.30	0.23	.38
b_2	.018 (.000+)	−.007 (.12)	.01 (.063)	0.01	0.01	0.02 (.381)	0.02	0.02	.34

§ $\ln(s^*D^e)$ is the (log) of the imputed expectation of the share of equilibrium demand the subject seeks. It is calculated from the estimated coefficients as $\ln(s^*D^e) = c/(1 - a_0)$; see Eqs. (5) and (9).

The model in all cases is: p_{it} = Constant + Subject$_i$ + Trial$_t$ + w_{it} + r_{it} + $w_{it} \times r_{it}$ + error, where p_{it} is the estimated parameter for trial t of the ith subject; w and r are the (log) strengths of the word of mouth parameter and replacement fraction, respectively. Significance levels (p-values of the F-statistic) for the effects are given in parentheses. The subject factor was significant for all estimated parameters at better than the 0.001 level.

casts). With experience, however, subjects learn approximately how big the peak and equilibrium values of demand will be. They rely increasingly on their knowledge of the demand levels reached in prior trials and become less responsive to the actual demand in the current trial. Similarly, initial demand and capacity levels are low compared to the peak and equilibrium values of demand, so initial expectations of demand in trial one, before any experience is gained, should be low but rise over trials. Indeed, the imputed prior expectation s^*D^e averages about 300,000 units in trial one; it doubles by the second trial, and rises to nearly 900,000 by trial five. These estimates also depend significantly on equilibrium demand (indicated by the significant effect of replacement fraction on s^*D^e) since the true equilibrium demand becomes clear about half-way through (see Figures 3–4).

The capacity acquisition lag requires subjects to forecast demand well into the future. Yet the regression results show that on average subjects are virtually unresponsive to the growth rate of demand. Though subjects do learn to respond to demand growth with successive trials, the effect is small (Table 4). In the first trial the mean estimate of the elasticity of target capacity with respect to market growth, α_1, is negative, indicating subjects expect demand to regress to prior values rather than grow further. By the fifth trial most have learned to extrapolate recent growth, but the mean elasticity has risen only to about 0.10 (similar shifts from regressive to extrapolative expectations under growth were found by Andreassen (1990a, 1990b)). Experience does lead subjects to anticipate market growth somewhat, but the improvement is so slight that even after five trials subjects show little ability to account for the capacity acquisition lag. Ignoring growth when lags exist inevitably results in insufficient capacity and lost revenue during the boom and slow reduction of excess capacity during the bust. The response of target capacity to the demand/supply balance, α_2, also increases with experience. The mean elasticity rises from 0.18 in trial one to about 0.5 in the last two trials. However, even with experience the average response is much less than optimal.

Worse, there is no evidence that subjects' pricing strategies evolve. In particular, the responsiveness of price to the demand/supply balance does not increase with experience. Subjects learn slowly to adjust capacity to demand, but do not learn to use price to clear the market, nor do they alter the average level of price. During the boom, price can be raised to both reap higher profit and to slow the growth of demand. During the bust, price can be cut to boost market share and stimulate industry demand, reducing losses. Subjects in general do neither, foregoing a critical opportunity to moderate the severity of the boom and bust dynamic and boost profitability.

Thus experience does not move subjects towards a greater appreciation of the feedback processes which create market dynamics. Rather, subjects seem to find the dynamics so hard to understand that they move towards a "ballistic" strategy in which prior beliefs about equilibrium demand are increasingly influential while outcome feedback about actual demand is increasingly ignored. The subject logs confirm the regression results. The following, describing a subject's strategy for the final trial, is typical:

> Since I know I can't beat my competitor during peak sales, I am going to ramp up early to the level that I believe might represent replacement sales. I can hopefully then capture that much of the market during the peak . . . , and the majority of the replacement market after sales peak. Price will be adjusted as necessary to maintain market share.

This subject immediately boosted capacity to about 2 million and held it constant through quarter 30, even though orders reached more than 5 million. Price was increased above the competitor during the boom, but not enough to prevent long delivery delays. During the bust, prices were cut, but not enough to prevent significant excess capacity.

Discussion

Prior work in dynamic decision making suggested that our mental models of dynamic environments are generally poor. Specifically, people do not account well for feedback loops, time delays, accumulation processes, and nonlinearities. However, much prior work did not explicitly vary the strength of feedback processes as treatments to establish how dynamic complexity influenced performance, nor did they include market institutions and opportunities for learning which might mitigate the errors. Many prior experiments used abstract tasks or tasks not relevant to the subjects' training and experience. The present experiment presents subjects with a common and realistic management task. Extensive opportunities for learning were provided—50 years of simulated industry experience with perfect, immediate outcome feedback. Despite these opportunities for excellent performance, the vast majority of subjects are outperformed by a naive behavioral rule, even though the benchmark rule utilizes a small subset of available information and combines these cues in simple ways, without recourse to optimization or game theoretic reasoning.

Consistent with the misperceptions of feedback hypothesis, the stronger the feedback processes in the environment the worse people do *relative to potential*. Subjects fail to account for a fundamental structural feature of durables markets: ceteris paribus, the faster sales grow, the sooner and more suddenly the market must saturate. The effect is not mere forecasting error. Subjects' own actions make the task more difficult by strengthening the positive feedback loops, generating a more vigorous boom and a more severe bust. Further, subject behavior is riddled with inconsistencies. Most subjects cut prices to match the competitor, even during the boom phase when they are unable to meet demand.

Most disturbing, there is no evidence that subjects improved their ability to manage the environments with high feedback complexity, despite improvement on average. Analysis of estimated cue weights revealed why. As they gained experience the subjects altered their strategies to use less, not more, outcome feedback on demand. Participants learned the basic pattern of market dynamics. They predicted the approximate size of the replacement market and quickly increased capacity to that level, largely ignoring the level and growth rate of market demand in the current trial. Because experience provided useful information on likely equilibrium demand, performance on average improved with trials. Because subjects were insufficiently responsive to the level and growth rate of the market and to the demand/supply balance, they did not improve their ability to handle the difficult feedback environments. The nature of subjects' learning is particularly remarkable in light of their poor overall performance: after five trials mean performance is just 60% of the naive benchmark, and only 17% of subjects beat the benchmark in their final trial.

Conditions for learning in the experiment are superior those in the real world, where outcome feedback is often missing, noisy, ambiguous and delayed; where other confounding factors are more numerous and demands on managerial attention are greater; and where the time scale for change can exceed the tenure of managers (Tversky and Kahneman 1987). Further, the learning that did occur in the experiment would be much less successful in the real world. By design, the experiment simplified the environment by holding the potential market constant across scenarios. In real markets the variation is much greater. Few managers could ignore market feedback, determining capacity primarily from the history of prior products and then failing to revise that decision despite the huge backlogs, angry customers and other stresses of rapid growth.

The results show subjects' mental models did not account well for the feedback processes, time delays, and nonlinearities that create the boom and bust dynamic. The striking correspondence between many first trials and the behavior of numerous actual firms suggests these misperceptions of feedback may play a significant role in the real world. Empirical studies contrasting the dynamics of firms facing high and low feedback complexity should be undertaken to test the generality of these findings. Existing studies (e.g., Zarnowitz 1985, Mosekilde et al. 1992) do show that markets characterized by long lags, strong positive feedbacks, accumulations, and nonlinearities (e.g., commercial real estate, shipping, capital goods) do suffer from more instability than those with less feedback complexity (e.g., soft goods, services).

Implications for Learning from Simulations and Games

The recognition that traditional pedagogy, stressing lectures and cases, often does not lead to improved decision making ability has long motivated the use of management games. In principle, games and simulations allow time and space to be compressed, allow rapid accumulation of "experience" and permit controlled experimentation. In practice, many management games are so complex they are played but once. Experimentation is difficult. Students are often expected to learn from outcome feedback. Consequently evidence on the effectiveness of traditional business games is mixed (see Graham et al. (1992) for a review). The present study offers an explanation for these mixed results and poses a challenge to designers and users of educational simulations.

If outcome feedback is not effective when dynamic complexity is high, how then might protocols for the use of simulations be modified to overcome the persistent misperceptions of feedback documented here? One approach is the use of cognitive feedback. Decision makers can be provided with *task information*, typically in the form of the optimal functional form and weights relating the available cues to a criterion. Alternatively *cognitive information* in the form of decision makers' own implicit cue weights or *functional validity information* allowing them to compare their perceptions of cue-criterion relations to the actual situation can be provided (Balzer et al. 1989). By alerting decision makers to the structure of the environment, their own decisions, or discrepancies between the two, it is hoped they can become more consistent and adjust towards a better weighting of available cues. Though the evidence is mixed, cognitive feedback appears to improve judgments. Task information seems to be more helpful than cognitive or functional validity information.

Cognitive feedback has been explored primarily in static tasks such as predicting grade point averages from cues like SAT scores. Such tasks have no dynamic complexity. The judge's decisions do not feed back to alter outcomes or system structure. There are virtually no studies of cognitive feedback in dynamic tasks. In one exception, Richardson and Rohrbaugh (1990) modified Sterman's (1989a) multiplier-accelerator simulation by adding the optimal decision rule to the information display, thus providing task information. Unfortunately, performance with cognitive feedback was not significantly different than with outcome feedback alone. In another recent study, Sengupta and Abdel-Hamid (1993) explored how subjects managed a simulated software development project. Subjects provided with a good decision rule (task information) outperformed subjects provided with limited outcome feedback, but were outperformed by subjects receiving more comprehensive information on the status of the simulated project. Clearly more research is needed to explore the efficacy of cognitive feedback in dynamic environments.

While the ability of cognitive feedback to boost *performance* in dynamic tasks is unclear, the use of cognitive feedback to stimulate *learning* about complex dynamics is even more problematic. First, to provide the optimal cue weights someone must determine the functional form of and weights for rules that provide superior performance. In complex nonlinear dynamic systems this is often no small task. Designing effective, robust rules consistent with the cognitive limits on decision makers requires insight into the feedback structure of the system, knowledge of nonlinear dynamical theory, and understanding of human decision making abilities (Forrester 1992). That is, the creation of effective, robust and useful policies requires good modeling skills. Unless decision makers learn how to do this for themselves they must rely on the counsel of outside experts.

Reliance on outside expertise, however, is not likely to lead to adoption of policy recommendations that conflict with deeply held mental models (Senge and Sterman 1992). In situations of high dynamic complexity people's mental models are grossly simplified compared to reality, and high-performing decision rules differ significantly from those most people bring to bear—often leading to rejection of the expert's advice. Indeed, some subjects in Richardson and Rohrbaugh's experiment apparently found the optimal rule "counterintuitive" and did not use it. More fundamentally, reliance on outside expertise will not generate deep knowledge of the structure or dynamics of complex systems. Without such knowledge, people are unlikely to transfer the lessons learned in one context to another, or from the classroom to real life (Bakken 1993).

These results suggest principles for the design of effective management simulations. The process should help people unearth the deeply held and often tacit habits of mind that lead to dysfunctional behavior and hinder learning. Protocols for game use should engage people in what Dewey called "reflective thought" and what Schön (1992) calls "reflective conversation with the situation." They should encourage an iterative learning cycle of observation, reflection, design and action. For that learning loop to operate effectively people must develop what Davis and Hogarth (1992) call "insight skills"—the skills that help people learn when feedback is ambiguous:

> the interpretation of feedback in the form of outcomes needs to be an *active* and *disciplined* task governed by the rigorous rules of scientific inference. Beliefs must be actively challenged by seeking possible disconfirming evidence and asking whether alternative beliefs could not account for the facts (emphasis in original).

Developing these skills takes effort and practice. Simulations can provide the "practice field" to develop them (Senge 1990).

Still, settings with high dynamic complexity can garble the reflective conversation between the learner and the situation. Long time delays, causes and effects that are distant in time and space, and the confounding effects of multiple nonlinear feedbacks can slow learning even for people with good insight skills. We suggest learning can be accelerated when the protocol for game use helps people learn how to represent complex feedback structures and understand their implications. To learn when dynamic complexity is high we need to become modelers, not merely players in a simulation. Recent advances in interactive modeling processes, tools for representation of feedback structure and simulation software make it possible for anyone to engage in the modeling process (Morecroft and Sterman 1992). To fulfill their promise of accelerated learning, games and simulations must be embedded in a structured learning environment—a learning laboratory—in which game play, elicitation and mapping of mental models, simulation, policy design, experimentation and discussion all take place. Experiments to test these hypotheses are now underway in diverse settings, from schools to top management teams, where dynamic complexity poses a growing challenge to individual and organizational learning.[12]

[12] The comments of John Carroll, Don Kleinmuntz, Rebecca Henderson, Robin Hogarth, Rogelio Oliva, George Richardson, Anjali Sastry, Paul Schoemaker, John Seeger, anonymous referees and seminar participants at MIT, Carnegie-Mellon, and SUNY Albany are gratefully acknowledged. Rod Paich did an excellent job programming the management flight simulator used in this study. This work was supported in part by the Organizational Learning Center, MIT Sloan School.

References

Andreassen, P., "Judgmental Extrapolation and the Salience of Change," *J. Forecasting*, 9 (1990a), 347–372.

——, "Judgmental Extrapolation and Market Overreaction: On the Use and Disuse of News," *Behavioral Decision Making*, 3 (1990b), 153–174.

Balzer, W. K., M. E. Doherty and R. O'Connor, Jr., "Effects of Cognitive Feedback on Performance," *Psychological Bulletin*, 106 (1989), 410–433.

Bakken, B., "Learning and Transfer of Understanding in Dynamic Decision Environments," Ph.D. Dissertation, MIT Sloan School of Management, Cambridge, MA, 1993.

Bass, F. M., "A New Product Growth Model for Consumer Durables," *Management Sci.*, 15 (1969), 215–227.

Beinhocker, E., "Worlds of Wonder (A) and (B)," Case study available from John Sterman, Sloan School of Management, MIT, Cambridge MA, 1991.

——, L. Newman, R. Henderson and J. Sterman, "A Behavioral Model of Learning Curve Strategy," Working Paper, MIT Sloan School of Management, Cambridge, MA, 1993.

Brehmer, B., "In One Word: Not from Experience," *Acta Psychologica*, 45 (1980), 233–241.

——, "Strategies in Real Time, Dynamic Decision Making," In R. Hogarth (Ed.), *Insights in Decision Making*, University of Chicago Press, Chicago, 1990, 262–279.

——, "Dynamic Decision Making: Human Control of Complex Systems," *Acta Psychologica*, 81 (1992), 211–241.

Broadbent, D. and B. Aston, "Human Control of a Simulated Economic System," *Ergonomics*, 21, 12 (1978), 1035–1043.

Camerer, C., "Do Biases in Probability Judgment Matter in Markets? Experimental Evidence," *American Economic Review*, 77, 5 (December), (1987), 981–997.

Carlson, E., "Fiberglass's Long Life Is Sinking Sailboat Producers," *Wall Street J.*, August 31 (1990), B2.

Davis, H. and R. Hogarth, "Rethinking Management Education: A View from Chicago," Selected Paper 72, University of Chicago, Graduate School of Business, 1992.

Diehl, E., "Effects of Feedback Structure on Dynamic Decision Making," Ph.D. Dissertation, MIT Sloan School of Management, 1992.

Einhorn, H. J., D. Kleinmuntz and B. Kleinmuntz, "Linear Regression and Process-Tracing Models of Judgment," *Psychological Review*, 56, 5 (1979), 465–485.

Forrester, J. W., "Counterintuitive Behavior of Social Systems," *Technology Review*, 73 (1971), 52–68.

——, "Policies, Decisions, and Information Sources for Modeling," *European J. Operational Res.*, 59, 1 (1992), 42–63.

Funke, J., "Solving Complex Problems: Exploration and Control of Complex Systems," In R. Sternberg and P. Frensch (Eds.), *Complex Problem Solving: Principles and Mechanisms*, Lawrence Erlbaum Associates, Hillsdale, NJ, 1991.

Gort, M. and S. Klepper, "Time Paths in the Diffusion of Product Innovations," *Economic J.*, 92 (1982), 630–653.

Graham, A. K., J. D. Morecroft, P. M. Senge and J. D. Sterman, "Model Supported Case Studies for Management Education," *European J. Operational Res.*, 59, 1 (1992), 151–166.

Hauthakker, H. S. and L. D. Taylor, *Consumer Demand in the United States*, Harvard University Press, Cambridge, MA, 1970.

Hax, A. C. and N. S. Majluf, *Strategic Management: An Integrative Perspective*, Prentice-Hall, Englewood Cliffs, NJ, 1984.

Hogarth, R., "Beyond Discrete Biases: Functional and Dysfunctional Aspects of Judgmental Heuristics," *Psychological Bulletin*, 90 (1981), 197–217.

——, B. Gibbs, C. McKenzie and M. Marquis, "Learning from Feedback: Exactingness and Incentives," *J. Experimental Psychology: Learning, Memory, and Cognition*, 17, 4 (1991), 734–752.

—— and S. Makridakis, "The Value of Decisionmaking in a Complex Environment: An Experimental Approach," *Management Sci.*, 27, 1 (1981), 93–107.

—— and M. W. Reder, *Rational Choice: The Contrast Between Economics and Psychology*, University of Chicago Press, Chicago, 1987.

Homer, J., "A Diffusion Model with Application to Evolving Medical Technologies," *Technological Forecasting and Social Change*, 31 (1987), 197–218.

Hoyt, H., *One Hundred Years of Land Values in Chicago*, University of Chicago Press, Chicago, 1933.

Kalish, S. and G. Lilien, "Market Entry Timing Entry for New Technologies," *Management Sci.*, 32, 2 (1986), 194–204.

Kampmann, C. and J. Sterman, "Do Markets Mitigate Misperceptions of Feedback in Dynamic Tasks?" Proceedings of the 1992 International System Dynamics Conference, Utrecht, The Netherlands, 1992.

Kleinmuntz, D., "Information Processing and Misperceptions of the Implications of Feedback in Dynamic Decision Making," *System Dynamics Review*, 9, 3 (1993).

—— and J. Thomas, "The Value of Action and Inference in Dynamic Decision Making," *Organizational Behavior and Human Decision Processes*, 39, 3 (1987), 341–364.

Klepper, S. and E. Graddy, "The Evolution of New Industries and the Determinants of Market Structure," *RAND J. Economics*, 21, 1 (1990), 27–44.

Mahajan, V., E. Muller and F. Bass, "New Product Diffusion Models in Marketing: A Review and Directions for Research," *J. Marketing*, 54, 1 (1990), 1–26.

—— and Y. Wind, (Eds.), *Innovation Diffusion Models of New Product Acceptance*, Ballinger, Cambridge, MA, 1986.

Morecroft, J., "Rationality in the Analysis of Behavioral Simulation Models," *Management Sci.*, 31, 7 (1985), 900–916.

—— and J. Sterman (Eds.), *Modeling for Learning*, Special Issue of *European J. Operational Res.*, 59, 1, May (1992).

Mosekilde, E., E. Larsen, J. Sterman and J. Thomsen, "Nonlinear Mode-Interaction in the Macroeconomy, In G. Feichtinger (Ed.), *Annals of Operations Res.*, 37 (1992).

Oster, S. M., *Modern Competitive Analysis*, Oxford University Press, New York, 1990.

Paich, M., "Boom and Bust: Decision Making in a Dynamic Market Environment," Ph.D. Thesis, MIT, Sloan School of Management, 1993.

Petre, P., "Jack Tramiel Is Back on the Warpath," *Fortune*, March 4, (1985) 46–50.

Porter, M., *Competitive Strategy*, Free Press, New York, 1980.

——, *Cases in Competitive Strategy*, Free Press, New York, 1983.

Prelec, D. and G. Loewenstein, "Decision Making Over Time and Under Uncertainty: A Common Approach," *Management Sci.*, 37, 7 (1991), 770–786.

Richardson, G. and J. Rohrbaugh, "Decision Making in Dynamic Environments: Exploring Judgments in a System Dynamics Model-Based Game," In K. Borcherding, et al. (Eds.), *Contemporary Issues in Decision Making*, North Holland, Amsterdam, 1990, 463–472.

Salter, M., *Tensor Corporation*, Case 370-041, Harvard Business School Publishing Division, Boston, MA, 1969.

Schön, D., "The Theory of Inquiry: Dewey's Legacy to Education," *Curriculum Inquiry*, 22, 2 (1992), 119–139.

Senge, P., "A System Dynamics Approach to Investment Function Formulation and Testing," *Socioeconomic Planning Sciences*, 14 (1980), 269–280.

——, *The Fifth Discipline: The Art and Practice of the Learning Organization*, Doubleday, New York, 1990.

—— and J. D. Sterman, "Systems Thinking and Organizational Learning: Acting Locally and Thinking Globally in the Organization of the Future," In T. Kochan and M. Useem (Eds.), *Transforming Organizations*, Oxford University Press, Oxford, 1992, 353–371.

Sengupta, K. and T. Abdel-Hamid, "Alternative Conceptions of Feedback in Dynamic Decision Environments: An Experimental Investigation," *Management Sci.*, 39, 4 (1993), 411–428.

Simon, H. A., *Models of Bounded Rationality*, The MIT Press, Cambridge, MA, 1982.

Smith, V., G. Suchanek and A. Williams, "Bubbles, Crashes, and Endogenous Expectations in Experimental Spot Asset Markets," *Econometrica*, 56, 5 (1988), 1119–1152.

Sterman, J. D., "Testing Behavioral Simulation Models by Direct Experiment," *Management Sci.*, 33, 12 (1987a), 1572–1592.

——, "Expectation Formation in Behavioral Simulation Models," *Behavioral Sci.*, 32 (1987b), 190–211.

——, "*People Express* Management Flight Simulator," Simulation Game (Software), Briefing Book, and Simulator Guide. Available from author, MIT Sloan School of Management, Cambridge, MA, 1988.

——, "Misperceptions of Feedback in Dynamic Decision Making," *Organizational Behavior and Human Decision Processes*, 43, 3 (1989a), 301–335.

——, "Modeling Managerial Behavior: Misperceptions of Feedback in a Dynamic Decision Making Experiment," *Management Sci.*, 35, 3 (1989b), 321–339.

——, "Teaching Takes Off: Flight Simulators for Management Education," *OR/MS Today*, October (1992), 40–44.

Tversky, A. and D. H. Kahneman, "Rational Choice and the Framing of Decisions," In R. M. Hogarth and M. W. Reder (Eds.), *Rational Choice: The Contrast Between Economics and Psychology*. University of Chicago Press, Chicago, 1987.

Wagenaar, W. and H. Timmers, "The Pond-and-Duckweed Problem: Three Experiments in the Misperception of Exponential Growth," *Acta Psychologica*, 43 (1979), 239–251.

Zarnowitz, V., "Recent Work on Business Cycles in Historical Perspective: A Review of Theories and Evidence," *J. Economic Literature*, 23 (1985), 523–580.

Accepted by Gregory W. Fischer; received June 22, 1992. This paper has been with the authors 4 months for 1 revision.

Part III
Corporate Policy and Management

Corporate Strategy

The corporate applications in this section range from operations to strategy, from controlling inventories to managing corporate transformations. The section begins with Roger Hall's classic study of the rise and fall of the old *Saturday Evening Post*. The paradox he explores is the observation that the initial crises of a number of large-scale publishing ventures occurred at the time of their greatest circulations and revenues. Hall traces these instabilities to interactions between advertising and subscriber revenue and to a particular self-reinforcing feedback loop linking total readership and advertising pages. He buttresses his model-based insights with reflections on data from the life cycle of the old *Saturday Evening Post* and suggests and tests a strategic orientation that could have averted the magazine's demise.

The next three studies explore other aspects of corporate strategic issues. In Chapter 14, Morecroft, Lane and Viita trace a modelling process studying corporate growth issues in a start-up firm. By describing the group modelling process as well as the substance of the problem in biotechnology, they give us a preview of Part V (in Volume II) which focuses on strategies and techniques of modelling *with* management.

Merten, Löffler and Wiedmann then present a sophisticated simulation-based tool to support strategic management. Their work links the Boston Consulting Group portfolio concept with a dynamic simulation model, resulting in a simulation tool that is capable of tracing and analysing the movement of corporate businesses in the BCG two-by-two matrix, from poor dogs and question marks to stars and cash cows. Their model-based tests of business portfolio management strategies reveal subtleties, not captured in static strategic analyses, which can lead to serious policy errors traceable to important feedbacks between the firm, its competitors and the economic environment.

Henry Weil, long-time principal in the consulting firm of Pugh-Roberts Associates, and health care consultant Leon White extend these strategic discussions to the management of business *transformations* for long-term survival. Transformations are nonincremental shifts in the ways companies do business. The authors describe a simulation-based study of the transformation of a major health insurance company as the United States moves to the 'managed care' structures in current health care finance plans. They show classic business strategies that fail in the transformation environment and others that succeed, and then outline a sophisticated, generally applicable eight-part strategy that has the highest likelihood of enabling a firm to flourish during its transformation period.

Forecasting

With Chapter 17 by Urban, Hauser and Roberts on prelaunch forecasting of new automobiles, we move from corporate strategy towards operations issues. The puzzle of prelaunch forecasting is the lack of history on which to base potentially vital corporate decisions about price and production capacity as well as the potential effects of increased advertising, changing the targeted market, dealer incentives and product availability. The authors describe the design, calibration and use of a management forecasting support tool in the form of a difference equation model of the stocks and flows of customers as they become aware of the new car, enter the market to buy, visit dealers and finally buy or exit the system. They trace the model's use in management decisions to change advertising copy and improve dealer training to entice potential customers in for dealer visits. They then evaluate the model's forecasts against ensuing actual sales.

Inventory Dynamics

The next two chapters address the dynamics of complex inventory management systems. Clark, Trempe and Trichlin focus on a multiechelon inventory system for the Air Force that includes multiple items, the possibility of breakdowns and repair, different operating procedures at different levels, and transportation among sites and stages. The authors describe the stock-and-flow/feedback structure of the system in overview and in detail, and outline the use of the model in analysing Air Force inventory management policies.

Morecroft's 'A Systems Perspective on Material Requirements Planning' (Chapter 19) focuses on integrated computer-based inventory control systems and strives to understand why MRP systems have not yielded the improvements expected of them. He creates a simulation model that interrelates production and labour planning and material ordering, and then tests both a manual order-point inventory control and MRP. Surprisingly the computer-based inventory control scheme is shown to cause more severe fluctuations in production, lower labour productivity and increased costs. Morecroft traces these dynamics to unanticipated changes in vendor lead times. In a significant use of simulation, he shows that predictions of improved performance are indeed rational and correct if one's mental model of the complex manufacturing environment omits or underestimates particular interdependencies, thus explaining both the promise and the disappointment in MRP systems.

Dynamics of Information in a Firm

These notions, that information in a management system is a significant source of its dynamics and that it is not likely to be completely known to actors in the system, appear significantly in the work of Clark and Augustine (Chapter 20), who use simulation to measure the value of information at different managerial levels of a firm. In a sophisticated analysis, they test the effects of the accuracy, reliability, timeliness and relevance of different kinds of information on the profitability, cost and efficiency of a simulated firm. Their experimental design treats three levels of the firm – operational, managerial and strategic – and is able to show the different information attributes that have strong effects on performance indicators at each of these three levels. Significantly, their analyses suggest that firms should be aggressive in investing in operational and managerial decision support systems and less aggressive in executive information systems.

The use of system dynamics modelling to study information systems recently received its most extensive treatment in Wolstenholme et al.'s significant work.[1]

Project Management

The next two chapters are excellent examples of the extensive use of system dynamics modelling in project management. Both address the ubiquitous and recurrent problem of overruns in large projects, and both represent prize-winning work. Cooper's study of the use of modelling and simulation in a litigious situation about overruns in naval ship production

(Chapter 21) won second prize in the 1980 Management Science Achievement Award competition sponsored by The Institute of Management Science. The paper describes the path-breaking work of the author and his colleagues at Pugh-Roberts Associates using a system dynamics model to help untangle the conflicting arguments in litigation about a $500 million overrun on a shipbuilding project. Two main sources of the overruns were in dispute: the US Navy argued that mismanagement of the extremely complex project caused the overruns, while Ingalls Shipbuilding argued that they stemmed from delays and disruptions caused by Navy design changes in all phases of the project. The author describes the model-building effort, particularly the subtleties involved in accounting for ripple effects of design changes, and documents how the model was used to help settle the claims out of court, a settlement estimated to be worth between $170–$350 million to Ingalls. Cooper then goes on to describe how the model developed into an on-going tool for project management – a seminal piece of system dynamics modelling work.

Chapter 22 by Abdel-Hamid and Madnick is one of a series of publications by these authors on software project management, culminating in their book *Software Project Dynamics*[2] which won the 1994 Jay Wright Forrester award from the System Dynamics Society for its outstanding contribution to the field. In this paper the authors address the issue of learning from past project management errors and show how a system dynamics simulation model can be used as a postmortem diagnostic tool. Their model integrates the planning, controlling and staffing functions of management with the software production activities of design, coding, reviewing and testing. Their model-based analyses shed new light on project management wisdom such as Brooks' Law and the use of past data to calibrate project estimates. Most significantly, their work shows the weaknesses of postmortem intuitions about project overruns and provides a sound model-based alternative capable of uncovering erroneous 'lessons' about project management.

Individuals and the Organization

The final two chapters in this Corporate Policy and Management section deal with the dynamics of people in organizations. Homer's classic essay on worker stress and burnout is an elegant and instructive example of model-based theory building. It focuses on the dynamics and interactions of an individual's energy level, expectations and performance. The model exhibits dramatic oscillations, much like the author's own intermittent periods of productivity and exhaustion during the writing of his dissertation. The modelling is instructive, particularly in its treatment of a number of 'soft' variables at the level of the individual; the policy conclusions are insightful and personally useful.

Kim and Senge complete the section by examining current thinking on organizational learning. The work forms part of the extensive efforts of these authors and others to understand and design learning organizations. In Chapter 24 they identify six breakdowns in the learning cycle which they trace to role constraints, ambiguities in how an individual affects an organization, superstitious inference, superficial analyses, fragmentation and opportunism. To improve our abilities to learn in and about organizations – to enable us to build learning organizations – they advocate a model-based approach employing what they call managerial practice fields. Simulation and serious management games (or 'flight simulators') can shorten inherent delays in reflecting on real-world experience and can provide flexible testing grounds for developing skills and theory.

This focus on the use of simulation to build learning organizations provides a framework for looking back on the essays of this section, each of which is an exemplary attempt to advance learning about the structure and dynamics of management organizations. It also anticipates Part IV of this collection, as its implications are as relevant for public sector organizations as for corporations.

Notes

1. E.F. Wolstenholme, S. Henderson and Allan Gavine (1993), *The Evaluation of Information Systems: A Dynamic and Holistic Approach*, Chichester: Wiley.
2. T. Abdel-Hamid and S. Madnick (1991), *Software Project Dynamics*, Englewood Cliffs, NJ: Prentice Hall.

A System Pathology of an Organization: The Rise and Fall of the Old *Saturday Evening Post*

Roger I. Hall

The peculiar circumstances surrounding the demise of mass circulation magazines, such as *Life, Look,* and the old *Saturday Evening Post,* are explained from a systems point of view. The methodology of System Dynamics together with a corporate framework is applied to modeling a typical large magazine publishing company. The advantages and pitfalls associated with this methodology are discussed. The assumptions built into the model are tested by an empirical study of the old *Saturday Evening Post.* Experiments with a simulation version of the model lead to an understanding of how the system reacts, both in the short and long run, to changes to the management control variables such as subscription and advertising "rates." This understanding of the dynamic relation among the parts of the publishing system is used as a basis for interpreting the phases of the rise and fall of the old *Saturday Evening Post.* Similarities to other magazines are noted and some implications are drawn for this method of studying the systemic pathology of organizations.[1]

Considerable interest has been generated in the plight of the large publishing firms. For instance, the Curtis Publishing Company was eclipsed in 1969 with the death of the *Saturday Evening Post* after a series of panic measures that included canceling subscriptions to reduce production costs (Friedrich, 1970; Culligan, 1970). The Cowles Communications Inc. announced a planned reduction in circulation and advertising rates of the *Look* magazine following a period of financial loss (Dougherty, 1970) and stopped publication in 1971. A similar move was made by the Time Inc. over its magazine, *Life,* following a poor reported financial performance *(Wall Street Journal,* 1970) before *Life* also was discontinued. Conflicting reasons have been given for the demise of these magazines: competition with other media, such as T.V., sharply rising printing and postal costs, substantial increases in the cost of acquiring additional readers, lost touch with readers, erratic behavior of advertisers, and plain bad management (Dougherty, 1969, 1970a, 1970b; *Saturday Review,* 1970; Friedrich, 1970).

At the time of its initial crisis, each of these magazines reported its highest circulation and largest revenue. There must be an explanation for such a paradoxical situation wherein a record circulation and revenue is associated with poor profit performance. It is hardly credible that a large number of the leading magazines were being mismanaged simultaneously. These magazines continued to grow in spite of keen competition with other large circulation magazines and other mass-communications media until they reached a critical point in their history. This suggests that the pathology of magazine publishing is, perhaps, a complex phenomenon.

The economics of a magazine publishing firm is complicated by the fact that its revenues come from two different but related sources—advertising revenues and circulation revenues. They are related by the number of readers of the magazine. Obviously, circulation revenues are directly related to the readership. Advertising revenues, on the other hand, are indirectly related to readership since the price that adver-

[1] The author wishes to thank Dr. Leslie L. Roos for his incisive comments on a previous draft.

tisers are prepared to pay for magazine advertising space depends, to a large extent, upon the exposure of their advertisements. Also, if companies tend to finance readership growth out of current revenues, then the level of readership is also dependent, over time, upon itself. This suggests that a magazine publishing company may be viewed as a rather complex system of parts dynamically related over time, and that a systems study of magazine publishing may provide a convenient starting point for analyzing the interplay of the various forces at work in shaping the destiny of a company. This study will attempt to discover how much the structure of the system accounts for the observed behavior of large firms.

METHODOLOGY

System Dynamics as a System Modeling Methodology

System Dynamics (Forrester, 1968a) and its complementary computer system simulation language, Dynamo (Pugh, 1970), have been designed primarily to aid the modeling and simulation of complex dynamic feedback systems. As the modeling-simulation package adopted for this study, it offers a number of advantages over other modeling approaches (Day, 1974). First, it enables the researcher to maintain a one-to-one correspondence between his verbal description of the real world system of cause and effect and the flow diagram representing this causal chain, and between his flow diagram and the set of equations in the computer program to simulate this model of causality. Second, the flow diagram provides an excellent vehicle for communicating with managers in various parts of the system in order to solicit their perceptions of how the system works. Third, the rapid feedback of results from the simulation program—in particular the similarity or dissimilarity of the behavior of the model to the real world system—provides further clues to the researcher as to the aptness of the emerging model. Four, the new insights into the structure and operation of the system gained by the process can be quickly incorporated by redrawing the flow diagram and modifying the simulation program—easily accomplished in the Dynamo language since parallel processing renders the order of the equations unimportant—by re-punching a few computer cards. Finally, the Dynamo language is very easy to learn, provides excellent diagnostics to the novice programmer and requires only very simple instructions to run, print tables, plot time-series of variables in the model, and gives the researcher the freedom to concentrate on conceptualizing the parts of the system under study and on mapping their interrelations. There is no necessity to make great mental leaps from the flow diagram of causality in the system to yet another flow diagram of the computational sequence in the computer.

However, the methodology is not without its critics. As Brewer and Hall (1973: 347), writing from a policy analysis framework, put it:

A model is a theory. Acceptance of a computer program as 'good' social theory is dependent upon one's acceptance of the responsible theorist and his assumptions. It is important to know both. To the extent that these assumptions are unreasonable, the validity of the model is decreased, and to the extent that a model contains formal theoretical relationships not empirically obtained, the relevance of the model is decreased.

System Pathology

Formal computer models appear to be quite scientific. Without adequate understanding of the empirical context, without full realization of the embedded assumptions, and without appreciation of the exclusions and omissions, a potential user is easily led down the garden path. The enormous difficulty of specifying a model is not to be lightly dismissed by the so-called 'system engineer' who can model anything, any time, any place, for anyone.

The criticism is directed more at the modeler who tries to draw inferences from an unvalidated model, than at the methodology per se. This study will try to avoid this criticism by making explicit the assumptions built into the model and by supplying the empirical evidence to validate them. It is inevitable that we shall commit some sins of omission. An all-inclusive model would, after all, be as complex and intractable as the real world system under study. A purpose of model building is to abstract and simplify the phenomenon under study to make it comprehendible. The necessity for closure at some point automatically dictates that omissions have been made. Whether further enrichments of the model would result in a more valid or complete model that would justify the extra research work needed is always a matter of judgment to be argued.

The Model Building Process

System Dynamics or the Theory of Structure (Forrester, 1968b), is based upon the concept of a bounded system in interrelated parts. These parts comprise the essential system states and activities that characterize the firm's gross behavior with its environment. For example, the level of readership of a magazine can be conceptualized as a system state that changes from one time period to the next in response to the system activities, such as the inflow and outflow of subscribers to the readership level. The movement of readers in and out of the level of readership might be a function of the magazine's volume, price, and appeal in comparison with other magazines. The dynamic feedback characteristic of the system is imparted by the component interrelationships. For example, the cost of producing the magazine can be described as a function of the volume of the magazine (number of pages), which in turn is related to the amount of advertising purchased, which in its turn is related to the level of readership, and so on. In this manner, a typical magazine publishing company can be conceptualized by a system of temporally interrelated parts. The art in this kind of modeling lies in choosing a level of conception and a system boundary that includes the smallest number of components that will adequately describe the system of the firm in its environment.

Once conceptualized the system can be analyzed as if it were a wiring diagram of a self-controlling electronic device. Concepts from control engineering can be borrowed to facilitate the analysis of the system. For instance, some of the system's dynamic behavior can be predicted by identifying positive feedback loops—groups of parts forming a closed circular pattern of interrelationships—that will cause unrestrained growth in response to a change in the system, and negative feedback loops that will tend to counteract or limit system changes. If the system is too complex for this kind of analysis alone, then one can resort to a computer simulation model. The programming language, Dynamo, provides a ready-made kit to assemble such a simulation model.

The System Dynamics view of a company and its environment leads to the notion that the structure of the system accounts for a large part of the company's own peculiar growth and development. Complex systems with many feedback loops can give rise to counter-intuitive situations, whereby the intuitive judgmental decisions made by people in the system may, on occasion, not correct an out-of-control situation and may even make it worse (Forrester, 1970). A magazine firm, when viewed as a complex dynamic information feedback system, may exhibit such situations.

A Corporate Modeling Framework

The usual approach to building System Dynamic models is to structure the model around the basic feedback loops of the system (Nord, 1963; Packer, 1964; Roberts, 1964; Meadows, 1970), thus facilitating the interpretation of the structurally determined time-dependent behavior. This approach becomes less feasible for complex systems with many interact-

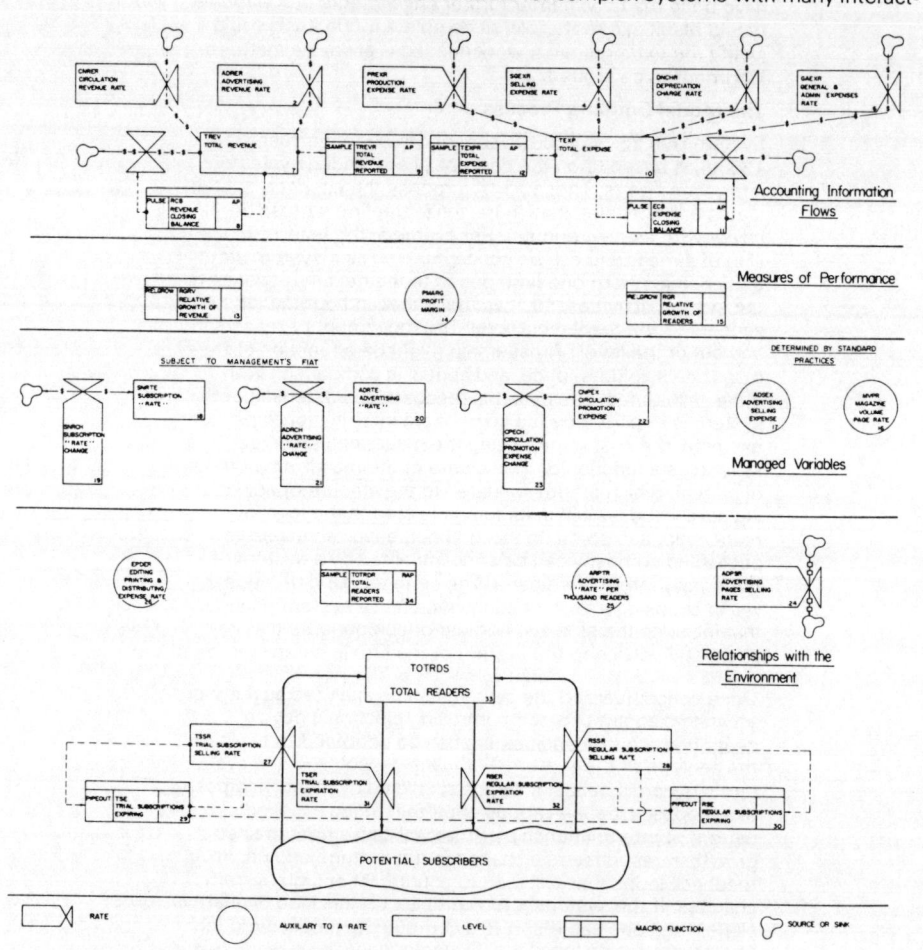

Figure 1. Corporate modeling framework.

System Pathology

ing components and intertwining feedback loops. In such circumstances it is replaced by a series of building blocks that partition the complex system into more tractable subsystems (Roberts et al., 1968; Forrester, 1969, 1971; and Meadows et al., 1972). Each subsystem can be built up independently from basic assumptions or empirical information about its inner workings, and connected to all the other similarly derived subsystems to form a complete system model. Due to the complexity of the magazine publishing system this latter strategy has been adopted and a corporate modeling framework used to subdivide the system into manageable portions.

The basic structure of the model of a magazine publishing firm is illustrated in Figure 1. It consists of four corporate building blocks: (1) accounting information flows, (2) measures of performance, (3) managed variables, and (4) relations of the firm with its environment.

The accounting information flows. This sector represents the accumulation of accounting information concerning total revenues and total expenses, the reporting of the end-of-year amounts, and the closing and clearing of the balances in the accounts so that the process may repeat itself in the following year. It is a simple analogue of the company's accounting processes.

The measures of performance. This sector represents the computation of three major performance indices thought to influence management decisions in magazine publishing companies: (1) the profit margin on total revenue as reported at year-end, (2) the relative growth of revenues, and (3) the relative growth of readers over the year in question.

The managed variables. This sector represents the major variables under the management's control: namely, the annual subscription "rate"[2] or price to be charged readers of the magazine, the advertising "rate" or price per page to purchase advertising space in the magazine, the annual circulation promotion expense for acquiring trial readers, the advertising selling expense, and the magazine volume (pages per year). It is assumed that the management can, if it so desires, manipulate these variables by a conscious decision-making process stimulated, perhaps, by changes in the measures of performance. Some of these variables are handled automatically. For example, it was discovered that both the advertising selling expense and the annual magazine volume are adjusted routinely by industry and company standard practices. Most magazines pay their advertising agents a standard commission on sales, so that the advertising selling expense varies directly with the advertising revenue earned. Similarly, magazines have editorial-advertising formulae which regulate the number of pages of text that the editor may publish for each page of advertising purchased in the magazine. The magazine volume, therefore, is related to the pages of advertising purchased. The other managed variables, that are subject to the management's fiat, are viewed as system states that remain unchanged unless the management makes a conscious decision to change them. For example, the subscription "rate" can be increased or decreased only by a subscription "rate" change decision. A similar representation

---

[2] The magazine publishing industry uses the word "rate" to connote "price." On the other hand, the same word is used in System Dynamics terminology to mean "rate of flow." To avoid any confusion between the two uses of the word, when "price" is implied the word "rate" will be written in quotation marks.

189/ASQ

is used to model changes to the advertising "rate" and circulation promotion expense. Since one of the unknowns in corporate simulation modeling concerns the mechanism by which the management of an organization decides how to change prices and promotion expenditures in response to changes in its measures of performance, these modeled decision points are used as experimental inputs. An arbitrary change, such as a 20 percent change in the subscription "rate," can be imparted to the model and its impact traced through the system to help understand the effect of these management controls on the system's performance.

Relationships with the environment. This sector represents the firm's interaction with its principal marketing and technical environment: namely, the flow of advertising pages purchased (advertising pages selling rate), the rate of expenditure on editing, printing, and distributing the magazine to the readers, and the rate at which subscriptions are sold or expire together with their effect on the total readers of the magazine. The rate of selling advertising pages is posited to be related to the unit price for advertising established by the industry (advertising "rate" per thousand readers). This in its turn is computed from the total readers reported at the year-end and the advertising "rate" per page set by the management. The dollar expenditure on producing and distributing the magazine is assumed to be a function of the total number of pages delivered to the readers, which in turn is computed from the magazine volume and the current total readers. The sale of trial subscriptions is assumed to be influenced by both the expenditure on circulation promotion and the magazine volume. Subscriptions are modeled as expiring one year after purchase. The sale of regular subscriptions are posited to be a function of the regular and trial subscriptions that are expiring and therefore potentially renewable, the magazine volume (number of pages in the annual volume) and the annual subscription "rate" charged. The total readers of the magazine are represented as a system state, the level of which changes in response to the flows of subscribers in and out of the system. The total number of readers is reported annually and provides the basis for computing the advertising "rate" per thousand readers.

The Completed Model

The informational linkages interconnecting the components of this corporate framework are shown in the completed model (Figure 2). These linkages consist of logico-mathematical relations and conversion relations. For example, component #2 (Figure 2), advertising revenue rate, is comprised of a simple mathematical extension of the components #24, advertising pages selling rate (pages per year) and #20, advertising "rate" ($ per page of advertising). When multiplied together, they determine the rate at which advertising revenue (dollars per year) is flowing into the total revenue account (#7). On the other hand, advertising pages selling rate (#24) is determined by the prices index, advertising "rate" per thousand readers (#25). It represents the decisional process of the advertisers in buying space in the magazine and involves the conversion of dimensions from dollars per page per thousand readers to pages per year. The conversion requires an empirical study of

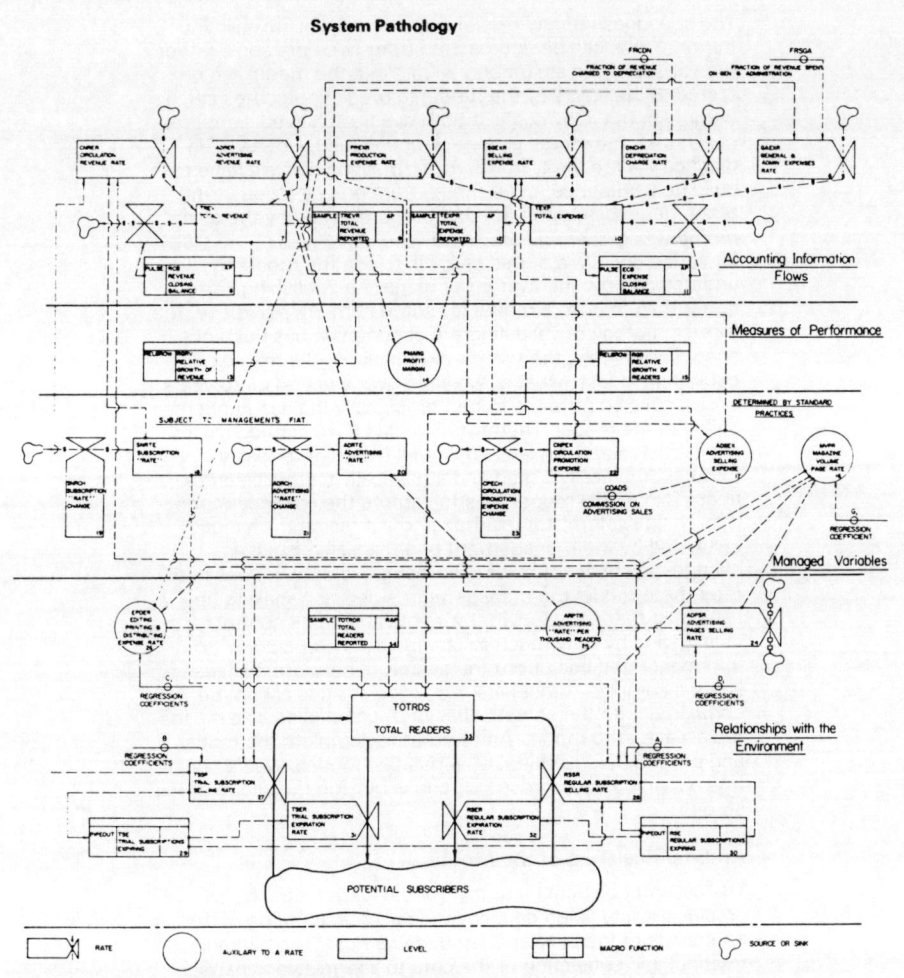

Figure 2. Model of a magazine publishing firm.

the buying behavior of advertisers to supply the needed coefficients of conversion. These conversion coefficients are shown in Figure 2 as the regression coefficients D_i. Figure 2, therefore, represents a working hypothesis of how a magazine publishing system functions and it requires testing before inferences can be drawn concerning how it behaves as a whole.

An Empirical Study

In contrast to many other System Dynamics studies, an attempt was made to base the model on statistically treated empirical data. As the authors of one such study note (Roberts, Abrams, and Weil, 1968: B-675):

> Empirical data were not available sufficiently to permit use of statistical techniques for deriving some critical market relationships . . . . Industrial Dynamics methodology does not insist upon such data availability, although added confidence in the model formulation does result when derivation of relationships can be enhanced by statistical analysis methods.

The soundness of any model, as measured by its ability to mirror reality, can be approached from two directions. Either the validity of the assumptions built into the model can be tested or the ability of the model to predict outcomes can be demonstrated. Obviously, if both can be achieved simultaneously, then the model is quite sound indeed. However, in practice we are rarely in this idyllic position and we have to build up confidence in our model from one direction or the other, depending upon the problem presented by the environment in gathering data and by the objectives of the study. Since the objective of this study is to use the model to understand how the system of magazine publishing works, rather than to build a model for some normative purpose, the former strategy of validating the assumption has been pursued. Fortunately, the wealth of data about the magazine publishing industry that is available over a period of 20 years or so, makes it possible to test empirically the assumptions built into the model. Therefore, we can have confidence in this partial model, because it is well fastened to reality through empirically based and statistically tested assumptions. This partial model tries to capture the essence of the publishing system; for example, how it reacts to changes instigated by the management of a magazine (such as changes to subscription or advertising "rates"). It *does not* attempt to model the management's decision-making behavior, as for example, what variables under its control to change and by how much to change them in response to information fed back from the system. Therefore, because it is not a complete model, its predictive abilities cannot be compared with the actual behavior of companies as a means of validating the model. An attempt to complete the model and perform this acid test of simulation models would constitute a major piece of research and is outside the scope of this study.

An Empirical Test of the Model

The assumptions built into this model were tested by an empirical study using data covering a 20-year period of the operations of the old *Saturday Evening Post*. The gathering, treating, and subjecting of the data to a regression analysis (Rao and Miller, 1971) was, itself, a considerable undertaking and is reported in detail elsewere (Hall, 1973). The values of the summary statistics, computed to assess the reliability of the estimates in the regression equations, lend credence to this model of a publishing firm as representing reality for the purpose in hand.

A measure of the strength of an assumption in a regression equation is the ratio of the coefficient of regression to the standard error of the coefficient: the higher the ratio, the more reliance can be put on the assumed relationships. In econometric studies, for example, a ratio of 1:1 is thought to be acceptable. For this study the smallest ratio exceeded 2.5:1 and the largest was of the order 30:1. The R-squared statistics, that estimate the proportions of observed behavior ascribed to these posited relationships, were all in the high .90s, the lowest being .95. Taking into account the number of data points available (usually 20) these results would seem to be acceptable.

System Pathology

Empirical Findings

The analysis did indicate that the major influence on trial subscription sales was the expenditure on circulation promotion (Figure 3). There is little to indicate that trial readers were becoming more expensive to acquire; on the contrary, from 1957 onwards, the technical revolution, brought about by new techniques of mass mailing reduced-price subscription offers, appears to have increased the efficiency of promoting the

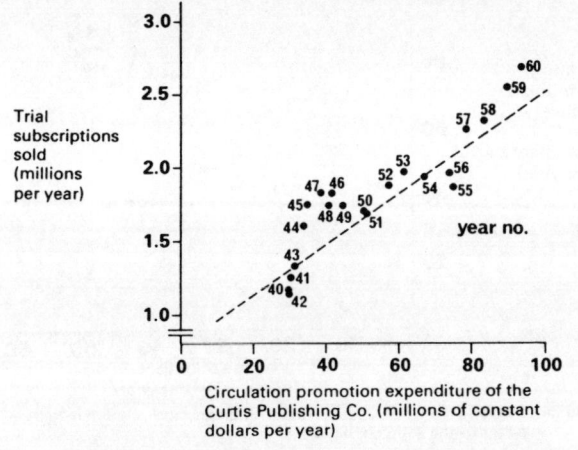

Source: Association of National Advertisers, 1961, 1969; Moody's Industrial Manual, 1940–1960; Hall, 1973.

Figure 3. Trial subscriptions sold vs. circulation promotion expenditure.

magazine. Also, the fraction of regular subscribers who renewed their subscriptions was found to be strongly related to the subscription "rate" charged, and that the fraction of trial subscribers who convert to regular readership was markedly affected by the number of pages in the magazine's annual volume.

Surprisingly enough, no effect of editorial policy or quality of editorial content could be found on the subscription renewal behavior of readers of the old *Saturday Evening Post*. This does not mean that the quality of the editorial content in the magazine was unimportant, but rather that, one way or another, it remained constant over the 20-year period covered by the empirical study. Friedrich (1970: 478) noted that any one of the diverse personalities who occupied the editorial chair of the old *Saturday Evening Post* was or could have been successful, but that no amount of editorial genius could have made up for, what he considered to be, bad management. Presumably, as long as the editorial flavor of the magazine does not become out-of-date and the editor is able to keep more-or-less abreast of the changes in the tastes and social mores of his readership, then he maintains a loyal or, at the very least, a satisfied clientele.

The yield of regular subscribers from the previous year's trial readers was found to be sensitive to the magazine's annual volume size. This suggests that the more articles published covering a broader range of subject matter, the greater the chance that the trial reader might find something of interest to him personally that will influence his decision to become a regular subscriber. Once a reader becomes a regular subscriber, it seems that he acts as a satisfier who renews his subscriptions more-or-less indefinitely until he becomes dissatisfied by the raising of the subscription "rate."

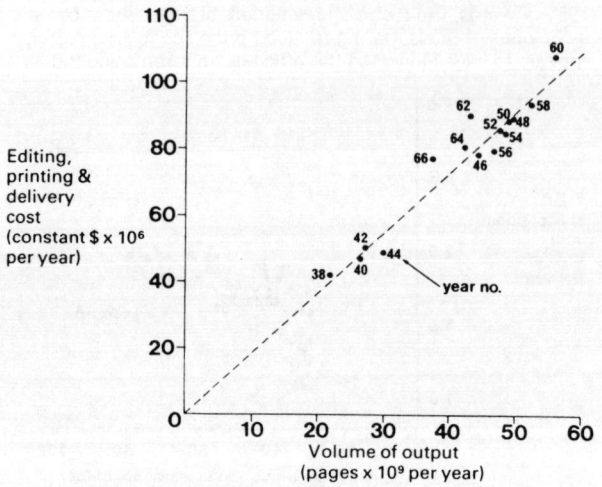

Source: Moody's Industrial Manual (1940–1960); physical count of magazine pages by the author (Hall, 1973).

Figure 4. Production costs vs. volume of output—the Curtis Publishing Co.

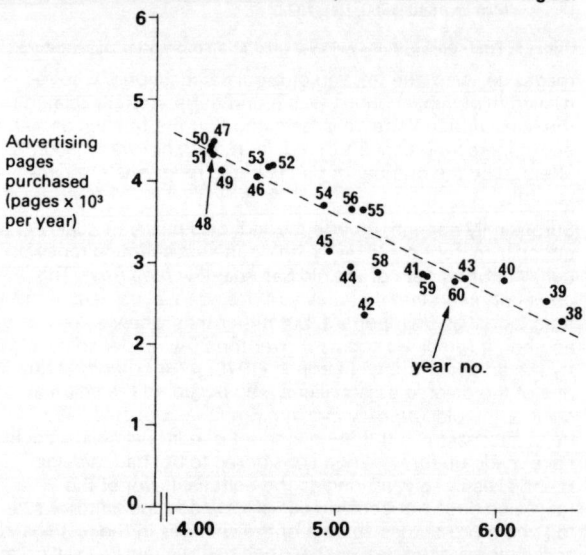

Source: Association of National Advertisers (1961, 1969); Advertising Age (1940–1960) & Hall (1973).

Figure 5. Advertising purchased vs. price of advertising—the old *Saturday Evening Post*.

System Pathology

The relationship of the company's production expenses to the volume of pages printed (Figure 4) suggest that, at least prior to 1960, increasing production costs per unit of output was not a factor to be considered. By 1960, however, the company was already in dire financial straits. Similarly, the relationship between advertising purchased in the magazine and the price charged for advertising (Figure 5) does not suggest capricious behavior by the advertisers, except for the year 1942 when an anti-Jewish article in the magazine incurred the displeasure of the advertisers who withdrew their support; thus forcing the resignation of the editor.

Of particular interest is the relation between pages in the annual volume and the amount of advertising purchased in the magazine, since this determines to a large extent the production costs and the renewal characteristics of trial subscribers. Friedrich (1970: 244) referred to it as the "traditional advertising-editorial formula, whereby an increase in the sale of advertising pages also permitted the publication of more editorial pages." The remarkable stability of this relationship over an extended period of the magazine's history is illustrated in Figure 6.

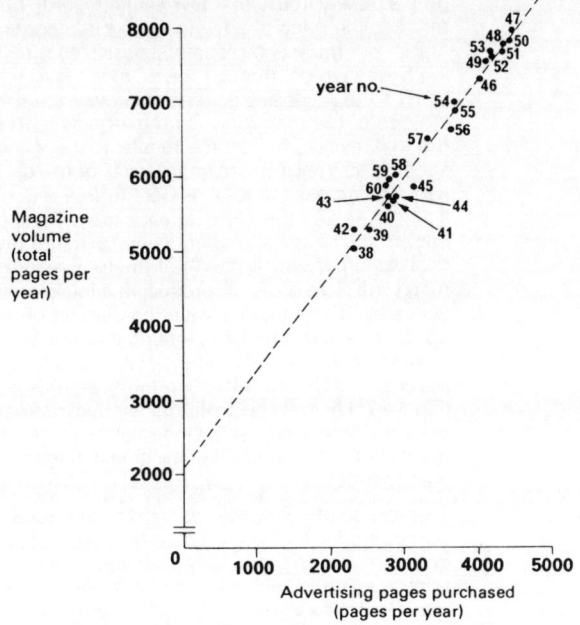

Source: Advertising Age (1940–1960) & physical count of magazine pages by the author (Hall, 1973).

Figure 6. Advertising-editorial relationship—the old *Saturday Evening Post*.

EXPERIMENTS WITH THE SIMULATION MODEL

Experiment #1 with a Free Running Model

The model was programmed in the Dynamo computer simulation language and run primed with the relationships uncov-

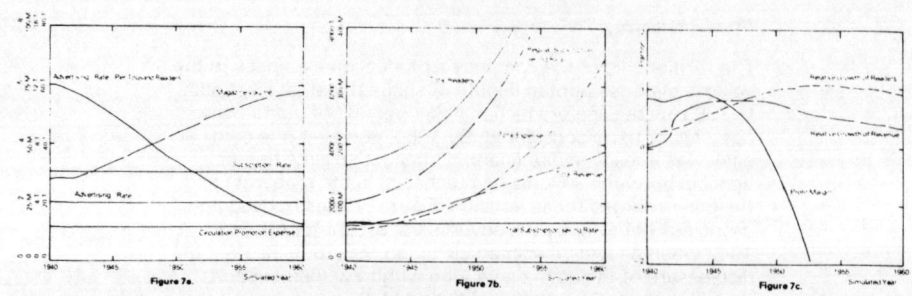

Figure 7. Experiment #1 response of free-running model.

ered in the empirical study and with the initial conditions appertaining to the old *Saturday Evening Post* in 1940. The results of this experiment are shown in the three plots of Figure 7. The three major managed variables of subscription "rate," advertising "rate," and circulation promotion expense in this experimental run, are fixed throughout the 20 simulated years (Figure 7a). However, since the circulation promotion expense is sufficient to acquire trial readers at a rate that more than offsets the natural loss of readers, the readership grows slowly in the first few years (Figure 7b). This growth reduces the price of advertising in the magazine (advertising "rate" per thousand readers), stimulates the sale of advertising pages which, through the editorial-advertising formula, causes the magazine volume to grow (Figure 7a). The increasing size of the magazine volume attracts a greater fraction of the trial readers to become regular readers and the regular subscription selling rate improves (Figure 7b). The consequent increase in total readers further reduces the price of advertising and the cycle repeats itself. This positive feedback in the cause and effect chain built into the model creates exponential growth of the total readers of the magazine. The effect of producing a thicker magazine and delivering it to an ever increasing number of readers, drives up the total expense of operating the firm at a rate that is faster than the increase in total revenues from circulation and advertising. The net effect on the measures of performance (Figure 7c) is that the profit margin declines very rapidly after the simulated year 1945. One might infer from this experiment that the system of publishing a magazine is potentially self-destructive.

The source of instability lies within the structure of the system in the form of the positive feedback loop, shown for greater clarity in Figure 8. Any change in the loop will be reinforced and feedback upon itself. Hence, an increase in readers, for example, will create a further growth of readers and a decrease in readers will cause a further reduction in readers. The system will have the tendency to grow or decay exponentially. If the system has this characteristic of running out of control, one would expect that it is difficult to manage.

Management's corrective actions. Since the profit margin is the only performance measure to go out of control, one might expect the management to initiate some sort of corrective action by manipulating the variables under its control. For example, revenues could be increased by (1) increasing the

System Pathology

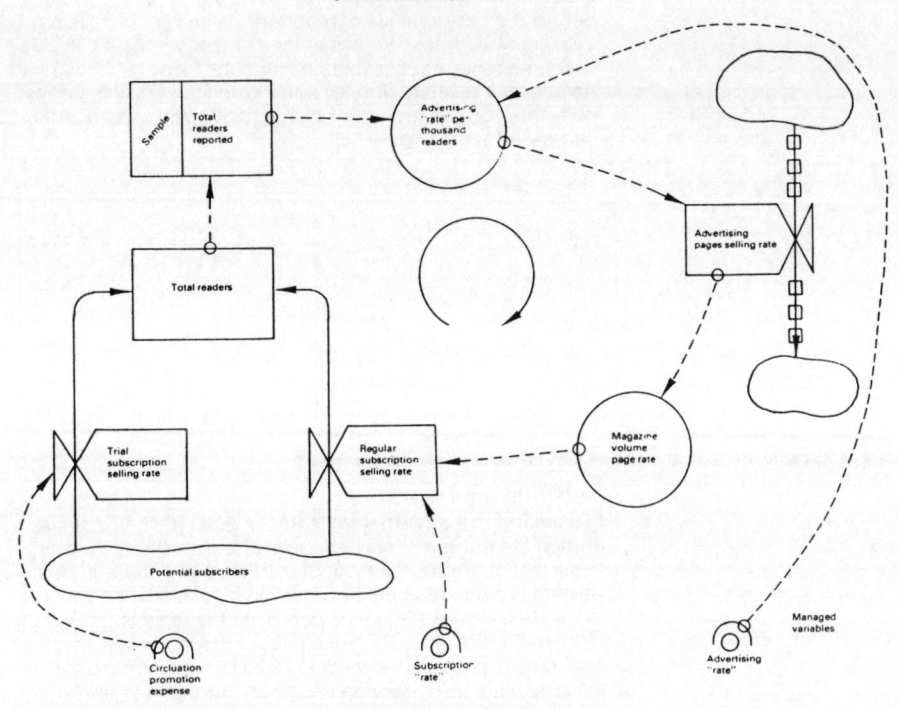

Figure 8. The source of growth, decay, and potential uncontrollability.

[3]
The experimental changes were introduced in the year that the profit margin began to decline, namely, the simulated year 1945. Choosing this year also circumvents a technical problem in simulation associated with a settling-down period for transient disturbances, caused by the initialization procedures (see Meier, Newell, and Pazer, 1969: 296–299).

subscription "rates" or (2) increasing the advertising "rates," or alternatively, expenses could be reduced by (3) decreasing the circulation promotion expenditure. The relationships of these variables to the aforementioned positive feedback loop are shown in Figure 8. In order to test the sensitivity of the system to adjustments in these managed variables, each variable was charged in turn by an amount equal to 20 percent of its initial value.[3] The results of these experiments are described as follows:

Experiment #2

Increasing the subscription "rate." (Figure 9a) has an immediate ameliorating effect on the profit margin (Figure 9c).

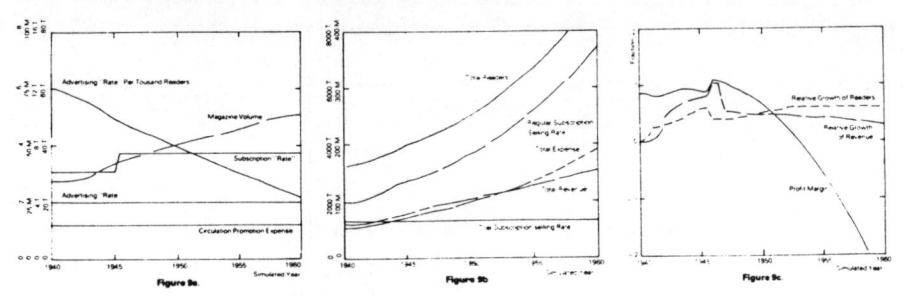

Figure 9. Experiment #2 response to a 20% increase in subscription "rate."

Unfortunately, this improvement lasts but for a few years before the performance deteriorates as before. Increasing subscription "rates" strikes at the company's most valuable asset, its regular subscribers (Figure 9b). Fewer subscribers means less revenue from circulation and advertising, so that both the long-run growth of readers and revenues are adversely effected (Figure 9c).

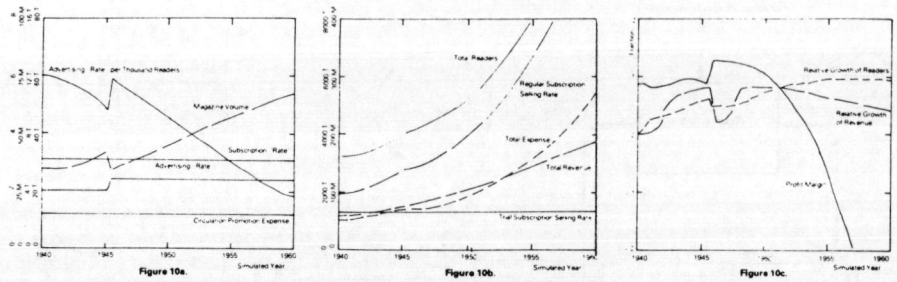

Figure 10. Experiment #3 response to a 20% increase in advertising "rate."

Experiment #3

Increasing the advertising "rate." Figure 10a has a similar immediate but transitory beneficial effect on the profit margin (Figure 10c). Perhaps a most unexpected and counter-intuitive relation is exhibited here between an increase in the advertising "rate" (Figure 10a) and a decline in the relative growth of readers (Figure 10c). This results from the increased advertising "rate" per thousand readers reducing the demand for advertising in the magazine and, then, through the time-honored editorial-advertising formula, reducing the magazine volume (Figure 10a). The temporarily smaller magazine volume becomes less attractive to trial subscribers and fewer buy regular subscriptions (Figure 10b) resulting in a decline in the relative growth of readers (Figure 10c). The temporary restraint on the growth of the magazine volume, however, reduces the printing costs—a major constituent of the total expense (Figure 10b)—and brings about the significant improvement in the profit margin (Figure 10c), albeit at the expense of the growth of regular readers.

Experiment #4

Decreasing the circulation promotion expenditure. This reduces the rate of selling trial subscriptions (Figure 11b). This in turn has a cumulative effect on the total readers because

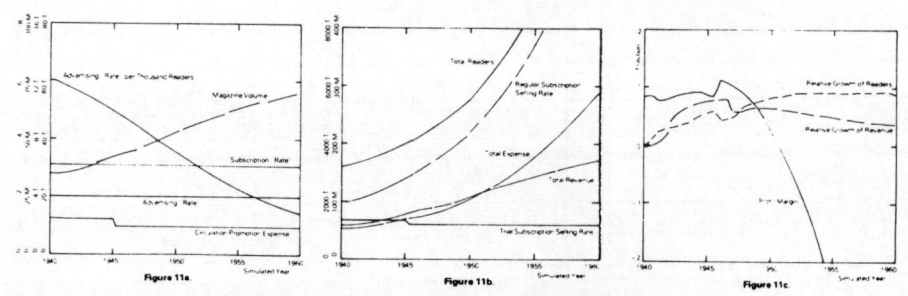

Figure 11. Experiment #4 response to a 20% decrease in promotion expenditure.

System Pathology

fewer subscribers are now being inducted into the system, which brings about a deceleration in the growth of readers through the mechanism of converting to regular readership in subsequent years. The growth process is further attenuated by the positive feedback loop described before. The reduced growth of readers slows the rate of decrease in the price of advertising which affects the advertising sales so that the magazine volume (Figure 11b) grows less quickly. This in its turn affects the fraction of trial subscribers who convert to regular subscribers, and so on. The net effect of these changes to the readership is to decrease significantly the relative growth of readers and to increase temporarily the profit margin (Figure 11c). The inevitable decline in the profit margin brought about by the firing-up of a positive feedback loop is delayed for about three years.

Management Decision Making in a Complex System

If the magazine's management is not aware of the complexity of these interrelations in the publishing system, it might easily be beguiled by the short-run, but transitory, corrective action of those variables under its control. For example, in competing against other magazines for readers, it might decide to substantially increase circulation promotion expenditure. To afford this strategy it might increase advertising "rates," which could result in a decrease in advertising pages purchased in the magazine, a decline in the magazine volume and a decrease in the yield of regular subscribers from trial subscribers. In order to achieve its growth goal, the firm might be prompted to further increase its circulation promotion expenditure and further increase its advertising "rates" to pay for this. Over an extended period of time, this could drive the firm from low to high circulation promotion expenditure and advertising "rate," and from publishing a thick to a skinny magazine. The firm, burdened with an extraordinarily high promotion expenditure to maintain the level of readership, is now vulnerable to such happenings as business cycles, inflation in production costs and increases in postal "rates." Any of these illnesses may strike the death blow to one already weakened by a wasting disease! The counterintuitive behavior of such complex systems was noted by Forrester (1959: 110):

With a high degree of confidence we can say that the intuitive solutions to the problems of complex social systems will be wrong most of the time. Here lies much of the explanation for the problems of faltering companies . . . .

THE RISE AND FALL OF THE OLD *SATURDAY EVENING POST*

By looking at some of the *Saturday Evening Post's* management's more significant decisions and by tracing their impact through the magazine publishing system, this section tries to explain the rise and fall of this distinguished magazine in terms of the dynamics of the entire system including the management decision processes. Tables 1 and 2 depict four distinct periods in the developmental history of the *Saturday Evening Post* between the years 1940 and 1960.

Phase 1: 1940–1944

During most of this period—the World War II years—the expansion of the company was inhibited by paper rationing.

Table 1

Revenues, Costs and Readers for the Curtis Publishing Company and the *Saturday Evening Post*

Year Ending	Total Revenue (c$m)	Circulation Revenue (c$m)	Fraction of Total Revenue	Advertising Revenue (c$m)	Fraction of Total Revenue	Production Costs (c$m)	Fraction of Total Revenue	Promotion Costs (c$m)	Fraction of Total Revenue	Total Readers (millions)
1940	97.4	23.4	.240	74.0	.760	46.7	.480	29.4	.302	3.25
1941	99.8	24.8	.248	75.0	.752	51.0	.511	29.8	.299	3.39
1942	89.7	28.3	.316	61.4	.684	51.2	.571	29.5	.329	3.33
1943	103.2	30.4	.294	72.8	.706	48.2	.467	30.9	.299	3.44
1944	110.7	32.6	.294	78.1	.706	48.5	.438	32.8	.296	3.39
1945	115.1	33.3	.290	81.8	.710	52.7	.458	33.7	.293	3.45
1946	146.9	40.7	.277	106.2	.723	78.2	.534	41.3	.282	3.78
1947	162.3	43.3	.267	119.0	.733	86.7	.534	37.9	.234	3.96
1948	163.1	47.0	.288	116.1	.712	89.0	.545	40.4	.248	3.90
1949	164.1	52.0	.317	112.1	.684	88.4	.539	42.0	.256	4.02
1950	177.9	60.1	.338	117.8	.662	88.5	.498	50.0	.281	4.03
1951	169.6	56.6	.334	113.0	.616	85.0	.501	50.6	.299	4.00
1952	175.9	59.1	.336	116.8	.664	86.0	.489	57.1	.325	4.22
1953	187.1	65.1	.348	122.0	.652	88.8	.475	61.1	.326	4.52
1954	184.9	66.0	.358	118.9	.642	84.4	.457	67.1	.364	4.59
1955	191.2	65.8	.344	125.4	.656	84.1	.440	74.6	.390	4.70
1956	192.2	66.1	.344	126.1	.656	79.5	.414	74.0	.385	4.91
1957	201.8	69.4	.344	132.4	.656	85.9	.426	78.6	.390	5.30
1958	200.7	72.9	.363	127.8	.637	93.0	.464	83.0	.414	5.75
1959	221.6	76.4	.345	145.2	.655	104.5	.472	89.3	.404	6.12
1960	225.2	78.2	.347	147.0	.653	107.9	.479	92.8	.412	6.30

Source: Association of National Advertisers (1961, 1969), Moody's Industrial Manual (1940–1960) & Hall (1973)
Money values expressed in millions of constant dollars (c$m)

The company raised the annual subscription "rate" from an average of approximately $3.00 to $4.80 constant dollars per subscriber; presumably as a device for simultaneously rationing the magazine, which was in great demand, and compensating for the loss of wartime advertising revenue. The combined effects of limiting the volume of the magazine to around 5,700 pages—thereby holding the production costs in check—and increasing substantially the circulation revenue, resulted in an unprecedented profit margin of 14 percent of revenues.

Table 2

A Summary of Performance Measures, Managed and Intervening Variables for the old *Saturday Evening Post*

At year ending	Relative growth of revenue	Profit margin	Relative Growth of readers	At year ending[•]	Subscription "rate" ($/year)	Advertising "rate" (10^3 $/page)	Circ. promotion expense (10^6 $/year)	Advertising "rate" per thousand readers ($/page/thou. readers)	Magazine volume (pages/year)
				Phase 1					
1940	.08	.08	.05	1941	2.93	18.7	29.8	5.54	5666
1941	.01	.05	.04	1942	3.52	17.3	29.5	5.18	5332
1942	−.10	−.04	−.02	1943	4.15	16.9	30.9	5.80	5628
1943	.15	.11	.03	1944	4.50	17.3	32.8	5.10	5700
1944	.07	.14	−.01	1945	4.79	17.1	33.7	4.96	5822
				Phase 2					
1945	.04	.13	.02	1946	4.86	17.1	41.3	4.52	7336
1946	.28	.07	.10	1947	5.21	16.9	37.9	4.26	7920
1947	.10	.11	.05	1948	6.02	16.5	40.4	4.24	7780
				Phase 3					
1948	.01	.08	−.01	1949	5.97	17.2	42.0	4.29	7568
1949	.01	.08	.03	1950	5.97	17.1	50.0	4.23	7808
1950	.08	.10	.00	1951	5.52	16.9	50.6	4.23	7664
				Phase 4					
1951	−.05	.08	−.01	1952	5.40	19.5	57.1	4.61	7600
1952	.04	.07	.06	1953	5.36	20.8	61.1	4.59	7644
1953	.06	.08	.07	1954	5.34	22.7	67.1	4.94	6992
1954	−.01	.06	.02	1955	5.36	24.2	74.6	5.16	6896
1955	.03	.05	.02	1956	5.28	25.6	74.0	5.21	6616
1956	.01	.08	.05	1957	5.10	27.4	78.6	5.34	6490
1957	.05	.06	.08	1958	5.00	30.3	83.0	5.27	6038
1958	−.01	−.01	.08	1959	4.93	34.1	89.3	5.57	5932
1959	.10	−.01	.06	1960	4.85	36.1	92.8	5.74	5910

Source: Hall (1973)

[•] Assumes that the management took action to change the managed variables during the year following the report of unsatisfactory performance

System Pathology

Phase 2: 1945–1947

During this time, the magazine underwent a period of almost unrestrained postwar growth. Its readership grew from 3.4 to almost 4 millions, its revenues grew from 115 to 162 million constant dollars, but its profit margin fell from 14 percent in 1944 to 7 percent of revenues in 1946. This phase of the magazine's history parallels experiment #1 with the free-running simulation model and can be interpreted as follows. The significant increase in readers lowered the price of advertising from $4.96 in 1944 to $4.24 constant dollars per page per thousand readers in 1947, which stimulated the advertisers to buy more pages of advertising in the magazine. This increase in advertising pages purchased was matched by an increase in editorial pages which caused a significant increase in the volume of the magazine. As can be seen from Table 2, the annual volume grew from 5,822 in 1944 to nearly 8,000 pages in 1946. As demonstrated in the model, an increase in annual volume will improve the yield of regular readers converting from trial readers; thus accelerating the growth of total readers. The net result of the larger readership and more voluminous magazine supplied to each reader was a crippling increase in the production costs from around 46 to 53 percent of annual revenues (see Table 1). Thus, the profit margin was depressed through the mechanism already described.

The management's action to counteract the drop in profit margin was to increase, quite substantially, the subscription "rate" from an annual average of $4.79 in 1944 to over $6.00 constant dollars per subscriber.[4] Why they should have adopted this policy is a matter for conjecture. Cyert and March (1963: 121) suggest one way organizations go about searching for a solution to a pressing problem:

> We assume that rules for search are simple minded in the sense that they reflect simple concepts of causality. Subject to learning . . . , search is based initially on two simple rules: (1) search in the neighborhood of the problem symptom and (2) search in the neighborhood of the current alternative. These two rules reflect different dimensions of the basic causal notions that a cause will be found "near" its effect and that a new solution will be found "near" an old one.

Applying these rules to the present case leads to the conclusion that the management would indeed choose the alternative of increasing the subscription "rate." For example, Table 1 shows that one symptom of the problem is that the fraction of total revenue supplied by the circulation revenue fell during the years 1946–1947. This would suggest increasing the subscription "rate," evidence being that the company had very successfully raised its profit margin during the war years by increasing the subscription "rate" making the increase in the subscription "rate" a current alternative solution.[5] The effect of increasing the subscription "rate," however, has been shown to have a detrimental effect on the fraction of regular subscribers who resubscribe (Figure 9). The growth of readers of the magazine, in consequence, leveled off. Hence this period of the magazine's history can be described as (1) unrestrained growth leading to a depressed profit margin, (2) management action based, presumably, on the symptoms of the problem and the most current alternative solution (namely, raising the subscription "rate"), rather than being based on the underlying causal structure of the problem (namely, the loss of control of the annual volume and the consequent

---

[4] Equivalent to about 12 (1970) dollars.

[5] This raises the exciting prospect that available theories of organizational decision making could be operationalized and pressed into service for simulating the collective intuitive corporate decision processes.

increase in production costs), and (3) stagnation in the growth of readers due to the drop in renewal rate of regular subscribers.

Phase 3: 1948–1950

This phase can be described as a period of "stagnation." In spite of an ever increasing expenditure of circulation promotion dollars (from $42.0 to $50.6 million constant dollars) the readership scarcely grew at all and in 1951 it actually declined. This can be explained in terms of the reduced renewal rate of regular subscriptions due to the high subscription "rate" and the reduction in the efficiency of selling trial subscriptions as the market returned to normal after the high appeal of the magazine during the immediate postwar period. This drop in efficiency offset the increased promotional expenditure, so that the company was faced with a significant increase in promotional effort just to keep its total readership steady.

Phase 4: 1951–1960

The fourth phase was a period of "forced growth." The decline in total circulation recorded in 1951 must have been of considerable concern to the management. Also, during this period the *Look* magazine began to catch up with the *Saturday Evening Post* and a circulation war erupted (see Figure 12). There seems to have been a sudden realization that readership was the key to unlock future growth, because the management undertook to reduce the subscription "rate" and to inject a massive quantity of promotional dollars. Circulation promotion expenditures increased over the period from around 57 to 93 million constant dollars per year and resulted in a forced growth of readers from 4 to 6.3 million.

Since increasing the subscription "rate" was no longer an acceptable means of raising extra revenue to pay for the ever increasing promotional expenditure, the only available alternative was to increase the advertising "rate." This "rate" was consequently raised from an average of $19.5 to $36.1 thousand constant dollars per page. Unfortunately, the rate of

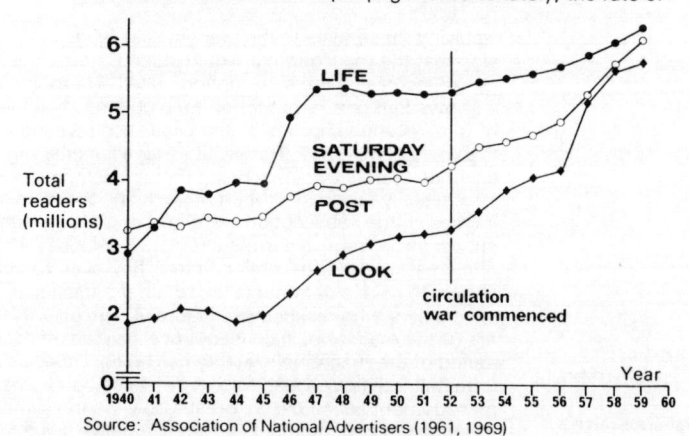

Source: Association of National Advertisers (1961, 1969)

Figure 12. A comparison of magazine readership.

System Pathology

increase in readers did not match the rate of increase in the advertising "rate." Hence, the real price of advertising rose from an average $4.61 to $5.74 constant dollars per page per thousand readers and the advertisers purchased fewer pages in the magazine.

Through the company standard practice of adjusting editorial pages to advertising pages, the editor was limited to fewer editorial pages and the magazine's issues grew thinner, from an annual volume of around 7,600 pages in 1951 to only 5,910 pages in 1960. The yield of regular subscribers from trial subscribers, which has been demonstrated to be dependent on the annual volume of the magazine, consequently dropped. This depressed the profit margin, since it led to the dangerous situation that readership could only be maintained by an ever increasing level of promotional expenditure. By this time, almost one-half of the total readers were trial readers and a smaller proportion of these readers was taking out regular subscriptions as the annual volume of the magazine declined in response to the ever increasing advertising "rate."

During this period, the magazine's readership grew from 4 to 6 million, the company's annual revenue grew from 170 to 225 million constant dollars but its profit margin fell from 8 percent of revenues to a loss position in 1958 and 1959. The company was on the brink of bankruptcy and never really recovered from this policy *cul-de-sac* of too high a subscription rate, too high an advertising "rate," a declining annual volume, and a too high promotional expenditure to solicit trial readers to replace the defecting readership.

The Death Throes

The final phase of the magazine's history is not covered by this study, but is mentioned here because the dramatic events that unfolded appear to be a direct result of the weakened financial position brought about by the interaction of the management's previous decisions with the magazine publishing system. The death throes of the ailing *Saturday Evening Post* are well documented by one of the last presidents of the Curtis Publishing Company (Culligan, 1970) and the last editor of the magazine (Friedrich, 1970). The reduction in the volume of pages published necessitated a reduction in the company's printing plant capacity which led to a disastrous strike at the plant. Also, the change to biweekly and then to monthly issues must have seemed threatening to the editors, whose skills lay in the production of a weekly magazine, because they revolted and approached the Board of Directors directly about the matter. In consequence, the president of the company was forced to resign (Culligan, 1970).

There was an attempt to reduce the circulation of the magazine, presumably to save production costs, but this seems to have failed to help its financial plight (Friedrich, 1970: 299). The company also changed its method of reporting its subscription income in the annual financial report to an accounting method that, in the short run, showed the company's operations in a better light (Friedrich, 1970: 65).

The editors resorted to sensationalism as a means of attracting and holding readers. Unfortunately, the company was successfully sued for libel and heavy damages were assessed in the favor of the parties defamed by the sensational disclosures published in the magazine (Friedrich, 1970: 41–45).

It would seem that the management never really understood the underlying causal structure of their problem and, hence, were never able to discover a satisfactory combination of the major variables under its control that would rescue the magazine. It was discontinued in 1969.

A POLICY FOR SURVIVAL

As mentioned earlier, the root cause of the sagging profit margin lies in the positive feedback loop relating the number of pages in the magazine, and hence its cost, to the number of readers (Figure 8): (1) as the readership increases, (2) the price of advertising decreases stimulating advertising sales, (3) the increased number of advertising pages leads to the addition of more pages of editorial content, (4) the increased volume of pages attracts more trial subscribers to convert to regular readership, which leads to accelerated readership growth and a feeding back of the outcome to further reducing the price of advertising, and so on, until (5) a feedback effect results in which costs rise more rapidly than the revenues and the profit margin is reduced.

If the management were aware of this process, then one might expect it to prevent the production costs from running away by controlling the number of pages in the magazine. Obviously some relationship between advertising and editorial content must be maintained, otherwise the magazine will become all advertising as the readership grows and the price of advertising declines. An obvious way out of this dilemma is to fix the amount of advertising by controlling the price of advertising. Keeping the advertising "rate" per thousand readers constant will achieve this. This is illustrated by experiment #5.

Experiment #5

In this experiment, the subscription "rate" and circulation promotion expense are held constant, but the advertising "rate" is adjusted every simulated year to effect a constant advertising "rate" per thousand readers. The results of this experiment are shown in Figure 13. It can be seen that the advertising "rate" is continually being revised in order to maintain a nearly constant advertising "rate" per thousand readers (Figure 13a). The performance measures do not now

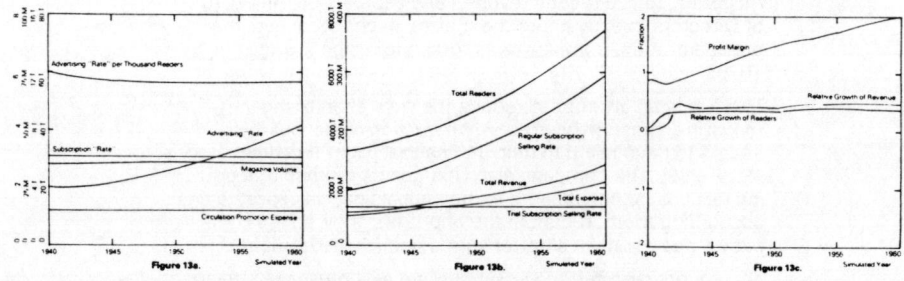

Figure 13. Experiment #5 response to a policy of **constant advertising price.**

System Pathology

deteriorate. The relative growth of revenues and relative growth of readers measures (Figure 13c) are nearly constant, albeit at a much smaller value than for experiment #1. The profit margin, on the other hand, grows steadily throughout the experiment. The conclusion, therefore, is that continually adjusting the advertising "rate" in order to maintain a constant advertising "rate" per thousand readers, leads to an increasing profit margin and constant revenue and readership growth. Growth of readers and revenues, however, is at a considerably lower level than for experiment #1. The management strategy built into this experiment leads to a profit maximizing rather than to a revenue maximizing behavior of the system.

Source: Advertising Age (January issues).

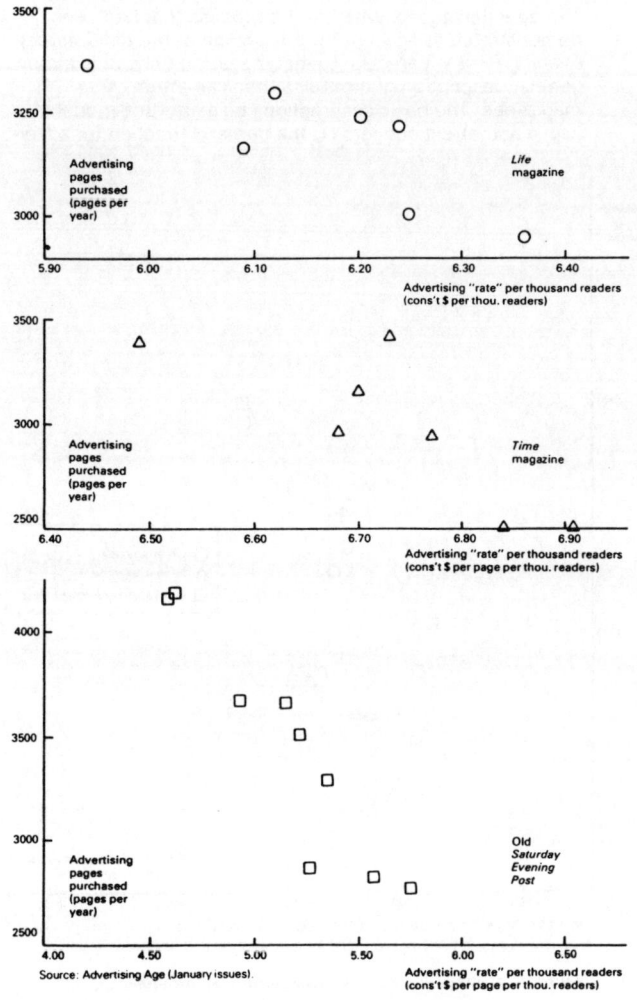

Figure 14. A comparison of advertising demand curves.

This policy is derived logically, albeit intuitively, from a systems analysis of magazine publishing. A more systematic method for discovering higher order policies, involving the year-by-year manipulation of several management variables at once in order to achieve satisfactory performance of a number of conflicting interactive goals has been suggested by Nelson and Krisbergh (1974). This method involves the interfacing of a sophisticated optimum-seeking search procedure, called Razor Search (Bandler, 1971) with a System Dynamics model. This seems to offer promise as a tool for optimal policy making in dynamic interactive multi-objective feedback systems that approximate to real world situations more closely than do the existing static models of the economist and management scientist.

PATHOLOGIES OF MAGAZINES

The question arises, whether the process that has been demonstrated to account for the decline of the old *Saturday Evening Post* is particular to that magazine only, or is a more general description of a malaise than can affect other magazines. The basic assumptions built into this model of cause and effect concern (1) the demand function for adver-

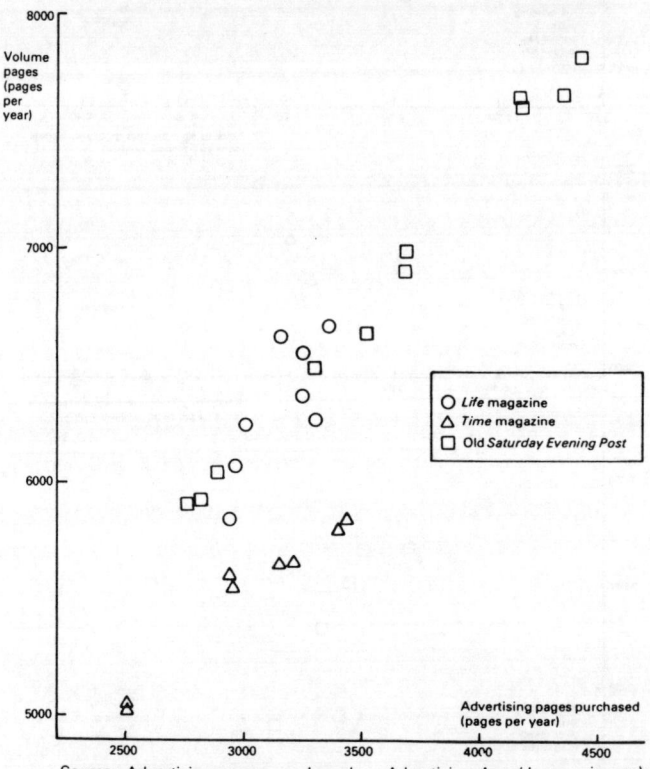

Source: Advertising pages purchased — Advertising Age (January issues); Volume pages — physical count of magazine annual volumes.

Figure 15. A comparison of advertising-editorial formulae.

System Pathology

tising in a magazine, (2) the editorial-advertising formula for a magazine, and (3) the determinants of the readership from the magazine's annual volume size and subscription "rate." These assumptions together with any evidence that has come to hand are used to compare these posited relationships for other magazines with those found for the old *Saturday Evening Post.*

The Demand for Advertising

The number of pages of advertising purchased in a magazine (pages per year) is posited to vary directly with the price of advertising charged by the magazine's publisher (advertising "rate" per thousand readers). Figure 14 compares the plots of advertising pages purchased versus the advertising "rate" per thousand readers for the old *Saturday Evening Post* and two other magazines, suggesting that the posited relationship exists for all three magazines.

The Editorial-Advertising Formula

A magazine's volume size (pages published per annual volume) is assumed to vary directly with the pages of advertising purchased (pages per year) in the magazine by the advertisers. The comparative plots of magazine volume size against advertising pages purchased are shown in Figure 15 for three magazines. This figure also suggests quite strongly that the relationship holds for the other magazines as well as the old *Saturday Evening Post.*

The Determinants of the Readership of the Magazine

The fraction of regular readers who renew their subscriptions and the fraction of trial readers who convert to the regular readership of a magazine are both posited to be a function of the subscription "rate" charged and its annual volume size. The empirical study of the *Saturday Evening Post* indicated a strong relationship between the fraction of regular readers renewing their subscriptions and the subscription "rate" charged. Also, the fraction of trial readers converting to regular readers was found to be markedly influenced by the annual volume size of the magazine. Unfortunately, data are not available in sufficient quantity to test these relationships on other magazines. It would be difficult to imagine, however, a magazine where at least the key relationship between subscription renewals and magazine volume size did not exist. It may not be a continuous variable, as the case of the *Saturday Evening Post,* but at least there must be a lower limit of magazine volume size at which point readers can no longer find enough editorial material of interest to them to make it worthwhile renewing their subscriptions. As long as such a relationship exists—and it would seem intuitively obvious that it would—then there is a possibility of a magazine's publisher getting caught up inadvertently in a series of events described by Forrester (1970: 55) as:

In other words, the known and intended practices of the organization are fully sufficient to create the difficulty, regardless of what happens outside the company or in the marketplace. In fact, a downward spiral develops in which the presumed solution makes the difficulty worse and thereby causes redoubling of the presumed solution.

A DISCUSSION OF SOME OMISSIONS IN THE STUDY

Two assumptions are implicit in this study: (1) that the quality of editorial content does not affect the sale of subscriptions and advertising, and (2) that the market of trial subscribers is limitless, are perhaps, difficult to accept.

The Quality of Editorial Content

The editorial direction of a magazine obviously must be of importance, particularly when a magazine is new. It is the editorial flavor of the magazine—its visceral appeal as one editor put it—that enables it to be launched successfully on the newsstands in the first place. However, this study does not cover the beginning or end events in the life of a magazine but rather the middle period when it enjoys a stable relationship with its environment. These stable relationships assume a stable editorial quality of the magazine. If the editor incurs the ire of his readers or advertisers, he is replaced, as was discussed earlier. The editorial direction of the magazine also determines, to a large extent, the characteristics of its audience. This in turn affects the demand for advertising. The different slopes of the demand curves for advertising for, say, the old *Saturday Evening Post* and the *Life* magazine (Figure 14) exemplify this phenomenon. The old *Saturday Evening Post* was reputed to appeal to readers who lived in small towns and rural communities, whereas the *Life* magazine appealed more to urban dwellers. The differences in the slopes of the advertising demand curves could be attributed to the desirability, on the part of the advertisers, to communicate their messages to one type of audience rather than to the other. Therefore, editorial direction and quality of content will affect indirectly the advertising sales, but this effect is a constant parameter embodied in the slope of demand curve as far as this study is concerned.

A Limitless Supply of Readers

The hidden assumption concerning a limitless supply of trial readers is justified because, over the 20-year period of the study of the old *Saturday Evening Post,* no sign of a saturating market could be discovered. In spite of references to the increasing cost of acquiring additional readers (see for example: "Editorial," *Saturday Review,* 1970), the exact opposite was found to apply to the old *Saturday Evening Post.* This was attributed to the increased technical efficiency of selling trial subscriptions by mass mailing reduced-price subscriptions offers. If the magazine had become slimmer then it might have become harder to retain readers. The management of the magazine must then spend more on circulation promotion to maintain the level of readers. It might easily be beguiled into thinking that the cost of acquiring each additional reader had increased, whereas in actual fact the cost remained constant and the yield of regular subscribers from trial subscribers had declined. The market for a magazine obviously cannot be limitless and must saturate some day, but by broadening its appeal and by bringing out foreign editions, mass-circulation magazines seem to find ways of putting off that day.

IMPLICATIONS OF THE STUDY

If this experimentation with model building and empirical validation can be performed successfully for a moribund magazine publishing firm, why cannot it be done for other magazine firms that are still in business? And if it can be done for

System Pathology

magazine publishing firms, why cannot it be performed on other firms in other industries? There would seem to be no reason for suggesting that this approach could not be applied more generally. This study might, therefore, point the way to systematizing the construction of corporate system simulation models.

The experiments conducted with such a constructed corporate simulation model might yield useful information about the long-run viability of the organization. One might ask of it such questions as, is the enterprise going to be difficult to manage? How robust is the system to sudden changes in business conditions? How will it grow—steadily or boom followed by bust? Are there any counterintuitive elements in the system that might beguile the management into, unknowingly, pursuing a path to destruction? Are there more optimal policies that the management doesn't know about? The management of the company and its investors would surely find the answers to these questions useful. If this be so, then we have the beginning of a tool for a more refined control of companies.

The methodology might have some merit, from an organizational research point of view, in such fields as leadership, comparative management and behavioral theories of firms. It allows one to contrast the underlying chain of cause and effect at work in the system with the symptoms generated by systemic problems, and then to trace the actions taken by the actors in the real-life drama that unfolds. For example, the various leaders of the Curtis Publishing Company were, to a large extent, the products of the situations that brought them into power. President Walter Fuller turned the company in the 30s and 40s into an integrated printing and publishing empire and his protegé, Robert A. MacNeal, pursued this vertical empire building philosophy by purchasing a paper company for $20-million in 1950. The model suggests that the symptom was rising production costs and the underlying cause was the magazine volume getting out of control. President Matthew Culligan, a man from the advertising industry, was hired to retrieve the sagging advertising sales (1962–1964) but, as we have seen the root cause was the high advertising "rate" driven up by the need to finance the promotion of subscriptions in the circulation war. President Mac Clifford (an expert cost-cutter with the nickname Mac-the-knife) was hired to perform the unpleasant surgical operation on the company's excess capacity (1964–1968), which stemmed from a loss of advertising pages and hence, through the advertising-editorial formula, a loss of editorial pages also. It would seem that the owners, by treating the symptoms of the problems that arose, rather than fathoming the real causes, possibly hired leaders with managerial skills that did not necessarily match the needs of the time, thereby compounding the problem.

The people who work in the magazine industry can be viewed as a group subculture. They meet each other formally and socially to exchange views, ideas and do business. The industry collectively established measures of performance to compare the magazines. Editors tend to compare thickness (number of pages), glossiness, and other more subjective measures of editorial content. Publishers tend to compare advertising pages and revenue. Presidents tend to look to total revenue, total assets and other measures of bigness. Pecking orders are established and there is a natural rivalry for top or near top positions in the pecking order. At times this competition can be intense and almost senseless. For instance, the circulation war between the big three magazines (Dougherty, 1970):

> And troubles for *Life* in the circulation war came in 1963, when *Look* which had passed *The Post* in 1961, moved into the number one spot. The figures were 7.49 million to 7.17 million . . . And, oh, how *Look* rubbed it in. It ran ads with headlines such as *"Look is bigger than Life"* . . . It was this sort of goading, several publishers thought, that led *Life* into taking what they considered a major tactical misstep . . . .

It would seem that when the corporate ego gets involved, a company can take hasty actions that reverberate through the system of publishing with catastrophic results. Tracing these events with a system model, and noting whether they are fed back to reinforce or discourage the original action, might provide valuable insights into the evolution of the distinctly different personalities of organizations found in the same industry.

Lastly, it might be worth noting that the missing link in corporate simulation models is the management decision making processes. Without this link, we cannot expect the model to generate realistic predictions of how a corporation will grow. Although the model gives us useful insights into how the system works and allows us to predict what will happen when certain management decisions are enacted, without a realistic model of management decision making we cannot use the system model to predict outcomes reliably.

If a submodel of the management's collective and intuitive decision making behavior could ever be developed and plugged into a systems model of the organization, then reliable simulations and predictions of the organization's future growth could be made. Developments in the theory of management decision making in an organizational context, within the last decade, have brought this within the bounds of possibility. It was demonstrated that Cyert and March's theory would have predicted correctly the raising of subscription "rates" by the management of the old *Saturday Evening Post* at a time when they would have been better advised to follow another course of action. *The construction of a simulation model of intuitive management decison making would constitute a significant breakthrough in corporate simulation modeling.*

Roger I. Hall is an associate professor in the Department of Business Administration, University of Manitoba.

REFERENCES

Advertising Age
1940–1960 Chicago: Crain Communications Inc., January issues.

Association of National Advertisers.
1961–1969 Magazine Circulation and Rate Trends. New York: Association of National Advertisers.

Bandler, J.W.
1971 "The razor search program." IEEE Transactions on Microwave Theory and Techniques, July: 667.

Brewer, Garry D., and Owen P. Hall
1973 "Policy analysis by computer: the need for appraisal." Public Policy, 21: 343–365.

Culligan, Mathew J.
1970 The Curtis-Culligan Story. New York: Crown Publishers.

Cyert, Richard M., and James G. March
1963 A Behavioral Theory of the Firm. Englewood Cliffs, N.J.: Prentice-Hall.

Day, Richard H.
1974 "On system synamics." Behavioral Science, 19: 260-271.

Dougherty, Philip H.
1969 "Magazines flaunt it." New York Times, November 17: 77.
1970a "Look leaves the numbers race." New York Times, April 21: 68.
1970b "Life-Look battle ends, but war goes on." New York Times, May 10 III., 15.

Forrester, Jay W.
1961 Industrial Dynamics. Cambridge, Mass.: M.I.T. Press.
1968a Principles of Systems. Cambridge, Mass.: Wright-Allen Press.
1968b "Industrial dynamics after the first decade." Management Science, 14: 388-415.
1969 Urban Dynamics. Cambridge, Mass.: M.I.T. Press.
1970 "Counterintuitive behavior of social systems." Technology Review, 73, 3: 52-68.
1971 World Dynamics. Cambridge, Mass.: Wright-Allen Press.

Friedrich, Otto
1970 Decline and Fall. New York: Harper and Row.

System Pathology

Hall, Roger I.
1973 A Systems Model of a Magazine Publishing Firm. Seattle: Unpublished doctoral dissertation, University of Washington.

Meadows, Dennis L.
1970 Dynamics of Commodity Production Cycles. Cambridge, Mass.: M.I.T. Press.

Meadows, Donella H., Dennis L. Meadows, Jorgen Randers, and William W. Behrens
1972 The Limits to Growth. New York: Universe Books.

Meier, Robert C., William T. Newell, and Harold L. Pazer
1969 Simulation in Business and Economics. Englewood Cliffs, N.J.: Prentice-Hall.

Moody's Industrial Manual
1940-1960 New York: Moody's Investors Service.

Nelson, Carl W., and Harold M. Krisbergh
1974 "A search procedure for policy oriented simulations: applications to urban dynamics." Management Science, 20: 1164-1174.

Nord, Ole C.
1963 Growth of a New Product. Cambridge, Mass.: M.I.T. Press.

Packer, David W.
1964 Resource Acquisition and Corporate Growth. Cambridge, Mass.: M.I.T. Press.

Pugh, Alexander L. III.
1970 Dynamo II User's Manual. Cambridge, Mass.: M.I.T. Press.

Rao, Potluri, and Roger L. Miller
1971 Applied Econometrics. Belmont, Calif.: Wadsworth Publishing Co.

Roberts, Edward B., Dan I. Abrams, and Henry B. Weil
1968 "A systems study of policy formulation in a vertically-integrated firm." Management Science, 14: B-674-B-694.

Saturday Review
1970 Editorial, "Report on SR." Saturday Review, November 7: 23-24.

Wall Street Journal
1970 "Time Incorporated Life magazine says it will cut circulation 1.5 million." Wall Street Journal, October 2.

[14]

Modeling growth strategy in a biotechnology startup firm

John D. W. Morecroft, David C. Lane, and Paul S. Viita

The top managers of a biotechnology startup firm agreed to participate in a system dynamics modeling project to help them think about the firm's growth strategy. The article describes how the model was created and used to stimulate debate and discussion about growth management. The paper highlights several novel features about the *process* used for capturing management team knowledge. A heavy emphasis was placed on mapping the operating structure of the factory and distribution channels. Qualitative modeling methods (structural diagrams, descriptive variable names, and "friendly" algebra) were used to capture the management team's descriptions of the business. Simulation scenarios were crafted to stimulate debate about strategic issues such as capacity allocation, capacity expansion, customer recruitment, customer retention, and market growth, and to engage the management team in using the computer to design strategic scenarios. The article

There is growing interest among system dynamicists about the process of creating and using behavioral simulation models. This interest stems in part from the realization that important learning about business and social systems occurs as the model is being built and that "client ownership" comes from active participation in the model's specification. Moreover, the data needed to specify a behavioral model come principally from the mental models of participants in the system, so the procedures used to elicit knowledge from mental models need to be better understood (Richardson et al. 1989).

Work by Vennix et al. (1990a) describes a modeling process, called the preliminary model approach, that was used in a project on the Dutch health care system. The approach began with a preliminary conceptual model designed by a small team of modelers and clients. Other health care experts were given the opportunity to criticize and improve the preliminary model through questionnaires, a series of workbook exercises (assigned to individuals), and structured group workshops, spread over weeks or even months. The process was specifically designed for public policy making, where the number of individuals to consult during model development is large (10, 20, or more people). However, it may be much more widely applicable. Originally the scope of the process was confined to model conceptualization, but more recently workbook exercises and workshops have been used to involve public policymakers in equation formulation, simulation experiments, and policy design (Vennix et al. 1990b).

Richmond's (1987) Strategic Forum is another process for engaging a group of policymakers (usually business executives) in model building and model use. At first glance, the approach is quite different from the one used by Vennix. It is aimed at small groups (average size of eight people) in the private sector, and the forum itself often takes place in two days or less, though preforum work may be spread over several weeks. Much emphasis is placed on parameter estimation and on simulation of partial models, which begin as simple open-loop models and increase in complexity as new feedback loops are added to represent real-life operating constraints. However, just like the Vennix approach, the Strategic Forum uses a mix of prebuilt models (which participants are encouraged to revise) and structured group workshops in order to capture participants' knowledge, stimulate critical thinking, and invite ownership.

This article adds to the small but important collection of publications that describe how models evolve, how project team members participate, how their ideas are captured and mapped, and how simulations are used to challenge the team's intuition about policy options and consequences. It traces the development of a model all the way from issue conceptualization with a management team to meetings in which the managing director manipulated the computer's mouse to graph his own strategic scenarios. The article complements the existing literature by documenting the way in which the management team's discussion was shaped during the early, precomputer stages of modeling in order to capture data for a first-

John Morecroft is associate professor of strategic management at London Business School. After obtaining degrees from London University (Imperial College) and Bristol University, he received a Ph.D. degree in management and system dynamics from the Massachusetts Institute of Technology in 1979 and served on the faculty there from 1980 to 1986. His research, teaching, and consulting work focus on strategic modeling and frameworks to aid strategic thinking in management teams. He is the associate editor for business policy and applications of the *System Dynamics Review*. *Address*: London Business School, Sussex Place, Regent's Park, London NW1 4SA, U.K.

David Lane received a B.Sc. degree in mathematics from Bristol University in 1983, an M.Sc. degree in mathematical modeling and numerical analysis from Oxford University in 1984, and a D.Phil. degree from Oxford in 1986 for work in mathematical modeling of biological phenomena.

concludes with comments on the impact of the project.

cut conceptual model (see also Morecroft and Van der Heijden 1990). In addition, it amplifies Richmond's point that modeling promotes communication and consistent thinking. It documents several examples of structural maps and simulations that provoked critical thinking and cross-functional discussion about the feasibility of the management team's growth objectives.

Background

Bio Industrial Products (BIP) is a startup biotechnology company based in Southeast England. The company ferments, blends, and packages naturally occurring microbes and sells them as commercial products. Among the company's product lines are grease cleaners used in the food service industry, silage additives used in farming, and sewage additives used in waste water treatment. The top managers of the company agreed to participate in a system dynamics modeling project to help them think about the firm's growth strategy.

The modeling project focused particularly on commercial grease-cleaning products, which are the company's largest and fastest-growing product line. These products are intended to unclog grease that accumulates in drainage pipes of large commercial kitchens in hotels and fast-food chains. Traditionally, powerful chemicals have been used to cut-through the grease in clogged pipes. But now biological products offer a gentler and more effective remedy. Kitchen workers receive sachets containing microbes and inert bran, much safer to handle than powerful alkalis. They add the contents of the sachet to water and pour the mixture into the kitchen sinks. The microbes go to work, devouring the grease and so clearing the pipes. Moreover, it is possible for a colony of microbes to grow inside the pipes and so prevent future accumulations of greasy deposits.

Although the end use of the products is far from glamorous, there is potentially a large market for microbiological cleaning products, particularly given increasing public concern over food hygiene and chemical cleaning agents. BIP is a small company within this fledgling industry, with revenues of approximately £500,000 per year in 1987 and expected growth of 30–50 percent per year over the next five to ten years (50 percent annual growth compounded over ten years would lead to revenues of approximately £30 million by 1997).

The project team and the effort

An important part of the project was to involve the management team closely in building and using the model. Indeed, our project was intended to explore how to structure the modeling process in order to secure involvement and commitment of the management team. Here the term *process* includes the agendas of meetings, the composition of the project team, and the use made of graphics, modeling symbols, and computer simulations.

The project team included the managing director, the head of manufacturing, the

After three years as a senior analyst in the business consultancy department of Shell UK Oil Ltd., he now serves as a business manager for Shell.

Paul Viita has 16 years' experience in international business and finance. From 1977 to 1989, he held a variety of posts with the Royal Dutch Shell Group and then joined one of the oldest venture capital firms in London, where he specializes in international investments and relations with large corporations. Educated at Harvard and Oxford, which he attended as a Rhodes Scholar, he holds degrees in mathematics and economics.

commercial manager (who was responsible for information systems and planning in this fledgling enterprise), and a new-ventures manager from the parent company. These individuals are the strategic decision makers of the company, not technical specialists assigned to a modeling task force. The same group of individuals would be involved in any important strategic decision for the company.

The project team also included an experienced system dynamics consultant and a model builder. The role of the consultant was to facilitate the project team meetings and to act as an interface between the management team and the modeling technology. The role of the model builder was to create a working simulation model from an outline of model structure provided by the consultant and endorsed by the project team as a whole.

The team brought together a unique combination of skills and knowledge that is a prerequisite for effective strategic modeling. The managing director, head of manufacturing and new-ventures manager provided a solid base of operating knowledge, including factory knowledge of how the products are made, marketing knowledge of how the products are distributed and sold, and industry knowledge of technology, customers, competitors, government legislation, and social trends. The consultant and the model builder provided facilitation and technical modeling skills. In addition, both the commercial manager and the new-ventures manager had attended an intensive one-week introductory modeling course and were able to play an important communication role at the interfaces between normal business debate, the model, and model-generated scenarios.

The project ran for a period of six months. During that time, there were five half-day working meetings of the full project team. The consultant worked 10 days, which included $2\frac{1}{2}$ days in project team meetings and $7\frac{1}{2}$ days in outlining the model structure and supervising the development of the algebraic model and model simulations. The model builder worked 40 days, attending meetings, making a fact-finding visit to the factory, gathering data, mapping, writing equations, doing simulations, and preparing for team meetings.

Tangible output from the project consisted of three STELLA[1] simulation models (a factory model, a customer based model, and a combined factory-customer model), a 37-page management report outlining the model and making recommendations, and a 50-page technical report containing diagrams, equations, and simulations of the three STELLA models.

Capturing management team knowledge

The agenda for the first working meeting of the project team is shown in the following checklist. The meeting lasted four hours and was intended to provide facts, ideas, opinions, and thoughts as the basis for building a simulation model.[2]

1. Discuss core strategic issue: growth
   a. Review growth history
   b. Review growth targets
   c. Discuss how growth targets will be met

2. Introduce model building
   a. Modeling a growth business: the market growth model
   b. Symbols for mapping operating structure
   c. Simulations of market growth
3. Discuss operating structure of the business
   a. Manufacturing capacity expansion and capacity allocation
   b. R&D and product development
   c. Expansion of sales effort
   d. Pricing
   e. Customer ordering
   f. Competitors
4. Outline next steps
   a. Process of model development
   b. Dates for future meetings

Opening the discussion – business and strategic issues

The team began by discussing the core strategic issue of growth. The commercial manager provided charts to trigger discussion. The charts showed quarterly historical revenues and costs by product line over the past five years and growth targets for the next five years. A striking feature of the growth targets was the assumption of 50 percent annual revenue growth with little or no increase in the major cost factor—sales and marketing expense. The result of growing revenue and stable expenses would, of course, be improving profitability, as reflected in the company's profit targets.

The charts provoked discussion about the growth prospects and profitability of the business. How does the market grow? Is a growth rate of 50 percent per year really sustainable? Why should revenue grow without a corresponding growth in selling expense? What factors will cause the cost structure of the business to change (the relative costs of production, R&D, packaging, administration, and marketing)? The managing director gave his personal opinions on the growth potential of different product lines, the likely impact of government legislation on market size, the methods and costs of selling, the difficulties of attracting new customers, the uncertainties of fermenting and blending technology, and the gaps in scientific and R&D knowledge about the effectiveness of microbial products.

Shaping the discussion – The modeling framework

The first hour of discussion yielded a great deal of descriptive information about growth management and growth prospects. Deliberately, modeling technology was absent. There was no computer in the room and, as yet, no diagrams.

Modeling was introduced as the second agenda item. The consultant selected Forrester's (1968) market growth model to illustrate how modeling and simulation can provide insight into growth management. The model has a compact and easy-to-explain feedback structure that interrelates marketing effort, capacity expansion, and customer ordering in a growing company.

The market growth model fulfilled several important functions in the meeting. It showed how a business can be represented in terms of decision-making processes and word-arrow diagrams. It also showed examples of simulation runs and the role they might play in a discussion of growth strategy. Most important, it showed the managers how their ideas would be captured in a model and played back to them as simulations.

The operating structure of the business

The third agenda item was a simple checklist used to organize discussion of the operating structure of the business. The items in the checklist were chosen with the lessons and structure of the market growth model in mind. The modelers wanted the managers to articulate their views on growth management. How much capacity does the business need? Under what conditions will capacity be expanded? What is the payoff to R&D and product development? How does the management team allocate resources to R&D? How is the product sold? How does management decide when and whether to expand the sales force and the sales effort? How are prices set and changed? What is a reasonable price for the product? What is the relation between price and manufacturing cost? How do customers learn about microbial products? What does it take to convince them that the product is worth trying and worth using? Why should customers change to using microbial products? Who are the major competitors in the business? What products and services do they offer?

The discussion based on the checklist lasted for approximately three hours and yielded descriptive information, anecdotes, and opinions that were vital to later model development. The consultant made handwritten notes for each checklist heading and used these notes (after the meeting) to draw an overview of BIP's business and to develop STELLA maps (Richmond, Peterson, and Vescuso 1987).

The overview is shown in Figure 1. It contains six boxes representing major conceptual units of the business. The three boxes on the left-hand side represent functional areas within BIP, and the three right-hand boxes represent parts of the market and distribution system. For each box, the modelers prepared a STELLA map, a diagram without algebra. The overview and the STELLA maps were used in the second working meeting to present the management team with a synopsis of the first meeting and to draw them into the modeling process.

Understanding and mapping sales and distribution (boxes 5 and 6 in Fig. 1)

BIP has a small sales force that sells mostly to distributors rather than directly to individual commercial kitchens. The distributors themselves each deal with several hundred commercial kitchens, supplying them with utensils, detergents, cleaners, and paper towels.

BIP's sales and marketing expenses were high in relation to sales revenue. The managing director believed this high expense-to-revenue ratio was necessary to

Fig. 1. Overview showing major conceptual units of BIP

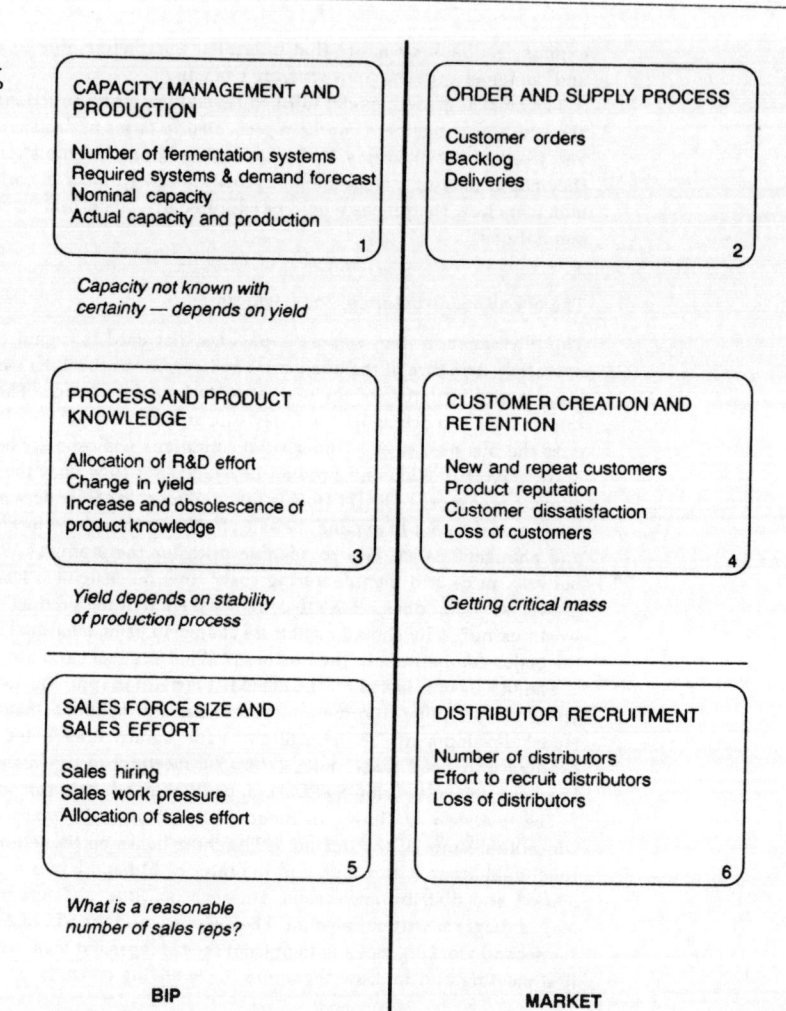

CAPACITY MANAGEMENT AND PRODUCTION

Number of fermentation systems
Required systems & demand forecast
Nominal capacity
Actual capacity and production

1

Capacity not known with certainty — depends on yield

ORDER AND SUPPLY PROCESS

Customer orders
Backlog
Deliveries

2

PROCESS AND PRODUCT KNOWLEDGE

Allocation of R&D effort
Change in yield
Increase and obsolescence of product knowledge

3

Yield depends on stability of production process

CUSTOMER CREATION AND RETENTION

New and repeat customers
Product reputation
Customer dissatisfaction
Loss of customers

4

Getting critical mass

SALES FORCE SIZE AND SALES EFFORT

Sales hiring
Sales work pressure
Allocation of sales effort

5

What is a reasonable number of sales reps?

DISTRIBUTOR RECRUITMENT

Number of distributors
Effort to recruit distributors
Loss of distributors

6

BIP   **MARKET**

establish BIP's position in the market. The management team felt that, in the future, sales would continue to grow without further additions to sales and marketing expense, thereby reducing the expense-to-revenue ratio and improving company profitability.

But how can the business grow if sales effort is held constant? Is the product becoming easier to sell? What are the limits to growth, given the current size of the marketing and sales organization? These were the kinds of questions the management team discussed with the help of STELLA maps.

Figure 2 shows the total marketing time available (TotalMktgTimeAvail). Suppose there are 80 marketing hours per month available. (Say, two sales reps spend 25 percent of their time in face-to-face meetings with distributors. The sales staff in the field is supported from central office by marketing and administrative staff.) How does this selling time get used, and what volume of sales can it generate?

In Figure 2, marketing time is divided between two principal activities: recruiting new distributors (MktgTimeToNewDist) and maintaining existing distributors

Fig. 2. STELLA map of marketing and distribution

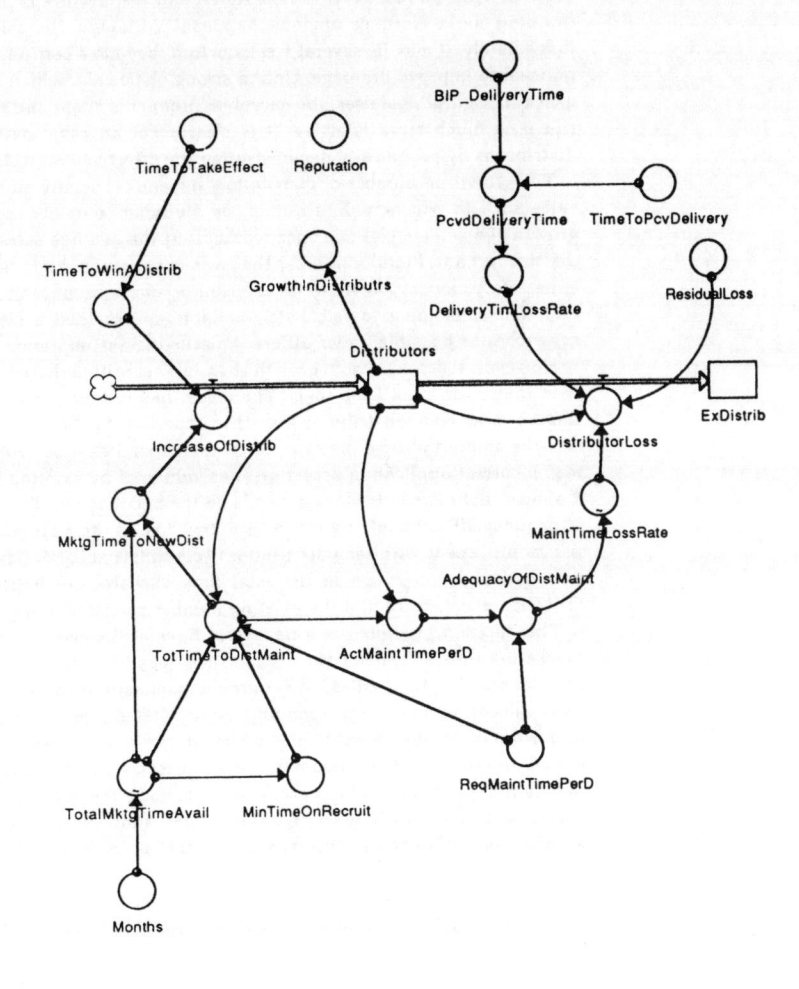

(TotTimeToDistMaint). Assume, for the time being, that maintenance time (time spent dealing with distributors' product and supply problems) is very small. Then sales reps are free to spend most of their time recruiting new distributors. How do they win new recruits? How long does it take?

A sales rep must locate distributors and then arrange site visits to explain and demonstrate the product. A convincing demonstration is not a simple matter. The sales rep appears at a site (a commercial kitchen, the customer of a selected distributor) with a handful of sachets full of harmless looking powder, claiming that it will improve drainage in the most grease-ridden pipes. Lukewarm water is added to the powder to reactivate the microbes, and the mixture is poured down a slow-draining sink. Nothing obvious happens! Although the microbes go to work immediately, it may be several weeks before they have consumed enough grease to noticeably improve drainage. Unlike strong chemicals, which often generate heat, gases, and gurgling noises, the microbial product is silent and slow. But in the long run it is much more effective. It is clearly not an easy matter to win over the distributor by graphically demonstrating the effectiveness of the product.

The growth in number of distributors depends crucially on the time it takes the sales staff to win new distributors. By studying company records of distributor growth the commercial manager worked out the average sales time (in hours per distributor) and found a number that was surprisingly high. So it is reasonable to expect only modest growth in the distributor's base because the product is difficult and time-consuming to sell. Later simulations provided a clearer picture of the growth rates possible under different marketing assumptions.

However, there is more to growth than just recruiting distributors. Once one has won them, one must keep them. The model focused management attention on the factors influencing distributor loss. One important factor is distributor maintenance—the amount of time the sales force must spend dealing with product problems (e.g. incorrect application procedures) encountered by existing distributors. Figure 2 shows that distributor loss depends on the adequacy of distributor maintenance (AdequacyOfDistMaint), which in turn depends on the maintenance time, in hours per month, spent with each distributor (ActMaintTimePerD). The maintenance time per distributor depends on the total time allocated to distributor maintenance (TotTimetoDistMaint) and the existing number of distributors.

The diagram prompted two important lines of discussion. First, how in fact is marketing time allocated? How much time goes to recruitment and how much to maintenance? Who decides? What are the implications for growth of changing the time allocation and, say, spending more time on maintenance? Second, how important is maintenance to the distributors; in other words, how sensitive is distributor loss to the amount of time the sales force spends on dealing with distributor problems? The process of developing the algebraic model gave more precision to these questions, and simulations allowed the team to see the consequences of different assumptions about the sensitivity of distributor loss and changes in time allocation.

Distributor loss also depends on BIP's delivery time. The management team felt that a delivery time of two months was acceptable to distributors. If the delivery time were to become much longer, say, four or six months, then eventually some distributors would become dissatisfied with the product (despite its effectiveness as a degreaser) and cease stocking it. Figure 2 shows that distributor loss depends on delivery time loss rate, which in turn depends on the delivery time perceived by the distributor (PcvdDeliveryTime). None of the managers knew exactly how sensitive distributors might be to delivery time. The diagram simply brought the issue into the discussion. Developing the algebra forced more careful thought about distributor sensitivity, and simulations allowed the team to see the consequences of different sensitivity assumptions.

Delivery time is a particularly important factor to consider because it couples the market to the factory. If the factory for some reason falls behind on deliveries, then eventually poor delivery will accelerate distributor loss and restrain the growth of the distributor base.

How the customer base grows (box 4 in Fig. 1)

Figure 3 shows the customer base. The rectangle labeled RepeatCustomers represents all the commercial kitchens that have tried microbial degreaser, think it effective, and are placing regular repeat orders with distributors. Customers increase through the sales and marketing effort of distributors. The distributor sales force must demonstrate the product and win over kitchen managers in much the same way that the BIP sales force first convinced the distributors. Figure 3 shows that an increase of customers depends on the number of distributors.

Fig. 3. STELLA map of the customer base

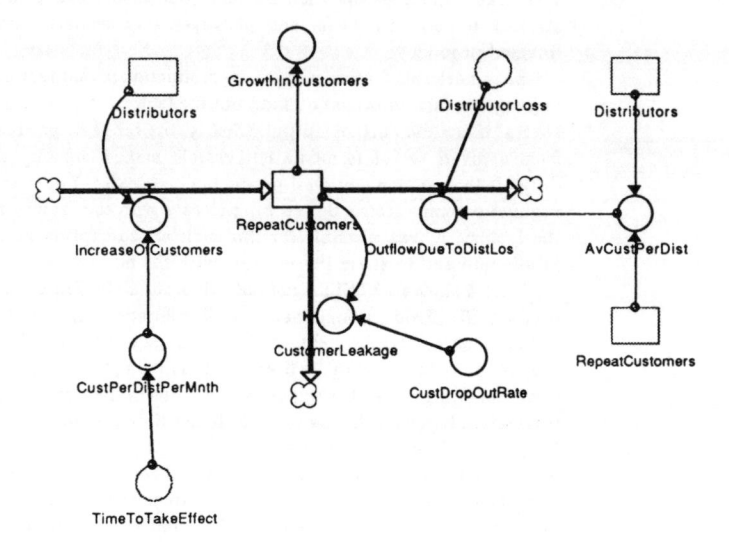

Each distributor serves a base of several hundred customers. It takes time to introduce the product to the entire customer base. The distributor sales reps select a few kitchens at a time and fit in site visits and demonstrations with their other selling and support tasks. Each distributor wins a certain number of new kitchens per month (represented in Figure 3 by CustPerDistPerMnth). This number of conversions decreases as the product's time to take effect increases.

Repeat customers decrease for two reasons. Some customers (a small percentage per year) drop out because they find the product difficult to use. Other customers drop out because the distributor that supplies them stops ordering the product and offers a conventional chemical alternative.

Zooming in on the factory (boxes 1 and 2 in Fig. 1)

The production of microbial products differs in important ways from the production of normal material products. The model forced the project team to think about the unique features of microbe production and to discover their strategic business implications (see Lyneis (1980) for examples of conventional production models).

A microbe factory uses fermentation vessels to brew batches of microbe-rich liquid. One can imagine the vessels as large metal containers, supported on frames, with pipes and wires entering and exiting. Each day the fermentation vessels are filled with a fresh charge of liquid and starter microbes. The microbe population is allowed to grow in the liquid medium for 24 hours. The batch is then drained off and the microbes are separated using powerful centrifuges. The resulting precipitate is transferred into trays, which are placed in ovens for a low-temperature bake. The baked microbes are then blended (the factory can produce several different strains), mixed with bran, and packaged into sachets ready to be shipped as finished product.

One remarkable feature of microbe production is that factory capacity is difficult to gauge. In fact, informed opinion put the factory's theoretical maximum output at several times the current output. Clearly, the range of production that is possible from a given set of fermentation vessels makes capacity planning much more difficult than in conventional production processes. But where does this range of production come from? By working closely with the factory manager and visiting the factory, it was possible for the modelers to capture and represent microbial production and to share the insights with the management team.

Figure 4 shows a STELLA map of BIP production. The current output of finished product (BIP_Production) depends on fermentation capacity, the number of batches run per month, microbe yield, and agreed bug density. Here fermentation capacity is thought of as the capacity, in liters, of the existing fermentation vessels. The yield of the fermentation vessels is measured in terms of the number of microbes grown per production batch (in thousands of billions). Finished output is measured in terms of kilograms of finished product (microbes plus bran) produced per month. The microbiological and blending processes that convert liters of liquid first to microbes and then to kilograms of finished product reveal why factory capacity is so uncertain. Microbe yield measures the number of microbes produced per liter of

Fig. 4. STELLA map of production—actual and theoretical

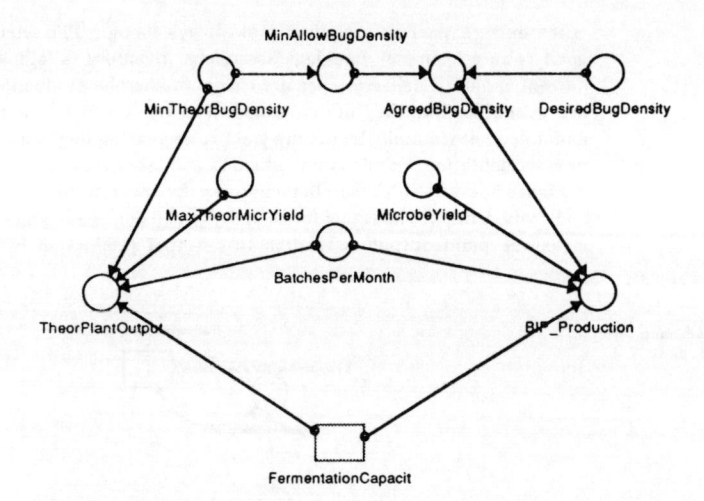

fermentation capacity. But yield depends on manufacturing conditions, and factory workers are still learning how to improve the conditions. The factory manager believed that the maximum theoretical microbe yield was considerably higher than the current yield.

Bug density measures the number of bugs that go into each kilogram of finished product. What concentration of bugs is needed for the product to work? For a microbial product, there are widely differing opinions, because the microbes reproduce when put to work in greasy pipes, so that only a seed colony need be applied. The product works at both low and high bug densities. However, at very low bug densities, it takes a long time (though no one knows for certain how long) for the product to cause a noticeable degreasing effect. At very high bug densities, the time to take effect is lower. The current bug density (shown as AgreedBugDensity in Figure 4) is considerably higher than the minimum theoretical bug density. In other words, factory output could in principle be increased by cutting the bug density from its current value to the minimum theoretical.

Figure 4 shows two different measures of plant output. On the right-hand side is BIP_Production, which comes from multiplying fermentation capacity, batches per month, microbe yield, and agreed bug density. On the left-hand side is theoretical plant output (TheorPlantOutput), which comes from multiplying fermentation capacity, batches per month, maximum theoretical microbe yield, and minimum theoretical bug density. In the model, theoretical plant output is much higher than current output because of the possibility of higher yield and lower bug density.

What are the strategic implications of a potential boost to factory output? One implication, of particular significance to a growing company, is the difficulty of gauging when and by how much to expand capacity. In most factories, it is clear when extra capacity is required (not always though; Forrester (1968) provides a good counterexample). Backlogs are rising, inventory is falling, forecasts exceed current capacity, delivery times are rising. In microbe production, all these signals are available. But they are overshadowed by the fact that production can be expanded substantially by raising yield or decreasing bug density. The need to add new fermentation vessels is less obvious and less pressing.

Figure 5 is a STELLA map that captures the uncertainties of capacity planning in a microbe factory. The signal for capacity expansion is adequacy of capacity, which measures plant output in relation to required production BIP_ReqProdn). Here

Fig. 5. STELLA map of capacity expansion

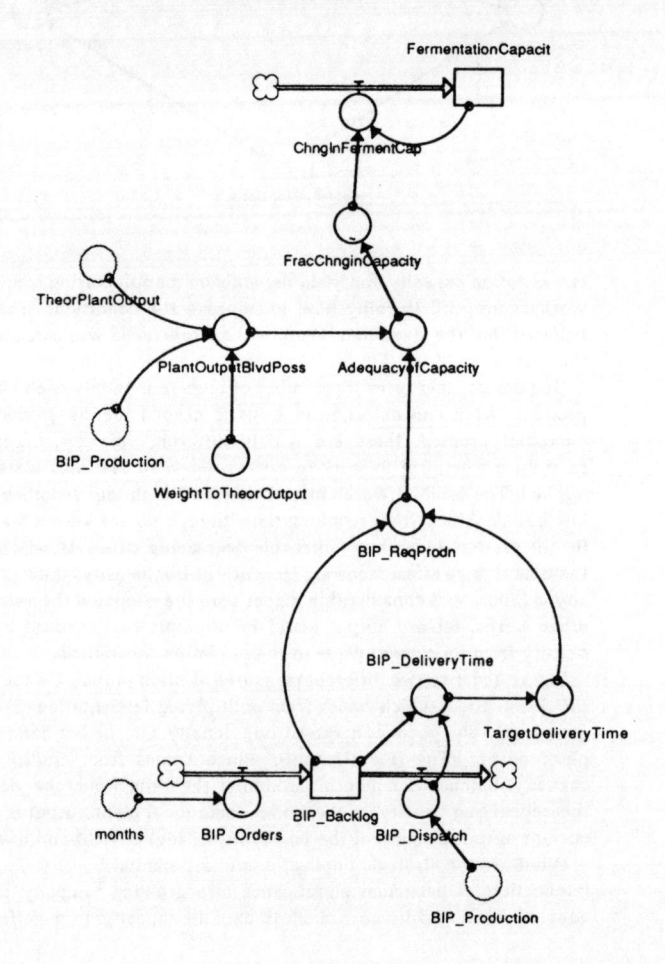

required production depends on the backlog of orders and the company's target delivery time. When the backlog is high, required production is high. The relevant measure of plant output is the output that is believed possible (PlantOutputBlvd-Poss) by the management team. This number is a matter of judgment but lies somewhere between theoretical plant output and current output (BIP_Production). The management team's judgment is the consensus deriving from the weight of opinion in favor of the theoretical output versus current output.

The factory model provided a forum to discuss the special characteristics of microbe production and to address the fundamental question: Does the factory have enough capacity? The managing director took a special interest in bug density. How and by whom is it determined? Is it really possible to dilute bug density so the factory can handle short-term (or even long-term) capacity shortages? What are the production and marketing trade-offs in using bug density as a lever in capacity management? How sensitive are distributors and customers to the strength of the product? Simulations of the model (in the fourth and fifth working meetings) enabled these questions to be explored and discussed in depth.

The management team also talked about microbe yield. What R&D efforts are being made to improve yield? What is the priority given to the R&D budget? Should the budget be larger? What would be the likely payoff in terms of yield and improved understanding of the product? Note that the STELLA map does not have to explicitly include R&D in order for R&D budgets and priorities to be discussed by the management team. The map and the simulation model are triggers for a wide-ranging discussion.

Use of "friendly" algebra

For most of the project, the management team saw the model as STELLA maps. However, the team occasionally took a look inside the STELLA icons to see the model's underlying algebra.

There is no reason why algebra should not be an integral part of such a modeling project, providing it can be read easily, uses phrasing that managers are familiar with, is well-documented, and is organized with a clear visual layout. The criteria for "friendly" algebra may sound like "motherhood and apple-pie," but they are of vital importance in models used for communication among nonexperts. It takes a good deal of effort to write algebra that conforms to these criteria. Figure 6 shows the algebra corresponding to the STELLA map of production (Fig. 4). The algebra is made readable by using straightforward English phrases for the variable names, numerical values, and simple algebraic operators; and by providing explanatory notes for each equation. The modelers used these notes to store important numbers and other pieces of information; they deliberately adopted a chatty style in writing them. When used with the STELLA maps, the algebra brought additional clarity to the team discussion, forcing people to think carefully about microbial production processes and establishing the factory manager's terminology as a part of the team's vocabulary.

Fig. 6. "Friendly" algebra representing the factory (numbers omitted for confidentiality)

FermentationCapacit = FermentationCapacit
INIT(FermentationCapacit) = 'A'
{Weighted average in litres per batch for the existing fermentation vessels in the factory initially}

AgreedBugDensity = MAX(DesiredBugDensity,MinAllowBugDensity)
{The agreed number of bugs to produce a Kg of finished product. Must be greater than or equal to MinAllowBugDensity}

BatchesPerMonth = 'B'
{Batches produced per calendar month}

DesiredBugDensity = 'C'   {The bug density the factory and management would like to use given the prevailing production pressure. Measured in thousand-billion bugs per Kg of finished product}

BIP_Production = BatchesPerMonth*FermentationCapacit
*MicrobeYield/AgreedBugDensity
{The mass (Kgs) of finished product produced per month.}

MaxTheorMicrYield = 'D'   {Maximum number of bugs that could possibly be produced per litre of capacity per batch under ideal manufacturing conditions: yield = max laboratory value : compare with 'E' below}

MicrobeYield = 'E'   {Number of Bugs produced per litre of capacity per batch -- averaged across all strains and all fermentation vessels}

MinAllowBugDensity = MinTheorBugDensity* 'F'   {'F' > 1 Minimum bug density, measured in number of bugs per kg of finished product, that management is willing to allow in its products. Must be a multiple of MinTheorBugDensity}

MinTheorBugDensity = 'G'   {Minimum theoretical bug density, measured in number of bugs per Kg of finished product, that could be used in a product}

TheorPlantOutput = BatchesPerMonth*FermentationCapacit
*MaxTheorMicrYield/MinTheorBugDensity   {The maximum mass (Kgs) of finished product that could theoretically be produced per month under ideal operating conditions and with perfect product knowledge}

Simulation scenarios and management team insights

The modelers designed simulations around several strategic issues. The customer base model (Figs. 2 and 3 combined) was used to examine sales growth and marketing time allocation. The production model (Figs. 4 and 5 combined) was used to explore capacity shortages and production parameters (yield and bug density). The combined customer base–production model, which included a financial subsystem, was used to explore the supply-demand balance in a growing business and the sensitivity of distributors to poor delivery times. Such a progression from partial model simulations is designed to improve understanding and communication of a model (Morecroft 1988; Sterman 1985).

Simulations were the centerpiece of the fourth and fifth working meetings. The meetings lasted for four hours each. The modelers spent the first half hour reviewing the STELLA maps to refresh the team members' memory of model structure and vocabulary (bear in mind that intervals of one or two months separated team meetings). The remaining time was divided equally between discussions of pre-prepared simulations and new simulations proposed by the management team.

A computer was installed in the meeting room to allow instant simulation. This real-time use of the computer proved to be popular with the management team and was certainly effective at drawing people into the discussion. For example, the managing director was curious about the relation between bug density, capacity, and sales growth, and proposed several simulations with different bug densities. The commercial manager was particularly interested in customer and distributor loss, and proposed simulations that involved changes in marketing time allocation.

We do not show all the simulations used in eight hours of management team meetings, nor do we review the full range of topics discussed. Instead, we present a few simulations to give the flavor of the meetings. (For ease of presentation, the simulations shown here are based on edited versions of the real company models; also, for confidentiality, all financial variables have been removed.)

Limits to growth from sales force size

Can the market grow without proportional growth in the sales force and sales expense? Understanding this question is vital if company profitability is to improve along with market size.

Figure 7 shows an optimistic growth scenario in which 100 percent of marketing time is allocated to distributor recruitment and there are no losses of distributors or customers. The top half of the figure shows the number of distributors and the number of repeat customers plotted over a 48-month time horizon. The lower half of the figure shows the annual fractional growth rate of distributors and customers.

The simulation starts with 12 distributors and 1,250 repeat customers. The number of distributors grows linearly (reflecting the steady recruiting efforts of the fixed sales force), reaching more than 30 by month 36. Interestingly, the number of customers grows more quickly, because customers are recruited in proportion to the number of distributors, which is steadily increasing. By month 36 there are more than 8,000 repeat customers. The simulations show there is a basis for optimistic sales growth opinions. Despite the long selling time and the need to restrain marketing costs, it is possible (admittedly under ideal conditions) to generate healthy growth of the customer base averaging around 50 percent per year for four years. A fixed sales force that leverages its effort through a distributor network can reach a large customer base.

There are, however, limits to growth with a fixed sales force, even under ideal conditions. The lower half of Figure 7 shows a steady decline in the growth rate of distributors and customers after month 24 (growth rate here is defined as an annual fractional increase). What is happening? Is this trend likely to continue? The growth rate of distributors (line 1) is bound to decline, since the fixed sales force recruits a *constant number* of distributors per month, which is a *declining*

Fig. 7. Optimistic growth scenario

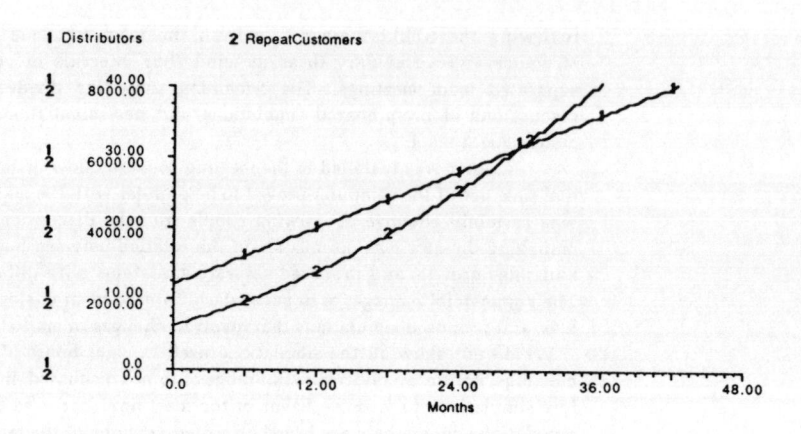

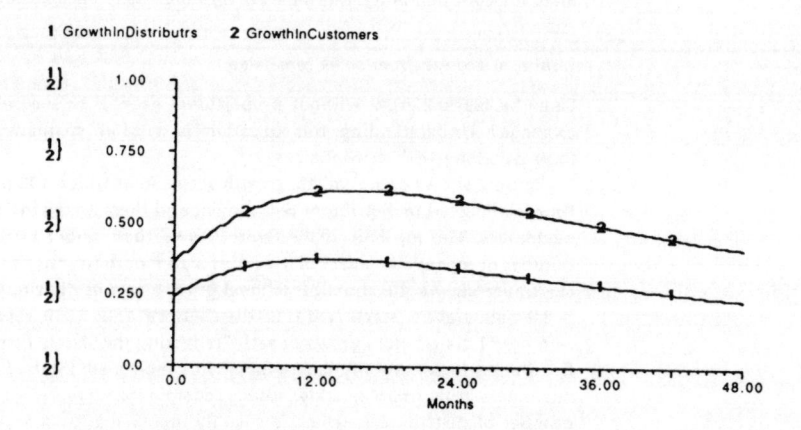

proportion of the growing distributor base. But, surely, extra distributors will guarantee a sustained high growth rate of customers? Strictly speaking, the answer is no. The distributor network only guarantees that, in the long run, the growth rate of customers exceeds the growth rate of distributors (line 2 above line 1). Both growth rates eventually decline as (intuitively) the efforts of the fixed sales force become proportionally ever smaller relative to the market size. However, for all practical purposes, a fixed sales force operating through a distributor network (with no losses) can sustain a high growth rate of sales. A 96-month (eight-year) simulation shows that the growth rate of the customer base always remains above 25 percent per year.

Limits to growth from distributor maintenance

The previous simulation shows the upper limit to BIP's growth rate, assuming that distributors require no maintenance. Distributor maintenance is a fact of life, however, and it puts practical limits on the market size possible to sustain with a fixed sales force.

Figure 8 shows a scenario in which the sales force allocates 50 percent of its time to recruitment and the remainder to distributor maintenance. The scenario also assumes that distributors will stop stocking the product if they feel they are being neglected by the sales force (questions not answered, phone calls not returned promptly, few site visits). In addition, 1 percent of distributors and 1 percent of customers are assumed to drop out each month because of unexplained loss of

Fig. 8. Growth limited by distributor maintenance

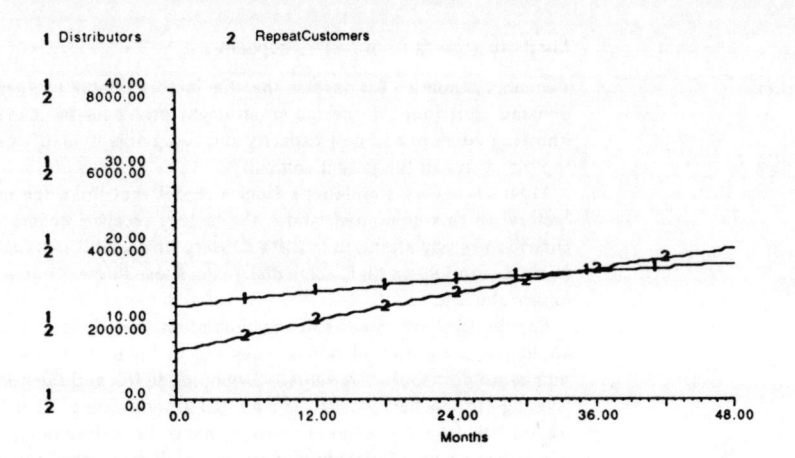

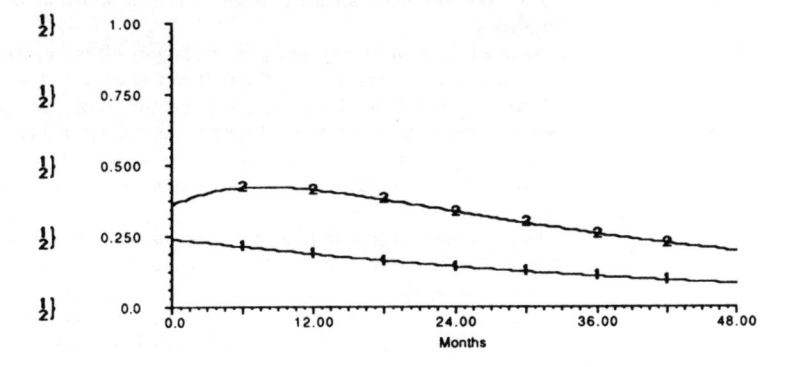

interest in the product. By comparison with Figure 7, the annual growth rate of distributors and customers is, on the average, 25 percent lower during the 48-month simulation. The result through compounding is a much lower customer base—about 3,000 customers in month 36 versus 8,000 in month 36 of the optimistic scenario.

The simulation focused management attention on the importance of distributor and customer retention, a topic that previously had not been appreciated. Discussion focused on marketing time allocation (the priority given to distributor recruitment versus maintenance) and on the sensitivity of distributors to maintenance (how much hand-holding do they really need?). Interestingly, the team members did not wrangle over the numerical accuracy of the simulations (e.g. will the customer base be 3,000 or 2,500 in month 36?).

Limits to growth from factory capacity

The simulations so far assume that the factory is able to keep pace with growing demand. But, one of the major strategic problems in managing the factory is knowing when to add new capacity and being able to justify capacity expansion to top managers in the parent company.

Figure 9 shows simulations from a model that links the customer base to the factory. In this combined model, the factory receives orders from the customers. Distributors pay attention to BIP's delivery time, and if it is high—say, four months or more—and stays high, some distributors lose interest in the product and will no longer stock it.

For the first six months of the simulation, distributors and customers grow at about the same annual rate as they did in Figure 8. However, by month 12 the number of distributors is actually beginning to fall and the number of customers is leveling off just below 2,000. The annual growth rate of distributors (lower half of figure) falls from 25 percent to zero by month 18 (it does not go to zero in month 12, when the number of distributors begins to fall, because the growth rate is averaged over a year.) From month 18 on, the number of distributors stays almost constant at about 2,000 and the customer base grows very slowly at an annual rate of less than 10 percent.

Meanwhile, what is happening in the factory? The top half of Figure 10 shows BIP's orders and production. At the start, orders are growing because of the growth of the customer base. Production lags behind, however, as shown by the gap between lines 1 and 2 over the first 12 months of the simulation. Shortly before month 18, production catches up, then overtakes orders as the factory works off the backlog it has accumulated. Then production declines and falls below orders once again.

Management finds it difficult to justify capacity expansion. The lower half of Figure 10 shows why. Line 1 is BIP's required production—the production rate the factory must achieve to ensure two-month delivery times. Line 3 is the plant output that top management believes is possible, taking into account uncertainties in yield and bug density. Only when required production exceeds line 3 is there factory

Fig. 9. Growth limited by distributor maintenance and by factory capacity

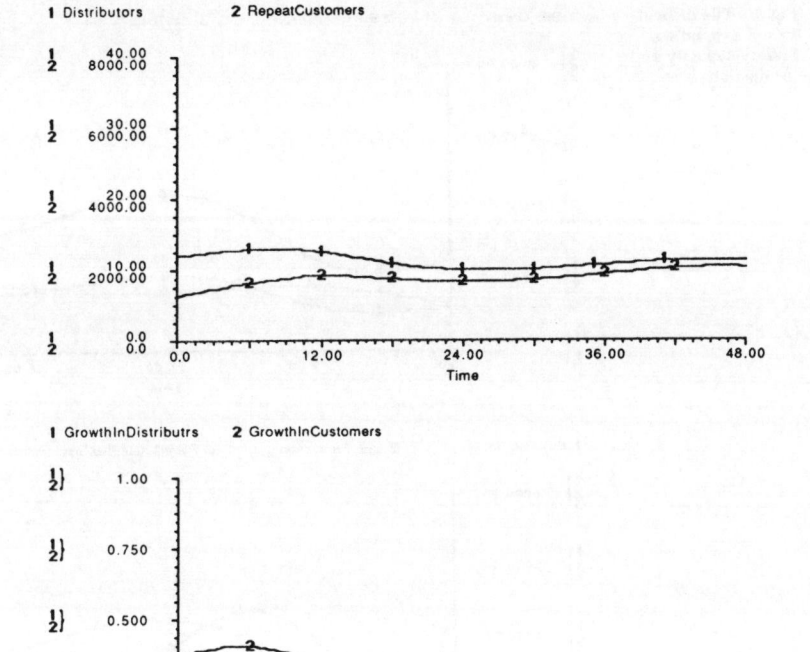

evidence to persuade top management to add new fermentation capacity. Inadvertently, the uncertainties of microbe production lead to a chronic shortage of fermentation capacity, so that BIP's production (line 2) is always less than required production. Distributors experience high delivery times, which peak at six months in month 12 and which average about four months. These sustained high delivery times accelerate distributor loss, making it impossible for the small fixed sales force to increase the size of the distributor base—monthly recruits are balanced by monthly losses.

This low-growth scenario is not a prediction of what will happen but rather a possibility of what could happen if the company lacks the conviction to expand capacity (because of uncertainties about yield and bug density) and if the sales force is held constant to improve profitability.

Fig. 10. The difficulties of expanding factory capacity and production

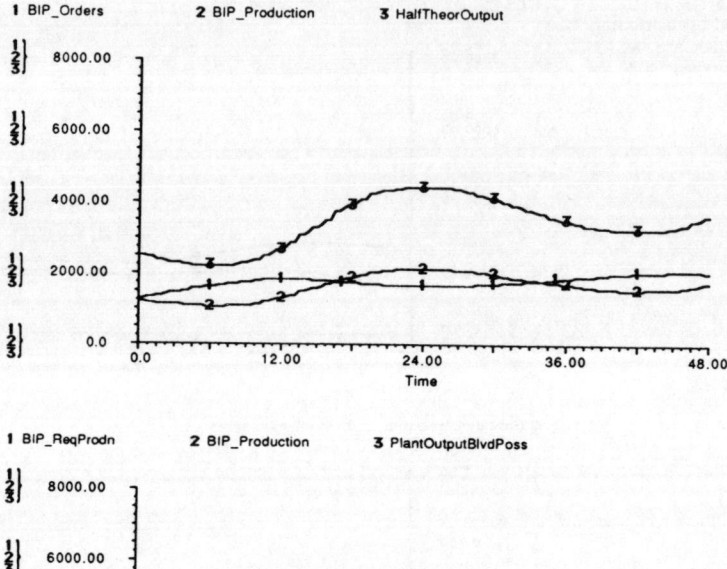

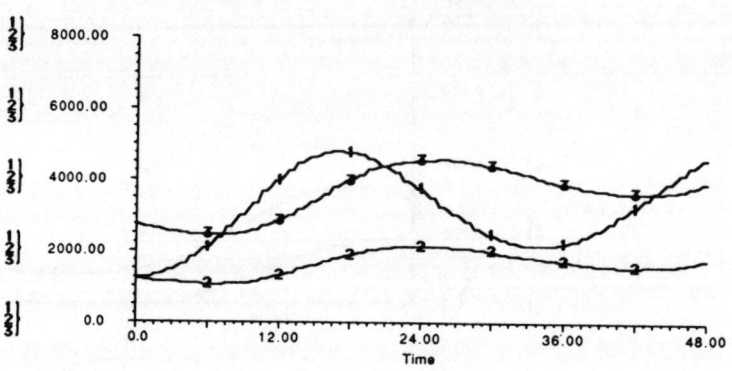

Factory simulations like the one described led the management team to think carefully about measuring the adequacy of factory capacity. Specifically, how should one account for changing microbial parameters (yield and bug density) in capacity planning? How sensitive are distributors to poor delivery times? The team probed these questions by making simulations with new values for yield, density, and delivery sensitivity.

Impact of the project

The last hour of the final meeting was set aside to obtain the opinions of the management team about the value and effects of the project. The managing director began the discussion. He admitted to having been skeptical about modeling at the start of the project. In particular, he believed that a computer model could not capture the flavor of his fledgling company. At the end, he acknowledged, the model did represent the business. Specifically, he felt that the project had raised his awareness of several strategic issues: the importance of microbial production parameters in capacity planning, the short time period before capacity constraints might stifle growth, the recognition that small improvements in production parameters can defer scarcity problems, and the importance of knowing distributors' sensitivity to delivery.

He said that the first two meetings had been frustrating because he felt he was giving more information than he was receiving. However, this negative feeling was outweighed by his positive views of the third, fourth, and fifth meetings, in which model simulations and hands-on sessions had provided him with new insights into the business. His overall conclusion was that he had learned a considerable amount about the business from the project, but he wondered whether a process of similar length but without the use of modeling and computer simulation would have yielded similar or equivalent insights.

The commercial manager said he had learned a lot about the factory from the project and had been made aware of the critical importance of distributor loss (and the factors that influence loss) in limiting the growth potential of the business. As a result, he had begun to monitor distributor loss, delivery times, and maintenance time. The new-ventures manager viewed the project as a test of the methodology in the special circumstances of a startup firm, where formal business data are scant and there are few established operating procedures. He felt that the process was a very useful way of getting everyone to understand how the business works. However, after the project, the model was not used regularly by the management team as he had hoped, mainly because of time pressures on management in a small company. According to him, the process proved more useful than the final model.

Insights from the project led to increased priority for two ongoing programs: product improvement and R&D. Product improvement was aimed at making an easier-to-use microbe mix, perhaps a liquid instead of powder. An easy-to-use product was viewed as important because (in addition to being more attractive to customers) it would stimulate growth by freeing up time spent in distributor maintenance. The result would be more time available for recruiting new distributors—a fact that the management team noted from simulations of the limits to growth. The R&D program was aimed at enhancing yields and was given higher priority by the head of manufacturing, who recognized, as a result of factory simulations, the market payoff from adequate capacity.

Lessons from interactive model building

Only recently have modelers (and more generally those working on decision support) begun to recognize the importance of the process that surrounds the building and use of computer models. The way that business problems are defined and represented affects the knowledge that is activated and the ease with which a problem can be solved (Weber and Konsynski 1988; Morecroft 1988). Even when a representation scheme is specified, as with a system dynamics model, there are many different ways to organize how knowledge is elicited and mapped (Richardson et al. 1989). Once a model exists, allowing users to experiment on the computer with easy-to-run partial models and games can influence the effectiveness of computer-based learning (Graham et al. 1989). The following sections report the main findings about the modeling process noted during the Bio Industrial Products project.

Need for devices to trigger and structure discussion

All management teams are loaded with business information, much more than could be included in a simulation model. Model builders need to obtain this knowledge selectively and to structure it.

In the BIP project, a checklist was deliberately used in the first meeting to organize team discussion of the operating structure of the business. Included in the list were broad topics like manufacturing capacity expansion, R&D, sales and marketing effort, which allowed the team members to participate in a seemingly broad-ranging discussion while providing the modelers with a rich flow of descriptive information that would fit a system dynamics model. The modelers made handwritten notes to record the information. It is likely that most strategic modelers and indeed most consultants use some similar visual or verbal framing technique to shape team discussion.

Retaining flexibility: maps and small models

It is important to retain flexibility—room for discussion, interpretation, and new ideas—within the boundaries defined by the model. In fact, at the start, the boundaries themselves should be flexible to allow for creative problem definition.

In the BIP project, the checklist, the six conceptual units in Figure 1, and the STELLA maps each provided flexible frames. However, the frames gradually tightened as the team homed in on a specific problem area. The STELLA maps made a much tighter frame for discussing growth management than the simple checklist had, but not nearly as tight as a fully specified algebraic model, which really nails down the logic and structure of the system.

A progression from loose to tight frames of discussion is probably vital for team modeling because team members feel involved at each stage of the discussion and play a central role in defining the scope and content of the model. Modeling processes that leap from the very unstructured (normal dialogue) to the very structured (large and complex algebraic models) bypass important steps in team communication and consensus building, and are likely to be viewed and treated as black boxes by the team.

The progression from loose to tight frames does not necessarily preclude the use of algebraic models and simulations at an early stage of team model building as long as the algebraic models are small and transparent and are used as partial models to illuminate a part of the broad team discussion rather than to stifle and restrict discussion. In the BIP project, versions of the customer base model were used to illustrate "friendly" algebra and simulation (meeting 2) and to trigger discussion of the limits to market growth (meetings 4 and 5).

Value of pre-existing models

Pre-existing models are useful in a new team project to provide a comprehensive set of in-depth questions for fueling discussion and structuring information gathering, particularly early in a project. Forrester's market growth model was well suited to the BIP project. The model raises a host of key strategic questions about growth management. How much capacity does a growing firm need? How do factory managers recognize a capacity shortage? Why do customers buy a product? How do they hear about it? How much marketing effort is needed? What coordinates the factory with sales and marketing? The list of questions is long and probes deeply into information channels, incentives, politics, and even the culture of the growing firm. Pre-existing models, and the generic structures that underlie them (Paich 1985), seem therefore to have a valuable role to play in framing team discussion and extracting valuable operating knowledge.

Notes

1. STELLA is a trademark of High Performance Systems, 45 Lyme Road, Hanover, N.H. 03755, U.S.A.
2. The first working meeting was preceded by two short conferences between the managing director and the new-ventures manager to define the terms of reference and the logistics of the project.
3. There are many ways to capture knowledge for models. A checklist with notes is very low-key and does not interrupt the flow of conversation yet imposes some structure on the discussion. More structured but still flexible is a discussion organized around major points of decision making. The agenda lists the decision-making processes to be discussed, and the facilitator draws and labels each decision-making process on a flipchart. The management team then discuss how decisions are made, the information to be used, the information to be ignored, and the goals and incentives of decision makers. Another approach is to draw word-arrow charts based on the management team's views of important linkages in the business (Wolstenholme 1990).

References

Forrester, J. W. 1968. Market Growth as Influenced by Capital Investment. *Sloan Management Review* 9 (no. 2): 83–105. Also in *Collected Papers of Jay W. Forrester*, 111–132. Cambridge, Mass.: Productivity Press. 1975.

Graham, A. K., J. D. W. Morecroft, P. M. Senge, and J. D. Sterman. 1989. Computer-Based Case Studies in Management Education and Research. In *Computer-Based Management of Complex Systems*, ed. P. Milling and E. Zahn, 317–326. Berlin: Springer-Verlag.

Kuipers, H. A., and J. A. M. Vennix. 1990. Organizing Home Care in the Future: Using System Dynamics to Assess Organizational Changes. In *Proceedings of the 1990 International System Dynamics Conference*, ed. D. F. Andersen, G. P. Richardson, and J. D. Sterman, 596–604.

Lyneis, J. M. 1980. *Corporate Planning and Policy Design: A System Dynamics Approach*. Cambridge, Mass.: Productivity Press.

Morecroft, J. D. W. 1990. Executive Knowledge, Models, and Learning. Discussion Paper GS-40-90, London Business School, Regent's Park, London NW1 4SA, U.K.

Morecroft, J. D. W., and K. A. J. M. Van der Heijden. 1990. Modeling the Oil Producers. In *Proceedings of the 1990 International System Dynamics Conference*, ed. D. F. Andersen, G. P. Richardson, and J. D. Sterman, 783–797. Also available as Working Paper GS-38-90, London Business School, Regent's Park, London NW1 4SA, U.K.

Paich, M. 1985. Generic Structures. *System Dynamics Review* 1: 126–132.

Richardson, G. P., J. A. M. Vennix, D. F. Andersen, J. Rohrbaugh, and W. A. Wallace. 1989. Processes for Eliciting and Mapping Knowledge for Model Building. In *Computer-Based Management of Complex Systems*, ed. P. Milling and E. Zahn, 341–357. Berlin: Springer-Verlag.

Richmond, B. M. 1987. *The Strategic Forum: From Vision to Operating Policies and Back Again*. High Performance Systems, 45 Lyme Road, Hanover, NH 03755, U.S.A.

Richmond, B. M., S. Peterson and P. Vescuso. 1987. *STELLA for Business*. Cambridge, Mass.: Productivity Press.

Sterman, J. D. 1985. A Behavioral Model of the Economic Long Wave. *Journal of Economic Behavior and Organization* 6 (no. 1): 17–53.

Vennix, J. A. M., J. W. Gubbels, D. Post, and H. J. Poppen. 1990a. A Structured Approach to Knowledge Elicitation in Conceptual Model Building. *System Dynamics Review* 6: 194–208.

Vennix, J. A. M., L. D. Verburgh, J. W. Gubbels, and D. Post. 1990b. Eliciting Group Knowledge in a Computer-Based Learning Environment. In *Proceedings of the 1990 International System Dynamics Conference*, ed. D. F. Andersen, G. P. Richardson, and J. D. Sterman, 1187–1198.

Weber, E. S., and B. R. Konsynski. 1988. Problem Management: Neglected Elements in Decision Support Systems. *Journal of Management Information Systems* 4 (no. 3): 63–81.

Wolstenholme, E. F. 1990. *System Enquiry Using System Dynamics*. Chichester, U.K.: Wiley.

[15]

Portfolio simulation: a tool to support strategic management

Peter P. Merten, Reiner Löffler, and Klaus-Peter Wiedmann

We show that a quantitative portfolio simulation model can be used effectively in the allocation of investment funds in multibusiness firms. The portfolio simulation model, which is formulated with an extended system dynamics approach, further allows us to show severe limitations of qualitative portfolio approaches, such as that of the Boston Consulting Group (BCG). The simulation experiments demonstrate that it can be extremely dangerous for diversified companies to follow the investment suggestions typically drawn from the BCG portfolio matrix if competitors choose a course of action that is contradictory to normative situations. The simulation runs additionally show that in an economic depression a more flexible positioning strategy can yield much better results than the fixed positioning strategy typically used by the BCG.

Peter P. Merten is wissenschaftlicher Angestellter at the Industrieseminar, Mannheim University, West Germany. He received master's and Ph.D. degrees in management science from Mannheim University. He has been teaching system dynamics

The allocation of investment funds in multibusiness firms is considered in this article as a complex strategic decision-making process that is located at the top management level of diversified companies (Simon 1981, 49). Qualitative portfolio approaches like the portfolio concept of the Boston Consulting Group (BCG) were developed to support this strategic decision-making process. However, *qualitative portfolio concepts* have severe limitations (Hax and Majluf 1984, 145–150). We show a newly developed *quantitative portfolio simulation model* that can overcome some of the methodological limitations typical of qualitative portfolio approaches. This quantitative portfolio simulation model is shown from three perspectives. First, we briefly describe the BCG approach to portfolio management. Second, we show the formal generic structures of the portfolio simulation model. Third, we present simulation results of the model that show different evolutionary development patterns of diversified firms and highlight severe limitations of the BCG approach.

The qualitative model of portfolio management: the Boston Consulting Group portfolio concept

The portfolio management process is a complex strategic decision-making process determined by several factors. These include the actual business situation of a conglomerate and its business units, its goals and the funds available for capital investment, the expected strategies and capabilities of major competitors, and the general economic situations of the countries where the business units are located. To solve the funds allocation problem, diversified companies normally use some kind of heuristics. One qualitative heuristic, which is used worldwide to support the portfolio management process in multibusiness companies, is the portfolio concept of the Boston Consulting Group (Henderson 1973; 1979).

The essence of the BCG approach is to represent the firm as a portfolio of businesses, each one offering a unique contribution with regard to growth and profitability. The firm is then viewed not just as a single monolithic entity but as a composite of largely independent units whose strategic directions are to be distinctively addressed (Hax and Majluf 1984, 127).

To visualize the particular role to be played by each strategic business unit (SBU), the BCG developed the *growth-share matrix*, in which each business is plotted on a four-quadrant grid (Figure 1). The horizontal axis corresponds to the relative market share enjoyed by a business—as a way of characterizing the strength of the firm in that business. A cutoff point separates businesses of high and low strength. The vertical axis indicates market growth, representing the attractiveness of the market in which the business is positioned. A cutoff point, defined by the company or its consultants, separates high-growth from low-growth businesses.

The SBUs of a company are positioned in the so-defined growth-share matrix, as shown by the circles in Figure 1. The circles show the contribution of the SBU to the

and international business management since 1979, and his main research interests are computer simulation, artificial intelligence, national and international strategic business management, technology transfer, and problems of Third World development.
Address: Industrieseminar, Universität Mannheim (LS: Prof. Dr. G. v. Kortzfleisch), 6800 Mannheim, West Germany.

Reiner Löffler is a financial analyst at Wang–Deutschland GmbH. He received master's and Ph.D. degrees in management science from Mannheim University. His main research interests are strategic management and computer simulation.
Address: Wang–Deutschland GmbH, 6000 Frankfurt a./M., West Germany.

Klaus-Peter Wiedmann is wissenschaftlicher Angestellter at the Institute of Marketing, Mannheim University, West Germany. He received a master's degree in management science from Mannheim University. He has taught marketing and strategic planning since 1980 and is a business consultant. His main research interests are strategic marketing, early warning systems, social marketing, value

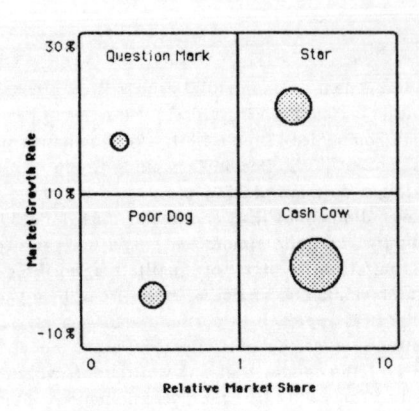

Fig. 1. The growth-share portfolio matrix of a diversified company

firm measured by sales or earnings, which are proportional to the area within the circles in the matrix.

One implication of this categorization is that the businesses in each quadrant (see Figure 1) have distinct characteristics with regard to cash flow (see Figure 2) (Hax and Majluf 1984, 131–133). The primary objectives of the corporation implicit in the BCG approach are growth and profitability (Henderson and Zakon 1980). The approach seeks to utilize the ability of a multibusiness organization to transfer cash from those businesses that are highly profitable but have a limited potential for growth to those that offer attractive opportunities for future growth and profit.

The BCG philosophy leads to an integrated management of the portfolio, designed to make the whole larger than the sum of the parts. For such synergy to be obtained, a fairly centralized resource allocation process is required to produce a balanced portfolio.

Another contribution of the BCG resides in their selection of market share and market growth to express the desired strategy for each business. The strategy suggestions drawn out of the growth-share matrix by the BCG are selective offensive strategies for Question Marks, offensive strategies for Stars, defensive strategies for Cash Cows, and divest or harvest strategies for Poor Dogs.

The portfolio approach of the BCG, however, has severe limitations (Hax and Majluf 1984, 145–150). The approach does not allow the assessment of financial and market implications of different strategies in a quantitative and dynamic way. "Relative market share" represents the competitive strengths and weaknesses as well as the market structures in a highly aggregated and therefore incomplete way. "Market growth" does not separate the general economic and political situations of the change, and business ethics. *Address:* Institut für Marketing, Universität Mannheim (LS: Prof. Dr. H. Raffée), 6800 Mannheim, West Germany.

	Question Marks	**Stars**
high	• Major untapped opportunities, which appear to be very attractive because of the high market growth rate. • Because of the low market share, large cash is needed for success. • Select most favorable "?" SBUs and invest sufficient funds to achieve a leading position in industry.	• Highly attractive businesses, because of the strong competitive position in a rapidly growing market. • SBUs in this position generate large amounts of cash but at the same time require a significant inflow of cash resources to hold the competitive position in the growing market. • Hold the position and invest: the deficit required from the overall organization is relatively modest.
	Poor Dogs	**Cash Cows**
low	• These SBUs are the "great losers": unattractive and weak. • They must be regarded as "cash traps": whatever little cash they generate is needed for maintaining their operations. • If there is no legitimate reason to suspect a turnaround in the future, the logical strategy to follow would be harvesting or divesting.	• Central sources of cash for the organization: because of their extremely high competitive strength in a declining market, they generate more cash than they can wisely reinvest into themselves. • Use the large positive cash to support the development of other businesses (Question Marks and partly also Stars). • The resource allocation process has to be centralized at a higher managerial level, otherwise the management of a Cash Cow will tend to reinvest in its own domain, suboptimizing the use of its resources.

Market Growth Rate

low — Relative Market Share — high

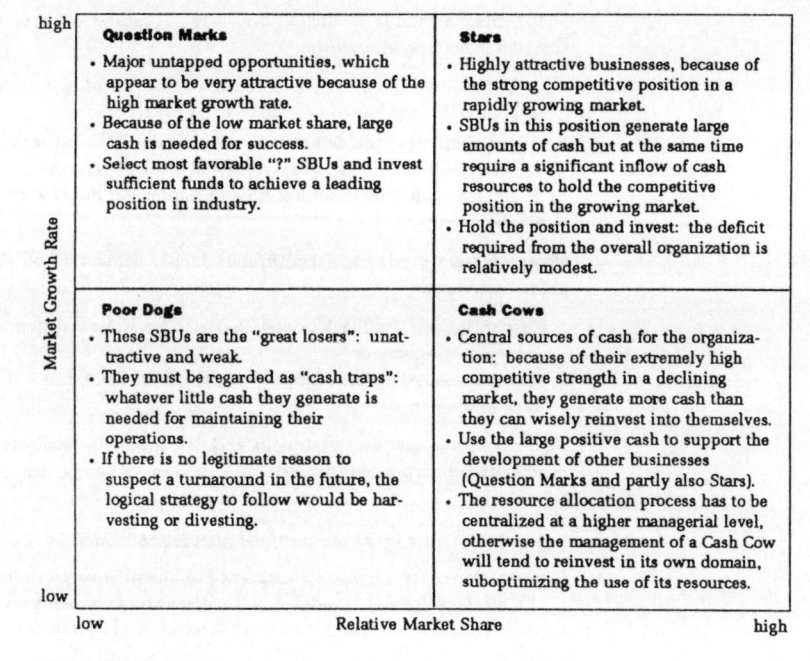

Fig. 2. Characteristics of the different portfolio positions

countries where the SBUs are located from their inherent potential. The time-invariant definition of the cutoff lines of the portfolio matrix by BCG is critical too, because general market and economic trends can change and thereby make a redefinition of the cutoff lines necessary.

The quantitative portfolio simulation model

The quantitative portfolio simulation model, developed with an extended system dynamics approach, incorporates the most useful features of the BCG approach and additionally overcomes some of the limitations of the qualitative portfolio approach. The continuous feedback loop concept of system dynamics is used to model the decentralized decision-making processes of the SBUs (Forrester 1961; Richardson and Pugh 1981). Discontinuous feedback loops are used to represent the rule-setting strategic decisions of the centralized portfolio management process (Merten 1985;

1986). Discontinuous feedback loops are composed of three sets of rules, which sometimes may be interwoven:

1. A decision rule that assigns when the critical load of a system is attained, i.e., a structural change has to take place (rule of critical load)
2. A decision rule that determines what to do if the critical load of the system is attained (rule of strategy generation and strategy selection)
3. A decision rule that describes how to implement the new strategy (rule of strategy implementation)

There are two kinds of discontinuous loops, depending on the kind of structural change generated:

1. Discontinuous feedback loops that add or delete system elements with their feedback connections
2. Discontinuous feedback loops that change feedback connections between existing system elements

Figure 3 shows how the continuous and discontinuous feedback loops can be used in combination to represent the decision structures in companies.

The generic structure of the portfolio simulation model

Figure 4 shows the generic structure of the quantitative portfolio simulation model.

The strategy level is modeled with discontinuous feedback loops and has four sectors: portfolio analysis, marketing strategies, production strategies, and strategic budgeting.

In the portfolio analysis sector the SBUs of the company are positioned in the portfolio matrix, and consequences for investments in new businesses and divestments of old businesses are derived from the portfolio structure. Strategic positioning of the SBUs is represented in the model with four rules of critical load. An SBU is qualified by the first rule of critical load as a Poor Dog position if its market growth is 10 percent per year or less and its relative market share is 1 or less (see Figure 1). A minimum capital investment is necessary in Poor Dog positions for the positioning of SBUs. SBUs with high market growth but a low relative market share are qualified by the second rule of critical load as Question Mark positions if the company already has investments in this business. SBUs are qualified as Star positions by the third rule of critical load if their market growth and their relative market share are high. Finally, SBUs with a low market growth and a high relative market share are positioned by the fourth rule of critical load as Cash Cow positions.

Investments in new SBUs with high market growth, where the company's present market share is zero, depend on the portfolio structure of the company. The company invests in a new SBU with high market growth if the portfolio structure shows too many "old" SBUs and if it does not already have a new SBU (Question Mark position). The company totally divests SBUs that are in Poor Dog positions if their losses exceed a maximum acceptable level. The company also divests Question Mark positions when they generate losses and the financial situation of the company is critical.

Fig. 3. The representation of a company with discontinuous and continuous feedback loops

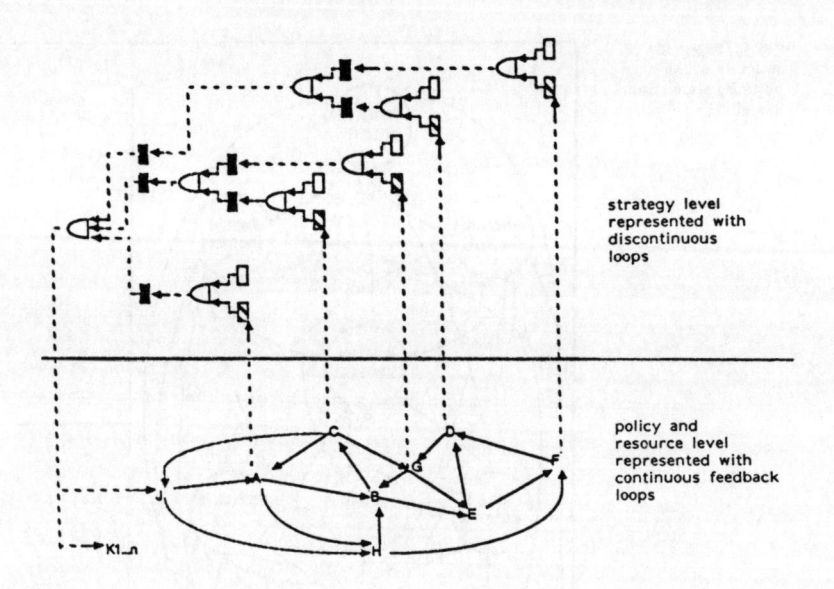

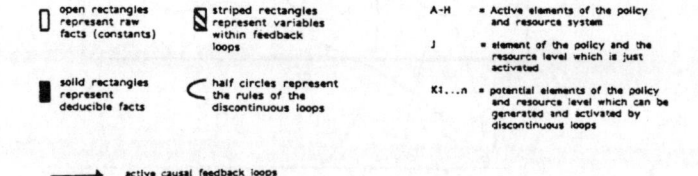

strategy level represented with discontinuous loops

policy and resource level represented with continuous feedback loops

open rectangles represent raw facts (constants)	striped rectangles represent variables within feedback loops	A-H = Active elements of the policy and resource system
solid rectangles represent deducible facts	half circles represent the rules of the discontinuous loops	J = element of the policy and the resource level which is just activated
		K1...n = potential elements of the policy and resource level which can be generated and activated by discontinuous loops

⟶ active causal feedback loops
─ ─ ▶ just activated causal feedback structure
- - -▶ information processing within discontinuous loops

Fig. 4. The generic structure of the portfolio simulation model

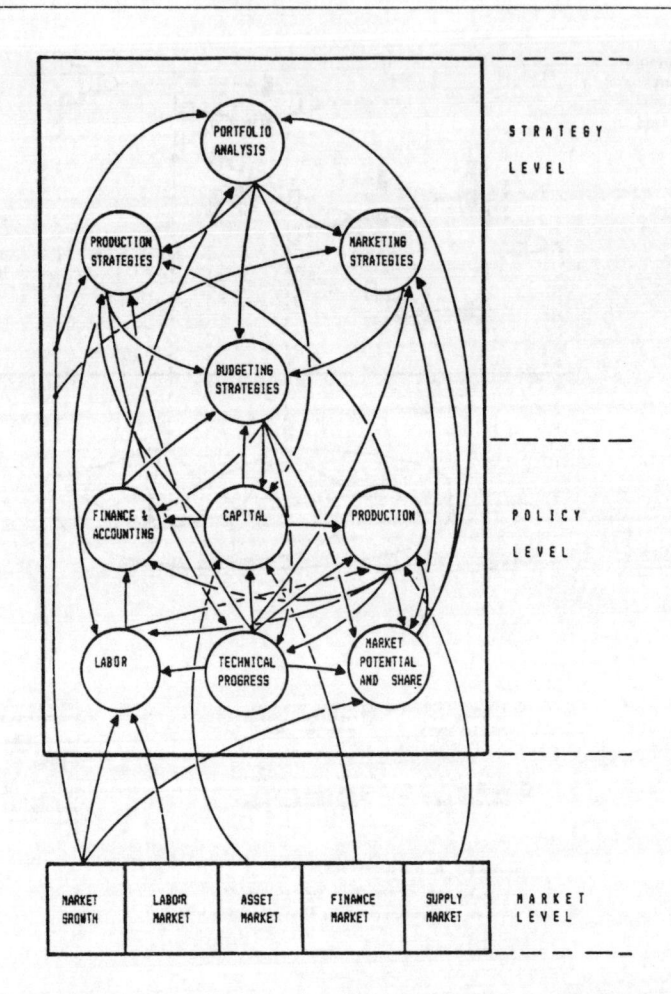

If an existing SBU is qualified by one of the four rules of critical load, a BCG strategy suggestion is activated (rule of strategy selection and strategy generation). For each of the four strategic problems, one BCG strategy is defined in the strategy sectors of the model. In the production strategy sector the investment strategies are defined for different (portfolio) situations. The marketing strategy sector is composed of the subsystems price, product, distribution, and communication strategy. Different marketing strategy sets are defined for different (portfolio) situations (Figure 5).

Fig. 5. Strategy sets for different portfolio situations

Identification	Policy Mix			
	Price Policy	Product Policy	Advertising Policy	Investment Policy
= 0 Attractive market without an active SBU Buildup strategy	—	Development of product-technical-competitive advantage	—	Buildup of a minimum production capacity
= 1 Question Mark Offensive strategy	Profit margin: 2.5% Maximum price: 5% under competitive level Minimum price: variable unit costs	Planned product-technical advantage: 85% over competitive level	Planned advertising budget: 20% over competitive level	Investment level as forecasted booking rate
= 2 Star Investment strategy	Profit margin: 5% Maximum price: competitive level Minimum price: 75% of total unit costs	Planned product-technical advantage: 75% over competitive level	Planned advertising budget: 5% over competitive level	Investment level as forecasted booking rate
= 3 Cash Cow Defensive strategy	Profit margin: 7.5% Maximum price: 5% over competitive level Minimum price: total unit costs + 3.75% profit margin	Planned product-technical advantage: 50% over competitive level	Planned advertising budget: competitive level	Investment level as forecasted booking rate
= 4 Poor Dog Disinvestment strategy	Profit margin: 10% Maximum price: 10% over competitive level Minimum price: total unit costs + 8% profit margin	Planned product-technical advantage: 0% over competitive level	Planned advertising budget: competitive level	Investment level as forecasted booking or disinvestment in case of monthly loss of DM 250,000
= 5 Unattractive market or disinvested SBU	—	—	—	—

In the strategic budgeting sector the product, distribution, communication, and investment budgets are defined on the basis of top-down and bottom-up information. The top-down generated production and marketing strategies alter the bottom-up generated budgets and functional policies of the SBUs, taking the financial constraints of the conglomerate into account (rules of strategy implementation). The bottom-up generated budgets are based on different kinds of information, such as forecasts of market development, information about competitors, and information about the company's costs and the capacities in the SBUs.

Besides the sectors of the strategy level there are six sectors of the policy level, which are modeled with continuous feedback loops and which are identical for all SBUs. In the accounting sector important indicators, such as costs per unit, turnover, and earnings, are calculated on a company and SBU level. The capital sector is divided into two subsectors: assets and financing of assets. In the labor sector hiring and firing of workers are modeled. The production process is modeled in the production sector. Experience effects in production are defined as a function of the accumulated production. The technical progress sector represents the technical progress in production and in products. The market sector defines the market potential and the market share. Market growth is given exogenously in the model. Market share and market growth as well as the earnings calculated in the accounting sector are the most important inputs in the strategic portfolio analysis.

On the procurement market side the prices are exogenously given. The demand of the company can be satisfied without limits in these markets.

Strategic feedback loops of the portfolio simulation model

The portfolio simulation model is based on the assumption that there are two companies competing in five different product markets (duopoly situation). The competitive feedback structure represented in the model is shown in Figure 6.

Both companies analyze the strategic positions of their SBUs with the BCG growth-share matrix, i.e., market growth and market share are used as indicators for strategic positioning. The growth and profitability goals inherent in the portfolio matrix determine together with the strategic positions of the SBUs the strategies of the competing companies. For Question Marks and Stars, offensive growth strategies become activated. Cash Cow positions are defended with defensive strategies. Poor Dogs are divested.

The discrete selected strategies (see Figure 5) determine together with the resources of the company and the policies of the competitor the policies of the company. The selected policy sets change the market share of the company in different ways: with buildup, offensive, and investment strategies the market share will rise; with a defensive strategy the market share will be constant; with disinvestment strategies the market share will decline.

The dashed lines in Figure 6 show two further assumptions of the portfolio simulation model:

1. The competitor generates its policies without information about the policies of the other company (Stackelberg dependence position).

Fig. 6. The competitive feedback structure of the portfolio simulation model

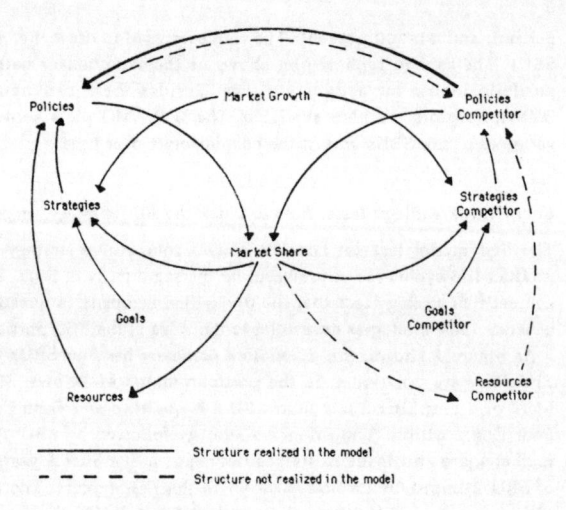

2. The resource system of the competitor is not represented in the model.

The consequence of the first assumption is that the competitor has to lose in competition if resources and strategies of the two companies are identical. The second assumption partly reduces this disadvantage of the competitor. Every strategy of the competitor can be realized without limitations from the resource system.

Selected results from the portfolio simulation model

The quantitative portfolio simulation model helps to explain the evolution of multibusiness firms in duopoly markets, and it also can be used as a simulation game and as a strategic decision support system. Further, the quantitative model allows the testing of different assumptions of the qualitative BCG portfolio model. The results of two model tests are presented here: (1) a competitive strategy test set, and (2) a company strategy test set (for the complete results, see Löffler and Wiedmann 1985).

To show the qualitative and quantitative changes typical of the development of diversified firms, we present the results of the portfolio simulation model in three types of plots. The comparative dynamic portfolio plots show the development of the SBUs in the portfolio matrix over a 20-year period in steps of 4 years. The sizes of the circles in these plots show us the percentage of earnings an SBU contributes to the total earnings of the conglomerate. There are four sizes of circles, which represent four different earning categories: 0–10 percent, 11–25 percent, 26–50 percent, and 51–100 percent. The numbers used to draw the circles characterize the SBUs. The second type of plot shows us the evolutionary paths of the SBUs in the portfolio matrix in a dynamic way. Besides these two new forms of plots, the DYNAMO plots are also available. The DYNAMO plots show the development of variables of the SBUs and of the conglomerate over time.

Competitive strategy tests: how to crack the BCG strategy suggestions

The first model test set consists of two competitive strategy tests. The exogenous product life cycles are assumed to be the same for both tests. We assume in the first competitive strategy test that the diversified company in question and its competitor generate their strategies according to the rules of the BCG portfolio heuristic.

As Figure 7 shows, the diversified company has four SBUs in the starting period. The SBUs are positioned in the portfolio matrix as follows: SBU 1 is in a Question Mark position; SBU 2 is a Star; SBU 3 is qualified as a Cash Cow; and SBU 4 is in a Poor Dog position. The offensive strategy followed by SBU 1 increases its relative market share and leads to its positioning as a Star after 4 years. The growth strategy of SBU 2 improves its Star position in the first 4 years. The Cash Cow position of SBU 3 can be held with a defensive strategy during the same period, and SBU 4 becomes divested as a Poor Dog. After 8 years the company consists of five SBUs, because a new SBU has been established in the fast-growing fifth market. After 12 years the company has four SBUs again. SBU 4 has been totally divested. After 20 years the company still has four SBUs: one is a Star (SBU 5) and the other three are Cash Cows. The extremely positive situation of the SBUs of the company can be explained predominantly by the competitive assumptions made in the model, i.e., the Stackelberg independence position of the company.

In the second competitive strategy test we assume that the competitor acts opposite to the investment suggestions typically derived from the portfolio matrix of the BCG. In this case, the competitor divests Question Mark positions; tries to hold Star positions; and invests in Poor Dog and Cash Cow positions.

Figure 8 shows that we have the same starting position as we had in the last test and that the development of the SBUs is also similar during the first 8 years. The declining demand in the markets of SBU 1 and SBU 2, generated by the exogenous product life cycles, leads to a repositioning of these two business units so that what were once Star products become Cash Cows and, for the competitor, what were once Question Marks become Poor Dogs. The atypical offensive strategies of the competitor in Poor Dog positions, together with the company's defensive strategies in Cash Cow positions, influence the development of the two business units and of the conglomerate in a negative way after 8 years. The competitor wins market shares in these two markets with offensive strategies. At the end of the simulation run, SBU 1 is in a Poor Dog position and is divested. SBU 2 is still in a Cash Cow position but with a strong tendency towards a Poor Dog position. The portfolio-atypical behavior of the competitor does not appreciably change the development of the Cash Cow position of SBU 3. The development of SBU 5 over the 20-year period is slightly better, because the defensive strategies of the competitor make it easier for the company to establish this SBU in a Star position.

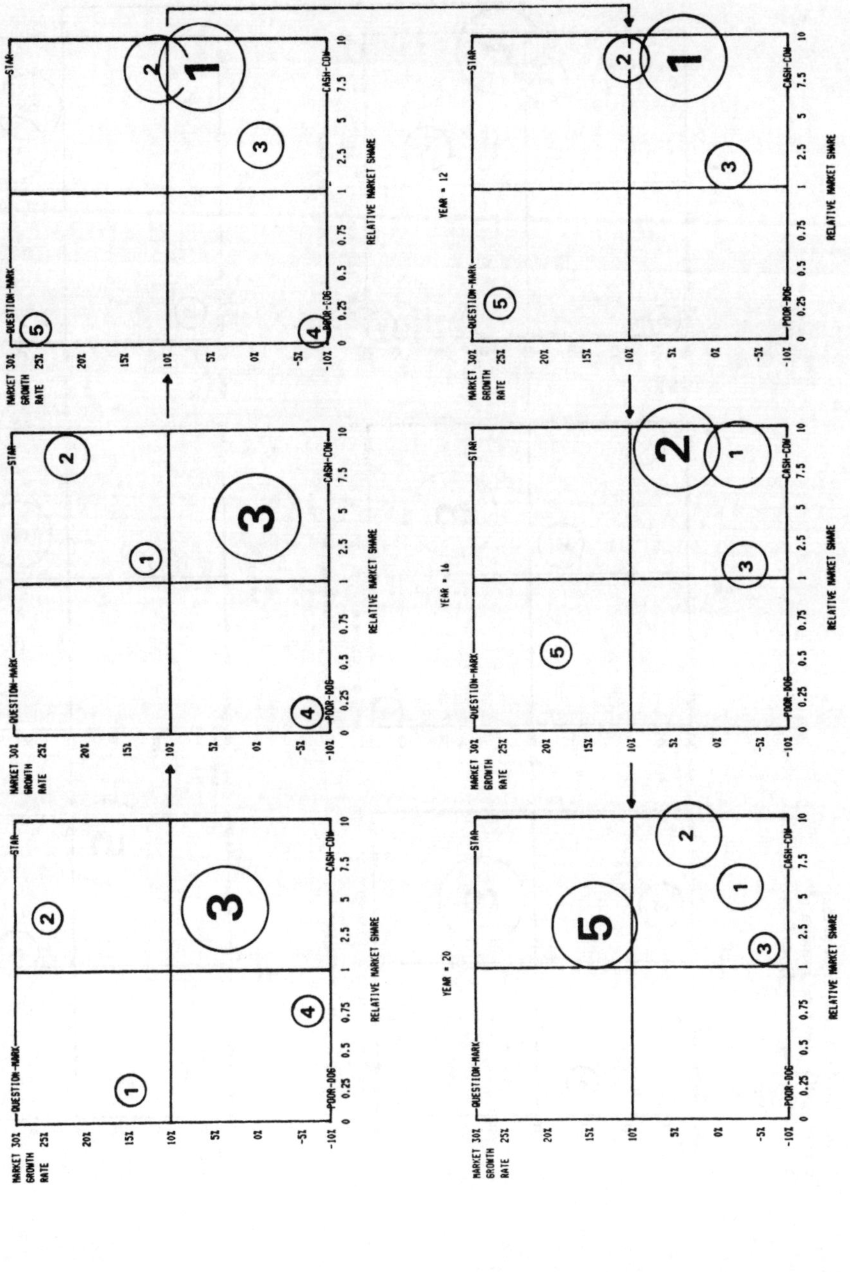

Fig. 7. Portfolio development in the case of portfolio-typical reaction of competitor (comparative dynamic view)

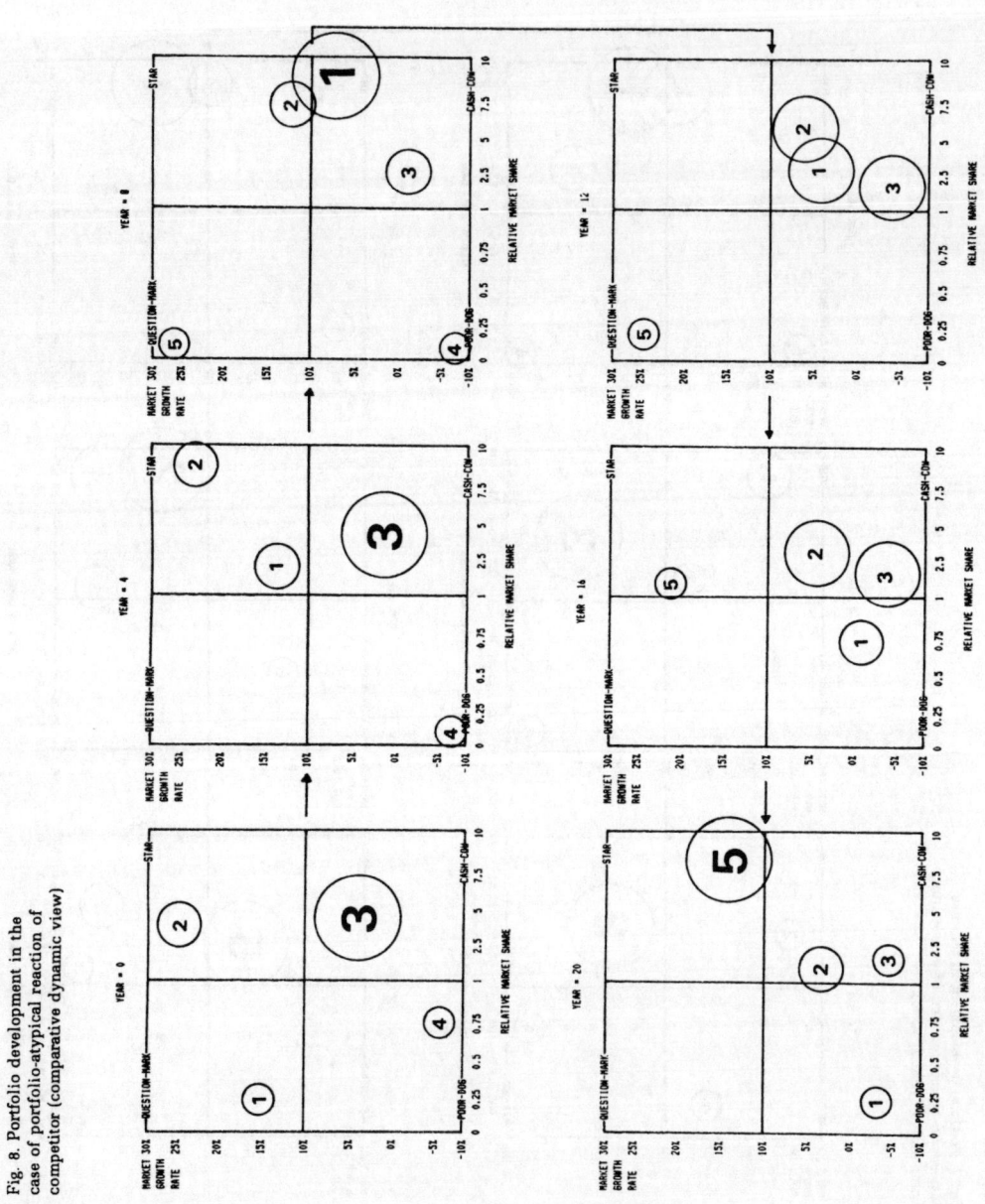

Fig. 8. Portfolio development in the case of portfolio-atypical reaction of competitor (comparative dynamic view)

Fig. 9. Portfolio development in the case of typical and atypical reactions of competitor (dynamic view over 20 years)

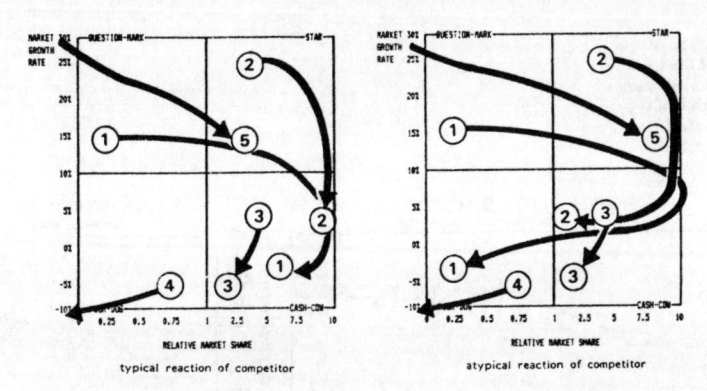

typical reaction of competitor   atypical reaction of competitor

If we now compare the results of the two competitive strategy tests (Figures 9–11), we can conclude that it may be extremely dangerous for a company to follow the investment suggestions typically drawn from the BCG portfolio matrix, because BCG strategy suggestions do not take into account reactions or feedback from the competitive environment.

Figure 9 shows the development of the diversified company in the case of typical and atypical reactions of the competitor in a dynamic view. With typical reactions of the competitor, the company has three Cash Cows (SBU 1, 2, 3) and one Star position (SBU 5) after 20 years. In the case of atypical reactions of the competitor, the company has one Poor Dog (SBU 1), one Cash Cow position drifting towards a Poor Dog position (SBU 2), one Cash Cow position (SBU 3), and one Star position (SBU 5).

Figure 10 shows the development of the turnover of the conglomerate for both competitive strategy tests. With typical reactions of the competitor, the total turnover of the conglomerate rises from 160 million German marks (DM) per month to DM 230 million per month in the 20-year period. In the case of atypical reactions of the competitor, the turnover of the company remains nearly constant and is DM 180 million per month after 20 years.

Figure 11 summarizes the results of the two competitive strategy tests. The indicators on company level and the company risk indicator show that the strategy suggestions of BCG fail in the case of atypical reactions of competitors in duopoly markets.

Company strategy tests: limitations of the BCG fixed cutoff point strategy in a depression

With the company strategy test set, we examine the influence of different portfolio positioning strategies on the development of the diversified company. The exogenous product life cycles are assumed to be the same for both tests, and we also assume that a depression of the whole economy negatively influences the market growth rates in all markets.

Fig. 10. The development of the turnover of the conglomerate in the case of typical and atypical reactions of competitor

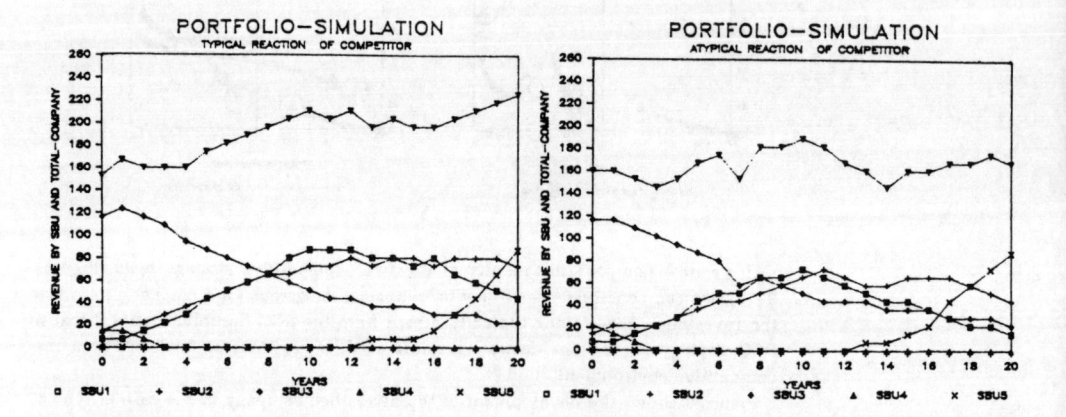

Fig. 11. Comparison of the consequences of different competitive strategy tests

	Behavior of Competitors	
	Portfolio-typical	Portfolio-atypical
PORTFOLIO STRUCTURE, YEAR = 20		
SBU 1	Solid Cash Cow position	Divested as a Poor Dog
SBU 2	Solid Cash Cow position	Tends to be a Poor Dog
SBU 3	Solid Cash Cow position	Solid Cash Cow position
SBU 5	Star/Cow perspective	Star/attacked by competition
INDICATORS ON COMPANY LEVEL, YEAR = 20		
Sales	DM 230 million/month	DM 180 million/month (= −25%)
Workers	15,000 workers	11,500 workers (= −25%)
Earnings	DM 24 million/month	DM 22 million/month (= −10%)
Accumulative earnings	DM 4.6 billion	DM 3.6 billion (= −25%)
Company risk	Sales, earnings, and employment risk are divided among the SBUs	Risk concentration on SBU 5: 55% of total sales 53% of total workers 90% of total earnings

In the first company strategy test, we further assume that the company follows the fixed cutoff point strategy of BCG, i.e., classifying SBUs with a market growth rate higher than 10 percent as Question Marks or Stars and SBUs with a market growth rate lower than 10 percent as Poor Dogs or Cash Cows. We assume additionally that the competitor follows a variable cutoff point strategy, i.e., reducing its cutoff point in case of a depression. The reduction of the cutoff point is based on the average growth rate of all markets.

Figure 12 shows that the diversified company has four SBUs in the starting period, which are in the same position as they were in the first test set. The offensive strategy followed by SBU 1 increases its relative market share and leads to its positioning as Star after 4 years. The growth strategy of SBU 2 improves its relative market share in year 4. The decreasing market growth rate of SBU 2 leads to its positioning as Cash Cow in year 12. The shift of SBU 1 and SBU 2 from Star to Cash Cow positions is a result of the fixed cutoff point strategy of the company and the decrease in the market growth rates of these two markets. The positioning of SBU 1 and SBU 2 as Cash Cows causes a change from growth strategies to defensive strategies for both businesses. The competitor, in contrast, reduces its cutoff point because of the declining market growth rates and positions SBU 1 and SBU 2 as Stars in period 144. The competitor therefore follows offensive strategies in SBU 1 and SBU 2.

The competitor wins market shares in these two markets with its offensive strategies. After 20 years SBU 1 and SBU 2 are therefore close to Poor Dog positions. SBU 4 is divested in year 12. There are also no investments in SBU 5 because of its small market growth rate and the relatively high cutoff point defined by the company. SBU 3 is after 20 years also in a Poor Dog position. After 20 years the company has only three SBUs; two of them are Poor Dogs and one is on its way to becoming a Poor Dog.

We have changed only one assumption in the second company strategy test. The company in question now also follows a variable cutoff point strategy.

Figure 13 shows that we have the same starting point as we had in the other model tests. The offensive strategies followed by SBU 1 and SBU 2 increase their relative market shares. After 8 years the company has a dominant market position in both businesses. Because of the depression of the economy the market growth rates of SBU 1 and SBU 2 decline. The decline in the market growth rate causes, because of the variable cutoff point strategy, a reduction of the cutoff point of the company, which can be seen in Figure 13. One consequence of the reduction of the cutoff point is that SBU 1 and SBU 2 are still qualified as Stars. With the growth strategies generated by the model in Star positions, the company can defend its market shares in SBU 1 and SBU 2 until the end of the simulation run.

A further implication of the reduced cutoff point strategy of the company is that SBU 5 is identified as an attractive market after 8 years and is positioned in year 12. Between year 8 and year 12, SBU 5 generates costs but no turnover. The offensive strategy followed by SBU 5 increases its relative market share and leads to its positioning as a Star in year 20. SBU 4 is in a Poor Dog position at the beginning of the simulation run and is divested in year 12. SBU 3 can defend its Cash Cow

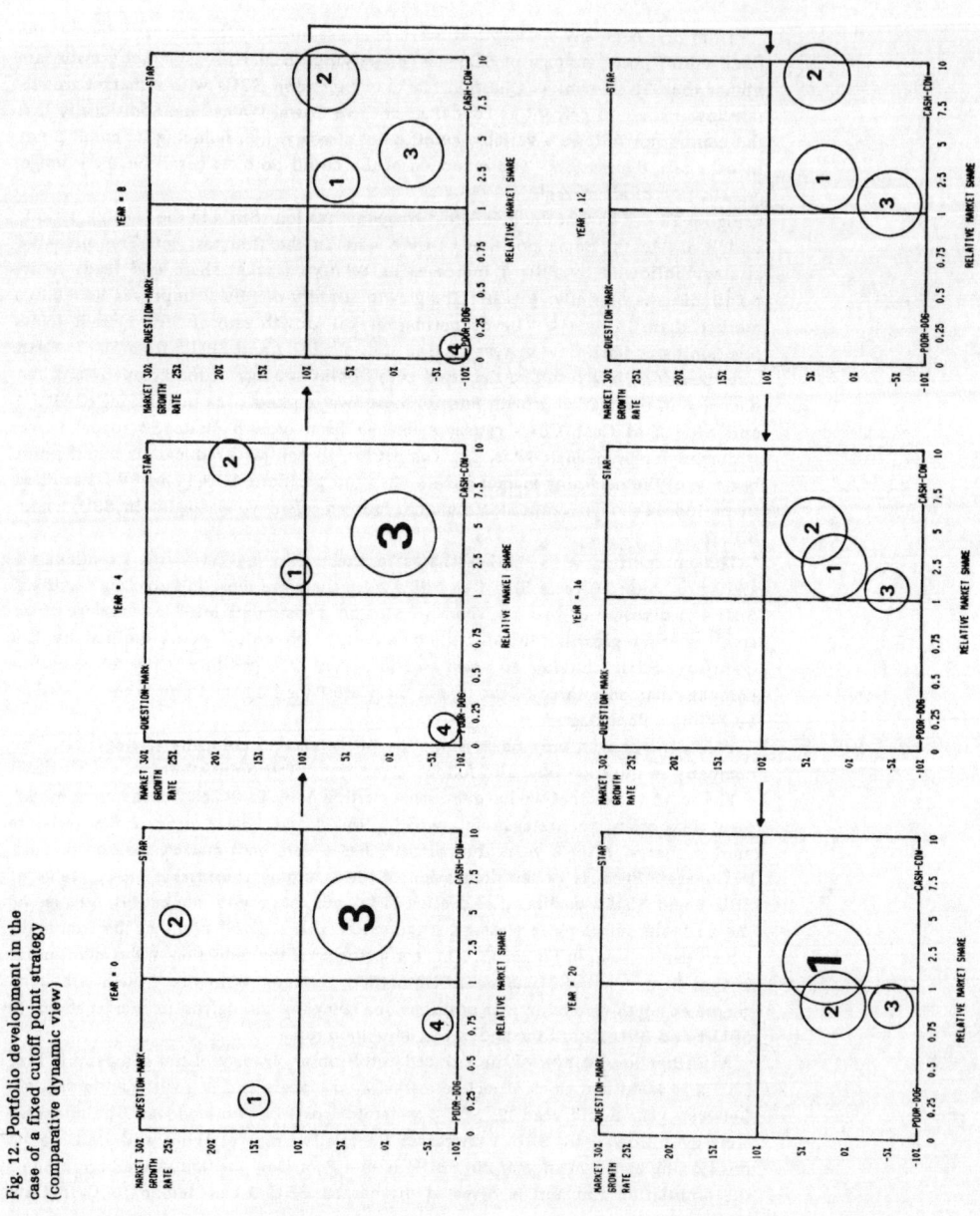

Fig. 12. Portfolio development in the case of a fixed cutoff point strategy (comparative dynamic view)

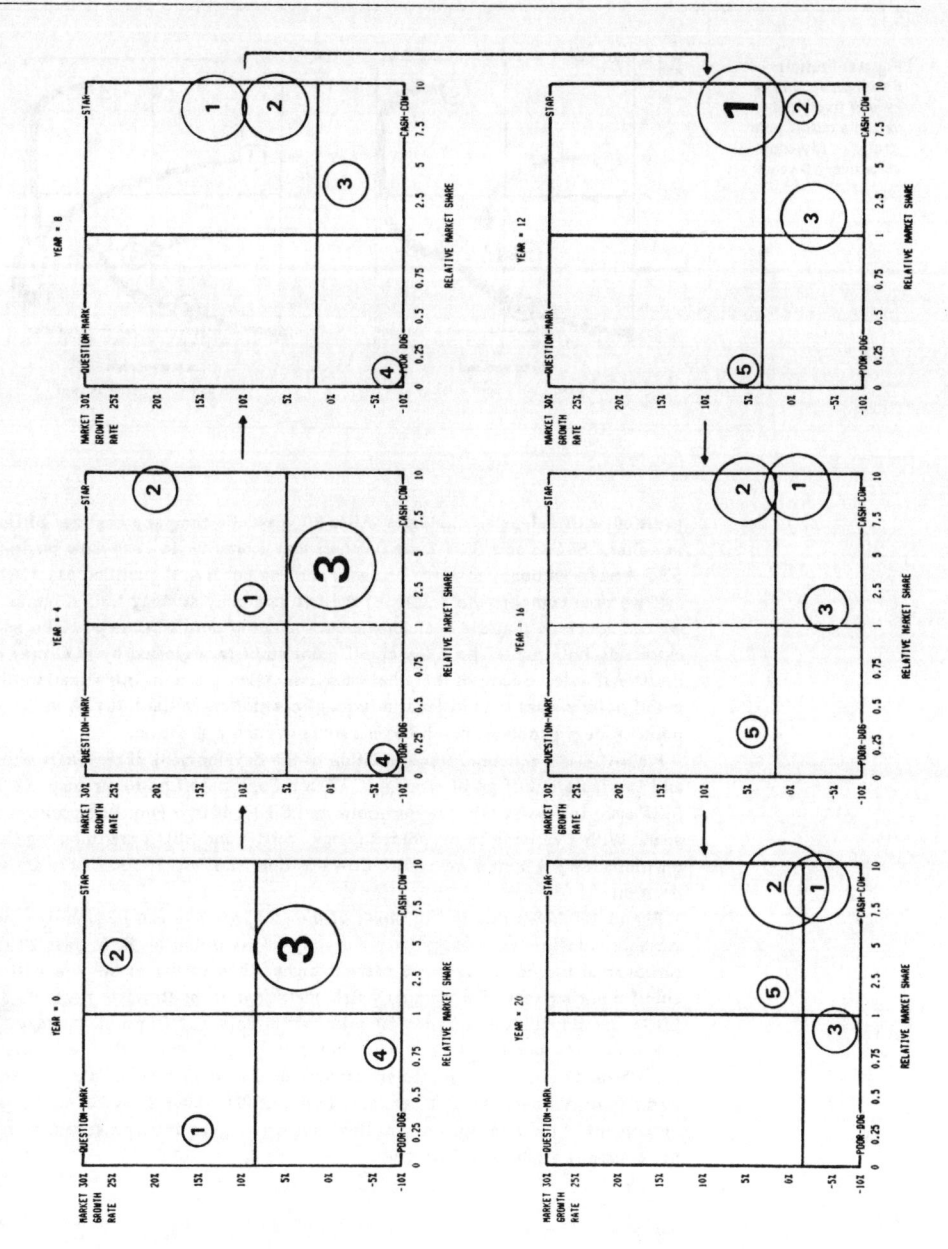

Fig. 13. Portfolio development in the case of a variable cutoff point strategy (comparative dynamic view)

Fig. 14. Portfolio development in the case of fixed and variable cutoff point strategies (dynamic view over 20 years)

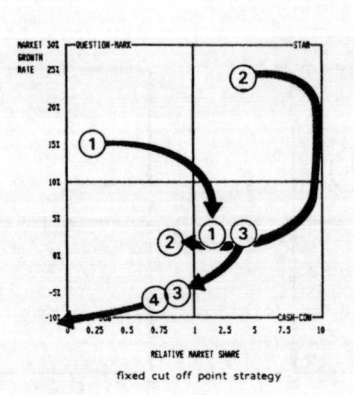

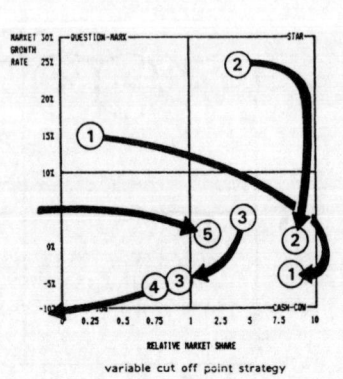

fixed cut off point strategy   variable cut off point strategy

position with defensive strategies. After 20 years the company has four SBUs: SBU 5 is a Star; SBU 1 and SBU 2 are on their way from Star to Cash Cow positions; and SBU 3 has a tendency towards being a Poor Dog but is still qualified as a Cash Cow.

If we now compare the results of the two company strategy tests (Figures 14–16), we can conclude that the decisions about the cutoff points in the portfolio matrix are extremely important. The fixed cutoff point strategy suggested by BCG may create a disaster if a depression of the whole economy takes place. In this situation, the fixed cutoff point strategy could lead to "wrong" positioning of the SBUs. A variable cutoff point strategy generates much better results in such a situation.

Figure 14 is a dynamic representation of the development of the SBUs with fixed and variable cutoff point strategies. With a fixed cutoff point strategy, SBU 1 and SBU 2 are in weak Cash Cow positions and SBU 3 is in a Poor Dog position after 20 years. With a variable cutoff point strategy, SBU 1 and SBU 2 are in strong Cash Cow positions, SBU 3 is in a weak Cash Cow position, and SBU 5 is in a normal Cash Cow position.

Figure 15 shows that the turnover of the conglomerate can be stabilized with the variable cutoff point strategy nearly exactly on its initial level. In year 20 the total turnover of the company is 55 percent higher than in the model run with a fixed cutoff point strategy. The company risk, measured at the turnover percentages of the SBUs, is distributed in year 20 with a variable cutoff point strategy. SBU 2 contributes 40 percent, SBU 1 contributes 36 percent, and SBU 3 and SBU 5 each contribute 12 percent to the total turnover of the conglomerate. With a fixed cutoff point strategy, there is a risk concentration on SBU 1 after 20 years. SBU 1 generates 50 percent of the total turnover of the company. Figure 16 summarizes the results of the company strategy tests.

Fig. 15. The development of the turnover of the conglomerate in the case of fixed and variable cutoff point strategies

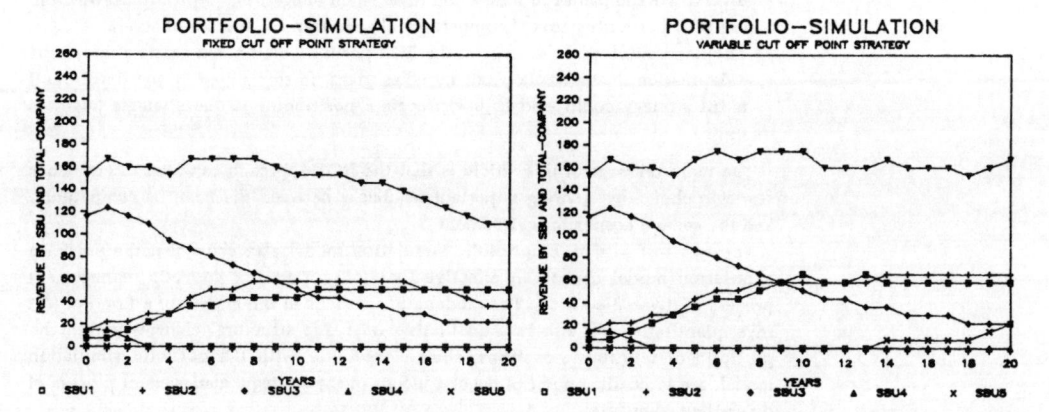

Fig. 16. Comparison of the consequences of different company strategies

	Company Strategy	
	Fixed cutoff point	Variable cutoff point
PORTFOLIO STRUCTURE, YEAR = 20		
SBU 1	Weak Cash Cow position	Solid Cash Cow position
SBU 2	Developing into a Poor Dog position	Solid Cash Cow position
SBU 3	Developing into a Poor Dog position	Tends to be a Poor Dog
SBU 4	Poor Dog/disinvested	Poor Dog /disinvested
SBU 5		Cash Cow position
INDICATORS ON COMPANY LEVEL, YEAR = 20		
Sales	DM 102 million/month	DM 159 million/month (= +55%)
Workers	7,500 workers	11,000 workers (= +50%)
Earnings	DM 5 million/month	DM 5.7 million/month (= +12%)
Accumulative earnings	DM 3.8 billion	DM 3.2 billion (= –15%)
Company risk	Risk concentration on SBU 1	Risk is divided between SBU 1, SBU 2, and SBU 5

Conclusions

The simulations show two severe limitations of the BCG portfolio approach:

1. The simulation experiments demonstrate that it can be extremely dangerous for diversified companies to follow the investment suggestions typically drawn from the BCG portfolio matrix if competitors choose atypical courses of action.
2. The fixed cutoff point strategy of the BCG portfolio matrix can create a disaster if a depression of the whole economy takes place. In this situation, the fixed cutoff point strategy could lead to inappropriate positioning of the strategic business units.

The main message of this article is that the BCG approach can lead to erroneous strategic choice by ignoring important feedbacks between the firm, its competitors, and the general economic environment.

The two test sets of the portfolio simulation model also show that the portfolio simulation model can be an effective tool to support the portfolio management process of diversified firms. The model allows a look at the growth of a firm not just in a quantitative but also in a qualitative way. The structural changes within the portfolio of multibusiness firms, shown explicitly with the portfolio simulation model, are typically a point of major concern in the strategic management process of diversified companies.

To broaden the applicability of the portfolio simulation model it is necessary to eliminate some of its limitations. The connections between the SBUs should be represented in the model. An improved version of the model should also represent the competitive situation in duopoly markets in a complete way.

References

Forrester, J. W. 1961. *Industrial Dynamics*. Cambridge, Mass.: MIT Press.
Hax, A. C., and N. S. Majluf. 1984. *Strategic Management: An Integrative Perspective*. Englewood Cliffs, N.J.: Prentice-Hall.
Henderson, B. D. 1973. The Experience Curve Reviewed. IV. The Growth Share Matrix of the Product Portfolio. *Perspectives*, no. 135. The Boston Consulting Group, Boston, Mass.
———. 1979. *Henderson on Corporation Strategy*. Cambridge, Mass.: Abt Books.
Henderson, B. D., and A. J. Zakon. 1980. Corporate Growth Strategy: How to Develop and Implement It, 1.3–1.19. In *Handbook of Business Problem Solving*, ed. K. J. Albert. New York: McGraw-Hill.
Löffler, R., and K.-P. Wiedmann. 1985. Portfolio Simulation als Ansatzpunkt der strategischen Unternehmensplanung. Working Paper 35. Institute of Marketing, Mannheim University.
Merten, P. P. 1985. *Know-how Transfer durch multinationale Unternehmen in Entwicklungsländer: Ein System Dynamics Modell zur Erklärung und Gestaltung von Internationalisierungsprozessen der Montageindustrien*. Berlin: Erich Schmidt.
———. 1986. The Simulation of Social System Evolution With Spiral Loops. Paper presented at the MIDIT 1986 Conference on Structure, Coherence, and Chaos in Dynamical Systems, Technical University of Denmark, August 1986; also available

as Working Paper WP-1800-86, Sloan School of Managment, M.I.T., Cambridge, Mass.

Richardson, G. P., and A. L. Pugh III. 1981. *Introduction to System Dynamics Modeling With DYNAMO.* Cambridge, Mass.: MIT Press.

Simon, H. A. 1981. *The Sciences of the Artificial*, 2d ed. Cambridge, Mass.: MIT Press.

Wiedmann, K.-P., and R. Löffler. 1985. Portfolio Simulation und Portfolio Planspiele als Unterstützungssysteme der strategischen Früherkennung, 419–474. In *Strategisches Marketing*, ed. H. Raffée and K.-P. Wiedmann. Stuttgart: Poeschel.

[16]
Business Transformation: The Key to Long-Term Survival and Success

Henry Birdseye Weil and *Leon S. White*

I. Introduction

The formula has always been simple. Provide a product or service that meets a need and can be sold at a profit and you can win in the marketplace. The difficulty is that, over time, products and services must respond to changing needs, and all three are impacted by changing organizational and environmental conditions. This complex series of interactions causes products, services and needs to affect each other in ways that are often difficult to predict. Consequently, businesses often focus on and better meet the needs of their customers in the short run.

Marketplace success over long time periods – years or decades – is a more challenging goal. The old adage that you can't rest on your laurels (read successful products or services) applies. Businesses that survive and succeed over the long run appear to redefine themselves and their relationships to their suppliers and customers over and over again. Ideas like 'if it ain't broke, break it', 'mass customization', 'lean production' and 'learning organization' all speak to the dynamics and imperatives of change in the marketplace. Today's business leaders are challenged to both recognize the need for change and successfully manage business transformations.

Kanter et al.[1] provide a kind of force-field characterization of the dynamics of organizational change that pits 'direction setting' leaders of a firm against three clusters of forces that 'create motions' in and around the organization. These forces, outside the control of management, often intensify over time and, if left unattended, may lead to abrupt crises followed by radical change. The first cluster is environmental, an all-encompassing set of external forces that includes competitive, economic, political, social and physical dimensions. The second cluster is 'organic' and relates to how an organization grows and, sooner or later, declines. The third cluster is political and is characterized by power struggles within and across the borders of an organization.

Environmental forces lie beyond the walls of the organization. As businesses interact with their environments, they both undergo change. Porter[2] characterizes a firm's competitive environment in terms of five forces: 'the entry of new competitors, the threat of substitutes, the bargaining power of buyers, the bargaining power of suppliers and the rivalry among existing competitors'. He believes that the success or failure of any business depends on 'competitive advantage' which, in his view, takes the form of either cost leadership or product differentiation that commands a premium price. He maintains that managerial tools, such as value-chain analysis, allow an organization to beat back the environmental forces and create and sustain superior performance.

Kaufman,[3] on the other hand, believes that management's role in assuring the continued success of an enterprise is limited at best. He sees the environment as something akin to a fisherman's net continuously sweeping through the sea of organizational entities. Even more invidious, the net's openings change their shapes and sizes constantly. Organizations try to avoid getting caught by changing themselves to metaphorically fit through the holes. Sometimes they succeed because of their actions; other times they succeed in spite of them. Sometimes they face holes so small that nothing they do will save them. In the end, Kaufman concludes, 'the survival of some organizations for great lengths of time is largely a matter of luck; ... such longevity comes about through the workings of chance'.[4]

If a business, through skill and/or luck, escapes the environmental net, it must still deal with internal forces that can threaten its survival. Small startups may have decent balance sheets, but succumb to the absence of cash flow. Mature firms may no longer be flexible enough to make needed changes. In addition to the challenges of the environment, business leaders must successfully manage the difficulties inherent in organizational growth and aging. Decisions about what to preserve and what to change in terms of products and services, human resources, business processes, policies and procedures, values and culture, are critical to long-term survival. But, as Kaufman[5] observes, such decisions are subject to contradictory judgments, ineffective decision making and imperfect implementation. The ability of a firm's executives to deal successfully with these handicaps appears to diminish as an organization ages. Such organic difficulties may slow the ability of a business to see either the opportunity or need for change. Young firms may die from lack of fluids, particularly cash; older firms may be toppled by blindness or other severe functional rigidities and disabilities. The existence of such organic forces gives support to the idea that organizations have 'life cycles'.

In addition to environmental and life-cycle forces, political forces within an organization can also affect longevity. Political models characterize business activity in terms of the interplay of interests between groups of individuals who are or desire to be organizational stakeholders. Businesses are seldom run as democracies where votes count equally. They are organized hierarchically and directed by dominant individuals or coalitions. From time to time the organizational leadership is subject to political challenge, the resulting power struggle sometimes making business page headlines. Political battles may also occur between organizational groups vying for limited resources, between labor and management or between suppliers or customers competing for the attention of the corporation. Powerful interest groups within or related to the business may support or oppose the course charted by current leaders. Consequently, power struggles, regardless of source or location, may enhance or detract from a firm's ability to deal with environmental or organic threats to its future.

II. A Model of Business Transformation

The central task of management is to contend with these three clusters of forces. In doing so, a firm's leaders are from time to time faced with the challenge of making non-incremental changes in the way they do business. Such changes may involve the development and introduction of new products or services and the phasing out of old ones, a global expansion of market territory, a merger with a former competitor or, more generally, any large-scale change required to meet a major environmental shift. The central character of such changes is that they are perceived to be needed to maintain the growth curve of the organization. If such changes are made successfully, sales and profits will continue to increase at satisfactory rates or a downturn will be reversed. When such changes fail to achieve their objectives, a firm's prospects dim. We shall refer to changes of this magnitude as *business transformations*.

The complexities of a business transformation are great and the stakes are extremely high. Success comes to the minority of companies that proceed correctly and confidently, learn effectively as they go, and make the necessary mid-course corrections. Failure can be the result of a misbegotten strategy or hesitation and lack of commitment. Business history is clear on this point. Very few major corporations successfully 'reinvent' themselves. Most either never see the need or can't pull it off.

Several leading companies in the financial services. telecommunications, aerospace and energy industries have used new planning approaches that stimulate systematic consideration of the requirements for transforming their current business and the process by which such fundamental changes can be achieved. Their planning combines the use of scenarios and simulation modeling. Scenario development is recognized as an effective means for anticipating shifts in competitive, market, technological, economic, political and social factors. Simulation modeling can make major contributions to strategy formulation, analysis of complex markets, risk assessment and contingency planning. The synergy between the two methodologies is very powerful, not only in analytical terms, but more importantly in impacting the thinking of executives involved in the process.

The formal process of scenario development and use is closely associated with the Shell group.[6] The motivation came from a study of businesses that survived and prospered over very long periods of time. The common denominator of their longevity was an unusual ability to adapt, quite often in radical ways, to major changes in their environments. Effective organizational learning was the key to their ability to adapt. Looking to the future, Arie de Geus (then Planning Coordinator at Shell) concluded: 'The ability to learn faster than your competitors may be the only sustainable competitive advantage'.[7]

Porter[8] defined a ten-step process for developing and using scenarios. It is very significant that the first three steps involve a systematic microeconomic analysis of the industry in question. What is its structure? How does it function? What are the major uncertainties that might affect the industry? What are the sources of these uncertainties? To address these questions, managers must rely on some type of model. A later step requires managers to project the competitive situation under each scenario. How are they to do this? Again, some type of model is needed. And the final step – monitoring key factors to anticipate changes in the industry – depends on an ability to identify valid 'leading indicators', to interpret their movements correctly and to know when to act. Here, too, managers inevitably employ some type of model.

Most managers rely on their professional knowledge and experience, organized as informal, qualitative, 'mental models'. These models should not be denigrated. They can be sophisticated and remarkably insightful. Important business decisions are based on such models every day. Nonetheless, mental models have serious weaknesses. They become increasingly deficient as problems grow more complex, as the environment changes more rapidly and as more people participate in key decisions. The alternative is to use some type of formal model. System dynamics models of the type described by Forrester,[9] Roberts,[10] Lyneis[11], Sterman[12] and Weil[13] are well suited for dealing with the issues of business transformation.

Such models can be used to:

- identify particularly significant sources of uncertainty and risk in the business environment;
- quantify the effect on the company's business performance of scenarios involving changes in these factors;
- test the consequences of alternative competitive strategies (including quite radical departures from 'business as usual') under various scenarios;
- define major requirements for transforming the business and the window of opportunity for achieving these changes;
- evaluate alternative strategies for achieving business transformation objectives;
- establish realistic performance targets for both the current core business and the new business;
- communicate the reasons for transforming the business, what to expect and what is at stake to employees, shareholders and government officials;
- develop 'leading indicators' of major changes in a company's business environment; and
- assess progress in the transformation process and the need for mid-course corrections.

Scenarios consider multiple futures and force unconventional thinking. They can cause a team of senior managers to be more creative about important aspects of the business. And in so doing, they can change the mentality of those managers. Scenario building requires managers to take a more coherent view of their business and the environment outside the company. The simulation model can help them to acquire this view.

Take, for example, the important question of how fundamental changes in the delivery and financing of health care in the US might impact a major provider of health insurance. Unlike many other countries, in the US large amounts of health services are paid for by private employer-sponsored plans which are sold and administered by large insurance companies. There is general agreement that 'managed care' is the wave of the future, i.e., a substantially different relationship among insurers, health care providers (physicians, hospitals, diagnostic laboratories, drug companies, etc.), employers and individual consumers, aimed at controlling costs.

But far more specifically, how fast is the managed care sector likely to grow? And therefore how quickly will the traditional health insurance business decline? As it covers a larger fraction of the population, how will the costs and profitability of managed care change? What will happen to the costs and profitability of the traditional business? How quickly does a player in the managed care business have to build market share to achieve economies of scale, a competitive cost structure and an appropriate return on the huge investments required to get into this game? What are the implications of moving too slowly? Is it possible to move too quickly? And most basically, how can a dominant company in the traditional health insurance business emerge as a leader in a radically different business?

A simulation model along the lines shown in Figures 1 and 2 was developed by the authors to assist a major US health insurance company with these issues of business transformation. It was developed using system dynamics in close collaboration with a team of managers responsible for the company's business strategy. The model represents the determinants of market

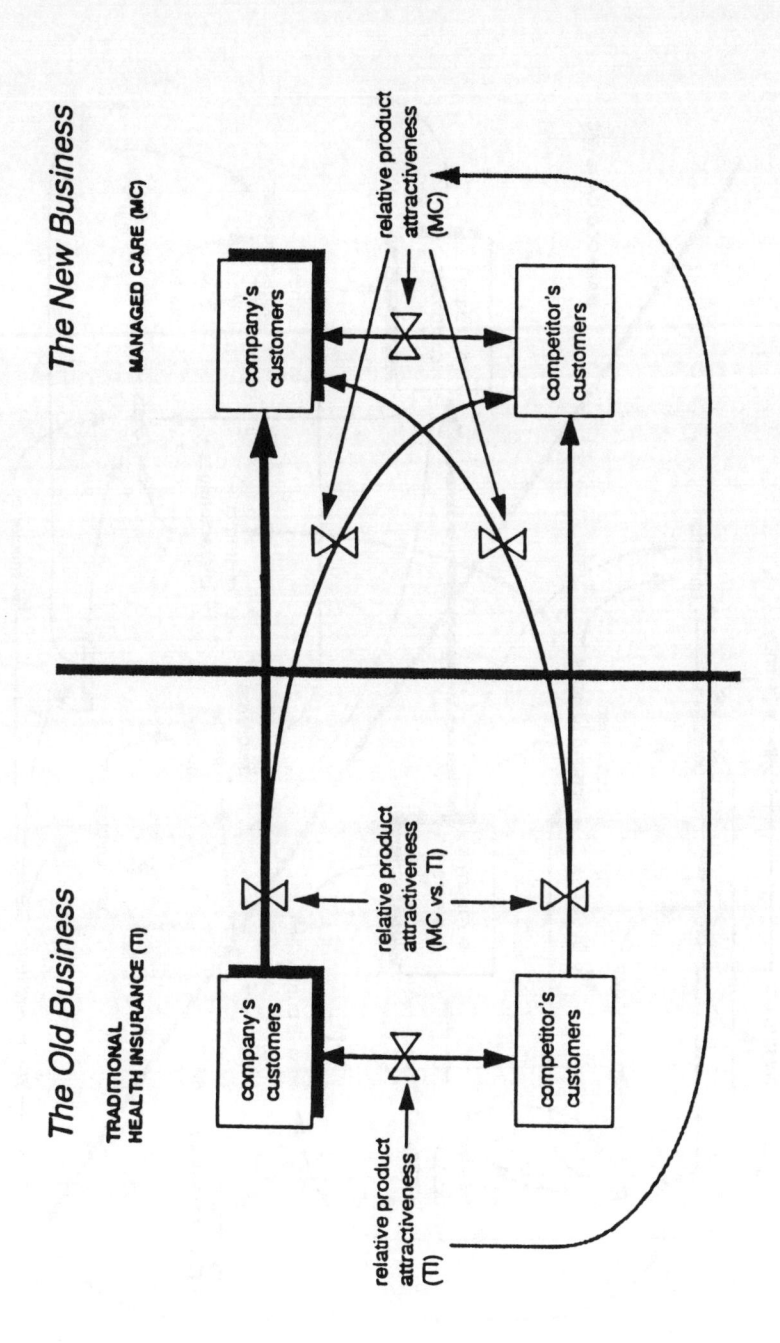

Figure 1 A model of business transformation – the flow of customers

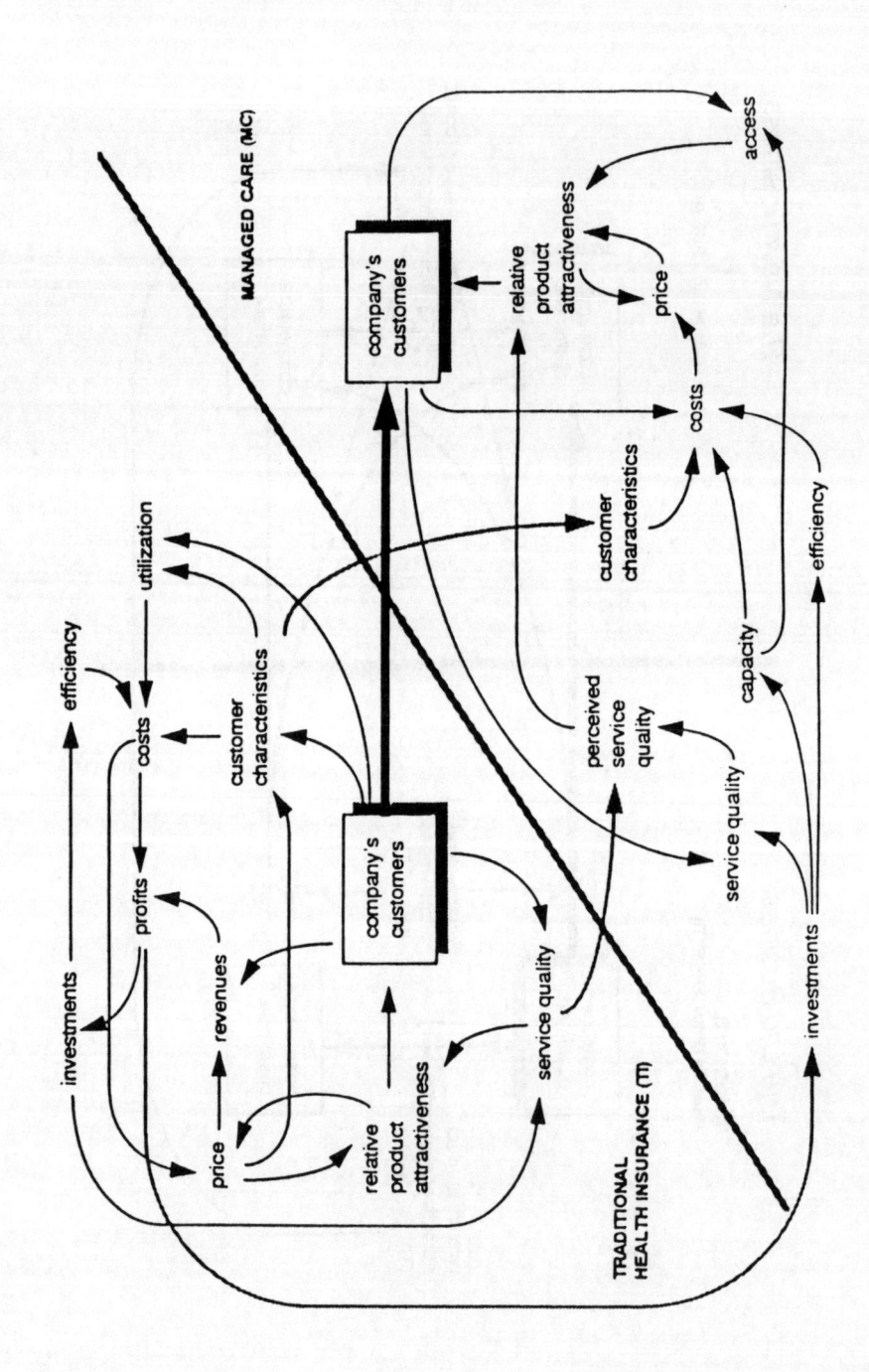

Figure 2 Key links between the old and new businesses

shares and profits in both the traditional business and managed care. Especially important parts of the model are:

- the components of product attractiveness, i.e., prices, service quality and access to health care providers;
- customers and their characteristics, retention or loss, and consumption of health services;
- investments in service quality, cost efficiency and building networks of health care providers; and
- the revenues and expenses associated with both businesses.

The model incorporates information from a wide range of sources. Financial data were used to establish cost factors, initialize the model and calibrate important parameters. Expert judgments from participating managers were used initially to quantify cause/effect relationships, e.g., the effects of product attractiveness on market shares. The calibration process then refined those estimates. The model also incorporates descriptions from senior executives of the company's management policies in areas such as pricing, investment and service standards. Key inputs come from scenarios regarding competitive conditions in both markets, changing customer and employer attitudes, the behavior of health care providers and government regulations.

Notice in Figures 1 and 2 the important flows and feedbacks that link the two businesses. In the simplest of terms, business transformation involves quite different but interdependent beings living together under the same corporate roof – the company's traditional core business and the one(s) into which it is transitioning. As with parents and children, there are inevitable culture gaps, paradigm disconnects, friction and frustrations. Thus there are many pressures to compartmentalize the business into the 'old' and the 'new', and for the new parts to be seen as exciting and glamorous while the old parts stagnate.

In fact, the strategic imperatives are quite different. Successful transformation depends, more than anything else, on capturing synergy between the current business and the business of the future. Specifically, the new business must effectively exploit key assets of the current business rather than ignoring or, worse, destroying them. The strategic role of the core business is to conserve those assets and, at the appropriate time, to pass them on.

Most of the key assets for business transformation do not appear on the company's balance sheet. They fall into several categories.

- *Market assets* — A substantial fraction of the current customer base should become customers for the new business. The alternative of building a new customer base is slower, more costly and riskier. The same holds for reputation and image. Letting quality slide in the core business will be devastating for the transformation process. Current customers and other potential customers of the new business will extrapolate their dissatisfaction, and what might have been an asset will become a major liability. An important element of a transformation strategy may well be a deliberate campaign to improve quality in the 'old' business.
- *Financial assets* — For a long time the traditional core business will be the primary source of the company's profits and cash flow. Indeed, it will bankroll the product and

service developments, new facilities, market penetration and start-up losses associated with the new business. Hence the structural profitability and cash-generating power of the core business must be preserved for as long as possible. This may well mean substantial on-going investments in cost reduction and product improvements in the business the company intends to de-emphasize.
- *Human assets* — To the greatest extent possible, a company must carry its workforce with it through the process of business transformation. These critical assets embody all the experience, know-how and competencies of the company. They represent an enormous investment. It is essential that the transformation process does not inadvertently undermine staff morale and productivity, cause many of the best people to leave, de-skill the company or work counter to drives for improved efficiency and quality.

These principles are illustrated with results from the model in the section which follows.

III. Strategies for Business Transformation

The computer simulation model described in the preceding section was used to test a range of strategies for business transformation. The ideas behind these tests and the key results are described below. First, however, it is necessary to establish a 'Base Case', i.e., the outlook for the company assuming a continuation of its current business strategy and management policies.

The Base Case

Figure 3 shows market shares in the traditional and new business areas. For the insurance company in question, these correspond to the traditional indemnity-type health plans (characterized by rather loose control of health care consumption and costs) and the managed care plans which are replacing them (a range of systems that all seek proactively to control the costs of health care). The company, once overwhelmingly dominant in the market, sees its 'traditional' share decline from about 65% to less than 20% over a 20-year period. However, its 'new' share never gets much above 20%. During this time, the traditional market shrinks to about one-fifth of what it was at the start of the simulation. While profits grow in nominal terms, real (deflated) profitability is stagnant until the later years of the simulation. The company is in serious trouble. Its traditional market is shrinking steadily in size and profitability. And the company has only moderate success in the rapidly developing new business area.

The underlying problem is evident in Figures 4 and 5. Product attractiveness is an index that combines components of the company's competitive position. In the traditional market, product attractiveness depends on relative price and service quality, with different weightings for various customer segments (e.g., young, healthy customers who do not expect to require non-routine care are quite price sensitive) and competitive situations (e.g., a large price differential will make relative service far less significant). The situation in the new business is more complex. Product attractiveness is a function of relative price and service, plus 'access', that is, the customer's choice and convenience in obtaining health care (e.g., proximity of providers, waiting times, ability to use providers of choice). Figure 4 shows the company's

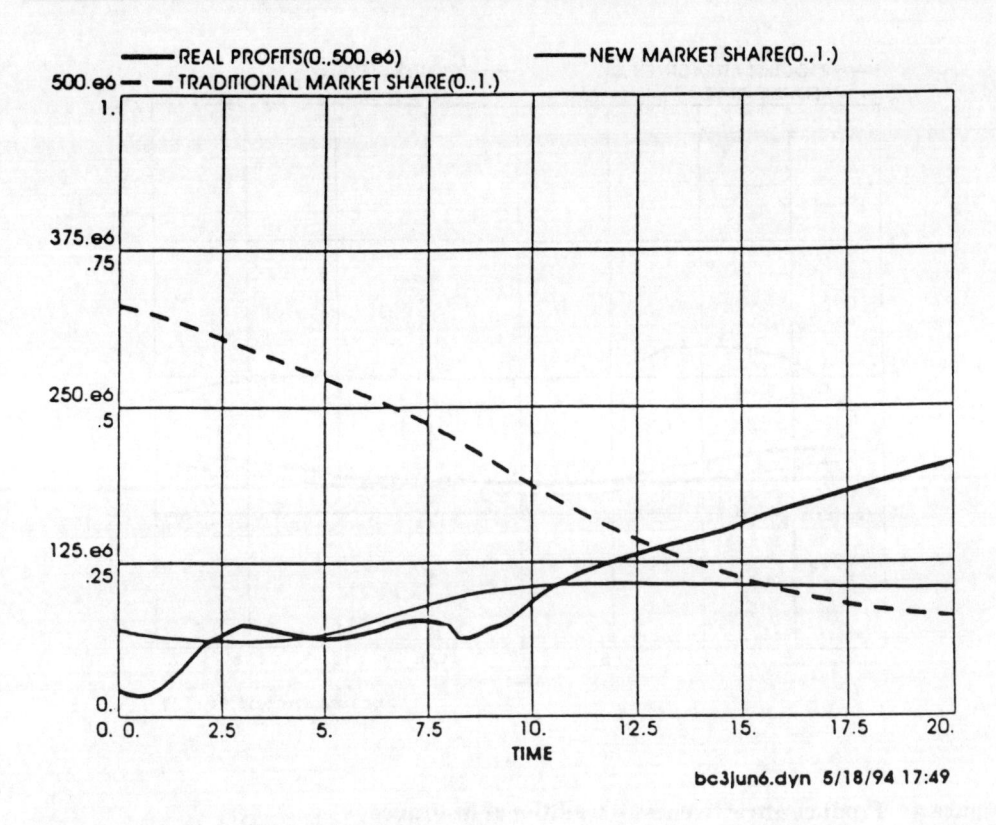

Figure 3 Overall performance measures

situation in its traditional market. Product attractiveness is below 1.0 during the entire period, causing continual loss of market share. Relative price obviously is a major problem. This is partially offset by a service quality advantage between years 2 and 7. Once the service advantage is lost, product attractiveness declines further and the loss of share accelerates. There is no practical way for the company to eliminate the price disadvantage, as it has (by a large margin) the highest cost structure; wherever it lowers prices, competitors can under-price.

Turning now to Figure 5, the company's product attractiveness in the new market initially is great but erodes rapidly after year 5 and later stabilizes slightly below 1.0. Unlike the traditional market where the company has a price disadvantage, here relative price is about 1.0 (i.e., very close to competitors' prices). For a period of time, the company gains significant competitive advantage from both service quality and access. By year 10, however, the service advantage has nearly disappeared and access has become a problem. What is going wrong for the company?

Delving deeper into the details of the simulation reveals a complicated set of causes. To summarize, the company is falling victim to:

- *Excessive caution* — The company's growth objectives and investment plans for the

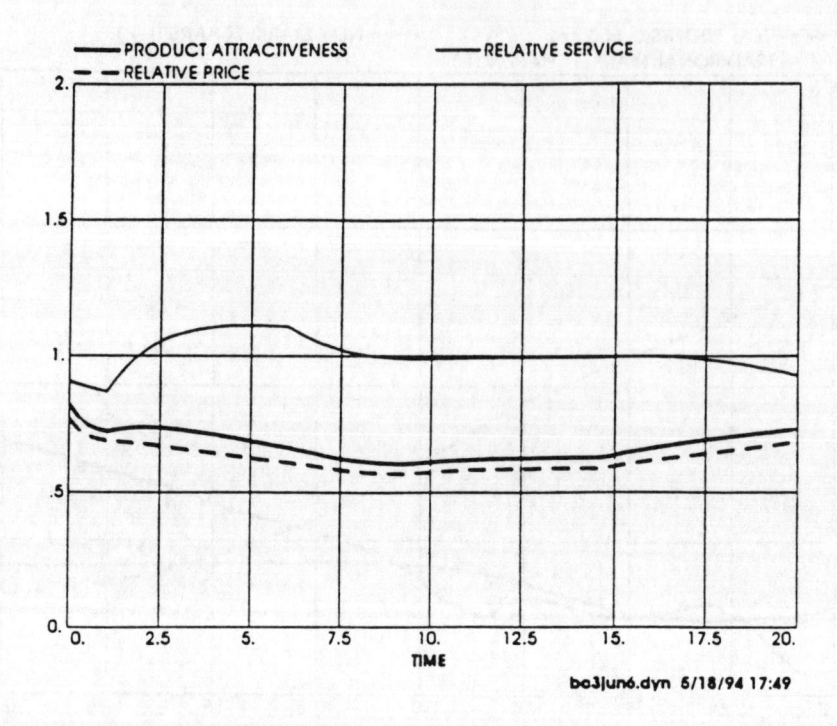

Figure 4 Product attractiveness – traditional insurance

new business seem ambitious, but actually translate into an assumed capture of only one out of three of their 'traditional' customers who shift to the new market. After an initial roll-out of service and access capacity, the company's planning simply reacts to the growth in customers actually achieved.
- *Self-fulfilling forecasts* — The service and access capacity put in place by the company ends up determining how many customers it can handle before relative service quality and relative access slip below 1.0. At that point, growth of market share slows and then stops. In the absence of continued growth in customers, the company's very cautious investment policies hold capacity approximately constant. This causes market share in the new business to stabilize.
- *Prematurely writing off the traditional business* — With the size and profitability of the traditional business steadily eroding, the company sees no reason to continue to invest in that area. The new business is growing in both size and profits; it commands the big investments. This narrow view of priorities fails to recognize that the traditional business remains the predominate generator of cash flow for many years; moreover, the company's reputation for service quality in that area strongly affects its capture of customers for the new business.

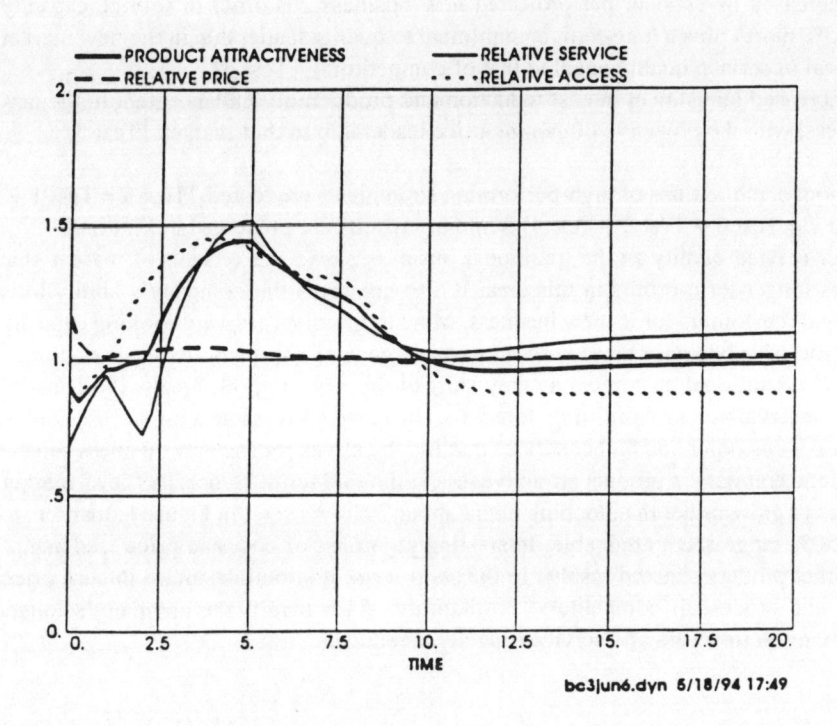

Figure 5 Product attractiveness – managed care

Alternative Strategies

Diagnosis of the Base Case simulation suggested a number of potential improvements in the company's strategy. What if the company focused on increasing its product attractiveness in the traditional market and capturing most of its customers as they shifted to the new market? What if the company set more ambitious targets and invested more aggressively in building its new business area? What if the company did both simultaneously?

To investigate these questions, a wide range of simulation tests were performed. The tests which produced the most interesting results are listed below.

- Increase desired service quality in the traditional business substantially (e.g., by 50%) and do not deliberately phase down quality as market share and profits in this area decline. [Test 1]
- Plan capacity in the new business area based on projected loss of customers in the traditional market and on a very aggressive target (e.g., 70%) for capturing them for the new business. [Test 2]
- Increased investment per projected new business customer in access capacity (e.g., 25% more). [Test 3]

- Increased investment per projected new business customer in service capacity (e.g., 25% more) plus a long-term commitment to quality leadership in the new market (vs. a goal of service quality equal to that of competitors). [Test 4]
- Increased investment in cost reduction and productivity enhancement in the new business, with the objective of gaining price leadership in that market. [Test 5]

In addition, combinations of high-performing strategies were tested. [Test 6 = Test 1 + Test 2 and Test 7 = Test 6 + Test 3 + Test 4] Summary results are presented in Figure 6.

Higher service quality in the traditional business slows the erosion of market share and improves longer-term profits in this area. It also enhances the company's ability to capture 'traditional' customers for its new business. More aggressive, forward-looking capacity planning in the new business area, with an explicit goal of capturing two out of three of the company's traditional customers as they shift to the new market, breaks the constraints of overly conservative, self-fulfilling forecasts. Increased investment in access and service capacity per customer and higher service quality objectives for the new business substantially improve the company's product attractiveness in the mid term. Hence, its 'new' market share continues to grow rather than topping out at about 20%. As seen in Figure 6, market shares in the 40–50% range seem attainable. Interestingly, pursuit of cost and price leadership in the new market produces mixed results. In the short term, it stimulates more intense price competition and erodes all competitors' profitability. As a result, the company's longer-term ability to invest in access and service capacity is reduced.

TEST	Year 10 Profits	Old Share	New Share	Year 15 Profits	Old Share	New Share
1	$59m	.40	.15	$125m	.29	.15
2	$112m	.38	.28	$202m	.23	.29
3	$120m	.37	.28	$214m	.22	.32
4	$152m	.37	.35	$314m	.22	.45
5	$60m	.38	.20	$140m	.23	.20
6	$73m	.40	.21	$169m	.28	.23
7	$116m	.39	.31	$346m	.27	.53
BASE	$90m	.37	.21	$155m	.22	.21

Figure 6 Summary of strategy test results

IV. Conclusions

As noted, very few major corporations successfully 'reinvent' themselves. Many do not understand the need. Others do not understand how. The strategic imperatives discussed in Section II are clearly illustrated by the simulation model: capturing the synergy between the current business and the business of the future; effectively exploiting key assets of the current business; conserving those assets and passing them on to the new business.

The simulation results point to several conclusions that seem to have general applicability:

- maintain product attractiveness in the core business, relying particularly on service quality rather than price competition;
- aim to capture a large percentage of core business customers with the new business;
- set market share targets for the new business consistent with an aggressive customer capture goal;
- roll out enough capacity to attract and generously satisfy expected demand;
- build product attractiveness in the new business based on capacity and service quality, not price;
- cost reduction and leadership are more important in the traditional core business, where margins are under greater pressure, than in the new business area;
- substantial sacrifice of near-term profitability is required to launch the new business 'properly' because of the need for aggressive investment in anticipation of volume growth; and
- delay and/or moderate price competition in the new business area for as long as possible, to slow 'commoditization' and enhance returns on the large investments required for successful transformation.

It may be time for companies to consider supporting permanent business transformation activities such as we have described. The business transformation group could play a role similar to that of the loyal opposition in a political system. Members would continually question the current attributes of corporate success. Their activity would be based on the premise that today's products and services will not assure long-term survival. Management would look to the business transformation group to challenge existing paradigms. The group could build scenarios and simulation models similar to those described above that raise the most difficult questions regarding current strategic thinking. They would engage the leadership in a continuing strategic dialogue aimed at anticipating and overcoming the destructive forces that could jeopardize the organization's future. A small investment in such boat-rocking activity could keep the corporate ship from sinking prematurely.

References

1. R.M. Kanter, B.A. Stein and T.D. Jick, *The Challenge of Organizational Change* (New York: The Free Press, 1992).
2. M.E. Porter, *Competitive Advantage* (New York: The Free Press, 1985), p. 4.
3. H. Kaufman, *Time, Chance, and Organizations*, 2nd edn (Chatham, NJ: Chatham House Publishers, 1991).
4. Kaufman (1991), p. 67.
5. Kaufman (1991).
6. P. Wack, 'Scenarios: Uncharted Waters Ahead', *Harvard Business Review*, September/October 1985, p. 72. P. Wack, 'Scenarios: Shooting the Rapids', *Harvard Business Review*, November/December 1985, p. 139. A.P. de Geus, 'Planning as Learning', *Harvard Business Review*, March/April 1988, p. 70.

7. A.P. de Geus (1988), p. 71.
8. M.E. Porter (1985), p. 449.
9. J. Forrester, *Industrial Dynamics* (Cambridge: MIT Press, 1961).
10. E.B. Roberts (ed.), *Managerial Applications of System Dynamics* (Cambridge: MIT Press, 1978).
11. J.M. Lyneis, *Corporate Planning and Policy Design: A System Dynamics Approach* (Cambridge: MIT Press and Pugh-Roberts Associates, Inc., 1980).
12. J.D. Sterman, 'Modeling Managerial Behavior: Misperceptions of Feedback in a Dynamic Decision Making Experiment', *Management Science*, 35 (1989), p. 321.
13. H.B. Weil and K.P. Veit, 'Corporate Strategic Thinking: The Role of System Dynamics' in P.M. Milling and E.O.K. Zahn (eds), *Computer-Based Management of Complex Systems* (Berlin: Springer-Verlag, 1989).

PRELAUNCH FORECASTING OF NEW AUTOMOBILES*

GLEN L. URBAN, JOHN R. HAUSER AND JOHN H. ROBERTS

*Sloan School of Management, Massachusetts Institute of Technology,
Cambridge, Massachusetts 02139*
*Sloan School of Management, Massachusetts Institute of Technology,
Cambridge, Massachusetts 02139*
University of New South Wales, Kensington, New South Wales, Australia

> This paper develops and applies a prelaunch model and measurement system to the marketing planning of a new automobile. The analysis addresses active search by consumers, dealer visits, word-of-mouth communication, magazine reviews, and production constraints—issues that are important in understanding consumer response to durable goods. We address these issues with a detailed consumer flow model which monitors and projects key consumer transitions in response to marketing actions. A test-vs.-control consumer clinic provides data which, with judgment and previous experience, are used to "calibrate" the model to fit the sales history of the control car. We illustrate how the model evolved to meet management needs and provided suggestions on advertising, dealer training, and consumer incentives. Comparison of the model's predictions to actual sales data suggests reasonable accuracy when an implemented strategy matches the planned strategy.
> (MARKETING—NEW PRODUCTS, PRODUCT POLICY, MEASUREMENT)

Consumer durable goods purchases (e.g., appliances, autos, cameras) represent a huge market, but relatively few management science models have been successfully implemented in this area of business. In this paper we attack the marketing problems of a subset of the durables market—automobiles—in an effort to understand the challenging issues in marketing durables and how they can be modeled.

Our purpose is to describe a model and measurement system developed for and used by the automobile industry managers. The system forecasts the life-cycle of a new car before introduction and develops improved introductory strategies. Such models are applied widely in frequently purchased consumer goods markets based on test marketing (see Urban and Hauser 1980, pp. 429–447 for a review) and on pre-test market measures (e.g., Silk and Urban 1978; Pringle, Wilson, and Brody 1982; and Urban and Hauser 1980, pp. 386–411). But standard models must be modified for premarket forecasting of new consumer durable goods such as an automobile.

After briefly highlighting some important modeling challenges in applications to autos, we describe two modeling approaches to forecasting the launch of a new model car offered by General Motors. We extend existing models for production constraints and measure customer reactions after conditional information that simulates word-of-mouth and trade press input; but our emphasis is on how state-of-the-art science models can be used to affect major managerial decisions.

Challenges in Modeling Automobiles

Automobiles represent a very large market; sales in the 1988 model year were over 100 billion dollars in the U.S. and over 300 billion world wide. A new car can contribute over one billion dollars per year in sales if it sells a rather modest 100,000 units per year at an average price of $12,000 per car. Major successes can generate several times this in sales and associated profits.

---

* Accepted by Jehoshua Eliashberg; received October 2, 1987. This paper has been with the authors 6 months for 2 revisions.

These potential rewards encourage firms to allocate large amounts of capital to design, production, and selling of a new model. Ford spent three billion dollars developing the Taurus/Sable line (Mitchell 1986). General Motors routinely spends one billion dollars on a new model such as the Buick Electra. Most of this investment occurs before launch; if the car is not a market success, significant losses result.

Rates of failure are not published for the auto industry, but many cars have fallen short of expectations. Most failures are not as dramatic as the Edsel which was withdrawn from the market, but significant losses occur in two ways. When sales are below forecasts there is excess production capacity and inventories. In this case, capital costs are excessive and prices must be discounted or other marketing actions undertaken to clear inventories. Losses also occur when the forecast of sales is below the market demand. In this case not enough cars can be produced, inventories are low, and prices are firm. The car is apparently very profitable, but a large opportunity cost may be incurred. Profits could have been higher if the forecast had been more accurate and more production capacity had been planned.

For those readers unfamiliar with the automobile industry we describe a few facts that will become important in our application.

Consumer Response

Search and Experience. In automobiles, consumers reduce risk by searching for information and, in particular, visit showrooms. Typically 75 percent of buyers test drive one or more cars. The marketing manager's task is to convince the consumer to consider the automobile, get the prospect into the showroom, and facilitate purchasing with test drives and personal selling efforts.

Word-of-Mouth Communication/Magazine Reviews. One source of information about automobiles is other consumers. Another is independent magazine reviews such as *Consumer Reports* and *Car and Driver*. Given the thousands of dollars involved in buying a car, the impact of these sources is quite large.

Importance of Availability. Eighty percent of domestic sales are "off the lot," i.e., purchased from dealer's inventory. Many consumers will consider alternative makes and models if they cannot find a car with the specific features, options, and colors they want.

Managerial Issues

No Test Market. Building enough cars for test marketing (say, 1,000 cars) requires a full production line that could produce 75,000 units. Once this investment is made, the "bricks and mortar" are in place for a national launch and the major element of risk has been borne. Therefore, test marketing is not done in the auto industry.

Replace Existing Model Car. Occasionally the auto industry produces an entirely new type of car (for example, Chrysler's introduction of the Minivan), but the predominant managerial issue is a major redesign of a car line such as the introduction of a downsized, front-wheel drive Buick Electra to replace its larger, rear-wheel drive predecessor.

When the management issue is a redesign, the sales history of its predecessor provides important information for forecasting consumer response to the replacement. Even when no direct replacement is planned, say, the introduction of the two-seated Buick Reatta, the sales history of related cars such as the Toyota Supra provides anchors to forecasts.

Production Constraints. The production capacity level must be set before any actual market sales data can be collected. Once the production line has been built, production is limited to a rather narrow range. The maximum is the plant capacity (e.g., two shifts with the machines in the plant and their maintenance requirements) and the minimum is one eight-hour shift of production unless the plant is shut down completely.

The need to make production commitments early in the new product development process produces a two-stage sequence of decisions. First, a market strategy is developed, advanced engineering specification and designs are created, consumer reaction is gauged, and a GO or NO GO production commitment is made. See, for example, Hauser and Clausing (1988). Because of the long construction times, this usually occurs three or more years before introduction. As market launch nears (24 months or less), the second set of decisions is made. A premarket forecast is generated and a revised marketing plan (e.g., targeting, positioning, advertising copy and expenditure, price, promotion, and dealer training) is formulated. In the first decision, production level is a variable, but in the prelaunch forecasting phase (the focus of this paper) the capacity constraints are taken as given.

"*Price*" *Forecasting Problem*. Production capacity is based on the best information available at the time, but as engineering and manufacturing develop the prototype cars, details change as do external conditions in the economy. At the planned price and marketing levels consumers may wish to purchase more or fewer vehicles than will be produced. The number of vehicles that would be sold if there were no production constraints is known as "free expression." Naturally, free expression is pegged to a price and marketing effort.

If the free expression demand at a given level of price and marketing effort is less than the production minimum, the company and its dealers must find a way to sell more cars (e.g., target new markets or change price, promotion, dealer incentives, and advertising). If the forecast is in the range, marketing variables can be used to maximize profit with little constraint. If free expression demand is above the maximum production, then opportunities exist to increase profit by adjusting price, reducing advertising, or by producing cars with many optional features.

Existing Literature and Industry Practice

Marketing Science

Marketing science has a rich tradition of life-cycle diffusion models which describe durable good sales via phenomena such as innovators, imitators, and the diffusion of innovation. These models focus on major innovations such as color TV or computer memory (Bass 1969, Robinson and Lakani 1975, Mahajan and Muller 1979, Jeuland 1981, Horsky and Simon 1983, Kalish 1985, and Wind and Mahajan 1986). However, for forecasting, these models require substantial experience with national sales (Heeler and Hustad 1980). In prelaunch analysis no national sales history is available for the new auto model. Thus, the parameters for initial penetration, diffusion, and total sales over the life cycle would need to be set based on judgment, market research, or analogy to other product categories. In our application we incorporate these "data" sources, but in a model adapted to the details of consumer response and the managerial situation in the automobile industry.

One model of individual multiattribute utility, risk, and belief dynamics has been proposed for use in prelaunch forecasting of durables (Roberts and Urban 1988). This model can be parametized based on market research before launch, but our experience with this complex model suggests that it is difficult to implement and does not deal with production constraints and the "price" forecasting problem.

Industry Practice

Industry practice has included market research to obtain consumer response to new durables. In the auto industry concept tests, focus groups, perceptual mapping, conjoint analysis, and consumer "clinics" have been utilized. The clinics traditionally collect likes, dislikes, and buying intent with respect to currently available cars. After exposure to a fiber-glass mockup of a new car in a showroom setting, free-expression "diversion" from the consumer's most preferred currently-available model is measured. (That is, consumers indicate which make and model car they would have purchased. The clinics measure the percentage of these consumers who would now purchase the new car.)

These analyses are useful in very early forecasting before the production commitment, but do not include search and experience, word of mouth, magazine reviews, life-cycle dynamics, and availability constraints. Nor do such analyses incorporate *traditional* marketing science concepts such as advertising response functions. Thus, it is difficult to use these traditional clinics to identify the best marketing strategy to maximize profit within the constraints of production.

Prelaunch Forecasting Clinic Design

We build upon the marketing science literature and industry practice to address the managerial problems of prelaunch forecasting. In keeping with the magnitude of the investment and the potential profit impact of prelauch decisions, our analyses are based on a heavy commitment to measurement to get consumer-based estimates of the relevant inputs. To build upon industry experience a clinic format is used; however, we add a control group to minimize response task biases. Usually the control group sees the existing car model which is being replaced. The control group does not see the new model. If the car does not replace an old one, the most similar existing car (or cars) is used for control purposes. The model structure is based, in part, on differences between the test and control group and the (known) sales history for the control car.

We apply marketing science concepts by modelling explicitly the consumer information flow (dealer visits, word-of-mouth, advertising) and production constraints. The method we use is a probabilistic flow model called macro-flow (Urban 1970, Urban and Hauser 1980, Chapter 15). This method is a discrete time analog of a continuous time Markov process (Hauser and Wisniewski 1982a, b) and represents an expansion in the number of states and flows of diffusion models such as that by Mahajan, Muller, and Kerin (1984), which includes positive and negative word-of-mouth. We begin by describing the sampling scheme and consumer measurement.

Sampling Scheme

If cost were not an issue we would select a random sample of consumers and gauge their reactions to the test and control vehicles. However, there are a large number of automobiles available (over 200), the automobile market is highly segmented (luxury, sport, family, etc.), and automobile purchases are infrequent. Not every consumer is in the market for a car or in the right segment. Random samples would be inefficient and very expensive. (A car model can do well if every year a few tenths of one percent of the American households purchase that model.)

To balance costs and accuracy we stratify our sample by grouping consumers by car model that they purchased previously. To get a representative sample that has a good chance of being interested in the automobile category (segment) being studied, we select the sizes of the strata in proportion to past switching to the target category. For example, if 2 percent of last year's category buyers had previously purchased Volvo 700 series cars, then 2 percent of the sample is drawn from these Volvo owners. If the managerial team is interested in "conquest" outside the target category, random or targeted strata are added. The names, addresses, and telephone numbers of these consumers are available from commercial sources (e.g., R. L. Polk and Co.).

Once selected, consumers are contacted via telephone, screened on interest in purchasing an automobile in the next year, and recruited for the study. Consumers who agree to participate are scheduled to come to a central location, a clinic, for a one-hour interview. They are paid $25–50 for their participation. If both spouses participate in the decision to buy a new car, both are encouraged to come.

Basic Clinic Design

Upon arrival two-thirds of the consumers are assigned randomly to the test car group and one-third to the control car group. In both cases they are told they are evaluating next year's models. (This is believable to consumers because most year-to-year changes in an automobile model are relatively minor.) (See Figure 1 for the basic measurement design.)

After warmup and screening questions, the consumer(s) is asked to describe car(s) that he (she or they) now own, including make, model, year, miles per gallon (if known), options, maintenance costs, etc. This task puts them in a frame of mind to evaluate cars and provides valuable background information.

They are next presented with a list of the 200 or so automobile lines available, along with abridged information on price (base and "loaded" with options), fuel economy and engine size, and asked to indicate which automobiles they would consider seriously. The modal consideration set consists of about three cars; the median is five cars. In addition, they indicate the cars they feel would be their first, second, and if appropriate, third choices. They rate these cars on subjective probability scales (Juster 1966) and on a constant sum paired comparison of preferences across their first three auto choices. These questions allow us to estimate "diversion," the percent of consumers who intended to purchase another car who will now purchase the target car.

Now the experimental treatments begin. Two-thirds of the consumers are shown concept boards (or rough ad copy) for the test car in an effort to simulate advertising exposure. One-third are shown concept boards (or rough ad copy) for the control car. They rate the concept on the same probability and preference scales as the cars they now consider.

In the market, after advertising exposure, some consumers will visit showrooms for more information, others will seek word-of-mouth or magazine evaluations. Thus, as shown in Figure 1, the sample is split. One half of each test/control treatment cell sees

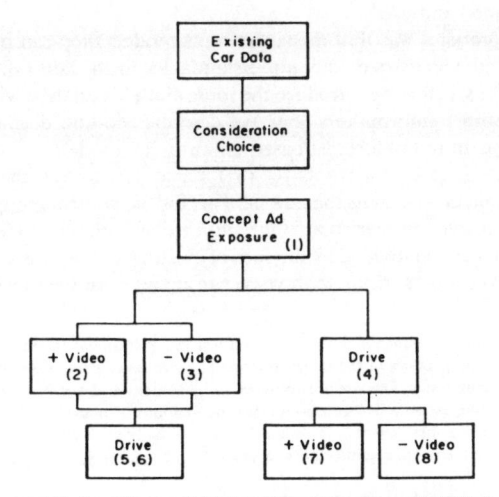

FIGURE 1. Experimental Design of Sequential Information Exposure in Clinic [(x) = Sequence Codes].

video tapes which simulate word-of-mouth[1] and evaluations which represent consumer magazine evaluations (e.g., *Consumer Reports*); the other half are allowed to test-drive the car to which they are assigned. The video treatment is divided into positive and negative exposure cells. Probability and constant-sum paired-comparison preference measures are taken for the stimulus car and the respondents' top three choices among cars now on the market. The half which saw the videotapes and magazine abstracts now test drives the car; the half which test drove is now exposed to the videotape and magazine information. Again probability and preference measures are taken. More elaborate designs can be used. For example, management needs may require splitting the sample further on two-door vs. four-door or adding measurement modules for consumer budget planning and/or conjoint analysis with respect to potential feature variations. It is also possible to split on alternative positioning strategies. All such options in the experimental design require tradeoffs with respect to sample size and length of interview. In the application we are describing, the design in Figure 1 was used.

A New Mid-Sized Car—Phase I Analysis

This application takes place in the Buick Division of General Motors. General Motors had made a strategic decision to downsize all of its luxury cars—its 1983 Electra/Park Avenue had been launched. In the fall of 1984, 18 months prior to launch, we began analysis of the next downsized car—the division's largest selling mid-sized model. Sales targets were set optimistically at 450,000 units—a 15 percent share of the mid-sized market. This represented doubling of current sales volume and a 50 percent increase in market share.

The clinic was run in Atlanta, Georgia. The sample size was 534 and drawn randomly from car registration data but stratified by current ownership: 119 from previous buyers of the target car. 139 from previous buyers of other cars from the division, 128 from other domestic cars, and 148 from imports.

Top-line Analysis

In 1970, Little studied how managers react to marketing science models. In that seminal article he proposed a "decision calculus," a set of guidelines marketing models should follow to be accepted and used.

A tenet of his proposal was that managers want models they can trust, which match their intuitions, and which are readily understandable. In the late 1980s managers have the same needs. Thus, before we introduce the more complex analysis with its probabilistic modeling of consumer information flow, we describe top-line diagnostic information from the clinic and an initial forecast based on an index model.

Our first diagnostic indicator is relative preference. Recall that the consumers rated three currently available cars plus the new car (or, for the control group, the control car) on constant-sum paired comparisons.[2] One indicator of relative preference is the preference value of the new car divided by the sum of existing and new cars. Another measure is the percent of consumers who rate the new car higher than the existing cars. We have

---

[1] The videotapes include a commentator and three consumers. Professional actors are used, but an attempt is made to match the demographics of the target market. The semantics come from earlier focus groups on prototypes of the car being tested. One script is positive in its content and another is negative. Both use the same actors. The magazine exposure is a mock-up from the fictitious "Consumer laboratories, Inc." and put in a format similar to *Consumer Reports*. The quantitative evaluations are chosen to match the qualitative video tapes. We have found through pretesting that consumers find the videotapes and magazine reports believable and realistic.

[2] A few consumers rated only two cars because that is all they considered.

found both measures give similar results, thus Table 1 reports only the relative measure. The test/control design is critical here. Exposure to concepts can be inflated (deflated) due to the specifics of the task, but such inflation should be constant across test or control. Thus, although each specific measure may be inflated, their ratio should be unbiased.

Table 1 was a disappointment to management. Although not all differences were significant, all test car values were below the control. It was clear that the test car would not do as well in terms of preference as the rear-wheel drive car it was scheduled to replace.

Furthermore, relative values of preference decrease when consumers have more information. They decrease from a ratio of 0.94 for concept only exposure to 0.88 for concept and positive word-of-mouth (wom) and magazine exposure, 0.87 for concept and drive, and 0.84 for full positive information. (The latter is the average of ratios of concept/exposure to drive and to positive word-of-mouth and magazine exposure in either order: (0.78 + 0.90)/2.) A doubling of sales volume did not look promising.

At this point it became important for managers to obtain a "ballpark" estimate of the potential sales shortfall. If it was sufficiently large, they would have to consider radical strategies. To obtain top-line, "ballpark" forecasts, we developed an index model similar to those used by Little (1975, 1979) and Urban (1968).

Top-line Forecasts

In an index model we modify a base sales level, in this case the sales history of the control car, by a series of percentage indices. From previous research (Silverman 1982), we knew that the sales pattern for mid-sized car models followed a four- to five-year "life-cycle" which had an inverted U-shape. Not until a sufficiently novel relaunch did the life-cycle restart. In this case management felt the new front-wheel drive car would restart the life-cycle and that the pattern, but not the magnitude, would be similar to the rear-wheel drive car.

Management felt that the sales of the new car t years after its introduction, $S(t)$, would follow the pattern of the sales history of the control car, $S_c(t)$, if all else were equal. We would modify this forecast by factors due to preference, $P(t)$ (defined as the ratio of preference of the new car to the control car) as measured in the clinic; industry volume, $V(t)$ as estimated by exogenous econometric models; and competitive intensity, $C(t)$ (nominally 1.0 if no new competition enters and less than one when new competitive

TABLE 1
Relative Preference Conditioned by Information Sequence

Information Sequence[△]	New Car (n = Sample Size)	Control Car (n = Sample Size)	Difference (New − Control)	Ratio (New/Control)
1. concept awareness	13.3 (336)	14.2 (167)	−0.9	0.94
2. concept then wom (+)	14.7 (85)	16.6 (82)	−1.9	0.88
3. concept then wom (−)	10.3 (86)	16.6 (46)	−5.3*	0.62
4. concept then drive	18.5 (165)	21.2 (82)	−2.7	0.87
5. concept → wom (+) → drive	16.4 (85)	21.0 (37)	−4.6*	0.78
6. concept → wom (−) → drive	14.0 (86)	23.1 (46)	−9.1*	0.61
7. concept → drive → wom (+)	16.7 (91)	18.5 (41)	−1.8	0.90
8. concept → drive → wom (−)	16.6 (74)	18.2 (46)	−1.6	0.91

* Significant at 10% based on comparison of means across subsamples.
[△] See Figure 1 for experimental flow diagram for sequence codes.

cars enter) as judged by the managers. (In other applications further indices are added as the situation demands.)

In symbols, the top-line forecast is given by:

$$S(t) = S_c(t) * P(t) * V(t) * C(t). \qquad (1)$$

The preference index was based on the clinic measures. Because information reaches consumers over the life-cycle, and because the preference ratios decrease in Table 1 as more information is gained, we felt it was reasonable for the preference indices to start near the concept level and decrease over the four years of the forecast. After discussion of the clinic results and based on the managers' automobile experience, management felt that an evaluation of 0.92, 0.90, 0.88 and 0.85 was reasonable for years 1, 2, 3, and 4 of this forecast. (No exact formula was used; rather the integration of data and judgment. More sophisticated analyses are described in the next section.)

From General Motors' econometric models, we obtained industry volume indices, $V(t)$, of 1.26, 1.61, 1.2, and 1.2 for years 1, 2, 3, and 4 of the car's life-cycle. The competitive index, $C(t)$, was based on judgment with regard to the impact of new competitive cars not now on the market and past conjoint studies done for other cars. The relevant indices of 1.0, 0.98, 0.94, and 0.86 were deemed reasonable by management.

Putting these indices together with historic sales of the control car gives the forecasts in Table 2.

Management Reaction

Management faced a marketing challenge. The shortfall from target was dramatic. Perhaps advertising could increase the consideration index and, perhaps, promotion and dealer incentives could increase the preference index. Furthermore, detailed examination of the data suggested that women who drive small cars were the best target consumers. The preference index was 1.17 for this group.

However, simulation of these changes (via judgment with the index model) and other sensitivity analyses suggested a major shortfall of sales versus planned production. Management faced a difficult decision. With demand likely to be well below production levels and with major redesign not possible in the short run, some action needed to be taken to keep the plants in operation. Management decided that the only potentially viable option to retain sales volume was to delay retooling of the existing car plant and to produce, temporarily, both the existing rear-wheel drive car *and* the new downsized front-wheel drive car.

At this point we see the managerial need for a more advanced model. The index model identified the need for managerial action, but could not forecast the effect of maintaining the existing car while producing the new car. Furthermore, it was clear that specific marketing actions would be necessary to decrease the shortfall. While management trusted their judgments for top-line "ballpark" forecasts, they became convinced of the need for greater detail on dealer visits, word-of-mouth, advertising, and production constraints in order to select the appropriate marketing strategy.

TABLE 2
Top-Line Forecasts for New Mid-Size Car

Year of Life Cycle	Sales	Share	Difference from Target
1	274,000	9.8	176,000
2	326,000	11.0	124,000
3	247,000	8.5	203,000
4	191,000	7.4	259,000

Probabilistic Flow Model for Dealer Visits, Word-of-Mouth Advertising, and Production Constraints

Detailed modeling, to forecast the effects of increased advertising, repositioning, dealer incentives, and the availability of both the old and the new cars, provides management with a tool to evaluate strategic decisions. Such modeling is also useful to monitor and fine-tune marketing decisions made throughout the launch.

Basic Modeling Methodology

Our more detailed structure is based on a probability flow model that has been used successfully in the test market and launch analyses of consumer frequently purchased goods (Urban 1970) and innovative public transportation services (Hauser and Wisniewski 1982b). The modeling concept is simple. Each consumer is represented by a behavioral state that describes his/her level of information about his/her potential purchase. The behavioral states are chosen to represent consumer behavior as it is affected by the managerial decisions being evaluated. We used the set of behavioral states shown in Figure 2; they represent information flow/diffusion theory customized to the automobile market.

In each time period, consumers flow from one state to another. For example, in the third period a consumer, say John Doe, might have been unaware of the new car. If, in the fourth period, he talks to a friend who owns one, but he does not see any advertising, he "flows" to the behavioral state of "aware via word-of-mouth." We call the model a "macro-flow" model because we keep track, probabilistically, of the market. We do not track individual consumers. For details of this modeling technique see Urban and Hauser (1980, Chapters 15 and 16). The flow probabilities are estimated from the clinic or industry norms, but supplemented by judgment when all else fails. For example, after consumers see the concept boards which simulate advertising, they are asked to indicate how likely they would be to visit a dealer.

In some cases the flow rates (percent of consumers/period) are parameters, say, X percent of those who are aware via ads visit dealers in any given period. In other cases, the flows are functions of other variables. For example, the percent of consumers, now

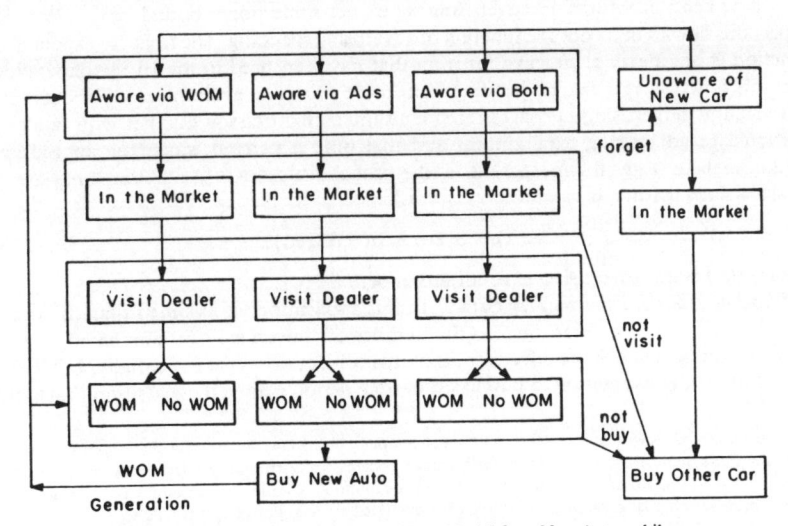

FIGURE 2. Behavioral States Macro-Flow Model for a New Automobile.

unaware, who become aware in a period is clearly a function of advertising expenditures. The exact functions chosen for a given application are chosen as flexible yet parsimonious, parameterized forms. Whenever possible, they are justified by more primitive assumptions. When we have experience in other categories we use that experience as a guide to choose functional forms.

Example Flows

Figure 2 requires 20 state equations to specify the 25 nonzero flows and the conservation conditions.[3] Rather than repeat those equations here we select one conservation equation and three of the more complex flows to illustrate the technique.

Conservation Equation. For every state in Figure 2 there is a conservation equation. That is, the number of people in a state at the end of a period equals the number in that state at the start of a period, plus the number who flow in during that period, minus the number who flow out during that period.

For example, let $N_{aa}(\tau)$ = the number aware via ads in period τ and let $N_u(\tau)$ be the corresponding numbers of consumers in the unaware state. Let $f_a(\tau)$ be the flow rate in period τ from unaware to aware via ads, that is, the probability of awareness given initial unawareness. Let $f_w(\tau)$ be the flow rate due to word-of-mouth, let $f_f(\tau)$ be the forgetting rate, and let $f_{ia}(\tau)$ be the flow into the market among those aware by ads only. Then,

$$N_{aa}(\tau) = N_u(\tau - 1) * f_a(\tau) * [1 - f_w(\tau)] + N_{aa}(\tau - 1) - N_{aa}(\tau - 1)$$
$$* f_f(\tau)[1 - f_{ia}(\tau)] - N_{aa}(\tau - 1) * f_w(\tau)[1 - f_{ia}(\tau)] - N_{aa}(\tau - 1) f_{ia}(\tau). \quad (2)$$

Other conservation equations are in this form. Their specification is tedious, but straightforward.

The next task is to flow people to new states. Most flow rates are a parameter indicating the rate of flow (e.g., the fraction of aware consumers who visit a dealer). A few equations are more complex. We now detail these more elaborate equations for advertising, word-of-mouth prior to dealer visit, word-of-mouth posterior to dealer visit, and production constraints.

Advertising Flow. At zero advertising this flow from the unaware to the aware state is zero percent; at saturation advertising we expect some upper bound, say α. We also expect this flow to be a concave function of advertising spending. The negative exponential function is one flexible, concave function that has been used to model this flow. Note that this function can also be justified from more primitive assumptions. For example, if we assume advertising messages reach consumers in a Poisson manner with rate proportional to advertising expenditures and that only α percent watch the appropriate media, then in a given time period, τ, the probabilistic flow, $f_a(\tau)$, from unaware to aware via advertising, is given by

$$f_a(\tau) = \alpha[1 - \exp(-\beta A(\tau))], \quad (3)$$

where $A(\tau)$ is the advertising expenditure in period τ.

Word-of-Mouth, Prior to Test Drive. In this application we assumed that: (a) word-of-mouth contact is proportional to the number of consumers who purchased in each previous period but (b) the effectiveness of this contact decays exponentially. If $M(\tau)$ is the number of consumers who purchased in time period τ, then these assumptions yield:

---

[3] The source code is written in "Stella", a personal-computer based, commercially available system dynamics language. For system disks contact High Performance Systems, 13 Dartmouth College Highway, Lyme, NH 03768. For the program of this auto model, contact the authors. A more cumbersome basic version in the BASIC programming language is also available for interested readers. For greater details see Goettler (1986) and Srinivasan (1988).

$$f_w(\tau) = \rho \sum_{i=1}^{\tau} [M(\tau - i)/M_\tau] \exp[\gamma(i - 1)] \qquad (4a)$$

where M_τ is the total number of potential customers.

Flows from advertising and from word-of-mouth are treated as independent probabilistically.

An alternative formulation, somewhat more attractive theoretically, assumes that: (a) Poisson incidence comes from consumers who purchased in each previous period; (b) the incidence is proportional to the number of people who purchased in that period and decays proportionally to the number of periods since purchase; (c) the incidences from each consumer are independent; and (d) only ρ percent of consumers are susceptible to word-of-mouth:

$$f_w(\tau) = \rho\{1 - \exp[-\gamma \sum_{i=1}^{\tau} M(\tau - i)/(\tau - i)]\}. \qquad (4b)$$

Future controlled experiments might improve these specifications and/or identify which specification is appropriate for which application. This research is beyond the scope of the present paper. Equation (4b) is preferred on theoretical grounds, but (4a) might be more robust empirically.

Word-of-Mouth Posterior to Test Drive. From qualitative research it was clear that once consumers visit dealers they seek advice from others more actively in order to evaluate their final decision. Management felt that this meant that word-of-mouth intensity would not decay posterior to test drive. For example, for the post-test-drive conditions analogous to equation (4a), the word-of-mouth flow, $f'_w(\tau)$, is given by:

$$f'_w(\tau) = \delta \sum_{i=1}^{\tau} M(\tau - i)/M_\tau. \qquad (5)$$

Equations (3)–(5) have a number of unknown parameters. We discuss calibration of these parameters and of the other flows after indicating how we handled production constraints.

Production Constraints

The forecast for the new, front-wheel drive, mid-sized car was below planned production capacity, but such is not always the case. In fact, the sales of the old, rear-wheel drive, mid-size car were constrained at many times in its sales history by availability. In auto industry terms, free expression was above production.

Ultimately, in a model year, a car model's sales will equal production. (Rebates, special incentives, end-of-model-year sales will be used if necessary.) However, our probabilistic flow model makes forecasts month-by-month. Thus, we used some special characteristics of the auto market to incorporate production constraints. In particular,

(1) As stated earlier, traditionally about 80 percent of domestic sales are "off the lot" or purchased from dealer inventory. If inventories are low, it is likely consumers will not find the specific features, options, and color they want and sales will be lost.

(2) Inventory is expensive in terms of interest, insurance, and storage. At high levels of inventory the dealers allocate effort and sales incentives to switch consumers to overstocked models.

(3) The numeraire for inventory is generally accepted by all concerned as "days supply," the number of units in stock divided by the current sales rate. It is this stimulus to which dealers react.

To incorporate these phenomena we expand the set of behavioral states to include availability. See Figure 3 for new and old car flows. In the model, the awareness shown in the Figure 3 boxes is broken down as shown in Figure 2, but for expositional simplicity this is not done in Figure 3. We then model the availability probability, $p(\tau)$, as:

$$p(\tau) = 1 - \exp(-\lambda D(\tau) - \theta) \tag{6}$$

where $D(\tau)$ is days supply at time period τ: λ and θ are parameters.

Days supply for the control car is observed from historical data and calculated for the new car. Initial days supply for the test car is based on management judgment and then calculated from the simulation results in later periods. Management acceptance of the $D(\tau)$ is critical. It must be consistent with the macro-flow forecasts as well as consistent with their own projected fine-tuning.

The number of people buying the car is now calculated as the fraction of all potential purchasers who want to buy the car "off the lot" multiplied by the availability $(p(\tau))$. Those who place a custom factory order and wait (usually 8–12 weeks) are not reduced by the availability probability.

Calibration and Fitting

The models shown in Figures 2 and 3 are practical models. They incorporate phenomena management feels are important in a way management can accept. Yet, the models are complex—we need many flow probabilities.

It is tempting to develop a clinic design so that each flow in Figure 2 (or 3) can be measured directly. However, clinics are expensive—they can cost upwards of a quarter-of-a-million dollars. Realistically, we must balance the tendency to prefer direct measures with the cost of obtaining those measures. We obtain directly those estimates that are available, say purchase likelihood given ad & drive. We approximate others; for example, we assume the purchase likelihood from a sequence of { wom → ad → drive → wom } is not much different from a sequence of { ad → drive → wom }. We obtain others from

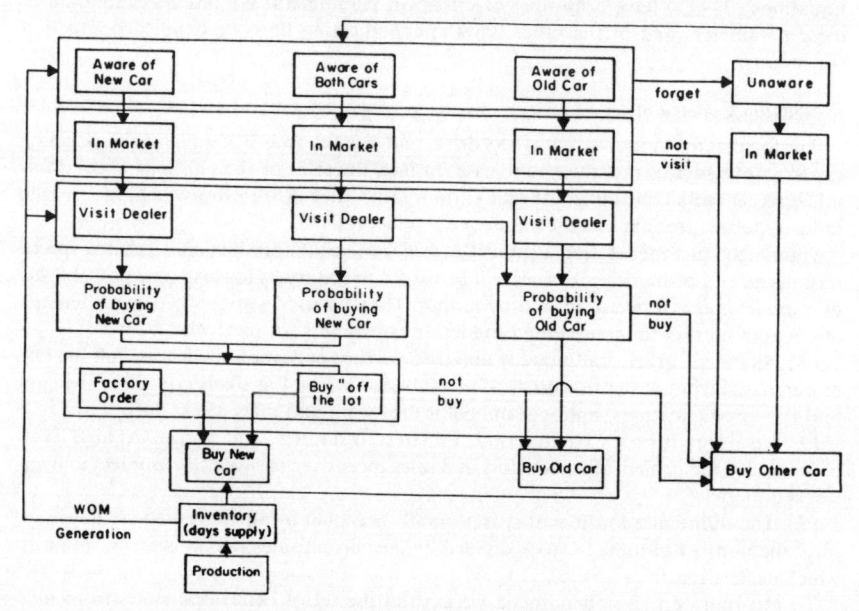

FIGURE 3. Production Constrained Macro-Flow Model for Two Cars.

internal studies, for example, the likelihood that a consumer will visit a dealer after an ad exposure. Still others are obtained from managerial judgment.

Table 3 lists the flows in Figure 3 and the data sources. Note that some of the flows are based on equations (3)–(5) which contain the unknown parameters, α, β, γ, ρ, δ,

TABLE 3
*New Inputs and Sources for Two-Car Model**

Inputs	Source
Target Group Size	Set in plan for number of buyers
Category Sales (monthly)	G.M. econometric forecasts
Awareness	
—advertising spending (monthly)	planned levels
—α, β, forgetting (flow from aware of ad, WOM, or both to unaware) (see equation 3)	fit to past awareness, spending and sales for control car and modify judgmentally for changes for new car
—aware of both cars	awareness proportion for new car times awareness proportion for old car
In Market	
—fraction of those aware who are in market	calculate as category sales divided by target group size for all awareness conditions
Visit Dealer	
—fraction who visit dealer given ad aware	clinic measured probability of purchase after ad exposure (see Figure 1)
—fraction who visit dealer given ad and WOM aware	clinic measured probability of purchase after WOM video tape exposure
—fraction who visit dealer given WOM aware	judgmentally set given above two values
—probability of visit dealer if aware of both cars	probability of visit for new car in clinic after awareness among those respondents who were aware of the old car before the clinic
Purchase	
—probability of buying new car given awareness condition:	
(1) ad aware before visit and no other awareness	clinic measure probability of purchase after ad exposure and test drive
(2) ad aware before visit and WOM	clinic measure probability of purchase after ad, test drive and WOM exposure
(3) ad and WOM aware before visit	clinic probability of purchase after ad, WOM and test drive
(4) ad aware before and after visit	judgmentally set based on (1), (2), (3)
(5) WOM aware before and no other awareness	judgmentally set based on (1), (2), (3)
(6) WOM before and after visit	judgmentally set based on (1), (2), (3)
—probability of buying new car if aware of new car and old car	probability of buying new car in clinic among those respondents who were aware of the old car before the clinic
Word of Mouth Communication	
—ρ, γ (equation 4a)	managerial judgment and fit to past data on fraction of awareness due to word of mouth and control car sales
—δ (equation 5)	past survey data, judgment, and fit to control car sales
—aware of ads and WOM	probability of ad aware times probability of WOM aware
Production	
—levels of production (monthly)	planned levels
—λ, θ (equation 6)	managerial judgment, fit to past data on control car sales, and past research studies
—fraction of buyers who want to buy "off the lot"	past studies and judgment

* Analogous procedures are used for control car based on control cell measures in the clinic and past data.

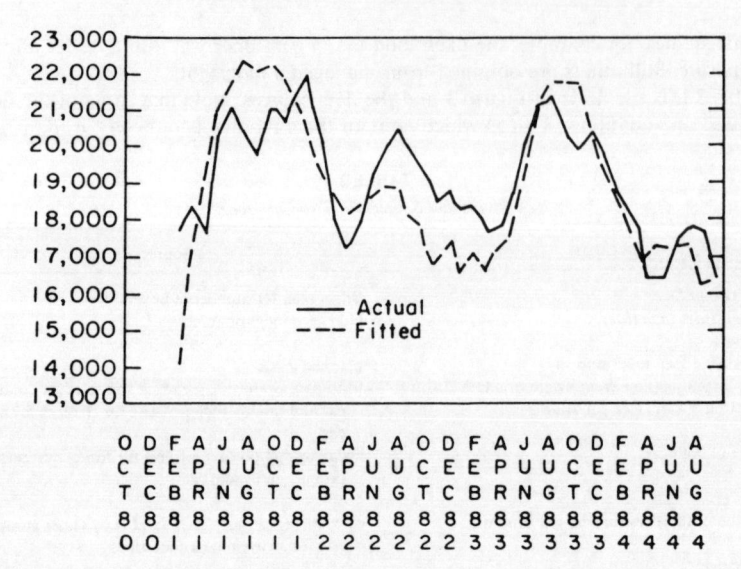

FIGURE 4. Actual vs. Fitted Sales of Control Car. Five-Month Moving Average with Production Constrained Macro-Flow.

λ, and θ. We "calibrate" the model by interactively selecting parameter values to maximize the fit to the actual sales for the control car.

The results of the calibration are shown in Figure 4. The "predicted" sales are simply the number of consumers who flow into the "buy new auto" state in each period, i.e., the fraction of consumers times the total potential market. It is obtained by running the model forward in time with the fitted parameter values.

The macro-flow model fits the data reasonably well with a mean percent error of 5.6% in the five-month moving average and the model appears to capture the major swings in the data, including the partial seasonal pattern.[4] This fit clearly outperforms simple three-parameter life-cycle models. (For example, they would not capture the double peak in sales.) But our model has many more parameters than a simple life-cycle model. We claim only that the model has face validity and that this fit is better than that which had been obtainable previously by the automobile division. To examine further whether or not the fit is adequate we compare predictions to actual data in a later section.

Two-Car Macro-Flow Model

The desire to examine management's decision to keep both the new and old models in production caused us to extend the flow model to include the effects of two competitive models on the market. Once the one-car production-constrained macro-flow model is calibrated, it is straightforward to expand the model to incorporate two cars. See Figure 3. Behavioral states are added for "awareness of both," "visit dealers given awareness of both," and "probability of buying given both." Clinic measures and judgment are used for preference among the test and control cars in this study (see Table 3). Only two-thirds of the people, who had prior awareness of the old rear-wheel drive car, preferred the new car to the old auto when exposed to the new front-wheel drive car.

[4] The five-month moving average of the actual data smoothes transient effects due to special rebate and interest programs. The behavioral states in Figure 3 do not model these effects explicitly.

Managerial Application of Flow Model

Table 4 reports forecasts based on the macro-flow model. The base case predictions are close to those in Table 2—still well below the production target.

The projected shortfall in sales put pressure on management to develop strategies that would improve free expression sales. We simulated three marketing strategies that were considered. The first strategy was a doubling of advertising in an attempt to increase advertising awareness (the model was run with advertising spending doubled). Table 4 indicates this would increase sales somewhat, but not enough. Given its cost, this strategy was rejected.

The next strategy considered was a crash effort to improve the advertising copy to encourage more dealer visits. Assuming that such copy would be attainable, we simulated 40 percent more dealer visits. (The model was run with dealer-visit flow-parameters multiplied by 1.4 for ad aware conditions). The forecast was much better and actually achieved the sales goals in year 2. Although a 40 percent increase was viewed as too ambitious, the simulation did highlight the leverage of improved copy that encouraged dealer visits. A decision was made to devote resources toward encouraging dealer visits. The advertising agency was directed to begin work on such copy, especially for the identified segment of women currently driving small cars.

The final decision evaluated was the effect of incentives designed to increase the conversion of potential buyers who visit dealer showrooms. We simulated a 20 percent increase in conversion (all dealer-visit flow were parameters multiplied by 1.2). The leverage of this strategy was reasonable but not as high as the improved advertising copy. This simulation coupled with management's realization that an improvement would be difficult to achieve on a national level (competitors could match any incentive program) led management to a more conservative strategy which emphasized dealer training.

The net result of the sales analysis was that management decided to make an effort to improve dealer training *and* advertising copy, but that any forecast should be conservative in its assumptions about achieving the 40 percent and 20 percent improvements.

The shortfall in projected sales, dealer pressure to retain the popular rear-wheel drive car, and indications that production of the new car would be delayed, led management to the decision (described earlier) to retain both the old and the new cars. Initial thinking was that the total advertising budget would remain the same but be allocated 25/75 between the old and new cars. Evaluation of this strategic scenario required the two-car macro-flow model.

The forecasts for the two-car strategy with the above advertising and dealer's incentives tactics are shown in Table 5. The combined sales were forecast to be higher than a one-car strategy in years 1 and 4, but lower in years 2 and 3. Overall the delayed launch caused a net sales loss of roughly 48,000 units over 4 years. This is not dramatic, especially given potential uncertainty in the forecast. However, the two-car strategy did not achieve the sales goal and made it more difficult to improve advertising copy and dealer training. Once the production decision had been made and the production delays were unavoidable,

TABLE 4
Sales Forecasts and Strategy Simulations (in Units)

Year	Base Case	Advertising Spending Doubled	Advertising Copy Improved 40%	Dealer Incentives Improved 20%
1	281,000	334,000	395,000	340,000
2	334,000	370,000	477,000	406,000
3	282,000	330,000	405,000	345,000
4	195,000	225,000	273,000	234,000

TABLE 5
Sales Forecasts for Two-Car Strategy (in Units)

Year	New Model	Old Model	Combined Sales
1	181,000	103,000	284,000
2	213,000	89,000	301,000
3	174,000	80,000	254,000
4	121,000	84,000	205,000

management was forced to retain the two-car strategy. Our analysis suggested that it be phased out as soon as was feasible.

This chain of events illustrates the value of a flexible, macro-flow model. The world is not static. Often, unexpected events occur (dramatic sales shortfalls, production delays) that were not anticipated when the initial model was developed. In this case we could not evaluate the overall two-car strategy with the Mod I analysis; management proceeded on judgment and the information available. Once we developed the two-car macro-flow model we could fine-tune the strategy to improve profitability and, in retrospect, evaluate the basic strategy. More importantly, we now have the tool (and much of the calibration) to evaluate multiple-car strategies for other car lines.

Predicted vs. Actual Sales

We turn now to a form of validation. Validation is always difficult because management has the incentive to sell cars, not provide a controlled laboratory for validation.

There are at least two components of deviations between actual and predicted sales. If planned strategies are executed faithfully, the model is likely to have some error and actual sales will not match predicted sales. To evaluate this model, we are interested in this first component of error. But as sales reports come in and unexpected events happen, management modifies planned strategies to obtain greater profit. This, too, causes predicted sales to deviate from actual sales. For example, excess aggregate inventories (across all car lines in the corporation) often encourages rebate or interest rate incentives. Both of these increase and/or shift sales. We are interested in these deviations to identify those actions which need to be added in future model elaborations.

To examine both components of deviations we report two comparisons of actual vs. predicted sales. In the first we compare predictions made prior to launch with sales obtained during launch. In the second we input managerial actions as they actually occurred and compare the adjusted predictions to actual sales. When any adjustments are made we are conservative and we include adjustments which hurt our accuracy as well as help our accuracy. Together, the two comparisons give us an idea of which deviations are due to model error and which deviations are due to changes in managerial actions.

In our application, the advertising allocation changed, industry sales were above the econometric forecast, special interest rate promotions were employed, and production

TABLE 6
Comparison of Actual Sales to Unadjusted Predictions

	1st 6 months	2nd 6 months	3rd 6 months	Total
Actual	97,000	119,000	90,000	306,000
Unadjusted prediction	133,000	151,000	162,000	446,000
Percent difference	37%	27%	80%	46%

was delayed further for the new car. We report first the unadjusted comparison and then a comparison adjusted for the changes in advertising, industry sales, incentives, and production.

Table 6 reports the unadjusted predictions. Actual sales for the two cars were well below the forecast. However, almost all of this deviation occurs when we compare predicted sales for the new car to actual sales. The forecasts for the existing car were close to actual. Recall the new car was production constrained while the old car was not.

We now attempt to decompose these deviations into deviations due to the model and deviations due to management decisions. We do this by computing the adjusted prediction.

The actual advertising allocation was 50/50 not 25/75 as planned. We modify the direct inputs to the macro-flow model accordingly (see equation (3)). Industry sales were above the economic forecasts. We modify the macro-flow inputs accordingly. (Note

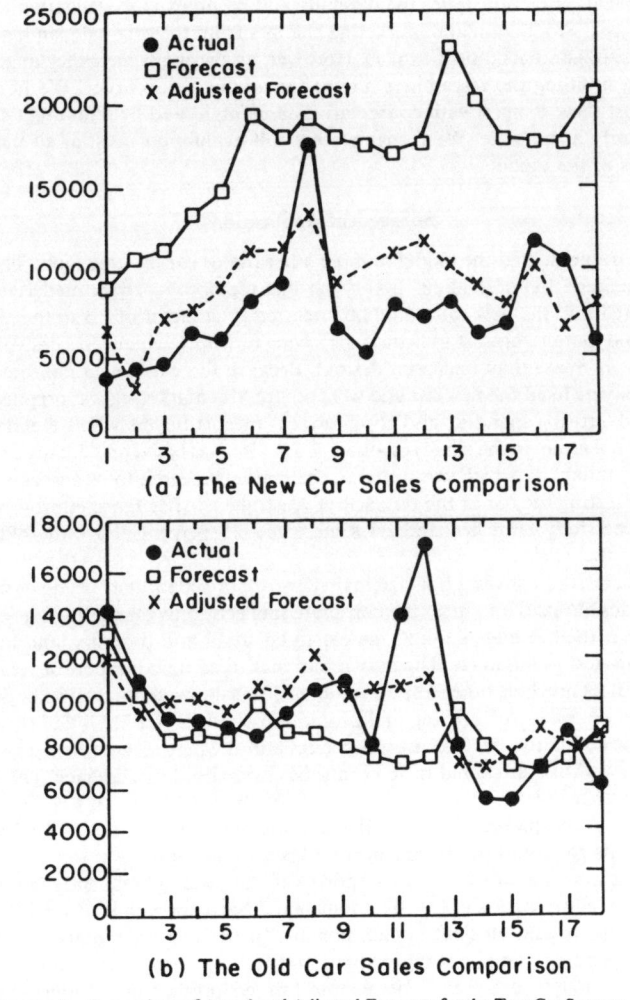

FIGURE 5. Comparison of Actual and Adjusted Forecasts for the Two-Car Strategy.

that this modification works against improving our fit.) There was a special interest rate incentive program for the old car in months 11 and 12. We have no way to include this explicitly, but will scrutinize months 11 and 12 carefully in the final comparison. Production of the new car was delayed significantly. Production problems reduced the availability of the popular V6 engines causing 80% of the old cars in months 13 to 18 to be produced with the less popular V8 engines; similar problems in months 13 to 18 caused a substitution of the less popular standard transmissions in 33% of the new cars. We make these adjustments with the production constrained model using the free expression preferences among engines and transmissions from periods 1 to 12.

The adjusted forecasts are shown in Figure 5. The agreement is acceptable—the mean model error for the 18 months is now 8.8% (down from 46% in the unadjusted comparison). The agreement would have been much closer had we been able to adjust for the incentive program on the old car in months 11 and 12. The overall cumulative predictive accuracy is good, but monthly forecasts would have to be used with some caution.

This application demonstrates the difficulty and complexity of validation for durable goods forecasts. Production and marketing changes from the original plan have a significant effect; adjustments must be made. However, adjustments have the danger of being ad hoc and fulfilling the researchers' desire for predictive accuracy. We have tried to guard against these dangers with conservative adjustment and by reporting these adjustments as fairly as possible. We recognize that full evaluation must await independent applications of the model.

Subsequent Applications

We have implemented the model in three other major car introductions. The first was a new downsized "top of the line" luxury car that replaced its larger predecessor. Clinic data indicated that the new car would be preferred by a factor of 1.1 to the old car and the detailed dynamic forecast indicated a 25 percent improvement in sales volume. But this was less increase than had been desired. Because the clinic data indicated that the old brand buyers liked the new car and were secure, the marketing was oriented through increased advertising spending and copy towards import-buyers who were identified as a high potential group in the clinic responses. Copy also was based on building a perception of improved reliability which was found in the market research to be a weak point (e.g., ads showed testing the car in the outback of Australia). After those improvements, the car was successfully launched and sales increased 25 percent above the old levels as predicted by the model.

The next car studied was a full-size luxury two-door sedan that was downsized in an attempt to double sales and meet the corporate fuel economy standards. The clinic data indicated that the old buyers found the car to be small and ordinary, and they would have little interest in buying it. The only group that liked it was import-buyers, but they did not like it as much as other import options. The sales were forecast to be 50% of the old car's level of sales. Advertising and promotion changes were of little help. Unfortunately for the company, the forecast was correct and the first 12 months were 45% of the previous levels. This car should have been repositioned but a subsequent change in the marketing management of the company just after the final forecasts were made caused the bad news to be ignored. The new division director wanted a success and wanted to believe that the car could be "turned around" before the launch.

The final car was a small two-door sports car that was subsequently launched successfully. The clinic data showed that sufficient "free-expression" demand existed to make an exclusive and efficient launch possible in the first six months. That is, large advertising spending would not be required and fully featured cars could be offered to those "lucky enough to get one" because of limited production volumes. Private car showings were arranged for target customers to position the launch as exclusive. Higher prices could be supported in the first 9 months when production capability was low, but management chose to keep a lower price initially to avoid the perception of distress pricing and to maintain the special tone of the introduction. Test drives were promoted because the clinic showed significant increase in probability of purchase after people experienced the comfortable and roomy, but sporty, ride and handling. After six months, sales are within one standard deviation of predictions.

The durable goods model proposed in this paper has also been implemented on a PC home word-processing system and on a new camera. In all cases the model, measures, and simulations were key components in management decisions on how to target, position, communicate, and price the new product.

Discussion

When we undertook the challenge to develop a prelaunch forecasting system for new automobiles we hoped to develop a deeper understanding of the managerial needs and the special challenges of durable goods forecasting. We feel we have learned a lot in the seven years of applications.

Durable goods do present unique problems. The "price" forecasting problem, validation of production-constrained forecasting, search and experience, and word-of-mouth (magazine reviews) are critical phenomena relevant to durable goods. Addressing these issues has been challenging and scientifically interesting. We hope that the applications described in this paper enable the reader to appreciate better the needs of automobile (durable goods) marketing managers. Clearly, many challenges remain. We summarize a few here.

Applications Challenges

Perhaps the biggest challenge is efficient measurement. Clinics are expensive—sites must be leased, cars obtained, cars maintained, videos produced, test drives set up, names obtained, consumers recruited, etc. Macro-flow models are data intensive. The advantage of making every flow explicit leads one to recognize the need for detailed (and expensive) consumer intelligence. In the applications described in this paper we made what we believed to be efficient tradeoffs among data needs and data costs. The industry would benefit from explicit cost/benefit analyses to optimize data collection.

We can foresee the use of a computer with video disk interface as a method to provide information more efficiently and effectively. Perhaps the word-of-mouth spokesperson could be selected from a number of candidates stored on the video disk. The spokesperson might be matched to demographic and attitudinal characteristics of respondents to simulate the availability to the respondents. The information would be respondent controlled and responses recorded simultaneously as the information is processed and perceptions and preferences change.

Another challenge is the cost of the vehicles. Hand-built prototypes can cost $250,000 or more. Such prototypes are built as part of the engineering development, but the operating division must obtain them for clinic. Work is underway in the industry to determine whether fiberglass mockups or other substitutes can be used to provide earlier forecasts of consumer response. For example, at MIT, holograms are being used as full-scale auto representations.

Scientific Challenges

Equations underlying the flow model (equations (3)-(5) and Figures 2 and 3) represent the authors' experience but they are still somewhat ad hoc. Research is needed on the best specifications of these flows. How many levels should be created and how much segmentation by awareness should be done?

In our applications to date we relied on "calibration" which mixed direct measurement, modeling, judgment, and fitting. As we gain clinic experience, one might consider constrained maximum-likelihood or Bayesian estimation. For example, work is underway at Northwestern University to adapt the continuous-time equations (Hauser and Wisniewski 1982a) to maximum likelihood estimation via super computers.

Extensions

A number of extensions are possible to our auto prelaunch forecasting model. For example, the two-car model could be extended to a full product-line formulation. A number of new phenomena could be added: dealer advertising, dealer visits without prior awareness, multiattribute effects on preference, risk, and consumer budgeting. These modifications are feasible, but they add to the complexity and increase measurement/analysis costs. In each case these extensions should be evaluated on a cost and benefit basis before embarking on a more complex model.

Perhaps the most important extension is the use of marketing science analyses for preinvestment as well as prelaunch decisions. Early modeling of the "voice of the customer" should prove valuable in integrating marketing, engineering, and production to develop automobiles that satisfy long term consumer needs.

The auto industry is now experimenting with test/control clinic methodologies to understand the causal links between engineering design features and attributes that consumers desire. Perhaps future macro-flow analyses can link design improvements, such as anti-lock brakes, to sales.

Although much research is suggested by our efforts, the initial results suggest customer-flow models are useful in capturing the unique aspects of durable goods marketing. The models can be calibrated empirically and implemented with managers.

References

BASS, FRANK M., "A New Product Growth Model for Consumer Durables," *Management Sci.*, 15, 5 (January 1969), 215–227.
GOETTLER, PETER N. "A Pre-market Forecasting Model for New Consumer Durables: Development and Application," Master's Thesis, Sloan School of Management, MIT, Cambridge, MA, 1986.
HAUSER, JOHN R. AND DON CLAUSING, "The House of Quality," *Harvard Business Rev.*, 66, 3 (May–June 1988), 63–73.
────── AND GLEN L. URBAN, "The Value Priority Hypotheses for Consumer Budget Plans," *J. Consumer Res.*, 12 (March 1986), 446–462.
────── AND KENNETH J. WISNIEWSKI, "Dynamic Analysis of Consumer Response to Marketing Strategies," *Management Sci.*, 28, 5 (May 1982a), 455–486.
────── AND ──────, "Application, Predictive Test, and Strategy Implications for a Dynamic Model of Consumer Response," *Marketing Sci.*, 1, 2 (Spring 1982b) 143–179.
HEELER, R. M. AND T. P. HUSTAD, "Problems in Predicting New Product Growth for Consumer Durables," *Management Sci.*, 26, 10 (October 1980), 1007–1020.
HORSKY, DAN AND LEONARD S. SIMON, "Advertising and the Diffusion of New Products," *Marketing Sci.*, 2, 1 (Winter 1983), 1–17.
JEULAND, ABEL P., "Parsimonious Models of Diffusion of Innovation. Part A: Derivations and Comparisons. Part B: Incorporating the Variable of Price," mimeo, University of Chicago, IL, June, 1981.
JUSTER, FRANK T., "Consumer Buying Intentions and Purchase Probability: An Experiment in Survey Design," *J. Amer. Statist. Assoc.*, 61 (1966), 658–696.
KALISH, SHLOMO, "New Product Adoption Model with Price, Advertising, and Uncertainty," *Management Sci.*, 31, 12 (December 1985), 1569–1585.
LITTLE, JOHN D. C., "Models and Managers: The Concept of a Decision Calculus," *Management Sci.*, 16, 8 (April 1970), 466–485.
──────, "BRANDAID: A Marketing Mix Model: Structure, Implementation, Calibration, and Case Study," *Oper. Res.*, 23, 4 (July–August 1975), 628–673.
──────, "Decision Support Systems for Marketing Managers," *J. Marketing*, 43 (Summer 1979), 9–26.
MAHAJAN, VIJAY AND EITAN MULLER, "Innovation, Diffusion, and New Product Growth Models in Marketing," *J. Marketing*, 43, 4 (Fall 1979), 55–68.

——, AND ROGER A. KERIN, "Introduction Strategy for New Products with Positive and Negative Word of Mouth," *Management Sci.,* 30, 12 (December 1984), 1389-1404.

MITCHELL, RUSSELL, "How Ford Hit the Bull's-eye with Taurus," *Business Week*, (June 30 1986), 69-70.

PRINGLE, LEWIS G., R. DALE WILSON AND EDWARD I. BRODY, "NEWS: A Decision Oriented Model for New Product Analysis and Forecasting," *Marketing Sci.*, 1, 1 (Winter 1982), 1-30.

ROBERTS, JOHN H. AND GLEN L. URBAN, "New Consumer Durable Brand Choice: Modeling Multiattribute Utility, Risk and Belief Dynamics," *Management Sci.*, 34, 2 (February 1988), 167-185.

ROBINSON, BRUCE AND CHET LAKHANI, "Dynamic Price Models for New Product Planning," *Management Sci.*, 21 (June 1975), 1113-1132.

SILK, ALVIN J. AND GLEN L. URBAN, "Pre-Test Market Evaluation of New Packaged Goods: A Model and Measurement Methodology," *J. Marketing Res.*, 15 (May 1978), 171-191.

SILVERMAN, LISA, "An Application of New Product Growth Modeling to Automobile Introductions," Master's Thesis, Sloan School of Management, MIT, Cambridge, MA, June, 1982.

SRINIVASAN, K. V., "Effect of Consumer Categorization Behavior on New Product Sales Forecasting," Master's Thesis, Sloan School of Management, MIT, Cambridge, MA, June, 1988.

URBAN, GLEN L., "A New Product Analysis and Decision Model," *Management Sci.*, 14, 8 (April 1968), 490-517.

——, "SPRINTER Mod III: A Model for the Analysis of New Frequently Purchased Consumer Products," *Oper. Res.*, 18, 5 (September-October 1970), 805-853.

—— AND JOHN R. HAUSER, *Design and Marketing of New Products*, Prentice-Hall, Englewood Cliffs, NJ, 1980.

WIND, YORAM AND VIJAY MAHAJAN, *Innovation Diffusion Models of New Product Acceptance*, Ballinger Publishing Co., Cambridge, MA, 1986.

[18]

COMPLEX MULTIECHELON INVENTORY SYSTEM MANAGEMENT USING A DYNAMIC SIMULATION MODEL

Thomas D. Clark, Jr.
Department of Operational Sciences, School of Engineering,
Air Force Institute of Technology, Wright-Patterson AFB, OH 45433

Robert E. Trempe
U.S. Air Force, DET OORC, USAFE (CM), APO New York, NY 09012

Herbert E. Trichlin
Royal Australian Air Force Support Unit, Russel Offices, Canberra 2600, Australia

ABSTRACT

A dynamic modeling approach to management of multiechelon, multi-indenture inventory systems with repair is addressed. The structure of the model follows that of the U.S. Air Force Reparable Asset Management System. The model is used as a vehicle to discuss the structure of typical multiechelon systems and to illustrate the advantages of a dynamic modeling approach to such systems.

Subject Areas: Logistics and Distribution, Inventory Management, and Simulation.

INTRODUCTION

A multiechelon inventory management system is one in which items at one location are stocked for use at another location. In their classic text on inventory management, Hadley and Whitin recognized the complexity of inventory systems that have multiple echelons [8]. Part of the complexity stems from different operating systems and procedures at different levels, and part of it comes from a transportation structure embedded in the typical multiechelon system. Multiechelon systems that handle multiple items are even more complex, as are multi-item, multi-echelon systems in which items are repaired for reuse. The most complex systems are created by the items having repair components supported by an inventory. The term multi-indenture is used to describe this situation. In such instances, a transportation structure and a repair structure are embedded in the system and they are called multiactivity structures [19]. These are typical in the airline industry and in military systems. Determining optimal inventory policy involves balancing the number of items, their transshipment, and repair among, in, and between the echelons.

Clark discusses the structure of the various types of multiechelon systems, making a distinction between those directed toward managing the everyday flow of material and those directed toward planning or evaluation problems [1]. In [1], where several approaches to use for analysis of the latter set of problems—including analytical techniques, servo-mechanism theory, and simulation—are outlined, it is concluded that "all analytic inventory control models suffer from constraining assumptions concerning the environment within which the inventory system operates" [1, p. 641]. Other approaches cannot, however, *solve* inventory problems in the same sense as analytical approaches. Techniques may be mixed to advantage. For example, analytically derived solutions can be tested in simulation models that incorporate a richer representation of the environment and decision structures for a given system. Simulation models also can provide mechanisms to evaluate integrated logistics management approaches that give a full appreciation of the interplay among operations, maintenance, transportation, and supply functions. The model presented in this paper is partially directed toward that end.

A variety of analytical approaches to the analysis of multiechelon structures exist [12] [21]. Especially useful in reviewing these approaches are the reference lists and articles in the book edited by Schwarz [21], which is part of the TIMS series on Studies in the Management Sciences, and the work by Clark [1]. Both works have extensive material that illustrates the range of approaches taken to multiechelon-system study. Typically the techniques employ optimization algorithms that minimize the overall expected backorders in the system or provide stock position goals that maximize equipment availability for given budget constraints [3] [4] [17] [22] [23]. Such models are capable of producing quantitatively accurate predictions of stockage levels, but they have the limitations noted by Clark and others [1] [7]. First, they are based largely on static tools of inventory and reliability theory and deal, therefore, with steady-state situations. For example, demand typically has been treated as a steady-state, independent, identically distributed stream or derived in a time-averaging technique. Steady-state approaches have been shown to have serious limitations, especially for low-demand items [18], since a critical factor in the system is the decision streams that are vital to system behavior over time. These decision elements, in particular, should be treated.

Second, the majority of these models have made simplifying assumptions to make them mathematically tractable. These assumptions usually relate to the nature of the embedded transportation and maintenance structures [7], which are treated as deterministic elements or are characterized by a single probability distribution aggregated over the system. In fact, such assumptions may not be warranted because the system structure changes from time to time, depending upon system state. For example, when routine resupply channels do not satisfy demand, priority routes are invoked or equipment is cannibalized for parts, creating shifts in repair distributions. Feedback mechanisms exist in the system which create these structural shifts.

Hillestad has addressed the steady-state problem in development of the DYNAMETRIC technique [11]. He accomplishes this by implementing a set of analytic mathematical equations describing the dynamic behavior of the component-repair queuing system. Also, recent work by Hausman and Scudder has addressed the structure and management of repair queues [10]. They show the importance of specifically considering the repair process structure of the system and the level of spares at various locations and echelons. Neither of these techniques specifically considers the information feedback mechanisms that exist.

A model that explicitly treats the complex interactions in the multiechelon, multi-item systems with repair elements would satisfy the criteria set forth by Graves and Keilson for an adequate approach to such systems. [7]. They believe an approach should be active and dynamic, concerned with the time-dependent behavior of the system, and should allow for repair and replacement of assets. Most importantly, a model should describe the time the system is in both acceptable and unacceptable states and be able to relate the states to the system's decision and policy structure at each echelon. The model and approach developed here illustrate how to satisfy these requirements.

The approach requires inclusion of assumptions and system structure in a way that they can be viewed and challenged [9]. The iterative process used in model development strengthens its face validity and helps ensure inclusion of critical systemic feedback relationships. A weakness of the approach is that it does not produce optimal solutions. Rather, it provides a method to find acceptable solutions when complexity clouds direct measurement of systemic elements. Although a number of other approaches are possible, most do not provide a vehicle to demonstrate directly the effects of policy decisions for specific echelons on the attainment of the system goals.

System models are excellent vehicles for quickly viewing the interactions among competing policy alternatives. They are, however, inefficient for use in establishing initial stockage requirements. Analytical probabilistic and deterministic methods, such as those mentioned, should be exercised for establishing initial requirements and inventory placement and the dynamic simulation used to assess the system under various repair structure alternatives and operating patterns. One approach cannot replace the other, but each can be used to mutual advantage.

The system used as an example in this study to illustrate the approach comes from the U.S. Air Force reparable-asset structure. It is an extremely complex multi-echelon, multi-indenture, multi-item system servicing, from six central points, hundreds of primary items in 138 locations worldwide. The model can be used to demonstrate the effects of various policy changes on the achievement of primary system goals. This system has been extensively modeled using mathematical programming techniques [2]. Models have been applied with varying degrees of success to initial provisioning problems, replenishment of spares determinations, and budget allocation. Major areas of concern still involve determination of stock levels for each location in the multilocation structure and in providing a vehicle for system structural study [2].

An abstract goal of the Air Force system is to maintain and sustain a "high level" of weapon (aircraft, missile) availability. A more specific goal is required, however, because availability or "readiness" must be related to the availability of serviceable assets where they are needed to sustain given "levels of effort" for given weapons at specific locations. The goal served will therefore be serviceable-asset availability at the point of use. This is analogous to the "minimization of backorders" goal and to Hillestad's criteria of "state of availability and preparedness of resources with respect to their planned wartime mission" [11, p. 1]. The model developed here demonstrates a range of policies to achieve this objective rather than using only inventory for control. System structure will be reviewed in detail and the effects of various policies given this structure explored.

SYSTEM STRUCTURE

The formulation of cause and effect relationships creates the foundation for a dynamic model of a feedback structure; understanding the logic behind the relationships provides the foundation for understanding system behavior [5]. In the case of the current research, gaining a clear understanding of how information about system variables and states influences decision making, and illustrating how the decisions affect reparable-asset-system behavior were the objectives that guided model development. The system relationships are explored in this section. Presentation of the structure in this manner places the methodology in the "refutationist" tradition of science [9]. Instead of defending conjectural hypotheses, an attempt to overthrow them is made.

The specific structure of the system was determined through observing it and interviewing managers responsible for system functions. It consists of two major levels with several important processes or sectors within the levels. Level 1 is the operating level for the end item; in this case, aircraft. In this system, Level 1 is an air force base. The aircraft contain reparable assets that are removed upon failure, replaced with serviceable assets from inventory, and forwarded to the Level 1 repair facility. The assets are either repaired there or forwarded to a central facility for repair. The central repair facility, a logistics center in the air force, constitutes Level 2 in the multiechelon system described here. The central facility also performs an inventory (warehouse) storage and control function. Assets removed from the aircraft contain components that can be removed from the assets, replaced with serviceable components from inventory, and forwarded to the central repair facility. The system is, therefore, multi-indenture. The system consists of six major processes within and between the two levels: demand generation, Level 1 repair, transportation, requisitioning, Level 2 repair, and resupply. Elements in these six major processes define the exact operating nature of the system. This is a typical structure for a complex multiechelon, multi-indenture system with repair.

Demand is a function of asset failure, which in turn is a function of the use of the aircraft in which the assets are installed. Because of its importance in driving system behavior, the demand function stems from the flying-hour program for a given aircraft. Such programs vary with operational and training requirements. The flying-hour program for a specific aircraft type was used as a key control variable of the model. System performance is measured by the number of serviceable assets stocked at Level 1 and the rate of flying-hour effort that this number of assets would sustain over various demand and repair patterns. The relationship of the major inventory levels and processes is depicted in Figure 1.

Causal Structure of Demand

The general relationships shown in Figure 1 provided the basis for further development of specific cause-and-effect relationships for the main processes of the system. The causal structure of the demand generation process is shown in detail in Figure 2. In posing such structural models, the hypothesized causal

FIGURE 1
Multilevel, Multi-indenture Inventory and Repair System

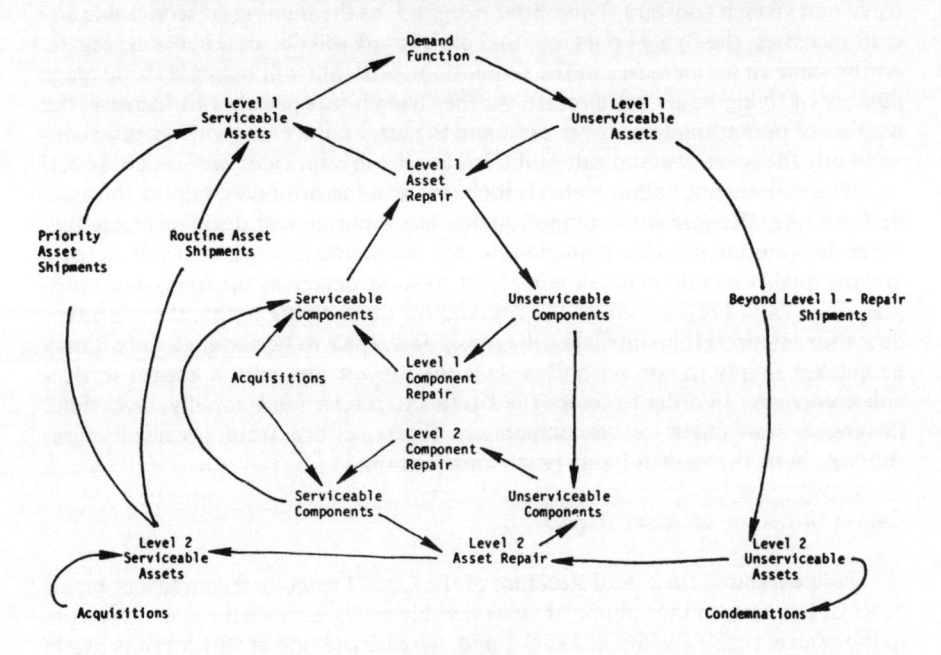

FIGURE 2
Causal Structure for Asset Demand Rate

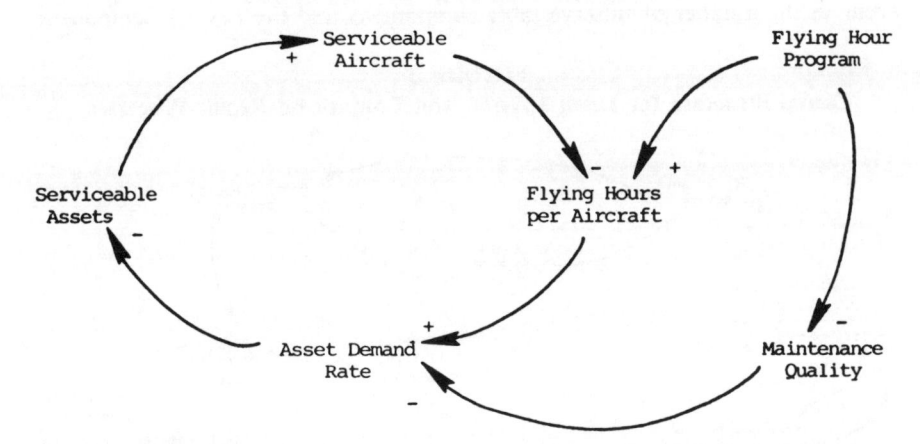

relationships between system elements are specified by considering two elements, one at a time. The + or − sign on the arrow indicates the hypothesized direction of movement taken by the response variable when the first variable increases. Figure 2 illustrates how the demand for serviceable assets drives several key decisions.

Starting with the variable "serviceable assets," the number of serviceable aircraft is directly related to the availability of operational assets. All other things being equal and given a constant flying-hour program, as the number of serviceable aircraft increases, the flying hours required per aircraft will decrease in the aggregate. At the same time, increases in the flying-hour program will increase the average number of flying hours per aircraft. As the flying hours per aircraft increase, the number of operational hours per asset and the asset failure rate will increase; consequently the asset demand rate will decrease the inventory of serviceable assets.

The maintenance quality also is included as a factor in determining the asset demand rate. Because maintenance quality is a separate and distinguishable factor in determining the asset demand rate, the maintenance work load will increase and the quality of maintenance will suffer to some degree as the flying-hour program increases. Further, under the demand for more flying hours, there is a tendency for on-aircraft maintenance diagnosis and repair to be curtailed since it may be quicker simply to remove and replace the suspect unit with a known serviceable component in order to return the aircraft to service more rapidly. Over time, this creates more unserviceable components. This is a critical factor because it causes shifts in both the demand and repair distributions.

Causal Structure of Asset Repair

Figure 3 shows the causal structure of the Level 1 asset- and component-repair process. Increases in the volume of unserviceable assets increase the asset shipments to the central repair facility at Level 2 and increase the rate at which faulty assets are diagnosed. The changes in the diagnosis rate result in similar changes in the number of unserviceable assets awaiting replacement components. Similar changes occur in the number of unserviceable components and the Level 1 component

FIGURE 3
Causal Structure for Level 1 Asset- and Component-Repair Processes

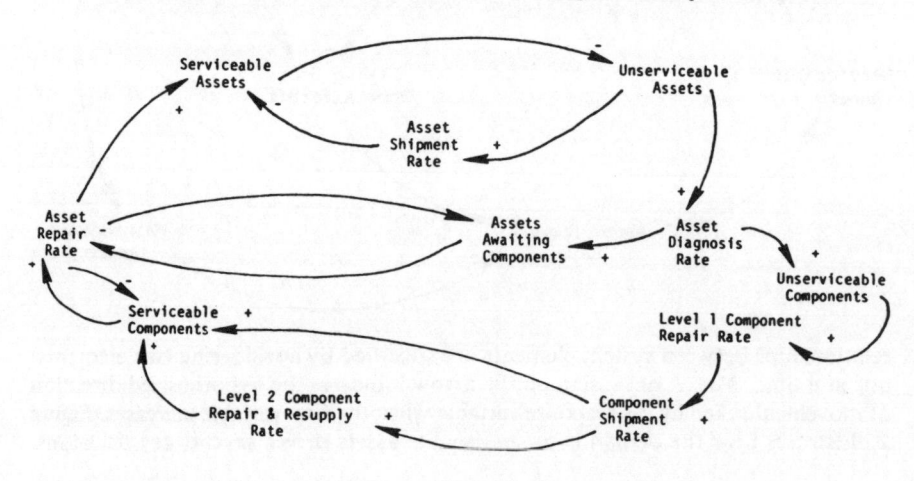

repair rate. Increases in the component repair rate will increase the volume of serviceable assets and the component shipment rate to the central repair facility. In response to changes in the component shipment rate, the Level 2 component repair and resupply rate will change in a like manner. Increases in the resupply rate increase the Level 1 stocks of serviceable components.

An increase in the number of assets awaiting replacement components causes an increase in the asset repair rate as maintenance personnel attempt to repair assets as quickly as possible. An additional consideration in the linkage between these two factors is the pressure by management to keep the level of assets awaiting components at or near zero. It is easy and quick to make the assets serviceable by installing available components. As a consequence, increases in the availability of serviceable components from either Level 1 or Level 2 actions will cause increases in the component repair rate. The availability of serviceable components could be one of the key limiting factors as primary demand increases.

The quality of maintenance work at Level 1 is a matter of continuing concern to policy makers. Inadequate maintenance during aircraft diagnosis and asset replacement reduces system reliability and availability and could conceivably result in the loss of an aircraft. Poor quality control in the maintenance workshop can reduce asset reliability. Reduced reliability will increase asset failure rates and, consequently, demand rates. The results are obvious.

A wide variety of technological as well as psychological factors appear to influence the quality of maintenance. In terms of system behavior these factors can be grouped into two major categories. The first is the impact that changes in the flying-hour program have on primary aircraft maintenance; the second is the impact that increased shop work rates have on the quality of output. The nature of these influences, in combination with the asset demand generation process and

FIGURE 4
Causal Structure of Maintenance Quality at Level 1

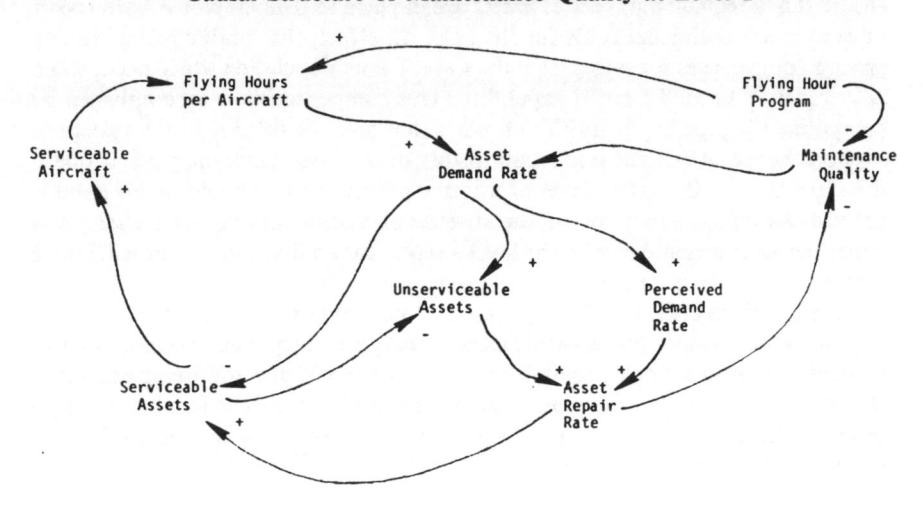

Level 1 asset-repair process, is illustrated in Figure 4. This figure provides further detail for the Level 1 repair process and illustrates how causal diagramming can be used to decompose a system for further detailed analysis.

With the addition of the maintenance quality factor, increases in the flying-hour program act two ways to increase the asset demand rate. First, by increasing the flying hours per aircraft and, second, by decreasing the quality of maintenance. This decrease in the quality of maintenance results from the tendency to curtail on-aircraft maintenance diagnosis and repair. The maintenance managers interviewed confirmed that as pressure to fly increases, a suspect asset is quickly replaced with a serviceable asset to return the aircraft to service rapidly. This "on spec" changing of assets has an obvious impact upon asset demand rates.

Increases in the asset repair rate also tend to decrease the quality of maintenance performed in the repair shops. As the pressure to increase the asset repair rate grows, managers and technicians tend to spend less time on each maintenance task, thereby increasing the likelihood of errors. At the highest levels of pressure, quality control procedures may even by curtailed in order to return the asset to serviceable stock rapidly. This decreased maintenance quality acts to increase the asset demand rate since the lower-quality components tend to malfunction or fail more frequently. In this situation the net effect of maintenance quality is to amplify changes in the asset demand rate. Such behavioral effects normally are not included in inventory optimization models. The ability to include them and to provide a device with which to test system sensitivity to them is an advantage of a dynamic modeling approach.

The Requisitioning Process

The Level 1 routine requisitioning process for assets provides the normal link between the Level 1 and Level 2 asset inventories. The requisitioning goal is to ensure that adequate numbers of assets are in place to balance stocks with repair rates to meet routine demands for the asset. In effect, the routine requisitioning process compensates for losses from the Level 1 asset population which occur when asset repair is beyond Level 1 capability. This compensation is accomplished by computing the pipeline quantities of assets that must be moving in the system to support the recent demand and repair history of the asset. Once the pipeline quantities are known, the safety level of uninstalled assets that should be on hand is derived. All things equal, and in the absence of significant long-term changes in either the asset demand rate or the level's repair capability, the system will create a requisition only in response to shipment of an asset.

Requisitions are tracked at both Level 1 and Level 2. Records of requisitions help managers monitor the reparable asset system performance and prevent "double ordering" against a single requirement. Level 1 records of requisitions are maintained until satisfied by shipment of an asset from Level 2. The number of backorders at Level 2 is an important measure of the response of the reparable asset system to long-term demand cycles.

FIGURE 5
Causal Structure of Level 1 Routine Requisitioning Process

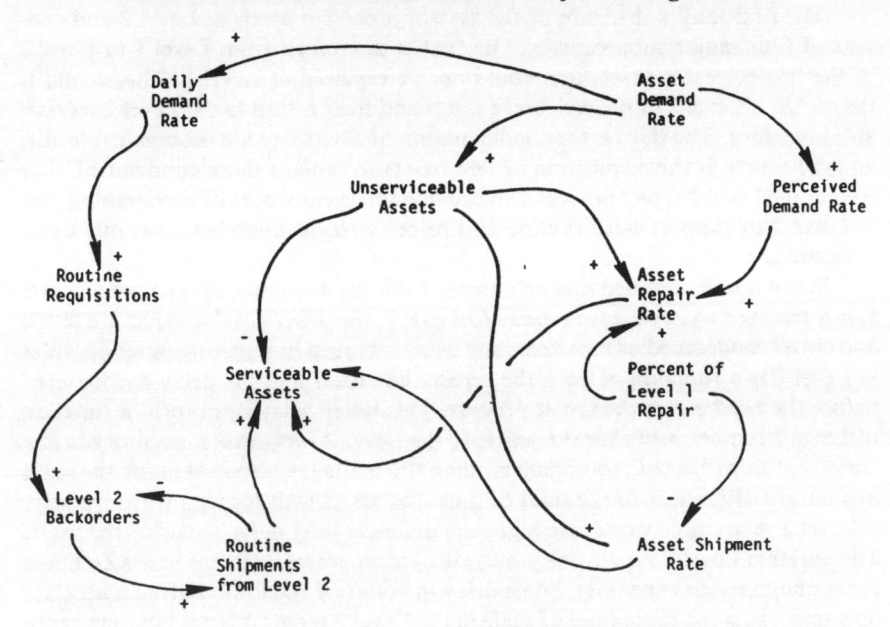

The causal structure of the Level 1 routine requisitioning process is illustrated in Figure 5. The major influences on the requisitioning process are the asset demand rate, the asset repair rate, and the asset shipment rate. The daily demand rate shown is not exactly the same as the asset demand rate. Rather, it is the arithmetic average of at least 180 days' asset demand data. Longer periods are used for low-demand items. Thus, only significant and lasting changes in the asset demand rate will affect the daily demand rate. At the same time, changes in the asset demand rate, acting through the repair and shipment rates, cause changes in the level of serviceable assets. The nature of these changes is mediated by the percentage of unserviceable assets that can be repaired at Level 1.

Routine requisitions are placed in response to the daily demand rate and the current level of serviceable assets. If the level of serviceable assets is insufficient to meet the current daily demand, a routine requisition is generated. This requisition, in turn, creates a Level 2 backorder. In response to the backorders placed with Level 2, shipments are made to Level 1.

Shipping an asset to a Level 1 location reduces the pressure created by the backorder. Receipt of the asset at Level 1 dampens the daily demand rate. The dampening influence that the level of serviceable assets has on the routine requisitioning process will prevent requisitioning serviceable stock in excess of that justified by the daily demand rate. This "self-leveling" nature of the asset requisitioning process prevents a location from holding excess stock indefinitely.

Level 2 Repair and Shipment Structure

The next major structure of the system processes assets at Level 2 and consists of four major subprocesses. The first is the return from Level 1 to Level 2 of the unserviceable assets that could not be repaired at Level 1. The second is the repair at Level 2 of unserviceable assets and their return to the Level 2 serviceable inventory. The third is the condemnation of assets beyond economical repair, and the fourth is the acquisition of new assets to replace those condemned. The goal of the Level 2 repair process is to provide sufficient stocks of serviceable assets at Level 2 to support both routine and priority requisitions from various Level 1 locations.

When it is determined that an unserviceable asset will not be repaired at Level 1, it is returned to Level 2 for repair. At Level 2, the unserviceable assets are tested and either condemned or repaired. Any delay incurred in repairing unserviceables at Level 2 is a function of both the repair time itself and the delay encountered before the asset enters the repair process. This latter delay is, in turn, a function of Level 2 requirements for the asset. If the Level 2 serviceable inventory is low compared to projected requirements, then the manager responsible for the asset in question will reduce the amount of time that assets wait for repair. Conversely, if Level 2 serviceable stocks are high, the manager may defer repair of the asset. The variable Level 2 repair delay may also occur when different assets compete for common repair capability. Some delay in initiating repair on a given asset class may result in some economies of scale in the Level 2 repair process but may cause serviceable asset shortages over the system.

Some assets will be beyond economical repair when they arrive at Level 2 and therefore will be condemned and leave the system. In turn, new assets are acquired from supplies to replace the condemned assets and to meet any new requirements. The newly acquired assets enter the system after a production lead-time delay. This delay can also contribute to shortages unless properly controlled.

The causal structure for the Level 2 repair process is shown in Figure 6. As the shipments from Level 1 increase, the Level 2 repair rate must also increase, or eventually shortages will occur across Level 1. The increase in the Level 2 repair rate leads to an increase in the serviceable inventory. If the serviceable inventory is at or near the desired level, there will be a tendency to reduce the Level 2 repair rate in order not to exceed the desired level. This is a critical system goal. Similarly, if the serviceable inventory should drop below the desired level, this will create pressure to increase the repair rate to restore the desired level of serviceable stock.

This typical process will occur under normal operating conditions. If, however, Level 1 locations should experience a sustained overload of their maintenance capability, the level of unserviceable inventory will increase steadily. Although this is an extremely rare occurrence, the system managers interviewed identified several situations in which the levels of unserviceable stock at Level 1 would become excessive. In this situation, there would be growing pressure within the system to divert some of the excess backlog to Level 2 for repair. This diversion would take place to prevent expensive and scarce assets from lying idle while awaiting repair.

FIGURE 6
Causal Structure of the Level 2 Repair Process

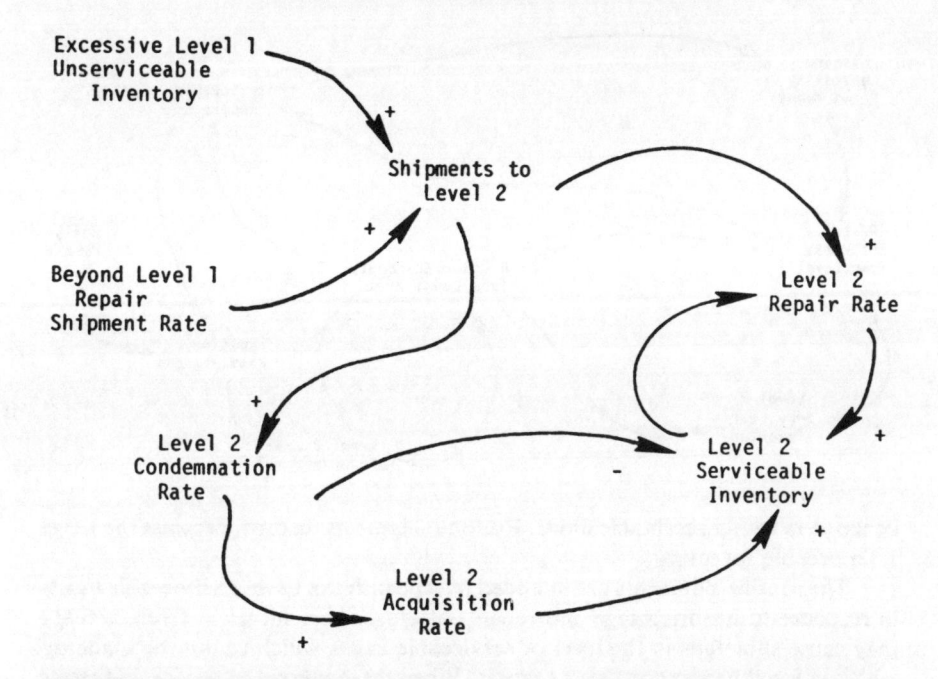

These diverted assets would then combine with the normal shipments to form the total shipments to Level 2. The condemnation rate would also be affected by increased shipments to Level 2 and thereby lower the serviceable inventory. Shortages created by condemnations would be made up by acquisition of the required number of items after some delay.

The Level 2 resupply process has two major components: priority and routine shipments. Taken together with the Level 1 routine requisitions, the Level 2 resupply process provides the physical and informational linkages between the Level 2 serviceable inventory of assets and the Level 1 serviceable inventory. The goal of this process is twofold. First, it must satisfy the routine requisitions that arise out of the normal Level 1 requisitioning process described earlier and, second, it must satisfy the high-priority mission capability requirements that arise when the routine system is unable to provide adequate numbers of assets to support the primary flying program. The resupply process sector then includes the determination of mission capability requirements and the response to both these and routine requirements.

The causal structure for the Level 2 resupply process is shown in Figure 7. For clarity, certain elements of the routine requisition process sector are included. As Level 1 backorders respond to routine requisitions, the rate at which routine shipments are made to Level 1 increases or decreases as needed to keep the Level 2

FIGURE 7
Causal Structure of the Level 2 Resupply Process

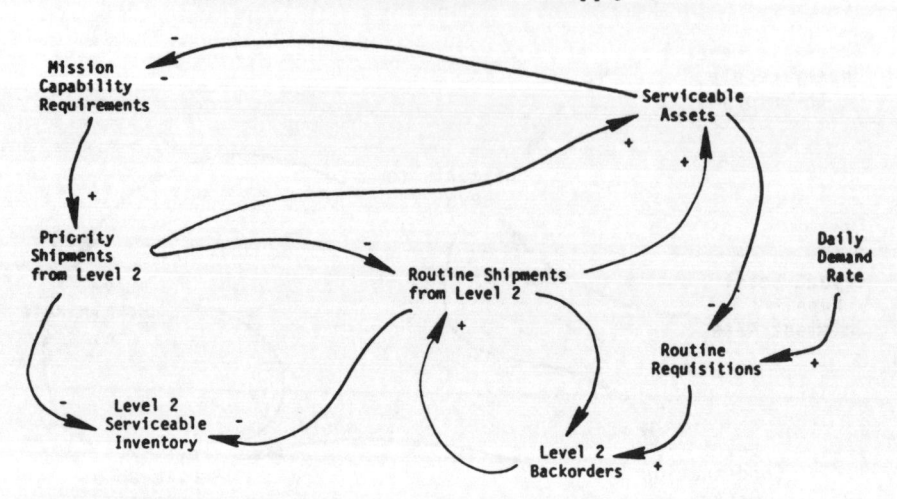

backorders within acceptable limits. Routine shipments, in turn, decrease the Level 1 serviceable inventory.

The routine shipments are intended to replenish the Level 1 serviceable assets in response to historic usage and repair patterns. Short surges in flying activity may cause shortfalls in the level of serviceable assets which cannot be made up with routine shipments or Level 1 repair. When these sources of serviceable assets cannot match the demand rate, the serviceable inventory decreases. At some point this decrease in the number of serviceables will affect the operational capability of the flying unit. In order to restore the aircraft, a "mission capability" demand is placed for Level 2. This requirement will be satisfied by priority shipment of a serviceable asset from the Level 2 serviceable inventory.

Both priority and routine shipments are made from and compete for the same Level 2 serviceable inventory so there is a point at which priority shipments will suppress routine shipments. This reflects the fact that the Level 2 serviceable inventory is segmented because priority requirements have claim on all of the depot inventory. Routine requirements may not be filled from certain segments of the Level 2 serviceable inventory. The nature of this competition and suppression is taken up in more detail in the discussion of the model developed for the system.

MODEL STRUCTURE AND OPERATION

The conceptual structure described was implemented mathematically using the system dynamics process and language, DYNAMO [20]. Such a model has several advantages. First, by explicitly showing the effects of policy decisions on the performance of the system in terms of aircraft availability, it provides a useful tool for investigating the effects of policies that are not limited to stockage levels and item placement. Second, it points out which variables in the system provide the best management indicators to gauge system performance over time. Finally, by explicitly showing how information influences managerial decision making and how the state of the system changes given certain decision streams, it permits the design of effective decision support systems. The model becomes the centerpiece of such a system [15]. A major limitation of the approach is the absence of an explicit criterion function to determine exactly the magnitude that policy or systemic changes should take [13]. Deterministic approaches and other simulation approaches attempt to provide such a function, and in cases where structures are not complex, these functions are well defined and useful. In the classic sense, validation of system dynamics models also is believed by some to be a limitation. A process that has evolved to deal with this issue will be discussed later.

Perhaps the major drawback of this approach is the large size of the model which results if large numbers of items with several levels of indenture at a number of locations are included. Computer resource requirements must be balanced carefully against the size of the model with the specific objective of a study using the model defining its size. Data processing limitations are, as always, considerations in analytical approaches [2].

The structure and behavior of the model were verified and validated through a series of tests outlined by Forrester and Senge for system dynamics models [6]. The strategy involved operating each sector of the model with simple, controlled inputs. The output from these operations was rigorously analyzed to ensure proper behavior by comparing model data to system data. With the verified model, a series of structured interviews were conducted with experienced logistics managers to provide further external validation of the structures in the model. The statistical tests and interviews provided sufficient confidence that the model performed properly and would be useful as a policy-analysis tool. Demonstration of its use is provided in a subsequent discussion. Full implementation of the model in the decision process, however, was delayed by data requirements. The model demonstrated the requirement for information that was not readily available in the management information system. Development is continuing.

The structure of the model using the accepted system dynamics symbols is presented in Figure 8. The structure described in the last section can be seen in the diagram. The major stocks of Level 1 are shown in the variables SINVL (serviceable assets); USINVL (unserviceable assets); and URINV3, URINV2, URINV1 (assets in various stages of repair). Shipments to Level 2 are shown through the two rates RNRTS (rate of shipments for assets beyond repair) and DTDR (diversions because of limited repair capacity). The demand structure is translated through the rate variable RDEM (rate of demand).

The repair of components is shown in the rate and level structure in the center of the figure and captured in the variables USSRUI (unserviceable components), BSRUI (serviceable Level 1 components), and DSRUI (serviceable Level 2 components). The Level 2 repair and stockage structure is shown at the bottom of the figure and captured in the variables DUI (Level 2 unserviceable assets), DSI

FIGURE 8
System Dynamics Flow Diagram

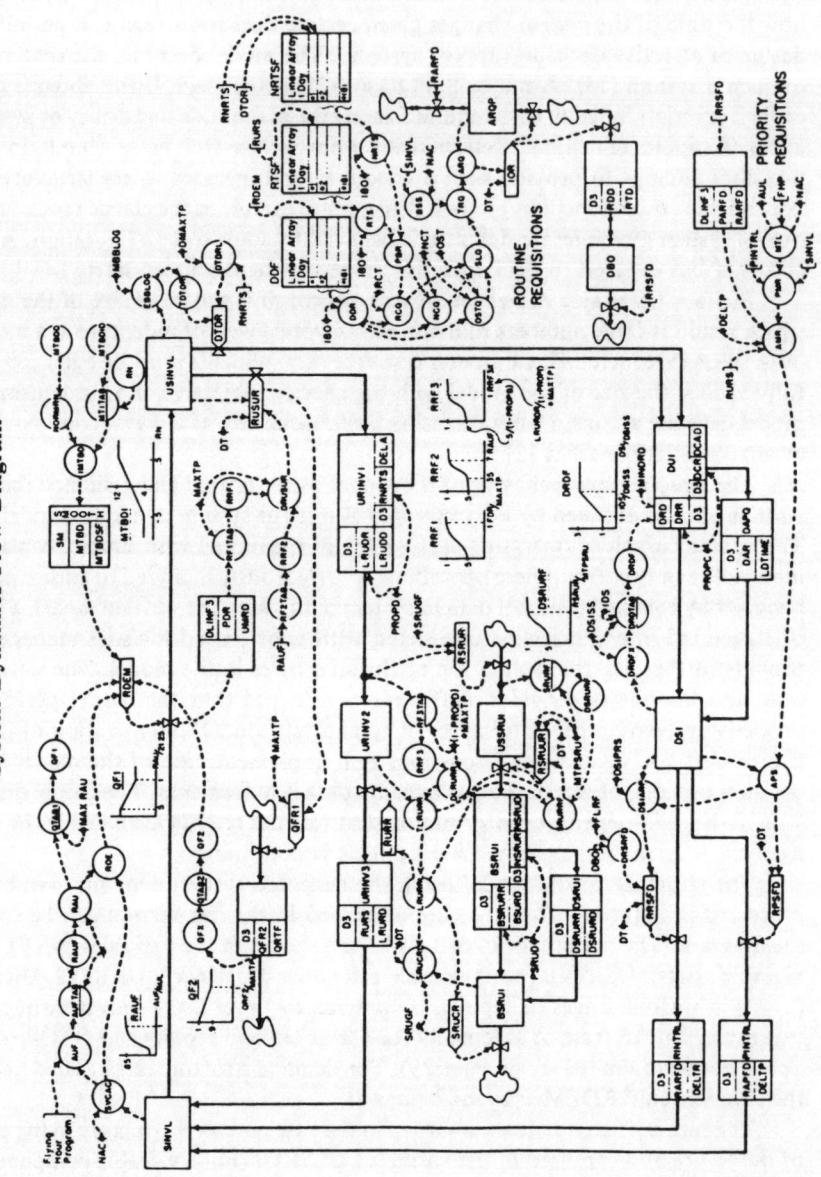

FIGURE 8 (cont.)
(Flow Diagraming Symbols)

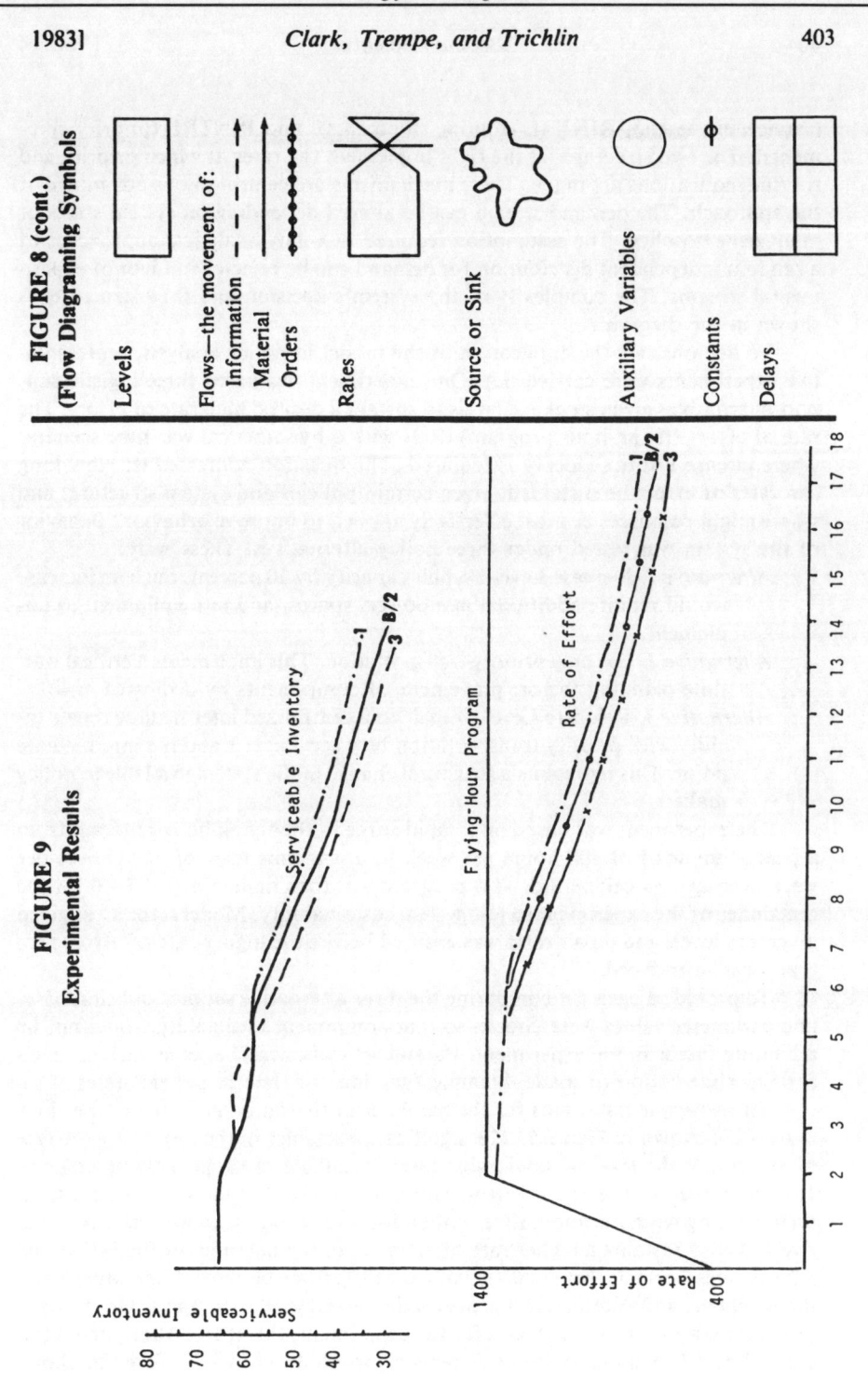

Levels

Flows—the movement of:
 Information
 Material
 Orders

Rates

Source or Sink

Auxiliary Variables

Constants

Delays

FIGURE 9
Experimental Results

(serviceable assets), RINTRL (routine shipments), and PINTRL (priority shipments). The two structures at the right implement the rates at which priority and routine requisitions are made. These mechanisms are central to one advantage of the approach. The demand stream can be altered depending on system states or management policy. The assumption required by many analytical approaches of a random independent distribution for demand can be rejected in favor of experimental streams. The complexity of the system's decision and flow structures is shown in the diagram.

To demonstrate the application of the model in policy analysis, representative experiments were carried out. One experiment evaluated three logistic support alternatives given stockage levels to sustain a desired high rate of effort. The rate of effort (flying-hour program) deals with a hypothetical war-time scenario where intense effort suddenly is required. The question addressed is: How long can rates of effort be sustained, given certain policies and system structure, and where might resources be most effectively applied to improve behavior? Behavior of the system was tested under three policy alternatives. These were:

Alternative 1. Increase Level 1 repair capacity by 30 percent. Such an increase would require additional manpower, spares, and test equipment to implement.

Alternative 2. Use only priority transportation. This implements a critical wartime planning factor: movement of components by dedicated airlift.

Alternative 3. Relocate Level 1 repair to a centralized intermediate repair facility with priority transportation between Level 1 and the intermediate point. This represents a structural change in the system available to policy makers.

The experiment was based on a rapid surge in the flying-hour program from a peace-time level of 400 hours per week to a war-time level of 1400 hours per week over a two-week period. This program was then maintained at 1400 for the remainder of the experiment to test system sustainability. Model stability at given inventory levels and repair rates was ensured before the higher-rate-of-effort program was introduced.

To provide a basis for comparing the three alternative support policies, baseline parameter values were chosen so that component availability would not be a limiting factor in the experiment. Parameter values can be set at various levels for experimentation or made dynamic functions of time or system states.

The experimental results for the baseline configuration and each of the alternatives are shown in Figure 9. The significant variables in the results are the rate of effort and the level of serviceable assets available to support flying at Level 1. Comparison of the rate of effort sustained shows that there is no significant difference between the alternatives until about week six. From week six, Alternative 1 always sustains a higher rate of effort than the baseline configuration and Alternatives 2 and 3; there is no significant difference between Alternative 2 and the baselines; and Alternative 3 provides the lowest level of support. On the basis of the evaluation criterion chosen for the experiment, therefore, Alternative 1 (increase Level 1 repair capacity be 30 percent) would be chosen. Before this choice would be made in reality, however, other criteria would need to be considered. For instance, is the difference in the rate of effort among the alternatives operationally significant? A more important result of this experiment may be that neither the baseline nor any of the alternatives is able to achieve the desired flying-hour program. This result shows that a much more fundamental change in the logistic support structure is required if a rate of effort of 1400 hours per week is to be achieved. For example, an anticipatory resupply structure instead of the current reactionary resupply structure may be needed. The model becomes very useful in evaluating alternatives for, and in the design of, such a support structure.

Although not significant with respect to the ability of the system to sustain a high rate of effort, in practice the behavior of the resupply rates may be significant in the final choice among alternatives. Each alternative exhibits a different sharing pattern between the routine and priority requisitioning structures. These differences may become significant if the planned transportation times cannot be achieved or the availability of transportation is not as planned. The model provides the means for assessing the impact of these contingencies.

Finally, the relatively poor support provided by Alternative 3 is due mainly to the intermediate repair facility being implemented with the same repair capacity as the Level 1 workshop in the baseline structure. The drop in support should therefore be anticipated because of the increase in transportation requirements. The experiment shows, however, that unless this drop in support is offset by the operational advantages of centralizing intermediate maintenance at a point away from the operational levels, the facility will need to have a significantly higher repair capacity. The model is useful in making the necessary tradeoffs between operational and logistics requirements.

Earlier it was suggested that a fundamental change in the support structure is required if the war-time flying program of 1400 hours per week is to be achieved and sustained for the required period. The experimental results do show there is an alternative that requires no changes to the baseline structure. The system is able to sustain a relatively constant high rate of effort until Level 2 reserve stock is exhausted (about week six). If the reserve stock in the system is high enough, the system would be able to achieve and sustain any desired high rate of effort for a given period. After that period, the system repair rate capability would determine the rate of decline in the achieved rate of effort. The model provides an excellent means of determining the best tradeoff between reserve stock and repair capability for any operational contingency. In addition, cost functions can be added to the model to investigate support alternatives within given budget constraints.

Although dealing with only a "hypothetical" war-surge scenario, this experiment has addressed some fundamental issues in the interdependency of operational and logistics inventory decisions. The alternatives evaluated were chosen to be representative of realistic policy alternatives. The implementation of them required only parameter changes and demonstrated the flexibility and adaptability of the model. The foregoing analysis of the experimental results also demonstrates the usefulness of the approach in policy analysis and system design. It satisfies the criteria outlined by Graves and Keilsen for an approach to multiechelon inventory systems [7]. Also demonstrated was the value of such a model in reaching decisions about allocation of inventory among the various levels. Hausman and Scudder believe such a vehicle is required to assess typical systems properly [10].

CONCLUSIONS

The research outlined demonstrates the system dynamics approach to multi-echelon inventory systems. The causal structure of the system is made explicit and used to design and implement a mathematical model that can be directly employed by managers. A model's exact structure is dependent upon the view of the system that a manager holds.

The model presented here addresses the major processes relevant to a multi-echelon inventory structure. Other elements need to be included to expand further the applicability of such models. The impact of component and part cannibalization on system availability should be included as well as the impact of a maintenance manager's decision process for allocation of resources among several competing items. Such embellishments are possible by using the array features of DYNAMO and adding decision structure at the appropriate points.

The multiechelon system used to illustrate the approach is a typical information-feedback structure that moves toward a recognizable goal. Despite wide agreement among logisticians about what the goal should be, there is less agreement about the methods to achieve the goal of the support system. The route to minimization of stockouts can take several forms. One can trade off repair capability, reserve stocks, transportation, and facilities to achieve the goal. The primary benefit of this research is production of a model that assists policy makers in evaluating current and future options. It is most useful in combination with other analytical techniques. [Received: September 2, 1982. Accepted: April 12, 1983.]

REFERENCES

[1] Clark, A. J. An informal survey of multi-echelon inventory theory. *Naval Research Logistics Quarterly*, 1972, *19*, 621-650.

[2] Demmy, W. S., & Presutti, V. J. Multi-echelon inventory theory in the air force logistics command. In L. B. Schwarz (Ed.), *Multi-level production/inventory control systems: Theory and practice*. New York: North-Holland, 1981.

[3] Feeny, G. J., & Sherbrooke, C. C. *A system approach to base stockage of recoverable items* (RM-4720-PR). Santa Monica, Cal.: Rand Corporation, December 1965.

[4] Feeny, G. J., & Sherbrooke, C. C. *The (s − 1,s) inventory policy under compound Poisson demand: A theory of recoverable item stockage* (RM-4176-PK). Santa Monica, Cal.: Rand Corporation, March, 1966.

[5] Forrester, J. W. *Industrial dynamics*. Cambridge, Mass.: MIT Press, 1961.

[6] Forrester, J. W., & Senge, P. M. Tests for building confidence in system dynamics models. In A. A. Legasto, Jr., J. W. Forrester, & L. M. Lyneis (Eds.), *Studies in the management sciences: System dynamics* (Vol. 14). New York: North-Holland, 1980.

[7] Graves, S. C., & Keilsen, J. A methodology for studying the dynamics of extended logistics systems. *Naval Research Logistics Quarterly*, 1979, *26*, 167-197.

[8] Hadley, Q., & Whitin, T. M. *Analysis of inventory systems*. Englewood Cliffs, N.J.: Prentice-Hall, 1963.

[9] Hall, R. I., & Menzies, W. B. A computer system model of a sports club using simulation as an aid to policy-making in a crisis. *Management Science*, 1983, *29*, 52-60.
[10] Hausman, W. H., & Scudder, G. D. Priority scheduling rules for reparable inventory system. *Management Science*, 1982, *20*, 1215-1232.
[11] Hillestad, R. J. *Dyna-METRIC: Dynamic multi-echelon technique for recoverable item control* (R-2785-AF). Santa Monica, Cal.: Rand Corporation, July 1982.
[12] Hillestad, R. J., & Carillo, M. J. *Models and techniques for recoverable item stockage when demand and the repair process are nonstationary—Part I: Performance measurement* (N-1482-AF). Santa Monica, Cal.: Rand Corporation, May 1980.
[13] Legasto, A. A., Jr., & Maciarillo, J. System dynamics: A critical review. In A. A. Legasto, Jr., J. W. Forrester, & J. M. Lyneis (Eds.), *Studies in the management sciences: System dynamics* (Vol. 14). New York: North-Holland, 1980.
[14] Miller, B. L. *A real time metric for the distribution of serviceable assets* (RM-5687-PR). Santa Monica, Cal.: Rand Corporation, October 1968.
[15] Morecroft, J. D. W. *System dynamics as a tool for information systems design* (System Dynamics Group D-2755-1). Unpublished manuscript, Massachusetts Institute of Technology, October 1977.
[16] Muckstadt, J. A. A model for a multi-item, multiechelon, multi-indenture inventory system. *Management Science*, 1973, *19*, 472-481.
[17] Muckstadt, J. A. A three-echelon, multi-item model for recoverable items. *Naval Research Logistics Quarterly*, 1979, *26*, 199-221.
[18] Muckstadt, J. A. *Comparative adequacy of steady state versus dynamic models for calculating stockage requirements* (R-2636-AF). Santa Monica, Cal.: Rand Corporation, November 1980.
[19] Nahmias, S. Managing reparable item inventory systems: A review. In L. B. Schwarz (Ed.), *Multi-level production/inventory control systems: Theory and practice*. New York: North-Holland, 1981.
[20] Pugh, A. L., III. *DYNAMO users' manual* (5th ed.). Cambridge, Mass.: MIT Press, 1976.
[21] Schwarz, L. B. (Ed.). *Multi-level production/inventory control systems: Theory and practice*. New York: North-Holland, 1981.
[22] Sherbrooke, C. C. *METRIC: A multi-echelon technique for recoverable item control* (RM-5078-PR). Santa Monica, Cal.: Rand Corporation, November 1966.
[23] Sherbrooke, C. C. *A management perspective on METRIC—Multi-echelon technique for recoverable item control* (RM-5078/1-PR). Santa Monica, Cal.: Rand Corporation, January 1968.

Thomas D. Clark, Jr., is Professor of Systems Management in the School of Engineering at the Air Force Institute of Technology. He received his D.B.A. degree in management from the Florida State University. He has published articles in a number of journals including *Behavioral Science* and *The Public Administration Quarterly* and is the author of two books dealing with application of computers in decision making and computer simulation. He has fifteen years of experience as an aircraft maintenance manager in the U.S. Air Force. His research interests are in the areas of computer simulation and information system design.

Robert E. Trempe is major in the U.S. Air Force. He holds an M.S. in logistics management from the Air Force Institute of Technology. He has had a variety of assignments in transportation management, with primary emphasis in air movement of cargo. He is currently a transportation requirements and systems analyst.

Herbert E. Trichlin is a squadron leader in the Royal Australian Air Force. He holds an M.S. in logistics management from the Air Force Institute of Technology. He has managed large inventory systems and has served as an engineering project officer for avionics and electronic warfare systems. He is currently assigned to the Australian Department of Defense Air Force Office as a plans officer and systems analyst.

[19]

Concepts, Theory, and Techniques

A SYSTEMS PERSPECTIVE ON MATERIAL REQUIREMENTS PLANNING*

John D. W. Morecroft, *Massachusetts Institute of Technology*

ABSTRACT

For many companies, the implementation of material requirements planning systems has failed to produce the expected improvements in manufacturing efficiency. This paper shows that MRP failure can occur in the common situation in which MRP is installed in a manufacturing environment that has evolved around manual methods of material control. A system dynamics simulation model is used to interrelate decision functions (policies) of a manufacturing firm. Simulation runs of the model operating with manual methods of material control show six- to seven-year fluctuations in production, ordering, and labor. A modified version of the model, changed only by the introduction of a requirements explosion to represent MRP, shows that MRP can actually cause more severe production fluctuations, resulting in lower average labor productivity and higher manufacturing costs. The major practical implication of the analysis is that the organizational environment that suits MRP (and utilizes its inherent strengths) is different from the environment that is likely to prevail at the time of implementation.

Subject Areas: Production/Operations Management, Inventory Management, System Dynamics, and Simulation.

INTRODUCTION

Over the past decade, there has been a remarkable growth in the use of integrated computer-based systems to help control inventory levels and material flows in manufacturing firms. Such computer-based systems, known generically as MRP (material requirements planning) systems, hold the promise of reducing manufacturing inventory levels and improving customer service. However, as Miller has pointed out,

For many companies, these supposedly modern systems offer little improvement over the manual systems that preceded them. [12, p. 145]

Miller cites survey information from Sirny [18] indicating that only 44 percent of manufacturing companies surveyed felt that their new computerized manufacturing control systems were cost effective, and from Shaw and Regentz [17] indicating that as many as 50 percent of companies expressed dissatisfaction over newly installed systems.

Many reasons have been advanced for the failure of MRP. At the technical level, inaccuracy of the data base supporting material ordering is often cited as a problem. Hall and Vollmann [8] have indicated the importance of management

---

*The author is indebted to Jay W. Forrester and two anonymous referees for comments received on earlier drafts of this paper, which was presented at the Twelfth Annual Meeting of the American Institute for Decision Sciences, November 1980. The analysis presented in this paper was supported by funds from a joint MIT/corporate research project. Preparation of the paper was supported by the System Dynamics Corporate Research Program of the Sloan School of Management, MIT.

commitment to the implementation of MRP. More recently Miller [12] has argued that manufacturing control system failure can be traced to the failure of managers to ensure that the systems developed are consistent with the strategic and organizational requirements of the company.

This paper presents an analysis that focuses on organizational issues, in the same spirit as Miller [12], but uses simulation modeling to develop insight into the likely causes of MRP failure. We are interested in the broad question of whether an efficient method of materials management (one that is, in principle, more efficient than manual methods[1]) will work effectively with the rest of the manufacturing organization in which it is placed.

From this "systems" perspective, materials management is but one part of a much larger decision-making process that involves in addition such activities as aggregate production planning, labor hiring, and vendor supply. The only *assured* changes in decision making that occur with the introduction of MRP are concentrated within materials management. The requirements explosion process forces a change in the channels of information used in all ordering and scheduling decisions. Decisions are based on a single, central source of information, the master schedule of production, rather than local usage information, as occurs in manual order-point systems. MRP, however, does not *guarantee* any change in the body of decision making that surrounds materials management, which, in the short run, is relatively "frozen" according to standard operating procedures.

Our purpose, then, is to understand what happens when MRP (defined as a requirements explosion) is introduced into an existing organization that has evolved around more primitive material management methods. This is the implementation environment that is likely to prevail in many real-world situations. If the rest of the manufacturing organization continues with its pre-MRP decision-making habits, do we necessarily have a better manufacturing system? What kinds of problems can we anticipate when simply planting MRP in a complex organizational setting?

The method of analysis involves the use of a system dynamics simulation model to interrelate the decision functions (policies) of a manufacturing firm. A base version of the model depicts the organization operating according to a manual order-point scheme. Simulation runs of the model show that the interaction of aggregate production planning, labor planning, and material ordering results in six- to seven-year fluctuations in production, material, and labor. A modified version of the model introduces a requirements explosion to represent MRP. The remainder of the decision making in the organization is unchanged. Simulation runs of the revised model show that MRP can actually *cause* more severe production fluctuations, lowering average labor productivity and driving up manufacturing cost. Furthermore, and of equal importance, the simulation model is used to show that there is a compelling rationale to *expect* improvements from the introduction of MRP but that these expectations are based on a mistaken and overly simple perception of the manufacturing environment.

---

[1]As Orlicky [16] has argued, the ability of MRP to distinguish truly random variations in derived demand from deterministic variations caused by lot sizing enables an MRP system to operate with less safety stock than an order point system and therefore to be intrinsically more efficient.

AN ORGANIZATIONAL SETTING FOR MRP

Materials planning does not take place in isolation. It is a decision-making process that is contingent upon decisions made elsewhere in the organization by many different people who are not necessarily aware of, or even concerned about, day-to-day activities in material control. These different people may include senior managers responsible for setting aggregate production plans, personnel managers responsible for hiring labor to support the production plan, and vendors whose main concern is with running their own organizations effectively. The point is that when MRP is introduced, it directly affects decision making only within the material control area of a manufacturing organization. The rest of the decision-making structure (perhaps 90 percent or more) is left entirely intact, operating according to the rules and traditions built up through the daily routine of company operations. To understand the impact of MRP, we must view it within the context of this "frozen" structure.

Figure 1 is a schematic representation of a manufacturing organization. It depicts four subunits that are intimately involved in the overall control of the manufacturing process. Material control is one of these subunits, and it is within material control that the MRP system is implemented.

At the top of Figure 1 is the subunit labeled production control. Here is located the aggregate production planning decision, usually made by senior managers in the organization. Their willingness to change production rates depends upon the organization's overall objectives for customer service standards (in terms of delivery response time) and finished inventory investment. A company that prides itself on prompt customer service and rapid inventory turnover is likely to operate with a volatile production schedule. Thus, the variability of production planning (which is an important part of the environment for MRP) is largely a function of company philosophy and tradition. There is no reason to believe that either philosophy or tradition will be influenced by the introduction of MRP.

On the right of Figure 1 is the subunit labeled labor management. Here are located overtime, hiring, and layoff decisions. The labor management subunit provides the labor to support the aggregate production plan. This subunit, however, must act within constraints set by company traditions that govern the rate at which the labor force can be increased or decreased (for example, the company may have a policy of decreasing labor force only through attrition) and contractual limitations on the amount of overtime that can be worked. The traditions and practices in the labor management subunit have likely evolved as a working compromise between short-term production needs and basic company attitudes toward labor. There is no reason to suppose any immediate change in these traditions with the introduction of MRP, even though the overall efficiency of manufacturing depends jointly on the availability of labor and materials.

On the left of Figure 1 is the subunit labeled material control. Within material control are located the activities of parts production and materials ordering. As the aggregate production plan changes, the material control subunit must vary the volume and mix of production parts, schedule parts production on the shop floor,

FIGURE 1
An Organizational Setting for MRP

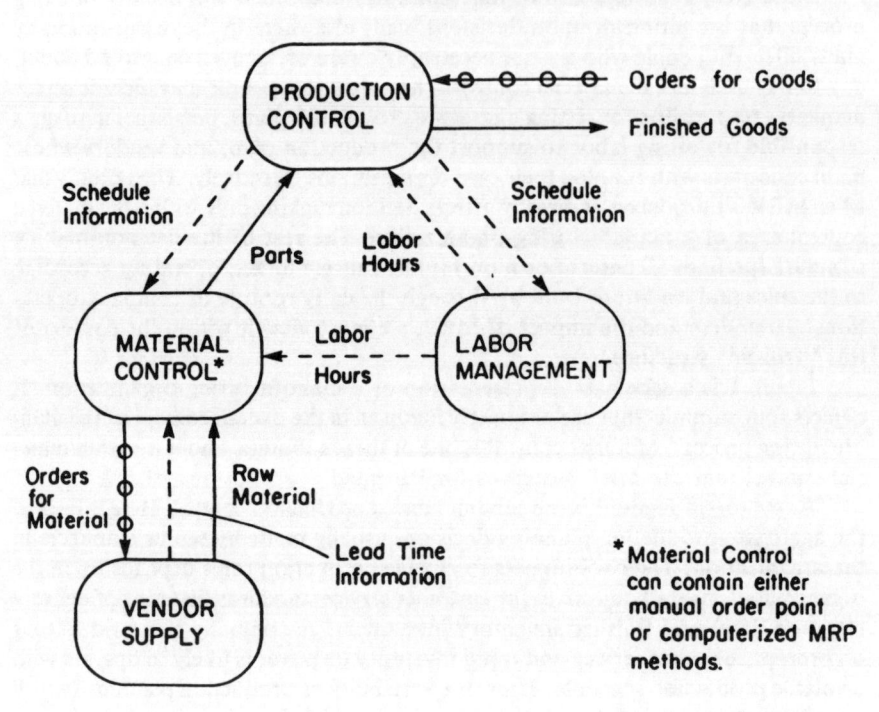

*Material Control can contain either manual order point or computerized MRP methods.

and place orders with outside suppliers. The way in which these decisions are made will depend in part on the company's philosophy of manufacturing inventory turnover, acceptability of stockouts, and required responsiveness to changes in the aggregate production plan.

On the lower left of Figure 1 is the vendor supply subunit. The vendor supply subunit represents a number of outside organizations that are receiving purchase requests from material control and shipping parts and materials in return. The responsiveness of vendor supply to the purchase requests of the upstream manufacturer depends on vendor traditions for service reliability and inventory investment. The introduction of MRP does not guarantee any change in vendor traditions.

In summary, our discussion has shown that MRP operates within a "frozen" environment consisting of established policies and procedures. The basic MRP mechanism, a requirements explosion, makes only a small change in the overall decision-making structure of the organization, and there is no guarantee that the change will be compatible with the remainder of the existing organization.

METHOD OF ANALYSIS

The vehicle for analysis is a simulation model of a manufacturing organization. The model can appropriately be viewed as an organizational process model [4] and should be distinguished from normative optimizing models that are often used in manufacturing systems. An organizational process model is aimed at understanding the interactions between existing decision rules that might account for inefficiencies. Usually an organizational process model will span several functional areas. By contrast, most normative optimizing models do not pay great attention to the existing decision rules and are more specifically focused on designing optimal decision rules within a single functional area.

The simulation model was constructed using the structuring principles of system dynamics as defined by Forrester [5] [6]. System dynamics is particularly appropriate since it readily lends itself to portraying the breadth of organizational structure (encompassing several interrelated functional areas) that forms the operating environment for material requirements planning. Furthermore, the formulation of a system dynamics model clearly identifies the goal-seeking aspect of decision making—in which the traditions and management philosophy of the company are reflected.

The model arose from a system dynamics research project conducted over several years with a manufacturer of heavy automotive equipment. At the time of the analysis the manufacturer was considering converting to computerized MRP from an essentially manual system. The model therefore portrays the traditions and manufacturing philosophy of one particular company but contains sufficient general characteristics of all manufacturing organizations to make the analysis of broad value and interest.

The analysis begins using a model of the organization the way it was before the introduction of MRP. There is not sufficient space to describe the detailed formulations of the entire model, but we can at least describe the broad characteristics of the organization as they are reflected in the formulation of decision functions. We take as our base for discussion the overview diagram in Figure 1. (See [14, pp. 62-87] and [7, pp. 2-111] for equation descriptions of the complete model.)

In the production control subunit, the policy of the company is generally to build to order and to maintain relatively low levels of finished inventory. Delivery times are regarded as an important competitive variable. As a result of these policy characteristics, aggregate production planning tends to respond quickly to changes in demand. In the labor management subunit, policy is oriented toward achieving a flexible workforce. Overtime can be used to increase capacity up to 25 percent above normal. Layoffs are used to bring about rapid downward adjustment of the work force, and hiring quickly responds to needs dictated by aggregate production planning. In the material control subunit, policy is dominated by a desire to restrain manufacturing inventory costs. Inventory is tightly controlled around a relatively small base level. The model portrays a manual materials planning process in which ordering is based on past usage—essentially an order-point system. In the vendor subunit, aggregate production planning portrays a ship-from-stock philosophy involving a substantial finished inventory investment. When vendor's inventory is insufficient to cover incoming orders, delivery delay can rise to two or three times the normal delay.

With this "base" model, the first step is to examine the production characteristics of the existing decision-making structure. Specifically, we examine how the manufacturing system as a whole adapts to a one-time 10 percent step increase in demand. From the base run, we are able to learn about the volatility and responsiveness of the environment into which MRP is inserted.

Next, the material control subunit is modified to represent the changes that occur in switching from order-point to MRP methods. The simulation runs are then repeated to see how MRP modifies the performance of the manufacturing organization.

SIMULATION ANALYSIS OF
THE ORIGINAL MANUFACTURING ORGANIZATION (EXPERIMENT 1)

The first simulation experiment shows the response of the manufacturing organization to an unexpected 10 percent step increase in customer demand. The experiment starts with the model in a state of equilibrium, as it would be following a long period of stable demand. Production at the different stages of manufacturing is taking place at a steady rate compatible with demand. Inventories throughout the manufacturing system are steady at levels that satisfy the inventory turnover objectives for the organization.

Figure 2A shows behavior in the material control subunit. Three progressive stages of derived demand are shown, starting with the aggregate schedule and progressing downward to a subassembly schedule and raw material order rate.[2] The response of the system is clearly oscillatory, with a time period of seven years. As time progresses, the oscillations gradually subside, so that scheduling and ordering settle at rates compatible with the new higher level of demand.

Figure 2B shows the behavior of direct labor, overtime, and labor productivity in the labor management subunit. In the short term, the labor subunit adjusts to increased demand by going on overtime—a condition that persists for almost two years. In the longer term, the level of direct labor is increased, but the pattern of adjustment is strongly oscillatory, periods of hiring being followed by layoff in an attempt to arrive at the appropriate level of labor. Labor productivity also moves in an oscillatory fashion, reflecting the availability of parts and

---

[2]The subassembly schedule and raw material order rate are measured in terms of finished unit equivalents. In other words, they show the number of finished units that could be assembled from the underlying parts and materials. The timing and amplitude of derived demand at the different stages vary because of inventory adjustments and lags in scheduling that are overlaid on the base customer demand.

FIGURE 2
Step Response of Original Manufacturing Organization Using Order-Point Methods

A. Material Control

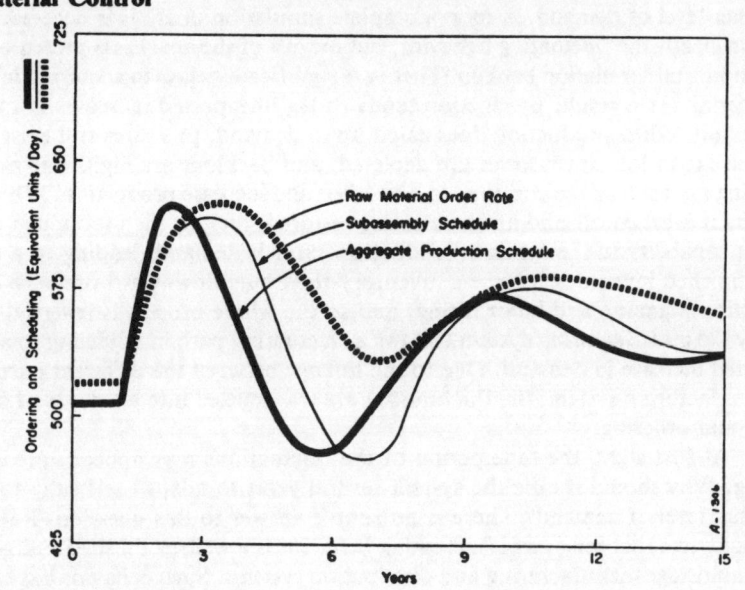

B. Labor Management

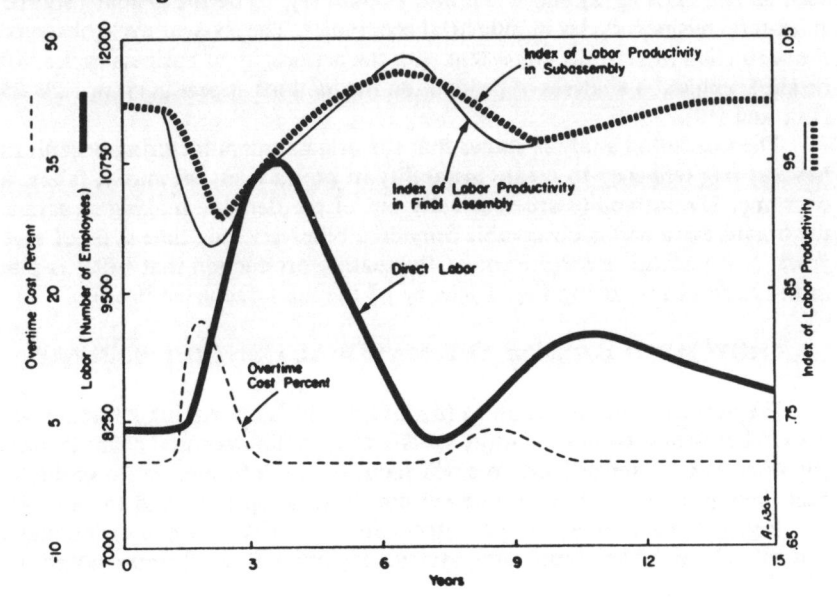

materials with which the labor force can work. During the initial phase of adjustment, productivity tends to fall as parts shortages develop. As the flow of parts and materials increases, the shortages are eliminated and then reversed to become excesses, thereby causing a rise in labor productivity.

The overall response is a rather sluggish and imprecise adjustment to the new higher level of demand. A more complete simulation analysis is necessary to explain clearly the fluctuating behavior, but the gist of the analysis is presented below without full simulation backup. There are significant delays in acquiring labor and material. As a result, production tends to lag unexpected increases in customer demand. When production does catch up to demand, pressures still exist to continue expansion. Inventories are depleted, and backlogs are high. The manufacturing system tends to continue to hire labor and increase production. When backlogs are worked off and inventories are restored, there is then too much production capability in the system. Production exceeds demand, leading to a buildup of finished inventories. Excess inventory then puts downward pressure on production planning and labor hiring, and so the whole process is reversed. In this way the manufacturing system follows a fluctuating path in adjusting to an unexpected increase in demand. Due to the linkage between the different parts of the manufacturing system, the fluctuations are transmitted into all stages of scheduling and ordering.

At first sight, the time period of the fluctuations may appear unreasonably long. Why should it take the system several years to adapt itself fully to a new, higher level of demand? There is no simple answer to this question. Rather, we should note that long-term fluctuating behavior is a well-established characteristic of multistage manufacturing and distribution systems. Such behavior has been empirically observed in the work of Mack [10] and is believed by many economists, such as Abramovitz [2] and Klein and Popkin [9], to be the primary source of short-term business cycles in industrial economies. The six-year cycle observed in the simulation run is quite consistent with the periodicity of business cycles. More detailed simulation analyses of production fluctuations appear in [5, pp. 253-257], [15], and [19].

The simulation analysis shows that the original manufacturing organization has a strong tendency to create instability in production, inventory, labor, and overtime. The instability arises directly out of the decision-making structure of the organization and is observable only on a relatively long time scale of several years. It is into this environment of fluctuating production that MRP is placed in the hope of improving the efficiency of the manufacturing process.

HOW MRP CHANGES THE MATERIAL CONTROL SUBUNIT

We now turn our attention to the internal decision-making structure of the material control subunit and, more specifically, to the structural changes that occur when MRP is introduced. We will focus on the information flows that connect the top of the manufacturing system to the shop floor and to vendors.

Figure 3 is a comparison of order-point and MRP versions of the material control subunit. The figure uses system dynamics flow diagram notation [5,

FIGURE 3
Comparison of Order-Point and MRP Methods in Material Control Subunit

A. Order-Point Material Control Subunit Showing Local Control

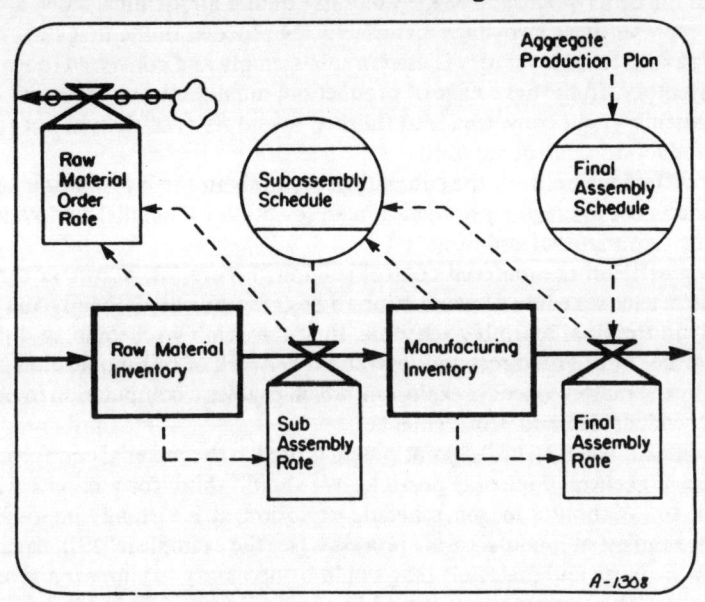

B. MRP Material Control Subunit Showing Central Control

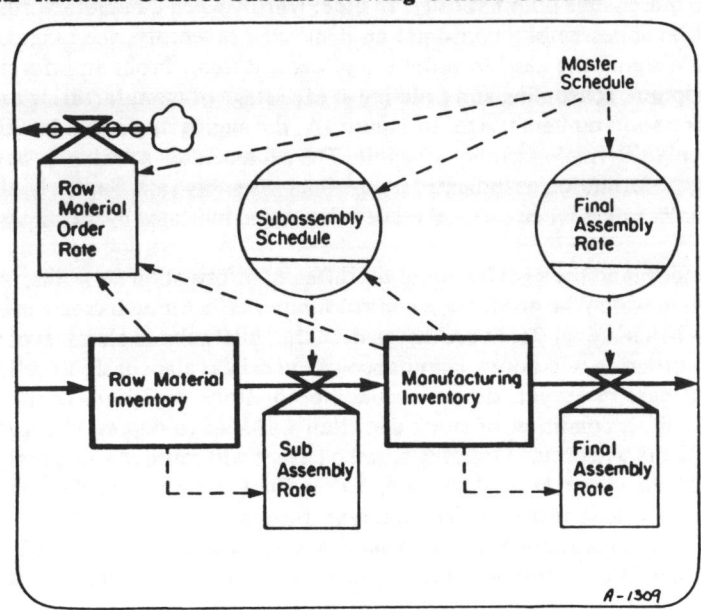

pp. 81-85] to depict the physical flow of parts and materials as well as the information network that controls the physical flows. Solid lines indicate physical flows of materials and parts. Broken lines represent information flows.

Both the order-point and MRP subunits contain an identical stock and flow network representing a two-stage manufacturing process. In the first stage of production, raw material inventory is used in subassembly and converted to manufacturing inventory. In the next stage of production, manufacturing inventory is used in final assembly and converted into finished inventory (not shown, but residing in the production control subunit).

The difference between the subunits lies entirely in the information network that connects the aggregate production plan (or master schedule) to downstream scheduling and material ordering.

Using MRP in the material control subunit, Figure 3B, allows information about the master schedule of production to be communicated directly and simultaneously to the final assembly schedule, the subassembly schedule, and the raw material order rate. This direct and centralized network of communication is made possible by the master schedule explosion, which enables a computation to be made of all dependent demand requirements.

In contrast, when an order-point system is used in the material control subunit, Figure 3A, no central control is possible. We should think for a minute why this should be so. Without a master schedule explosion, it is virtually impossible, in all but the simplest of manufacturing processes (see the example in [13]), to calculate manually the parts and materials that would be necessary to support a given production plan. The computations would be too time-consuming and cumbersome to be used routinely. It is better and easier to allow usage to "unravel" dependent demand requirements automatically. In other words, when a manufacturing process (such as subassembly) consumes an item from inventory, the usage of that item should signal the need to order a replacement item. From an information-flow standpoint, scheduling and ordering at each stage of manufacturing use only local information on item usage. In Figure 3A, the aggregate production plan influences only the final assembly schedule. The subassembly schedule is based on local usage information as indicated by the final assembly rate. Similarly, the raw material order rate is based on local usage information indicated by the subassembly rate.

To understand the significance of the different information networks, imagine a situation in which the production control subunit calls for an increase in output at a time when material stocks are depleted. In the MRP subunit all stages of scheduling and ordering will adjust simultaneously and instantaneously to reflect the desired increase in output, despite a condition of stock depletion. In the order-point subunit, a condition of stock depletion will lead to depressed usage rates since stockouts will occur. Ordering based on usage will cause raw material ordering to fall below the real needs dictated by the final assembly schedule, resulting in sluggish response to the desired increase in output.

MRP has one additional effect on material control which is not visible in Figure 3 but which is of great importance. An MRP system is able to keep very accurate track of vendor lead times. The system is able to detect when lead times are rising and factor that information into future purchase recommendations. By contrast, a manual system is unlikely to have access to such timely information (due again to the clerical load involved) and is more likely to detect a condition of rising lead time through an unexpected stockout.

In summary, the discussion has shown that MRP has two important effects on the information network in material control. First, it replaces the network of local control typical of order-point systems with centralized control emanating directly from the master schedule of production. Second, it provides more timely information on vendor lead times.

THE FROZEN STRUCTURE SURROUNDING MRP

As we indicated earlier, structure is tied to the traditions and established procedures of an organization that have evolved over many years of operation. It is important, however, to be clear in a more formal sense about the meaning of the frozen structure surrounding MRP. Does a frozen structure, for example, imply that all decisions outside material control will be totally unaffected by MRP? The answer is no. Many decisions will be different, but the criteria for decision making will not (or need not) be changed.

Structure refers to the network of information channels supporting company policy and the interpretation given to that information. Structure does not, however, refer to the message content of specific information channels. For example, one channel of information entering the aggregate production-planning policy is the status of finished inventory. An unusually high level of finished inventory will bring about a downward adjustment of the production plan. The magnitude of the downward adjustment depends upon the urgency with which a condition of excess inventory is viewed—hence, upon the interpretation of the inventory status in the production-planning policy. The introduction of MRP does not change the criteria for decision making within the policy. The policy still uses finished inventory information and still interprets a condition of excess with the same urgency it would if order-point methods were in use. However, MRP does change the *variability* of finished inventory by making manufacturing more responsive to demand changes. Therefore, the content of the inventory information channel is changed. As a result, the stream of decisions coming out of the aggregate production-planning policy is changed, even though the structure of the policy is frozen. The same idea applies elsewhere in the system. The structure of the labor-hiring policy is frozen, but the content of the information it uses is changed by the introduction of MRP. The structure of vendor-supply policies is frozen, but the material-ordering information that drives them is changed by the introduction of MRP.

SIMULATION ANALYSIS OF THE MANUFACTURING ORGANIZATION USING MRP (EXPERIMENT 2)

In the second simulation experiment, shown in Figure 4, we again look at the response of the manufacturing organization to an unexpected 10 percent step

FIGURE 4
Step Response of Original Manufacturing Organization Using MRP

A. Material Control

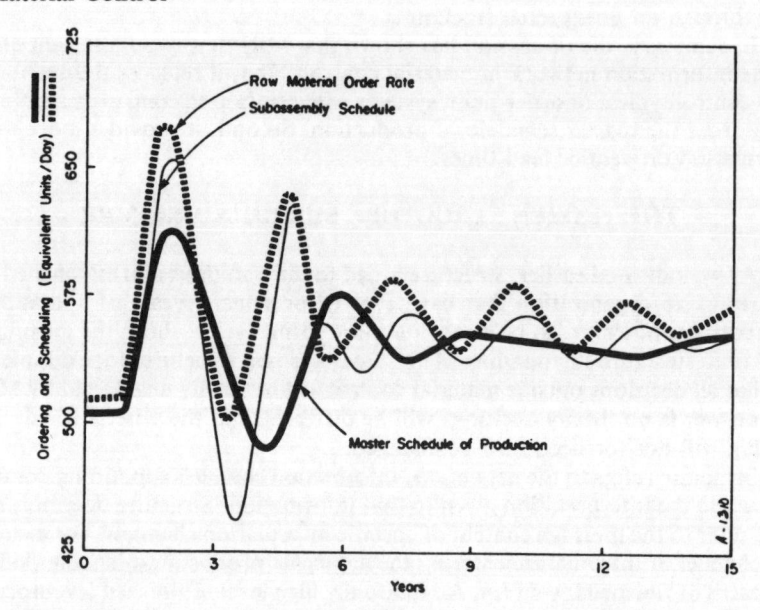

B. Labor Management

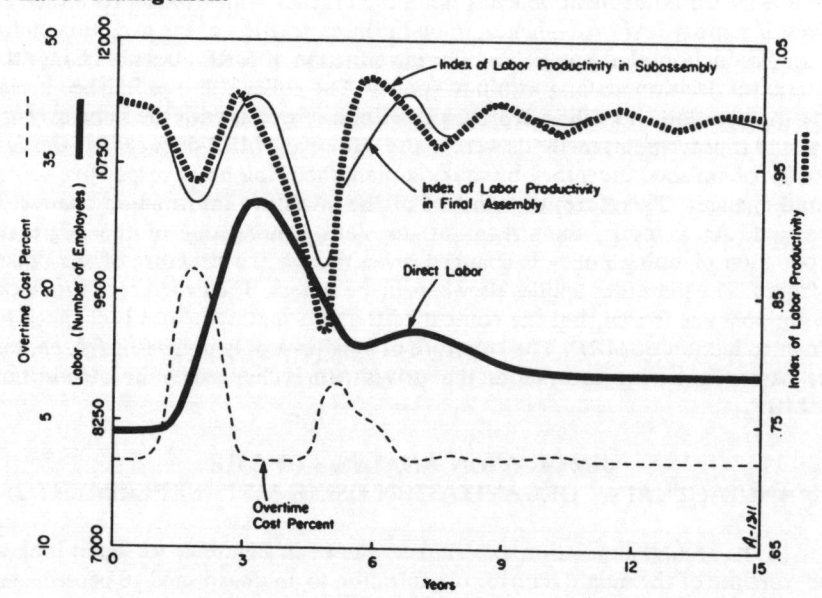

increase in demand, but now under the assumption that the MRP requirements explosion has been implemented. We assume that the remainder of the manufacturing system is unchanged. The policies governing aggregate production planning, labor management, and vendor supply are the same as in Experiment 1. We are therefore seeing an organization adopt MRP into a frozen policy environment that is geared to order-point methods of material control.

In Figure 4A we see that MRP actually worsens the fluctuations in scheduling and ordering by comparison with Figure 2A. The raw material order rate and subassembly schedule both show more variability than in Figure 2A, indicating that MRP has more tendency to amplify demand variations than order-point methods. In addition, the time period of the fluctuation (the time between peaks) is greatly reduced, from seven years to approximately three years.

In Figure 4B, we see how the effects of MRP are transmitted into the labor management subunit. Perhaps the most important effect is that labor productivity is more variable than in the order-point system and, on the average, lower. The greater variability in productivity results from material shortages that are directly attributable to volatile ordering and scheduling induced by MRP. Overtime usage is also higher on the average than in the order-point system—both as a result of more volatile scheduling and more variable productivity.

Manufacturing cost is likely to have risen with the introduction of MRP due to the fall in labor productivity. Moreover, it would not be easy in a real manufacturing firm to blame the productivity changes directly on MRP. If we consider the symptoms that are observed, we see there is every reason for assigning the blame elsewhere. Supplies from vendors are more variable than in Experiment 1, so the fluctuations in material availability could easily be blamed on vendors. The aggregate production schedule is more variable than in Experiment 1, so shortages of material could easily be blamed on inadequate forecasting or more capricious ordering habits of customers. Finally, the time scale of the fluctuating behavior is sufficiently long (3 years) to lead to the conclusion that the fluctuations are not associated with the short-term logistics of MRP.

EXPLAINING THE EFFECTS OF MRP

On the face of it, we might expect MRP to improve rather than worsen the behavior of the manufacturing system in which it is placed, even if that manufacturing system does not change its policies to accommodate MRP. After all, centralized control of scheduling and ordering and more timely vendor lead-time information would appear to be prerequisites for responsive and efficient manufacturing.

The rationale for expected improvement is compelling but is based on a mistaken and overly simple perception or "mental model" of the manufacturing environment. In this section, we will use a simplified version of the simulation model to reconcile our intuition about MRP with the observed effects shown in Experiment 2. The analysis should improve understanding of MRP and increase confidence in the model.

FIGURE 5
Step Response of Original Manufacturing Organization Using MRP with Fixed Vendor Lead Times

A. Material Control

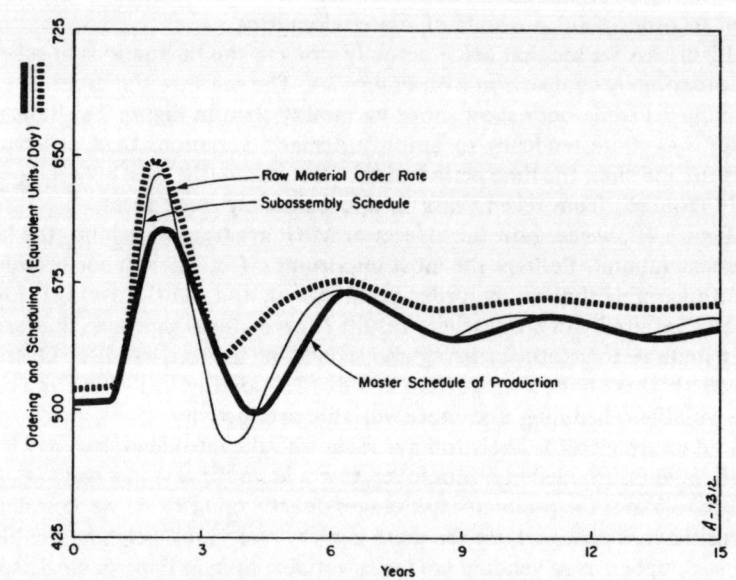

B. Labor Management

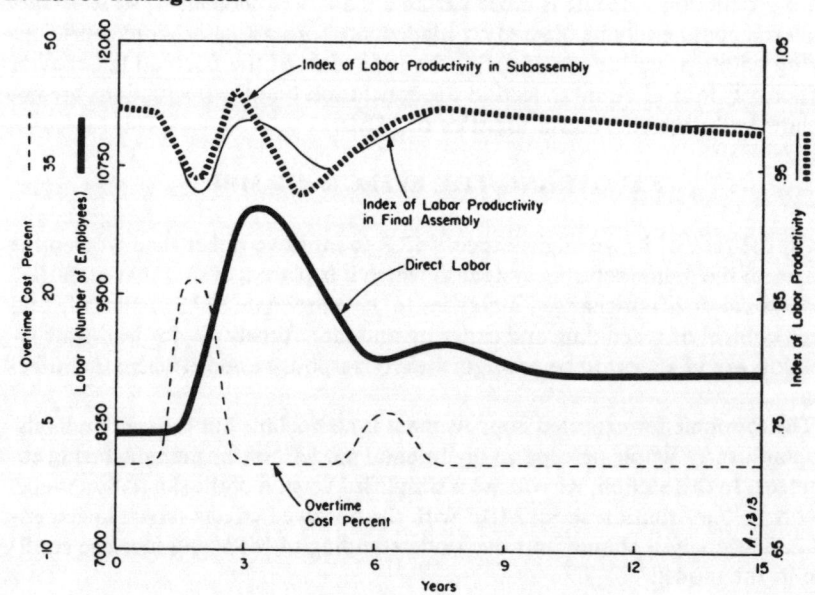

The analysis hinges upon the load variations that MRP places on the shop floor and vendors. We imagine a situation in which the shop floor and vendors can supply any load with fixed lead time—in other words, a situation in which there are no short-term capacity constraints. In the model, average vendor lead time is held at a fixed value, but otherwise conditions are identical to those in Experiment 2. Figure 5 shows the step response of the manufacturing organization using MRP under the assumption of fixed vendor lead times. The reader should compare this figure with Figures 4 and 2.

In Figure 5A, the trajectories of scheduling and ordering are shown. By comparison with Figure 4A, the trajectories are more stable, indicating a more orderly adjustment to the demand change. By comparison with Figure 2A, the time period of the fluctuation is reduced, but with no increase in instability. The behavior agrees with our intuition about the likely effects of MRP. Centralized control of ordering and scheduling enables the manufacturing system to respond more quickly than the local control of order-point methods and to reach a new equilibrium more quickly.

In Figure 5B, the trajectories of labor productivity, direct labor, and overtime are shown. By comparison with Figure 2B, labor productivity is on the average higher and recovers more quickly after an initial decline, reflecting the advantage that MRP has over order-point methods in increasing the flow of parts and materials. The simplified model leads to the conclusion that MRP is better than order-point methods and supports our intuition that MRP should improve productivity by reducing the likelihood of stockouts.

Why then does this advantage disappear when vendor lead times are no longer fixed (or, more generally, when there are limits on short-term capacity)? In realistic situtations, lead times are a function of load—the greater the load, the longer the lead time.[3] As lead times rise, MRP rapidly updates its lead-time estimates and orders more materials further ahead to compensate. (Remember that the order-point system is not capable of rapidly updating lead times.) As a result, load on the vendor grows still further, well beyond the "base" requirements dictated by the master schedule. The MRP system readily becomes locked into a vicious spiral of speculative overordering. But the vendors have no way of knowing that some of the orders are speculative and continue to respond to the order stream according to established manufacturing and planning procedures. Only when the vendors have substantially increased supply (which often cannot be done without a delay of several months), is the vicious spiral broken and reversed. The reversal causes underordering of materials and eventual material shortage. The speculative ordering tendency of MRP, imposed on the frozen production-control and supply procedures of the vendor, actually induces fluctuations in material ordering and material stocks, which are then transmitted throughout the rest of the manufacturing system. Fluctuations in material stocks are transmitted into labor

---

[3]In this model, lead times are actually more accurately portrayed as a nonlinear function of load. Small increases in load can be readily accommodated by vendors by drawing down finished inventory with no increase in lead time. If inventory is depleted, however, lead times will necessarily rise.

productivity and production rates. Production rates influence the status of finished inventory and backlog and thereby transmit the fluctuations into aggregate production planning and labor hiring.

Our argument reconciles the apparent advantage to be gained from MRP with its observed disadvantages in Experiment 2. MRP improves the stability and efficiency of manufacturing in the situation where the lead time of parts and materials is not contingent on the load. Then, faster responding schedules result in faster responding supplies. By contrast, when the lead time of parts and materials is a function of load, faster responding schedules result in more variable lead times which, coupled with rapid MRP lead-time updating, cause self-induced inventory cycles and a lowering of manufacturing efficiency.

IMPLICATIONS OF THE ANALYSIS

The analysis casts a new perspective on the evaluation of MRP. MRP should be seen and evaluated as part of a larger manufacturing system. The manufacturing system as a whole has a tendency to create long-term instability and fluctuation in production rates and labor force independent of the precise form of material control used. MRP intervenes in this structure, providing more timely information for the control of materials without altering a substantial part of the decision-making structure of the organization. Surprisingly, more timely information causes a deterioration of manufacturing performance. MRP causes the inherent fluctuations of the manufacturing system to be intensified and shortened in period. A manufacturing system using MRP appears to be particularly vulnerable to recurrent over- and underordering of materials on a three- to four-year time scale. The resultant fluctuation in material stocks causes average labor productivity to decline, thereby driving up manufacturing costs.

The major practical implication of the analysis is that the typical environment into which MRP is installed is likely to cause MRP to be troublesome, costly, and, in the long run, a failure. Furthermore, the environment is a function of a wide-ranging set of policies spanning many functional areas. Since the policies are remote from the detailed concerns of material control, they are not likely to be changed by the introduction of MRP.

The analysis should not be taken to mean that MRP is inherently worse than the systems that preceded it. Rather, the organizational environment that suits MRP and utilizes its inherent strengths is different from the environment that is likely to have evolved around manual material control systems. This result is consistent with the recent behavioral analyses of White [20] and Blasingame and Weeks [3], who stress the importance of educating and reorienting the entire organization when MRP is introduced. By extending the simulation analysis it is possible to pinpoint policy improvements that will produce an organizational environment supportive of successful MRP [14, pp, 126-183].

The analysis also has some rather interesting implications at the broader level of industry and economic performance. MRP changes policy structures that at the level of the firm cause production fluctuations and at the level of the entire economy cause short-term business cycles. Since MRP has been widely adopted in U.S. manufacturing industry we might expect to be able to observe its impact on aggregate economic data such as inventory investment. Furthermore, analysis of such data should give some indication of whether MRP implementation is, in the aggregate, being effectively accomplished.

In a recent analysis of the manufacturing and trade industries, Able and Bechter [1] showed that inventory investment over the post-1975 period is both lower and more volatile than during a pre-1975 period of equal duration. In particular, inventory sales ratios for materials and work in progress declined by 50 percent while the volatility of inventories increased by 100 percent. The 100 percent increase in inventory volatility, though not positive validation of the analysis presented in the paper, is consistent with the experimental observation that MRP induces strong fluctuations in material stocks. Moreover, such an interpretation of Able and Bechter would indicate that, in the aggregate, MRP systems are being ineffectively implemented. [Received: January 26, 1981. Accepted: July 8, 1982.]

REFERENCES

[1] Able, S. L., & Bechter, D. M. Inventory recession ahead. *Economic Review of Federal Reserve Bank of Kansas City*, 1979, *64*(7), 7-19.

[2] Abramovitz, M. *Inventories and business cycles*. New York: National Bureau of Economic Research, 1950.

[3] Blasingame, J. W., & Weeks, J. K. Behavioral dimensions of MRP change: Assessing your organization's strengths and weaknesses. *Production and Inventory Management*, 1981, *22*(First quarter), 81-95.

[4] Cyert, R. M., & March, J. G. *A behavioral theory of the firm*. Englewood Cliffs, N.J.: Prentice-Hall, 1963.

[5] Forrester, J. W. *Industrial dynamics*. Cambridge, Mass.: MIT Press, 1961.

[6] Forrester, J. W. *Principles of systems*. Cambridge, Mass.: MIT Press, Wright-Allen Series, 1968.

[7] Forrester, J. W., & Mass, N. J. *The production sector of the system dynamics national model—Equation description* (System Dynamics Group Working Paper D-2486-3). Cambridge, Mass.: Massachusetts Institute of Technology, Sloan School of Management, 1976.

[8] Hall, R. W., & Vollmann, T. E. Planning your material requirements. *Harvard Business Review*, 1978, *56*(5), 105-112.

[9] Klein, L. R., & Popkin, J. An econometric analysis of the postwar relationship between inventory fluctuation and change in economic activity. *Publications of Joint Economic Committee* (Part 3), 1961, pp. 71-86.

[10] Mack, R. P. *Information, expectations and inventory fluctuation*. New York: National Bureau of Economic Research, 1967.

[11] Mass, N. J. *Economic cycles: An analysis of underlying causes*. Cambridge, Mass.: MIT Press, Wright-Allen Series, 1975.

[12] Miller, J. G. Fit production systems to the task. *Harvard Business Review*, 1981, *59*(1), 145-154.

[13] Miller, J. G., & Sprague, L. G. Behind the growth in material requirements planning. *Harvard Business Review*, 1975, *53*(5), 83-91.

[14] Morecroft, J. D. W. *Influences from information technology on industry cycles*. Unpublished Ph.D. dissertation, Massachusetts Institute of Technology, 1979.

[15] Morecroft, J. D. W. *Structures causing instability in production and distribution systems* (System Dynamics Group Working Paper D-3244-2). Cambridge, Mass.: Massachusetts Institute of Technology, Sloan School of Management, 1980.

[16] Orlicky, J. A. *Material requirements planning*. New York: McGraw-Hill, 1975.
[17] Shaw, R. J., & Regentz, M. O. How to prepare users for a new system. *Management Focus*, 1980, *27*(2), 33-36.
[18] Sirny, R. F. The job of the P and IC manager—1975. *Production and Inventory Management*, 1977, *18*(Third quarter), 100-119.
[19] Ward, E. E. Improve production planning with an inventory adjustment policy. *Production and Inventory Management*, 1981, *22*(First quarter), 1-14.
[20] White, E. M. Implementing an MRP system using the Lewin-Schein theory of change. *Production and Inventory Management*, 1980, *21*(First quarter), 1-12.

John D. W. Morecroft is Assistant Professor of Management at the Alfred P. Sloan School of Management, Massachusetts Institute of Technology. He received his Ph.D. from MIT in system dynamics; an M.Sc. in management science from London University, Imperial College, England; and a B.Sc. from Bristol University, England. He has published in *OMEGA* and is a member of AIDS and TIMS.

[20]

Using system dynamics to measure the value of information in a business firm

Thomas D. Clark, Jr., and Fred K. Augustine, Jr.

The primary focus of the research reported in this article was on measuring the value of information in a business firm. A five-sector system dynamics model was developed and calibrated to an average firm in the U.S. metal-can production industry. The model was used to test several propositions about the economic value of information. A framework in which to assess information value was developed, and the performance of the firm was assessed using cost, profitability, and efficiency measures for the information attributes of accuracy, timeliness, relevance, and reliability at the strategic, managerial, and operational decision-making levels of the firm.

Thomas D. Clark, Jr., is professor and chairman of information and management sciences and director of the Center for Information Systems Research at the Florida State University College of Business. He has extensive operational and consul-

Like other vital resources, information must be managed to ensure that its cost is justified by the benefits that accrue to an organization from its possession. Since information systems are the tools for the "acquisition, use, retention, and transmission of information," (Wiener 1948), these resources must be managed in the same way as an organization's material, financial, and personnel resources. In order to accomplish this, resource managers must have a means of measuring both the cost and the benefits of an information system. It is generally accepted that it is much more difficult to measure the benefits of information in an enterprise's decision system than to quantify its costs.

Benefit assessment has been a fairly straightforward process for specific transaction-processing systems, because value can be equated to reduced administrative and personnel costs. The value of information has, however, been extremely difficult to quantify for decision support and control systems, especially when all systems are viewed as the information infrastructure of an organization. Since the benefits of information in an organization's decision structure should be measured in analogous ways to the cost/benefit approach used in assessing the value of transaction-processing information, several methods for assessing the value of information in the organizational context have been suggested.

Approaches to establishing the value of information

Four major approaches have been proposed for evaluating the value of information. The *information economics approach* employs statistical decision theory to determine the incremental cost of information associated with a specific set of benefits, generally for a specific decision. The assessment of benefit is usually made using the utility preference of a single decision maker, a set of available alternatives, a set of possible system states (outcomes), and alternative information patterns, all of which must be known a priori. Zmud (1978) found the approach theoretically appealing but believed that its rigid assumptions limited its applicability with respect to the complex, dynamic environments that exist in organizations.

Since user satisfaction has been widely used as a measure of information systems success (or failure), it follows that it should also be an appropriate measure of system benefits. The *perceived or utility value approach* solicits the opinions of users about an information system. This technique is highly subjective in nature and suffers from the limitations of techniques that attempt

Received March 1991
Accepted December 1991

ting experience in government management and policy development. His current research involves study of the nature and evolution of decision support systems, the value of information in decision processes, and the effects of outsourcing on information system functions. *Address:* Thomas D. Clark, Jr., Department of Information and Management Sciences, College of Business, Florida State University, Tallahassee, FL 32306, U.S.A.

Frederick K. Augustine. Jr., is assistant professor of information systems in the department of accounting and information systems, School of Business Administration, Stetson University. His research interests include the value of information, the management of systems, and the behavior of complex management systems. He has extensive management and computer systems experience. He holds M.B.A. and Ph.D. degrees from Florida State University.

to assign numeric values to entities (such as attitudes) which cannot be directly measured. Melone (1990) has discussed this limitation as well as others in using satisfaction as a measure of value. A clear link between value and user satisfaction has been difficult to establish. As with information economics, this approach usually focuses on a specific system rather than on the whole information infrastructure of an enterprise.

The *economic value approach* utilizes a somewhat similar method to that of user perception. Information system users are asked to appraise the monetary value of the information provided by the system. This method suffers from the difficulty of assigning meaningful dollar values to system attributes that are essentially intangible and from differences in users' perceptions of appropriate dollar values for the same information (Zmud 1978).

A *general systems approach* to assessing the value of information systems has been proposed by Swanson (1971), demonstrated by Morecroft (1979), and tested by Jones (1981). This approach utilizes simulation modeling in an attempt to overcome the limitations of the valuation methods previously discussed and to extend the evaluation from a single decision maker to the enterprise level. The simulation modeling approach attempts to assess the benefits of information by examining the merits of certain information attributes in terms of their impact on overall system performance. The approach has used only the attributes of timeliness and accuracy, and has not been specifically directed at a business organization's decision system.

Wolstenholme et al. (1990) followed the modeling approach in assessing an information system in the defense environment. They proposed a three-stage process applied in a holistic framework that focused on the effectiveness of an entire information system. Our approach is quite similar to theirs. It differs in how information attributes are treated and how specific decision patterns are modeled. The Wolstenholme study does confirm that use of a modeling methodology seems to be a worthwhile approach to the complexity of information value assessment.

To pursue a modeling methodology, we must identify a complete and relevant set of information attributes, assign different dimensions to these attributes, and test the performance of the system on these several dimensions. The benefit of any performance gain must then be related to the cost of providing the information to establish economic value. The application of this experimental approach assumes the existence of a valid model that effectively incorporates the decision-making and information-processing structures of the organization. The research reported in this article extends the systems approach by developing an expanded set of attributes, formulating multidimensional performance measures, and directly addressing an organization's specific decision system.

The quality of information

The quality of information can be expressed in terms of a set of attributes that define its nature. Any information will possess certain attributes that determine its usefulness in a given decision process. The value of information can therefore be established by assessing (formally or informally) the contributions to a decision system made by the several attributes under various conditions. The body of literature addressing this topic is limited, especially with respect to empirical research aimed at determining the attributes that adequately describe information. One notable exception is the study by Zmud (1978). As a result of his empirical analysis, an eight-factor attribute structure was suggested to describe information. The eight attributes of information were divided into four groups: (1) its overall quality, (2) its relevance, (3) how well it is presented, (4) how well it conveys meaning. This scheme is shown in Table 1.

O'Reilly (1982) and Swanson (1987) provide support for assessing information quality via attributes; both suggest approaches similar to the structure shown in Table 1. Feltham (1972) and Marder (1979) believe that the value of information is related to its usefulness, which they evaluate using similar attributes. The problem is quantification of the attributes. Appropriate ratio scales, or even interval scales, for information attributes are difficult to develop. What must be

Table 1. Information attributes

Attribute group	Attribute	Description
1. Overall quality	Relevance	Applicable Significant
2. Relevance	Accuracy	Accurate Believable Factual True
	Quantity	Complete Sufficient
	Reliability	Reliable Valid
	Timeliness	Timely Current
3. Presentation (format)	Arrangement	Orderly Precise
	Readability	Clear Readable
4. Meaning	Reasonableness	Logical Sensible

Adapted from Zmud (1978).

done, then, to establish the value of information in an organization is to assess its impact on overall system performance, the approach taken by Wolstenholme et al. (1990). Different levels of the attributes must be postulated and system performance measured in these different scenarios. Assuming that decision makers in the organization are consistently operating within appropriate decision structures in these scenarios, the value of information is indicated by differences in organization performance. The economic value of any performance gain may then be compared to the cost of providing the information, and a net value of the information for the organization may be determined.

Morecroft (1983) found the use of system dynamics for organizational performance assessment particularly appropriate, since "it lends itself to portraying the breadth of organizational structure encompassing several interrelated functional areas." Even for single decision makers, a major limitation of the information economics, utility value, and economic value approaches to valuing information has been the degree of abstraction and simplification of the decision environment necessary to create models that are manageable in terms of complexity and computations. According to Forrester (1961), such models are far too complex (thousands of variables would be necessary) to yield analytical solutions. In addition, if a system is nonlinear, as modern organizational systems are, mathematics can achieve analytical solutions to only the most simple problems.

Morecroft (1983) and Coyle (1977) have demonstrated the validity of the system dynamics approach for modeling the complex structures necessary to simulate organizational system behavior. Thus, its use is especially applicable to the evaluation of the information infrastructure of an enterprise. If the specific information attributes are to be related to overall system performance, any intervening variables or exogenous factors that could affect this performance must be eliminated or controlled. A classical experimental design that attempts to control for such factors would quickly become too complex. The intervening factors can, however, be incorporated into a system dynamics model and controlled to allow examination of the effects of information quality on system performance. The system dynamics simulation of industrial firms for purposes of problem and policy analysis has proved its worth. Numerous examples of system dynamics models of industrial organizations can be cited (Hall 1976; Hall and Menzies 1983; Lyneis 1980; Morecroft 1983; Roberts 1978).

Research focus and model structure

Decision-making activities are the means by which managers control the flow and effective use of resources in pursuit of organizational objectives. Information about the status of organizational processes, resources, and capabilities, and a set of objectives for these entities are essential inputs for managerial decision making. The quality of the information provided by the organizational information system is critically important. Gorry and Scott-Morton (1971) recognize this in their discussion of the negative consequences to the organization of a mismatch between information requirements and the information supplied.

The complexity of organizations and their decision-making structures causes the outcomes of one decision to serve as inputs for a second decision. The outcomes of the second decision may in turn provide inputs to the first process in a subsequent iteration of the decision-making activity in an information feedback structure (Kleinmuntz 1985; Morecroft 1983; Sterman 1989). Thus, the dynamic feedback nature of organizational decision making must be incorporated into the structure of any model used to examine the effects of information quality on system performance.

Our model, then, is a dynamic one that incorporates the decision-making and information-processing structures of a typical manufacturing firm. The feedback structure of such an organization is illustrated by the causal model shown in Figure 1. This diagram depicts the interrelations present in the major functional areas of the firm. The structure of the model is based on previously validated models of manufacturing firms discussed by Morecroft (1983) and Roberts (1978) and on specific structures in the metal-can production industry.

Model sectors and exogenous inputs

The sectors of the model represent the major decision-making structures of a typical manufacturing firm (Amrine et al. 1982). Using a generic structure for a typical manufacturing firm was helpful in calibrating the model to a specific industry and in employing actual industry data to validate the model. The functional form of organizational structure was chosen because it is by far the most common basis for subdividing organizational activities. Because there are hundreds of variables and parameters in the model, a detailed and documented listing of the model is not included here but will be furnished upon request. An overview of each sector follows:

- *Finance and Accounting Sector.* This sector includes the major financial decision-making functions of funds allocation and budgeting, accounts receivable, and capital budgeting for capacity expansion.
- *Sales and Marketing Sector.* The decision-making functions of demand forecasting, advertising and promotion, and product distribution are included in this sector. Exogenous factors (demand) originate in this sector and drive sales.

Fig. 1. Sectors and key variables of the system dynamics model of a manufacturing firm

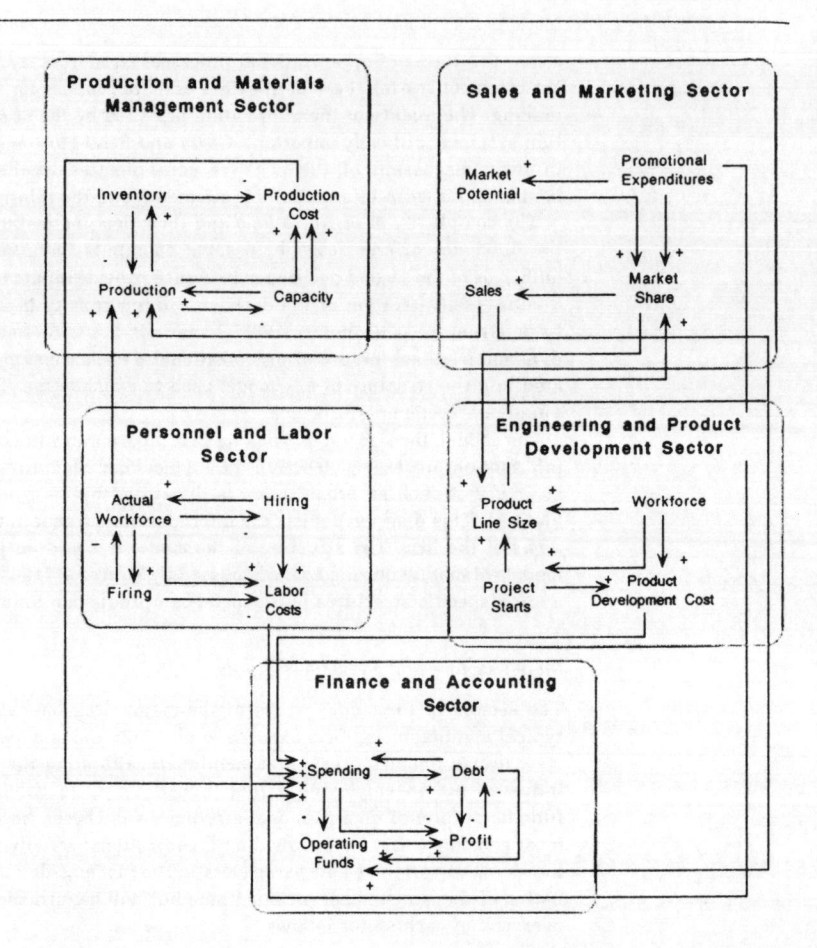

- *Engineering and Product Development Sector.* This sector includes the research and development and new product development functions. These functions are driven by market factors and pressures stemming from the firm's sales effectiveness.
- *Personnel and Labor Sector.* The decisions that control the labor supply for the firm are represented in this sector.

Production and Materials Management Sector. The production, inventory, and purchasing functions of the firm are represented in this sector. Key decisions include setting output objectives, production scheduling, inventory management, and raw materials acquisition.

Exogenous inputs that affect the firm are incorporated into the model structure, including market factors, economic factors, capital market factors, labor market factors, and raw materials availability.

Performance measures

The use of this type of model for the purpose of organizational analysis is predicated on the development of systemic measures of an organization's performance that will allow the evaluation of alternative decision rules and organizational policies. The structure of the model and the multidimensional nature of organizations suggest that a single measure would be inadequate to describe performance. The literature does not indicate the existence of any single systemic measure of performance (Steers 1975), but it does propose a set of performance measures. We have used a set of performance measures based on those identified in the literature as specifically relevant to manufacturing firms (see Table 2). These performance measures are assigned to three categories for the purpose of presenting the results of our experiments: profitability, cost, and efficiency of resource utilization.

Managerial levels of decision making

To adequately assess the effects of information quality on performance, the simulation model includes the specific decision structures necessary for operating a manufacturing firm.

We locate the decision-making activities of the firm at three managerial levels—strategic planning, managerial control, and operational control. These are based on Anthony's (1965) framework and his criteria for the types of decisions that might be made at each managerial level. The decision points at each managerial level, across all sectors of the model, are shown in Table 3. Selection of the decision points was based on a survey of literature dealing with the operation of firms (Bowlin et al. 1990; Jones 1981; Kotler 1988; Krajewski and Ritzman 1990; Morecroft 1983; Robbins 1990; Roberts 1978; Stevenson 1990).

The decision points were modeled in the typical system dynamics manner by which rate and level variables are combined in an information feedback structure. Information about variables in the structure is used at various places in the model. How varying patterns of information are tested in this framework is discussed in the next section.

Table 2. Performance measures

Model sector	Performance measure	Literature source

Finance and accounting	Rate of return
	  Return on equity
	  Return on investment
	  Times interest earned
		a, b, c

	Profitability
	  Net income
	  Profit margin
	  Average collection period
		a, d

Sales and marketing	Sales	d, e, f
	Market share	b, f
	Demand forecast effectiveness	f
Production and materials management	Production capacity utilization	f
	Output	b, f

	Inventory
	  Level
	  Cost
	  Utilization
		b, e, f

Engineering and product development	Product development cost	b, f

Personnel and labor	Human resources
	  Employee turnover
	  Labor cost
		b, f

a. Price b. Kilmann and Herden c. Campbell
d. Reimann e. Bonini f. Sloma

Experimental structure

Our research was structured to control the comparison of different levels of information quality across the three managerial levels of decision making in the firm. Different levels of the attributes accuracy, timeliness, reliability, and relevance (see Table 1) were tested at each managerial level (operational, managerial, and strategic). Table 4 shows this design.

These attributes were chosen because they are representative and the ones most amenable to implementation in the context of our simulation experiments. Accuracy is implemented by imposing a random noise function on information, varying it by 1 percent (level 1), 10 percent (level 2), or 20 percent (level 3). Timeliness is implemented by delaying decision *input* information by 1 (level 1), 6.5 (level 2), or 13 (level 3) periods. Relevance is implemented by delaying decision *output* information by 1 (level 1), 6.5 (level 2), or 13 (level 3) periods. The difference between timeliness and relevance is subtle, given the manner in which they are implemented. Since the output information is transmitted throughout the model to other decision points, its significance at a point in time is reduced. Zmud's (1978) discussion of relevance was used as a basis for implementing this component. Reliability is implemented by sampling information at the differing times of 1 (level 1), 8.5 (level 2), or 17 (level 3) periods, thus making it different (inconsistent) at certain points. The choice of these particular attributes and experimental values was based partly on the work of Swanson (1971) and Kleijnen (1980).

Each of the four information attributes was set at level 1, 2, or 3 for a given managerial level, a model run was completed, and the firm's performance was measured and analyzed with respect to profitability, cost, and efficiency. The levels of the attributes were then changed and another model run was carried out. After all the runs were done, the results were compared.

Base performance for the model was established using weighted average (based on sales) data about the metal-can production industry taken from the Industrial Compustat data base. The four major firms in the industry are American Can Corporation (0.63 weight), Crown Cork and Seal (0.30 weight), Zero Corporation (0.02 weight), and Heekin Can, Inc. (0.05 weight). The parameters needed for calibration of the model to this industry were averaged over the most current three years of data and their values used for the base model run.

The model was extensively validated using the methods suggested by Forrester and Senge (1980) and by Richardson and Pugh (1981). Over 100 model runs were completed, and the model was adjusted until we had a high degree of confidence that the model was useful for its designated purpose and that analysis of the output would yield valid results. For an extensive and detailed discussion of the verification and validation testing, see Augustine (1989).

The number of possible combinations for the 4 × 3 × 3 design shown in Table 4 is large. Since our purpose was to assess information quality effects across all managerial levels of decision making, an exhaustive search of the entire experimental response surface was not necessary. Thus, model runs were chosen to isolate the effects on performance of varying information quality (represented by attribute levels) at given decision points in a managerial level.

Each of the four attributes was varied from its lowest to its highest level across the three managerial levels. Runs were completed to ensure that all three levels of each attribute were tested at all three managerial levels. The experimental structure also allowed isolation of overall information quality effects at each managerial level. Each set of information attributes was tested over a simulation period of 200 weeks (approximately four years).

The reference behavior of the model for 15 performance measures is shown in Figure 2. The behavior was established, of course, without delays or distortions of the information attributes. There is a brief initial period of instability before

Table 3. Decision points in the model

Sector → Managerial Level	Production and Material Management	Personnel and Labor	Sales and Marketing	Finance and Accounting	Engineering and Product Development
Operational	· Finished Goods Inventory Level · Production Start Rate (Fig. 2) · Production Rate · Deliveries from Factory · Desired Finished Goods Inventory · Actual Production Capacity · Order Delay · Work-in-Process Inventory · Safety Stock · Materials Ordering Rate · Level of Materials Desired · Level of Materials on Hand · Expected Back Orders · Current Materials Inventory Level · Desired Materials Inventory Level · Materials to Finished Goods Conversion Factor	· Workers Leaving the Work Force · Current Work Force Size · Work Force Size Desired · Training Completion Rate · Normal Work Force Turnover Rate · Prevailing Level of Worker Satisfaction · Training Period Required · Labor Desired · Labor Change Desired · Level of Qualified Work Force	· Promotional Expenditures Adjustment Rate · Desired Change in Promotional Expenditures · Current Level of Promotional Expenditures · Current Credit Sales Rate · Accounts Receivable Collection Factor		· Engineering Work Force Adjustment Rate · Current Engineering Work Force Level · Desired Engineering Work Force Level · Limitations on the Size of the Engineering Work Force · Current Project Start Rate · Level of Engineering Effort · Desired Level of Project Starts · Current Project Backlog · Project Start Rate · Project Completion Rate · Normal Project Completion Delay
Managerial	· Production Rate · Forecast Sales Level · Expected Back Order Level · Current Back Order Level · Anticipated Scrap/Rework/Defective Products · Production Process Materials Handling Times · Production Start Rate · Desired Finished Goods Inventory · Actual Production Capacity · Delivery Rate · Actual Sales · Current Finished Goods Inventory Level · Current Delivery Delays	· Level of Actual Work Force · Work Force Cost · Labor Desired · Training Completion Rate · Rate of Employees Leaving the Work Force · Hiring Rate · Work Force in Training · Labor Change Desired	· Level of Promotional Expenditures · Desired Level of Promotional Expenditures · Current Level of Promotional Expenditures · Change in Promotional Expenditures Desired · Promotional Expenditures Adjustment Rate	· Earnings Retention Rate · Current Period After-Tax Profit · Normal Earnings Retention Percentage · Normal Earnings Retention Fraction · Dividend Payment Rate · Current Earnings Retention Rate · Normal Percentage of After-Tax Profit Paid Out as Dividends · Normal Dividend Payment Rate · Degree of Leverage · Current Level of Debt · Desired Level of Debt · Cost of Debt · Desired and Actual Degree of Leverage	· Level of Engineering and Product Development Work Force · Current Work Force Adjustment Rate · Current Engineering Work Force Level · Management's Desired Work Force Level · Level of Engineering Effort Required · New Product Introduction Rate · Rate of Project Completions · Product Line Size Limitation · Current Size of the Product Line · Product Introduction Delay · Desire for Product Deletions

Sector →	Production and Material Management	Personnel and Labor	Sales and Marketing	Finance and Accounting	Engineering and Product Development
Managerial Level Managerial (continued)	· Finished Goods Inventory · Physical Capacity Addition Rate · Desired Capacity Level · Allowable Increase in Capacity · Physical Capacity Depreciation Rate · Level of Capacity Investment · Desired Capacity Increase			· Level of Debt · Rate of Increasing Debt · Desired Debt · Desired Increase in Debt · Level of Accounts Receivable · Current Credit Sales Rate · Accounts Receivable Repayment Rate · Accounts Receivable Default Rate · Normal Credit Sales Percentage · Current Accounts Receivable Level · Credit Sales Rate · Current Sales Levels · Firm's Normal Credit Sales Percentage · Revenue Deficit · Normal Credit Sales Fraction	
Strategic	· Production Capacity Level · Current Actual Capacity · Rate of Adding Capacity · Desired Capacity Level · Rate at Which Capacity Can be Added · Current Physical Depreciation Rate on Capacity · Actual and Forecasted Production Levels · Desired Increase in Capacity			· Retained Earnings · Current Level of Retained Earnings · Current Retention Rate · Current Dividend Payment Rate · Current Level of Cumulative Retained Earnings · Level of Debt · Upper and Lower Limits for the Level of Debt · Current Level of Debt · Level of Debt Desired by Management · Degree of Leverage · Rate of Increasing Debt · Rate of Retiring Debt · Desired Increase in Debt · Desired Debt · Rate at Which to Decrease Debt · Cost of Debt	· Size of One Variable Product Line · Current New Product Introduction Rate · Product Deletion Rate · Current Product Line Size · Current Market Pressures for New Product Introductions

Table 4. Experimental design

	Information attribute			
Managerial level	Accuracy	Timeliness	Reliability	Relevance
	1 2 3	1 2 3	1 2 3	1 2 3
Operational				
Managerial	*Measures of the firm's performance:*			
Strategic	*profitability, cost, efficiency*			

the feedback structures in the model stabilize the output at target levels. This behavior is common, indicating initial transient effects with global stability. The resulting behavior represents an equilibrium between the goals of the system and the behavior possible to attain given the structure of the system. In the absence of any external stimuli, the equilibrium conditions will continue for an indefinite period. The ability to stabilize performance is an important reason for using simulation to isolate the effects of selected experimental conditions. The stabilized performance illustrated in Figure 2 is a reasonable behavior for a typical firm in the metal-can production industry.

The profitability performance of the firm is indicated by the values for return on equity, return on investment, average profit, profit margin on sales, and times interest earned. Return on equity peaks at about 0.8 percent per week with an equilibrium value of about 0.4 percent. Return on investment stabilizes at about 15 percent annually. The average pre-tax net profit peaks at around $25,000 per week with an equilibrium value of $12,000–$13,000 per week. The firm's profit margin on sales has an equilibrium value of about 9 percent, and the times interest earned is in equilibrium at a ratio of about 4 to 1.

Cost performance is indicated by the variables for average labor cost, average product development cost, and inventory holding cost. Average labor cost stabilizes at about $75,000 per week, average product development cost gradually rises to an equilibrium value of about $13,000 per week, and inventory holding cost gradually declines to a stable value of about $7,000 per week.

The efficiency with which the firm employs resources is indicated by the difference between actual and desired finished goods inventory, the difference between actual and desired production, inventory utilization, employee turnover, capacity utilization, demand forecast efficiency, and average market share. As with the other measures, an initial transient period is followed by stable behavior. It is this reference behavior against which the experimental results are compared.

Experimental results

Method of analysis

With the reference behavior as the basis for analysis, the results were examined to determine (1) which attributes of information had the strongest or weakest effect on performance, and (2) whether different attribute levels had different effects on performance at each managerial level.

To illustrate the analysis process, the profitability, cost, and efficiency performance measures for the timeliness attribute are used. The experimental runs for profitability using the *least* timely information (input delay of 13 periods) across all managerial levels is shown in Figure 3. The return on equity peaks at slightly less than 0.8 percent per week (40 percent annually). This is similar to the peak value of the reference behavior (see Fig. 2), but the peak occurs at a much later time (week 122 versus week 50). This performance shows a great deal more cyclic variation, reflecting instability, than does the reference mode for this variable. The result is greater uncertainty about performance. This uncertainty can affect not only internal decision behavior but external market reaction to the firm's performance.

The experimental runs for return on investment, average profit, and cost show similar fluctuating behavior. For example, average labor cost (see Fig. 3) is less stable and has a higher peak under conditions of untimely information than in the reference mode (see Fig. 2).

The measures that reflect resource utilization efficiency are consistent for inventory utilization and capacity utilization, which never reach stability over the four-year simulation period. Actual and desired levels of production never come into balance.

To assess the overall effect on performance of the experimental runs for timeliness, accuracy, reliability, and relevance, the strength of effect for each change in information quality was subjectively assigned a value from relatively strong to relatively weak. Using this method was necessary because the results of the output streams could not be strictly quantitatively compared. The plots of behavior (like those in Figure 3) were evaluated, first, in terms of the maximum, minimum, and equilibrium performance results; second, for the relative timing of the changes (periodicity); and third, in terms of the overall stability of performance. Table 5 illustrates the outcome of this procedure.

Table 5 shows the effects on performance of systematically decreasing information quality. The table is interpreted by looking at the arrangement of the individual information attributes (accuracy, reliability, timeliness, and relevance) with respect to the three measures of performance (profitability, cost, and efficiency): the *order* of listing in each column indicates the relative strength of

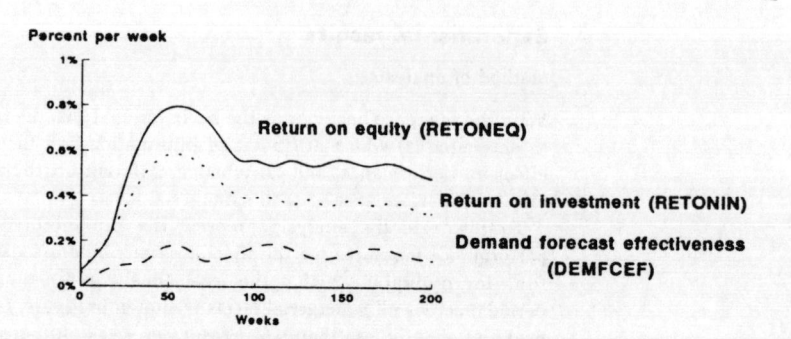

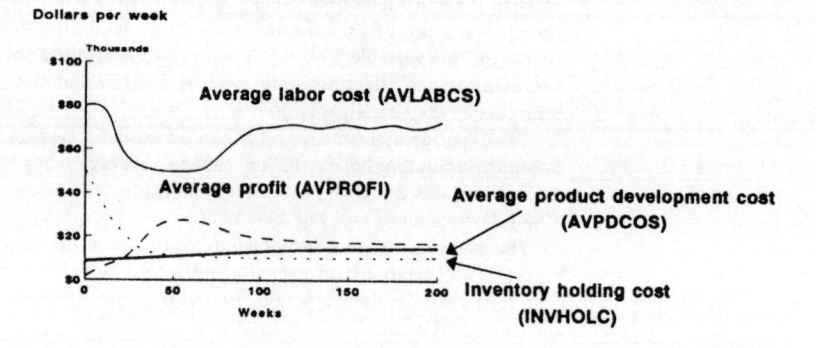

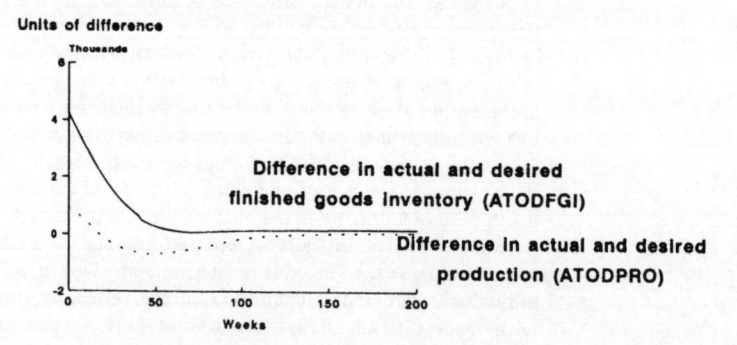

Fig. 2. Reference behavior modes

Fig. 2. Reference behavior modes (continued)

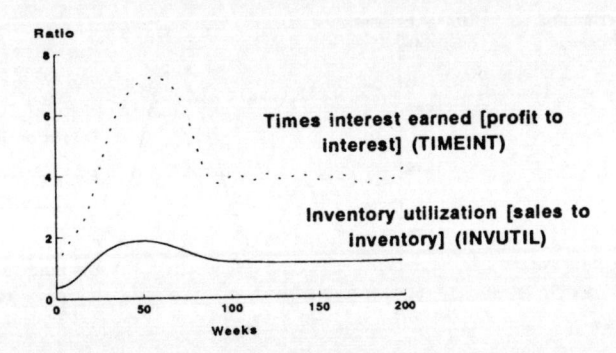

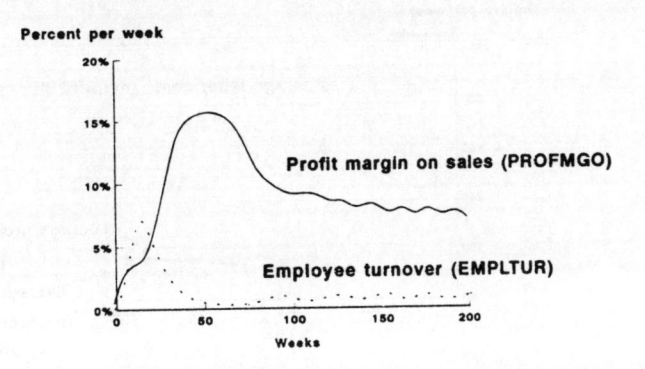

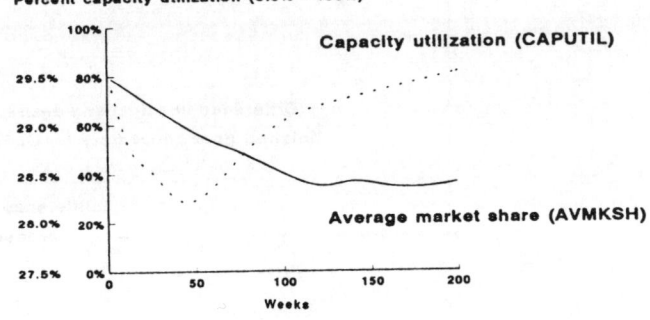

Fig. 3. Experimental runs: timeliness attribute

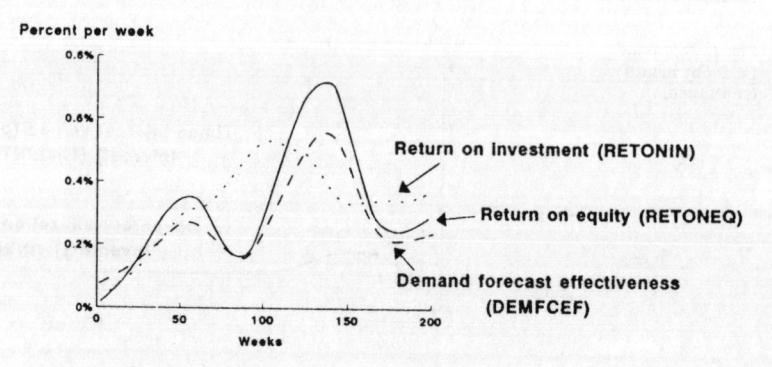

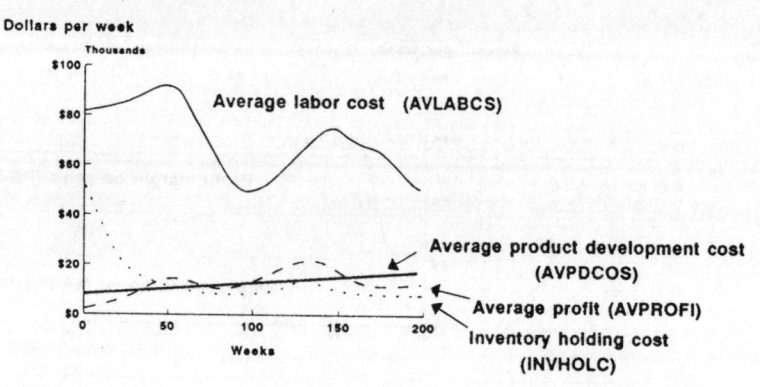

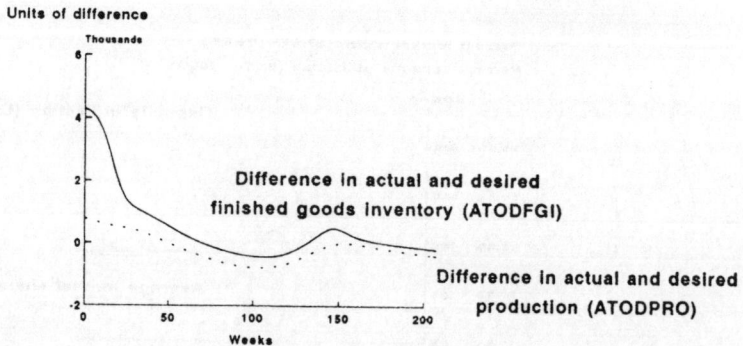

Fig. 3. Experimental runs: timeliness attribute (continued)

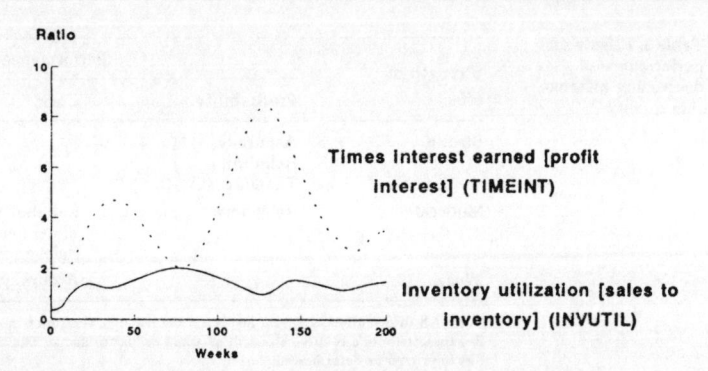

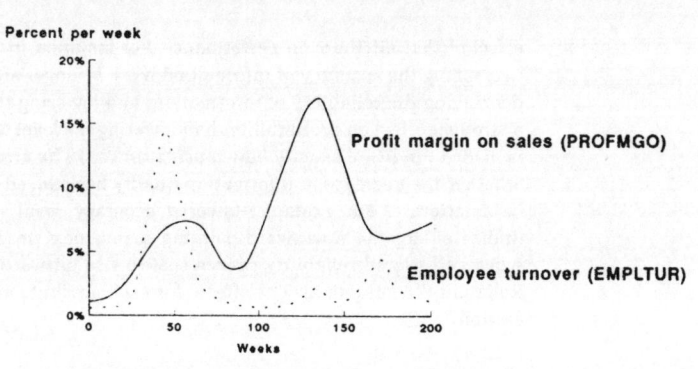

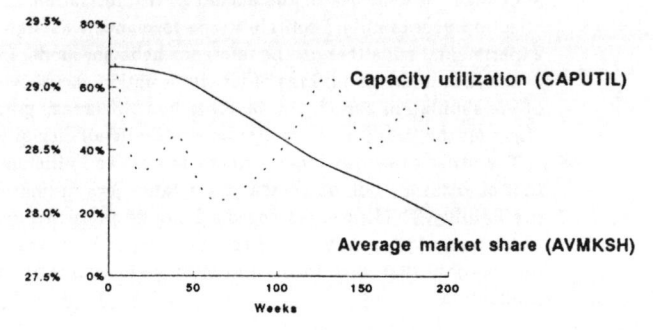

Table 5. Effects on performance of decreasing information quality

Strength of effect	Performance measure		
	Profitability	Cost	Efficiency
Strong	Accuracy ↓ Reliability ↓ Timeliness ↓		
Moderate	Relevance ↓	Reliability ↑ Timeliness ↑ Relevance ↓	Relevance ↓ Timeliness ↓ Reliability ↓
Weak		Accuracy ↓	Accuracy ↓

Note: All information attribute levels are decreasing. The order in which the attributes are listed signifies the attribute's *relative* strength of effect on performance. The arrows indicate whether performance has improved or deteriorated.

effect of that attribute on performance. For instance, in the Profitability column, decreasing the accuracy of information has a stronger effect on profitability than decreasing the reliability of information; and lowering the level of reliability has a stronger effect on profitability than lowering the level of timeliness. (No attempt is made to indicate exactly *how much* stronger.) The arrows in the table indicate whether the decrease in information quality has caused performance to improve or deteriorate. For example, lowered accuracy results in poorer profitability (indicated by the downward-pointing arrow next to Accuracy in column 1), whereas lowered reliability causes cost to rise (upward-pointing arrow next to Reliability in column 2). The effects for each attribute are discussed in the next section.

Overall attribute effects

ACCURACY. A decrease in the accuracy of information had the greatest overall effect on profitability. Profitability performance was significantly poorer in the experimental runs than in the reference behavior mode. In fact, the profitability of the firm under conditions of low information accuracy was negative for most of the simulation period. On the other hand, decreasing accuracy had very little effect on the firm's cost performance or on its efficiency (see Table 5).

The other three attributes' effects on cost and efficiency were stronger than that of accuracy but, as shown in the table, less dramatic than their effects on profitability. The firm experienced a major decrease in market share and capacity utilization. Apparently, the firm has made decisions (based on inaccurate information) that have focused on cost performance at the expense of revenue production.

RELEVANCE. Decreased relevance of information affects profitability negatively but less so than decreased accuracy does (see Table 5). Indeed, receiving irrelevant information had only a moderate effect on the firm in all three performance categories, although decreased relevance impaired efficiency more than did decreased levels of all other attributes.

TIMELINESS. Decreased timeliness of information impairs all three areas of performance only moderately—profitability slightly more than the other performance categories (see Table 5). Its effects show up in terms of model stability rather than in the absolute values of performance. Contrasting the reference behavior with the experimental plots reveals changes in the timing of peak and minimum periods of performance. For instance, when the timeliness of information is decreased, the peak periods of profitability occur much later in the simulation period and no real equilibrium is achieved.

RELIABILITY. Decreased reliability of information exhibited a relatively strong negative effect on profitability in terms of both absolute values of performance and model stability. In addition to decreased stability, periods of lower profitability and higher cost were evident (see Table 5). Efficiency also suffered moderately.

Effects of varying information quality at different managerial levels

Using the same kind of analysis as before, we assessed the effects of providing low- and high-quality information at the three managerial levels (operational, managerial, and strategic). To do this, the levels of all four attributes were set so that high- and low-quality information input as a whole was tested at each managerial level. The system's performance was then compared to the reference behavior. The results of these experimental runs are summarized in Table 6.

OPERATIONAL LEVEL. Low-quality information received by operational managers had the strongest (negative) effect on the firm's profitability (see Table 6). With respect to cost and efficiency, receiving low-quality information at the operational level had a moderate effect. High-quality information to operational managers had a weak effect for all three performance categories. The only experimental runs for individual attributes that exhibited a weaker effect were those combining low-quality information to strategic managers with high-quality information to operational and managerial decision makers.

MANAGERIAL LEVEL. For these decision makers, neither the combination high managerial–low strategic–low operational nor the combination low managerial–

Table 6. Effects of high-quality and low-quality information on performance at different managerial levels

Strength of effect	Performance measure		
	Profitability	Cost	Efficiency
Strong	Low operational ↓		High strategic ↓
	High strategic ↓		
	High managerial ↓		
Moderate	Low managerial ↓	High strategic ↑	Low operational ↓
		Low operational ↑	High managerial
		High managerial ↑	
Weak	High operational ↑	High operational ↓	Low managerial ↓
	Low strategic ↑	Low managerial →	High operational →
		Low strategic →	Low strategic →

Note: "Low" and "High" refer to information quality. The order in which the information quality–managerial level pairs are listed signifies the information quality's *relative* strength of effect on performance at that managerial level. The arrows indicate whether performance has improved, deteriorated, or remained essentially the same.

high strategic–high operational (see Table 6) produced performance that compared favorably with the reference behavior. Low-quality information provided to managerial decision makers caused a deterioration in performance, but the effect was weaker than that observed when low-quality information was supplied to operational decision makers. The changes in information quality at the managerial level had the strongest effect on profitability. For the cost and efficiency performance measures, the effects were relatively weak.

At the same time, for overall performance, high attribute settings at the managerial level produced model behavior that was worse than the reference behavior and than the experimental run for the combination High Operational–Low Managerial–Low Strategic. Apparently, the effect of providing high-quality information to managerial decision makers does not compensate for low-quality information at other managerial levels in the same way as providing high-quality information to operational decision makers would.

The results indicate a strong negative effect on the firm's overall performance when low-quality information is provided to operational managers. This effect is so strong that providing high-quality information at the strategic and managerial levels can neither compensate for it nor prevent the deterioration of the firm's performance.

STRATEGIC LEVEL. The effect of providing low-quality information to strategic managers is very weak (see Table 6). Surprisingly, compared to the reference case, profitability performance actually improved slightly when strategic managers received low-quality information and deteriorated when they received high-quality information. Cost and efficiency performance remained virtually unchanged with receipt of low-quality information by strategic managers. The effects on profitability, cost, and efficiency are weakest for the individual attribute experimental runs in which strategic decision makers received low-quality information and the managerial and operational decision makers received high-quality information.

On the other hand, the strategic level's receiving high-quality information does not prevent the serious deterioration in performance that occurs if the operational and managerial levels receive low-quality information. High-quality information supplied at the strategic level actually caused performance to be worse than in the reference case, and this effect is relatively strong. These results suggest that strategic decision makers do not require the same quality of information as managerial and operational decision makers do and that the marginal benefit of providing better information to strategic decision makers is not as great as it would be for the managerial and operational levels. There seems to be some base level of acceptable quality of information for the strategic (and, in fact, for the managerial and operational) managers; once this base level is reached, little benefit seems to derive from expenditures to raise the quality of information at the strategic level. This is not to say that low-quality information should be supplied to strategic managers. Inappropriate stategic-level decisions can have a greater adverse impact of longer duration than those made by managerial and operational decision makers. It does appear, however, that strategic managers process less information and make fewer decisions requiring highly accurate, relevant, reliable, and timely information. Our results support the view in the literature that decision makers at different levels of the firm require information of different quality and also that there exists some minimum acceptable level of information quality for decision-making activities.

The results of this experiment are interesting and certainly counterintuitive, but caution should be exercised in projecting them beyond this study. The model contains a definition of strategic decision making based on literature sources and previous models of production firms but does not specifically address what may be broad strategic-level policy issues that could affect performance. For example, the effects of market performance and long-term structural and organizational changes are not included.

Summary

The results of our experiments, summarized in Tables 5 and 6, show how a firm's overall performance is affected by different levels of information quality. They point to a differential effect, depending on the information attribute and the managerial level at which the information is used.

Some general conclusions were developed about the effects of information quality on organizational performance. They are grounded in empirical evidence produced through experimentation with the model developed in this research. It would be difficult to project them beyond this empirical setting, but our conclusions do raise some interesting points about the value of information to a firm. It seems feasible to use the described method to study the topic of information value further. Some of the results could have been expected, but some proved counterintuitive. Both types offer insight into the nature of information value in organizational decision structures.

- Decreases in information quality (expressed in terms of the accuracy, relevance, reliability, and timeliness of that information) adversely affect the performance of the organization in terms of profitability, cost, and efficiency of resource utilization.
- At each managerial level of decision making, a decrease in a different information attribute appears to cause the greatest deterioration in organizational performance. Decreases in the quality of information provided at the strategic level have the weakest overall effect on organizational performance, while decreases in the quality of information provided at the operational level have the strongest overall effect on organizational performance.
- There exists a base, or normal, operating range for the quality of information (in terms of its attributes) required by the organization for its decision-making activities, below which the performance of the organization is adversely affected and above which the marginal benefit of acquiring better information may be exceeded by its marginal cost.
- The requirements for information used in decision making are so diverse that no single attribute of information has a consistently stronger or weaker effect on the performance of the organization when this performance is viewed in terms of each of the three performance measure groups.
- The greatest overall effect on performance because of the decrease in the quality of information in terms of a specific information attribute at a single managerial level occurs as a result of decreasing the reliability of information provided to operational managers.
- The smallest overall effect on performance occurs for the decrease in the timeliness of information used in strategic-level decision making.

Implications and conclusions

As noted, the results of this study raise interesting questions about information value within the decision context developed in this research. Also produced are some interesting implications regarding management of information resources. Although these implications and questions arise from the specific results of this research and should not be projected beyond it without care, they do present a different view than is held by some regarding the use of information at the various decision-making levels of the firm. As such, they provide a point of departure for discussion of the topic.

It has long been assumed that the implementation of a computer information system would provide benefits to the organization and improve its overall performance. Unfortunately, in most situations, management has not been able to catalog the benefits better than to account for the cost of such systems. This is especially true with decision support and control systems, where benefits cannot be associated directly with personnel savings. Since these systems are oriented toward supporting managerial decision-making activities (as opposed to operative and clerical activities), the benefits of these systems have been less tangible.

Since information provided to decision makers in the organization is not provided without cost, and the cost of information provided by an information system tends to increase as its quality (measured in terms of its attributes) increases, any increase in the timeliness, accuracy, relevance, or reliability of information produced by the system means an increase in cost. Of course, a benefit is assumed to result from an increase in the quality of information. It is the nature of this relation that was addressed in this research.

One very clear result of the experiments is that decreases in the quality of information (beyond a base level) provided to decision makers can adversely affect the performance of the organization in terms of profitability, cost, and efficiency of resource utilization. Each organization has a certain investment in information technology. Thus, management cannot afford to use an information system that provides information of a substandard quality or value to its decision makers.

These results, however, cannot be interpreted to imply that information of the highest possible quality (and therefore cost) must be provided to decision makers at all levels of the organization. Indeed, the experimental results suggest that information of a lower quality in terms of certain attributes at the strategic level of decision making can actually enhance performance, assuming that the organization's base or minimum information requirements have been met. Given these results, a more appropriate strategy might be for an organization to continue its investment in providing higher-quality information to operational managers and to devote fewer resources to its strategic-level information technology investment. This means a stronger investment in operational- and managerial-level decision support systems and a less aggressive investment strategy for executive information systems.

The results here also support the notion that organizations should design and implement integrated information systems that provide the appropriate levels of support at the levels of the organization where they are required and should use the level of technological and applications sophistication appropriate to each function provided. In addition to providing insights, the findings demonstrate the value of systems modeling to assist organizations in evaluating their information requirements. The approach is not only feasible but appears to be of great potential benefit in the design, implementation, and continuing use of information systems.

References

Amrine, H. T., J. A. Ritchie, and C. L. Moodie. 1982. *Manufacturing Organization and Management*, 5th ed. Englewood Cliffs, N.J.: Prentice-Hall.

Anthony, R. N. 1965. *Planning and Control Systems: A Framework for Analysis*. Cambridge, Mass.: Harvard University Press.

Augustine, F. K. 1989. Validation and Verification of an Industrial Manufacturing Model. Working Paper 89–2, Center for Information Systems Research, College of Business, Florida State University, Tallahassee, FL 32306.

Bonini, C. P. 1962. *Simulation of Information and Decision Systems of the Firm*. Englewood Cliffs, N.J.: Prentice-Hall.

Bowlin, O. D., J. D. Martin, and D. F. Scott. 1990. *Financial Analysis*, 2d ed. New York: McGraw-Hill.

Campbell, J. P. 1977. On the Nature of Organizational Effectiveness. In *New Perspectives on Organizational Effectiveness*, ed P. S. Goodman and J. M. Pennings, 13–35. San Francisco: Josey-Bass.

Coyle, R. G. 1977. *Management System Dynamics*. New York: Wiley.

Feltham, G. A. 1972. *Information Evaluation*. Studies in Accounting Research. Vol. 5. Sarasota, Fla.: American Accounting Association.

Forrester, J. W. 1961. *Industrial Dynamics*. Cambridge, Mass.: Productivity Press.

Forrester, J. W., and P. M. Senge. 1980. Tests for Building Confidence in System Dynamics Models. In *System Dynamics*, ed. A. A. Legasto, Jr., J. W. Forrester, and J. M. Lyneis, 209–228. TIMS Studies in the Management Sciences. Vol. 14. New York: North-Holland.

Gorry, G. A., and M. S. Scott-Morton. 1971. A Framework for Management Information Systems. *Sloan Management Review* 13 (1): 55–70.

Hall, R. I. 1976. A System Pathology of an Organization: The Rise and Fall of the Old Saturday Evening Post. *Administrative Science Quarterly* 21 (1): 185–211.

Hall, R. I., and W. B. Menzies. 1983. A Corporate System Model of a Sports Club: Using Simulation as an Aid to Policy Making in a Crisis. *Management Science* 29 (1): 52–64.

Jones, J. W. 1981. Application of a Performance-Based Approach to Economic Valuation of Information. *Journal of the Operational Research Society* 32 (11): 967–977.

Kilmann, R. H., and R. P. Herden. 1976. Toward a Systematic Methodology for Evaluating the Impact of Interventions on Organizational Effectiveness. *Academy of Management Review* 1 (3): 57–98.

Kleijnen, J.P.C. 1980. *Computers and Profits: Quantifying Financial Benefits of Information*. Reading, Mass.: Addison-Wesley.

Kleinmuntz, D. N. 1985. Cognitive Heuristics and Feedback in a Dynamic Decision Environment. *Management Science* 31 (6): 680–702.

Kotler, P. 1988. *Marketing Management*, 6th ed. Englewood Cliffs, N.J.: Prentice-Hall.

Krajewski, L. J., and L. P. Ritzman. 1990. *Operations Management*. Reading, Mass.: Addison-Wesley.

Lyneis, J. M. 1980. *Corporate Planning and Policy Design: A System Dynamics Approach*. Cambridge, Mass.: Productivity Press.

Marder, C. 1979. *Information Systems: Technology, Economics, Applications, Management*. Chicago: Service Research Associates.

Melone, N. P. 1990. A Theoretical Assessment of the User-Satisfaction Construct in Information System Research. *Management Science* 36 (1): 76–91.

Morecroft, J.D.W. 1979. An Integrated Approach to Industrial Dynamics. Working Paper, Sloan School of Management, MIT, Cambridge, MA 02139.

———. 1983. A Systems Perspective on Materials Requirements Planning. *Decision Sciences* 14 (1): 1–18.

O'Reilly, C. A. 1982. Variation in Decision Makers' Use of Information Sources: The Impact of Quality and Accessibility of Information. *Academy of Management Journal* 25 (2): 756–771.

Price, J. 1972. The Study of Organizational Effectiveness. *Sociological Quarterly* 13 (1): 3–15.

Reimann, B. C. 1982. Organizational Competence as a Predictor of Long-Run Survival and Growth. *Academy of Management Journal* 25 (2): 323–334.

Richardson, G. P., and A. L. Pugh III. 1981. *Introduction to System Dynamics Modeling with DYNAMO*. Cambridge, Mass.: Productivity Press.

Robbins, S. P. 1990. *Organization Theory*, 3d ed. Englewood Cliffs, N.J.: Prentice-Hall.

Roberts, E. B., ed. 1978. *Managerial Applications of System Dynamics*. Cambridge, Mass.: Productivity Press.

Sloma, R. S. 1980. *How to Measure Managerial Performance*. New York: Macmillan.

Steers, R. M. 1975. Problems in the Measurement of Organizational Effectiveness. *Administrative Science Quarterly* 20 (3): 546–558.

Sterman, J. D. 1989. Modeling Managerial Behavior: Misperceptions of Feedback in a Dynamic Decision-Making Experiment. *Management Science* 35 (3): 321–339.

Stevenson, W. J. 1990. *Production/Operations Management*. Homewood, Ill.: Irwin.

Swanson, C. V. 1971. Evaluating the Quality of Management Information. Working Paper, Sloan School of Management, MIT, Cambridge, MA 02139.

Swanson, E. B. 1987. Information Channel Disposition and Use. *Decision Sciences* 18 (1): 131–145.

Wiener, N. P. 1948. *Cybernetics*. New York: Wiley.

Wolstenholme, E. F., A. Gavin, K. M. Watts, and S. Henderson. 1990. The Design of Dynamic Methodology for the Assessment of Computerized Information Systems. *Proceedings of the 1990 International System Dynamics Conference*, ed. D. F. Andersen, G. P. Richardson, and J. D. Sterman. III: 1346–1354.

Zmud, R. W. 1978. An Empirical Investigation of the Dimensionality of the Concept of Information. *Decision Sciences* 9 (2): 187–195.

0883–7066/92/020149–25$17.50
© 1992 by John Wiley & Sons, Ltd.

NAVAL SHIP PRODUCTION: A CLAIM SETTLED AND A FRAMEWORK BUILT

Kenneth G. Cooper

Pugh-Roberts Associates, 5 Lee Street, Cambridge, Massachusetts 02139

ABSTRACT. Program overruns, contract disputes, and legal confrontation between defense contractors and the government escalated seriously over the 1970's. The author led the development and application of a computer simulation model to resolve a $500 million shipbuilder claim against the US Navy. By using the model to diagnose the causes of cost and schedule overruns on two multibillion-dollar shipbuilding programs, Ingalls Shipbuilding quantified the costs of disruption stemming from Navy-responsible delays and design changes; in June 1978, the Navy agreed out of court to pay $447 million of the claim. Use of the model (which was the basis for at least $200-300 million of the settlement) broke new legal ground, providing the defense and legal communities with a means by which adversary relationships can be avoided and equitable settlements of contract cost disputes achieved.

Ingalls Shipbuilding (a division of Litton Industries, Inc.) now has extended the model to aid strategic decision making in managing its shipyard operations. Each phase of several shipbuilding programs — acquisition and utilization of manpower, scheduling and performance of work, and managerial decisions throughout the program — can be accurately simulated. Executives find it valuable as a test bed for evaluating the consequences of alternative policies in bidding and marketing, contract management, program work scheduling, resource management, and cost forecasting. Also, it provides a needed technique in the avoidance of contractor claims.

Ingalls Shipbuilding in Pascagoula, Mississippi, is a division of Litton Industries, Inc., an international, broadly diversified industrial corporation with annual revenues of three to four billion dollars. Over the past several years, some 15 to 20% of Litton's sales typically arose out of marine engineering and production operations at Ingalls. During the mid-1970's, the division's sales ranged from $500 million to $800 million annually [Litton Industries, 1974-1977], with employment of approximately 20,000.

Ingalls is one of the largest shipyards in the world, by any measure — size, capabilities, employment, sales volume. As with most major US shipyards, the bulk of its business is typically the design and construction of vessels for the Navy. Since 1968, the Navy has contracted all of its new shipbuilding to private US shipyards. For the shipyards, this combines the opportunities and difficulties of building the most complex, sophisticated ships in the world. It is, indeed, this situation that led quite directly to the development of the model for Ingalls Shipbuilding.

BACKGROUND

How Overruns Occur

Procurements of major defense systems have often experienced cost and schedule overruns. The temptation is to explain them simply by laying all the blame on contractor mismanagement, inflation, or government interference. One may,

---

PROJECT MANAGEMENT; SIMULATION

however, categorize the multiplicity of causes of program overruns into two general classes: (1) inaccuracies in the original estimate of the work content, and (2) circumstances subsequent to contracting which change the cost requirements of doing the work.

The original cost estimate reflects not only a technical appraisal of work content, but business judgments as well. For large defense systems such as combatant ships, there are several paths by which inaccuracies may enter the original estimate. First, the technical content of the work that is necessary to do the job is often uncertain at the time of contracting; to varying degrees, the ships are first-of-a-kind systems for which no directly comparable experience exists. Also, pressures exist on the Navy to place the expected costs of defense systems in a palatable range for a scrutinizing Congress. Finally, equally appropriate competitive pressures among shipbuilders usually foster an optimistic view for bid estimates.

It is extremely difficult to anticipate accurately salient events and their impacts on program performance over five to ten years in the future. Circumstances that can change subsequent to contracting must somehow be considered in the original contract or through contract amendments. Perhaps the best example of a *desirable* change is the incorporation of the most technologically up-to-date equipment available. For a combatant ship, the systems (e.g., navigation, detection, weapons) to be employed are often not fully developed when the ship is contracted. Hence, system design changes or unexpected completion delays are likely, and these affect the design and construction process (and the costs) for the ship itself. Of course, changes in the design or the scope of work for the ship may arise from sources other than technological change. An entire lexicon of terms has developed to describe the origin, form, and disposition of design changes on Navy-contracted ships. Indeed, the issues of delays and design changes are central to the discussion of contractor claims against the Navy, and the long-range higher-order impacts of design changes have been the focal point of technical and managerial debates over those claims.

More circumstances that can increase cost and time requirements include those that are actually beyond the control of the Navy or the shipbuilder, such as unexpected inflation in unit labor or material costs, skilled labor shortages (shipbuilding is highly labor intensive), or material scarcities. Fully *within* the contractor's control is the final example of influences on the cost and time of building ships — the host of decisions made by the contractor in running the program. The scheduling and sequencing of multiple interdependent activities, the acquisition and deployment of resources, and the priorities set by management all affect the performance and cost of the program. Even these basic managerial functions are not cut and dried: the complexity of the process and the product makes shipbuilding one of the most difficult program operations to manage. The industry has changed substantially in the past 30 years. The ships themselves are more complex, the processes more sophisticated, the work force more mobile, the shipyards less specialized, government and corporate administrative requirements more extensive, and the time span of programs longer (thus allowing for more changes in design and personnel). These developments have greatly increased the demands on program and shipyard management.

In no aspect of defense procurement have these issues and causes of cost and schedule overruns been cast in such starkly black-and-white terms as in contractor claims against the Navy. In many claims, the builder lays all the blame for overruns squarely at the feet of the Navy, while some in the Navy counter with charges of the builder "buying in" on the contract, or contractor mismanagement. Along with others' efforts, part of the model-based work was aimed directly at changing that contradictory set of views.

Two Blockbuster Programs

In early 1969, Ingalls was awarded a firm-fixed-price contract by the Navy to design and build nine (subsequently reduced to five) amphibious assault ships (LHA's). The LHA is something like a downsized aircraft carrier, capable of deploying 2000 fully equipped Marines and 200 combat vehicles via landing craft and 30 large helicopters. The LHA is 20 stories high and the length of three football fields. It is, according to the Navy, "the largest, fastest, and most versatile vessel in the history of American amphibious warfare." The LHA program was one of two Navy shipbuilding programs contracted as a "Total Package Procurement," meaning the shipbuilder was provided only with performance specifications, and was thereafter solely responsible for all system design, detailed design, material procurement, planning, testing, and construction.

The only other naval program ever contracted as a Total Package Procurement was the 30-ship destroyer "DD963" program, also awarded to Ingalls (in mid-1970). Current Navy policy is to use a cost-type contract with a shipyard to design and build the first ship of a series before the contractual commitment to subsequent ships in the series. Also, the Navy has again assumed more explicit responsibility for the early design stages and for the delivery of major equipment items such as weapon systems.

The design and construction of the new, complex LHA's and the DD963 Spruance-class destroyers (twice the size of destroyers of the prior generation) dominated the operations at Ingalls throughout the 1970's. Either of the LHA or DD963 programs would have required a significant facilities and manpower expansion for any shipyard; Ingalls more than doubled its workforce for the two programs. During this time there were periodic nationwide material shortages, and a critical scarcity of skilled shipbuilding labor. A new form of organization for ship design was being used by Ingalls and the Navy. Formal requirements were instituted for integrating with the usual design effort the consideration of vessel maintainability, reliability, logistics support, manning, and more.

It was in this setting that thousands of design changes on the LHA were received by Ingalls from the Navy.

The Claim

It is difficult to conceive of an effort that is much more consuming of managerial, technical, legal, and professional time and talent, and one that is entirely outside the business at hand — building ships — than the preparation and resolution of a shipbuilding claim. For major shipbuilders, claims assumed monumental proportions, growing from $300 million in 1971 to over $2.7 billion in unsettled claims in 1977; the Annual Reports of Litton Industries, Inc., for the years 1974-1977 concentrate heavily on the implications of unresolved claims against the Navy.

Ingalls approached Pugh-Roberts Associates in January 1976, convinced that the major contributing factor to anticipated overruns of $500 million was the disruption that had been evident in every phase of the programs. Further, Ingalls felt that Navy-responsible delays and design changes had contributed to the disruption, and had affected many areas which otherwise would not have experienced difficulties.

This argument, with attendant detail, formed the basis of a claim against the Navy.* However, the character of previous contractor claims had been questioned and criticized, and a new "more solid" approach was needed.

Claims against the Navy have evolved to a form in which two major segments can be identified. First, the direct impact, or the "hard-core" costs, of a design change or delay are estimated. While there are always legal questions of entitlement, these costs are not difficult to understand, and can be quantified — for example, the number of man-hours required to effect the change in a design drawing, and the man-hours needed to implement the immediate change in the construction of the ship. The second segment of the claims consists of "delay and disruption" costs — the second- and third-order "ripple effects" of dealing with the direct changes. (These are traditionally the most difficult issues to quantify and justify.) In concept, they are the "snowballing" effects within a work phase, among work phases, and between programs, such as altered work sequence, conflicting facilities and manpower requirements, skill dilution, undetected work errors, and more. The ultimate consequences for program performance include the additional cost and time required to accommodate the full range of effects of the direct changes.

> Historically, the shipbuilders and the Navy have not found it difficult to agree on the hard-core costs of a change ... The pricing of delay and disruption costs has been a major impediment to the settlement of Navy shipbuilding claims.
> [*Naval Ship Procurement Process Study,* 1978].

Some examples of the so-called "ripple effects" of design changes should (a) help to clarify the meaning of "delay and disruption," and (b) point out the difficulty traditionally encountered in attempts to quantify, substantiate, and effectively control those "ripple effects."

(1) *Within a Design Phase.* An altered design element first increases engineering and drafting time (and costs) to alter design drawings. This alters the sequence and timing of work and lessens designer productivity, increasing errors and omissions.

(2) *To Successive Phases of the Same Program.* The need to "rip out and rework" costs material and manpower. Resultant confusion creates further errors and work done out of sequence increases manpower needs, lowers productivity, and increases cost.

(3) *To Other Programs.* Manpower diverted from other program activities disrupts work flow and requires additional hiring in a constrained labor market, lowering the average skill level and hence reducing productivity (and raising costs) on those programs as well.

Clearly, all these effects work together, and feed upon one another in vicious circles that continue to exaggerate the cost and schedule impacts of design changes far beyond the time and stage of work directly affected. This is the essence of "delay and disruption."

THE MODEL

The contracted role with the Litton claim was to develop and use a methodology that would (a) correctly quantify Navy-responsible delay and disruption costs in the design, procurement, planning, and production stages of the programs, and (b)

---

*Ed. Note: Another successful OR-supported claim is described in Nahmias, *Interfaces* Vol. 10, No. 1, 1980, pp. 1–12.

demonstrate the cause-effect relation of the costs to the items cited in the "hardcore" segment of the claim.

In the analysis, we developed a computer simulation model of the engineering, procurement, and production operations of Ingalls Shipbuilding Division, describing in considerable detail the workings of the LHA and DD963 programs. It contains thousands of equations which represent the acquisition and utilization of manpower, the scheduling and performance of tasks, and managerial decisions at different levels within the organization. The model traces through a complex web of technical and organizational interrelationships to simulate the behavior of the programs and the shipyard as a whole.

Five important reasons for using computer simulation were that it permitted:
(1) Direct answering of "What if" questions; in this case, "What if the Government interventions had not occurred?"
(2) More complete representation of the organizational and technical phenomena in a large and complex organization
(3) Clear and defensible attribution of impacts to specific sources
(4) Forecasting and diagnosing the total costs through program completion
(5) The organization of massive amounts of data in a comprehensive, logically consistent structure.

The model we designed was, in essence, a replica of the management decisions and operations of the company. The single, important, intended use was quantification of the comprehensive impacts of customer changes and delays. We did this by comparing the results of two simulations of the model. Each of these simulations calculated the number and timing of man-years expended in each program phase from the beginning of the programs to completion. In the first simulation, all of the Navy-responsible changes cited in the hard-core claim items were included. This simulation recreated and forecast the *actual* work schedules and expenditure of man-years on the LHA and DD programs. (With four years of work remaining on the programs at the time, the model forecasts of ship delivery times and man-year expenditures have proven to be quite accurate.) The second simulation was identical to the first with *one* exception. All inputs to the model that represented the Navy-responsible changes cited in the hard-core claim items were removed. This second simulation estimated the man-years and schedule which *would have* occurred had the government not intervened in the LHA program. The resulting quantification and diagnosis of costs was submitted to the government in October 1977, and was the sole technical basis for the majority of the claim.

Ingalls and the Model Today

With the settlement of the claim and the approach of the completion of the LHA and DD963 programs, the senior management of Ingalls turned its attention toward obtaining new business for the shipyard, and managing it profitably. But despite the declining workload, Litton and Ingalls were wary in their marketing efforts. The 1977 Annual Report stated:

> New contracts will be pursued when it can be determined that sufficient opportunity to earn a reasonable profit exists and when contractual terms are acceptable. In the future, Ingalls does not intend to take on high-risk shipbuilding contracts which fail to provide a satisfactory balance in the risk-reward relationship.

Ingalls decided to use "the model" to aid in the analysis of prospective shipbuilding program costs. For the first step outside the claims arena, a revised version of the model was developed to focus on several potential new programs. In a pilot effort that was separate from but parallel to Ingalls' in-house cost estimation process, "benchmark" cost estimates for several new programs were produced by exercising the revised model. These estimates were consistent with the results of the in-house process. With the benchmark simulation estimate as a base, the model then was put to a more significant use to obtain information that was not otherwise possible to get in a timely fashion. By posing to the model a series of "what if" questions, we produced several different simulations of program performance and costs.

Examples of situations tested included different work schedules, scenarios of material availability, labor market changes, and different shipyard manning possibilities. Through these tests, we identified conditions to which future programs' cost performance would be most sensitive, and quantified the impact of each. Ingalls then was able to assess the risk associated with any specific level of bid cost by judging the likelihood of the different conditions.

New program bidding is one of several areas to which Ingalls senior management affords most attention; others are contract management, scheduling, resource management, and work estimation. While analytical techniques that assist detailed operations proliferate in these areas, Ingalls sought previously unavailable analytical aid on the strategic, higher-level issues. Several examples illustrate the distinction between *operational* details and the *strategic* issues that most concern Ingalls senior managers on their new and prospective programs:

Bidding
   Operational: Estimate work content.
   Strategic: How the new program and current programs will affect each other.
   How external factors such as labor availability will affect the cost.
   The risk associated with alternative competitive bid levels.

Contract Management
   Operational: Quantification of direct, immediate impacts of change.
   Strategic: Second- and third-order effects, cross-impact in downstream phases and in related and concurrent work.
   Possible overruns and legal disputes.

Scheduling and Resource Management
   Operational: Detailed task scheduling.
   Strategic: Sensitivity of cost and performance to scheduling and sequencing.
   Implication of uncertain future conditions.

Work Estimation
   Operational: Learning and "S" curves to forecast man-hour requirements.
   Strategic: Impact of alternative managerial policies or future conditions.

To aid the timely assessment of these strategic problem areas, about 20 Ingalls senior managers were trained in the capabilities and use of the model. In December 1979, two versions of the model were set up on Ingalls computer facilities for this implementation effort. One is a full-blown model of all major Ingalls activities, with several programs represented explicitly. The second is a rapid-access, condensed, and simplified model for the purpose of demonstration and preliminary analyses. The latter, which focuses on a single shipbuilding program, has come to be known as the "vest-pocket model." Both models are now in use, and are maintained and operated by Ingalls personnel.

The models are to be used for three basic functions: program cost/schedule forecasting and diagnosis; shipyard business planning; and support for negotiation with other corporate entities and customers. For all of these, the "What if" capability of the simulation models is the most pervasive form of use. The results provide: (a) a family of forecasts which present a range of cost and time possibilities; (b) information regarding the relative attractiveness of different managerial strategies; and (c) a quantification of the risks associated with different external circumstances.

The Dual-Use Model

In the first use of the model, key problems to be resolved were:
- The adversary relationship between Ingalls and the Navy over the claim
- Several hundred million dollars of net income at stake for Litton
- Ingalls' concern for future business with the Navy
- Definition of delay and disruption and lack of confidence in traditional attempts to quantify the resulting costs
- The technical complexity of the ship design and construction process, and the massive amount of historical data and information that needed to be integrated
- The necessity for treating managerial and legal issues.

In extending the model instead to strategic issues of shipyard and program management at Ingalls, the key business problems tackled were:
- Corporate and division management's concern over the costs and risks of potential new business
- The need to demonstrate profitable performance in the shipbuilding business
- Uncertainties regarding the consequences of alternative managerial actions on high-cost, complex shipbuilding operations
- Senior managers' need to coordinate multiple, interdependent, often conflicting shipyard activities
- The impacts of once again operating under conditions of skilled manpower shortages and critical material delays
- The need to improve capabilities for anticipating the full, comprehensive costs of delays and design changes on current programs
- The degree of potential for corrective managerial actions to control the impacts of design changes.

The appendix describes the generic structure of the model developed to help address these problems.

THE DEVELOPMENT AND IMPLEMENTATION PROCESS

The process by which the model was developed has been crucial to the success of its applications.

A key element at the start was the fact that Ingalls had a specific, urgent problem. We worked closely and regularly for two years with a small working team, including managers from all phases of shipbuilding, and a lawyer expert in government contracts and litigation.

In the early conceptual design of the model four years ago, the Ingalls project team guided and reviewed the decisions of what elements to include in the model, and with what measures and in what detail to include them. For a more detailed model formulation, dozens of individuals in all stages of shipbuilding, from workers through vice presidents, were interviewed. They offered qualitative and quantitative observations on ship design and construction. As the design of the model began to gel, the numerical data requirements were clarified; a massive data collection effort, in concert with other elements of the claim, was undertaken. These data and information provided enough material to assemble a preliminary mathematical model of a single work phase. The equations, parameters, and detailed output were reviewed and critiqued by the project team, and several model modifications made.

Preliminary output being generated by the model was compared with historical data on the shipbuilding programs. Extensive statistical testing of the model began, and continued throughout the next year. Three iterations of model refinement were done. Further, in those areas determined to be weak or sensitive, more hard data and expert opinion were obtained, more tests performed, and model improvements implemented. One such area was the setting and adjustment of master work schedules: several refinements in the formulation were made in order to capture accurately within the model the complex sets of considerations made by management in the decisions to adjust program schedules.

In the end (for the claim analysis), the model replicated quite accurately the vast amount of detailed information on the programs' histories. Further, the model reasonably simulated phenomena for which no "hard data" existed. In short, the output of the model was consistent with all available information. In order to assure, however, that the model performed correctly for the correct reasons (imperative for its intended use), several other procedures were employed.

First, we established at the outset explicit limits of reasonableness for each numerical parameter in the model; these would not be violated in order to achieve a more "accurate" simulation. Further, the numerical parameters in different sections of the model were required to be consistent with one another in terms of relative magnitude. These guidelines of relativity were never violated. The model was also subjected to a series of "shock tests" to assess robustness in responding as the company would to radically different circumstances. Finally, several different plausible combinations of equations and parameters were tested to explore "alternative models" that might accurately represent Ingalls operations. The result of these procedures was a model that, over several more applications in and outside of Ingalls, remained remarkably stable and accurate.

Throughout this process, the hallmark of the claim effort was the extraordinary degree of involvement and commitment of Ingalls managers. It was to enhance greatly the technical validity and managerial acceptance of the subsequent applications of the model.

In bringing the model outside the claims arena to address more constructive and forward-looking managerial concerns, the same process continued. However, many new managers became involved. For them to accept, implement, and believe the model, some retracing of our steps was called for. Again, the work began with several rounds of discussions; these identified three principal areas of concern on the part of the ultimate users of the model:
- The detailed contents
- The managerial problems that could be addressed
- The logistics of in-house use at Ingalls.

A project team at Ingalls was established to continue the process of detailed technical reviews and subsequent small modifications. However, with the somewhat more ambitious range of issues addressed, and the objective of in-house implementation, a larger group was involved; key senior managers, their representatives, and individuals who were designated to maintain the model at Ingalls were included. Procedures were defined for use and updating, and the equivalent of a college semester of formal hands-on training and documentation was provided to the entire project team.

IMPACTS AND IMPLICATIONS

Immediate Impacts

The short-term consequences of the Ingalls Shipbuilding model applications stem primarily from the analysis in support of the LHA claim. In the settlement reached in June 1978, Ingalls received from the Navy a net increase in income of $447 million. It was the first time that the Navy had given such substantial consideration to a delay and disruption claim.

In addition to facilitating the settlement as a whole, the dollar value of the delay and disruption segment constituted the majority of the claim. Because the claim was settled out of court as an adjustment in the contract value, there is no formal breakdown identifying the dollar value of delay and disruption, but managers' and lawyers' estimates place the model's dollar contribution to the settlement between $170-350 million. Indeed, senior managers have clearly pointed out that without the model there could have been no such resolution of the claim; without that resolution the future of the division and the corporation was uncertain.

Aside from obtaining income from the settlement, the direct dollar costs of continuing the claim effort were avoided. Even more significant, however, was the vast amount of managerial and professional time and talent (an entire "claim organization" of over 100 Ingalls personnel) that would have continued to be spent on something other than ship design and construction.

Above all, the elimination of the adversary relationship between Ingalls and its best customer was a milestone achievement. The skills of Ingalls and Navy management ultimately resolved the sensitive and complex issues of the claim. Management Science can take credit in providing a comprehensive, justified explanation of cost and schedule overruns; thus, the basis was laid for a reasonable settlement. Fortunately, mature discussion at senior levels, as reflected in the *Naval Ship Procurement Process Study* [1978], is spurring some real improvements in contract administration procedures. At the same time, a broader spectrum of program and contract management improvements is possible, and it is toward that end that more recent applications of the model are being directed.

With the resolution of the claim, and with the experience on the two contracts in mind, Ingalls and Litton management exercised great care in seeking appropriate new business opportunities. In support of their effort, another version of the model provided information in the form of a risk analysis of new and prospective programs. That analysis further confirmed the validity of in-house cost and schedule estimates that were used in bids for programs won by Ingalls. Also, it later provided forecasts of cost variability under different conditions that might be experienced.

Long-Term Implications

Necessarily less quantitative at this time are the implications for continuing use of the models now set up for senior managers at Ingalls, benefits of which will eventually be seen as dwarfing the high-visibility claim impact. Ingalls managers are using the model for analyzing and helping in the selection of managerial actions that have been demonstrated to exert as much as 20% leverage on costs and schedules. Very specific uses in monitoring and forecasting program performance are improving the quality and timeliness of information for Ingalls management. Overall business and shipyard planning are benefiting from use of the model to assess alternative business mixes and resource management policies.

The analyses that are being conducted by the shipbuilder fall into two categories of questions posed to the model:
- *What if something happens beyond my control?*
(Range of impacts on costs and schedules of current and prospective programs)
- *What if I take some specific action in scheduling or managing resources?*
(Near- and long-term effects and cross-program impacts; cost/benefits)

An example of this line of analysis, and the benefits realized, is provided by comparing the results of three simulations:

Case (1). Made under the conditions assumed in the original program plan
Case (2). Made with a specific series of design changes and delayed equipment deliveries
Case (3). Made with a specific shift in schedule and reallocation of manpower to accommodate the changes in Case (2).

Case (2) creates a 10% cost increase and four-month schedule slippage over Case (1). Case (3) reduces the costs from Case (2) by 15%, as well as reducing schedule slippage by one month. This kind of test provides guidelines and specific information on which the manager can base decisions in controlling programs budgeted for many hundreds of millions of dollars, as well as affording a comprehensive overview of companywide operations.

Ingalls' marketing efforts in the past two years have added seven sophisticated Navy combatant ships — two cruisers and five destroyers — to their business backlog. With the new shipbuilding programs now in progress, Ingalls has taken a major step to fully implement "the model" as an in-house Management Science system for aiding senior shipyard and program management.

Other Long-Term Implications

The same benefits that are being seen by Ingalls are applicable in other corporate settings. Three other firms have employed variants of the model; the model structure has shown itself to be highly transportable to other situations of ship design and construction. Eight different shipbuilding programs totalling 55 ships and approximately $7 billion of business have been modeled. We anticipate further applications in related settings of large-scale design and construction programs, particularly in other defense procurements such as aircraft and major electronic systems.

While the forward-looking managerial applications offer promise, we are not abandoning the use of the model in legal and contractual disputes. It provides a most comprehensive and fair-minded approach for aiding their resolution. Steven L. Briggerman, of the law firm of Sellers, Conner, and Cuneo, who advised us throughout the claim work and was responsible for the preparation of the delay and disruption claim, has stated (in a letter to the Chairman of the CPMS Competition):

> ... the advantage of the modeling technique from the point of view of the lawyer is that it permits presenting to the judge the totality of the factual setting without overwhelming him so that no meaningful evaluation can take place ...
>
> My experience with the use of computer simulation techniques has largely been in the area of the litigation of large complex claims. However, it seems to me clear that the implications of the use of computer simulation techniques are far broader than this. If a computer model can be used to resolve a dispute, then it fairly clearly can be used to avoid the dispute in the first place. In any major federal or private program it would seem that the model could be used both as a planning tool and as a method of monitoring actual performance ...

... I believe the use of the Pugh-Roberts techniques represents the "wave of the future" in the litigation of complex claims in both government and commercial disputes. Further, and probably more significantly, their use as a planning and monitoring tool on major projects seems almost unlimited.

The *avoidance* of contractor claims against the government was cited as a high-priority objective in the procurement process study prepared under the Secretary of the Navy. Given the inevitability of contract and design changes on complex defense systems, the challenge is to deal effectively and finally with them at the time they are first considered, not in a claim several years later. Far more than a technical methodology is required, and significant contracting improvements are already being implemented; still, a technique *is* required for comprehensive analysis. Progress on implementing what is seen as a fundamental change in the system is slow. No formal approval or acceptance of the model has been obtained from the Department of Defense, nor should it be, necessarily. The manner of dealing with contract changes is, in shipbuilding, left largely to the individual shipyards and the resident Navy Superintendents. Our intent is to demonstrate in these settings the value of the model not just in forecasting cost impacts, but also as a mechanism for exploring realistic ways to *alleviate* the impacts and reduce costs. Ultimately, the reduction of costs and the elimination of defense contractor claims benefits both the Navy and the US taxpayer.

ACKNOWLEDGEMENTS

The author's colleagues at Pugh-Roberts Associates, Henry Weil, David Peterson, Mark Keough, Bill Hohensee, and Alex Makowski, contributed vitally to the success of this work. Steve Briggerman, of Sellers, Conner, and Cuneo, helped significantly. Our clients at Ingalls and Litton deserve recognition for a series of bold steps in pioneering Management Science applications to extremely sensitive and financially vital issues. Individuals to whom we are especially indebted are Archie Dunn, Rich Goldbach, J.B. Rawlings, John Landry, Frank Burger, Dick Marler, Conway Davis, and their associates.

REFERENCES

Assistant Secretary of the Navy, Manpower, Reserve Affairs and Logistics, 1978, *Naval Ship Procurement Process Study: Final Report*, Department of the Navy, Washington, DC.
Litton Industries, Inc., Annual Reports for the Fiscal Years 1974-1978.

APPENDIX: MODEL DESCRIPTION

Of the different versions of the model that have been developed and used, we focus this description on the full shipyard model of multiple programs. It is this version of the model that the claim analysis and most managerial analyses have used.

Overview

The model, in the form of a computer program, describes in considerable detail the workings of multiple shipbuilding programs. For each of several program phases, the model represents the acquisition and utilization of manpower, the scheduling and performance of work, and managerial decisions at different levels within the organization. Equations in the model describe cause-effect relationships between the variable aspects of the programs. The computer keeps track of all the ways in which the many variables relate to one another over time; it traces through the specified interrelationships to simulate the behavior of the shipyard operations.

Each program is modeled as a multiphase process of engineering, planning, procurement, and construction. Management functions represented in the model include performance monitoring, the establishment of priorities, budgets, and schedules, and the acquisition and allocation of manpower and materials. The diagram in Figure 1 provides a schematic overview of the model structure.

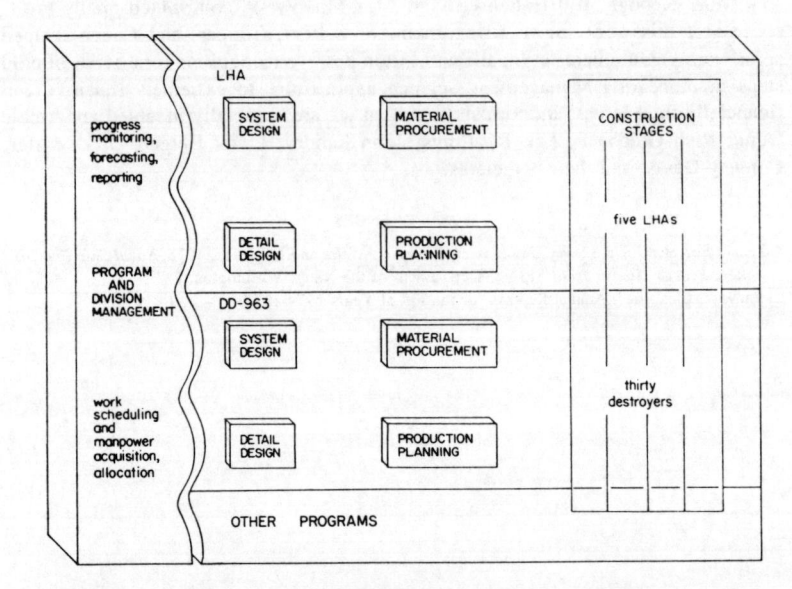

FIGURE 1. OVERVIEW OF MODEL STRUCTURE.

Within each program, all major phases of activity are modeled: system and detail design, material procurement, production planning and control, and four stages of ship construction. In each appropriate phase, we represent the utilization of labor, the accomplishment of work and rework, manpower productivity, technical requirements, and work progress monitoring. The hiring, lay-off, attrition, deployment, and attributes of six different categories of manpower are simulated by the model.

The activities in the work phases affect one another in many ways, as illustrated in the sequence of diagrams in Figure 2. First of all, (A) the schedules of all phases are interdependent. Variations from the planned schedule of "upstream" activities — in the form of late drawings, work plans, or material — may cause difficulties in properly completing "downstream" activities on time. Impending (or actual) downstream schedule slippages, in turn, cause significant pressures to be exerted on upstream schedules by management.

FIGURE 2. KEY RELATIONSHIPS.

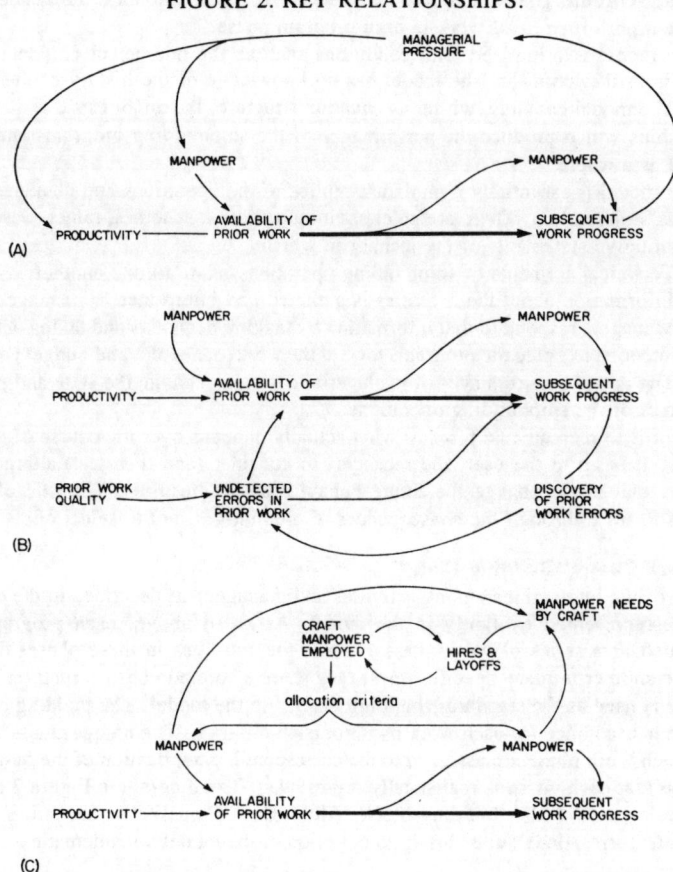

A second form of interaction (B) among phases centers around the quality of work performed. Out-of-sequence, incomplete, and/or incorrect work have serious impacts on the performance of subsequent work. The need for rework (because work is discovered to be incomplete or incorrect) may delay or impair dependent work in subsequent phases. Indeed, the need for rework may remain undiscovered until progress in a subsequent phase becomes directly dependent on the required work.

Third, the various phases of work compete with one another, to some extent, for resources (C). Schedule slippages and the resultant greater overlapping of phases exacerbate this competition. Among the different *programs* there also is direct competition for any constrained resources, such as particular categories of skilled labor. Hence, work schedules in different programs affect one another, and need to be coordinated by management to the extent that individual programs' goals permit.

The managers of each program and of the company act on the basis of information obtained from monitoring the performance of engineering, production planning, procurement, and construction. The resulting information is used to formulate priorities, schedule goals, and resource decisions. These, in turn, influence the subsequent performance of work in each program phase.

The model is initialized with conditions such as the number of engineers on board. From that point on, the model has no knowledge of the history of the programs. The model contains, within its equation structure, the major cause and effect relationships which produce the performance of the shipbuilding programs and the shipyard as a whole.

The model is essentially a miniature replica of the operations and management of Ingalls Shipbuilding. There are no explicit optimization schemes; rather, descriptive quantitative statements of the manner in which:

- Technical elements of shipbuilding operations relate to one another
- Information about the activities is gathered and interpreted by management
- Managers respond to that information by making decisions and taking actions intended to guide the programs toward the work, schedule, and budget goals
- The actual consequences of managerial decisions change the state and progress of the shipbuilding operations.

The intent is to recreate and forecast what actually happens over the course of time, and why. It is up to the user, the manager, to consider (and then test) alternative strategies that might change the future behavior of the business. The role of the model is to trace through the consequences of alternatives, not to select one.

The Work Phase "Building Block"

All of the interactions among activities and management described in the overview are represented explicitly in the model. As noted above, each program is represented as a series of work phases. While the activities in these phases differ from one another in many specific ways, they share a common basic structure. This structure is used as the standard "building block" in the model. The building block structure is used once for each work phase of each program. The unique characteristics of each work phase are assigned to the corresponding application of the building block, so that each phase is realistically represented. The diagram in Figure 3 illustrates basic parts of that building block. Although still qualitative in nature, this framework corresponds quite closely to a portion of the model's mathematical equation structure.

FIGURE 3. WORK ACCOMPLISHMENT.

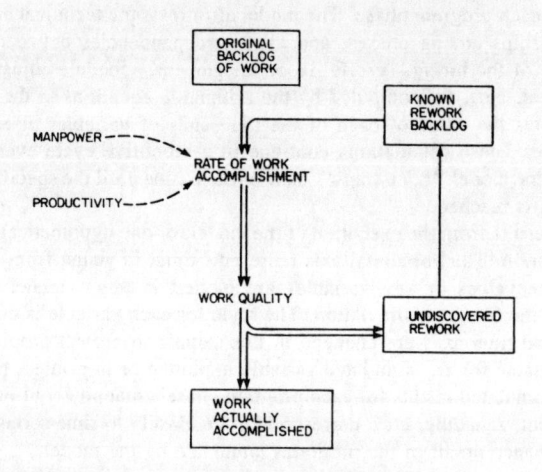

The work accomplishment sector of the building block keeps an account of the work that has been performed and the work that remains to be done within a program phase. For example, a design phase has two pools of work to be completed. They are:
1. The backlog of initial issues still to be accomplished. The drawings in this backlog are those which have not been started.
2. The backlog of rework. The drawings in this backlog are those that have been identified as requiring revision for any reason.

There are two pools of "work accomplished":
1. Undiscovered rework. The drawings in this pool have been issued and will require revision, but have not yet been identified as requiring revision. After the need for rework is perceived, these drawings become part of the recognized backlog of rework.
2. Work actually accomplished. This pool represents drawings that have been completed, issued, and will not require revision.

The rate of accomplishment of work decreases the work backlogs and adds to the levels of accomplished work. The rate of accomplishment (in terms of drawings per year) depends upon the number of people working in the phase and the average productivity of those people (in terms of drawings per man-year). As work is accomplished, it flows to "undiscovered rework" or "work actually accomplished" depending on "work quality." Quality, by our definition, represents the fraction of work that will *not* require rework. The model simulates within its structure the behavior of the principal factors affecting quality and productivity in each different program phase, such as: manpower skill levels, out-of-sequence work, prior-stage work availability and correctness, vendor design and material availability, managerial pressures, and other organizational conditions. All of these factors are, in turn, the result of other phenomena simulated by the model.

Sample Results

The model description has focused on a few key elements of the model's representation of each program phase. The model also treats the technical and organizational relationships among phases, and the interdependencies between concurrent programs. All of the hiring, layoffs, labor assignment, schedule adjustment, work accomplishment, etc., are computed by the arithmetic equations in the model. The model calculates the value of each of the thousands of variables at each point in simulated time. These calculations continue in a repetitive cycle every simulated month so that the model "bootstraps" itself through time until the specified length of the simulation is reached.

Sample results from the execution of the model for one hypothetical scenario are shown in Figure 4. The horizontal axis represents time, in years, from mid-1979 to mid-1983. The values of key variables are plotted in approximately two-month intervals over the five-year simulation. The scale for each variable is on the vertical axis (scales and time axes are changed in this sample to protect proprietary data). Output is available for any simulated variable in plotted or in printed, tabular form. The model's simulated results for each program phase's manpower utilization, work accomplishment, schedule, etc., correspond quite closely to time-series data on the actual performance on all of the programs simulated by the model.

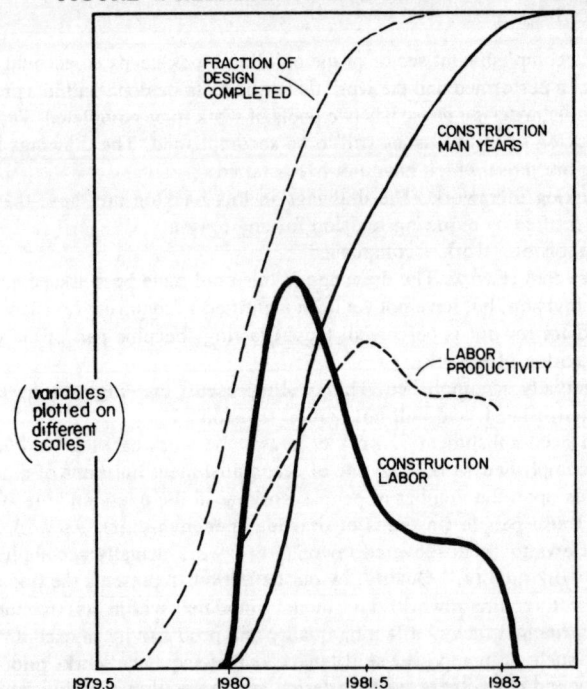

FIGURE 4. REPRESENTATIVE SIMULATION OUTPUT.

Beyond the few sample variables illustrated in Figure 4, a great deal more detailed diagnostic information is available, such as time-series output of individual influences on work phases' productivity and quality. This information is especially useful in comparing and diagnosing the differences between two or more simulations performed under different managerial policies or shipyard conditions. The forecast output available from the simulation for each shipbuilding program includes plotted and tabular output for Ingalls Shipbuilding Division (ISD) on:

Manpower on the Program and the Total Manpower for ISD
Design Work Accomplishment
Design Manpower and Cumulative Man-years
Design Manpower Determinants
Design Effort Diagnostics
Design Productivity and Determinants of Productivity
Design Productivity Diagnostics
Design Quality and Determinants of Design Quality
Material Procurement Performance
Construction Manpower and Cumulative Man-years
Scheduled Date of Ship Delivery
Scheduled Date of Ship Delivery Diagnostics
Construction Manpower and Technical Feasibility
Construction Productivity and Determinants of Productivity
Construction Work Quality and Determinants of Work Quality
Overall ISD Yard Manpower

The Elusive Silver Lining: How We Fail to Learn from Software Development Failures

Tarek K. Abdel-Hamid
Stuart E. Madnick

Naval Postgraduate School
MIT Sloan School of Management

AS MODERN organizations struggle with increasingly complex challenges, every experience — win, lose, or draw — is a valuable organizational asset that can be exploited. Managers must be willing to view failures as opportunities to learn rather than as embarrassing moments to be quickly forgotten. Yet, discerning the lessons is not always easy. Abdel-Hamid and Madnick have developed a postmortem diagnostic tool to do just that.

Sloan Management Review

39

Fall 1990

EVERY FAILURE has its silver lining. For only through experience and costly errors can managers develop effective intuitive judgment. As Neustadt and May have written, "Good judgment is usually the result of experience. And experience is frequently the result of bad judgment."[1]

So why don't we learn from project failures? First, we rarely try. People tend to hide mistakes rather than report and evaluate them. Second — and this is often missed — the important lessons are almost never readily apparent; they need to be extracted from deep within the project experience. In this article we will show how and why the silver lining often eludes us. To illustrate, we will focus on the information technology field, using a case study of an actual software project.

Software technology is playing an ever greater role in formulating business strategy, in determining how an organization operates and creates products, and indeed in reshaping the product itself.[2] Yet, to the dismay of system professionals and business executives, this formidable dependence on software technology has not been matched by a corresponding maturity in the capability to manage it. We continue to produce too many project failures, marked by cost overruns, late deliveries, poor reliability, and user dissatisfaction.[3]

Failure to learn from mistakes has been a major obstacle to improving software project management. Boddie argues:

> We talk about software engineering but reject one of the most basic engineering practices: identifying and learning from our mistakes. Errors made while building one system appear in the next one. What we need to remember is the attention given to failures in the more established branches of engineering.[4]

We will demonstrate the utility of a system dynamics tool for conducting a postmortem diagnostic analysis of a software project.

The Challenge of Software Development

It has been estimated that U.S. expenditures for software development and maintenance will grow by 1995 to more than $225 billion domestically and more than $450 billion worldwide.[5]

This growth in demand for software has not, however, been painless. The record shows that the software industry has been marked by cost overruns, late deliveries, poor reliability, and user dissatisfaction, which are collectively referred to as the "software crisis."

As early as November 9, 1979, a report to Congress by the Comptroller General cited the dimensions of the software crisis within the federal government. The report's title summarizes the issue: "Contracting for Computer Software Development — Serious Problems Require Management Attention to Avoid Wasting Additional Millions." The

---

Tarek K. Abdel-Hamid is Associate Professor of Information Systems at the Naval Postgraduate School. Stuart E. Madnick is the John Norris Maguire Professor of Information Technologies and Leaders for Manufacturing Professor of Management Science at the MIT Sloan School of Management.

Software Development

40

Abdel-Hamid
& Madnick

report concludes, "The government got for its money less than 2 percent of the total value of the contracts."[6]

More than a decade later, the problems persist. An article in the December 18, 1989, issue of *Defense News* describes the software problems with the Peace Shield project, which was then four years behind schedule and estimated to be up to $300 million over budget.[7]

Although many of the largest and most completely documented examples of the software crisis are found in military projects, these problems are by no means confined to projects developed by or for the federal government. Private sector organizations experience similar problems.[8] For example, DeMarco cites some startling statistics:

- Fifteen percent of all software projects never deliver anything; that is, they fail utterly to achieve their established goals.
- Overruns of one hundred to two hundred percent are common in software projects.

So many software projects fail in some major way that we have had to redefine "success" to keep everyone from becoming despondent. Software projects are sometimes considered successful when the overruns are held to 30 percent or when the user only junks a quarter of the result. Software people are often willing to call such efforts successes, but members of our user community are less forgiving. They know failure when they see it.[9]

Personal computer software development is not immune to these problems. This May 11, 1990, headline in the *The Wall Street Journal* says it explicitly: "Creating New Software was Agonizing Task for Mitch Kapor Firm."[10] The article is subtitled: "Despite Expert's Experience, Job Repeatedly Overran Time and Cost Forecasts." The issues cited in the article have been repeated for decades in both public and private organizations and in large and small companies (Kapor's company had less than thirty people).

It is likely that only a small portion of these problems are ever publicly reported, given the embarrassment and bad publicity that follow. Kapor, the founder of Lotus Development Corporation, agreed to describe the experiences in his new company, ON Technology, Inc., "because he believes that software design must be improved and the development process better understood."[11] Disclosing the failure is only the first step, learning from the failure is the critical next step.

A Case Study

Consider the case of NASA's DE-A software project. The project, conducted at the Systems Development Section of the Goddard Space Flight Center (GSFC) in Greenbelt, Maryland, was established to design, implement, and test a software system for processing telemetry data and providing attitude determination and control for the DE-A satellite. In planning and managing this project, NASA allocated approximately 85 percent of the total project cost to development (design and coding) and the remaining 15 percent to testing. A relatively large portion (30 percent) of the development effort was allocated to quality assurance (QA), a level significantly higher than the industry norm.[12]

Initially, NASA estimated the project size to be 16.000 delivered source instructions (DSI), costing 1,100 man-days and requiring 320 working days to complete. Figure 1 depicts the values of these and other DE-A project variables over the duration of the project. Because NASA's launch of the DE-A satellite was tied to the completion of the DE-A software, serious schedule slippages could not be tolerated. Specifically, all software was required to be accepted and frozen three months before launch. As the project slipped and this date approached, management reacted by adding new people to the project to meet the strict launch deadline, as evidenced by the rising workforce curve in Figure 1. The actual final results: 24,400 DSI; 2,200 man-days; and 380 working days.

Obviously the DE-A project was not a total success. The project overshot its schedule by 20 percent and its cost by 100 percent. On the positive side, the end product was reported to be of high quality—reliable, stable, and easy to maintain.[13]

If we rely on conventional wisdom, we might attribute NASA's problems and successes to the following:

- **Staffing.** Obviously, the DE-A policy of adding people late in the project is not cost effective. Indeed, Brooks suggests that by adding new people to the late DE-A project, management actually delayed it further![14] Thus, in the future NASA should limit hiring to the early phases only.
- **Undersizing.** Another obvious culprit is the initial 35 percent underestimation of the product's size. Schedule estimation models are only as accurate as the sizing information that goes into them. On the DE-A project, an initial 35 percent underestimation of project size led to an underestimate

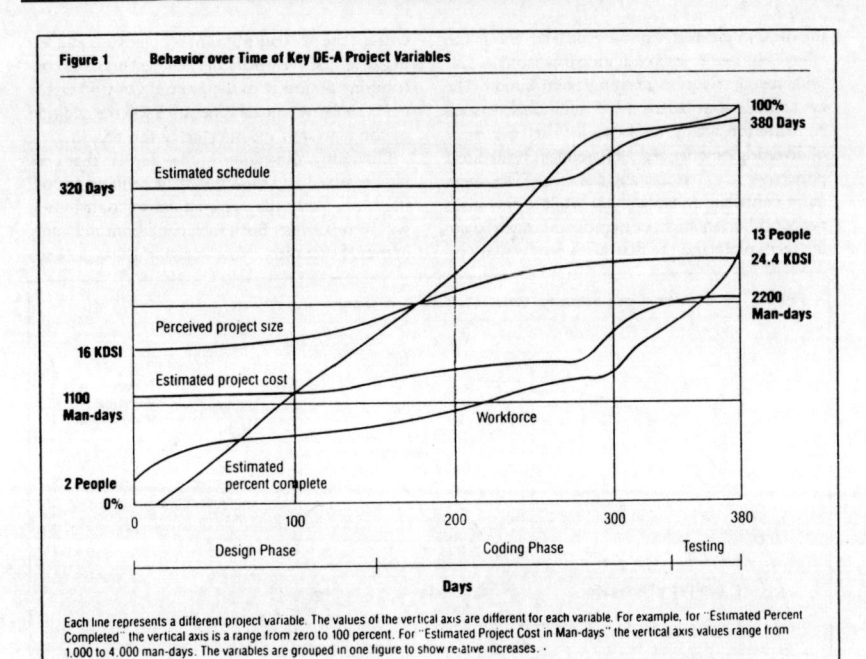

Figure 1 Behavior over Time of Key DE-A Project Variables

[Figure showing curves for Estimated schedule (reaching 380 Days / 100%), Perceived project size (reaching 24.4 KDSI / 13 People), Estimated project cost (reaching 2200 Man-days), Workforce, and Estimated percent complete, over Days 0–380, across Design Phase, Coding Phase, and Testing.]

Axis labels: 320 Days, 16 KDSI, 1100 Man-days, 2 People, 0%

Each line represents a different project variable. The values of the vertical axis are different for each variable. For example, for "Estimated Percent Completed" the vertical axis is a range from zero to 100 percent. For "Estimated Project Cost in Man-days" the vertical axis values range from 1,000 to 4,000 man-days. The variables are grouped in one figure to show relative increases.

of the project's labor and time requirements. In future projects of this type, the budgeted project size, man-days, and time requirements should be increased to match the actual results of this project.
• **Quality Assurance.** The high level of quality assurance activity appears to have been worthwhile and should be continued in the future.

A number of published articles have advocated these kinds of responses, relying on "conventional wisdom," but we have not found them to be necessarily accurate. We recommend a more systematic approach.

Arguments for a Formal Diagnostic Tool

Did DE-A's aggressive staffing policy in fact contribute to the project's schedule delays? To most students of the DE-A project, the answer is: "Yes, obviously." Brooks's law—adding manpower to a late software project delays it further—is intuitively palatable because we know that new hires are not immediately productive and, furthermore, they consume the time of experienced people, who must train and assist them. Since its publication, Brooks's law has been widely endorsed in the literature for all kinds of projects—systems programming projects and applications projects, both large and small.[15] This, in spite of the fact that it has not been formally tested.

We tested the applicability of Brooks's law to the DE-A project.[16] Our results indicate that while adding people late in the lifecycle did increase the project cost, it did *not* delay the project.

Our result is not necessarily as counter-intuitive as it might appear. In fact, Brooks made no claim to the universality of his law. He quite explicitly limited the applicability of his insights to what he called "jumbo systems programming projects."[17] Such projects are significantly more complex to develop and manage than smaller applications projects, like the DE-A.

When a staff increases, in projects such as the DE-A, the team's average productivity decreases because of additional training and communication overhead. However, for the schedule to also suffer,

Software Development

42

Abdel-Hamid & Madnick

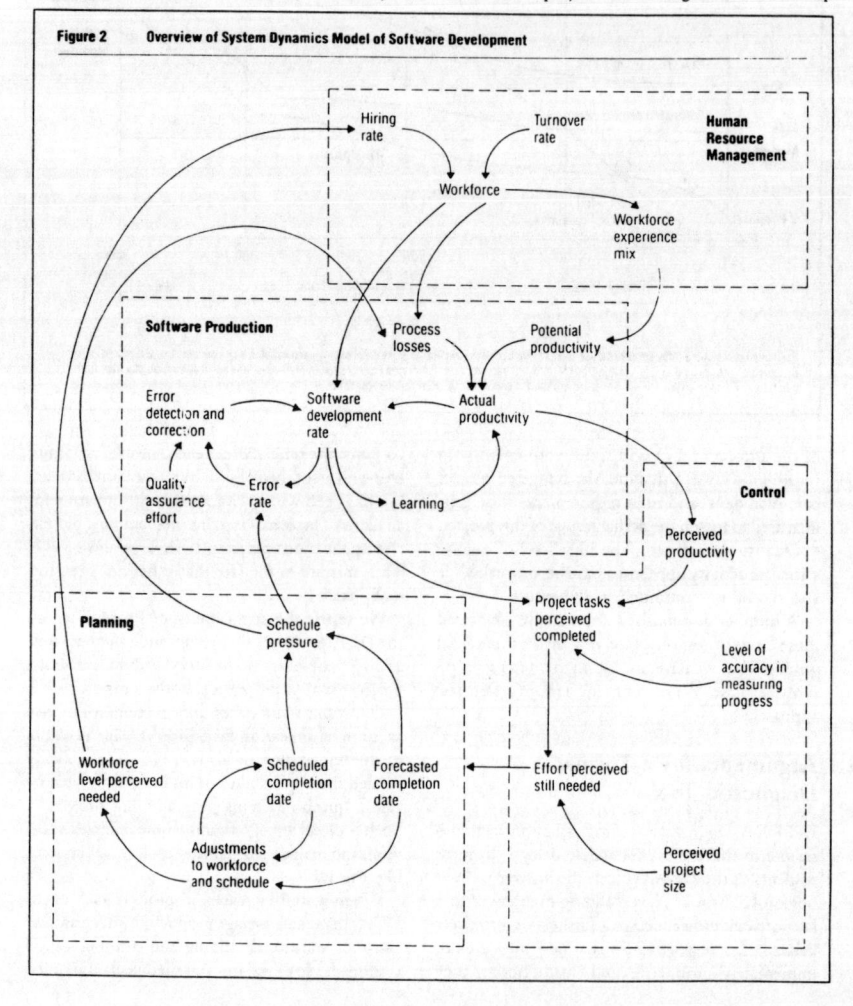

the drop in productivity must be large enough to effectively render each additional person's *net cumulative* contribution a *negative* contribution. The *net* contribution balances the additional person's contribution against the losses incurred as a result of diverting experienced staff members from direct project work to training and assistance. The *cumulative* contribution shows that while a new hire's net contribution might be negative initially, as training takes place and the new hire's productivity increases, the net contribution becomes less and less negative, and eventually the new person starts contributing positively to the project. Only when the net cumulative impact is negative will the addition of the new staff member delay the project.

Obviously, the earlier in the lifecycle that people are added and the shorter the training period, the more likely the net cumulative contribution will turn positive. Both such conditions did apply in the DE-A project. Note in Figure 1 that the steep

Figure 2 Overview of System Dynamics Model of Software Development

rise in the workforce level commenced early in the coding phase. Also, the training and assimilation period needed to bring new hires up to speed was relatively short. There are two reasons for this. First, the software developed was similar to the telemetry software developed by the GSFC organization for previous NASA satellites. Second, NASA had made an arrangement with the Computer Sciences Corporation (CSC) to draw from its pool of software professionals for recurrent work assignments on NASA projects. These software professionals have, over the years, gained a lot of experience with the NASA project environment, and get up to speed quickly on new projects.

The above observations, then, demonstrate the real dangers of overgeneralizing about software project management. Our results suggest that the impact of adding staff to a late software project will depend on the particular characteristics of the project. Because these project characteristics interact in a complex non-linear fashion, relying on human intuition alone can be perilous.[18]

Engineers turn to laboratory experiments to understand the behavior of complex engineering systems. Why, then, do we not use the same approach of making models of social systems and conducting laboratory experiments on them? Controlled laboratory experiments on managerial systems are indeed possible with computers that can simulate social systems:

> Model experimentation is now possible to fill the gap where our judgment and knowledge are weakest—by showing the way in which the known separate system parts can interact to produce unexpected and troublesome overall system results....The manager, like the engineer, can now have a laboratory in which he can learn quickly and at low cost the answers that would seldom be obtainable from trials on real organizations.[19]

A System Dynamics Model of Software Project Management

Abdel-Hamid and Madnick developed a comprehensive system dynamics simulation model of software development as part of a wide-ranging study of the software development process.[20] The model integrates the multiple functions of the software development process, including both the management functions (e.g., planning, controlling, and staffing) and the software production activities (e.g., designing, coding, reviewing, and testing). Figure 2 depicts a highly aggregated view of the model's four subsystems and their interactions, namely: (1) human resource management; (2) software production; (3) control; and (4) planning.

The human resource management subsystem captures the hiring, training, assimilation, and transfer of the project's human resources. Such actions are not carried out in a vacuum, but, as Figure 2 suggests, are affected by the other subsystems. For example, the project's hiring rate is a function of the workforce level needed to complete the project on a certain date. Similarly, the available workforce has direct bearing on the allocation of human resources among the different activities in the software production subsystem.

The four primary activities in the software production subsystem are development, quality assurance, rework, and testing. The development activity comprises both the design and coding of the software. As the software is developed, it is also reviewed for errors. Errors detected through quality assurance activities are then reworked. Not all errors are detected and reworked at this phase, however. Some escape detection until the end of development (e.g., until the system testing phase).

The control subsystem compares the actual progress of the project with the planned schedule. Its assessment of the project's status becomes an important consideration for the planning function.

In the planning subsystem, managers make initial project estimates, and then revise them, when necessary, throughout the project's life. For example, to handle a project that is perceived to be behind schedule, managers can revise plans to hire more people, extend the schedule, or both.

A full discussion of the model's structure, its mathematical formulation, and its validation is available in other reports.[21] The DE-A project case study, which was conducted after the model was completely developed, constituted an important element in validating model behavior. In Figure 3, actual DE-A project results are compared with the model's simulation output.

Project Underestimation Revisited

While undersizing is obviously a serious problem in software development, identifying it as *the* culprit may not be very helpful to the practicing software manager, and indeed it may even be harmful. First, the software manager might not be able to avoid undersizing. Second, blaming undersiz-

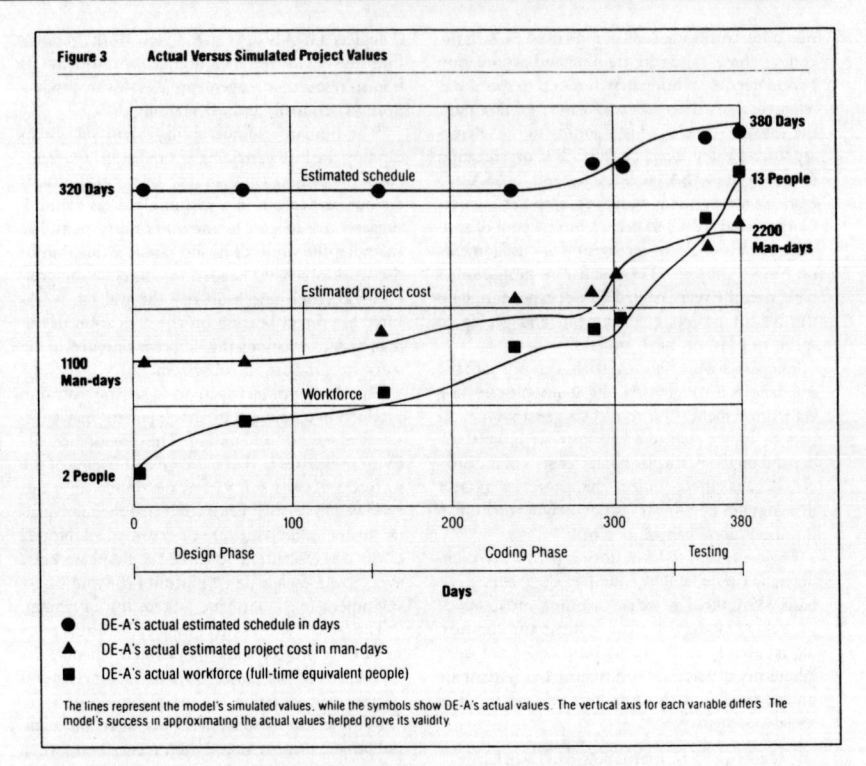

Figure 3 Actual Versus Simulated Project Values

- ● DE-A's actual estimated schedule in days
- ▲ DE-A's actual estimated project cost in man-days
- ■ DE-A's actual workforce (full-time equivalent people)

The lines represent the model's simulated values, while the symbols show DE-A's actual values. The vertical axis for each variable differs. The model's success in approximating the actual values helped prove its validity.

ing can only numb organizational curiosity, depriving management of the opportunity to appreciate the multitude of factors that can and do contribute to cost and budget overruns.

While the industry's predisposition to exaggerate the sins of undersizing may not be a shocking revelation, that organizations consistently underexploit the undersizing lesson should be. Recall that DE-A's final results were as follows:

Project size	24,400 DSI
Development cost	2,200 man-days
Completion time	380 working days

The standard procedure in the industry (as well as at NASA) is to incorporate project results such as the above into a database of historical project statistics to support the development, calibration, and fine tuning of software estimation tools as depicted in Figure 4(a). The underlying assumption here is that such project results constitute the most preferred and reliable benchmark for future estimation purposes. After all, they are *actual* values.

However, from our earlier discussion of the DE-A project history, we must suspect that its final cost of 2,200 man-days may *not* be a desirable benchmark for future estimates. Such a value reflects the inefficiencies incurred in staffing the project, which were a result of its initial undersizing. Thus, if a new project like the DE-A comes along, and if planners estimate the size correctly from the start (as we must assume when estimating for any new project), then a more effective staffing plan can be devised to avoid DE-A's last-minute staff explosion. As a result the new project *should* require less than 2,200 man-days to accomplish.

However, if planners adopt DE-A's (inflated) 2,200 man-days value as the benchmark *and* more accurately estimate project size, they may not in fact realize any savings. The reason: the self-fulfilling prophecy of Parkinson's law. Work on a software project can expand in many different forms to fill the available time. For example, work expansion could take the form of goldplating (e.g., adding features to the software product that make the job bigger and more expensive, but which provide little utility to the user or maintainer) or an increase in slack-time activities.[22]

We need a strategy that allows us to fully capitalize on DE-A's learning experience by "wringing" out those man-day excesses caused by undersizing; we need a set of *normalized* cost and schedule estimation benchmarks (see Figure 4(b)). The system dynamics model provides a viable tool for such a task. It allows us to experiment by keeping all factors constant except for one, then replaying the project to see how that factor affected the outcome.

Specifically, we can simulate the DE-A project with *no* undersizing. In order to determine the extent of the man-day excesses, we conducted not one but several simulation runs. In all runs we held the initial schedule estimate constant at 380 days, while gradually decreasing the man-day estimate. Figure 5 shows the results of such an experiment. The X-axis depicts the different initial man-day estimates, while the Y-axis depicts the project's final (simulated) cost in man-days.

The results indicate that using DE-A's raw value of 2,200 man-days is indeed wasteful. As the initial man-day estimate for the project is gradually lowered, wasteful practices such as goldplating and unproductive slack-time activities gradually decrease. This continues until reaching the 1,900 man-day level. Lowering the project's initial man-day estimate below this point, however, becomes counter-productive, as the project not only sheds all its excess, but becomes understaffed and is forced to build its staff later in the cycle. It becomes, in effect, an underestimated project.

The above results clearly indicate that the widely held notion that *raw* historical project results constitute the most preferred benchmark for future estimation is not only flawed, but can be costly as well. In the case of NASA's DE-A project, a 1,900 man-day value is a more preferred benchmark for inclusion in the normalized database of historical project results than the raw 2,200 value; it would save NASA 234 man-days—a 10.6 percent cost saving. In view of the pervasiveness of the under-

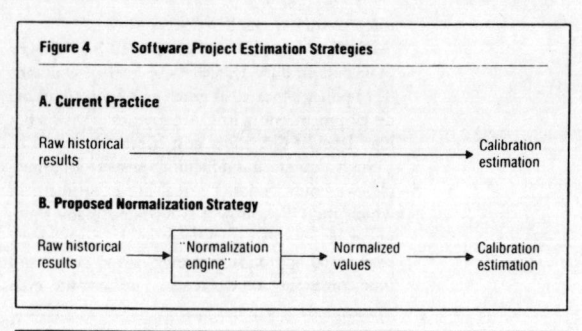

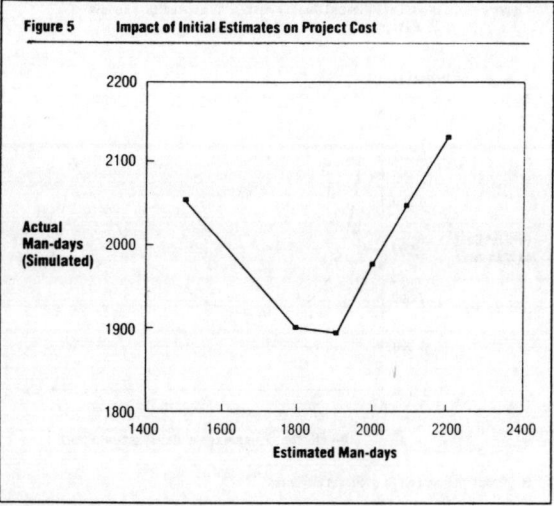

Figure 4   Software Project Estimation Strategies

A. Current Practice

Raw historical results ——————————————→ Calibration estimation

B. Proposed Normalization Strategy

Raw historical results → "Normalization engine" → Normalized values → Calibration estimation

Figure 5   Impact of Initial Estimates on Project Cost

sizing problem in the software industry, we can only suspect that the potential for such savings is not only realizable, but indeed abounds in the software industry.

A False Sense of Security?

Our focus so far has been on problems, their causes, and the lessons we derive from them. Now we will focus on success and the lessons we can gain "in spite of it." Such a quest is rarely, if ever, undertaken. Organizations do not look for problems until someone is dissatisfied.[23] When goals are accomplished, the system often deludes us into a false sense of security that may not be justifiable or wise. It may breed complacency and possibly even reinforce dysfunctional behavior.

DE-A's success lay in the reported high quality of its end product. Its aggressive quality assurance (QA) policy allocated as much as 30 percent of the development effort to QA activities. Was such a high level of QA effort cost-effective?

Such a question is difficult to answer. In principle, we could conduct a real life experiment in which the DE-A project is repeated many times under varied QA expenditure levels. Such an experimental approach, however, is too costly and time consuming to be practical. Furthermore, even when affordable, the isolation of the effect (cost) and the evaluation of the impact of any given practice (QA) within a large, complex, and dynamic social system such as a software project environment can be exceedingly difficult.[24] Simulation modeling, on the other hand, does provide a viable alternative for such a task.

We used our system dynamics model to investigate the impact of different QA expenditure levels on the DE-A project.[25] Figure 6(a) plots the impact of QA expenditures (defined as a percentage of total man-days) on the project's *total* cost. At low values of QA, the increase in total project cost results from the high cost of the testing phase. However, at high values of QA expenditures, the excessive QA effort is itself the culprit. The reason: As QA expenditures increase beyond the 15 to 20 percent level, they reach a level of "diminishing returns," as shown in Figure 6(b). Such behavior is not atypical. "In any sizable program, it is impossible to remove all errors (during development)...some errors manifest themselves, and can be exhibited only after system integration."[26]

It is quite clear from Figure 6(a) that the QA expenditure level has a significant influence on the total cost of the project. Specifically, DE-A's cost ranged from a low of 1,648 man-days to a high of 5,650 man-days over the range of QA policies tested. It is also obvious that DE-A's actual 30 percent QA allocation level is not optimal; it yielded a total project cost of 2,200 man-days. The same quality of project could have been achieved in 1,648 man-days, with a 15 percent QA allocation. (Under the different QA policies tested, the quality of the software end product was controlled to remain the same through increased testing phase activities. The increased testing costs are reflected in total project cost figures above.)

The significance of the above result is not in deriving a particular optimal QA allocation level, since this cannot be generalized beyond the specific DE-A project, rather it is in the value of the system dynamics simulation modeling approach. Except for costly and time-consuming controlled experimentation, as far as the authors know this model provides the first capability to quantitatively analyze the economics of QA policy. In this case it allowed us to discern the overspending that would have gone unnoticed in the period of post-project self-congratulation at having achieved the quality goals. When such inefficiencies are not detected and

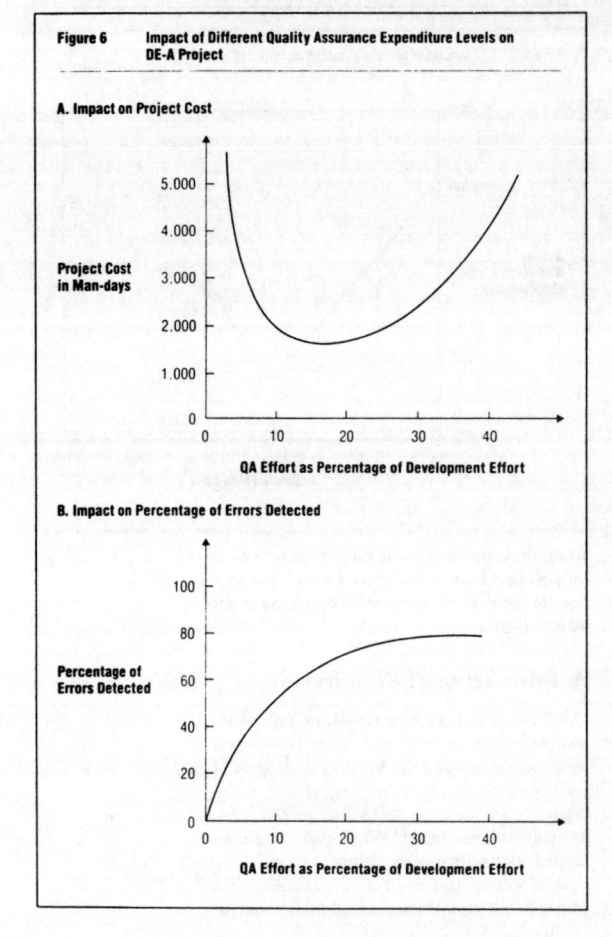

Figure 6 Impact of Different Quality Assurance Expenditure Levels on DE-A Project

A. Impact on Project Cost

B. Impact on Percentage of Errors Detected

quickly corrected, they tend, over time, to be institutionalized into organizational fat that is then very difficult and often painful to shed.

Conclusions

Our system dynamics modeling of the NASA project produced three insights. First, intuition alone may not be sufficient to handle the complex and dynamic interactions characterizing the software project environment, and may indeed mislead us into deriving the *wrong* lesson (Brooks's law in the DE-A environment). Second, the model can help managers learn from what continues to be a seriously *underexploited* software project lesson: undersizing. And third, the model can uncover *disguised* lessons, in this case the excessive expenditures on QA.

In general, without an effective postmortem diagnostic exercise to identify problems and their causes, managers cannot adequately scrutinize project deficiencies, and may repeat errors on future projects. The payoff from an effective postmortem is a smarter organization that truly learns from its failures. ∎

References

1
R.E. Neustadt and E.R. May, *Thinking in Time* (New York: The Free Press, 1986).

2
M.E. Porter and V. Millar, "How Information Gives You Competitive Advantage," *Harvard Business Review*, July-August 1985. See also:
C.F. Bales, "The Myths and Realities of Competitive Advantage," *Datamation*, 1 October 1988.

3
J.P. Newport, Jr., "A Growing Gap in Software," *Fortune*, 28 April 1986, pp. 132–142.

4
J. Boddie, "The Project Postmortem," *Computerworld*, 7 December 1987.

5
B.W. Boehm, "Improving Software Productivity," *Computer*, September 1987.

6
Report to Congress by the Comptroller General, FGMSD80-4j, November 1979.

7
C. Baker and D. Silverberg, *Defense News*, 18 December 1989.

8
R.W. Zmud, "Management of Large Software Development Efforts," *MIS Quarterly*, June 1980, pp. 45–55.

9
T. DeMarco, *Controlling Software Projects* (New York: Yourdon Press, Inc., 1982).

10
P.B. Carroll, "Creating New Software Was Agonizing Task for Mitch Kapor Firm," *The Wall Street Journal*, 11 May 1990.

11
Ibid.

12
B.W. Boehm, *Software Engineering Economics* (Englewood Cliffs, New Jersey: Prentice-Hall, 1981).

13
NASA, "Software Development History for Dynamic Explorer (DE) Attitude Group Support System," NASA/GSFC Code 580, June 1983.

14
F.P. Brooks, *The Mythical Man Month* (Reading, Massachusetts: Addison-Wesley, 1975).

15
R.S. Pressman, *Software Engineering: A Practitioner's Approach* (New York: McGraw-Hill, 1982).

16
T.K. Abdel-Hamid, "The Dynamics of Software Project Staffing: A System Dynamics Based Simulation Approach," *IEEE Transactions on Software Engineering*, February 1989, pp. 109–119.

17
Brooks (1975).

18
Abdel-Hamid (1989).

19
J.W. Forrester, *Industrial Dynamics* (Cambridge, Massachusetts: MIT Press, 1961).

20
T.K. Abdel-Hamid, "The Dynamics of Software Development Project Management: An Integrative System Dynamics Perspective" (Cambridge, Massachusetts: MIT Sloan School of Management, unpublished Ph.D. dissertation, January 1984).

21
Ibid;
T.K. Abdel-Hamid and S.E. Madnick, *The Dynamics of Software Development* (Englewood Cliffs, New Jersey: Prentice-Hall), forthcoming.

22
Boehm (1981).

23
R.L. Glass, *The Universal Elixir and Other Computing Projects Which Failed* (Seattle: R.L. Glass, 1977).

[24] B. Hedberg, "How Organizations Learn and Unlearn," in *Handbook of Organizational Design*, eds. P.C. Nystrom and W.H. Starbuck (Oxford, England: Oxford University Press, 1981).

[25] T.K. Abdel-Hamid, "The Economics of Software Quality Assurance: A Simulation-Based Case Study," *MIS Quarterly*, September 1988, pp. 395–411.

[26] M.L. Shooman, *Software Engineering: Design, Reliability and Management* (New York: McGraw-Hill, 1983).

Reprint 3213

Software Development

48

Abdel-Hamid & Madnick

[23]

Worker burnout: a dynamic model with implications for prevention and control

Jack B. Homer

This paper explores the dynamics of worker burnout, a process in which a hard-working individual becomes increasingly exhausted, frustrated, and unproductive. The author's own two-year experience with repeated cycles of burnout is qualitatively reproduced by a small system dynamics model that portrays the underlying psychology of workaholism. Model tests demonstrate that the limit cycle seen in the base run can be stabilized through techniques that diminish work-related stress or enhance relaxation. These stabilizing techniques also serve to raise overall productivity, since they support a higher level of energy and more working hours on the average. One important policy lever is the maximum workweek or work limit; an optimal work limit at which overall productivity is at its peak is shown to exist within a region of stability where burnout is avoided. The paper concludes with a strategy for preventing burnout, which emphasizes the individual's responsibility for understanding the self-inflicted nature of this problem and pursuing an effective course of stability.

In this world there are two tragedies. One is not getting what one wants, the other is getting it. (Oscar Wilde)
The survival of mankind as a species may well depend on the successful management of stress. (Greenwood 1979, xii)

The negative consequences of unrelieved stress have become increasingly evident over the last few decades. In a fast-moving, achievement-oriented society, individuals may easily become worn down and unable to function effectively if they are not careful. Excessive stress can lead not only to chronic fatigue but also to a wide variety of psychological, medical, and behavioral problems ranging from irritation, depression, and loss of appetite to violence, alcoholism, mental illness, and heart disease (Cherniss 1980; Greenwood 1979, 117–163; Holt 1982, 427–433). These problems affect both the individual and the society at large and have had a clear depressive effect on economic productivity in the United States. It has been estimated that output could be boosted by at least 10 percent if the work loss and impaired job performance attributable to mismanaged stress were eliminated (Greenwood 1979, 128–163; Ivancevich 1980, 18). As most executives surely now realize, the connection between distress and the bottom line is indeed real.

Since work plays a central role in the lives of most people, it should not be surprising that a great deal of potentially harmful stress originates in the workplace. In recent years many researchers in the area of occupational safety and health have turned their attention to the issue of occupational stress. Potential sources of stress at work are many and include irritants in the physical or social environment, problems of role or responsibility, poor job fit, inadequate rewards or support, and deadline pressure (Greenwood 1979, 103; Holt 1982, 420–427; Ivancevich 1980, 96). Some jobs tend to be more stressful than others; studies have shown, for example, that air traffic controllers are much more susceptible to stress-related diseases and behavioral problems than the average person. The same is probably true for lawyers, doctors, social workers, and salespeople (Ivancevich 1980, 171). But because tension may arise in any situation where personal needs are not being satisfied, every job has the potential for being stressful (NDACTRD 1980, 225).

When work-related stress becomes severely debilitating, the affected individual may be said to be "burned out." Burnout has been defined broadly as "a process in which individuals become exhausted by making excessive demands on energy strength" (NDACTRD 1980, 1). It is generally agreed that at the root of the problem is the individual's own overcommitment to frustrating work. The source of a burnout victim's frustration is the inability to attain high expectations set by others or, more frequently, by the individual. The entire process may take weeks, months, or years (Freudenberger 1980, 13–16; Greenwood 1979, 47; NDACTRD 1980, 1, 125). Some have said that organizations or even entire societies may burn out if they push themselves too hard (Greenwood 1979, 126).

The burnout process begins when the individual attempts to meet unmet expectations by working longer hours. Longer hours mean more exposure to the normal stress

System Dynamics Review 1 (no. 1, Summer 1985): 42–62. ISSN 0883-7066. © 1985 by the System Dynamics Society.

Jack Homer is assistant professor of systems science at the University of Southern California. His model-based doctoral dissertation at M.I.T. explored the emergence of new medical technologies. His research in system dynamics spans a variety of industrial, social, and personal applications. *Address:* Jack B. Homer, Dept. of Systems Science, Institute of Safety and Systems Management, University of Southern California, University Park, Los Angeles, CA 90089.

of work and consequently more of a drain on the individual's finite store of "adaptation energy" and less time available for recovery of that lost energy (Greenwood 1979, 31–43; Ivancevich 1980, 176; Selye 1974, 38–40). This drain of energy may, in turn, render the individual weaker and less capable of reaching his or her goals. The response to continued inadequacy of performance is to work harder, which depletes energy further (Freudenberger 1980, 5–6). In addition, the worker's growing frustration at work increases the very stressfulness of that work, so that energy is drained still more rapidly (Greenwood 1979, 47; Selye 1974, 78, 96). If the individual refuses or is unable to take time out to recover, the vicious cycle of frustration-exhaustion-dysfunction will ultimately produce chronic and severe problems which *force* him off the job, a burned-out ember of his former self (Ivancevich 1980, 96; NDACTRD 1980, 151).

The ideal context for burnout combines a workaholic personality type with a disagreeable, and therefore highly stressful, job. In general, a nonworkaholic will simply be unwilling to work unusually long and stressful hours and certainly will not seek out such a position. Workaholics or high achievers, on the other hand, create conditions of work overload for themselves and feel uneasy when they are not working (Ivancevich 1980, 177; Machlowitz 1980, 87; McClelland 1961). They compete most strongly with themselves, essentially expanding their goals whenever necessary to maintain the challenge they inherently need; current accomplishments are never quite enough (Freudenberger 1980, 49; Machlowitz 1980, 27, 122). The fact that most workaholics can push themselves this way for many years without burning out speaks well for their ability to find work that is so fulfilling as to minimize the wear and tear of long hours (Machlowitz 1980, 103, 117). But put a self-driven workaholic in a disagreeable work setting—for example, one lacking in tangible rewards—and the prescription for burnout is complete: Unmet goals become more of a burden than a motivating challenge (Freudenberger 1980, 42; Machlowitz 1980, 109; NDACTRD 1980, 128).

It is worth looking more closely at the workaholic personality. Workaholism is a way of life for perhaps 5 percent of American adults. Beneath their energetic and intense surface lies an obsessive perfectionism associated with the fear of failure or boredom (Machlowitz 1980, 6, 26–32, 41–46). Their inability to relax, compromise, seek assistance, or admit limitations often arises first in childhood, reflecting in part the internalization of family values regarding the importance of determined effort, self-reliance, and self-improvement (Freudenberger 1980, 11, 32; Machlowitz 1980, 39; NDACTRD 1980, 108). But the relatively recent phenomenon of workaholism is not attributable solely to the American work ethic, which, after all, goes back many generations. The difference in America today is that with the rapid and widespread erosion of traditions and support systems, few activities outside of the workplace continue to give the individual the sense of meaning and control that they once did. As a result, ". . . our expectations from work become disproportionate to what, in most cases, it can provide" (Freudenberger 1980, 186, 198). Since workaholics invest little of themselves outside work, they risk losing all if work itself ceases to be rewarding.

Strategies for the prevention and amelioration of burnout are as numerous as the writers who propose them. But they all seem to fall into one of three categories: (1) work less, (2) minimize the stress of work, and (3) relax more effectively when not working. Working less may involve working fewer hours per day or taking more frequent vacations (Freudenberger 1980, 158; Machlowitz 1980, 133; Selye 1974, 40). Minimizing work stress may involve shifting tasks or reducing expectations or learning through techniques such as assertiveness training and "stress inoculation" consciously to defuse and to redirect potentially stressful situations (Cameron 1982, 702; Freudenberger 1980, 158, 175; Holroyd 1982, 29; Ivancevich 1980, 230; Janis 1982, 82; NDACTRD 1980, 192; Stoyva 1982, 754). Minimizing stress also may require action by the supervisor or employer, such as clarifying goals or roles, providing more rewards and "strokes," allowing for more personal initiative, and generally improving the work climate (Ivancevich 1980, 207–214; Kiefer 1982, 6; Machlowitz 1980, 133–137, NDACTRD 1980, 192–202). More effective relaxation may involve exercise, hobbies, loafing, close friendship, meditation, biofeedback, body realignment therapy, or any of several techniques specifically designed to elicit the calm state of "passive attention" (Greenwood 1979, 175–211, 229; Freudenberger 1980, 136, 206; Ivancevich 1980, 176, 217; NDACTRD 1980, 186–191; Stoyva 1982, 749–753).

Because the sources of stress are manifold and varied, there exists no single panacea for this complex problem. But each of the preceding techniques can be helpful; in contrast, palliatives that are themselves addictive, such as drinking and gambling, clearly are not effective in managing stress and may only worsen the situation (Freudenberger 1980, 99; Greenwood 1979, 171; Maslach 1978). The prevention of burnout ultimately depends on maintaining a healthy balance of activities, giving adequate time to both active coping and rest (Freudenberger 1980, 210; Greenwood 1979, 220–221; Stoyva 1982, 746).

While the literature provides graphic descriptions of the process of burnout and offers many pieces of advice, it does little to address the question of what actually happens following burnout, that is, during and after recovery. Presumably, the individual can regain lost energy during the time off from work, but what then? If he or she returns to stressful work following recovery, without adopting measures to manage energy more effectively, another round of burnout would seem likely.

Although repeated cycles of burnout are apparently undocumented in the literature, they were, in fact, my experience from 1981 to 1983, the two years of researching and writing my doctoral thesis. Perhaps four times during this long and often lonely effort, I experienced periods of moderate burnout, the symptoms including exhaustion, confusion, anger, headaches, stomach pains, and depression. My productivity plummeted during these periods, and I would finally take time off to recover my strength. When I returned to work, I would not only feel refreshed but also have a more relaxed attitude toward work, with lower expectations for my weekly output. I could meet these new goals without working too hard, but soon I would find my expectations rising and work hours increasing, true to the workaholic profile. First, my evenings disappeared, then my weekends, and it was only a matter of time before I would start to feel tired and confused again.

Purpose and approach

The purpose of this paper is to present a dynamic model of worker burnout, consistent with both the literature and with my personal experience, which can suggest guidelines for attaining greater stability and higher productivity. The model is tested to determine whether stabilizing policies do in fact raise overall accomplishment: uncertainty on this point arises because the ways of the burnout candidate are precisely those of the high achiever. Can one actually push less and achieve more?

The next section describes the structure of the small (four-level, nineteen-equation) system dynamics model used for the subsequent analysis, first in overview and then in detail. This is followed by an investigation of model behavior: First, a description and causal-loop explanation of the base run; and second, an exploration of policies to prevent and control burnout cycles, culminating in the idea of an "optimal work limit." The paper concludes with a general strategy for fighting worker burnout, based on insights provided by the model.

Model structure

Overview

The model of worker burnout presented here focuses on the psychological dynamics underlying the problem, namely, the dynamics of workaholism. (See the Appendix for a complete model listing.) The model has four major elements: (1) accomplishments per week, the outcome measure of interest; (2) expected accomplishments per week, the outcome goal set by the worker; (3) hours worked per week, also adjusted by the worker and one determinant of the weekly accomplishment rate; and (4) energy level, which determines hourly productivity, this being the other factor determining weekly accomplishment. The energy level is depleted by the stress of work and replenished during periods of rest; thus, longer hours at work lead to faster depletion and slower recovery of energy. The frustration that comes from accomplishment falling short of expectations can also accelerate energy depletion. If current accomplishment seems adequate or nearly so, the textbook workaholic will increase expectations; the worker's goals drift downward only if they appear far too high given current output. On the other hand, he or she will tend to work longer hours if accomplishments are perceived to be inadequate; and will decrease hours only if goals are exceeded or if the energy level is so low as to make time off unavoidable.

The model does not attempt to account for the individual's basic approach to and compatibility with his work. Thus, the factors that define the workaholic personality are exogenous, as is the worker's normal level of stress. Also beyond the model's boundary are those personal and environmental factors that determine the individual's basic ability to relax. In addition, hourly output at a given energy level, determined in real life by such factors as preparation for the task at hand, native intelligence, and assistance from others, is exogenous. The model is not concerned with learning curves or organizational dynamics. This is not to say that changes in the individual or the surroundings are not important; indeed, the role of sensitivity testing is precisely to analyze the importance of various exogenous factors. Rather, the model is intended to show how the workaholic syndrome can by itself lead to burnout, without the aid of other dynamic factors. One need not examine changes in the individual's career goals, for example, in order to explain the month-to-month dynamics of burnout, though such longer-term changes may be central to an explanation of a midlife "achievement crisis" (Dabiri 1979).

Equation description

A note on parameter values: The values ascribed to constants and table functions in the baseline model are entirely based on logic and considered judgment. The numerical data of interest are simply not to be found in the literature, nor have I attempted to measure these parameters myself. The numbers were drawn primarily in an impressionistic fashion from my own experience as a victim of burnout. Note that the burnout cycle reference mode itself was presented in descriptive, not numerical, terms. Thus, lacking numerical data on both structure and behavior, attempts at historical accuracy or prediction are obviously out of the question. Still, if the endogenous structure is potent enough, one can learn much about the generic process through careful model testing. The baseline set of parameters is treated simply as a takeoff point for investigating model behavior under a variety of circumstances. The results can thereby be considered applicable to a whole spectrum of individuals and work settings.

```
AW.K = (AH.K)(HWW.K)                    A, 1
AH.K = TABLE(TAH,EL.K,0,1,.2)           A, 2
TAH  = 0/.2/.4/.6/.8/1                  T, 2.1
       AW  = Accomplishments per week (A-units/week)
       AH  = Accomplishments per hour (A-units/week)
       HWW = Hours worked per week (hours/week)
       TAH = Table for accomplishments per hour
       EL  = Energy level (0-1)
```

The worker's weekly output is the product of hourly productivity and number of hours worked per week. Output is measured in units of accomplishment (A-units), the meaning of which depends on the kind of work involved. For simplicity's sake, it has been assumed that the worker can produce at most one accomplishment per hour. Hourly productivity is determined by the worker's energy level: When one's energy level (and correspondingly, one's levels of rationality and self-esteem) is low, one is easily distracted from the task at hand and prone to erratic performance and poor decision making (Greenwood 1979, 125; Ivancevich 1980, 201; Janis 1982, 69, 99). Indeed, hourly accomplishment might be thought of as an operational definition of the energy level, implying the linear relationship depicted in Eq. 2.1. When the worker has no energy at all, he produces nothing, while at full energy he produces at maximum hourly rate.

```
HWW.K = HWW.J + (DT/TAHWW)(IHWW.J -                    L, 3
   HWW.J)
HWW = HWWI                                             N, 3.1
HWWI = 40                                              C, 3.2
TAHWW = 1                                              C, 3.3

IHWW.K = MIN(LHWW,HWW.K*EELHW.K*EPAHW.K)               A, 4
LHWW = 80                                              C, 4.1

   HWW   = Hours worked per week (hours/week)
   HWWI  = Hours worked per week, initial (hours/week)
   TAHWW = Time to adjust HWW (weeks)
   IHWW  = Indicated hours worked per week (hours/week)
   LHWW  = Limit on hours worked per week (hours/week)
   EELHW = Effect of energy level on hours worked
   EPAHW = Effect of perceived adequacy on hours worked
```

The number of hours worked per week, initialized at a standard value of 40, is adjusted by the worker toward an "indicated" value more in line with his perception of the current situation. It is assumed here that hours are flexible and the adjustment can be made within one week's time. The indicated workweek may be longer than the current workweek if output is perceived as inadequate and may be shorter if output is perceived as more than adequate or if the energy level is low (see Eqs. 5 and 6 following); but the workweek is assumed never to exceed some upper limit (or to exceed it so rarely as to be insignificant). This weekly work limit may be determined by the worker or by others and may be explicit or implicit; in any case, it represents the maximum workweek the individual is willing to put in, on a continuous basis if need be. Many people regularly work 60 to 90 hours per week (Ivancevich 1980, 17); the baseline model assumes a work limit of 80 hours per week.

```
EELHW.K = TABLE(TEELHW,EL.K,0,1,.2)                    A, 5
TEELHW = 0/.4/.7/.9/1/1                                T, 5.1

EPAHW.K = TABLE(TEPAHW,PAA.K,0,1.6,.2)                 A, 6
TEPAHW = 2.3/1.9/1.6/1.35/1.15/1/.9/.8/.75             T, 6.1

   EELHW  = Effect of energy level on hours worked
   TEELHW = Table for EELHW
   EL     = Energy level
   EPAHW  = Effect of perceived adequacy on hours worked
   TEPAHW = Table for EPAHW
   PAA    = Perceived adequacy of accomplishment
```

Figure 1 shows the "time off" effect that a low energy level may have on hours worked. The function becomes steep only in the region of lower energy, reflecting the workaholic's natural reluctance to break away from work unless the situation is desperate. Workaholics feel guilty and anxious about leaving work and so tend to skip or shortchange vacation time (Machlowitz 1980, 93–99). But should the worker's

Fig. 1. Table for effect of energy level on hours worked

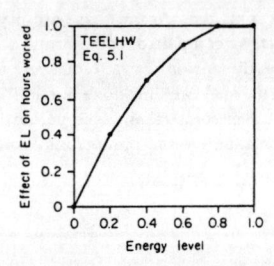

Fig. 2. Table for effect of perceived adequacy of accomplishment on hours worked

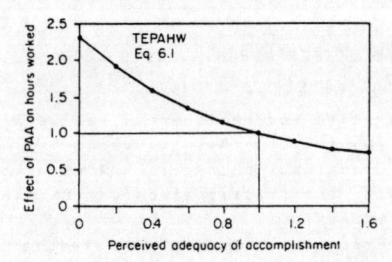

energy drop toward zero, a vacation will become a matter of necessity rather than choice.

Figure 2 depicts the "work harder" response to performance that falls short of one's goals; studies have shown that the further the goal is, the harder people will work to achieve it (Welford 1973). Experience and the logic of symmetry suggest that achievement exceeding one's goals tends to call forth a more relaxed attitude with fewer hours worked. The concave function used here represents a response roughly proportional to the perceived degree of inadequacy or surplus for values of input in the normal range, but considerably less than proportional in the region of very low adequacy. The latter reflects a natural resistance to radical increases in the workweek over a short period of time.

```
PAA.K = PAW.K/XAW.K                              A, 7

PAW.K = PAW.J + (DT/TPAW)(AW.J - PAW.J)          L, 8
PAW = AW                                         N, 8.1
TPAW = 1                                         C, 8.2

     PAA  = Perceived adequacy of accomplishment
     PAW  = Perceived accomplishments per week (A-units/
            week)
     XAW  = Expected accomplishments per week (A-units/week)
     AW   = Accomplishments per week (A-units/week)
     TPAW = Time to perceive accomplishments per week
            (weeks)
```

The worker's satisfaction with his performance has both psychological and behavioral consequences and reflects a comparison of perceived accomplishment with expected accomplishment. The dimensionless ratio measure used here seems a reasonable approximation to the informal calculus done in real life. The worker assesses his output rate by averaging it over some recent time period; the smoothing time of one week used here reflects the attentive self-observation typical of a high achiever.

```
XAW.K = XAW.J + (DT)(XAW.J*FCXAW.J)           L, 9
XAW = XAWI                                     N, 9.1
XAWI = 40                                      C, 9.2

FCXAW.K = BFCX + FCXPA.K                       A, 10
BFCX = .1                                      C, 10.1

FCXPA.K = TABLE(TFCXPA,PAA.K,0,1.6,.2)         A, 11
TFCXPA = -.7/-.5/-.35/-.2/-.1/0/.1/.25/.4      T, 11.1

    XAW = Expected accomplishments per week (A-units/week)
    XAWI = XAW, initial (A-units/week)
    FCXAW = Fractional change in XAW (1/week)
    BFCX = Bias for fractional change in expectations
           (1/week)
    FCXPA = Fractional change in expectations from per-
            ceived adequacy (1/week)
    TFCXPA = Table for FCXPA
    PAA = Perceived adequacy of accomplishment
```

The worker's expectation for weekly output, initialized to equal actual output, is adjusted up or down in response to the perceived adequacy of his performance. The high achiever pushes to expand his goals once they have been met. This is represented in the model by a bias causing the increase of expected output whenever perceived adequacy is neutral (PAA = 1). When accomplishment is more than just satisfactory, the worker will feel encouraged to expand his goals even faster than this bias, as shown in Figure 3. Conversely, when output is inadequate, the individual will nat-

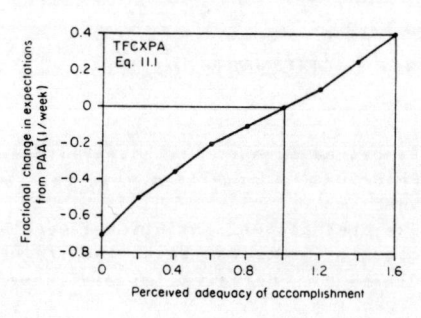

Fig. 3. Table for fractional change in expectations from perceived adequacy of accomplishment

urally be tempted to draw back his goals somewhat to avoid undue frustration.[1] In the baseline model this reaction overcomes the upward bias and causes an actual shrinking of expectations whenever perceived adequacy is less than 0.8.[2] Figure 3 indicates that this response becomes stronger as the worker's dissatisfaction becomes more acute.

```
EL.K = EL.J + (DT)(ER.JK - ED.JK)              L,  12
EL = ELI                                        N,  12.1
ELI = 1                                         C,  12.2

ER.KL = (ERN)(EHWER.K)(EHEFR.K)                 R,  13
ERN = .3                                        C,  13.1

EHWER.K = TABLE(TEHWER,HWW.K,0,120,20)          A,  14
TEHWER = 1.3/1.2/1/.7/.5/.35/.25                T,  14.1

EHEFR.K = TABHL(TEHEFR,EL.K,.8,1,.05)           A,  15
TEHEFR = 1/.9/.7/.4/0                           T,  15.1

    EL = Energy level (0-1)
    ELI = Energy level, initial (0-1)
    ER = Energy recovery (1/week)
    ED = Energy depletion (1/week)
    ERN = Energy recovery normal (1/week)
    EHWER = Effect of hours worked on energy recovery
    TEHWER = Table for EHWER
    HWW = Hours worked per week (hours/week)
    EHEFR = Effect of high energy on further recovery
    TEHEFR = Table for EHEFR
```

The individual's energy level, initialized at its maximum value of 1, is affected by rates of depletion and recovery. The state of low energy known as exhaustion or fatigue is generally associated with other psychological problems, which may include irritability, sadness, detachment, disorientation, and low self-esteem (Freudenberger 1980, 17–18; Holt 1982, 427–433).

Energy is recovered during periods of leisure, relaxation, and of course, sleep. The recovery rate is normalized at a point where the individual is working 40 hours per week and has an energy level lower than 0.8; the recovery rate in this situation is 30 percent per week. But a longer workweek leaves less time for recovery and therefore a slower rate of recovery, as indicated in Figure 4 (Breznitz 1982, 5; Ivancevich 1980, 176). This effect becomes proportionately greater as the workweek increases to cut into evenings, weekends, and even late nights. When the energy level exceeds 0.8, the "effect of high energy on further recovery" acts to suppress the recovery rate somewhat, simply because not much lost energy remains to be recovered. This effect becomes stronger as the energy level approaches 1, at which point the recovery rate must equal zero.

Fig. 4. Table for effect of hours worked on energy recovery

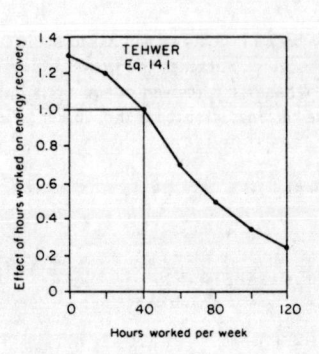

```
ED.KL = (EDN)(EPAED.K)(EHWED.K)(ELEFD.K)      R, 16
EDN = .06                                      C, 16.1

EPAED.K = TABLE(TEPAED,PAA.K,0,1.6,.2)          A, 17
TEPAED = 5/4/3.1/2.3/1.6/1/.6/.4/.3             T, 17.1

EHWED.K = TABLE(TEHWED,HWW.K,0,120,20)          A, 18)
TEHWED = .3/.6/1/1.5/2/2.5/3                    T, 18.1

ELEFD.K = TABHL(TELEFD,EL.K,0,.2,.05)           A, 19
TELEFD = 0/.4/.7/.9/1                           T, 19.1
```

```
ED = Energy depletion (1/week)
EDN = Energy depletion normal (1/week)
EPAED = Effect of perceived adequacy on energy deple-
        tion
TEPAED = Table for EPAED
PAA = Perceived adequacy of accomplishment
EHWED = Effect of hours worked on energy depletion
TEHWED = Table for EHWED
HWW = Hours worked per week (hours/week)
ELEFD = Effect of low energy on further depletion
TELEFD = Table for ELEFD
EL = Energy level (0-1)
```

Energy is depleted as the result of repeated exposure to stress. The depletion rate is normalized at a point where the perceived adequacy of accomplishment is neutral, the workweek is 40 hours, and the energy level is greater than 0.2; the depletion rate in this situation is only 6 percent per week. But should the work become frustrating or the hours at work increase, the normal stress of work can be greatly compounded, as illustrated in Figures 5 and 6 (Greenwood 1979, 42, 47; Howard 1965; Ivancevich 1980, 77, 176; Lazarus 1979; NDACTRD 1980, 1; Selye 1974, 96).

Fig. 5. Table for effect of perceived adequacy of accomplishment on energy depletion

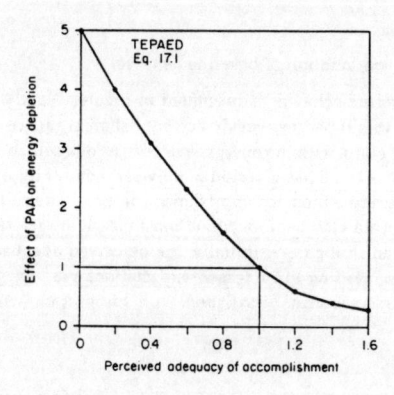

Fig. 6. Table for effect of hours worked on energy depletion

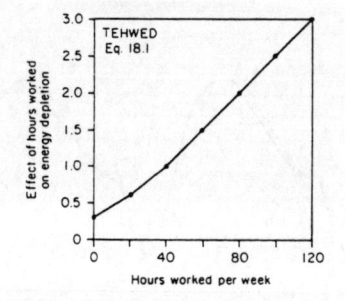

Frustration has been defined as the result of experiencing "undue delay in the fulfillment of a desired goal" (Greenwood 1979, 85), which may be interpreted here as a perceived inadequacy of accomplishment. Figure 5 indicates that as frustration increases, so too will its draining effect on energy. Figure 6 indicates that as the workweek increases, so will the exposure to work-related stressors, again resulting in faster depletion of energy. But note that energy depletion occurs even when the individual is not working at all, as a result of frustration, guilt, or boredom (Machlowitz 1980, 114; Selye 1974, 73; Weiman 1977). After all, "Ability brings with it the need to use that ability" (Albert Szent-Györgi, quoted in Selye 1974, 73). When the energy level falls below 0.2, the "effect of low energy on further depletion" acts to suppress the depletion rate somewhat, because not much energy remains to be lost. This effect becomes stronger as energy falls to zero, at which point the depletion rate must also equal zero.

Model behavior

Description and explanation of baseline behavior

The model's baseline behavior is presented in Figures 7 and 8, over a 75-week time horizon. During this time, the weekly accomplishment rate rises three times, only to fall precipitately along with the energy level as part of a self-sustaining burnout cycle. The observed limit cycle has a period of 30 weeks, one-third of this period being the decline phase during which accomplishment drops to one-sixth of its peak value.

The burnout cycle may be understood most clearly by referring to the causal-loop diagram presented in Figure 9. Initially, the perceived adequacy of accomplishment is relatively high, leading to increased expectations via loop 2. Rising expectations keep the worker somewhat dissatisfied with his output, which drives the "work

Fig. 7. Base run: accomplishment and hours worked per week

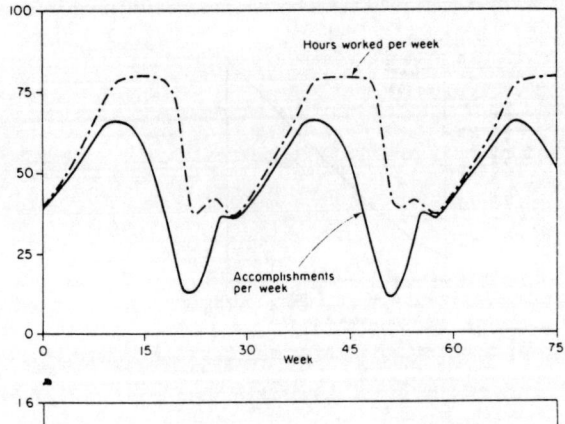

Fig. 8. Base run: energy level and perceived adequacy of accomplishment

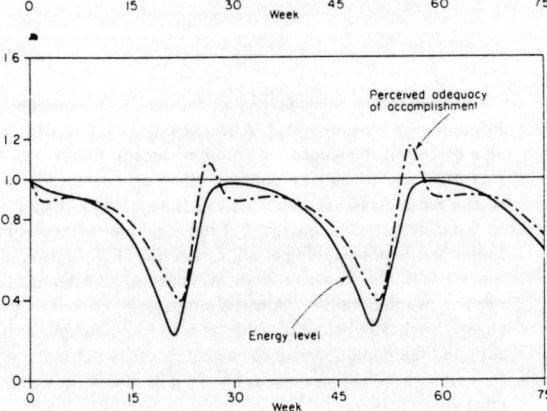

Fig. 9. Causal-loop structure underlying burnout cycles

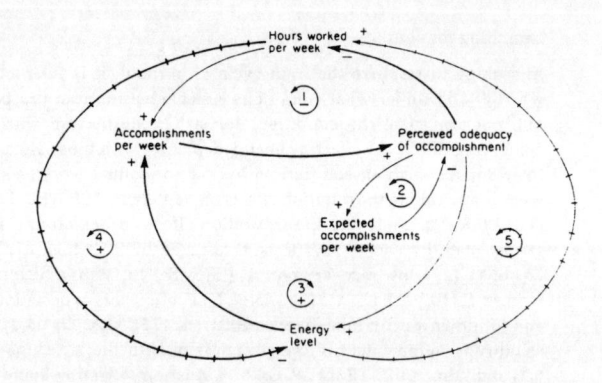

harder" response of loop 1. Weekly accomplishment rises accordingly and continues to do so as loops 1 and 2 combine to "bootstrap" the workweek upward toward its limit.

But as the hours worked increase, so does the stress of work, causing the energy level to decline. Falling energy puts a damper on output, leading to greater dissatisfaction and the beginnings of frustration. Dissatisfaction causes the individual to continue working hard, while frustration makes work even more stressful, both of which further speed the drain of energy. If the vicious cycles just described, seen in Figure 9 as positive loops 3 and 4, grow strong enough relative to the individual's ability to recover energy during nonwork periods, then a collapse of energy and output like that seen in the base run will result.

Recovery from burnout is made possible by less work and reduced expectations. When energy falls to a low enough level, the individual finally breaks free of the addictive "work harder" response and reduces hours at work; in the base run, hours worked per week fall rapidly from their peak of 80 to a trough of about 40.[3] This "time off" response finally stems the decline of energy, as suggested by loop 5, and indeed allows lost energy to be reclaimed. While the workweek has been reduced, so have achievement expectations. Loop 2 now counters dissatisfaction by bringing output goals down to a level more in keeping with the exhausted worker's depressed capability.

The final stage of the cycle comes when modest expectations and rising energy enable the worker to achieve at a rate that is satisfying without having to put in a lot of hours to do so. As seen in the base run, the perceived adequacy of accomplishment actually bounces back to exceed the neutral level of 1, at a time when the individual is working a relatively short workweek. But this euphoric period of "coasting" is short-lived, lasting only a couple of weeks (as corroborated by my own experience). Why? Because satisfaction is unnatural for workaholics and only encourages them to expand their goals and begin the cycle once again.[4]

Searching for stability

In seeking to stabilize the limit cycle of burnout, it is instructive to examine first whether and under what conditions a stable equilibrium can be found. As it turns out, one can state the conditions for stable equilibrium with a single inequality comparing the forces affecting energy depletion with those affecting energy recovery. Interestingly, such an equilibrium has the individual working steadily at his or her work limit. Taking the duration effects on depletion (TEHWED, Eq. 18.1) and recovery (TEHWER, Eq. 14.1) and the frustration effect on depletion (TEPAED, Eq. 17.1) as givens, stability can be said to be threatened by (1) a high depletion normal (EDN, Eq. 16.1); (2) a low recovery normal (ERN, Eq. 13.1); (3) a high upper limit on hours worked (LHWW, Eq. 4.1); (4) a large bias to expand expectations (BFCX, Eq. 10.1); and (5) downwardly inflexible expectations (TFCXPA, Eq. 11.1). On the other hand, stability is independent of the steepness of both the "work harder" (TEPAHW, Eq. 6.1) and "time off" (TEELHW, Eq. 5.1) functions affecting hours worked per week.[5]

Model tests verify that these five factors can be adjusted to stabilize the burnout cycle. The results of one such test, in which the energy depletion normal is reduced by 20 percent, from 0.06 per week to 0.048 per week, are shown in Figure 10. Although a limit cycle is still observed, its amplitude is considerably less than that of the base run (weekly accomplishment falls by less than 60 percent, compared with more than 80 percent in the base run), and its period is considerably longer (39 weeks versus 30). Another noticeable difference is that the decline phase now accounts for more than two-thirds of the entire cycle, compared with one-third in the base run. In effect, the vicious cycles causing burnout have been rendered less vicious, so that the decline is a slower and milder one, and one requiring less time off for recovery. As a result, weekly accomplishment averaged over the full 75 weeks of output is raised by 17 percent relative to the base run.[6]

Fig. 10. Energy depletion normal reduced by 20 percent

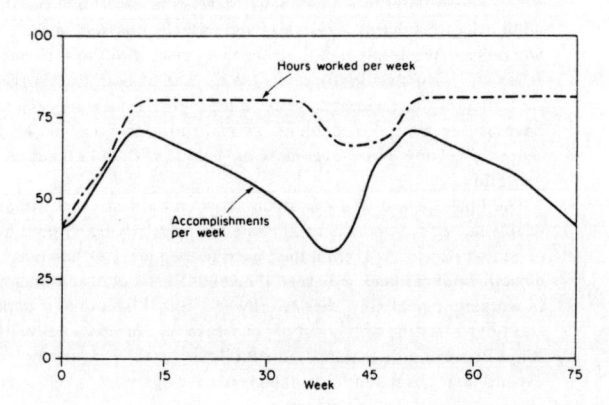

Fig. 11. Steeper effect of energy level on hours worked

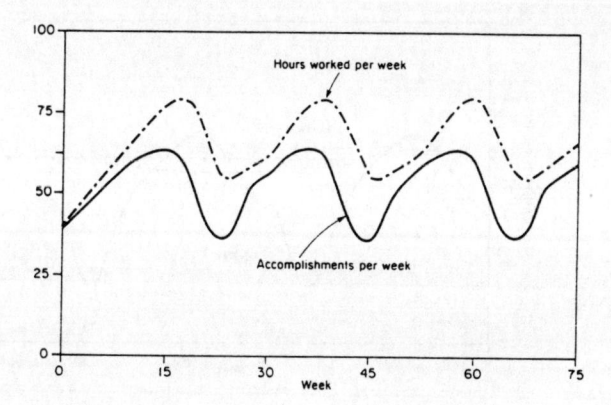

The results of this test are similar to the results of all those tests in which the described stability condition is closer to being satisfied. The limit cycle becomes smaller in amplitude. longer in period. more drawn out in the decline phase. and faster in the recovery phase. The average workweek increases. as does average weekly accomplishment. If the stability condition is actually satisfied. the limit cycle is replaced by a critically damped oscillation. with significantly higher average weekly accomplishment over the 75 weeks. For example. by reducing the energy depletion normal to 0.04 instead of 0.048 (a 33 percent reduction from the baseline instead of 20 percent). average weekly accomplishment is raised by 42 percent relative to the base run (instead of 17 percent) and a consistent 80-hour workweek is maintained. Thus. stabilizing policies do have the effect of increasing overall accomplishment. permitting the individual to work longer hours and to spend less time recuperating from exhaustion.

If the "time off" response to exhaustion does not affect the condition for stable equilibrium. one might wonder what effect this reasonable-sounding policy does have on behavior. Figure 11 shows the results of a run in which the individual is less reluctant than in the base run to break away from work during periods of reduced energy; in other words. the "time off" function falls more steeply than that seen in Figure 1.[7] As in the previous test. the limit cycle's amplitude is significantly reduced relative to the base run. a direct result of acting earlier to escape the vicious cycles of collapse. But this earlier response also leads to a cycle of shorter period. though similar in shape to the base run's cycle. The general impact is to shrink and speed up the cycle. rather than to stabilize it. In terms of overall output, though. this impact is beneficial: average weekly accomplishment is 12 percent higher in this test run than in the base run.

While a policy to reduce work hours in response to lower energy cannot stabilize the burnout cycle. a policy that reduces the limit on hours worked (LHWW) can: recall that this limit enters the condition for stable equilibrium. The essential differ-

Fig. 12. Three tests with reduced limit on hours worked per week

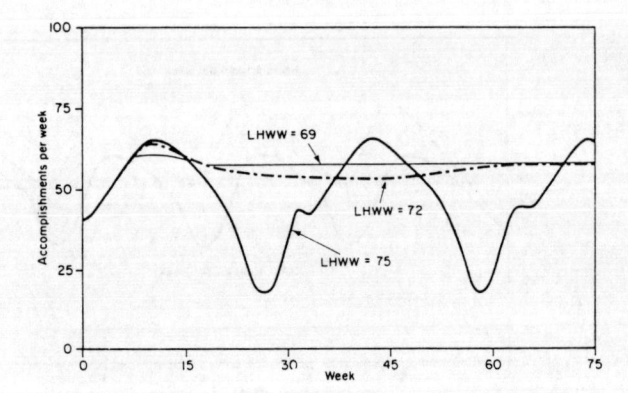

ence between these two workweek policies is that the former is reactive, responding only when a problem has already surfaced, while the latter is proactive and preventive in nature. Also, as a practical matter, it may be easier to implement a shorter work limit (perhaps, as Machlowitz (1980, 133) suggests, by locking the office doors after certain hours) than to fight the workaholic's natural reluctance to take time off to relieve fatigue. Figure 12 shows the results of three test runs in which the work limit has been reduced from its baseline value of 80. When LHWW = 75, a limit cycle is still produced, though it has a smaller amplitude and longer period than the base run cycle. When LHWW = 72, the limit cycle is replaced by a damped oscillatory mode that achieves stable equilibrium by week 60, after an initial overshoot and protracted undershoot. When LHWW = 69, the behavior is even more stable, consisting of a single small overshoot and virtual equilibrium soon after week 15. In terms of average accomplishment, stability again wins out: the first run improves on the base run by only 1 percent, the second run by 20 percent, and the third by 23 percent.

Figure 13 offers a broader view of the effect of the work limit (LHWW) on overall results.[8] Three 75-week summary statistics—average accomplishments per week to date, average hours worked per week to date, and average accomplishments per hour to date—are graphed against values of LHWW ranging from 50 to 90.[9] These graphs show clearly the difference between stability and instability, as far as total output and hours worked are concerned. Within the region of stability (where LHWW ≤ 72.2 hours per week),[10] a longer work limit means more hours worked (since HWW = LHWW in equilibrium) but also lower hourly productivity (since longer hours reduce the energy level). Because the depressive effect of longer hours on average energy, small at first, accelerates as the region of instability is approached, a point of maximum average weekly accomplishment exists: given all other baseline parameter values, this "optimal work limit" is approximately 69 hours per week.

A tradeoff of hours and energy no longer exists once the region of instability is entered. A longer limit on hours worked does not increase the average number of

Fig. 13. 75-week summary statistics as affected by work limit

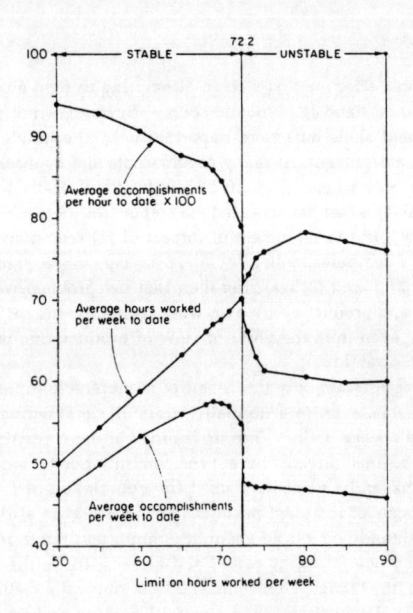

hours worked in this region. Instead, its effect is to increase the amplitude and decrease the period of the limit cycle; that is, to destabilize the behavior further. In fact, changes in the work limit have little effect on any of the cumulative measures shown in Figure 13. It is only in the transition from stability to instability that major differences appear: both average accomplishment and average hours worked drop significantly when the burnout cycle is introduced. Burnout both reduces available energy and requires more time off from work. The advantages of stability are underscored by the following sort of comparison: As shown in Figure 13, the individual can accomplish more on the average with a work limit of 55 hours per week than with a work limit of 75 hours per week, while actually working fewer hours per week on the average.

In noting that the optimal work limit is found within the region of stability but not far from the critical point of transition to instability, one is led to an important conclusion: The more advantageous the other parameters affecting stability are, the higher the *critical* work limit will be, so the higher the *optimal* work limit will be as well. In concrete terms, this means that if the individual can (1) reduce stress at work (by finding ways to make the basic tasks more enjoyable, or by adopting a less pushy or more flexible approach to setting goals), or (2) relax more effectively when not working, then he will be able to work longer hours and accomplish more without risking burnout.

Conclusion

Probably the most effective first step in attempting to fight a complex problem like burnout is to understand its dynamic source. Burnout is not caused by a stressful work environment alone but, more importantly, by the individual's workaholic response to that environment. As many psychiatrists and counselors would agree, real progress begins only when the client has understood clearly his or her own role in creating the problems and has accepted the responsibility to adopt healthier behavior. I can personally attest to the powerful impact of (1) seeing my own burnout cycles reproduced by a computer model, (2) adjusting behavioral parameters until a stable solution was found, and (3) realizing then that my problem was not inevitable but, to a large degree, a product of my own work habits. It was particularly enlightening to discover that even from the point of view of productivity, psychological stability is preferable to instability.

The model suggests not only that stability is preferable to instability but that it is generally attainable, even in a normally stressful work setting, through proper adjustment of one's work limit.[11] Chronic feelings of moderate tiredness or irritability at work must be met directly by a firm commitment to reduce one's maximum workweek permanently, or at least until the completion of a particularly stressful project. If the signs of incipient burnout later return even at this lower work limit, then the limit should be reduced again. It is important not to return to the old work limit, even when one is feeling rested and alert again; as the model demonstrates, vacations alone (the "time off" response) do not prevent a recurrence of burnout.

The model also demonstrates the potential benefit of reducing the normal stress at work, or relaxing better when not working, through methods such as those described at the beginning of this paper. By adopting ways that make one less vulnerable to the negative consequences of stress, one expands the region of stability described in the previous section. This means that one can work longer hours without risking burnout and so accomplish more. An increased ability to (1) anticipate and counteract potential sources of stress, (2) relax without feeling guilty, or (3) adopt more realistic and flexible goals, can do much to make life as a high achiever more enjoyable and satisfying and return to the individual a sense of control.

Appendix: Worker burnout model listing

```
*   WORKER BURNOUT CYCLES
    NOTE BY J. B. HOMER, APRIL 1984
 1  A  AW.K=(AH.K)(HWW.K)
 2  A  AH.K=TABLE(TAH,EL.K,0,1,.2)
    T  TAH=0/.2/.4/.6/.8/1 A-UNITS/HR
 3  L  HWW.K=HWW.J+(DT/TAHWW)(IHWW.J-HWW.J)
    N  HWW=HWWI
    C  HWWI=40 HRS/WK
    C  TAHWW=1 WK
 4  A  IHWW.K=MIN(LHWW,HWW.K*EELHW.K*EPAHW.K)
    C  LHWW=80 HRS/WK
 5  A  EELHW.K=TABLE(TEELHW,EL.K,0,1,.2)
    T  TEELHW=0/.4/.7/.9/1/1
 6  A  EPAHW.K=TABLE(TEPAHW,PAA.K,0,1.6,.2)
    T  TEPAHW=2.3/1.9/1.6/1.35/1.15/1/.9/.8/.75
 7  A  PAA.K=PAW.K/XAW.K
 8  L  PAW.K=PAW.J+(DT/TPAW)(AW.J-PAW.J)
    N  PAW=AW
    C  TPAW=1 WK
 9  L  XAW.K=XAW.J+(DT)(XAW.J*FCXAW.J)
    N  XAW=XAWI
    C  XAWI=40 A-UNITS/WK
10  A  FCXAW.K=BFCX+FCXPA.K
    C  BFCX=.1 PER WK
11  A  FCXPA.K=TABLE(TFCXPA,PAA.K,0,1.6,.2)
    T  TFCXPA=-.7/-.5/-.35/-.2/-.1/0/.1/.25/.4
12  L  EL.K=EL.J+(DT)(ER.JK-ED.JK)
    N  EL=ELI
    C  ELI=1
13  R  ER.KL=(ERN)(EHWER.K)(EHEFR.K)
    C  ERN=.3 PER WK
14  A  EHWER.K=TABLE(TEHWER,HWW.K,0,120,20)
    T  TEHWER=1.3/1.2/1/.7/.5/.35/.25
15  A  EHEFR.K=TABHL(TEHEFR,EL.K,.6,1,.05)
    T  TEHEFR=1/.9/.7/.4/0
16  R  ED.KL=(EDN)(EPAED.K)(EHWED.K)(ELEFD.K)
    C  EDN=.06 PER WK
17  A  EPAED.K=TABLE(TEPAED,PAA.K,0,1.6,.2)
    T  TEPAED=5/4/3.1/2.3/1.6/1/.6/.4/.3
18  A  EHWED.K=TABLE(TEHWED,HWW.K,0,120,20)
    T  TEHWED=.3/.6/1/1.5/2/2.5/3
19  A  ELEFD.K=TABHL(TELEFD,EL.K,0,.2,.05)
    T  TELEFD=0/.4/.7/.9/1
    NOTE SUMMARY STATISTICS
20  A  AVAWD.K=AD.K/(TIME.K+1E-7)
21  L  AD.K=AD.J+(DT)(AW.J)
    N  AD=AW*1E-7
22  A  AVHWWD.K=HWD.K/(TIME.K+1E-7)
23  L  HWD.K=HWD.J+(DT)(HWW.J)
    N  HWD=HWW*1E-7
24  A  AVAHD.K=AD.K/HWD.K
    NOTE CONTROL STATEMENTS
    SPEC DT=.25/LENGTH=75/PLTPER=1.5/PRTPER=15
    PRINT AVAWD,AVHWWD,AVAHD
    PLOT AW=A,HWW=H(0,100)
    PLOT EL=E,PAA=P(0,1.6)
    RUN BASE
```

Notes

1. This response of accommodation is known in the stress literature as syntoxic, in contrast with the catatoxic, or fighting, response of working harder to meet one's goals. Both responses are considered homeostatic, because their purpose is to reduce potentially harmful stress. See Selye (1974, 41, 47).
2. For values of PAA less than 0.8, BFCX + FCXPA < 0. Equilibrium can occur only when PAA = 0.8.
3. In this case of moderate burnout an extended full-time vacation is not needed.
4. In postscript to the explanation of the burnout cycle, it should be noted that loops 3 and 5—the "frustration" and "time off" loops— are not strictly necessary for generating the cycle. Model tests show that if the work is normally disagreeable enough (i.e., if the energy depletion normal EDN is large enough), the draining power of long hours can generate a collapse without the added stress of mounting frustration. But in the baseline model (with its relatively small value of EDN), removal of the aggravating effect of loop 3 does result in stable behavior. Other model tests show that when the individual does not respond to exhaustion by taking time off, expectations eventually fall so low that they can be satisfied even while working less. The resulting respite from work permits a recovery of energy and a renewal of higher accomplishment. But the removal of loop 5 does delay the recovery, resulting in a considerably more severe and protracted period of burnout.
5. Equilibrium requires that hours worked per week (HWW), expectations of weekly accomplishment (XAW), and the energy level (EL) all be unchanging. An equilibrium at which HWW is less than its limit (LHWW) can be shown to exist under certain circumstances, but this equilibrium is unstable in the sense that any small perturbation of certain exogenous parameters will trigger a limit cycle. The condition for a stable equilibrium requires that HWW = LHWW. Labeling EHWED as f, EHWER as g, and EPAED as h, the condition may be stated as follows:

   EDN * h(PAA') * f(LHWW) ≤ ERN * g(LHWW)

   where FCXPA(PAA') = −BFCX

   In the baseline model the left-hand side of the inequality equals 0.19, while the right-hand side equals 0.15: The condition for stable equilibrium is not met and a limit cycle results.
6. Average accomplishments per week to date, or AVAWD, increases from the baseline value of 47.0 to 55.1.
7. In the test run, TEELHW = 0,.3,.5,.7,.9/1, compared to the base run's TEELHW = 0,.4,.7/.9/1/1.
8. This figure summarizes the results of a number of model tests, like those in Figure 12, in which the work limit was altered. Recall that LHWW = 80 in the base run.
9. DYNAMO equations for these three summary statistics may be found in the Appendix, listed as AVAWD, AVHWWD, and AVAHD, respectively. AVAWD is computed by integrating accomplishments per week (AW) over time and then dividing by the total time elapsed. AVHWWD is similarly computed by intergrating hours worked per week (HWW) and then dividing by time elapsed. AVAHD is found by dividing cumulative accomplishments (accomplishments to date, AD) by cumulative hours worked (hours worked to date, HWD).
10. The analytic stability condition is satisfied in this region. When LHWW = 72.2, the left-hand (depletion) side equals the right-hand (recovery) side.
11. The person-environment fit may conceivably be so poor that the optimal work limit is less than a standard workweek or even nonexistent. In such cases, an individual in search of full-time work is best advised to find it elsewhere. Why court disaster?

References

Breznitz. S.. and L. Goldberger. 1982. Stress Research at a Crossroads. In *Handbook of Stress*. ed. L. Goldberger and S. Breznitz. New York: Free Press.

Cameron. R.. and D. Meichenbaum. 1982. The Nature of Effective Coping and the Treatment of Stress-Related Problems: A Cognitive-Behavioral Perspective. In *Handbook of Stress*.

Cherniss. C. 1980. *Staff Burnout: Job Stress in the Human Services*. Beverly Hills. Calif.: Sage.

Dabiri. H. E. 1979. Dynamics of Human Development: Achievement Crisis. Sloan School Working Paper WP-1043-79. Sloan School of Management. M.I.T.. Cambridge. Mass.

Freudenberger. H. J.. and G. Richelson. 1980. *Burn-Out: The High Cost of High Achievement*. Garden City. N.Y.: Anchor Press.

Greenwood. J. W.. III. and J. W. Greenwood. Jr. 1979. *Managing Executive Stress*. New York: Wiley.

Holroyd. K. A.. and R. S. Lazarus. 1982. Stress. Coping. and Somatic Adaptation. In *Handbook of Stress*.

Holt. R. R. 1982. Occupational Stress. In *Handbook of Stress*.

Howard. A.. and R. A. Scott. 1965. A Proposed Framework for the Analysis of Stress in the Human Organism. *Behavioral Science* 10 (2):141–160.

Ivancevich. J. M.. and M. T. Matteson. 1980. *Stress and Work*. Glenview. Ill.: Scott. Foresman.

Janis. I. L. 1982. Decision-Making Under Stress. In *Handbook of Stress*.

Kiefer. C.. and P. M. Senge. 1982. Metanoic Organizations in the Transition to a Sustainable Society. System Dynamics Group Working Paper D-3360-3. Sloan School. M.I.T.. Cambridge. Mass.

Lazarus. R. S. 1979. Positive Denial: The Case For Not Facing Reality. *Psychology Today* 13:44–60.

Machlowitz. M. M. 1980. *Workaholics: Living With Them. Working With Them*. Reading. Mass.: Addison-Wesley.

Maslach. C. 1978. Job Burnout: How People Cope. *Public Welfare* 36.

McClelland. D. C. 1961. *The Achieving Society*. Princeton. N.J.: Van Nostrand.

NDACTRD (National Drug Abuse Center for Training and Resource Development). 1980. *Trainer Manual: Staff Burnout*. NDACTRD Publication No. 80-00115. Washington, D. C.

Selye. H. 1974. *Stress Without Distress*. Philadelphia: Lippincott.

Stoyva. J.. and C. Anderson. 1982. A Coping-Rest Model of Relaxation and Stress Management. In *Handbook of Stress*.

Weiman. C. G. 1977. A Study of Occupational Stressors and the Incidence of Disease/Risk. *Journal of Occupational Medicine* 19:119–122.

Welford. A. T. 1973. Stress and Performance. *Ergonomics* 16:567–580.

[24]

Putting systems thinking into practice

Daniel H. Kim and Peter M. Senge

The dynamic systems perspective illuminates some of the core challenges in organizational learning. If learning occurs through experience, there are good reasons why organizations often fail to learn. In particular, large organizations face a class of systemic decision-making situations in which learning is extremely unlikely. The systems perspective teaches us that cause and effect are often not close in time and space, that obvious interventions do not always produce obvious outcomes, and that long time delays, and systemic effects of actions can make it almost impossible to judge the effectiveness of those actions. This article presents a framework for organizational learning, outlines several breakdowns that thwart the learning process, and discusses how systems thinking can play an important role in helping organizations overcome the learning breakdowns through the design and implementation of managerial practice fields.

Diverse methodologies of systems thinking have been developed over the past 40 years. Yet, despite widespread recognition of the growing importance of understanding interdependency and change, there has been relatively little penetration of these methods into the mainstream of management practice. Managers talk about "the big picture," yet there are no established tools to guard against myopic strategies and policies. Everyone acknowledges the sins of short-term profit maximization, yet planning continues to focus on simple, short-term goals for business performance rather than on high-leverage areas for systemwide redesign and significant improvement. Useful methodologies like system dynamics (Forrester 1961; Richardson and Pugh 1981; Richmond et al. 1987) and Ackoff's (1981) idealized design planning have been in existence for 30–40 years and yet are still taught in only a small fraction of management schools.

Especially problematic is the inability to deal with dynamic complexity, when cause and effect are not closely related in time and space, and obvious changes do more harm than good (see Senge 1990, 71–72). Planning often recognizes detail complexity by taking into account multiple market segments and complex product lines. But dynamic complexity is more challenging because it requires us to think in terms of complex causal interdependencies involving multiple sources of delay and nonlinearity, and evolving patterns of change over time. Very often, recognizing dynamic complexity demands changes in prevailing mental models. Few organizations, in our experience, have the capability to build shared understanding of dynamic complexity—yet this is precisely what characterizes the most important policy and strategy issues.

Organizational learning dilemma

For the past ten years, we have found it helpful to view our efforts at MIT to foster the practice of systems thinking as part of a larger challenge, the challenge of organizational learning. By organizational learning we mean the development of new organizational capabilities. To learn, for an individual, group, or larger organization, is to enhance one's capabilities in reliable and reproducible ways.

Thinking in terms of organizational learning illuminates why so little headway has been accomplished in getting systems thinking into practice. Methodologists have viewed their task as how to get their methodologies into use. This

Daniel H. Kim is the Learning Lab research project director at the MIT Center for Organizational Learning and publisher of The Systems Thinker newsletter. *Address:* Sloan School of Management, MIT, E40-294, Cambridge, MA 02139, U.S.A.

Peter M. Senge is the director of the MIT Center for Organizational Learning and author of *The Fifth Discipline*.

puts the cart before the horse. The first rule of all learning is that the learner learns what the learner wants to learn. (Violation of this rule has been the bane of traditional schooling.) Managers are much more interested in improving product development, building more effective partnerships with customers, or reducing cycle time in complex supply chains than they are interested in learning systems thinking. Rather than focusing on the implementation of a set of tools and methods, it is necessary to focus on the aspirations, goals, and challenges faced by real managers.

This, of course, is precisely the perspective taken by consultants: consultants help managers in addressing practical problems. But consulting rarely results in learning for the client organization. While the consultants' clients may come to understand particular issues, they rarely develop significant new capabilities for understanding similar issues in the future. In fact, making their clients highly proficient in new skills and capabilities is often contrary to consultants' goals.

Herein lies the dilemma. Organizations are in great need of new learning capabilities if they are to thrive in an increasingly complex, interdependent, and changing world. Yet managers' attention is naturally focused on addressing their most important practical problems. Even when those problems are met successfully, there is little to guarantee that new capabilities have been developed to address similar problems more effectively in the future. We settle for fish rather than learning how to fish.

This dilemma is especially vexing when the capabilities in question, like systems thinking, take years rather than weeks to master. This renders any sort of typical training and development process to develop these new skills impractical. Recently an engineering manager in one of our working sessions at the MIT Learning Center said:

> It has taken me a long time to begin to get what this new worldview is all about. I'm beginning to feel like I felt in my freshman calculus class. After months of confusion, I began to get it. Within a year, I had begun to develop some competence. Within four years, the basic tools and way of thinking were an integrated part of my professional skills.... The problem is, if calculus were invented today, our organizations could never learn it. We would send everyone off to the three-day crash course and then tell them to go off and apply it. After three months we'd check if it was working. Since little would have been achieved, we'd conclude that there really wasn't much there, and we'd move on to the next program.

We believe that there is another way for getting systems thinking into practice, which is neither traditional consulting nor training and development. This approach is based on the concept of managerial practice fields, settings where teams who need to take action together can learn together. In practice fields, organizational teams, like their counterparts in sports or the performing arts, experiment, rehearse, and reflect. They not only envision new possibilities, they try them out. They can, as learning theorist Donald Schön observes, speed up or slow down time, simplify complexity, and make what is irreversible in real life reversible (see Schön 1987, 75–76). Most of all, they can make lots of mistakes, which is just what no one would ever do intentionally in a real managerial setting. Over time, they eventually develop new capabilities, not because they are being trained, but as a by-product of how they are learning. Systems thinking gets into practice through practice.

Developing and implementing successful managerial practice fields will, we believe, represent a basic innovation in management practice. Our own efforts over the past two years at the MIT Learning Center are just beginning to scratch the surface of what is possible. In this article, we discuss the basic sources of breakdown in organizational learning and share how this understanding is helping in the creation of first-generation managerial practice fields, which are beginning to demonstrate significant effects.

Breakdowns in organizational learning: incomplete learning cycles

Organizations, like individuals, learn through experience, through taking actions and, as a result of those actions, developing new insights and behaviors that enable more effective future actions. The problem is that taking action is no guarantee of learning, either for individuals or organizations (March and Olsen 1975).

Organizational learning cycle
Kim (1993b) presents an integrated framework of organizational learning where individual learning is linked to organizational learning through the concept of mental models as the transfer mechanism. By mental models, we mean internalized maps (Bostrom et al. 1992), schemas (Fiske and Taylor 1984), beliefs and assumptions, stories (Pennington and Hastie 1991), scripts (Schank and Abelson 1977), and routines (Argyris 1990) that influence perception and action. Mental models are held by individuals, but they can also be shared. Often they are tacit, and even at odds with what people say about their assumptions or beliefs. For example, a manager may say that he believes in collaborative decision making yet consistently make decisions unilaterally. Figure 1 presents this framework of organizational learning, in which six potential learning breakdowns are identified.

Fig. 1. Organizational learning cycle (adapted from Kim 1993b)

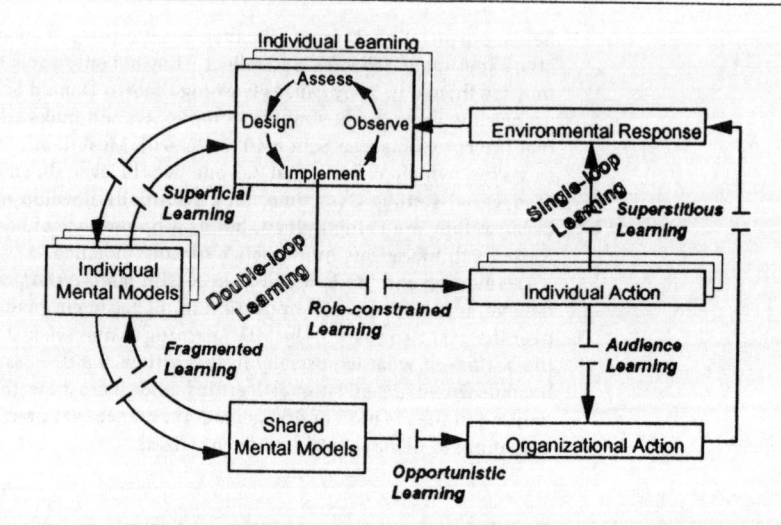

Individual learning is a necessary but not sufficient element of organizational learning. In Figure 1, the process of individual learning is represented through the OADI cycle of observation, assessment, design, and implementation (Kofman 1992). Like many other characterizations of the learning process, the OADI cycle directs our attention to the fact that all learning occurs over time, as we move between a domain of reflection (assess and design) and action (implement and observe consequences of our actions) (Kolb 1984). The process of individual learning is embedded in a larger feedback process whereby individual learning interacts with individual mental models. What data we as individuals see and how we make sense of our observations are conditioned by our cognitive frames (Fiske and Taylor 1984; Schank and Abelson 1977). The actions we take are shaped by our internalized behavioral routines (Argyris 1990; Argyris et al. 1985). Potentially, these mental models can change, although there is much evidence that this often does not occur. When mental models do change, there is a more complex learning process, which has often been termed second-order learning or double-loop learning (Argyris and Schön 1978; Kim 1993b).

Individual mental models are often strongly influenced by shared mental models. Individuals with assumptions and behaviors that are at odds with their larger social milieu experience many forms of pressure to conform. In turn, it is possible that changes in individual mental models may lead to changes in shared mental models—indeed, this is the only way that shared mental models ever change.

In an organizational setting, individual action is distinct from organizational action, both of which are influenced by mental models. Individual mental models shape individual actions through individual learning. In addition, organizational actions are directly influenced by shared mental models. This happens most often through standard operating procedures and operating policies, established ways of making decisions in organizations (Forrester 1961). Like individual mental models, shared mental models and operating policies may be tacit and unrecognized, even by the people whose actions are being influenced by them. The preceding framework recognizes that both individual action and organizational action may lead to an environmental response.

Tracing around the outer loop in Figure 1, we see the most basic loop of organizational learning: individual actions lead to organizational action, which in turn produces an environmental response, leading to individual learning and new individual actions.[1] If the environmental response is static and unchanging, individual beliefs, actions, and therefore organizational actions will also remain unchanged. If there are changes in the environment, there are two basic learning possibilities: individuals adjust their actions based on new information, with no adjustment in underlying mental models (single-loop learning), or there is an adjustment in mental models and actions (double-loop learning). If changes in individual mental models occur, this may also lead to changes in shared mental models, which could then lead to further changes in organizational actions. This would represent organizational double-loop learning.

Breakdowns in the learning cycle

Of course, there is also the possibility that no learning will occur. In fact, there are multiple points of potential breakdown in organizational learning. March and Olsen (1975) identify three breakdowns that can produce incomplete learning cycles. *Role-constrained learning* occurs when an individual is unable to take actions she sees as necessary because she is not permitted to do so within the organization. In other words, changes in individual observations or assessments have no effect on individual action because of constraints imposed by the individual's role. *Audience learning* occurs when the individual affects organizational action in an ambiguous way.

A third breakdown is *superstitious learning*, where individuals are unable to make valid sense of environmental response. Thus, actions are taken, responses are observed, inferences are drawn, and "learning" takes place, but there is no real basis for the connections made between organizational action and environmental response. For example, sales may increase after a new marketing program is implemented, which leads to the conclusion that the program was effective when, in fact, sales would have increased without the marketing program because of other changes, such as declining availability of a competitor's products.

Superstitious learning is especially likely in situations where there is dynamic complexity. The reason is the growing evidence that human beings have great difficulty making valid causal inferences when cause and effect are not close in time and space. For example, Sterman (1989) has generated substantial experimental evidence of "misperceptions of feedback," which suggests that decision makers consistently misperceive the consequences of their own decisions in situations where there are significant delays and more than one or two feedback loops. When undesired results occur, "most subjects," according to Sterman, "attribute the dynamics to external variables which they believe to be closely correlated in time and space with the (problematic) phenomenon to be explained."

In addition, Kim (1993b) identifies three additional types of incomplete learning cycles that affect organizational learning: superficial, fragmented, and opportunistic. An individual encounters a problem, improvises on the spot and solves the problem, and moves on to the next task. *Superficial learning* occurs when there are adjustments in behavior without any corresponding adjustment in mental model. The resulting single-loop learning may be perfectly appropriate in many situations—in fact, most learning is single-loop because our prevailing mental models serve well in most situations. Superficial learning is a special case of single-loop learning where changes in mental models are called for but do not occur. An example would be an interpersonal situation where an individual is stuck in a behavior that is ineffective but is unable or unwilling to bring about a deeper change in assumptions, beliefs, or frame needed to become unstuck. Another example of superficial learning occurs when there is an effective change in behavior that should lead to change in the person's mental models but does not. So the learning has no long-term impact. Such situational learning may occur because of lack of reflection or because the individual sees the situation in question as idiosyncratic, as not being relevant to other similar situations. Since the individual's mental model is not changed, the organization does not have a way of absorbing the learning either. Many examples of superficial learning fall under the broad category of crisis management, where each problem encountered is solved, but no learning is carried over to the next case.

There are many instances where individuals learn deeply, but the organization as a whole does not. When the link between individual mental models and shared mental models is broken, *fragmented learning* occurs. Organizational learning is fragmented among isolated individuals (or groups). One consequence is that loss of the individuals from the organization means loss of the learning as well. Universities are a classic example of fragmented learning. Professors within each department may be the world's leading experts on management, finance, operations, and marketing, but the university as an institution cannot apply their learning to the running of its own affairs. Very decentralized organizations that do not have the requisite networking capabilities to keep the various parts connected are also susceptible to fragmented learning. Individual mental models are changing, but those changes are not reflected in the organization's memory, and thus there is no cohesive picture of what is occurring at the individual level.

Not all disconnects are bad. There are times when organizations purposely bypass standard organizational procedures and succeed in producing collective actions that might work. Such *opportunistic learning* is characterized by new organizational actions that deviate from prevailing shared mental models (i.e., traditional values and beliefs or standard operating procedures). For example, "skunkworks" are examples where groups deviate from established ways of doing things because they think there is a better way. Sometimes such experiments are sanctioned by senior management, often out of frustration with established procedures. Such experiments can be very exciting. But even when they succeed, there is little guarantee of longer-term change. The use of "skunkworks" to develop the IBM personal computer is a good example. Consciously bypassing normal bureaucratic structure and creating an entirely separate dedicated team led to developing the PC in record time, but there is little evidence that the PC team had much impact on IBM, just as is the case today with General Motors' Saturn, an entire "skunkworks division." The same problem of broader learning occurs even with famous, extraordinarily successful "skunkworks." Much of this opportunistic learning remains as fragmented learning among the individuals, leaving the organizationally shared mental models unchanged.

Such cases of successful opportunistic learning are among the most puzzling and important breakdowns in organizational learning. They are testimony to the failure of the "better mousetrap" theory of innovation. Even when new experiments are successful, that is no guarantee that new insights and practices will spread. Often there is a complete absence of any mechanisms to reflect on and transfer new, better ways of doing things. Action-oriented managers are often too busy moving on to the next project to clearly articulate what established norms and procedures they violated and why. Even if they did, this would be little guarantee of change in shared mental models. After all, just because the daring experiment worked does not necessarily mean that those involved understand fully why it worked, or that the conditions for its success can be replicated. Clearly, transcending opportunistic learning would require a systematic process of articulating emerging new theories for improvement and designing further experiments to test those theories. The absence of such a learning process is an indictment of results-oriented senior management.

Understanding the breakdowns

These multiple breakdowns suggest theoretical reasons why deep organizational learning is difficult. If there is doubt that these theoretical concerns matter, one need only consider the conclusion of the Royal Dutch Shell study, which found the life expectancy of large successful corporations to be roughly 30–40 years, that is, half the life expectancy of individuals in those organizations (de Geus 1988). In concert, the theoretical and empirical evidence leads to a humbling sense of the prospects for genuine organizational learning.

Another way to look at these ideas is that enabling learning will require a multifaceted effort and management commitment. Compelling speeches and increased training budgets will not work. There will need to be a serious, sustained commitment (on our part as well) to changes in culture, infrastructure, and people. As one CEO involved in the Learning Center put it, "When I understood the problem, I saw that it was me." Understanding the sources of the breakdowns in learning can be an important step in focusing that commitment.

In our work, we have found three bodies of theory especially relevant for understanding why the learning breakdowns occur and what can be done about them. All three play a major part in present research projects at the Center, while we concurrently explore additional theoretical lenses. The first has already been cited—the dynamic systems perspective, which suggests that little learning is likely to occur when facing systemic decision-making situations in which the consequences of decisions are distant in time and space. This helps in understanding causes of superstitious learning, and can help in overcoming fragmented learning by providing tools for capturing and transferring particular insights.

A second body of theory concerns why individual mental models are unlikely to change in learning situations. In particular, the action science perspective developed by Argyris and his colleagues focuses on the reasons for nonreflectiveness within individuals and defensiveness in teams (Argyris 1990; Argyris et al. 1985), providing a powerful perspective on the causes of superficial learning. Last, an emerging theory and practice of dialogue is providing insight into fragmented learning by clarifying the subtle processes of collective thinking, whereby individual mental models might come into greater harmony and shared mental models might evolve (Bohm 1990; Bohm and Edwards 1991; Isaacs 1993).

Most important, these bodies of theory carry with them methods that can be used to address the breakdowns in organizational learning. In systems thinking, there are a variety of tools, starting with reflectively simple methods of conceptualizing dynamic feedback processes up to complex computer simulation models and management flight simulators, which can foster shared understanding of dynamically complex policy and strategy issues (Kim 1992; Morecroft 1988; Richardson and Pugh 1981; Richmond et al. 1987; Senge 1990; Sterman 1988; Vennix 1990). Action science also incorporates a variety of methods for fostering greater awareness of how one's mental models operate and influence, and for developing skills in bringing mental models more into the open and for challenging them without invoking defensiveness (Argyris et al. 1985). Finally, several methods for nurturing a "container" wherein deep shared assumptions emerge and change are being developed in current research on dialogue (Isaacs 1993).

From theory to practice: the role of managerial practice fields

Managerial practice fields can play a vital role in helping to address these breakdowns in learning and, in certain situations, help accelerate the whole learning process. However, in order to find broad application they must be championed, designed, and facilitated by the managers who will benefit from their presence. This requires, first, a way of framing the role of practice fields in a managerial context. The diagram in Figure 2 simplifies the breakdowns presented in the preceding section and conveys the essential strategy represented by the practice field.

The outer loop shows the basic organizational learning loop, in which processes of dialogue, discussion, and debate eventually lead to changes in strategy, structure, and particular decisions, new consequences, which feed back to lead to improved mental models and improved decisions. Supposedly, learning occurs through observing and interpreting the consequences in the real world arising from those changes. The problem, however, is that this loop rarely functions effectively for all the reasons cited in the previous section.

The most important breakdowns to pay attention to in the design of practice fields are those that occur (1) because the consequences of changes in strategy, structure, and particular decisions are impossible to observe unambiguously in a world characterized by long delays and external confounding factors (superficial learning); (2) because common processes whereby individuals interpret

Fig. 2. Learning in the virtual world (adapted from Morecroft 1988)

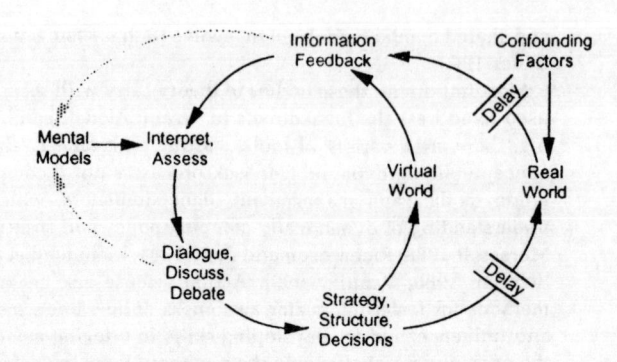

information and come together to debate alternatives do not bring underlying mental models into the open, to be examined and improved (superficial learning); and (3) because whatever changes in individual mental models do occur are rarely diffused broadly enough to affect shared mental models (fragmented learning).

Each of these breakdowns can be overcome in practice fields that

- Speed up time so that people can experience long-term, systemic consequences of decisions
- Slow down time so that people can observe and reflect more deeply on habitual ways of interacting
- Lead to explicit theories of the systemic causes of problem situations that represent shared mental models within the team

For example, a team at Ford is developing a "car product development learning laboratory" with the intention that it will eventually be used widely to augment the traditional car development process and to steadily improve that process. An interactive management flight simulator[2] offers participants in initial sessions an opportunity to test their assumptions and to viscerally experience the consequences of their actions. Suddenly, long-term consequences become real. Working in pairs, participants are encouraged to make explicit the reasoning behind their decisions, the mental models driving their decision making. Typically, they discover, for example, that their assumptions about the right pace of staffing and coordination between product and process engineering lead to missing all three targets: cost, quality, and timing. This sows the seeds for questioning well established but superstitious learnings.

Interactions with the simulator are just one facet of the practice field sessions. There is considerable work on examining in depth what happens intrapersonally and interpersonally when team members interact in ways that compromise learning. For example, using an action science tool called the left-hand column case, team members in an early session discovered that there were two very different sets of assumptions between finance and program management. The unspoken assumptions made it difficult for each to see and appreciate the other's view. By stepping off-line on the practice field, those assumptions were surfaced and acknowledged in a way that would not have happened in the day-to-day performance field.

There is also considerable work on conceptualizing feedback interactions that operate in car product development. In initial learning lab sessions, conceptualization is aided by elementary system archetypes, as presented in Senge (1990) and Kim (1992). To illustrate, consider tragedy of the commons, an archetype with much insight for car development (Zeniuk 1993). In a tragedy-of-the-commons structure, each individual pursues actions that are individually beneficial but that over time result in a worse situation for everyone involved because the individuals are depleting a common resource that is limited. At Ford, individual component teams were competing for the limited amount of alternator power output in the designs they were creating. It made sense for each component team to draw as much power as it required to maximize the functionality of its part. The collective result was an impasse in the design process, since no team was willing to concede what benefited its own component. Individual attempts to resolve the issue were unproductive.

What happens in typical projects as a result of this dynamic is that teams continue to struggle among themselves for resources, until at some point the program timing is jeopardized and the program manager has to step in and dictate what each team can have from the common resource. This makes the teams unhappy because a decision is imposed on them and because some of them did not get what they wanted. The manager is not happy because he had to intervene when he had expected the teams to work more cooperatively on their own. Typically, people conclude that this was just an instance of poorly aligned teams or a heavy-handed manager. There is no general framework for them to learn from; superficial, fragmented learning is the inevitable result.

In this case, once the tragedy-of-the-commons structure was recognized and conceptualized by team members, they realized that they were stuck in a situation where none of them, acting individually, would likely solve the problem. Only a collective governing body or an individual with the authority to impose constraints on all the teams could resolve the situation. They elected to give the program manager all the component designs and ask him to make the decision on how much power to allocate to each of the components. Those who had to give up some functionality did not like it, but they understood why it was necessary—because the alternative of laissez faire individual decision making made everyone lose. In subsequent sessions, team members looked at other common resources, such as available torque, and realized that they too fell into the tragedy-of-the-commons category. These examples provide a systemic explanation of why a program manager with wide authority over the entire car program makes sense and why most Japanese car programs are structured that way.

This example shows how making explicit a tacit understanding can lead to a new shared mental model and alternative collective action. This explicit dynamic theory would not have been possible without the right tools to express such a theory, such as the system archetype mapping method. Once this theory was articulated and understood by everyone, it was obvious that some new action was needed.

Moreover, the managers involved did not stop there. As they have begun to internalize the basic capabilities needed to do left-hand column cases and system archetypes, they have continued to apply and extend their learning. For example, team members have identified several other core dynamic structures that have traditionally undermined car development, such as how component teams ensconced in organizational "chimneys" create vicious cycles linking "shifting the burden" structures: where one component team's quick fix exacerbates another's basic problems, leading the second group to its own quick fix, which exacerbates the first group's problems.

Prototype practice fields are also being developed in concert with the Federal Express global sales organization, Philips Display components (a division of Philips North America), National SemiConductor, and other Learning Center member companies. The specific issues may vary, but the underlying theory and basic methods are the same in each case. While it is too early to assess the overall effectiveness of these experiments, initial results are very encouraging.

Conclusions

Overcoming the multiple breakdowns in organizational learning will not be easy. It will require basic innovation in how organizations operate. We believe that managerial practice fields can be such an innovation. As a by-product, we are seeing that they go much further than traditional consulting or training in bringing systems thinking principles and tools into the mainstream of management practice.

In this article, we have tried to lay out the motivations for managerial practice fields in terms of the basic breakdowns in organizational learning. We have also summarized our basic strategy for positioning systems-oriented practice fields as part of an improved organizational learning process. In subsequent publications, we will develop the design principles and practices for such practice fields in more depth.

Notes

1. This loop is similar to the basic model of organizational learning offered by March and Olsen (1975). The main difference here is that we distinguish individual learning from change in mental models in order to distinguish single-loop from double-loop learning.
2. Management flight simulators are interactive decision-making computer games based on a system dynamics model of a particular domain of interest, such as product development, service quality, and product life cycle.

References

Ackoff, R. L. 1981. *Creating the Corporate Future: Plan or Be Planned For.* New York: Wiley.

Argyris, C. 1990. *Overcoming Organizational Defenses.* Wellesley, Mass.: Allyn and Bacon.

Argyris, C., R. Putnam, and D. M. Smith. 1985. *Action Science.* San Francisco: Jossey-Bass.

Argyris, C. and D. Schön. 1978. *Organizational Learning: A Theory of Action Perspective.* Reading, Mass.: Addison-Wesley.

Bohm, D. 1990. *On Dialogue.* Ojai, Calif.: David Bohm Seminars.

Bohm, D., and M. Edwards. 1991. *Changing Consciousness.* San Francisco: Harper-Collins.

Bostrom, A., B. Fischhoff, and G. M. Morgan. 1992. Characterizing Mental Models of Hazardous Processes: A Methodology and an Application to Radon. *Journal of Society* 48 (4): 85–100.

de Geus, A. 1988. Planning as Learning. *Harvard Business Review* (March–April): 70–74.

Fiske, S. T., and S. E. Taylor. 1984. *Social Cognition.* New York: Random House.

Forrester, J. W. 1961. *Industrial Dynamics.* Portland, Ore.: Productivity Press.

Isaacs, W. 1993. Taking Flight: Dialogue, Collective Thinking, and Organizational Learning. *Organizational Dynamics* (Fall).

Kim, D. H. 1992. *Toolbox Reprint Series: Systems Archtypes.* Cambridge, Mass.: Pegasus Communications.

———. 1993a. A Framework and Methodology for Linking Individual and Organizational Learning: Applications in TQM and Product Development. Unpublished dissertation, Sloan School of Management, MIT, Cambridge, MA 02139, U.S.A.

———. 1993b. The Link Between Individual and Organizational Learning. *Sloan Management Review* 35 (1): 14.

Kofman, F. 1992. Lecture Slides. Sloan School of Management, MIT, Cambridge, MA 02139, U.S.A.

Kolb, D. A. 1984. *Experiential Learning: Experience as the Source of Learning and Development*. Englewood Cliffs, N.J.: Prentice Hall.

March, J. G., and J. P. Olsen. 1975. The Uncertainty of the Past: Organizational Learning under Ambiguity. *European Journal of Political Research* 3: 147–171.

Morecroft, J.D.W. 1988. System Dynamics and Microworlds for Policymakers. *European Journal of Operational Research* 35: 301–320.

Pennington, N., and R. Hastie. 1991. A Cognitive Theory of Juror Decision Making: The Story Model. *Cardozo Law Review* 13: 519–557.

Richardson, G. P., and A. L. Pugh III. 1981. *Introduction to System Dynamics Modeling with DYNAMO*. Portland, Ore.: Productivity Press.

Richmond, B., P. Vescuso, and S. Peterson. 1987. *An Academic User's Guide to STELLA*. High Performance Systems, 45 Lyme Rd., Hanover, NH 03755, U.S.A.

Schank, R. D., and R. Abelson. 1977. *Scripts, Plans, Goals, and Understanding*. Hillsdale, N.J.: Erlbaum.

Schön, D. A. 1987. *Educating the Reflective Practitioner*. San Francisco: Jossey-Bass.

Senge, P. M. 1990. *The Fifth Discipline*. New York: Doubleday/Currency.

Sterman, J. D. 1988. Strategy Dynamics: The Rise and Fall of People Express. Sloan School of Management, MIT, Cambridge, MA 02139, U.S.A.

———. 1989. Modeling Managerial Behavior: Misperceptions of Feedback in a Dynamic Decision-Making Experiment. *Management Science* 35 (3): 321–339.

Vennix, J.A.M. 1990. Mental Models and Computer Models: Design and Evaluation of a Computer-Based Learning Environment for Policy Making. Ph.D. dissertation, Catholic University of Nijmegen, Netherlands.

Zeniuk, N. 1993. Learning to Learn: A New Look at Product Development. *The Systems Thinker* 4 (1).

Name Index

Abdel-Hamid, Tarek 246, 443–52
Abelson, R. 92, 477, 478
Able, S.L. 397
Abramovitz, M. 388
Abrams, Dan I. 257
Ackoff, R.L. 119, 475
Adam, Jack 148
Adams, Henry 89
Allison, Graham T. 194
Amrine, H.T. 403
Andersen, D.F. 68
Anderson, P. 112
Andreassen, P. 243
Anthony, R.N. 405
Argyris, Chris 94, 110, 111, 143, 147, 477, 478, 482, 483
Aston, B. 231
Augustine, Fred K. 399–423
Axelrod, R. 92, 105

Bakken, B. 113, 230, 246
Balzer, W.K. 245
Bandler, J.W. 272
Bass, Frank M. 231, 341
Bateson, Gregory 50
Baum, Esther 144
Bechter, D.M. 397
Beinhocker, E. 234
Blasingame, J.W. 396
Boddie, J. 443
Boggs, Wade 109
Bohm, D. 483
Bostrom, A. 477
Boulding, Kenneth 120
Bower, G. 92
Bowlin, O.D. 405
Bowman, E.H. 222
Brehmer, B. 102, 226, 230, 231, 240
Brewer, Garry D. 252–3
Breznitz, S. 461
Broadbent, D. 231
Brody, Edward J. 339–59
Brooks, F.P. 445, 451
Bruckmann, Gerhart 19, 21, 110
Bruner, J.S. 98
Buonaparte, Napoleon 36
Burke, N. Warner 149, 150

Camerer, C. 220
Cameron, R. 455
Carlson, E. 230
Carroll, J.S. 115
Carter, Jimmy 10
Cavana, Robert Y. 194
Checkland, Peter xi, 118, 196
Cheng, P. 92
Cherniss, C. 453
Churchill, Winston 230
Cicerone, R. 98
Clark, Thomas D. jr 361–79, 399–423
Clausing, Don 341
Clifford, Mac 275
Cline, H.F. 117
Cobb, J. 97
Coleman, J.S. 210
Cooper, Kenneth G. 425–41
Copernicus, Nicolaus 109
Coyle, R. Geoffrey 68, 194, 196, 402
Crenson, M.A. 10
Crissey, B.L. 10
Culligan, Matthew J. 251, 269, 275
Cyert, Richard M. 10, 11, 75, 212, 267, 276

Dabiri, H.E. 457
Daley, H. 97
Dangerfield, B. 194
Davis, H.L. 108, 212, 246
Day, Richard H. 252
De Geus, Arie 135, 139, 198, 327, 482
DeMarco, T. 444
Deming, W. Edwards xi, 135
De Pree, Max 139
Dewey, John 91, 246
Dickens, Charles 181
Diehl, E.W. 32, 103, 107, 230, 233
Dörner 230
Dostoyevsky, Fedor M. 109
Dougherty, Philip H. 251, 276
Draper, F. 32

Eckstein, Otto 14, 18
Eden, Colin 118, 196, 203
Edwards, M. 483
Einhorn, H.J. 106, 108, 212, 240
Emshoff, J.R. 75

Farman, J. 98
Fast, Patricia 99–100
Feltham, G.A. 401
Festinger, Leon 50
Fiddaman, T. 115
Fiske, S.T. 477, 478
Fitzgerald, H. 120
Flint, Brilsford B. 197, 202
Ford, Henry 135
Forrester, Jay W. xii, xiii, 10, 11, 12, 21, 48, 53–4, 56, 64, 65, 69, 75, 90, 92, 95, 101, 106, 107, 110, 119, 120, 129–32, 138, 153, 154, 162, 191, 192, 198, 201, 202, 230, 246, 252, 253, 254, 255, 265, 273, 282, 290, 305, 327, 373, 385, 402, 407, 475, 479
Frankel, J.A. 219
Freudenberger, H.J. 454, 455, 461
Friedman, M. 112
Friedrich, Otto 251, 259, 261, 269, 270
Froot, K.A. 219
Fuller, Walter 275
Funke, J. 230, 231

Gentner, D. 92
Gödel, Kurt 109
Gorbachev, Mikhail 36
Gore, Bill 144
Gorry, G.A. 403
Gort, M. 229
Gould-Kreutzer, J. 117
Graddy, E. 229
Graham, Alan K. 21, 117, 245, 300
Graves, S.C. 362, 377
Greenberger, M. 120
Greenleaf, Robert 140
Greenwood, J.W. III 453, 454, 455, 457, 462
Greenwood, J.W. jr 453, 454, 455, 457, 462

Ha, Y. 108
Habibe, Tommy O. 202
Hadley, Q. 361
Halford, G. 92
Hall, Roger I. 76, 105, 194, 196, 202, 225, 251–77, 402
Hall, R.W. 381
Hampden-Turner, C. 146
Hansen, A.H. 224
Hastie, R. 477
Hauser, John R. 339–59
Hausman, W.H. 362, 378
Hauthakker, H.S. 232
Hax, A.C. 233, 303, 304
Heeler, R.M. 341

Henderson, B.D. 303, 304
Hernandez, K. 113
Hicks 50
Hillestad, R.J. 363
Hitler, Adolf 36
Hogarth, Robin M. 4, 91, 106, 108, 109, 194, 209, 212, 225, 226, 231, 233, 242, 246
Holroyd, K.A. 455
Holt, R.R. 453, 461
Homer, Jack B. 119, 120, 231, 453–73
Horsky, Dan 341
Howard, A. 462
Hoyt, H. 113, 230
Hustad, T.P. 341

Isaacs, W.N. 118, 483
Ivancevich, J.M. 453, 454, 455, 457, 461, 462

Janis, I.L. 110, 111, 455, 457
Jarmain, W.E. 113
Jeuland, Abel P. 341
Joan of Arc 36
Johnson, E.J. 212
Johnson, Robert W. 138
Johnson-Laird, P. 92, 108
Jones, J.W. 400
Jorgenson, D.W. 14
Judge 220

Kahneman, D. 4, 108, 194, 209, 212, 225, 245
Kaldor, Nicholas 15
Kalish, Shlomo 231, 341
Kampmann, C. 104, 231
Kanizsa, Gaetano 93
Kanter, R.M. 325
Kapor, Mitch 444
Kaufman, H. 326
Keen, Peter G.W. 73, 203
Keilson, J. 362, 377
Keller, Helen 183, 184
Kennedy, John F. 175
Kerin, Roger A. 342
Keynes, John Maynard 50
Kiefer, C. 455
Kim, Daniel H. xi, 21, 165–88, 475–88
King, Martin Luther 36, 137
Klayman, J. 108
Klein, Lawrence R. 13, 18, 388
Kleinmuntz, D.N. 102, 226, 230, 231, 403
Klepper, S. 229
Kofman, Fred 93, 94, 96, 478
Kolb, D.A. 478
Konsynski, B.R. 300

Kotler, P. 405
Krajewski, L.J. 405
Kreutzer, David P. 201
Krisbergh, Harold M. 272
Krushchev, Nikita 175
Kuhn, Thomas S. 98

Lakani, Chet 341
Land, Frank 203
Lane, David C. 118, 119, 279–302
Langley, P. 120
Lazarus, R.S. 462
Leamer, E. 100–1
Leontief, Wassily 18
Levine, R. 120
Lilien, G. 231
Little, John D.C. 345
Löffler, Reiner 303–23
Lucas, Robert 16, 112
Lyneis, J.M. 75, 288, 327, 402

McClelland, D.C. 454
Machiavelli, Nicolà 101
Machlowitz, M.M. 454, 455, 458, 463, 468
Mack, R.P. 388
MacKinnon, A. 226
MacNeal, Robert A. 275
Madnick, Stuart E. 443–52
Mahajan, Vijay 231, 341, 342
Majluf, N.S. 233, 303, 304
Makridakis, S. 233
Malthus, Thomas R. 50
Mandinach, E.B. 117
March, James G. 10, 11, 212, 267, 276, 477, 479
Marder, C. 401
Maslach, C. 455
Mason, R.O. 75, 139
Mass, Nathaniel J. 82, 117, 198, 199
May, E.R. 443
Meadows, Dana 25
Meadows, Dennis L. 98–9, 197, 201, 202, 225, 254
Meadows, Donella H. 3, 8, 19, 21, 37, 98–9, 106, 115, 153, 255
Melone, N.P. 400
Menzies, W.B. 402
Merten, Peter P. 303–23
Merton, Robert K. 50
Miller, J.G. 382
Miller, Lawrence 141
Miller, Roger L. 258
Minsky, Marvin 205
Mintzberg, Henry 139

Mitchell, Russell 340
Mitchell, T.W. 224
Mitchell, W.C. 224
Mitroff, Ian I. 75, 139, 140
Molina, M. 98
Morecroft, John D.W. 9, 11, 21, 58, 73–87, 117, 118, 189–208, 212, 225, 233, 246, 279, 280, 292, 300, 381–98, 400, 402, 403, 405, 483
Morecroft, Linda E. 206
Morrow, D. 92
Mosekilde, E. 245
Muller, Eitan 341, 342
Myrdal, Gunnar 50

Nelson, Carl W. 272
Nelson, R. 112
Neustadt, R.E. 443
Nisbett, R. 92
Nord, Ole C. 254

O'Brien, William 136, 138, 148–9
Olsen, J.P. 477, 479
O'Reilly, C.A. 401
Oster, S.M. 233

Packer, David W. 254
Paich, Mark 101–2, 103, 202, 229–48
Papert, Seymour 115, 206
Pennington, N. 477
Peterson, S. 32, 283
Petre, P. 229
Phelps-Brown, E.H. 15, 18
Pindyck, R. 17
Plott, C.R. 209
Plous, S. 98
Popkin, J. 388
Porter, Michael E. 229, 230, 233, 325, 327
Postman, L.J. 98
Powers, W. 90–1
Pringle, Lewis G. 339–59
Probert, D.E. 76
Pugh, Alexander L. III 252, 305, 407, 475, 483

Randers, J. 98–9
Rao, Potluri 258
Reagan-Cirincione, P. 118
Reder, M.W. 209, 231
Regentz, M.O. 381
Remus, W.E. 226
Richardson, George P. 37, 47–72, 90, 191, 245, 246, 279, 300, 305, 407, 475, 483
Richardson, John 19, 21, 110

Richmond, Barry M. 21, 25–45, 118, 191, 192, 199, 200, 203, 206, 279, 280, 283, 483
Ritzman, L.P. 405
Robbins, S.P. 405
Roberts, Edward B. 69, 76, 120, 254, 255, 257, 327, 402, 405
Roberts, John H. 339–59
Roberts, N. 36
Robinson, Bruce 341
Robinson, J. 109
Rohrbaugh, J. 245, 246
Rosenhead, J. 118
Ross, L. 106
Rowland, F.S. 98
Rubinfeld, D. 17

Sagaria, S. 107
Salter, M. 230
Samuelson, P. 50
Sashkin, M. 149, 150
Sastry, A. 120
Schank, R.D. 92, 477, 478
Schein, Edgar 110, 138, 150
Schkade, D.A. 212
Schneiderman, A. 95
Schön, Donald A. 75, 90, 110, 115, 117, 246, 477, 478
Schwarz, L.B. 362
Scott-Morton, Michael S. 73, 203, 403
Scudder, G.D. 362, 373
Selye, H. 454, 455, 462, 463
Selznick, Philip 138
Senge, Peter M. xi, 15, 21, 69, 118, 120, 135–51, 201, 203, 231, 233, 246, 373, 407, 475–88
Sengupta, K. 246
Sentz-Györgi, Albert 463
Shakespeare, William 100
Shannon, D. 115
Shaughnessy, D. 109
Shaw, George Bernard 141
Shaw, R.J. 381
Shewhart, W. 91
Shiba, S. 91
Silk, Alvin J. 339–59
Silverman, Lisa 345
Simon, Herbert A. 4, 9, 16, 74, 75, 105, 107, 194, 195, 198–9, 209, 212, 230, 233, 303
Simon, Leonard S. 341
Sirny, R.F. 381
Sloan, Alfred 135
Slovic, P. 4, 209
Smith, Adam 50
Smith, V.L. 102, 209, 230

Stalk, George 136
Steers, R.M. 405
Stenberg, L. 69
Sterman, John D. 3–23, 69, 89–128, 129, 194, 196, 197, 199, 200, 201, 204, 209–27, 229–48, 292, 327, 403, 480, 483
Stevens, A. 92
Stevenson, W.J. 405
Stohbaugh, Robert 13
Stolarski, R. 98
Stoyva, J. 455
Swanson, E.B. 400, 401
Swanson, M. 32

Taylor, L.C. 232
Taylor, S.E. 477, 478
Thomas, J. 102, 230, 231
Thornton, L. 113
Thurow, Lester 18
Timmers, H. 107, 242
Tinbergen, Jan 13
Toda, M. 112
Trempe, Robert E. 361–79
Trichlin, Herbert E. 361–79
Trow, D.B. 75
Trump, Donald 115
Tsu, Lao 150
Tufte, E.R. 205
Tversky, Amos 4, 194, 209, 212, 225, 245

Urban, Glen L. 339–59

Van der Heijden, K.A.J.M. 280
Vapenikova, O. 194
Venn, John 50
Vennix, J.A.M. 92, 279, 483
Vescuso, P. 283
Viita, Paul S. 279–302
Vollmann, T.E. 381

Wack, Pierre 139
Wagenaar, W. 107, 242
Wason, P. 108
Watson, Tom 135
Wearing, A. 226
Weber, E.S. 300
Weeks, J.K. 396
Weil, Henry B. 69, 257, 325–38
Weiman, C.G. 463
Weizenbaum, J. 21
Welford, A.T. 459
White, E.M. 396
White, Leon S. 325–38
Whitin, T.M. 361
Wiedmann, Klaus-Peter 303–23

Wiener, N.P. 399
Wilde, Oscar 453
Wilson, R. Dale 339
Wind, Yoram 231, 341
Winter, S. 112
Wisniewski, Kenneth J. 342, 347, 358
Wolstenholme, E.F. 68, 118, 120, 196, 400, 402
Wriston, Walter 136

Yergin, Daniel 13

Zakon, A.J. 304
Zarnowitz, V. 224, 245
Zeniuk, N. 485
Zimbardo, Philip 41
Zmud, R.W. 399, 400